WATCHING TV

Four Decades of American Television

**Harry Castleman
and
Walter J. Podrazik**

McGRAW-HILL BOOK COMPANY
New York St. Louis San Francisco Auckland Bogotá
Guatemala Hamburg Johannesburg Lisbon London
Madrid Mexico Montreal New Delhi Panama Paris
San Juan São Paulo Singapore Sydney Tokyo Toronto

12345678 M U M U 87654321

LIBRARY OF CONGRESS CATALOGING IN PUBLICATION DATA

Castleman, Harry.
   Watching TV—four decades of American television.

   Includes index.
   1. Television broadcasting—United States.
I. Podrazik, Walter J.   II. Title.
PN1992.3.U5C3   791.45'0973   81–5967
ISBN 0–07–010268–6   AACR2
ISBN 0–07–010269–4 (pbk.)

BOOK DESIGN BY NANCY DALE MULDOON

NOTES ON THE FALL SCHEDULE GRAPHS

* The schedules are arranged according to Eastern time.
* A title set entirely in UPPER CASE indicates a new program making its first appearance on network television.
* A network time period split by a horizontal line between program titles indicates that the shows alternate each week in the same slot. If one title is preceded by the @ symbol, that program appears only once each month.
* The ¢ symbol indicates a program carried only on the network's Midwestern stations.

Contents

President Dwight D. Eisenhower takes the oath of office on January 20, 1953. *(National Archives)*

Jackie Gleason, Audrey Meadows, Art Carney, and Joyce Randolph: The Honeymooners. *(Photo by Viacom, Hollywood)*

INTRODUCTION

Three Stars in the East

JANUARY 19, 1953, was a Monday. It was the day of a subtle but significant shift in twentieth-century-America. Though it had been almost thirty years since Charles Francis Jenkins had demonstrated the world's first experimental television, fifteen years since the first American TV sets had gone on sale, and nearly five years since Milton Berle had become the first television superstar, it was not until January 19, 1953, that three separate events marked the point at which television became synonymous with American popular culture.

As they did every Monday night, millions of Americans turned to CBS at 9:00 P.M. to watch the top-rated show in the country, *I Love Lucy*. That night the audience for the program was greater than usual because Lucy Ricardo was to become a mother. This development was set in the fictional world of situation comedy, but, at the same time, it was also very real. On *I Love Lucy* that evening, Lucy Ricardo gave birth to a healthy baby boy, nicknamed "Little Ricky" after his father, Ricky Ricardo. Earlier that very same day, Lucille Ball, who played Lucy Ricardo, gave birth herself to a real life healthy baby boy, named Desi Arnaz, Jr. after *his* father, Desi Arnaz. Interest in the two births had steadily grown over the previous three months through baby-related plots on the weekly series and in publicity photos and feature articles in popular magazines. The widespread attention paid to the double drama of celluloid TV pregnancy and real life pregnancy practically overshadowed the other big news story of the day: the inauguration of Dwight D. Eisenhower as president and Richard M. Nixon as vice president.

January 19, 1953, was the last day in office for President Harry Truman and it ended twenty years of uninterrupted leadership by Democratic presidents, who had taken the country through a major depression and a world war. The new Republican administration marked not only a significant shift in political style and priorities, but also a dramatic change in the election process itself. The Eisenhower-Nixon ticket was the first to reach national office by the deliberate and successful use of television. Eisenhower owed his nomination to the dominant presence of television at the 1952 Republican convention and to the skillful use of the new medium by his campaign managers. Richard Nixon, Eisenhower's running mate, had saved himself from an almost certain dumping from the Republican slate by responding to charges of maintaining a "secret slush fund" with an unprecedented personal appeal to the country, via television, in his famous "Checkers" speech. Appropri-

ately, the Eisenhower inauguration on January 20, 1953, was the first to be televised live, coast-to-coast, giving millions of Americans their first glimpse at the pageantry and ceremony in the American style of transferring power.

The fact that all three births (Desi Arnaz, Jr., Little Ricky, and the Eisenhower administration) came within twenty-four hours of each other was coincidental, but it serves as a convenient landmark in the history of television. The ascension of Eisenhower and Nixon ended the medium's long struggle to be taken seriously by government officials and important newsmakers. The nationwide attention lavished on the *I Love Lucy* birth episode was solid evidence that the American viewing public had totally accepted television's Hollywood-flavored sitcom characters as part of its daily life. By January 19, 1953, television had become the most powerful mass medium in the land.

The appearance of Little Ricky and Desi Arnaz, Jr. (the first by-products of television's premiere couple) also ushered in a brand new generation of Americans, the first to spend their entire lives growing up in the world of video images. Under the influence of the nation's new electronic babysitter, these children acquired a video vision of life which made it increasingly difficult for them to differentiate between the shape and makeup of the fantasy world they observed on the tube and the hopes and dreams they nurtured for the real world they lived in. While watching TV, the new video generation grew up with perfect parents such as Ozzie and Harriet, Donna Reed, and Fred MacMurray; perfect heroes such as the Lone Ranger and Superman; perfect buddies such as Howdy Doody and the Mouseketeers; and the generation's own personification—the perfect kid—Jerry Mathers as the Beaver. In the immediacy and intimacy of television, these fantasy characters became as real, if not more real, than the world itself. Unlike any previous form of entertainment, television brought lifelike images directly into homes throughout the country by the mere flick of a switch, allowing people thousands of miles apart to see, share, and learn the same things together. This simple fact made television the ultimate miracle of twentieth-century technology.

Since the first major experiments in television during the 1920s, ecstatic visionaries had been struck by the near miraculous technical nature of the new medium and they had painted rosy pictures of television as the "savior of our culture." Once TV arrived, nearly everyone marveled at the amazing process itself and watched almost

Lucille Ball and Desi Arnaz *(c.)* as Lucy and Ricky Ricardo, America's #1 sitcom couple, along with Vivian Vance as neighbor Ethel Mertz and Richard Keith as Little Ricky. *(Photo by Viacom, Hollywood)*

anything that aired, from roller derby to serious drama, yet it quickly became clear that the high expectations had ignored the hard realities of the business interests that had worked to develop television.

Television was conceived by the same people responsible for commercial radio. Like radio, television was structured around just a few programming networks, paid for by commercial advertisers, and dedicated to attracting the largest possible audience. At heart, TV was just a very fancy new way to present mainstream entertainment and sell some soap at the same time. This came as a rude shock to the visionaries and, within a few years, they were calling television a mental wastebasket for the dregs of American creativity. Like their original great expectations, this later letdown was far removed from reasonable reality.

To be understood, American television must be viewed as the embodiment of contradiction—a miracle of spectacular technical achievement imprisoned by the demands of its mundane day-to-day operations. So-called "high class" programming almost always competes with mass appeal presentations because, with 365 days a year to fill, programmers cannot possibly stock each moment of each day with uplifting culture. In spite of all its limitations, this mundane miracle still produces great moments of popular culture and, to varying degrees, special moments of brilliance that rekindle the awe felt by the first TV owners. Yet, in the game of American television, the bottom line has always been high ratings and, to this day, it still is.

Watching TV in Mayberry, North Carolina. (From *l.*) Gomer (Jim Nabors), Andy (Andy Griffith), Aunt Bee (Frances Bavier), and Opie (Ron Howard). *(Photo by Viacom, Hollywood)*

1. The World Is Waiting for the Sunrise

FOR A long time people were, and felt, apart from each other. Communication between cities and countries took time and, as late as the nineteenth century, people's lives and global events moved at a very slow pace. Then, almost within one lifetime, in one amazing century (1840–1940), the whole concept of communication was turned inside out.

The upheaval began on the afternoon of May 24, 1844, when Samuel Morse, sitting in the United States Supreme Court building in Washington, tapped out a series of electric dots and dashes on his new telegraph machine. Forty miles away, assistants in Baltimore received and decoded the message sent through the telegraph wires stretched between the two cities. Morse's first message was "What hath God wrought?" It was an appropriate comment on the entire revolution in communication that was just beginning.

Implications of the Morse message were staggering. For the first time in human history, people in two separate cities could converse with each other instantaneously. The new invention spawned a network of telegraph cable that covered the country within a few years and soon thereafter spanned the oceans. News became a same day medium. Using dots and dashes sent over wires, people could learn of events within twenty-four hours of their occurrence anywhere in the Western world. Yet this was only the beginning. Thirty-two years after Morse's breakthrough, Alexander Graham Bell provided the next communication link, the telephone. With this, the human voice itself could be sent over the wires.

The new-found ability to bridge great distances and bring people together tickled the imaginations of nineteenth century romantic visionaries. Ignoring the more pragmatic side of human nature, they naively predicted that the new technology would be developed and expanded for great humanitarian and social reasons. Soon, it was said, leaders of the world would be linked by cable and, with such channels of instant communication open, permanent world peace would naturally result. Instead, the new inventions were used to make money. Through such major companies as Western Union and American Telephone and Telegraph, both the telegraph and telephone became a means for private communication in which, for a fee, customers could send personal and business messages. Though this was a much less exalted purpose than the overnight end to all war, it provided an equally important change in the social pattern of society. With an ever expanding flow of information, world events grew increasingly complex and, consequently, individuals, businesses, and governments wanted to communicate even faster and farther.

In 1896, Guglielmo Marconi, a young Italian working in London, demonstrated the next step in communication technology, the wireless telegraph. This device could flash dot and dash messages limited distances through the air without any connecting cable. Wireless communication was perfect for situations which could not be handled by regular telegraph and telephone wires, such as ship-to-shore contact. In July, 1897, the Marconi Wireless Telegraph Company was formed in Britain and, two years later, a branch office was established in America.

As the new century began, the Marconi company led the way in commercial message wireless service and, by the outbreak of World War I in 1914, wireless telegraphy was a thriving business in the United States. Other companies such as General Electric and Westinghouse became involved in wireless research and development as well, though they all assumed that the most lucrative aspect of wireless communication would be transmitting personal messages for customers, like the telegraph and telephone.

At the same time, there were also thousands of amateur "ham" operators who took the basic wireless design and built home machines, tapping out their own messages into the dark. A few intrepid souls such as Reginald Fessenden and Lee De Forest began crude wireless voice broadcasts, a process dubbed "radio," and, within a few years, voices filled the air as well as dots and dashes. Wireless fanatics sat for hours at their equipment, listening for distant messages and sending their own. Some young executives such as American Marconi's David Sarnoff saw great potential in the dedicated listenership and proposed that the communication giants expand beyond private messages into the area of free informational and entertainment voice broadcasting. Such suggestions were ignored because there did not seem to be any great profit in this.

When the United States entered World War I, the military took over all important wireless transmitters for use in the war effort. Following the armistice of November, 1918, the administration of President Woodrow Wilson toyed with the idea of retaining governmental control of all broadcast facilities, but the private enterprise spirit won out and commercial wireless service was restored. An important part of the plan to end governmental control of broadcasting was the promise by American Marconi to separate itself from its "foreign" (British) roots. In the fall of 1919, General Electric set up the Radio Corporation of America (RCA), which absorbed American Marconi that November. When commercial wireless service resumed in February, 1920, RCA was the largest broadcasting company in America.

Looking for a competitive edge in the postwar marketplace, the Westinghouse company hatched a scheme to expand the market for its wireless equipment by producing ready-made wireless receivers. Instead of restricting itself to the limited world of dedicated amateurs, Westinghouse aimed for the general public. In late 1920, Westinghouse set up a rooftop broadcasting station (KDKA) in Pittsburgh to provide free entertainment and information programs that could be picked up by home radio receivers. For its inaugural broadcast, KDKA carried up-to-the-minute results of the presidential race between Warren Harding and James Cox, using information telephoned in by reporters from a Pittsburgh newspaper office. Leo H. Rosenberg, a Westinghouse public relations man, read the reports on the air. In the weeks preceding the broadcast, Westinghouse launched an intense publicity campaign for both the election night coverage and its "easy to operate" radio sets. The enthusiastic response to both was much stronger than anticipated and Westinghouse went ahead with a followup to the election night program—nightly radio broadcasts running at least an hour and featuring talk, music, speeches, and some sports. The success of KDKA convinced the major industrial firms that free radio broadcasting could be used to increase sales of radio equipment dramatically. Over the next few years, Westinghouse, General Electric, American

Telephone and Telegraph, and RCA set up radio broadcasting stations in major cities across the nation.

The phenomenal growth in equipment sales that resulted from the free broadcasts turned radio into a spectacular moneymaker. Yet almost immediately the costs of providing enough entertainment to fill the stations' expanding program schedules began to escalate as well. Searching for a way to meet rising costs and further increase profits, broadcasters soon realized that a veritable gold mine of a different sort lay at their feet. Instead of merely selling tubes and radio sets, the companies operating radio stations could sell the air itself. They could charge other companies for the privilege of inserting commercial messages into their entertainment programs. With the acceptance of radio advertising by the general public, radio as a profitable commercial medium became economically feasible, with no apparent limit to its possible growth.

With the potential for so much money and power at stake, hundreds of individuals and corporations quickly set up their own radio stations throughout the country, with very little governmental oversight. By the mid-1920s, broadcasting had deteriorated into a series of vicious battles as station owners jockeyed for choice frequency allocations and arbitrarily increased their transmitting signal strength. They wanted to round up as large an audience as possible in order to attract and satisfy advertisers. For more than a year there was near chaos in the radio spectrum. At last, in desperation, the industry itself asked the government to step in and, in early 1927, Congress passed legislation establishing the Federal Radio Commission to sort out the broadcasting mess. In doing so, the government set up a basic conflict in American broadcasting that would remain present throughout its further development: the battle between "crass" commercial interests and "class" programming.

Rather than assigning individual station owners permanent control of particular frequencies as expected, the Radio Act of 1927 took a dramatically different approach and defined the airwaves as belonging to the public. It authorized the FRC to issue only limited licenses which permitted the temporary use of, but not the actual ownership of, the airwaves. Station owners were required to apply for renewal of their licenses every few years. In granting a renewal, the FRC was to judge whether, overall, the station owner had used the frequency assigned to serve the "public interest, convenience, and necessity." Though the commission was also forbidden by law to act as censor on specific programs and in day-to-day operations, this licensing procedure gave it a powerful tool of influence. Previously, profit had been the sole motivation behind

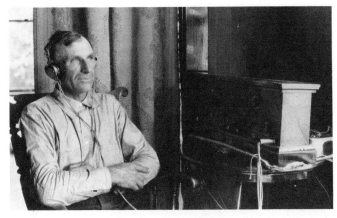

The earliest radio listeners needed headphones to hear the few stations on the air. *(National Archives)*

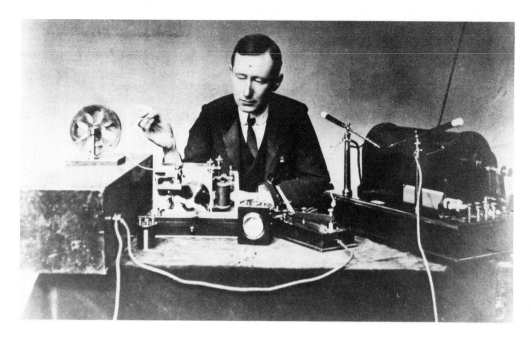

Young Guglielmo Marconi and one of his "black boxes." *(Smithsonian Institution)*

broadcasting. With the FRC sitting in judgment, station owners were forced to also make concessions to the public good that they could point to at renewal time, even though some of these concessions might not be profitable at all.

Just before the FRC was established to bring order to the airways, the major communication companies were busy themselves developing a system to meet the growing demand for radio programming across the country. AT&T, GE, RCA, and Westinghouse had been fighting each other throughout the decade for control over the various lucrative aspects of radio broadcasting and its hardware. In July, 1926, they hammered out their differences and set up the mechanism for a national source of radio programming, a "network." RCA, GE, and Westinghouse, the major producers of radio equipment, formed the National Broadcasting Company (NBC), based in New York City, to offer commercial entertainment and information programs to stations across the country. AT&T, which completely withdrew from actual station operation, provided the vital cross-country telephone cable link that made a national network possible. Programming was "fed" over AT&T lines for simultaneous broadcast by the individual stations subscribing to the NBC service. As a result, the opportunity for profit was established at each stage: equipment, commercial time, and cable use. In turn, listeners throughout the country were treated to highly professional New York based entertainment.

NBC actually consisted of two separate networks, called NBC Red and NBC Blue. Though governed by the same company, they featured different programs and could be sold to different radio stations in the same reception area, or "market." Less than a year after NBC's first broadcast in November 1926, a rival network service was organized, the Columbia Broadcasting System (CBS). The new network began operating in September, 1927, on shaky economic footing and was virtually bankrupt the night of its debut. Less than two months later, Columbia Records, its chief financial backer, pulled out of the venture. The network floundered for nearly a year before William Paley, the twenty-six-year-old son of a Philadelphia cigar manufacturer that was one of CBS's few regular sponsors, bought a controlling interest in the network and became its president. Within a few years, Paley's careful budgeting and emphasis on popular entertainers put CBS on stable financial footing.

By 1938, CBS was even strong enough to purchase Columbia Records as a wholly-owned subsidiary.

Though CBS consistently took second place to NBC in both number of hit shows and the number of listeners, the two systems were set up in essentially the same way. NBC and CBS used both "owned and operated" stations (so-called O&Os) and independent "affiliates" in their respective networks. The O&O stations, located in the major metropolitan areas, were the most valuable. The net-

April 14, 1912
David Sarnoff, a twenty-one-year-old American Marconi wireless operator, picks up a distress signal: "S.S. Titanic—Ran Into Iceberg—Sinking Fast." For seventy-two hours, the sole link to the disaster is Marconi's wireless station atop New York's Wanamaker Department Store. Wireless receives an important publicity boost with its role in the crisis.

October 17, 1919
General Electric sets up the Radio Corporation of America, which on November 20 takes control of American Marconi. David Sarnoff is RCA's commercial manager.

November 2, 1920
Westinghouse's KDKA in Pittsburgh reports on the Warren Harding-James Cox presidential race, ushering in a new approach to radio.

August 28, 1922
WEAF, AT&T's New York City radio station, broadcasts the first radio commercial: a pitch for a suburban housing development.

November 14, 1922
Just as America is beginning commercial radio, Britain goes non-commercial. The government assumes control over all broadcasting stations, setting up the British Broadcasting Corporation (BBC) to run the system without the need for advertising support.

December 1, 1922
Edward Belin gives a public demonstration of "tele-vision" in Paris. His system transmits flashes of light a few feet.

works themselves ran these as a major source of network revenue and an important outlet for network programming. Affiliates were independent stations around the country which contracted to broadcast as much of the networks' programming as they felt like, or could be pressured into accepting. Through the affiliates and O&Os, NBC and CBS maintained a virtual hammerlock over radio station programming from coast to coast. By 1930, just ten years after the KDKA breakthrough, the pattern of American network broadcasting had taken shape. The networks had become the country's primary source of radio programming, presenting top stars singing, telling stories, acting out dramas, and reporting the latest headline news.

Almost as soon as NBC and CBS began network operations, industry insiders felt a need to measure how one network was faring against the competition. Unlike newspapers and magazines, radio networks could not count how many people were steady customers, so an unofficial system of measuring audience size was instituted at the end of the 1920s. Archibald Crossley's research organization began to compile program "ratings" by calling homes and asking what radio station, if any, the folks there were listening to. It was impossible to call everyone in the country, so instead Crossley contacted people in carefully targeted small sample areas, usually consisting of several hundred or sometimes a few thousand households. Their answers were extrapolated into an estimate of how many listeners a show probably had nationwide. There was a margin of statistical error inherent in such a procedure but, for want of anything better, everyone in radio accepted "the Cross-

leys" as literally true. The early ratings confirmed the obvious— NBC was far ahead of CBS. Because a network's advertising rates depended on its popularity as determined by the Crossleys, ratings soon became crucial in decisions on what shows stayed and what shows were axed.

The most important finding of the first ratings was that radio listenership had enlarged tremendously in the late 1920s, confirming radio's status as a national mass medium. It joined two other entertainment forms that had also experienced dramatic growth in the Twenties, phonograph recordings and motion pictures. Phonographs, pioneered by Thomas Edison about the time of the birth of the telephone, began appearing in the homes of millions of Americans in the Twenties along with easy to operate and relatively cheap playback machines called "victrolas." Motion pictures, which had attained tremendous popularity without the benefit of sound since the turn of the century, made a dramatic leap forward in 1927 with the development of sound-on-film movies, called "talkies."

All three young media, to varying degrees, sought to remove the barriers between average people and popular entertainment. Yet, all three were flawed. Phonographs were severely limited in length, radio was entertainment for the sightless, and movies could only be seen at a neighborhood theater. By the mid-Twenties, enterprising scientists had developed a working model of a greater wonder, a device which could bring both sight and sound to the home virtually free of charge. It was called television.

2. Shadows in the Cave

AT THE turn of the century, the inventors who had sent first dots and dashes, then spoken words, into the air proclaimed that they were on the verge of doing the same for moving images. Over the years, the arrival of this tantalizing process, called "television," was constantly postponed. By the early 1920s, scientists had only developed methods of transmitting shadows, not detailed pictures. Nevertheless, on April 5, 1923, David Sarnoff, then RCA vice president and general manager, confidently declared to a meeting of the RCA board of directors that soon "television will make it possible for those at home to see, as well as hear, what is going on at the broadcast station." He urged the company to enter the potentially lucrative new field, predicting that eventually television would be in the home of every American. A decade before, executives had fumbled the lead in radio broadcasting by ignoring a Sarnoff memo proposing entry into that field, and RCA did not intend to repeat the mistake for television. Along with General Electric and Westinghouse, the company began to invest more and more money in television development and research.

Ironically, an outside independent American inventor, Charles Francis Jenkins, beat these powerful companies and produced the world's first working television on his own. On June 13, 1925, Jenkins brought Curtis Wilbur, the Secretary of the Navy; Stephen Davis, the Acting Secretary of Commerce; and other dignitaries to his laboratory at 1519 Connecticut Avenue in Washington. There, they watched moving images, transmitted from an old Navy radio station five miles away, appear on a ten-by-eight-inch screen. The action sequences were simple: one consisted of scenes from a motion picture film; another showed the vanes of a small Dutch windmill rotating in the air. Four months later, an independent Scottish inventor, John Baird, performed a similar experiment in his London studio. His system carried the image and sound of a fifteen-year-old boy and "Stookie Bill," a ventriloquist's puppet.

These first television systems were based on a mechanical process that used rapidly spinning disks containing spiral perforations to transmit the action. The spinning disks in the camera and receiving unit would "see" a rapid succession of tiny flashes of reflected light through the perforations. If the disks were spinning fast enough, the tiny flashes would be perceived by the human eye as forming a coherent, moving image. The process was akin to the techniques used to create the illusion of movement in film, where a series of still photos flashed by so quickly that the subjects appeared to move. Though very awkward and bulky, mechanical television was only slightly more complicated than the radios of the day and, as late as 1930, amateur mechanics magazines included instructions on how to build television sets at home from scratch. It was generally felt that if television progressed at the same rapid rate as radio, within five years the system could easily be in homes throughout the country. Such predictions appeared to be more than idle speculation in the late 1920s, when it seemed that science fiction could barely stay ahead of science fact.

In March, 1927, Fritz Lang's German film concerning life in the future, "Metropolis," opened in New York City. Among the film's many special effects was an elaborate television-telephone system used by the industrial wizard who ruled the fictional city. A mere thirty days later, such a system was used in real life, tying together New York, New Jersey, and Washington. This intercity transmission was viewed at the Bell Telephone labs in New York City. Secretary of Commerce Herbert Hoover delivered an opening congratulatory message from Washington via cable (his voice was carried by telephone) and then a comedy skit was sent over the air from nearby New Jersey. In this, a vaudevillian named A. Dolan told a few Irish jokes, then donned blackface and told "darky" jokes. Sent out as a moving image made up of eighteen horizontal "lines of resolution," the entire show appeared as a bluish-green hazy picture on a two-by-three-inch screen. Nonetheless, on April 8, 1927, the *New York Times* proudly proclaimed in a front page headline: "Far Off Speakers Seen As Well As Heard Here." A subheadline added: "Like a Photo Come to Life."

The excitement expressed by the *New York Times* infected the electronics industry as a whole. David Sarnoff called the event inspiring and said that it proved television had "passed the point of conjecture . . . the possibilities of the new art are as boundless as the imagination." The Federal Radio Commission optimistically declared that "visual radio is just around the corner" and set aside frequencies for the new medium, just above the AM radio band.

At first, it seemed as if all the enthusiasm was justified. In January, 1928, GE and RCA held the first public demonstration of home television sets, in Schenectady, New York. David Sarnoff appeared on the promotional show, calling it "an epoch-making development." Though at that point GE had produced only three of the bulky, spinning disk sets for home use, a larger number did go on sale later that year for $75 each. In May, 1928, General Electric's Schenectady station, W2XCW (later WRGB), became the world's first regularly operating television station, simulcasting the FRC to lift the ban on commercial television broadcasting, but the commission disagreed. Though continuing to encourage experimentation and expansion in television, it felt that approval of commercial broadcasting on a par with radio would have to wait for further technical improvements as well as a significant increase in station operation and set sales. Broadcasters felt that such developments hinged on commercial backing, but the argument soon became irrelevant as two factors combined to stop the television boom cold: the introduction of a new television system and the beginning of the Great Depression.

Since 1919, Vladimir Zworykin, a Russian immigrant, had been hard at work for Westinghouse and, later, RCA developing an alternative method of transmitting TV pictures, the all-electronic television system. In 1925, he demonstrated an early model iconoscope, the "eye" of an electronic TV camera and, by 1928, Zworykin had perfected the receiving end of the process, the kinescope. The all-electronic television system used an electron gun to "spray" tiny flashes of light into very thin horizontal lines of resolution, from the top to the bottom of a TV screen. This accomplished the same task as the spinning disk, but with a much smaller device that provided greater clarity. Because the electronic system operated at a faster rate than the mechanical one, less light was needed to illuminate the subjects in the studio and the resulting picture appeared better defined and more lifelike. As television technology improved, the number of lines used to form the picture increased, and the images became even sharper.

From the start, mechanical television had been awkward, bulky, and incapable of a very sharp picture. The new electronic system solved all these problems but imposed one new one: the two systems were incompatible. A mechanical TV set could not pick up the images sent out by an electronic system, and vice versa. Because the electronic system provided a more saleable product in the long run, it was only a matter of time before the industry would adopt it. As a short term result, all the mechanical spinning disk TV

programs with General Electric's Schenectady radio station, WGY, for a half-hour three days a week. At this point, television was primarily viewed as an adjunct to radio, not a competitor. In the experimental simulcasts by RCA and GE, television was literally visual radio, merely adding pictures to the audio then being broadcast on radio.

Throughout 1928 and most of 1929, enthusiasm for the new medium continued to grow. W2XCW broadcast the first outdoor scene, the first television play, and even covered the acceptance speech by Democratic presidential candidate Alfred E. Smith from Albany, New York. In July, John Baird, in London, successfully sent out the first color television images: a red and blue scarf and a man sticking out his tongue. The Federal Radio Commission began issuing noncommercial television station licenses so that an expanded schedule of experimental broadcasts could be conducted. RCA received one of the first licenses and, in the fall of 1928, W2XBS (later WNBC) went on the air in New York City. Because no human could stand extended stretches under the intense light needed for the experimental broadcasts, W2XBS used a statue of Felix the Cat, which slowly revolved on a platter, as its moving test pattern.

By the fall of 1929, John Baird had begun regular television service in London and twenty-six stations were operating in America, including five in the New York area. Programming was spotty and set sales were slow, but broadcasters felt the possibility for real economic growth in television was almost at hand. They urged

One of General Electric's early experiments with the cumbersome "spinning disk" mechanical television system. *(Smithsonian Institution)*

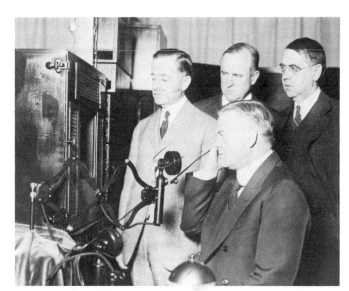

Secretary of Commerce Herbert Hoover (seated) takes part in the first public inter-city television broadcast. *(Reproduced with permission of AT&T Co.)*

sets were doomed to obsolescence and this meant at least a five-year hiatus in the expansion of television into American homes. Consumers and station operators might have been able to absorb such an expensive television adjustment without too much trouble, if not for the Great Depression.

The Wall Street "crash" of October, 1929, sounded the death knell for early television. Financing for experimentation and set construction evaporated. Most American station owners could not afford the changeover from the mechanical to the electronic system, so they went off the air. No new sets were being produced and there was little chance that very many people outside New York City would be watching anyway. Only the two giants of American radio broadcasting, NBC and CBS, could afford to keep television alive.

With personal income plummeting, radio became the average citizen's cheapest source of entertainment. Situation comedies such as *Amos and Andy* and *The Rise of the Goldbergs,* soap operas such as *One Man's Family,* and entertainers such as Rudy Vallee kept people glued to their radios and kept the networks in the black. NBC and CBS used the income from their successful network radio operations to subsidize flashy moves in television. In 1931, NBC received permission to build a large, powerful TV antenna atop the Empire State building. CBS opened its own New York TV station, W2XAB (later WCBS) with New York Mayor Jimmy Walker presiding at the ceremony, and Kate Smith and George Gershwin providing the music. W2XAB then seized the initiative from NBC's W2XBS and commenced a fairly regular schedule of entertainment and discussion programming in the evening for those few in New York who had receivers. CBS television even covered the 1932 presidential election.

On October 11, 1932, the "stage and screen division" of the Democratic National Committee held a thirty-minute political rally on W2XAB. Master of ceremonies Wayne Pierson introduced celebrities who, in turn, explained why they were supporting Franklin Roosevelt. On election day, November 8, the *New York Times* exalted:

> . . . television set owners, believed to be a few hundred, will catch a glimpse of the future when they see the way Americans will get the election returns in the '40s. W2XAB will

televise pictures of the candidates and bulletins, beginning at 8:00 P.M.

Two weeks before Roosevelt's inauguration, though, W2XAB suspended broadcasts when it became impossible to overcome the effects of the worsening depression. Though CBS was in solid financial shape overall, television was proving to be a dead-end investment for the time being. The problem was the lack of sets. Almost everyone already had a radio, but only a handful of people possessed TV sets. Even though RCA probably could have begun mass production of commercial electronic televisions by 1935, very few people would have been able to afford one.

The healthiest Western economy in the mid-1930s was that of Germany under Adolf Hitler. There, the National Socialist (Nazi) Party was strongly committed to propaganda efforts in the popular arts and mass media, and it set up the first relatively public electronic television system in the world. On March 22, 1935, after six months of extensive testing, the Reichs Rundfunk in Berlin began three-day-a-week broadcasts, at 180 lines, using the world's first mobile TV units. The Reich, like RCA, was capable of producing TV sets for home use in 1935, but wanted to wait until the price could be reduced enough to put television in the reach of the average German. In place of home sets, the Nazis temporarily compromised by setting up eleven viewing rooms in Berlin, where members of the public, after obtaining a free ticket, could view one of the ninety-minute film programs broadcast via television. By January, 1936, transmissions consisting of live and filmed segments were increased to one hour each day (with repeats). In August, the Berlin Olympics were televised to twenty-eight public viewing rooms. The Germans used three cameras and two mobile vans, but it is not known how they handled play-by-play and color commentary. The announcers were no doubt shamelessly biased

---

January 3, 1930
   David Sarnoff becomes president of RCA.

July 21, 1931
   CBS begins its television operation with the birth of W2XAB in New York.

February 15, 1932
   The George Burns and Gracie Allen Show. (CBS Radio). After some well-received guest appearances on NBC in 1931, George and Gracie are snapped up by CBS for a radio show of their own.

May 2, 1932
   The Jack Benny Program. (CBS Radio). The master of comic timing takes to the air. Benny popularizes the concept of a "family" of supporting players for a comedy-variety program, adding Don Wilson in 1934 and both Eddie "Rochester" Anderson and Dennis Day in 1937.

January 30, 1933
   The Lone Ranger. Tales of the Western masked man establish a new radio network. The program starts out on just one station, WXYZ in Detroit, but is soon picked up by other major independents, including WGN in Chicago and WOR in New York. In 1934, they form the Mutual Broadcasting System (MBS).

February 23, 1933
   CBS's W2XAB suspends television broadcasts.

March 22, 1935
   The Nazi TV network goes public.

A mid-1930s German prototype of home television sets. *(National Archives)*

for the home team, and, like Hitler himself, had to be publicly humiliated when the record-breaking performance of black American Jesse Owens triumphed over the best of Germany's "Aryan" athletes.

German home TV sets went on sale in July, 1939, but the outbreak of war two months later prevented many sales. However, telecasting in Berlin was soon increased to six hours a day in order to boost war morale and entertain the soldiers in hospitals. The Berlin broadcasts did not cease until Allied bombing destroyed the German transmitter on November 23, 1943, though Nazi-controlled telecasts continued from the Eifel Tower in Paris until August 16, 1944.

Right behind the Germans in bringing electronic television to the public were the British. The government-run British Broadcasting Corporation (BBC) had taken over John Baird's fuzzy thirty-line mechanical television operations in August, 1932. Three years later, the BBC signed off to retool for high definition, all-electronic television. The necessary new receivers went on sale in London in August, 1936, as the BBC resumed test broadcasts. On November 2, 1936, the BBC officially inaugurated its electronic television service, operating each weekday for an hour in the afternoon and an hour in the evening. It acquired its first mobile vans in May, 1937, in time to cover the coronation parade of King George VI. Three cameras sent the scene to an estimated 50,000 people watching on 3,000 sets. Before World War II intervened, France, Russia, Italy, and Japan also commenced high-definition electronic television service, with Japan broadcasting the first televised baseball game eight years before America.

As a result of the length and severity of the Depression in America, the United States lost the lead in television development to Europe. In the mid-1930s, television in the U.S. was largely moribund, having almost shut down completely after the "false start" of mechanical TV. It took a very powerful company and a very persistent man to pump some life back into the industry in the middle of the Depression. The company was RCA and the man was David Sarnoff.

3. The Dawn

JUST as Nazi Germany began its regular television broadcasting service in 1935, David Sarnoff, by then president of RCA, acted to revive television in America. Though the lingering economic depression made mass market set sales impractical, he was determined to keep the idea of television before the public while firmly establishing RCA and NBC as the unquestioned leaders in the medium. At a meeting of RCA stockholders on May 7, 1935, Sarnoff announced a $1 million program to take television "out of the lab" and "around the corner," saying that:

> In the sense that the laboratory has supplied us with the basic means of lifting the curtain of space from scenes and activities at a distance, it may be said that television is here. But as a system of sight transmission and reception, comparable in coverage and service to the present nationwide system of sound broadcasting, television is *not* here, nor around the corner.

Sarnoff's plan called for experimental broadcasts that would showcase the dramatic technical and artistic breakthroughs in the quality of television and, at the same time, generate public curiosity and excitement. Television was to put aside the 1920s concept of radio simulcasting and present its own programming instead. Picture quality was set at the much sharper transmitting signal of 343 lines and new receivers were to be placed in highly visible locations for easy public viewing. RCA was practically the only company in America capable of mounting such an expansive campaign then, due largely to the continued success of its network radio operations. Even though the end of simulcasting was, in effect, the quiet declaration that television and radio were to go their separate ways, radio would continue to pay for the very expensive experiments in television for nearly two decades.

After fourteen months of construction and testing, NBC's W2XBS began the all-electronic, high definition phase of American television on July 7, 1936. David Sarnoff presided over a special telecast, which featured comedian Ed Wynn. There was no effort to rush electronic TV sets onto the market because both the technical engineers and program producers wanted to use the experimental phase to discover what would and would not work on television. Besides, the government's ban on commercial TV was still in effect, though this "limitation" actually helped NBC's program producers. They could run any film and stage any play they wished without having to worry about paying for commercial authorization. As a result, over the next three years, W2XBS aired a wide range of material.

Even though RCA did not push set sales during this experimental phase, executives still felt that it was very important to keep news about television constantly before the public, so every few months reporters were brought to NBC's New York studios in Rockefeller Center to witness another test broadcast. During 1937 and 1938 they saw Gertrude Lawrence's play "Susan and God" (with the original Broadway cast), humorist George Ade's vaudeville act "The Mayor and the Manicure," Claudette Colbert in the film version of "I Met Him in Paris," and an adaptation of a Sherlock Holmes short story, "The Adventure of the Three Garridebs." Just before Christmas, 1937, W2XBS obtained America's first two mobile TV vans and they immediately began to roam within twenty-five miles of New York City, sending signals back to the studio transmitter via microwave. For the time, these telecasts were quite newsworthy and the press usually came away suitably impressed (reviewers called the mobile broadcast of a fire "very graphic"). Often, though, the writers swallowed whole the NBC press relations material that touted television as a force that would soon revolutionize entertainment, if not the world. A typical news report described the medium as:

> [a] vital new form of electronic theater that augurs an exciting and challenging new cultural era . . . the imperishable wonders of a vibrant and articulate stage will be spread to the far corners of the land . . .

They were falling into the same trap as their predecessors. Telephones were going to bring world peace, but instead brought pay phones. Radio was going to bring grand opera and learned discussion into the home, but instead delivered cigarette and soap commercials. Television's cultural visionaries saw the amazing tube as nothing less than the savior of the nation's artistic soul, while television's business planners saw it as a moneymaker potentially more lucrative than network radio.

Even though W2XBS was the only New York City station operating in 1937, technicians were already hard at work on a system that would make possible a national television network similar to the existing radio network. Due to technical limitations, television could not use regular AT&T phone lines for long distance hookups as radio did, so it was necessary to devise a thicker, more complex cable, called a "coaxial cable," and construct an alternate cable system throughout the country. In November, 1937, the first AT&T coaxial cable link was established, connecting New York with Philadelphia, which also had one television station in operation. The Philco company's W3XE (later KYW) began to occasion-

November 2, 1936

The BBC officially inaugurates its high definition, all-electronic television service. England is the first country in which home sets capable of receiving the improved signal are actually put on sale.

January 25, 1937

The Guiding Light. (NBC-Red Radio). The start of one of the few top radio soap operas to survive the challenge of television. In the early 1950s, it makes a smooth transition to video.

November 9, 1937

The first link in the chain. The New York to Philadelphia television coaxial cable opens.

March 13, 1938

CBS World News Roundup. (CBS Radio). Edward R. Murrow makes his first on-the-air broadcast for CBS's new daily news show, which emphasizes on-the-spot reporting.

July 20, 1938

The Department of Justice sues the eight major Hollywood studios for anti-trust violations, claiming they unfairly control both the production and the projection of movies.

August 8, 1938

Paramount Pictures, one of the eight major Hollywood studios, buys an interest in DuMont Labs.

October 29, 1939

CBS's New York TV station, W2XAB, returns to the air.

January 12, 1940

General Electric's television station in Schenectady is linked to New York, via microwave.

ally share programs with W2XBS via the cable, though it was usually a New York-to-Philadelphia sharing.

NBC's W2XBS practically monopolized domestic television progress through the late Thirties. In August, 1937, CBS served notice that, after letting its New York City license lie dormant for more than four years, it would reinject network competition into the television market by soon resuming its telecasts. It announced plans for constructing television studios in Grand Central Station, though CBS's W2XAB did not actually return to the air until October, 1939. During that time, David Sarnoff moved NBC and RCA into the next phase of their expansion initiative.

By early 1939, the American economy had picked up and RCA felt it was time to launch a full-scale drive to promote home television set sales. W2XBS was technically capable of presenting reasonably high quality signals and programming from both in the studio and on remote, so Sarnoff decided to put the station on a regular daily broadcast schedule which could be effectively publicized. As a dramatic kick-off event, NBC covered the opening of the 1939 New York World's Fair.

At 12:30 P.M. Sunday, April 30, 1939, the 200 television sets already in use in New York City and the twelve special receivers at the RCA Pavilion at the fair, carried a milestone in American broadcasting. Producer Burke Crotty directed the one-camera program, opening with a graceful view of the Trylon and Perisphere (the symbols of the fair), sweeping over to the Court of Peace, and resting on the opening day crowd and assembled VIPs. President Franklin Roosevelt (the first president to appear on television) delivered an opening address, as did many other dignitaries, but once again it was David Sarnoff of RCA who captured the moment:

Now we add sight to sound. It is with a feeling of humbleness that I come to this moment of announcing the birth, in this country, of a new art so important in its implication that it is bound to affect all society. It is an art which shines like a torch in the troubled world.

It was such prose that, four years later, earned Sarnoff the title Father of American Television.

On Monday, May 1, the day after the fair opened, the first American electronic television sets went on sale. There were twenty-five models, ranging from $200 to $1,000. Throughout the fair, an NBC mobile van remained stationed at the RCA exhibit, attracting large crowds of curious viewers who delighted in seeing themselves on television. However, there was no immediate rush to buy home sets. Though not as awkward as the old mechanical models, the new sets were still rather large and bulky. Many included a complicated tilted-mirror viewing device because it was feared that looking directly at the screen itself could cause radiation damage to the eyes. NBC confidently pressed on with its expanded broadcasting schedule anyway and, during the next few months, W2XBS racked up numerous television firsts: first baseball game on American TV; first TV professional baseball game; first TV prize boxing bout; first TV football game; first TV professional football game; first TV college basketball game; first TV professional hockey game; and the first televised circus.

These events were usually covered by one NBC mobile van which was severely restricted by the limitations of the equipment. There was only one television camera in a van and no means for the announcer to monitor the on-air signal. As a result, it became very difficult to coordinate the descriptions and pictures in complicated wide-open team sports such as baseball and hockey. Boxing and wrestling, on the other hand, were much easier to follow because both involved only two contestants and took place in small, well-lit arenas. Announcers such as Bill Stern, Dennis James, and Ben Grauer could sit ringside, reasonably certain that their descriptions would match the actions on the screen. Consequently, early television favored the one-on-one boxing and wrestling contests over major team sports, and sports announcers became some of the first familiar television personalities, turning up throughout the broadcast day—even on non-sports events. In addition to his play-by-play duties, Dennis James hosted two weekly shows, *Dennis James Sports Parade* and *Television Roof* (scenery and interviews from atop the Rockefeller Center). Ben Grauer did the special "play-by-play" report on the festivities surrounding the New York premiere of "Gone With the Wind" on December 19, 1939.

In spite of NBC's many well-publicized events and the return to the air of CBS's W2XAB in October, fewer than 1,000 TV sets were sold in New York by November, 1939. The Federal Communications Commission (successor to the FRC) analyzed the lack of public support for television and concluded that people would not buy sets until there were more stations and better programs available. NBC felt the best chance for such growth in the industry rested in commercial television, but the FCC felt that there were a number of vexing technical problems still to be worked out before opening up TV for sponsors. CBS, having just returned to active television broadcasting, was inclined to support the FCC's more cautious approach. Executives at both NBC and CBS did agree that one of the major stumbling blocks to popular acceptance of television was its monochrome nature—television pictures appeared only in black and white. Most agreed that television in color would be more appealing and saleable, but just how and when to add color to the system posed a perplexing problem.

The television industry's uncertainty over color was similar to problems the movie industry faced thirty years before in adding sound and color to film. When movies were developed at the turn of the century, some argued that commercial motion pictures should be withheld until the entire system was perfected and color, sound, and depth could be incorporated into the projection process. Others felt that the public would be willing to accept silent black and white two-dimensional films until something better came along, and this view prevailed. It proved to be an astute business decision and, as a result, the film industry made a great deal of money on silent pictures while color and sound techniques were worked out.

In television, successful but crude color broadcasting had been demonstrated in 1928, only three years after the first black and white transmissions, but the development of a system for acceptable high quality color images proved to be a very difficult next step. With initial black and white set sales very slow in 1939, the industry faced the question: Should it delay the promotion and mass production of black and white sets until a color system could be developed? Tackling the problem head on, RCA unveiled a prototype color system to the FCC in February, 1940. Seven months later, CBS proposed its own system. The two differed in various technical aspects but were identical in one vital respect: they were incompatible with black and white television sets. Both proposed color systems were based on the spinning disk method used for television in its mechanical era. The electronic black and white sets then in use would merely pick up static when trying to tune in a color broadcast. This meant that unless a compatible system could be devised, one day home owners would have to buy new sets specifically designed for color. In early 1941, when NBC and CBS began test color broadcasts, the prospect of junking all the TV sets then in use did not appear to be a distasteful solution. There were only 3,000 black and white TV sets in New York City and far fewer in other major cities. Throughout the country, there were fewer than ten TV stations on the air.

The debate over the proposed color TV systems was just the latest battle in the decade-long rivalry between the two major radio networks, NBC and CBS. All through the 1930s virtually all the important progress in American television had come from either one network or the other. Though some other major industrial firms were involved in local television operations (Zenith in Chicago, Philco in Philadelphia, and General Electric in Schenectady), it was generally assumed that the two big radio chains would monopolize any future system of network television. One company, however, dared to challenge NBC and CBS on their own turf, DuMont Labs.

Allen B. DuMont, who had worked with Charles Jenkins in the earliest days of television, had set up his own research corporation in New Jersey in 1931 and, during the decade, DuMont became an important electronics manufacturer. When NBC and CBS appeared ready to resume full-scale TV operations in the late 1930s, DuMont announced that it would join them—as a full-fledged television broadcasting power mass producing TV sets, applying for its own stations across the country, and setting up its own national network. Such a grandiose plan required more financial backing than the healthy, but limited, electronics base of DuMont, so in August, 1938, DuMont sold about 40% of its stock to Paramount Pictures. With this influx of capital, DuMont's TV sets were right beside RCA's in the department store showrooms when TV sets went on sale in May, 1939. That same year, DuMont applied for a TV station in New York City to serve as headquarters for its network operations.

DuMont faced two critical problems, aside from financial resources, as it tried to start its own television network. The company had no established stars and no experience in running any broadcast stations. NBC and CBS had a ready-made pool of radio talent (performers, producers, technicians) that could be shifted to television when the time came. DuMont had a ready-made pool of technicians, but had to start from scratch in finding creative programming talent. In the crucial area of signing up affiliates for a television network, NBC and CBS also held a tremendous advantage because they had been in radio since the 1920s. Most of the firms beginning local TV operations were companies that owned radio stations. They were used to dealing with NBC and CBS and they expected to do so again as soon as network television became feasible. DuMont had to first become a broadcaster itself, then develop a working relationship with the other broadcasters in order to win a large number of TV affiliates in the future.

Essential to the DuMont strategy was a healthy string of owned and operated stations located in key cities. These formed the nucleus of any network because they allowed it to showcase programs and stars for potential affiliates. Once commercial television began turning a profit, the O&Os would also serve as an important source of income for the network. Though DuMont lacked the program experience and radio network income of NBC and CBS, at this early stage of television its entry into the field was a realistic business gamble. It was already a feisty competitor to RCA in the manufacture and sale of sets and, once it obtained its O&Os, DuMont

March 23, 1940

Truth or Consequences. (NBC-Red Radio). Ralph Edwards becomes radio's number one gamesman as the host of a slick stunt show. Contestants who fail to answer simple quiz questions must "suffer the consequences" and participate in some outlandish, usually slapstick, "punishment."

April 13, 1940

The FCC grants DuMont its first television station license: W2XWV in New York.

June 24, 1940

The Republican National Convention opens in Philadelphia and becomes the first convention to be televised.

February 20, 1941

NBC begins on-the-air tests of its color television system.

July 1, 1941

Commercial television begins in the United States with Lowell Thomas, *Truth or Consequences,* and *Charades.*

October 14, 1943

NBC sells its Blue radio network to Edward Noble. In 1945, Blue is officially renamed ABC.

October 18, 1943

Perry Mason. (CBS Radio). Erle Stanley Gardner's literary sleuth turns up as a foppish playboy in a sudsy daytime serial starring Bartlett Robinson.

April 27, 1944

CBS asks the FCC to kick television "upstairs" to UHF in order to facilitate the shift to color broadcasting.

May 21, 1944

DuMont's New York TV station, W2XWV, at last goes commercial as WABD.

By 1937, television had won a spot in London's home entertainment showrooms alongside radio. *(National Archives)*

could develop its own stars and be ready to flourish when television really caught on.

Into all this, a monkey wrench was thrown to jam DuMont's expected growth. On May 8, 1940, RCA claimed to the FCC that DuMont was trying to get inferior technical standards adopted for television to protect the film industry because DuMont was really controlled by Paramount Pictures, its major stockholder. The immediate charge went nowhere, but the underlying claim stuck. Paramount Pictures, though not owning a majority of Du-Mont stock, was strong enough to elect half of the eight-member board of directors and the FCC ruled that, under its definition, Paramount controlled DuMont. Therefore, the FCC would treat the two companies as one entity. This distinction had important ramifications because the commission had set an ownership limit of five O&Os for any television broadcaster. In 1940, DuMont had already obtained a license for New York and was applying for one in Washington. Paramount had applied for licenses in Los Angeles and Chicago. These three applications were granted in June, 1940, but, according to the FCC, if either company received another television license, the DuMont-Paramount "combine" would reach its limit of five O&Os. After that, neither would be granted licenses for any more stations. Paramount and DuMont contended that they were not the same organization and so deserved more stations. DuMont pointed out that if it was to become a creditable national television network, it had to have a full slate of O&Os operational in the major cities as soon as possible. As long as the FCC stuck to its interpretation of DuMont's ties with Paramount, those hopes were mortally wounded.

Despite the complications facing experimental television at the

beginning of the 1940s, spurts of technical and program expansion continued. DuMont's first station, W2XWV in New York, signed on in October, 1940. In June, NBC used a "network" of three television stations to cover a major news event, the Republican National Convention in Philadelphia. Four NBC cameras sent twenty-five hours of political shenanigans live over Philco's station in Philadelphia, via coaxial cable to NBC's W2XBS in New York, and then over the new microwave link to the General Electric station in Schenectady. As the general public watched (if the elite few who then owned TV sets could be called general), the convention delegates selected a dark horse candidate, Wendell Willkie, as their presidential nominee. The Democratic convention was held in Chicago, far from any coaxial cable connection, so television was limited to newsreel reports of the renomination of President Franklin Roosevelt. Election night television coverage in November, though, was the first to go beyond merely posting vote totals. NBC even brought in as announcers radio news star Lowell Thomas and veteran broadcaster Leo Rosenberg (who had performed in the vanguard radio election night coverage on KDKA in 1920).

Through 1941, NBC continued to urge the FCC to approve commercial television, feeling that it was the only way enough money would ever be available to develop entertaining programs to attract a larger audience. In May, 1941, the commission at last agreed and announced that commercial television could begin in America on July 1, 1941. To qualify for commercial status, stations were required by the FCC to be on the air for at least fifteen hours a week and to broadcast at an improved transmitting signal of 525 lines. The FCC also authorized new call letters to take effect when the stations began commercial telecasts. In New York, the only city in which all three fledgling networks were already in direct competition, NBC's W2XBS would become WNBT, CBS's W2XAB would become WCBW, and DuMont's W2XWV would become WABD.

Appropriately, W2XBS, the main pioneering force in American television, was the first to make the changeover, transforming itself into WNBT at 1:30 P.M. on July 1, 1941. WNBT's first commercial rates were $120 an hour during the evening and $60 for an hour during the day. The first day's broadcast schedule contained nothing momentous—the station did not have the money for it yet—and the first commercial was very simple. During a time, temperature, and weather report, a watch bearing the name Bulova was shown ticking for sixty seconds. That was it. No catchy jingle. No pretty girls. Just a ticking watch.

The programming itself was equally primitive. Lowell Thomas read the news, but, without accompanying visuals, his newscast was essentially just a radio program. In contrast, quiz and game shows offered very cheap and easy visual action (slapstick, stunts, excited contestants), so the day's schedule was overflowing with them. Ralph Edwards hosted a test video episode of *Truth or Consequences,* sponsored by Ivory Soap. *Uncle Jim's Question Bee,* another quiz show, followed. Soon thereafter came *Charades,* the animated parlor game which quickly became a television cliché—it was what every run-of-the-mill programmer instinctively thought of when ordered to come up with something "new and visual" for television.

NBC soon applied for permission to upgrade to commercial status its stations in Washington, Philadelphia, and Chicago. Throughout the country, twenty-three television stations were either on or in the process of construction, including Paramount's Chicago station, WBKB (later WLS). Television seemed ready to take off at last. Once again, though, outside forces intervened to put the medium back into the freezer.

On May 27, 1941, just after the FCC authorized commercial television broadcasts, President Roosevelt declared an "unlimited national emergency" as America found itself being drawn into World War II. War came to the United States on December 7, 1941, when the Japanese bombed Pearl Harbor in Hawaii. CBS's WCBW broadcast an unprecedented nine-hour news special on the attack, anchored by Dick Hubbel, but then television practically shut down. American industry was ordered to cut down on unnecessary production and devote itself to the huge war effort. Station construction was halted. All but nine stations went off the air, and those that remained drastically cut their schedules. The three network stations in New York went from broadcasting on four nights a week to just one. By the end of 1942, NBC and CBS had locked their studios, falling back on filmed shorts, a few live sports remotes, and civil defense instruction films. Hospitals requisitioned as many TV sets as they could find for the entertainment of wounded servicemen. Police stations acquired sets so that the men could take notes on the generally dull civil defense flicks. All production of home TV sets ceased. The few thousand who owned sets had to treat them with love and care because anybody with enough technical skill to fix a TV set had been absorbed by the military. If a set stopped working, it had to sit idle "for the duration."

During the war years, the most important development in American broadcasting was the government-induced divestiture by NBC of its Blue radio network. The process began one day after the

FCC approved the beginning of commercial television in 1941, when the commission issued a proposed new set of rules to govern the relations between radio networks and their affiliates. The FCC felt that NBC and CBS enjoyed a near monopoly of the airwaves, so most of the new rules were aimed at loosening the hold the networks had on the operation of local stations. The radio networks could not prevent their affiliates from airing a few shows offered by other networks, and the duration of contracts tying a station to a particular network was reduced from five to two years. The networks were also ordered to give local stations more advance warning (fifty-six days) before exercising their "option" to reserve a time slot for a network program (a process called "option time").

In giving affiliates a stronger voice in their own affairs, the FCC hoped to encourage the growth of new networks. Its final rule went a step further and, in effect, ordered the creation of a new network by stating that no network could operate two competing chains at the same time. This section applied solely and specifically to NBC which, for years, had run both its Red and Blue networks, maintaining itself as number one in the radio ratings. NBC fought this ruling in the courts for two years, but lost. In October, 1943, NBC sold the Blue network to Edward J. Noble for $8 million. In June, 1945, it was renamed the American Broadcasting Company (ABC). Although Blue-ABC was a new network in a legal sense, it retained most of its old identity, hit programs, and top personalities in the transfer of owners. It even came equipped with three radio O&Os. For television, the arrival of ABC meant that

"Now we add sight to sound." The symbols of the 1939 New York World's Fair: (c.) The Trylon and Perisphere. (Reproduced with permission of AT&T Co.)

there was a new competitor applying for television stations, though ABC had to play "catch-up ball" for years—it was even behind DuMont.

The tide of World War II turned in favor of the United States and its allies in 1943 and, under the glow of this optimism, the networks began to awaken television from its nearly comatose state. The three New York TV stations had each been operating only one night of the week (NBC's WNBT on Monday; CBS's WCBW on Thursday; and DuMont's W2XWV on Sunday), but by New Year's, 1944, all three had expanded their broadcast hours to fill each night of the week (DuMont on Sunday, Tuesday, and Wednesday; NBC on Monday and Saturday; and CBS on Thursday and Friday).

NBC and DuMont were especially optimistic about launching full-scale network television operations as soon as the war ended. DuMont was anxiously awaiting the FCC's go-ahead to change W2XWV from experimental to commercial status and, in preparation, it was trying hard to gather performing and production talent. The network brought in Broadway producer Irwin Shane to organize a regular live dramatic series, *Television Workshop,* which won critical praise for its version of "Romeo and Juliet." Doug Allen acted as host of another studio program, *Thrills and Chills.* The title was slightly misleading, though, because Allen merely conducted interviews with studio guests who narrated their own travel films.

Through the war years, DuMont was the only network doing any live-in-studio productions but, on April 10, 1944, NBC at last reopened its TV studios after two and one-half years of old films and remote broadcasts. Network and FCC dignitaries were on hand to introduce what was boldly billed as the first world premiere movie on television, "Patrolling the Ether." It turned out to be a turgid two-reel MGM short which dramatized the FCC's work in tracking down illegal radio transmitters. Still, a brand-new film short for television was something to brag about in 1944. Since television's earliest days, and especially during the slow war years, programmers had plugged in virtually any film, regardless of subject matter or age, just to fill dead spots in the schedule.

On May 25, little more than a month after resuming studio programming, NBC was involved in one of the first instances on record of television censorship. Eddie Cantor, one of the first big radio stars to appear on television, was in the middle of a duet with Nora Martin on "We're Having a Baby, My Baby and Me," when the sound was cut off. The song was considered "suggestive." As Cantor commenced a hula-type dance, the cameraman was ordered to change the focus of the picture to a soft blur.

CBS reopened its studios on May 5, 1944, with the premiere of the *CBS Television News* (hosted by Ned Calmer), a fifteen-minute wrapup of news headlines using newsreel film. Under the direction of a recently hired producer, Worthington "Tony" Miner, CBS also began to develop entertainment shows. Miner's strategy was simple: He took successful CBS radio shows (usually game shows) and brought them to TV to see if they worked with video added. Lacking NBC's years of television program experience, CBS would have preferred a few more years of experimentation while the technicians, bureaucrats, and producers sorted out television's teething pain problems: program development, frequency allocation, and color. CBS urged that color be added to television before any postwar expansion took place, feeling that it would be best to abandon the few thousand TV sets then in service and move television to a new set of frequencies which would be more adaptable to color broadcasting. Though it developed some new shows, CBS maintained that television was still in the "experimental" stage. Consequently, it did not join in the early bidding for new television station licenses in other cities and limited television operations to its sole outlet in New York City.

A milestone in reverse took place in the summer of 1944 as the two major political parties staged their presidential nominating conventions and, for the last time, disregarded television. Both conventions took place in Chicago, even though the city was not yet connected to the minuscule coaxial cable system. Just as in the 1940 Democratic convention, East Coast viewers had to be satisfied with just same-day newsreel coverage. The established newsreel firms (RKO-Pathé and 20th Century-Movietone), which were actually more concerned with producing reports for the nation's movie theaters, flew the footage to New York for the special broadcasts. Only one concession was made to television at the 1944 conventions: Republican Governor Earl Warren of California pre-filmed his keynote address so that it could be aired on the three-station NBC network as he was delivering it in Chicago.

While the politicians practically ignored television that summer, major advertisers were beginning to seriously consider the commercial possibilities of the medium. There had not been much chance to dabble in commercial television before the war but, once peacetime began and things returned to normal, Madison Avenue felt that video advertising might be worth trying. The first major ad man to publicly display his faith in the future of commercial television was J. Walter Thompson, head of one of radio's largest advertising and program production firms. In the summer of 1944, he personally took charge of his company's premiere foray into television, "The Peanut Is a Serious Guy." This light hearted fifteen-minute opus on DuMont was nothing more than an entertaining plug for peanuts. Nonetheless, Thompson felt that such basic TV experience would prove invaluable in a few years because, he stated flatly, television was going to be "the biggest ad medium yet."

4. We Want to Find Out First Where TV's Goin'

ON FRIDAY, September 29, 1944, the first successful long lasting commercial network television program premiered, *The Gillette Cavalcade of Sports*. That evening, Steve Ellis, the announcer for the Gillette Razor Company's radio sportscasts, did the blow-by-blow description as world featherweight champion Willie Pep easily defeated Chalky Wright in fifteen rounds. The entire NBC television network—New York, Philadelphia, and Schenectady—carried that first program and the series became a Friday night fixture on NBC, lasting sixteen years.

The Gillette Cavalcade of Sports was an outgrowth from radio. Gillette had joined with Mike Jacobs's 20th Century Sporting Club in the late 1930s to present weekly boxing matches over the NBC radio network, which met with considerable success. In October, 1943, NBC television began occasional sports broadcasts from Madison Square Garden for servicemen in hospitals, carrying such events as the rodeo and boxing. By mid-1944, it was clear that television boxing and wrestling were quite popular. Telecasts from Madison Square Garden, local semi-professional matches, and a few professional prize fights drew a strong response. With hordes of servicemen expected back soon from the war, Gillette felt it might be wise to expand its sports coverage and get in on the ground floor of television by adding a TV version to its regular radio broadcasts. It scheduled telecasts for three nights of the week: boxing from St. Nicholas Arena on Monday, wrestling from the same spot on Tuesday, and, the main draw, boxing from Madison Square Garden on Friday.

Gillette's commitment to weekly television sponsorship, coming so soon after J. Walter Thompson's initial entry into television over the summer, gave the video industry a much-needed shot of respectability among the hard-to-impress skeptics on Madison Avenue. It proved that advertising on television was no longer a far-fetched fantasy for the future, but rather a daily commercial reality.

The success of Gillette's sports show (with its roots in radio) also showed that, while radio and television had ostensibly gone their separate ways a decade before when NBC ended its reliance on simulcasts, the two media were still inexorably tied. Not only did radio provide the funds to pay for television expansion, it also supplied ideas for shows. Programmers would look at established radio hits and restage them for television, hoping to attract a similar loyal following of fans to the new medium. Besides sports, radio

stunt and game shows in the style of *People Are Funny* and *Truth or Consequences* had the most obvious visual appeal. The format consisted of handsome interchangeable male hosts using the lure of cash or gifts to lead unsuspecting, eager, basically naive average Americans through demeaning yet undeniably funny shenanigans. In these audience participation programs, the antics were much more entertaining when seen rather than merely described.

The first network radio game show to be made into a weekly television series was *Missus Goes A' Shopping*. Actually, CBS had brought it to the air two months before the premiere of NBC's Gillette boxing, but because it was unsponsored the program was not considered as important to television's progress. Host John Reed King, a veteran of much the same sort of thing from radio's *Double or Nothing* game, presented such stunts as a woman trying to slide a quarter off her nose without moving her head and a 250-pound truck driver trying to squeeze into a girdle. CBS producer Worthington Miner added some clever visual production bits to this generally undistinguished show and perhaps it was his touch that won *Missus Goes A' Shopping* rave reviews. One critic wrote: "This removes all doubts as to television's future. This *is* television."

Simple stunt and game shows were the easiest choice among radio programs being considered for television and were especially appealing to CBS (which still treated TV as chiefly experimental) and the newly established Blue (ABC) network. In fact, the first television program by ABC-Blue was a TV version of a mediocre radio game show, *Ladies Be Seated* (hosted by Johnny Olson), which aired on February 25, 1945. Five months later, Blue was officially renamed the American Broadcasting Company, though it still did not have a home base for its television operations. It had applied for stations in New York, Chicago, and Los Angeles, but the FCC had put a halt to processing applications for the duration of the war. As a result, ABC was forced to bicycle around the East Coast, producing television shows in the studios of General Electric's WRGB in Schenectady and DuMont's WABD in New York. Among the productions in this jerry-rigged television operation were a video version of radio's *Quiz Kids* and a ten-week variety series, *Letter to Your Serviceman,* with the incongruous line-up of Joey Faye, Burt Bacharach, and Helen Twelvetrees.

DuMont did not have a stable of radio shows to draw from,

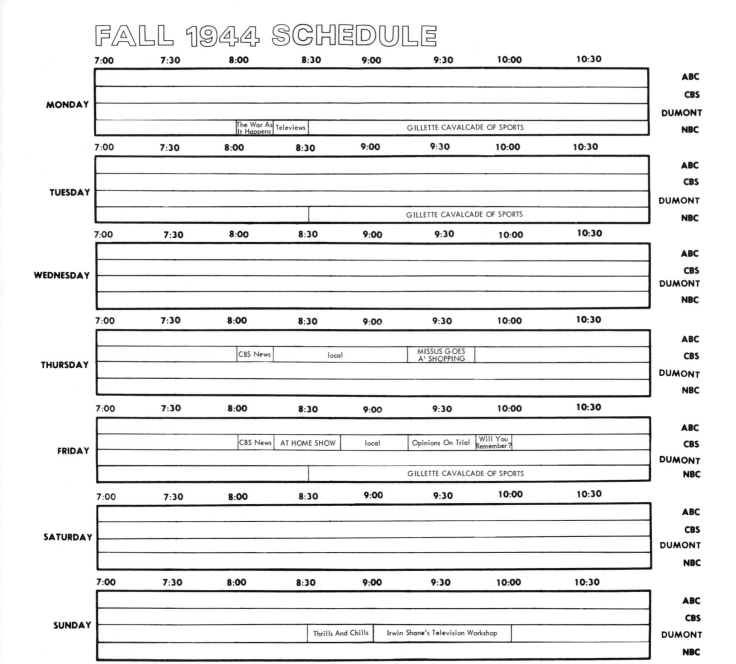

so it put more emphasis on formats specifically designed with video in mind. Instead of radio game shows, the network dabbled in travelogue presentations such as *Magic Carpet* and breezy cooking instruction such as *Shopping with Martha Manning*. Like game shows, these were cheap, visual, and easy to produce, though the subject matter of travel and cooking ultimately proved just as dull and trivial. However, because they were so simple, such programs proliferated for years on all the networks, serving as inexpensive filler with such appropriate titles as *The World in Your Home* and *I Love to Eat*.

When striving for class and recognition, however, DuMont continued to concentrate on drama and achieved mixed success. In the fall, DuMont presented the first televised version of "A Christmas Carol" by Charles Dickens as well as the first full-length musical comedy specifically written for television, "The Boys from Boise." "A Christmas Carol" was well received but "The Boys from Boise" (staged by the Charles M. Storm Theatrical Company)

suffered from the technical shortcomings of mid-1940s television. The cameras could focus clearly on only a limited area of action and so, on the small TV screen, movement seemed very cramped. As a result, the life and bounce of a wide-open stage show was absent and the meager plotline typical of such musical-comedy efforts wore through very quickly.

All of the TV networks were anxious to develop a successful TV format for music because music and musicians were the essential ingredient of radio. Programmers assumed that, to a degree, the same would hold true for television. CBS launched its own modest efforts at television music with a special fifteen-minute solo program featuring Victor Borge, a recent Danish emigre, and a weekly variety show hosted by Paquita Anderson, *At Home*, which featured regular appearances by singer-guitarist Yul Brynner. Developing musicians with TV experience seemed vital because, in network radio, most of the big stars had begun as singers or instrumentalists, and even the comedy giants included musical bits or singing sidekicks in their comedy-variety shows for a change of pace. In fact, that fall CBS radio promoted to top billing just such a pair of second bananas—Ozzie and Harriet Nelson.

Ozzie and Harriet had become man and wife in the mid-1930s, three years after Harriet Hilliard joined Ozzie Nelson's band. While later becoming the symbols of middle-aged parenthood at its best, at that time Harriet was quite a beautiful young singer and Ozzie was a very popular dance band leader. The two gained national recognition during their 1941–44 supporting stint on Red Skelton's new radio comedy show. Their relaxed ribbing of each other concerning marital spats and their young children made them well-liked radio personalities who showed they could handle comedy as well as music. When Skelton was drafted into the Army, the Nelsons received their own show.

Billed as "America's favorite young couple," Ozzie and Harriet began their radio series on October 8, 1944, their ninth wedding anniversary. Over the years, their personal and professional lives had become intertwined in the public's mind, so their program was structured to continue that impression. On *The Adventures of Ozzie and Harriet,* Ozzie Nelson, band leader, portrayed a fictitious Ozzie Nelson, band leader. In both worlds, he and Harriet had two young sons, eight-year-old David and four-and-one-half-year-old Eric (known later as Ricky). At first, child actors (Tom Bernard and Henry Blair) played David and Ricky, but by 1948 the real Ozzie Nelson allowed his real sons to portray their fictional counterparts.

This "I-Me-Mine" sitcom approach (as it might be labeled) placed a celebrity into a setting in which the fictional character was almost identical with real life. Thus, the very relaxed and natural personality that listeners had come to enjoy could be easily recognized by the audience in the new show. Top radio comedian Jack Benny had developed this style in the 1930s by playing a comedian, surrounded by a talented supporting cast, trying to stage a radio comedy show aided by a talented supporting cast. In Benny's program, though, showbiz life usually remained the focus and what emerged was a very funny comedy-variety show about putting on a comedy-variety show. Ozzie and Harriet shifted the emphasis almost completely to family home life in California, with occasional nods to the professional work that made the comfortable lifestyle possible. Their program was really a domestic situation comedy about a very likable family and their friends and neighbors. *The Adventures of Ozzie and Harriet* was a pioneering innovation and a tremendous success. The format carried them through both long radio and, later, television runs. It served as the model for other television performers in the mid-1950s, such as Danny Thomas in *Make Room for Daddy,* who wanted to place their show business characters into warm family settings.

Whatever plans the networks may have had for increasing the amount of music on TV were dealt a severe setback at the start of 1945 by James C. Petrillo, president of the American Federation of Musicians, the largest of the musicians' unions. Petrillo had become one of the most powerful men in American broadcasting by using radio's reliance on music as an effective bargaining tool. He had won fat pay raises for "his boys" in the radio orchestras by calling crippling musician walkouts during protracted contract negotiations throughout the late 1930s and early 1940s. Petrillo claimed the large raises were necessary to rectify the inordinately low-paying labor contracts that had been signed by his predecessors when radio was not yet a lucrative mass medium. He had no intention of falling into the same trap himself with television, so in February, 1945, before any bad video contract precedents could be set, he decided to put a total ban on all television appearances

WTOP's Arthur Godfrey covers the Independence Day ceremonies at Arlington National Cemetery, July 1945. *(National Archives)*

by any AFM musicians. Before making any deals, Petrillo said, "We want to find out first where TV's goin'!"

The Petrillo ban, which lasted three years, was a crippling blow to television at this stage because it eliminated some of the most popular radio talent, techniques, and formats, such as musical-variety shows and shows with famous singers. Without live music, television would never get off the ground. The few musical-variety shows tested on television after the Petrillo ban went into effect demonstrated the futility of such ventures without live musicians. Performers on a test TV version of ABC radio's popular *Breakfast Club* with Don McNeill tried to mime (or "lip sync") records, but the results were disastrous. Until the networks and Petrillo came to an understanding, television had to restrict itself to boxing, drama anthologies, cheap film shorts, cooking instruction, game shows, and, to a very limited extent, news.

The television networks had made little effort to establish any sort of news service by 1944 because television as a whole was not yet profitable and there seemed no reason to spend money in such a low return area. Instead, the networks used theatrical newsreel companies as the cheapest source of newsfilm, even though most of these reports barely qualified as news. The newsreels were light, upbeat, and oriented toward highly visual events such as far-off natural disasters, the christening of a new ship, or the finals of a beauty pageant. There was very little on-the-spot sound and no in-depth reporting. Instead, an announcer delivered breezy narration in stentorian tones while hokey "appropriate" music matched the action (a newsclip of an earthquake in Japan would be accompanied by oriental-style music).

In the 1930s, there had also been a similar scarcity of news on the radio, with most reports consisting of a few headlines supplied by the major newspaper wire services, or leisurely observations by commentators such as Lowell Thomas (NBC) and H. V. Kaltenborn (CBS). The outbreak of World War II changed all that as CBS made a concerted drive to become the top radio news service. Emphasizing on-the-spot coverage, the network built a solid corps of battle-trained correspondents (led by Edward R. Murrow) who brought their sharpened reporting skills back to the States when the war ended.

The same sort of style was impossible in the early 1940s for television, which lacked the technology, personnel, and finances for on-the-spot coverage. In the first half of 1945, as the war in Europe ended and the leadership of many major powers changed hands, world events moved much too quickly for newsreel orientation, yet the networks continued to rely on them. Television could

only pretend that it was covering the news. On V-E Day, May 7, 1945, not one television network had its own news-gathering operation.

That day, all three networks managed to assemble specials on the end of the war in Europe, but most of the coverage consisted of live pickups of the celebrating crowds in New York City's Times Square. A week after V-E Day, NBC decided to get the jump on its television competition and established the NBC Television News Film Department. It was a lovely title, but all the department consisted of was a few cameramen who made extensive use of a 35mm camera "borrowed" from the government. For news anywhere outside New York, NBC continued to purchase newsreels.

On August 8, 1945, NBC presented the first network produced television news show, *The NBC Television Newsreel,* but it was virtually indistinguishable from the coverage provided by the theatrical newsreel companies. For example, as the country celebrated the end of the war against Japan one week later, the program merely featured more live pickups of cheering crowds at Times Square. Since mid-1944, CBS had been presenting fifteen minutes of news on the nights that the network was on the air, but *The CBS Television News* relied solely on material purchased from the newsreel firms. Anchor chores on the CBS newscast fluctuated for over two years until late 1946 when twenty-nine-year-old Douglas Edwards became the regular anchorman (a post he held for more than fifteen years). Edwards resisted the assignment at first because he feared that television news was a dead-end occupation. In the mid-1940s, the only road to broadcast news stardom was on radio, which had made a celebrity out of Ed Murrow and, more recently, Arthur Godfrey.

Godfrey began his radio career as "Red Godfrey, the warbling banjoist" on Baltimore's WFBR in 1929. During the 1930s, he served a long stint as a disk jockey on CBS affiliate WTOP in Washington, where he pioneered a "natural" style of announcing. Godfrey tried to sound like a "regular Joe" rather than an officious announcer mechanically hustling some sponsor's products. He presented himself as an honest fellow who ad-libbed and talked directly to each individual listener, sharing just what was on his mind. The stuffy commercial scripts that shamelessly plugged the sponsors' products frequently served as a springboard for his comments, and Godfrey became infamous within the radio industry for his on-the-air ribbing of advertising men ("Boy, the stuff they ask me to read!"). The audience grew to love Godfrey and because he directed his comments at the commercial presentation rather than the product itself, their support kept nervous sponsors and programmers at bay.

National newspaper columnist Walter Winchell ran some complimentary reviews and this gave Godfrey a national reputation. Godfrey served a brief stint on the small Mutual radio network in the late 1930s and, in 1941, he secured a morning slot on CBS radio's local New York station. He handled this new assignment while still remaining in Washington by pre-recording the New York show. After finishing his early morning chores at WTOP, Godfrey would start all over again and record onto disk (or "transcribe") another music and gab show which would be shipped up the East Coast for airing the following morning. By early April, 1945, Godfrey was a radio workaholic, on the air ten hours a week from WTOP and sending another seven and one-half hours to New York. Though Godfrey was popular locally, the CBS radio network was not sure whether he could be sold nationally. It decided to give him a test run in the spring and summer of 1945, when the network's *American School of the Air* (a highly acclaimed educational show) took a summer vacation. CBS ran the educational

---

September 29, 1944

Gillette Cavalcade of Sports. (NBC). The first successful, long-lasting commercial network television series.

October 8, 1944

The Adventures of Ozzie and Harriet. (CBS Radio). "America's favorite young couple" begin twenty-two years of weekly shenanigans.

December 11, 1944

Chesterfield Supper Club. (NBC Radio). Perry Como's first musical-variety series, in which he follows Bing Crosby's formula of easy, natural singing.

January 15, 1945

House Party. (CBS Radio). After a year as sole host of *People Are Funny,* Art Linkletter adds a second show, one with less slapstick and more interviews.

February 25, 1945

Though it has no "home base" station of its own, the Blue network gamely begins television operations with a video version of its radio game show *Ladies Be Seated.*

April 15, 1945

NBC Television Theater. (NBC). Producer Edward Sobol begins Sunday night television drama on NBC, with Robert Sherwood's "Abe Lincoln in Illinois." Twenty-nine-year-old production assistant Fred Coe takes over as producer in 1946.

April 30, 1945

Arthur Godfrey Time. (CBS Radio). Slotted as an unsponsored summer filler, the "old redhead" stays on for twenty-seven years.

April 30, 1945

Queen for a Day. (MBS). Distraught women vie for fabulous prizes by describing their personal crises (on cue). Jack Bailey becomes emcee to this tearfest in January, 1946.

May 13, 1945

NBC sets up its own television newsfilm department.

June 7, 1945

The Adventures of Topper. (NBC Radio). Roland Young recreates his movie role as host to a pair of ghosts.

June 15, 1945

The Blue network officially becomes the ABC network.

July 2, 1945

Beulah. (NBC Radio). After a stint on the Fibber McGee and Molly show, the popular character of Beulah, a black maid, begins her own program. Though the "queen of the kitchen," Beulah is actually played by a small white man, Marlin Hurt.

The funeral procession for President Roosevelt. *(National Archives)*

program on a "sustaining" (unsponsored) basis anyway, so Godfrey was given the weekday morning network show unsponsored. If he caught on, it might be possible to snare a brave national sponsor and keep the show going on its own in the fall. Just two weeks before Godfrey's scheduled network debut, President Roosevelt died.

Franklin D. Roosevelt had been in the White House for twelve years and he was the only President many Americans had ever known. "FDR" engendered very deep emotions in almost everyone—he had helped the country out of the Great Depression and had led it to the brink of victory in World War II. Though his death was not totally unexpected—he had been quite ill for awhile—it was still a jolt.

On April 14, 1945, the whole country turned to radio for coverage of Roosevelt's funeral in Washington. Arthur Godfrey, as top man at CBS's WTOP, had the assignment of narrating the network's radio coverage of the slow caisson parade down Pennsylvania Avenue. Like everybody else, Godfrey was overcome with emotion that day, but, unlike his broadcasting brethren, he let those emotions show. As the parade moved slowly by, Godfrey talked of the millions of people listening who were "getting ready for suppertime." When the car carrying the new President passed, Godfrey choked as he spoke of the man who "just had such burdens fall upon him, God bless him, Harry Truman!" As Roosevelt's coffin came into sight, Godfrey broke down and sobbed into the microphone, "Oh God, give me strength!" It was a natural reaction for a man whose radio style was based on naturalness. Nobody else on the air that day better captured the way the country felt. When Godfrey began *Arthur Godfrey Time* on April 30, he already seemed like a close friend to many listeners.

Arthur Godfrey remained a daily fixture in broadcasting for the next thirty years, though he had no exceptional performing talent (his banjo and ukulele playing were only average and his jokes only mildly humorous), and his program (standard musical-variety with comedy) was different only in that it was ad-libbed. Years before the heyday of television, though, Godfrey had discovered the secret of longevity that would prove so important in the decade to come: personality. Because he was not tied to an act or theatrical style, Godfrey could remain on the radio day after day, year after year, and still not use up his material or overstay his welcome. People did not tire of him because he was an interesting person to listen to. He was himself.

Advertisers noted that, despite Godfrey's reputation for ribbing the sponsors' scripts, his approach to commercials was very effective. He was not just selling something, he was recommending it to his radio friends. Listeners enjoyed visiting with Godfrey, trusted him, and bought what he asked them to. He was the ideal pitchman.

5. After the Storm

WHEN World War II officially ended on September 2, 1945, there were fewer than 7,000 working television sets in the United States. There were only nine television stations on the air: three in New York City, two each in Chicago and Los Angeles, and one each in Philadelphia and Schenectady. Programming on all of them was spotty. Yet within sixty days, three events occurred which signalled the approaching expansion of television and the end of this torpid era of American broadcasting.

On October 8, the government lifted its wartime ban on the construction of new television stations and television sets. Over the previous four years, the FCC had received several applications for television station licenses, but had taken no action because most of the country's industry was occupied with War Department contracts. With wartime restrictions at an end, manufacturers could start to gear up for the production of TV station equipment and home sets on a mass market scale. People began to take an active interest in acquiring commercial television stations again and the FCC received a steady stream of applications, chiefly from major cities in the East and Midwest. Though the commission's own bureaucratic procedures kept it from moving very fast on processing the requests, within a year television managed to expand its base to areas outside New York, Chicago, and Los Angeles.

Near the end of October, Gimbel's Department Store in Philadelphia held the first large-scale television demonstration in years. Aside from the RCA Pavilion display at the 1939 New York World's Fair, most Americans had never seen a working television system close up. More than 25,000 people came to Gimbel's over three weeks for a chance to watch NBC programs from New York and local shows sent out by Philco's Philadelphia station. Because the major set producers had not yet retooled for domestic work, it would be another eleven months before large numbers of postwar sets reached the stores, so most of the sets on sale in 1945 were actually RCA and DuMont prewar models. Nonetheless, the public's response to even these old sets demonstrated great potential for television sales and it brought TVs back into store showrooms for the first time in years.

In October, RCA held its first public demonstration of a brand new type of television camera, the image orthicon, the first major improvement in TV cameras since Vladimir Zworykin's iconoscope of the late 1920s. The image orthicon was 100 times as sensitive as the other cameras then in use. This not only produced a sharper picture overall but also extended television's "depth of field." Previously, television cameras could show clearly only a relatively small area of stage or playing field. With the image orthicon, much more remained sharply in focus, so television producers could present indoor productions that occupied an entire stage, and outdoor events that were spread over large playing fields.

The first tangible benefits from the new camera turned up in the field of sports. The networks stepped up their interest in wide-open team sports. NBC began regular Saturday afternoon telecasts of college football games in the fall of 1945 and, the next summer, it made professional baseball an important part of its local New York programming. NBC also realized that the image orthicon camera allowed the already very popular one-on-one boxing matches to be presented with crystal clarity. With a sharp new product to display, NBC and Gillette staged what was billed as the first "television sports extravaganza," the Joe Louis-Billy Conn heavyweight fight at Yankee Stadium in June, 1946.

The Louis-Conn fight was heavily promoted in the East Coast television cities as both an important sports event and a special television program. By the time it aired, Washington had been connected to the East Coast coaxial cable network, so NBC added DuMont's experimental Washington station, W3XWT (later WTTG), to its four-city ad hoc fight network. Even though the program was an NBC exclusive, there was no reluctance to include a DuMont O&O in the hook-up because it was the only way the event could be seen in Washington. In the immediate postwar years, competing network affiliates in a market were rare, so any station on the coaxial cable would be offered a show if it was the only outlet in a new TV city.

The fight was a tremendous success, with an estimated audience of 150,000 watching over 5,000 TV sets, as Louis defeated Conn in eight rounds. Announcer Ben Grauer compared the event to the 1921 Jack Dempsey-Georges Carpentier bout which, as the first heavyweight championship fight on radio, generated similar excitement in its time. Tube veterans and television novices raved about the new clarity provided by the image orthicon camera. One reviewer said, "This is the sort of event that'll make people buy televisions, not the endless boring cooking shows that seem to turn up on every channel."

Gillette had proved its point—there was a huge potential audience for TV sports. For every TV set tuned to the fight, there were, on the average, thirty people watching, many of whom were seeing an event on television for the first time. NBC inserted frequent references to Gillette's weekly *Cavalcade of Sports* show, hoping that the excitement over the Louis-Conn fight might trans-

RCA's new image-orthicon cameras allowed better coverage of sporting events. *(National Archives)*

and Mrs. North," adapted from a Broadway show taken from a radio series based on magazine articles—with Efrem Zimbalist, Jr. in a bit part. Critics who had barely heard of television just months before began to praise NBC's television drama productions as being as good as or better than anything running on Broadway. Under Fred Coe, the performers, scripts, and direction were top notch and, almost singlehandedly, Coe made NBC the leader in serious TV drama for a decade. He was NBC's equivalent to Worth-

late into a greater number of regular TV viewers. The chief stumbling block to this strategy was that, aside from sports, no other program format had shown itself to be a sure-fire video hit, worthy of a sponsor's support or a viewer's investment in a home set.

Network programmers turned again and again to radio for precedents and ideas, but not all radio translated well into video. Game shows continued to appear all over television, both as clones of radio hits and as original video productions, but none could capture a sponsor. In the 1945–46 season, television presented such short-lived experiments as *Cash and Carry* (with Dennis James), *Play the Game* (more charades), and *See What You Know* (with Bennett Cerf). NBC's suspense radio thriller, *Lights Out,* failed in its attempt to cross over to TV in 1946. On radio, the program used spooky sound effects and the power of suggestion to create masterpieces of audio horror. During a few test television episodes, equivalent video tricks were either impossible or too expensive. As a result, the stories in the television version emerged as much too tame to match the reputation of the original.

NBC was more successful with *The NBC Television Theater,* a weekly drama series launched in April, 1945. Following DuMont's lead, NBC turned to the stage for inspiration, presenting drama productions with firm roots in the legitimate theater rather than radio. By 1946, Fred Coe had taken over production chores for the series, and he displayed a tremendous understanding of drama as both a serious and entertaining form. In its first year, *NBC Television Theater* presented: Noel Coward's "Blithe Spirit"; "Angel Street," a ninety-minute thriller using the entire Broadway cast of four people—an ideal size for the television staging; and "Mr.

September 29, 1945
NBC begins regular Saturday afternoon telecasts of college football games, featuring the few Eastern schools that will allow television coverage. In the first game, Columbia defeats Lafayette, 40 to 14.

October 5, 1945
Meet the Press. (MBS). Martha Rountree and Lawrence Spivak lead weekly, unrehearsed radio interviews with newsmakers. The first guest is U.S. Chamber of Commerce president Eric Johnson.

October 8, 1945
The war-induced freeze on handling new station applications ends. ABC officially files for three television O&Os, including one in New York.

October 25, 1945
NBC unveils its new image orthicon camera.

October 27, 1945
Harry Truman makes his first live television appearance as President: a Navy Day speech in New York's Central Park.

December 1, 1945
Army beats Navy (on NBC) in their annual football contest, the first event to be televised with the new image orthicon camera.

January 9, 1946
William Paley, president of CBS since 1928, moves up to chairman of the board. Frank Stanton is named the new president.

February 12, 1946
Washington is linked to the East Coast television network. General Dwight Eisenhower is shown laying a wreath at the Lincoln Memorial.

April 15, 1946
The DuMont television network is officially inaugurated and becomes the first TV network to have two O&Os on the air, connected by coaxial cable.

May 9, 1946
Hour Glass. (NBC). Vaudeville comes to television and it seems to work.

June 6, 1946
Here's Morgan. (ABC). Radio's reigning bad boy, Henry Morgan, tries out television, taking advantage of the visual nature of the medium. To illustrate his monologue largely devoted to the intense light necessary in a TV studio, Morgan—on camera—strips to the waist.

June 19, 1946
Joe Louis overcomes Billy Conn in television's first "sports extravaganza."

July 2, 1946
Arthur Godfrey's Talent Scouts. (CBS Radio). Godfrey enters prime time, as host of an amateur talent show.

FALL 1945 SCHEDULE

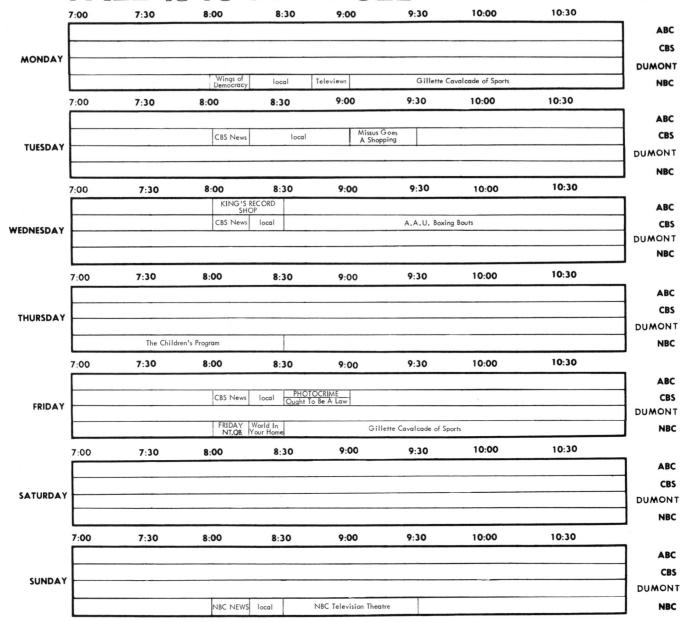

	7:00	7:30	8:00	8:30	9:00	9:30	10:00	10:30	
MONDAY									ABC
									CBS
									DUMONT
			Wings of Democracy	local	Televiews	Gillette Cavalcade of Sports			NBC

	7:00	7:30	8:00	8:30	9:00	9:30	10:00	10:30	
TUESDAY									ABC
			CBS News	local	Missus Goes A Shopping				CBS
									DUMONT
									NBC

	7:00	7:30	8:00	8:30	9:00	9:30	10:00	10:30	
WEDNESDAY			KING'S RECORD SHOP						ABC
			CBS News	local	A.A.U. Boxing Bouts				CBS
									DUMONT
									NBC

	7:00	7:30	8:00	8:30	9:00	9:30	10:00	10:30	
THURSDAY									ABC
									CBS
									DUMONT
	The Children's Program								NBC

	7:00	7:30	8:00	8:30	9:00	9:30	10:00	10:30	
FRIDAY									ABC
			CBS News	local	PHOTOCRIME / Ought To Be A Law				CBS
									DUMONT
			FRIDAY NT,QB	World In Your Home	Gillette Cavalcade of Sports				NBC

	7:00	7:30	8:00	8:30	9:00	9:30	10:00	10:30	
SATURDAY									ABC
									CBS
									DUMONT
									NBC

	7:00	7:30	8:00	8:30	9:00	9:30	10:00	10:30	
SUNDAY									ABC
									CBS
									DUMONT
			NBC NEWS	local	NBC Television Theatre				NBC

ington Miner at CBS—a producer with superb television instincts.

The NBC Television Theater ran Sunday night, usually starting about 9:00 P.M. (NBC devoted the time slot to drama for the next twelve years) and, from the beginning, the network had high hopes for the series. Though it remained unsponsored for more than three years, the critical acclaim given to *The NBC Television Theater* served as a reminder to viewers that television could expand beyond theretofore typical fare such as newsreels, games, cooking, film shorts, and sports. Just like Broadway, television could present high quality entertaining stories.

While pleased at the artistic success of its unsponsored Sunday night drama, NBC was still searching for a formula that could generate a commercial television hit. Comedy-variety and musical-variety programs were among the network's most successful radio shows then on the air, so in May, 1946, despite the continued ban on live music by James Petrillo's musicians union, NBC and Standard Brands, one of the major advertisers on radio, gambled

with the first big budget TV variety show, *Hour Glass*.

In adapting the variety format to television, *Hour Glass* took a very simple approach: On each program a host introduced four or five performers (nonmusical) who stood in front of the curtain backdrop or a simple set, did their individual acts, and departed. The show was really nothing more than a series of vaudeville routines staged before a camera, yet *Hour Glass* served as an important experiment in TV programming. Though this pioneer television vehicle rarely could afford a "name" act, its weekly talent budget, $4,000, was far higher than any previous video series. There was also money for better lighting, sets, props, and writers.

Because *Hour Glass* was the first program of its type on television, it started out ragged and uncertain. Singer Evelyn Eaton, the program's first host, had to lip-sync her records because of the Petrillo ban. During the show's first weeks, the pretty young women showing off the sponsor's products frequently forgot their lines and the ads often dragged on for five minutes, but, by the fall, the

Congressmen gather at the Statler Hotel in Washington to view the first "television sports extravaganza": the Joe Louis–Billy Conn heavyweight fight. *(Historical Pictures Service, Inc., Chicago/ Harris & Ewing Photo)*

show had tightened up and such fluffs were rare. Actress Helen Parrish took over the hosting chores and she proved more adept at projecting her personality through television and catching the imagination of viewers. Parrish became one of the first performers to be stopped in the streets of New York City and recognized as a television personality. *Hour Glass* attracted a loyal following and soon Edgar Bergen, one of radio's biggest stars, did a guest spot.

Hour Glass was the only commercial success of the TV season, yet it lasted less than a year. The program was the most expensive television production at the time and there were not enough stations, sets, and viewers to justify such a costly experiment after it had proved its popularity with the viewing public. Standard

Brands could not point to any dramatic increase in sales as a result of its television advertising and there seemed to be no end in sight to the stagnant situation in live television music and, more importantly, to the FCC's continuing indecision on color—which was serving as a deterrent to new station applications. In early 1947, the program was canceled. *Hour Glass* had been just slightly ahead of its time.

Yet *Hour Glass* set very important programming precedents in its brief run and became the model for future television variety shows. It demonstrated the surprising fact that the simple vaudeville format—long judged passé on stage—seemed tailor-made for the home screen.

6. TV Gets the Green Light

NETWORK radio was at the height of its golden age in the fall of 1946. The nation was resuming peacetime activities. More people had radios than ever before, and they spent more time than ever listening. There seemed to be an almost perfect mixture of news, familiar entertainment programming, and promising new series available. Network news operations, staffed with battle-trained correspondents, were given a larger share of the weekly schedule. Nationally known commentators such as Walter Winchell, Ed Murrow, and H. V. Kaltenborn had very popular regular slots in the early evening. In the ratings for evening entertainment shows, Jack Benny was number one, closely followed by Bob Hope, Fibber McGee and Molly, and Edgar Bergen. The strength of relative newcomers such as Red Skelton and Arthur Godfrey augured well for the future.

The NBC network was the unquestioned champion of radio. Through the early 1930s, the Crossley ratings showed NBC far ahead of CBS. In 1935, the Hooper organization supplanted Crossley as the most respected radio ratings source, and NBC continued its healthy lead in "the Hoopers." Even the government-induced sale by NBC of its Blue network (later called ABC) in 1943 had not shaken NBC's financial stability and dominance in the ratings. Though many stars such as Jack Benny and Fred Allen hopscotched between NBC and CBS in constant search of the best contract deal, NBC always maintained the strongest roster of programs. As the fall of 1946 approached, NBC had claims on Jack Benny, Bob Hope, Edgar Bergen, Bing Crosby, Fred Allen, Perry Como, Red Skelton, Kay Kyser, Dennis Day, Burns and Allen, Abbott and Costello, Eddie Cantor, Alan Young, and Art Linkletter, plus such popular continuing programs as *Amos and Andy, Fibber McGee and Molly, Life of Riley, DuPont's Cavalcade of America, The Voice of Firestone, Bell Telephone Hour, Dr. I.Q., Mr. and Mrs. North, The Great Gildersleeve, Duffy's Tavern, Mr. District Attorney, The Aldrich Family, The Kraft Music Hall, Truth or Consequences,* and *The Grand Ole Opry.*

NBC's schedule included several popular sitcoms as well as a few high caliber drama and music shows (usually financed by large industrial corporations in order to promote a positive company image), but the network based its ratings strategy on the strength of its line-up of established singers and comedians. NBC favored the variety format to showcase its stars and used them as hosts of comedy-variety and musical-variety vehicles. CBS's radio sched-ule was structured essentially the same way, but without as many big names. At CBS, there were such celebrities as Kate Smith, Frank Sinatra, Dinah Shore, Jimmy Durante, and Arthur Godfrey, plus a smattering of musical and dramatic programs such as *Texaco Star Theater, Lux Radio Theater, Suspense, The Thin Man,* and *Your Hit Parade.*

In January, 1946, William Paley, president of CBS since 1928, was promoted to the position of chairman of the board. During the war Paley was away from broadcasting, serving as head of the government's Department of Psychological Warfare, and, upon his return to civilian life, he was eager to begin a concerted drive to move CBS ahead of NBC and into the role as America's number one network. Paley chose Frank Stanton, a man who had worked his way up the CBS corporate ladder over nine years, to succeed him in the post of president, and the two began their task by analyzing CBS's strengths. CBS has earned the reputation for superiority in radio news during the war by pioneering the on-the-spot style of reporting. In an equivalent move in the entertainment field, the Paley-Stanton team decided that, instead of merely trying to imitate NBC's approach to programming, they would give CBS a distinctively different "feel" from the competition. At NBC, sitcoms were generally passed over in favor of variety formats, so CBS began to encourage ideas for popular sitcoms, adding to the handful—led by *The Adventures of Ozzie and Harriet*—it already had on the air. The network also attempted to break from the accepted practice of program control by advertisers and their production companies and to produce some shows completely on its own instead.

In the early 1930s, the radio networks had willingly turned over artistic and production control of their programs to the sponsors. At the time, the networks needed the advertising revenue to fund the fledgling but rapidly expanding operations, and felt relieved that some of the production burden had been removed. The sponsors, in turn, did not usually hire the talent and organize the shows themselves, but instead contracted with advertising agencies such as J. Walter Thompson and Young & Rubicam, which actually put the shows together. Soon it became clear that the networks had lost control of what they were broadcasting. For all practical purposes, popular shows on competing networks often sounded the same because the same agencies had done them. With the additional levels of production, the networks also lost a substantial

In late 1946, the postwar television production lines were rolling at a record pace. (National Archives)

share of the program profits. Because this policy was very lucrative to the "outside" producers, the networks found it next to impossible to eliminate on established shows. The only way around the status quo was to retain control on new programs and hope that they became big hits as well.

The sponsor-agency combination turned out very slick packages that worked well in popular comedy, adventure, music, and variety formats. These were light entertainment vehicles perfect for showcasing the sponsors' products and big name stars. Applying the same standards to drama, however, tended to eliminate any serious or controversial productions. Shows such as *The Lux Radio Theater* usually settled for fluffy star-laden melodrama. Appropriately, one of the first series in CBS's postwar independence drive was an ambitious drama anthology, *Studio One*. Under the direction of Fletcher Markle, the program began in April, 1947, with a poignant and exciting adaptation of Malcolm Lowrey's "Under the Volcano," a masterpiece on the alcoholic mind. Subsequent productions of *Studio One* continued to emphasize high quality writing rather than glamorous stars, giving CBS a clearly different radio offering. The network hoped that such distinctive network-controlled programs, combined with its established shows and stars, would eventually push it to the top. As long as NBC had so many big name stars under its banner, this was about the best strategy CBS could pursue.

The battle for supremacy in network radio was between NBC and CBS. Far behind, but still turning profits in this golden age of radio, were the two other networks, ABC and the Mutual Broadcasting System (MBS). Mutual was the third oldest independent radio network, formed in 1934 by owners of a few powerful radio stations not affiliated with either NBC or CBS. As a self-proclaimed "voluntary association of independent broadcasters" (thus the name "Mutual"), the network allowed its local affiliates much more con-

trol over network programming decisions and did not even have any owned and operated stations. While the individual stations did quite well, as a network Mutual was always on very shaky financial grounds and could rarely afford to stage high budget series.

Since the mid-1930s, Mutual had been playing an unsuccessful game of catch-up with the other networks and, in 1946, found itself last in the network radio ratings race, suffering the inherent frustrations of that position. Any hit shows developed by Mutual were inevitably snatched by the competition, so the network lost such programs as *Dick Tracy, The Lone Ranger, It Pays to Be Ignorant, Kay Kyser's Kollege of Musical Knowledge, Juvenile Jury, The Green Hornet,* and *Roy Rogers.* In the other direction, Mutual served as the dumping ground for network shows on their last legs such as *Lights Out, Sergeant Preston of the Yukon,* and *Sky King.* Nonetheless, even Mutual found gold during this era of broadcasting prosperity, chiefly with flashy but inexpensive game and quiz shows such as *Queen for a Day* and *Twenty Questions.*

The prestige program of the Mutual network was *Meet the Press,* a simple panel show with an important innovation. Previously, most radio interview programs consisted of tame reporters lobbing softball questions at that week's guest. Items of substance were rarely covered. In 1945, thirty-year-old Martha Rountree, a freelance writer, and Lawrence Spivak, editor of the magazine *American Mercury,* convinced Mutual to try a different interview approach, an unrehearsed interrogation with bite. Each week on *Meet the Press* an important, often controversial, public figure was grilled by some of the nation's top reporters. During the give and take between the guests and the questioners, important revelations and admissions sometimes slipped out and soon the national news services were covering *Meet the Press* as a legitimate news event itself. On one program, for instance, labor leader John L. Lewis

	7:00	7:30	8:00	8:30	9:00	9:30	10:00	10:30	
MONDAY									**ABC**
									CBS
					BOXING FROM JAMAICA ARENA				**DUMONT**
			Your Esso Reporter	Televiews	Gillette Cavalcade of Sports				**NBC**

	7:00	7:30	8:00	8:30	9:00	9:30	10:00	10:30	
TUESDAY			Play The Game						**ABC**
									CBS
					Serving Through Science				**DUMONT**
									NBC

	7:00	7:30	8:00	8:30	9:00	9:30	10:00	10:30	
WEDNESDAY									**ABC**
									CBS
			Magic Carpet	local	FARAWAY HILL	BOXING FROM JAMAICA ARENA			**DUMONT**
									NBC

	7:00	7:30	8:00	8:30	9:00	9:30	10:00	10:30	
THURSDAY			CHARM SCHOOL	local	Ladies Be Seated				**ABC**
			CBS News	Judge For Yourself / Ought To Be A Law	SPORTS FROM MADISON SQUARE GARDEN				**CBS**
					Cash And Carry				**DUMONT**
		In Town Today	Your Esso Reporter	Hour Glass					**NBC**

	7:00	7:30	8:00	8:30	9:00	9:30	10:00	10:30	
FRIDAY									**ABC**
									CBS
					WRESTLING FROM JAMAICA ARENA				**DUMONT**
			Friday Nt. Q B	YOU ARE AN ARTIST	I LOVE TO EAT / World In Your Home	Gillette Cavalcade of Sports			**NBC**

	7:00	7:30	8:00	8:30	9:00	9:30	10:00	10:30	
SATURDAY									**ABC**
			Week In Review	SATURDAY REVUE	King's Party Line				**CBS**
									DUMONT
									NBC

	7:00	7:30	8:00	8:30	9:00	9:30	10:00	10:30	
SUNDAY									**ABC**
			CBS News	Shorty	SPORTS ALMANAC	SPORTS FROM MADISON SQUARE GARDEN			**CBS**
									DUMONT
			Face To Face	Geograph. Speaking	BROADWAY PREVIEWS				**NBC**

unveiled a threat of a national coal strike. For a while, Mutual toyed with the idea of entering television, but its loose organization and meager financial resources eventually forced it to ignore video altogether. *Meet the Press,* however, was brought to television in late 1947 by NBC.

The ABC radio network ran ahead of Mutual in the ratings, coming in a distant but still respectable third. Even though it was technically the newest independent radio network, ABC's network roots (as NBC Blue) stretched back twenty years. As a result, ABC had a much stronger and more formal network organization than Mutual. Though it could not possibly match the depth of programming by NBC and CBS, ABC carried as varied a selection as possible, including comedy and adventure staples such as *Lum and Abner, Gangbusters,* and *The Lone Ranger,* as well as prestige programs such as *The Theater Guild of the Air* (later *The U.S. Steel Hour*), *The American Town Meeting of the Air,* and commentary by political gadfly Drew Pearson. Like Mutual, however, ABC

turned increasingly to quiz shows for its most successful popular programming. In 1947, ABC had the most popular quiz show on the air, *Break the Bank,* which handed out the largest prizes (up to a then astronomical $9,000) and offered one of the most enthusiastic quiz hosts, Bert Parks. He displayed an amazing knack for getting caught up in the quiz itself, urging contestants through their paces, and sounding as if he truly cared whether or not they won.

Television did not enter into the overall broadcast picture very much going into the fall of 1946, and seemed as distant a threat to radio's supremacy as ever. Few television stations were on the air, very few TV sets were in people's homes, broadcast schedules were brief and irregular, and there were next to no hits or stars to attract an audience. The debate over the adoption of a color TV system seemed to go on forever and there was even a move still afoot to discard all the TV sets then in use and move television to a different set of broadcast frequencies.

Beneath this apparent weakness, there was a dramatic expansion building. Special events such as the Louis-Conn boxing match in June, 1946, and regular series such as *Hour Glass* had demonstrated the public's interest in television. In September, 1946, the first large batch of postwar television sets rolled off the assembly lines and into department stores. For the first time ever, interest in TV began to translate into sales. People began to buy television sets in great numbers.

The rise in television set production that fall was nothing short of phenomenal. In the first eight months of 1946, only 225 TV sets were produced in the United States. In September, 3,242 were turned out. On November 4, RCA put its first postwar models on sale and, to pump up interest, NBC-TV aired a star-studded special edition of *In Town Today,* with Bob Hope, Edgar Bergen, and Ben Grauer. By January, 1947, the monthly TV set production figure had jumped to 5,437 and, by May, it reached 8,690.

This sudden surge of TV set production added a sense of urgency to resolving the important technical questions that still faced the industry. The central problem was color. Because both RCA and CBS's proposed color systems used the mechanical spinning disk concept, they were incompatible with electronic black and white sets. Since 1940, the FCC had been cautiously considering the wisdom of ordering the few TV sets then in use to be junked in favor of new ones designed for color reception. At mid-decade, however, the color question become entangled in yet another problem: frequency allotment.

In the late 1930s, the FCC had assigned television stations space on the VHF (Very High Frequency) band (channels 1 to 13), even though, practically speaking, this could accommodate only about 400 TV stations across the country without cross-signal interference. This was barely enough to support two national networks with affiliates in all major American cities and certainly could not provide outlets for three or four networks.

In April, 1944, CBS executive vice president Paul W. Kesten suggested that both the color and frequency problems could be solved in one fell swoop by "kicking TV upstairs" into the UHF (Ultra High Frequency) band (channels 14 to 83). In UHF, there would be room for four times as many TV channels, and broadcasts in spinning disk color could commence at once. In 1944, with the war still on and no new television sets in production, the transition could be relatively easy. The few people who owned TV sets would have to buy new ones but, Kesten said, in the long run it would be worth it.

Most of the other important television powers disagreed and CBS was virtually alone in supporting this plan. RCA-NBC, Du-Mont, Philco, and General Electric were already heavily committed to TV stations in VHF and to the promotion of black and white TV sets. They saw such a radical proposal as harmful to their own best interests and an unnecessary delay to the arrival of commercial television in America. Once the war ended, they observed, network operations would begin in earnest as TV station construction and set production resumed. CBS countered that color was essential to television's success and that the move to UHF offered the best solution to the problem. The network insisted that television was still only "experimental" in its monochrome stage and, to show that it was serious, CBS restricted itself to broadcasts on its sole outlet, WCBW in New York City.

During 1945 and 1946, the FCC held lengthy hearings on CBS's suggestion. RCA insisted that the CBS color system would not be ready for five to ten years, while CBS countered with a string of "surprise" demonstrations of progress in its color system, which it claimed would be ready by mid-1947, at the latest.

The psychological turning point of the struggle came at the end of October, 1946, when RCA held its own "surprise" demonstration of a brand new color system that would make the CBS spinning disk version obsolete. The new RCA color system was all-electronic. More importantly, the system was partially compatible with black and white sets. When a converter was attached to an existing set, RCA's system would allow reception of shows sent out both in black and white and in color. This meant that the TV sets already in operation could be kept and, with a flick of a switch, could be used no matter what sort of program was sent. RCA promised the FCC that, within five years, further improvements would make the RCA color sytem totally compatible with black and white sets, and the bulky converters would be unnecessary. Without any new equipment at all, owners of old TV sets would then see color shows in black and white, and those who bought RCA's color sets could see black and white shows without any problem.

RCA's promised compatible system involved far fewer headaches for the TV industry and for TV set owners, but CBS's noncompatible system seemed the closest to being ready for mass use. When sales of black and white VHF sets began multiplying in the fall of 1946, it became clear that the time for some sort of decision was at hand. If the CBS plan was to succeed, it had to be approved as soon as possible, before sales of monochrome sets increased further. In March, 1947, the FCC issued a ruling, stating that, despite the promises, CBS's color system was not yet ready for commercial use. The commission added that, in the meantime, there was no reason to prevent Americans from buying and using black and white television sets. This fateful statement relieved manufacturers and potential station applicants, who were worried over the possibility that the entire television system could be pulled

September 22, 1946
Broadway Preview. (NBC). Fred Coe, with help from the Dramatists Guild, presents television "sneak previews" of plays under consideration for Broadway runs.

October 2, 1946
Faraway Hill. (DuMont). Television's first regular soap opera series stars Flora Campbell as Karen St. John, a young city widow who moves to the country and finds a new love. This vanguard effort fades by Christmas.

October 17, 1946
CBS begins televising sports (other than boxing) from Madison Square Garden, opening with a rodeo contest. John Henry Faulk, a new CBS acquisition from Texas, handles the announcing chores.

November 1, 1946
WCBW, CBS's New York TV station, becomes WCBS.

January 3, 1947
Television covers Congress for the first time, carrying its opening day ceremonies live. Three days later, President Truman's state of the union address before the House and the Senate is also broadcast.

January 9, 1947
ABC temporarily ceases television programming in order to sink its money into station construction.

May 7, 1947
Kraft Television Theater. (NBC). New York says "cheese" and Kraft smiles.

out from under them in a sudden move to color. The FCC simply put aside the pesky color question for the foreseeable future and, in effect, made black and white VHF the approved television system for America. The path seemed clear at last for a rapid expansion in TV growth because, intended or not, the FCC had given commercial TV the green light.

Almost immediately following the FCC decision, applications for stations began pouring in. Within a few months, the number of stations on the air more than doubled. Most of the new licenses were for cities that previously had no TV stations at all, such as St. Louis, Detroit, Baltimore, Milwaukee, and Cleveland.

As more TV stations signed on across the country, local non-network programs began to reach a fair level of quality and talented local personalities began to emerge from cities other than New York. By mid-1947, WBKB, in still far-off Chicago, had developed several performers who would later become network stars. Young Dave Garroway, a former NBC page, added a touch of humor to *Remember the Days,* a weekly thirty-minute sustaining series that consisted of old silent films. As host, Garroway not only read the subtitles but also gently poked fun at the stylized flicks. One reviewer thought that the show was too cute, asking, "Won't we be doing the same thing to 1947 television one day?" A few months later, Fran Allison, who played the gossipy Aunt Fannie on radio's *Breakfast Club,* and Burr Tillstrom, a puppeteer, began a daily kiddie show on WBKB, *Junior Jamboree* (sponsored by RCA). The program focused on Fran's interaction with a group of puppet characters, especially Kukla, a well meaning little bald man, and Ollie, a scatterbrained dragon. Allison's gentle good humor and Tillstrom's imaginative puppet characterizations made the team regional celebrities and soon won *Kukla, Fran, and Ollie* a network slot on NBC.

By the end of 1947, Washington, Philadelphia, and Baltimore had joined New York City, Chicago, and Los Angeles in having more than one TV station on the air. Stations connected to the East Coast coaxial cable began establishing regular network affiliations, though most stations continued to accept programs from two, three, or even four networks—for the time being. With its long head start in video programming, NBC was the most successful in signing up TV affiliates.

CBS, the apparent loser in the color TV shuffle, had been caught napping. Expecting its color system to be approved and television "kicked upstairs" to UHF, the network had been lax in developing regular programming, seeking out sponsors, signing up TV affiliates, and applying for other owned and operated TV stations outside New York City. Grudgingly accepting the fact that black and white VHF TV was here to stay—at least for a few years—CBS applied for a Chicago O&O.

Two months after the FCC's "no go" to color, CBS began an ill-fated drive to make up for lost time in TV programming and to leapfrog into the TV lead by adopting a distinctively different "feel" from the competition. The network closed its TV studios at Grand Central Station in favor of all on-location ("remote") and filmed broadcasts. CBS announced plans to sharply increase, in the fall of 1947, telecasts of live sports events such as college football, basketball, hockey, track and field, and the rodeo. In addition, cooking shows would originate from famous restaurants, drama shows would come from theaters, and children's shows would be staged in parks throughout New York City. Douglas Edwards's news broadcasts would continue, but with Edwards relegated to the role of off-screen newsreel narrator.

CBS touted its outside-the-studio broadcasts as a great leap forward in television. The other networks merely televised the inside of a studio, which, it was said, was too much like radio with pictures. CBS promised to bring the world—or at least New York City—directly into viewers' living rooms. CBS's move was, at best, ill-timed and highly unrealistic. Television's bulky technology was not yet ready for extensive out-of-the-studio broadcasting and, with little preparation, CBS had nothing special to offer potential sponsors and potential viewers with its new format.

DuMont adopted a much more reasonable middle ground. The network also could not match NBC's in-studio expertise, but, unlike CBS, DuMont launched a more limited series of remote telecasts. The network copied NBC's already successful prime time sporting schedule and began an extensive series of on-location sports telecasts in the fall of 1946, with a series of Monday-Wednesday-Friday boxing and wrestling matches from New York's Jamaica Arena. NBC had aired a number of wrestling matches, but it had always concentrated on boxing, so DuMont emphasized wrestling, and turned it into a national fad. Like boxing, wrestling was confined to a small space and limited to just a few contestants at a time, which made it ideal for television coverage. Unlike boxing, wrestling had been a sport of only marginal interest until the arrival of television. Very quickly, the promoters of wrestling began to emphasize the theatrical values of the contests above the sport itself, which TV insiders soon nicknamed "flying beef." Before and after matches, the wrestlers threatened each other in pre-planned interviews and confrontations. Once in the ring, such colorful characters as Haystack Calhoun, Gorilla Monsoon, and Gorgeous George played every stomp, scream, and painful grimace to the audience for maximum effect. DuMont's ringside wrestling announcers patterned their actions to fit this style. Dennis James added such touches as snapping chicken bones next to his microphone when a wrestler was put in a particularly painful-looking hold. As wrestling grew increasingly popular, James became known for his trademark phrase, "OK, Mother . . ." which he used to begin explanations of the sport directed toward housewives in the audience.

DuMont's on-location sports programming was a rousing success and wrestling remained a part of the network's schedule through the next decade. Unlike CBS, DuMont continued to try in-studio program formats as well, achieving mixed results. *Faraway Hill,* network television's first soap opera series, was short-lived, but *Small Fry Club,* starring "Big Brother" Bob Emery, became television's first hit children's show. By April, 1947, *Small Fry Club* aired Monday through Friday, 7:00–7:30 P.M., beginning the television day with kiddie games and clowns for the small fry lucky enough to have a TV set at home. (After a successful five-year network run, Emery relocated on a local Boston station where he remained a comforting uncle figure to yet another generation of children.)

NBC continued to televise college football on Saturday afternoons and boxing matches in the evening two nights a week, but its primary focus remained on attracting advertisers for in-studio programming. The Borden Milk company sponsored a series of variety programs that served as try-outs (or "pilots") for formats that might work on TV, all without live music (the Petrillo ban was still in effect). Fred Coe beefed up the Sunday night drama show with assistance from the Dramatist's Guild. For a while, the lead-in to the drama slot was *Geographically Speaking,* starring world traveler Mrs. Carveth Wells, who narrated films of her world trips. The show ended abruptly after twenty-six weeks when she ran out of films.

The radio talk show duo of Tex and Jinx made a more conscious effort to adapt to television, experimenting with three different program forms that season on NBC. John Reagan "Tex" McCrary (newspaperman turned commentator) and his wife, Eugenia Lincoln "Jinx" Falkenburg (tennis player-swimmer-glamour girl), had been on NBC's local New York radio outlet since early 1946, leading a lowkey, intelligent celebrity talk show program. On April 27, 1947, they brought their successful format to television in *At Home with Tex and Jinx.* From a studio set resembling a fancy apartment, Tex and Jinx entertained their famous friends and showed home movies (apparently they took trips, too).

During the summer of 1947, Tex and Jinx took a brief vacation, but NBC wanted to continue their Sunday evening broadcasts, so, in spite of the network's preference for live programming, a filmed series was shown in its place. The new format, *Ringside with Tex and Jinx,* moved the show's locale from the couple's "apartment" to their favorite club haunts, where they continued to hob nob with their celebrity chums.

The success of the duo's Sunday evening program earned them an additional assignment, the first commercial network daytime television program. On May 16, *The Swift Home Service Club* began a one-year residency on NBC, Friday from 1:00 to 1:30 P.M. Geared toward the housewife audience, the show featured Tex and Jinx (especially Jinx) giving tips on interior decorating and home economics, while their ever-present celebrity friends tossed *bons mots.* Apparently Tex's chief responsibility was to sample, with relish, Swift's taste-tempting meat products specially prepared for the show. Because television broadcasting still required enormous amounts of light, the resulting heat wreaked havoc on the food. The mayonnaise went bad often enough that an off-screen bucket was kept close at hand so that Tex could immediately vomit if necessary.

The longest-running and most important program that NBC brought out in the 1946–47 season was *The Kraft Television Theater,* which began in May. NBC and Fred Coe had been staging weekly unsponsored dramas for some time, but the Kraft dramas were different. Not only were they sponsored by a major national concern, they were also produced by an outside firm, the J. Walter Thompson agency. All the early NBC and CBS video productions were "in-house," so it came as quite a surprise to the industry that NBC would allow its first major sponsored TV drama series to be run by outsiders.

Kraft and J. Walter Thompson had been long-time partners in staging *The Kraft Music Hall* on radio, so the television arrangement made good business sense. It also offered NBC a ready-made, sponsored vehicle to plug into its slowly expanding schedule. If the Kraft series caught on, the network might have an easier time finding support for its own drama series. In spite of network fears that the agency would turn out a slick and shallow *Lux Radio Theater* style drama series, *The Kraft Television Theater* maintained a remarkably consistent, high quality over the years. The show was rarely stupendous but was constantly quite good. Though the first presentation of the series, the slightly dull melodrama "Double Door," did not receive rave notices, another part of the program did.

Kraft's new McLaren's Imperial Cheese had been introduced to the market in early 1947 but, at one dollar a pound, was doing quite poorly in sales. Kraft subscribed to the notion that television might be an excellent advertising medium on a par with radio and decided to use Imperial Cheese as the acid test. For the first two weeks, all of the ads run on Kraft's show were for McLaren's Imperial Cheese. For two weeks, pretty model Dana Wyatt demonstrated the tastability of the cheese. For two weeks, the ever-convincing voice of Ed Herlihy expounded on the wonders of this new cheese marvel. By the third week, every package of McLaren's Imperial Cheese available in New York City had been sold.

Now this was news! Mrs. Carveth Wells could show all the travelogues she wanted, but this was something to make Madison Avenue sit up and take notice. Everyone had always suspected that television, with its combined visual and aural appeal, would probably be the "biggest ad medium yet," but until Kraft, nobody had proved it.

7. Vaudeville Is Back

IN SEPTEMBER, 1926, RCA placed a full page ad in the nation's major newspapers announcing the birth of NBC and the beginning of network radio broadcasting:

The day has gone by when the radio receiving set is a plaything. It must now be an instrument of service. . . . The purpose of [NBC] will be to provide the best program[ing] available for broadcasting in the United States.

Only two years later, NBC began operating an experimental television station, but it was not until January 5, 1948, that the follow-up ad appeared, announcing network TV:

1948—TELEVISION'S YEAR

. . . an exciting promise is now an actual service to the American home. After twenty years of preparation, the NBC television network is open for business.

NBC proudly spoke of the four TV stations already programming its network material, with stations in Boston and Baltimore to open soon. In 1947, it was pointed out, the number of TV sets operating in America had increased by more than 2,000 percent, from 8,000 to 170,000.

Nineteen forty seven marked the end of television's interim period. Nineteen forty eight marks TV's appearance as a major force.

In almost awe-struck tones the ad concluded:

The greatest means of mass communications in the world is with us.

The excitement that followed Kraft's successful entry into TV in the summer of 1947 had continued into the fall as more and more sponsors invested money in television entertainment. Throughout the fall, the networks launched new television vehicles and the quality of their programming began to rise noticeably. In October, DuMont presented gossip columnist Jack Eigen in a nightclub setting, surrounded by glamour girls. For fifteen minutes, Eigen talked about the latest showbiz rumors and chatted with whatever celebrity he could corral. (Both Frank Sinatra and Fred Allen were on the show, but only via a telephone hookup.) In November, NBC brought Mutual radio's popular *Meet the Press* interview program to TV, after convincing a sponsor, General Mills, that the show was not too controversial for television. Fred Coe enlisted help for his NBC Sunday night drama presentations from two respected Broadway organizations, the Theater Guild and the American National Theater Academy (ANTA). In December, DuMont restaged "A Christmas Carol," using twelve sets and a cast of twenty-two.

Still, it was another sports remote that produced the most exciting television in the fall of 1947—baseball's annual World Series contest, the first to be televised. All eight TV stations on the East Coast coaxial cable broadcast the seven game "subway" series between the New York Yankees and the Brooklyn Dodgers, two bitter cross-town rivals. With Gillette and the Ford Motor Company as sponsors, CBS, NBC, and DuMont organized a "pool" coverage system in which the three networks each carried all of the games but took turns on the play-by-play and camera chores. Bob Stanton of NBC was the broadcast voice for games one and seven, Bill Slater took games two, five, and six for DuMont, and Bob Edge handled games three and four for CBS. Close-up cameras presented viewers at home and in bars with sharp, clear pictures of every phase of the game: the antics of baseline coaches giving complicated signals, the challenging stance by a batter waiting for a pitch, and the dejection on the face of a pitcher taken out of the game. Television, in effect, provided the best seats in the house and gave the dramatic championship match a greater sense of theater than ever before as the Yankees won the series, four games to three.

Viewer response to the World Series was even greater than the reaction to the Louis-Conn fight of the year before. The TV audience was estimated to be at least 3.8 million, and retailers reported a sharp increase in TV set sales during early October. Welcome as this news was, the World Series was merely another short-term special event. The TV networks were still searching for regular weekly hit series to solidify their position as the primary source of video programming. They were a bit anxious to find such material because the very concept of national live TV networks was under attack from the West Coast.

In June, 1947, Jerry Fairbanks, a former producer of film shorts at the Paramount studios in Hollywood, announced that he was setting up a TV film unit. He promised to supply regular weekly filmed programs to individual stations directly through the mail for airing at their pleasure (a process called "syndication"). Not only did this represent a considerable saving when compared to the potential cost of using AT&T's coaxial cable, but, with coast-to-coast network TV hookups still years away, Fairbanks offered a ready supply of programs to new TV stations not yet connected to the cable. He filmed seventeen episodes of a crime drama series, *Public Prosecutor* (at the unconventional length of twenty minutes per episode), but the networks were able to pressure the local TV station managers into ignoring the service. The networks feared that if local stations began to obtain filmed shows directly from a syndicator, they might eventually decide not to use network programming at all. Stressing that television should be *live*, not filmed, the networks assured the locals that once the cable connections were made, stations would receive much better material if aligned with a national network. In the meantime, for those in the hinterlands, DuMont supplied the stopgap solution when it announced development of a method of preserving live TV shows by filming them directly from a television monitor. These kinescope recordings, popularly known as "kines," meant that while a local station waited for the arrival of live network TV in its area, it could still obtain network programs, albeit delayed a week or two. Though the kines were often grainy and hard to hear, they allowed the TV networks to beat Fairbanks at his own game. Finding no buyers, Fairbanks dropped the idea and, as a result, his *Public Prosecutor* series stayed on the shelf until the early 1950s.

The success of the networks in scuttling the Fairbanks film proposal had as much to do with the standoffish attitude of Hollywood to television, and vice versa, as their own influence on the locals. All the major film studios considered TV to be a prime competitor for the future, and they refused to allow any of their feature films, producers, directors, or stars to appear on television in any form. Consequently, they also gave Fairbanks no support in his scheme. Their strategy was to treat the upstart television with disdain and not give it any help or support, hoping that it would just fade away.

While Hollywood viewed television as a possible economic threat in the future, the movie industry had to concentrate on handling a more immediate crisis in the fall of 1947: the growing fear that Hollywood films might be used to spread Communist propaganda. Only two years after World War II had ended, the new "cold war" between the United States and the Soviet Union dominated the nation's thinking. Many Americans truly felt that the country was in danger of being infiltrated by sinister forces. They looked with suspicion at the many pro-Soviet organizations in America, which had been formed during the Depression of the 1930s and the war camaraderie of the 1940s, and regarded them as a subversive fifth column that could not be counted on in the seemingly inevitable struggle with communism.

Newsletters and magazines, such as *Counterattack* (founded in May, 1947, by two former FBI agents), sprang up to publicize the names of Americans suspected of having ties to communism. Congressional committees such as the House Un-American Activities Committee (HUAC) held public hearings designed to document Red collusion wherever it could be found. One of the first targets of HUAC was the film community of Hollywood, which possessed the most popular system for capturing the nation's attention in an effective, entertaining manner. The committee feared that Communists seeking to subvert the national will would logically try to take over various parts of the film industry as a quick way to reach the American public.

In October, 1947, HUAC opened public hearings to prove that Communists had been writing, producing, and starring in "suspicious" Hollywood films for years. The hearings, which featured some of Hollywood's leading producers and stars, were broadcast live by many stations along the East Coast television coaxial cable. These were the first important congressional hearings ever to allow television coverage and they provided the first national television exposure for a young first term congressman from California, Richard M. Nixon, a HUAC member. At first, Hollywood's bigwigs treated the hearings as a joke, but they soon realized that, in the national climate of fear and suspicion, the committee was looking

for a scapegoat. Fearing that a lack of cooperation might lay the industry open to a governmental takeover, the movie moguls offered up for sacrifice the "ten unfriendlies," ten writers with leftist and Communist connections who had refused to cooperate with HUAC. The writers' refusal to answer questions on their political backgrounds had infuriated the members of HUAC, who loudly observed that they "must be hiding something." The ten unfriendlies were suspended from their jobs and "blacklisted," that is, nobody in Hollywood would hire them any more because they had been linked to communism. Soon, blacklisting spread from these ten to others who worked in movies. In each case, the mere accusation of leftist ties was tantamount to being pronounced guilty, and the blacklisted artists were rarely given a chance to try and "clear" themselves. Writers, producers, directors, and actors suddenly found themselves out of work because of unsubstantiated charges made by unseen accusors. At first, television was mostly untouched by blacklisting because it was felt that TV in 1947 was not even worthy of infiltration.

As television continued to expand through the fall and winter, though, that situation was rapidly changing. Applications for stations, which had been crawling in at one or two per month the year before, averaged three a week by the end of 1947. Set sales were climbing and the January, 1948, declaration by NBC that network television had arrived served as a signal that the time had come for serious efforts at regular weekly programming.

Less than two weeks after the NBC ad, DuMont revived the long-successful radio variety standard, *The Original Amateur Hour*. Major Edward Bowes had run the series on radio from the early 1930s until it ended in 1945, just before he died. Bowes had assumed a wholesome, fatherly, yet realistically critical role introducing new talent to the nation. The possibility of rags-to-riches stardom had made the show very successful on radio and DuMont had high hopes for the TV version. Ted Mack, who had worked under the tutelage of Bowes, took charge, adopting the same approach in welcoming the aspiring performers. Though DuMont took a chance and slotted the program earlier than practically anything else then on (Sunday night, 7:00–8:00 P.M.), it became a very popular video hit. But how popular?

Television was being run by people familiar with radio formats and strategies and, as they began to develop more expensive new video series, they felt the need for program ratings just as in radio. Less than one month after *The Original Amateur Hour* premiered, the Hooper organization, radio's most respected ratings service, conducted the first television rating sweep, in New York City. Ted Mack's show walked away with the number one slot, registering a 46.8% rating (that is, of the televisions in the homes contacted, 46.8 percent were on and tuned to *The Original Amateur Hour*). The J. Walter Thompson agency, an early believer in TV advertising, was the first ad agency to subscribe to Hooper's rating service.

In early 1948, NBC also found itself with a hit show, though it took a while longer to catch on. *Puppet Television Theater* had begun at Christmastime, 1947, as a one-hour children's show running Saturday afternoons at 5:00 P.M. By April, 1948, two weekday episodes were added and the series was renamed *Howdy Doody* after the main puppet character. The idea behind the show was simple: a few kids, a few puppets, a clown, and some music. What made it click was the personality and verve of the program's ringmaster, "Buffalo" Bob Smith, a former New York disk jockey who had previously been the host of a relaxed Arthur Godfrey-type morning radio show for adults. Smith seemed to enjoy the children present in the "peanut gallery" and his efforts to entertain them came out in an ingratiating but not condescending form.

FALL 1947 SCHEDULE

MONDAY

	7:00	7:30	8:00	8:30	9:00	9:30	10:00	10:30	
									ABC
									CBS
	Small Fry Club	Doorway To Fame	SHOWCASE	Swing Into Sports	Boxing From Jamaica Arena				DUMONT
		NBC News	local		Gillette Cavalcade of Sports				NBC

TUESDAY

	7:00	7:30	8:00	8:30	9:00	9:30	10:00	10:30	
									ABC
									CBS
	Small Fry Club	PHOTOGRAPHIC HORIZONS	LOOK UPON A STAR	local	MARY KAY &JOHNNY	Boxing From Park Arena			DUMONT
									NBC

WEDNESDAY

	7:00	7:30	8:00	8:30	9:00	9:30	10:00	10:30	
									ABC
					Sports From Madison Square Garden				CBS
	Small Fry Club	local	CAFE DE PARIS	local	JACK EIGEN				DUMONT
		Kraft Television Theatre		In The Kitchen	local	CURRENT OPINION			NBC

THURSDAY

	7:00	7:30	8:00	8:30	9:00	9:30	10:00	10:30	
									ABC
			CBS News	TO THE QUEEN'S TASTE	Sports From Madison Square Garden				CBS
	Small Fry Club	Birthday Party	local	CHARADE QUIZ	local	WRESTLING FROM JEROME STADIUM			DUMONT
		NBC News	MEET THE PRESS	MUSICAL MERRY-GO-ROUND	You Are An Artist				NBC

FRIDAY

	7:00	7:30	8:00	8:30	9:00	9:30	10:00	10:30	
									ABC
									CBS
	Small Fry Club	THE GAY COED	local	Magic Carpet	local	Wrestling From Jamaica Arena			DUMONT
		Campus Hoopla	World In Your Home	Gillette Cavalcade of Sports					NBC

SATURDAY

	7:00	7:30	8:00	8:30	9:00	9:30	10:00	10:30	
									ABC
			CBS News	THE SCRAPBOOK	Sports From Madison Square Garden				CBS
									DUMONT
									NBC

SUNDAY

	7:00	7:30	8:00	8:30	9:00	9:30	10:00	10:30	
									ABC
	SCRAPBOOK, JUNIOR EDITION	local	Week In Review	Sports From Madison Square Garden					CBS
									DUMONT
		Author Meets The Critics	THEATER GUILD TELEVISION THEATER A.N.T.A. PLAYHOUSE		REVIEW OF THE NEWS				NBC

He supplied the voices to most of the puppets (such as Howdy Doody, Phineas T. Bluster, and Captain Scuttlebutt), giving each an individual personality. The live characters such as Princess Summer-Fall-Winter-Spring and the mute clown Clarabell (played by Bob Keeshan, later renowned as Captain Kangaroo) shared his enthusiasm and helped make the humans as warm and friendly as the puppets. By the fall of 1948, the program aired Monday through Friday.

Howdy Doody was one of television's first superstars. Small fry seized control of the family TV set in the late afternoon and demonstrated that they could become quite devoted to a television character. Mothers were not upset because, when the kids were occupied with *Howdy Doody,* they could relax. In the postwar baby-boom era, television had a practical function—it was an excellent babysitter. As a result, the late afternoon and very early evening "after school" time slots were recognized as prime "kidvid" hours—

perfect for programming geared toward children, whose parents were still too busy to settle down and watch.

Television was becoming an item of interest to more and more households. Newspapers began accepting the medium as a fact of life and grudgingly agreed to print daily broadcast schedules for no charge—just as they did with radio. CBS, which had been airing only remote telecasts for almost a year, realized that NBC and DuMont had seized the initiative in television programming. Having attracted only a few sponsors for its outdoor broadcasts, the network conceded defeat in February, 1948, by announcing that it would soon reopen and greatly enlarge its studios at Grand Central Station. ABC, which had abstained from TV production for a year while waiting for its home base in New York to be constructed, decided not to wait until the August completion date but geared up instead for a mid-April kick-off, using its affiliates on the East Coast.

All the networks realized that if their new program drive was to go anywhere, they would need live music. They at last came to terms with James C. Petrillo's American Federation of Musicians and the total ban on live television music ended. Within hours, CBS and NBC staged a nip-and-tuck race to be the first network to present live music on television. CBS won by ninety minutes. Eugene Ormandy and the Philadelphia Orchestra hit the air at five in the afternoon on March 20, while Arturo Toscanini and the NBC Orchestra weighed in at 6:30 P.M. These orchestral presentations, however, were not really representative of the future of live television music. Soon, pop-oriented musical programs appeared, modeled after the popular radio music shows, which showcased singers in either an all music format (usually a fifteen-minute slot) or more elaborate musical-variety shows (a half-hour or an hour long).

Though CBS was far behind NBC in developing studio entertainment programming and signing up new TV stations as affiliates, once it decided in earnest to reenter in-studio commercial television the network quickly became the chief competitor to NBC, leapfrogging the competition. This was a reflection of CBS's radio strength. It was a very strong number two in radio behind NBC and the two were generally regarded as the powerhouses of broadcasting. As television stations decided to align themselves with a network, it made sense to go with one of the two biggest in radio.

CBS's only holdover from its all-remote concept was the network's first effort in theatrical drama, *Tonight on Broadway*. Producer Worthington Miner took TV cameras to New York theaters in order to present hit Broadway plays, beginning with "Mr. Roberts," starring Henry Fonda. Miner treated the series like any other remote event and positioned the cameras so that the entire stage was visible at all times on the TV screen. While dead center, thirty-five rows from the front, might have been perfect for a patron at the theater, it was disastrous to viewers at home who tried to follow the action on their eight-inch screens (opera glasses were not much help). The tiny figures were lost in the open expanse

of stage, but it was felt that this was the only way to correctly convey the feel of theater. The cameras were there to present the event exactly as a member of the audience would see it. Home viewers were, in effect, sneaking in for free.

The resurrected ABC also dabbled in drama with its first new series in April, *Hollywood Screen Test*. Originating at first from Philadelphia, the program was a combination drama-anthology and talent show in which two performers who had Broadway experience, but who were not yet stars, appeared in a scene with a celebrity veteran. Just as in *The Original Amateur Hour* there was the lure of seeing stars-in-the-making, but the overall quality of production was much higher. The show was set up as if it were an actual West Coast "screen test," which not only served as an innovative format but also covered up the lack of expensive scenery. The series lasted five years for ABC, with veteran Neil Hamilton acting as host for all but the first few months.

Through the spring of 1948, the networks' TV schedules expanded tremendously to include elementary versions of basic entertainment formats that were popular on radio. NBC presented *Barney Blake, Police Reporter,* starring Gene O'Donnell as a reporter-as-cop. On DuMont, real-life husband and wife Johnny and Mary Kay Stearns faced the humorous trials and tribulations of married life in the appropriately titled situation comedy, *Mary Kay and Johnny*. Kyle MacDonnell, one of the first singing stars to make a name on television, hosted a series of pleasant fifteen-minute musical vehicles for NBC: *For Your Pleasure, Kyle MacDonnell Sings,* and *Girl About Town*. All the networks had quizzes such as *Americana Quiz* and *Charade Quiz*. DuMont offered the imaginative *Court of Current Issues,* in which actors would argue a case in a courtroom setting and the studio audience acted as jury. This seemed the perfect setting for a television discussion show.

While television developed its selection of entertainment vehicles in an effort to duplicate some of the attraction of network radio, a dramatic—and symbolic—change took place in radio program-

Milton Berle, the first host of *Texaco Star Theater,* soon became known as Mr. Television. *(Smithsonian Institution, Allen B. DuMont Collection)*

October 27, 1947
You Bet Your Life. (ABC Radio). After several misfired flops, Groucho Marx, the great ad-libber, finds a successful radio format under producer John Guedel. The setup is simple: Groucho acts as host of a quiz show that devotes most of its time to his jokes.

November 13, 1947
Boston is connected to the East Coast network, though it does not yet have any television stations on the air.

November 18, 1947
Mary Kay and Johnny. (DuMont). Television's first weekly situation comedy.

February 9, 1948
The Frederick W. Ziv Company, radio's largest program syndicator, sets up a television film branch to help fill the many programming gaps on the local TV stations.

February 16, 1948
Camel Newsreel Theater. (NBC). Fox-Movietone produces NBC's first nightly television news show.

April 15, 1948
ABC resumes television broadcasting, using as its temporary headquarters WMAL in Washington and WFIL in Philadelphia.

April 28, 1948
CBS resumes in-studio television broadcasts as the Douglas Edwards news show becomes a Monday through Friday production. By fall, twenty-five-year-old Don Hewitt becomes the program's first regular producer.

May 3, 1948
The Supreme Court upholds the anti-trust decision in the ten-year-old "Paramount Case." The eight major movie studios must begin to divest themselves of their theater chains.

ming. On March 21, the day after the Petrillo ban ended for television music, *Stop the Music* premiered on ABC radio. It was a musical quiz show conceived by Louis G. Cowan, directed by Mark Goodson, and slotted in one of the toughest time periods of the radio week: Sunday night against Edgar Bergen and Fred Allen. Surprisingly, within months, Fred Allen, a member of radio's top ten for a decade, had dropped to thirty-eighth place. By the end of the year, Edgar Bergen took his Sunday night show off the air for a season. *Stop the Music* had beaten them both.

Quiz and game shows had been a part of radio for years, but *Stop the Music* was different. It was a quiz that directly connected entertainment with the personal greed of listeners at home, offering prizes for merely tuning in. The contest was simple: Phone numbers from across the nation were selected at random. While host Bert Parks dialed a number, the show's musical regulars began performing a popular song. As soon as the home contestant picked up the phone, Parks would say "Stop the music!" and ask the listener to identify the song that had just stopped playing. If correct, the listener would win a prize and a chance to identify a much more difficult "mystery melody" worth as much as $30,000. Though the odds against being called were astronomical, listeners felt it was wise to tune in and be prepared—just in case. Besides, the music was good, Parks was energetic as ever, and the show was entertaining in its own right.

In the fall of 1948, Allen offered insurance (up to $5,000) to any listeners who lost out on winning on *Stop the Music* because they were tuned in to him. "In other words," Allen said, "my listeners

can only lose thirty minutes." That was not quite true—with a top prize of up to $30,000 on *Stop the Music* they could lose up to $25,000. But in any case, the offer came too late. Large numbers of similar giveaway shows appeared, at the expense of both established comedians such as Allen and youngsters such as Danny Thomas and Jack Paar. By June, 1949, Allen quit radio in disgust.

At the time radio was about to meet television in a head-to-head battle for advertising dollars, *Stop the Music* demonstrated that a game show could topple a highly paid star. This offered radio sponsors an attractive way to cut costs yet still have a top rated show. Even with all that fancy prize money, quiz show budgets were much less than the salaries of top radio stars who at the time made as much as $30,000 a week. A subtle shift in priorities began to take place. Though radio was still regarded as important to sponsors, the high-class high-budget formats had become expendable if necessary. Lower-budget quizzes could pull in high radio ratings while advertisers directed more of their money to television.

The giveaway quiz show fad did spill over into TV in mid-1948, but none of the programs became big hits. Video production budgets were still relatively small so the TV quiz programs looked cheap rather than magical and glamorous. The shows simply did not appear as visually exciting as the equivalent radio programs sounded. They remained just one more experimental format for television programmers in search of hit shows and prestige events.

The 1948 presidential race provided the networks with an excellent opportunity to boost television's stature. President Harry Truman, who had assumed office when Franklin Roosevelt died, was running for his first elected term and the Republicans felt certain they could beat him. As the race heated up through the spring and summer, the networks devoted as much air time as possible to the various campaigns. Most of the stories appeared on the fifteen-minute nightly newsreel shows that the networks had established over the previous year in an effort to upgrade the image of their news departments. DuMont had been first in the summer of 1947 with Walter Compton's *News from Washington.* NBC soon followed with *Camel Newsreel Theater,* a ten-minute collection of newsreels completely produced by Fox-Movietone (which even took responsibility for hiring the show's off-screen announcing trio of Ed Thorgensen, George Putnam, and Helen Claire). In April, 1948, as part of its return to in-studio broadcasts, CBS brought Douglas Edwards back on camera and retitled the daily program *Douglas Edwards and the News.* ABC joined the others in the summer with *News and Views,* which used a rotating anchor crew, including TV's first anchorwoman, Pauline Frederick.

In addition to coverage on the newsreel shows, that summer CBS gave thirty-minutes of time to a different presidential candidate each week on *Presidential Timber.* Republican Harold Stassen was the first to appear. At the time, the radio networks banned the "dramatization of political issues," so most political forays into radio were generally dull discussions and speeches by either the candidate or a chosen representative. Television had no such ban, so Stassen hired an ad agency to produce a thirty-minute film to run in his segment of *Presidential Timber.* Actually, the film did not spend much time on "the issues" at all, but instead served as a warm pictorial biography meant to promote Stassen as a "nice guy" rather than just a speechmaker.

The planners of both party nominating conventions had noted the staggering growth of television set sales in 1947 and realized that a city connected to the Eastern coaxial cable network offered the opportunity for a tremendous publicity boost at convention time. Both parties chose Philadelphia and, by the time the first

Paul White *(l.)*, who helped create the CBS news organization in the early 1930s, and Douglas Edwards. *(CBS News Photo)*

gavel fell, there were eighteen stations from Boston to Richmond sending out the proceedings to ten million viewers watching on 300,000 sets.

There was little to distinguish one network's convention coverage from another's because all four used the same pictures, provided by a common pool camera set up to focus on the main podium. There were no additional pickups from roving floor reporters, though NBC did set up a small studio off the convention floor ("Room 22") in which Ben Grauer conducted on-the-spot, off-the-cuff interviews with political bigwigs. To anchor coverage of the proceedings, the networks rotated among their top reporters. CBS featured Ed Murrow, Quincy Howe, and Douglas Edwards, while NBC had H. V. Kaltenborn and Richard Harkness. ABC made extensive use of Walter Winchell, while DuMont, which had no formal news staff, hired Drew Pearson as its main commentator.

The Republican convention was generally uneventful and dull as Governor Thomas Dewey from New York easily beat Harold Stassen, but the Democrats staged a drawn-out free-for-all. Minnesota's Hubert H. Humphrey, a candidate for the U.S. Senate, led a floor fight over inclusion of a civil rights plank in the party platform and, in response, Southern Democrats walked out and formed their own splinter party (popularly known as the Dixiecrats). The Democratic nominee, President Harry Truman, fell victim to the floor wrangling along the way and his acceptance speech was delayed until 2:00 A.M. By then most viewer-voters were asleep and consequently missed a truly electrifying presentation. Though Truman was a horrible reader of prewritten speeches, when he started speaking ad-lib from the heart, his oratory was close to perfection. This was the style he used for his acceptance address and it resulted in one of the best speeches of his life.

It was also a very good television speech. By not reading from a script, Truman could look the camera (and the voter) in the eye, without the distracting pauses and downward glances of most speechreaders. He came across on TV as a sincere natural man who was not so much the President as "one of the guys." Truman's speech vividly demonstrated the personal intimacy possible through television. Sharp politicians sensed that television might be even more important than first suspected, but they were not yet ready to incorporate the medium into a full-scale presidential campaign. That fall, Governor Dewey turned down an advertising agency's suggestion to concentrate on short "spot announcements" for television, and he and President Truman restricted their use of TV to a few live pickups of large political rallies. It was generally agreed that television played very little part in Truman's come-from-behind victory.

While politicians were just beginning to experiment with television, the era of testing had passed for entertainment programming. The networks and sponsors were ready for a dramatic breakthrough to tie it all together. Kraft's McLaren Cheese promotion demonstrated how effective television advertising could be. The top-rated Ted Mack show proved that viewers liked variety. The vaudeville styled *Hour Glass* had attracted a devoted following in 1946 without any live music, and now the Petrillo ban was lifted. The total number of TV sets in the country was doubling every four months. It was time to move!

On pages 26 and 27 of the May 19, 1948, issue of the entertainment trade weekly *Variety*, the William Morris talent agency placed a two-page ad with a large headline:

VAUDEVILLE IS BACK

The Golden Age of variety begins with the premiere of *The Texaco Star Theater* on television, Tuesday, 8:00–9:00 P.M. E.D.T., starting June 8 on NBC and its affiliated stations in New York, Washington, Boston, Philadelphia, Baltimore,

---

May 6, 1948
    The FCC takes away channel one from television, giving the military use of the frequency instead.

July 5, 1948
    My Favorite Husband. (CBS Radio). Lucille Ball plays a wacky wife whose zany escapades make life difficult for her banker husband and his short-tempered boss (played by Gale Gordon). Jess Oppenheimer produces this "in-house" CBS radio sitcom.

July 19, 1948
    Our Miss Brooks. (CBS Radio). In another successful home-grown CBS radio sitcom, Eve Arden plays Connie Brooks, a level-headed, believable teacher at mythical Madison High School. She is backed by the omni-present Gale Gordon as the blustery principal, Osgood Conklin.

July 26, 1948
    The Bob Howard Show. (CBS). Piano-playing Bob Howard becomes the first black to host a network television series, appearing in a fifteen-minute weekday evening musical show.

August 10, 1948
    ABC at last gets it own home-base television station as WJZ (later WABC) goes on the air in New York.

August 11, 1948
    News and Views. (ABC). Six different anchors handle ABC's first television news show.

Richmond, and Schenectady. WANTED—Variety artists from all corners of the globe. Send particulars to the William Morris Agency.

A radio version of *The Texaco Star Theater* had played since the fall of 1938, but that mixed variety and drama under a succession of celebrity hosts (including Ken Murray, Fred Allen, James Melton, Alan Young, and Gordon MacRae). The new television version was conceived as a throwback to the vaudeville houses (such as New York City's famed Palace Theater), which had thrived from the turn of the century until the advent of radio and talkies.

In vaudeville, a few acts would appear on stage, perform, and step off, beginning with the unknowns and working up to the headliners. An emcee would introduce the performers and attempt to give the show some continuity. NBC felt that a big budget television version of the vaudeville form might catch on, just as *Hour Glass* had done in its brief run. With imaginative production, a good selection of talent, and a strong host, *Texaco Star Theater* could be a big hit. Finding the right host was the most difficult part of the formula, so the network decided to spend the summer giving a few candidates trial runs. It quickly settled on Milton Berle to open the series. Berle was a successful nightclub comedian who had been a flop in numerous attempts to make it on network radio, but he had brought down the house on a heart fund auction program televised by DuMont on April 7. It seemed that the added visual nature of television was just the extra plus Berle needed and, on June 8, he stepped out for the first *Texaco Star Theater.* It was as if television had been reinvented.

Reviewers were ecstatic: "Television's first real smash!" "Let the hucksters make way for the show folk!" As emcee, Berle delivered a cleaned-up version of his nightclub routine, with visual mannerisms impossible to convey over radio, then introduced a succession of acts (including Pearl Bailey). Yet that was just the beginning. Berle also had an amazing sense of timing and pacing. When he saw the show was lagging, he would dash on stage and ham it up, holding the program together with the force of his personality. Unlike old-time vaudeville and every other variety show previously on television, Berle's *Texaco Star Theater* opened fast, stayed fast and tight, and finished fast. Even the one commercial—known as the middle ad—was integrated into the act as a funny plug by pitchman Sid Stone, whose "tell ya' what I'm gonna do . . ." come-on soon became a national catch phrase.

Instead of staging the show for the studio audience, the producers were more interested in giving the viewers at home a sharp, clear picture. The camera was taken out of the infamous thirty-fifth row and placed on stage. The resulting closeups produced an immediacy and intimacy unmatched by radio and theater. This marriage of vaudeville and video techniques produced a new form, vaudeo.

There had never been anything else like it on television.

NBC had hoped for success, but had not expected a hit of such proportions. After Berle's three appearances in June and July, a rotating group of emcees took over (including Henny Youngman, Morey Amsterdam, and George Price), but none could generate anything near the excitement of Berle. The format and his personality had meshed perfectly. After frantic importunings by NBC, Berle signed to become permanent host of *Texaco Star Theater* beginning in September.

Twelve days after Berle's June premiere, CBS unveiled its own television vaudeville show, *Toast of the Town,* with Ed Sullivan as host. Sullivan had been a Broadway newspaper columnist for almost twenty years and his Broadway contacts made him the perfect choice to head a variety show drawing on new talent. CBS producer Worthington Miner first spotted the somewhat dour, low-key Sullivan as a potential for television, and chose him to emcee the 1947 Harvest Moon Ball, staged and televised in Madison Square Garden by CBS and the *New York Daily News.* He used him again in a 1948 Easter Sunday variety benefit, and *Toast of the Town* soon followed.

Coming so soon after Berle's spectacular, Sullivan's June 20 debut suffered in comparison. He was judged by the same standards even though Berle had been chosen for his abilities as a performer and Sullivan for his skills as an off-stage producer who could unearth new talent. *Toast of the Town* itself was much closer to a traditional vaudeville set up than *Texaco Star Theater,* as Sullivan merely introduced a succession of acts and stepped aside. At first, even the camera placement was back at the thirty-fifth row.

Jack Gould of the *New York Times* called the selection of Sullivan as emcee "ill advised," saying: ". . . his extreme matter-of-factness and his tendency to introduce friends in the audience add up to little sparkling entertainment."

In a medium centered on performing talent and warm intimacy, Sullivan was the permanent exception to prove the rule—he had neither, but his knack for finding talent on the verge of making it big was uncanny. In fact, two of the seven performers on the opening show were the then unknown "zany comic" team of Dean Martin and Jerry Lewis (paid $200 for their appearance). Nonetheless, jokes about Sullivan's stage mannerisms never ceased, even after the show became a big success. Budding impressionists cut their teeth on mimicking his scrunched stance and his frequently repeated phrases such as "And now, right here on our stage . . ." and "really big shew." Husbands would turn to their wives in the glowing dark and opine, "He's got no talent. He'll never last." It was Sullivan who had the last laugh as his program ran for twenty-three years. Fred Allen explained the incongruity: "Ed Sullivan will stay on television as long as other people have talent."

8. The Freeze

THE EXPANSION of television during the first nine months of 1948 was nothing short of miraculous. Set manufacturers could hardly keep up with the demand for new product. The FCC could hardly keep up with the paperwork of applications for new stations. All four television networks planned major program premieres in the fall, treating the new TV season with the same respect as a new radio season. To the television industry, the era of "the greatest means of mass communications in the world"—also known as "the biggest ad medium yet"—had arrived at last. There seemed to be no limit to the coming boom. At the end of September, though, a long festering technical problem cast a chill over this euphoria.

In the 1930s, when the FCC had first set technical standards for television broadcasting, it frankly had no idea how far apart stations assigned to the same channel should be. If they were too close to each other, signals would clash and many home viewers would receive a jumble of images. In 1945, the commission set 150 miles as the minimum distance between stations on the same channel but, during 1948, when the number of TV stations on the air almost tripled, there were more and more reports of cross-station interference. The FCC felt impelled to do something quickly because unlike the question of color, which could be postponed indefinitely, signal interference was an obvious, irritating, and immediate problem which would only get worse as more stations signed on. Yet the FCC really needed time to study the situation and work out new standards, so on September 30, 1948, the commission put a freeze on processing applications for new stations.

When the freeze was announced, there were thirty-seven stations on the air in twenty-two cities, with eighty-six other stations already approved and in the process of preparing to sign on. These new stations would be allowed to go on the air, but the 303 station applications sent in but not yet acted on were filed away until the FCC could work out the frequency problem. The commission said that the freeze would be in effect for only a short time (approximately six months), so the networks took no immediate notice of it. At worst, they felt, there would be a slight pause in the rapid rise of television. Instead, the freeze extended three and one-half years and placed television in a peculiar state of suspended animation, just on the verge of expanding into a national mass medium. From 1948 to 1952, advertisers and programmers were given the opportunity to refine their formats and techniques while serving a large, but limited audience. While part of the nation continued to wait breathlessly for the long-postponed arrival of television, people in the rest of the country became caught up in the new focus of popular entertainment.

The most exciting event of the new season was the return of Milton Berle, the uncrowned king of television, to the *Texaco Star Theater*. Milton was back and NBC had him. What's more, he was still "boffo!" The magic chemistry that had powered Berle's few summer appearances continued to charge his fall shows. When the first ratings came in, Berle and Texaco were so far out in front that the number one slot was virtually conceded to them, and the other networks lowered their sights and aimed for number two. By November, *Texaco Star Theater* had an 86.7% rating (meaning that of all sets, including those not turned on, 86.7% were tuned to Berle on Tuesday) and a 94.7% share (meaning that of all sets then being used, 94.7 percent were tuned to Berle). Milton Berle had a hammerlock on the Tuesday-at-8:00 P.M. time slot that he would keep for almost eight years.

It soon became quite clear that any program slotted against Berle was going to lose big. A sponsor would have to be crazy to buy into a show on versus Berle—nobody would watch it. So, the other networks began filling early Tuesday evening with extremely weak programming (usually unsponsored) that had little hope of catching a large audience anyway. One of the first to do so was DuMont, which moved out its promising *Court of Current Issues* and moved in *Operation: Success,* a program of self-help tips for crippled veterans.

Milton Berle's program seemed irresistible with its fast-paced tempo aimed directly at the home audience. Gradually, the program evolved from standard vaudeville into an even stronger vehicle for Berle's dominating personality, a "sketch" show. This formalized Berle's habit of butting into routines by adding as a regular feature scenes with Berle and his guests performing together. This provided better continuity as well as the assurance that Berle would appear throughout the show as often as possible. Although sometimes he seemed to be staging a one man production, Berle also introduced some very talented performers as *Texaco Star Theater* became one of the prime television showcases for new talent. Sid Caesar, a rising young comic, appeared on one of the early shows to recreate an airplane skit he had performed in the feature film "Tars and Spars." In March, band leader Desi Arnaz soloed with his hot bongo drumming.

Number two in the ratings behind Berle was Ed Sullivan's *Toast of the Town,* which also served as a television springboard for new talent. In February, Jackie Gleason, who was then starring

FALL 1948 SCHEDULE

MONDAY

	7:00	7:30	8:00	8:30	9:00	9:30	10:00	10:30	
	News And Views	local	Kiernan's Corner	ON TRIAL	¢ VAUDEO VARIETIES		¢ SKIP FARRELL SHOW	local	ABC
	local	Places, Please	CBS News	Face The Music	local		Sports From Madison Square Garden		CBS
	Doorway To Fame	Camera Headlines	local	Champaign Orchids	local	Swing Into Sports	local	Court of Current Issues	local	DUMONT
	¢ KUKLA, FRAN AND OLLIE	American Song	Camel Newsreel	CHEVROLET ON BROADWAY	Americana Quiz		Gillette Cavalcade of Sports		NBC

TUESDAY

	7:00	7:30	8:00	8:30	9:00	9:30	10:00	10:30	
	News And Views	local	CHILD'S WORLD	local	AMERICA'S TOWN MEETING		¢ TOMORROWS CHAMPIONS [to 12 Midnite]		ABC
	ROAR OF THE RAILS	local	CBS News	Face The Music	local	We, The People	Straws In The Wind People's Platform	local	CBS
	OFF THE RECORD	Camera Headlines	INS Telenews	OPERATION: SUCCESS	local		Boxing From Park Arena		DUMONT
	¢ KUKLA, FRAN AND OLLIE	MUSICAL MINIAT.	Camel Newsreel	Texaco Star Theatre	MARY MARGARET McBRIDE SHOW		Gillette Cavalcade of Sports		NBC

WEDNESDAY

	7:00	7:30	8:00	8:30	9:00	9:30	10:00	10:30	
	News And Views	local	JERRY BERGEN	local	Club Seven	Quizzing The News	Wrestling From Washington		ABC
	local	Places, Please	CBS News	Face The Music	KOBB'S KORNER	Winner Take All	local	TOURNAMENT OF CHAMPIONS	CBS
	Birthday Party	Camera Headlines	local	Photographic Horizons	THE GROWING PAYNES	Boxing From Jamaica Arena		DUMONT
	¢ KUKLA, FRAN AND OLLIE	You Are An Artist	Camel Newsreel	Girl About Town	PICTURE THIS	PHIL SILVERS ARROW SHOW	Kraft Television Theatre	NBC News	The Village Barn	NBC

THURSDAY

	7:00	7:30	8:00	8:30	9:00	9:30	10:00	10:30	
	News And Views	local		FASHION STORY	Critic-At-Large	ABC FEATURE FILM		local	ABC
	local	CBS News	Face The Music	To The Queen's Taste	Sports From Madison Square Garden		CBS
	ADVENTURES OF OKY-DOKY	Camera Headlines	Jack Eigen	local	Charade Quiz	Wrestling From Park Arena		DUMONT
	¢ KUKLA FRAN	Paris Fashions	MUSICAL MINIAT.	Camel Newsreel	NBC Presents	Nature of Things	Lanny Ross Swift Show	BOB SMITH'S GULF ROAD SHOW	DUNNINGER AND WINCHELL	local	NBC

FRIDAY

	7:00	7:30	8:00	8:30	9:00	9:30	10:00	10:30	
	News And Views	local	RED CABOOSE	local	Candid Microphone	Gay 90s Revue	BREAK THE BANK	¢ MUSIC IN VELVET	local	ABC
	YOUR SPORTS	Places, Please	CBS News	Face The Music	What's It Worth	Capt. Billy's Music Hall	local		CBS
	Key To The Missing	Camera Headlines	Television Fashions On Parade	local	Wrestling From Jamaica Arena		DUMONT
	¢ KUKLA, FRAN AND OLLIE	Musical M.-G.-R.	Camel Newsreel	NBC Presents	Stop Me If You've Heard This One	I'D LIKE TO SEE	Gillette Cavalcade of Sports	GREAT FIGHTS	NBC

SATURDAY

	7:00	7:30	8:00	8:30	9:00	9:30	10:00	10:30	
	News And Views	local	Joe Hasel Sports	3 About Town	local		¢ STAND BY FOR CRIME	¢ SUPER CIRCUS	local	ABC
	local		Sports From Madison Square Garden		CBS
	local		DUMONT
	local		SATURDAY NIGHT JAMBOREE	Television Screen Magazine	local		NBC

SUNDAY

	7:00	7:30	8:00	8:30	9:00	9:30	10:00	10:30	
	local	THE SOUTHERNAIRES	Hollywood Screen Test	ACTOR'S STUDIO	¢ ABC TELEVISION PLAYERS		local		ABC
	Week In Review	local	STUDIO ONE FORD TELEVISION THEATER HOUR		DENNIS JAMES CARNIVAL	Toast Of The Town	AMERICA SPEAKS	local	CBS
	Original Amateur Hour		local		DUMONT
	Mary Kay & Johnny	Review Of The News	WELCOME ABOARD	Author Meets The Critics	Meet The Press	PHILCO TELEVISION PLAYHOUSE		local	NBC

on Broadway in "Along Fifth Avenue," delivered a comedy monologue about a man in love with a juke box. Later that month, young nightclub comic Larry Storch did some hilarious impersonations and, in June, Sam Levenson, a former schoolteacher, presented his view of life in New York City in a monologue that drew strong critical praise. Sullivan also arranged for the first television appearances by established stars such as Faye Emerson, Rosemary Clooney, Vaughn Monroe, Peter Lind Hayes, Skitch Henderson, the Baird Puppets, Frankie Laine, and Frank Fontaine. Unlike Berle, Sullivan continued to present his guests in a pure vaudeville format, always stepping aside once the introductions were finished. He also included a greater variation in types of guests than Berle, placing concert singers, circus animal acts, ballet troupes, and acrobats alongside more traditional comedy and pop music performers. Sullivan boasted that he put on a show with something for everybody in the family.

Even though Berle and Sullivan had only been on the air since June, their shows had become the standards other television series tried to copy. The makeup of the program schedule for the fall of 1948 made it quite clear that television had adopted yet another radio trait—mass imitation. Nervous radio sponsors, desiring the largest possible audience for their programs, tended to choose carbon copies of already successful formats rather than risk audience rejection with an untested concept. The same was holding true for television. Berle and Sullivan had vividly demonstrated the popularity of vaudeo shows, so the airwaves were filled with similar programs trying to cash in on this proved path to video success. Combined with the expected deluge of new musical-variety shows launched after the Petrillo ban was lifted, these gave viewers their first overdose of a hit formula.

Russ Morgan hosted *Welcome Aboard,* which was ostensibly set aboard a ship, and featured numerous guest appearances by Sullivan's first finds, Dean Martin and Jerry Lewis. Frank Fontaine and later Jan Murray hosted *Front Row Center,* while Morey Amsterdam's show brought forward the talents of second banana Art Carney. NBC slotted Phil Silvers to host *The Arrow Show* but, because he was also starring in "High Button Shoes" on Broadway at the time, Silvers had to rush from the studio immediately after his live TV program in order to appear live on stage. After a few months of this madness, Silvers gave up *The Arrow Show.* NBC placed Perry Como's casual fifteen-minute *Supper Club* after the fights on Friday, marking the first attempt at late night network programming.

Band leader Fred Waring conducted the classiest musical-variety show of the season—and the most expensive at the time ($20,000 each week). Waring rarely used guests, relying instead on his sixty-five-member family of dancers, singers, and musicians. In contrast, some of the season's weaker vehicles included ABC's *American Minstrels of 1949,* which placed twenty-six-year-old Jack Carter and the blackface duo of Pick and Pat into a cumbersome mix of the vaudeville era and the minstrel age; *Paul Whiteman's TV Teen Club,* which presented only mildly uptempo big band dance music; Bob Smith's attempt at a weekly half-hour of song and chat, similar to his pre-*Howdy Doody* Godfrey-esque radio show; and the unwieldy team of Dunninger the mind-reading mentalist and ventriloquist Paul Winchell.

The prime exponent of pure and simple variety was "the old redhead," Arthur Godfrey, who quickly became as much of a workaholic on television as he was on radio. Godfrey's first television series was a simulcast of his Monday night radio hit, *Talent Scouts,* in which he played the genial Ted Mack role. A month later he added *Arthur Godfrey and His Friends,* a Wednesday night television version of his popular morning radio show in which he headed a close knit "family" of musical performers. Like Godfrey, the show was extremely lowkey. Guests came on, engaged in chit-chat, and sang a song or two. One of the program's regulars performed a number. Godfrey recommended some products he truly believed in, played his ukulele, told a few slightly ribald jokes, and said goodnight. His warm, sincere personality carried over to television perfectly and he transformed such potentially boring routines into entertaining visits with an old friend. Both shows immediately became top ten hits and remained so for years.

One vaudeville format that failed miserably in the transition to television was the hellzapoppin' humor of Ole Olsen and Chic Johnson, the hosts of *Fireball Fun-For-All,* Milton Berle's summer replacement. For three decades, Olsen and Johnson had specialized in cornball punchlines and comic anarchy, including exploding scenery, stooges in gorilla suits, pop-up midgets, seltzer bottles, and gobs of custard pie. Their very busy productions worked well with a live audience in a large theater, but they were stopped cold by television. Even though the writers worked out detailed scripts and camera shots in advance, the very nature of the act—which Olsen and Johnson brought unaltered to television—made it impossible for the camera crews to follow close up, so the action was generally shown in long shots. As a result, the complicated bits were completely lost to the home audience watching on eight-inch screens. Without the impact of the visuals, Olsen and Johnson's cornball humor bombed.

In the summer of 1949, one year after Berle and Sullivan had first appeared, DuMont launched its big effort in vaudeo, *Cavalcade of Stars,* with Jack Carter as host. By then, there had been so many others like it already that *Cavalcade of Stars* was almost lost in the crowd. The only unique feature of the program was its unorthodox time slot—Saturday night at 9:00 P.M. The other networks did not place any of their stronger programs on Saturday because it was assumed that on "date night" the home audience would put television aside (as it had done with radio) and go out. Instead, more people stayed at home with the TV set than the networks had expected, so *Cavalcade of Stars* built a moderate (but not overwhelming) following and served as a training ground for comedians such as Jerry Lester, Jackie Gleason, Larry Storch, and Jack Carter, who went on to success with other networks after a stint with the show.

The less-than-spectacular performance by *Cavalcade of Stars* even against weak competition was a grim disappointment to Du-Mont, which badly needed a smash hit show. Though all the networks had ignored the FCC-imposed freeze at first, after the flurry of fall premieres it became apparent that, as a result of the freeze on new stations, the competition for affiliates would be tighter than ever before. During the freeze, there were many cities with only one television station, and, consequently, these stations found themselves besought by all four networks to air programs. Broadcasters in one-station markets regularly took programs from all the networks, depending on which shows were doing the best. DuMont and ABC were especially hurt by this situation because NBC and CBS, the leaders in network radio, had the biggest names and already occupied the top of the TV ratings. By the middle of 1949, the two major networks dominated the airtime on most stations, at the expense of the two smaller networks. *Cavalcade of Stars* demonstrated how difficult it was to break this cycle, even with a pretty good show. ABC and DuMont needed smash hits just to catch the attention of local programmers and get them used to airing their material. This became a circular "Catch-22" situation because if local stations regularly chose the most popular programs, how could any new show build an audience and become a hit? Soon, DuMont realized that the tight market limitations of the freeze had also provided it with one important weapon to fight back, the city of Pittsburgh.

Before the freeze took effect, DuMont had won FCC approval for its third O&O station, WDTV (later KDKA-TV), the first television station in Pittsburgh. During the freeze years, this gave the network the only television outlet in one of the nation's largest markets and sponsors who wanted to be seen in Pittsburgh had to play ball with DuMont. This monopoly over the Pittsburgh airwaves soon became one of the network's most important assets and it won sponsors for a number of DuMont shows that would have been otherwise ignored. One of the most peculiar program deals took place in early 1949 when Admiral agreed to run its *Admiral Broadway Revue* on DuMont as well as NBC (which had more affiliates than any other TV network) in order to get into Pittsburgh. The simultaneous placement allowed DuMont to tout the program to local stations as a DuMont show and to try to interest them in its other network offerings. This short cut to credibility failed because broadcasters considered *The Admiral Broadway Revue* an NBC program anyway, so it never became the "DuMont hit" the network so desperately needed.

NBC had its own problems with *The Admiral Broadway Revue,* chief among them the fact that its Broadway-based producer, Max Liebman, concentrated on the theatrical presentation itself and did not take the vital next step of directing the stage action toward the audience at home. He brought together a talented group of young performers—comics Sid Caesar, Imogene Coca, and Mary McCarthy as well as dancers Marge and Gower Champion—and each week staged a very funny Broadway-style revue that worked well in the theater but came across as choppy and distant on the TV screen. Instead of demanding intimate camera placement, Liebman was content to let the crews shoot the whole stage from out in the audience (the infamous thirty-fifth row). *The Admiral Broad-*

Washingtonians watch the 1949 World Series on a set displayed in a store window. *(National Archives)*

way Revue ended after a thirteen-week run when Admiral pulled out as sponsor, though Liebman learned from his mistakes and had considerably more success the following season when he restructured the program as *Your Show of Shows.*

When the FCC approved DuMont's request for a TV station in Pittsburgh, the commission reiterated its belief that DuMont was controlled by its major stockholder, Paramount Pictures, and said that it would not grant any more TV licenses to either Paramount or DuMont. The FCC had set an ownership limit of five TV stations for any one group and because it classified Paramount and DuMont as one organization, it counted the two Paramount stations (WBKB in Chicago and KTLA in Los Angeles) and three DuMont stations (WABD in New York, WTTG in Washington, and WDTV in Pittsburgh) as reaching that limit. Both companies refused to accept the FCC's decision as final and planned to continue the fight once the freeze was lifted. Paramount wished to establish TV stations in Boston, Detroit, and Dallas, while DuMont intended to push for O&Os in Cincinnati and Cleveland. With the battle over network TV affiliates already so intense, DuMont felt that it needed five O&Os as a solid base for expanding its network. Paramount also felt that it badly needed the income from some extra television stations because the end of a decade-long legal case had jeopardized the entire financial structure of the big Hollywood studios.

In 1938, the Department of Justice had filed an anti-trust suit against eight major film studios (including Paramount), claiming that they were monopolizing the movie business by controlling both the production and projection of films. The "big eight" not only created most of the movies in Hollywood, but also owned and ran large national chains of movie theaters, which routinely obtained exclusive screening rights to the latest films. By 1948, the Supreme Court ended the marathon suit (popularly called "The Paramount Case") by siding with the government and ordering the eight studios to end their production-exhibition arrangement. Along with the others, Paramount had to unload its chain of theaters, a major source of the company's revenue.

In 1949, Paramount Pictures, Inc., split in two. The Paramount Pictures Corporation was set up to continue making movies. It also kept control of KTLA and about 30% of DuMont. A separate company, United Paramount Theaters, was created to manage the movie theaters and run WBKB. The Justice Department was satisfied that Paramount had complied with the Supreme Court's ruling, but the FCC was not so sure. Preoccupied with the freeze, the commission refused to say whether it accepted the Paramount-United Paramount split as total. Until it did decide, it would continue to assume that DuMont and the two Paramounts were one organization that owned five TV stations and would get no more.

The FCC's slow pace in sorting out technicalities placed broadcasters in a squeeze between their day-to-day business reality and the commission's decision process. Without the expansion of television into new markets, the smaller networks found themselves consistently lagging behind as NBC and CBS solidified their hold in TV. Potential station applicants and investors across the country were forced to scuttle their television plans because they had no idea when the freeze would end. Yet during the freeze period, important growth did take place within the areas already served by television. Set sales continued to climb and the size of the home audience expanded. Both advertising and production budgets increased. Producers worked out some of the rough spots in such formats as variety and drama. The networks tried out programs in other time periods such as the morning and early afternoon. Through all this, work on the cross-country coaxial cable continued, bringing the industry closer to live, nationwide TV.

In September, 1948, a Midwest coaxial cable network began operations, connecting Chicago, St. Louis, Detroit, Milwaukee, Toledo, Buffalo, and Cleveland. On January 11, 1949, the Philadelphia-Pittsburgh-Cleveland link connected the Midwest cable with the East Coast network (Boston to Richmond) so that, for the first time, one quarter of the nation's population was within reach of live network programming. One of the first shows on the East-Midwest hookup was the inauguration of President Truman. Ninety-one-year-old Luther Parsons, who had seen the March 4, 1889, inauguration of Benjamin Harrison, watched the Truman ceremony on television and declared that seeing it from his home in Philadelphia was "the much more comfortable way."

One month after the inauguration broadcast, NBC took over control of its nightly news show, bringing in a live on-camera announcer, John Cameron Swayze, a comparatively fancy set, and a new title, *Camel News Caravan*. The new program soon passed Douglas Edwards and became the number one network news show, remaining so for seven years. At heart, though, both Edwards and Swayze were doing essentially the same thing and neither program could match the depth of network radio news coverage. Television still relied on the newsreel organizations for films of news events that were more visual than newsworthy. There was very little on-the-spot reporting and important, but more complex, stories were usually left for sketchy summaries by the news anchors. In his reports, Swayze would chirp, "Let's hop-scotch the world for headlines!" and then read a few bulletins taken from the wire services.

While news was still regarded as the domain of radio, much was expected of live television drama. New York based critics—surrounded by theater—viewed drama as one of the best forms television could present. Yet in 1948 and 1949, television drama was still far from their expectations. Original stories were rare and producers still needed to develop their production techniques. The biggest problem, however, was the sheer bulk of material required. Each week there were eight or nine programs, with no reruns.

Television writers turned to previously written plays, books, and short stores for scripts, but even these required a great deal of work. Everything had to be adjusted to television's limitations and cut down to fit a sixty- or thirty-minute format. In addition, the Hollywood studios applied as much pressure as possible to try and keep television away from hot Broadway property that was under consideration for film. Hollywood lawyers even argued that the studios' exclusive rights to film adaptations of some shows meant that the television kinescope recordings could not be allowed because they were really *films* of the productions. Just to be safe, TV producers usually concentrated on material the Hollywood studios did not care about or had no legal claim to.

CBS had assigned its top producer, Worthington Miner, the task of developing a major dramatic program for the fall of 1948 and he responded with a TV version of *Studio One*. The program consisted of the usual book and theater adaptations, but Miner's production skills transformed the material into high quality television drama. He adapted most of the first season's stories himself and used both theater veterans and fresh talent (including young Charlton Heston) in the casts. In his adaptation of William Shakespeare's "Julius Caesar," Miner demonstrated just how effective television drama could be. Using *Studio One*'s tight budget to his advantage, Miner staged the story in modern dress, an approach successfully used on stage by Orson Welles and the Mercury Theater Company in 1937. As a result, the television production had

an immediate, eye-catching punch that made the story instantly accessible. The Roman legions, dressed in pseudo-Nazi attire, clearly suggested the recent battle against fascism in World War II and brought the themes of totalitarian oppression and political conspiracy from ancient Rome to contemporary society. In one very effective sequence, Miner moved the camera into a tight closeup on the eyes of one of the Roman conspirators and played the actor's prerecorded voice to reveal his inner thoughts. Viewers experienced the unnerving but exciting sensation that they had jumped inside the man's mind as he thought about the assassination of Caesar. That was something even Broadway could not do! Viewers who had considered Shakespeare too highbrow and inscrutable found the program comprehensible and exciting. Critics praised the production as an example of the high quality television drama they had been hoping for.

At NBC, the Philco corporation signed on in the fall of 1948 as the first sponsor for the network's three-year-old Sunday night drama showcase, which became *The Philco Television Playhouse*. Producer Fred Coe's first efforts for Philco were adaptations of Broadway productions and classic plays. In the second season he shifted to adapting books and presented the program as a novel-a-week. Gradually, as Coe turned more and more to original scripts rather than adaptations, the program improved and eventually became known as the most innovative drama series on television.

The obvious solution to the adaptation problem was original material. In 1948, however, TV writers felt it was tough enough just turning out the adaptations on a weekly basis. Soon, out of practical necessity, the thirty-minute anthology programs were forced to come up with original scripts. Adaptations used on the thirty-minute anthologies such as *Chevrolet on Broadway*, *Colgate Theater*, and *Actor's Studio* required extensive, time-consuming ed-

October 3, 1948
The National Football League becomes the first professional sports organization to allow regular weekly network television coverage. As with radio, the Sunday afternoon NFL contests are on ABC, because both NBC and CBS do not consider pro football worth covering. On this first Sunday telecast, Joe Hasel does the play-by-play as the Washington Redskins defeat the New York Giants, 41 to 10.

October 22, 1948
Break the Bank. (ABC). Radio's big money quiz show fad is transplanted to television by ABC, the network that started the trend on radio. Bert Parks is emcee of what becomes ABC's first top ten television show.

November 22, 1948
Columbia Records releases the first *I Can Hear It Now* album, an audio montage of news events between 1933 and 1945. CBS's Ed Murrow narrates and NBC Radio's Fred Friendly produces.

December 17, 1948
The Morey Amsterdam Show. (CBS). Amsterdam brings his comedy-variety format to television from CBS Radio, playing the smart-mouthed emcee of the "Golden Goose' nightclub. He is aided and abetted by his bumbling doorman (played by Art Carney) and a dumb cigarette girl (played by Jacqueline Susann).

December 24, 1948
Supper Club. (NBC). Perry Como pioneers late night television as host to a fifteen-minute music show aired Friday nights at 11:00 P.M.

iting anyway and usually the finished product barely resembled the original work. The producers realized it could be cheaper and faster to use original scripts. Most of these vanguard efforts were horrible, but it really did not matter. Critics, who could barely keep up with all the television drama, had quickly dismissed the thirty-minute form and devoted most of their attention to the sixty-minute anthologies. There were fewer hour shows, they had bigger budgets, and they seemed more worthwhile and important. Though the thirty-minute showcases sometimes featured high quality productions, they were left practically unnoticed by critics and instead served as unheralded television training for aspiring writers such as young Paddy Chayefsky.

The thirty-minute dramas were also in the vanguard of the use of film. A few anthology series such as *Your Show Time* and *Fireside Theater* either began as all-film operations or turned to film after a brief live stint. The networks were still a bit leery about putting filmed shows on the air, and the hour dramas were restricted to just a few film clips for transitions and for some outdoor action shots that could not be staged in the studio. Producers learned that combining live action and film always held a danger of an embarrassing technical flub. For example, one script called for a quick cut from an actor jumping through a studio prop window live to a film of a figure falling to the ground. Instead, the film clip came in two seconds too late and viewers saw the actor hit the safety of the studio floor and scamper away.

The networks generally favored live action over cheap-looking film formats because, from a practical viewpoint, live television emphasized the networks as a source of original programming. The programs themselves seemed more intimate and immediate, presenting the home viewers the opportunity to follow the action as it happened. For instance, in the Chicago-based *Stand By for Crime* on ABC, a fictional police homicide chief would narrate a story in flashback, list the suspects, and then ask home viewers to call in with their guesses as to who was guilty.

In spite of television's progress, with the freeze in effect network radio remained the only means for advertisers to reach consumers throughout the country at once, and it was still the main entertainment force in television cities as well. The major comedy and variety performers shied away from any serious commitments to television, and radio was still regarded as the main stage for the continuing battle for network primacy between NBC and CBS.

Since World War II, CBS has been engaged in a concerted drive to break out of its perennial number two slot. The network chipped away at NBC's radio lead with a string of lightweight situation comedies such as *My Friend Irma* (with Marie Wilson as the archtypical dumb blonde) and *My Favorite Husband* (with Lucille Ball as the archtypical scatterbrained housewife), but NBC still had the top comics. With its virtual monopoly on popular big name humor, NBC seemed well insulated from even the most imaginative CBS program strategy. Determined to move his network into the top spot, CBS chairman William Paley came up with an ingenious ploy to lure NBC's comedy talent to CBS.

In September, 1948, Paley convinced *Amos and Andy*'s creators Freeman Gosden and Charles Correll that by selling CBS the rights to the characters of Amos and Andy (for $2 million), they could substantially reduce their taxes. By treating the program as a business package, which they happened to perform in, Gosden and Correll declared much of the income from the show's sale as a capital gain on an investment, and their tax rate dropped from 77% to 25%. NBC doubted the legality of Paley's maneuver and failed to make equivalent offers to its other stars. Soon Jack Benny, Edgar Bergen, Groucho Marx, Burns and Allen, and Red Skelton rode "Paley's Comet" to the opposition.

It was the biggest programming coup in radio history. CBS had

The popular ethnic humor of *The Goldbergs* came to television with: (from *l.*) Eli Mintz as Uncle David, Gertrude Berg as Molly Goldberg, and Philip Loeb as her husband Jake. *(CBS, Inc.)*

captured the core of NBC's big name star roster and seemed ready to take over as number one after two decades of effort. CBS radio was the immediate beneficiary of the shift but, as Paley later recalled in an interview with the industry magazine, *Broadcasting:*

I was not only thinking of radio, where I wanted to bolster our standing and please our audience . . . I wanted people who I thought would be able to transfer from radio to television.

Development of television vehicles for the new CBS property and stars would take a few years, especially with situation comedy formats such as *Amos and Andy.* In the meantime, CBS brought its reliance on situation comedy over to television with a strong video version of another popular radio show, *The Goldbergs.* CBS's ace producer, Worthington Miner, developed the program for television and it became the network's first major TV situation comedy.

Since 1929, *The Goldbergs* had run as a popular radio show presenting the members of a Jewish immigrant family as they grew up and adjusted to life in their new home, the East side of New York City. Gertrude Berg, who played Molly Goldberg, wrote, produced, and directed the radio program, which was one of several very successful "ethnic" comedies that thrived during the 1930s and 1940s, including *Lum and Abner* (Arkansas hillbillies), *Amos and Andy* (blacks in Harlem), and *Life with Luigi* (Italians in Chicago). The characters in these obviously reflected ethnic stereotypes, usually in their dialect and misspoken English ("It's time to expire" for "Let's go to sleep"), but within their settings, they were natural and homey.

In the transition to television in January, 1949, *The Goldbergs* retained its rich ethnic flavor and concern for everyday family problems. Unlike the brash, snappy vaudeo shows of the time, the program drew its humor from the complications that evolved as the characters faced generally realistic working class situations. Molly managed the household while her husband, Jake (Philip Loeb), ran a small clothing business. Though they worried about keeping the family solvent, their chief concerns were domestic. Jake was a strong father who loved his children yet did not hesitate to punish them when they deserved it. Molly served as both peacemaker and family gossip, always on the lookout for a "perfect match" for either their teenage son, Sammy (Larry Robinson), or daughter, Rosalie (Arlene McQuade). Molly's Uncle David (Eli Mintz) also lived with the family, tossing in homey aphorisms. For the latest in neighborhood news, Molly leaned out the window and summoned her upstairs neighbor by yelling, "Yoo-hoo, Mrs. Bloom!"

While drama programs at the time followed the anthology-adaptation format, the situation comedy of *The Goldbergs* presented viewers with slices of life involving familiar characters they could return to week after week, like old friends. Within six months, CBS added another warm family comedy to its schedule, *Mama,* which caught on and ran for eight years.

Mama presented the growing pains and light humor in the lives of a Norwegian immigrant family in San Francisco during the first years of the twentieth century. The series was based on the book by Kathryn Forbes, *Mama's Bank Account,* which had been turned into a play and theatrical film earlier in the decade (both called "I Remember Mama"). Each episode of the series opened with the family's oldest child, Katrin, looking at the family photo album, thinking back to her childhood and the people and places she had known so well. She remembered many things: "I remember the big white house . . . and my little sister Dagmar, and my big brother Nels, and, of course, Papa. But most of all, I remember Mama."

January 12, 1949
    Kukla, Fran, and Ollie. (NBC). Chicago's first major contribution to network television arrives on the East Coast.

January 21, 1949
    Your Show Time. (NBC). The first all-film series on network television dramatizes one-act plays, with Arthur Shields as narrator. Naturally, this venture comes from Los Angeles.

January 25, 1949
    The first Emmy Awards are handed out by Walter O'Keefe at the Hollywood Athletic Club. *Pantomime Quiz,* a local Los Angeles show, is named "Most Popular TV Program."

April 9, 1949
    The telethon is born. Milton Berle stays on the air for fourteen hours to raise $1.1 million for cancer research.

May 5, 1949
    Blind Date. (ABC). Arlene Francis transfers her successful radio game show to television. Anxious bachelors, hoping to be picked for a night out, take turns trying to woo a beautiful female hidden from their sight by a studio wall.

May 5, 1949
    Crusade in Europe. (ABC). Time-Life produces television's first documentary series, a study of World War II.

July 7, 1949
    Dragnet. (NBC Radio). Jack Webb dramatizes real life police cases, presenting policemen not as glamour boys or boobs, but as dedicated professionals.

Like *The Goldbergs, Mama* focused on down-to-earth problems faced by an immigrant family, and both series extolled the family as the most important force in a decent society. "Mama" Hansen (Peggy Wood), like Molly Goldberg, kept a watchful eye on the household while "Papa" Hansen (Judson Laire) worked to support his family. Neither the parents nor their children were always right and members of the family occasionally grew frustrated, angry, and confused with each other. Though the turn-of-the-century pacing was sometimes extremely slow, *Mama* lasted longer on television than any of the other ethnic series of the Forties and Fifties, as viewers followed it almost like a soap opera. Its Broadway-based cast performed each episode live until the series was canceled in 1956.

Television grew a great deal during the first year of the freeze, establishing important foundations in comedy, drama, and variety. Nonetheless, there was still very primitive programming through most of the broadcast day and, as the networks expanded into new time periods, they ran anything they could.

Two fifteen-minute programs designed to showcase model railroads premiered in the fall of 1948. *Roar of the Rails,* on CBS, used a model railroad train going around and around the same track to illustrate stories told by a narrator about the railroads. ABC's *Tales of the Red Caboose* ran *films* of a model railroad train going around and around the same track while a narrator told stories about the railroads. They were sponsored by the makers of American Flyer and Lionel model trains, respectively.

In November, DuMont tried expanding its schedule to run from 10:00 A.M. until 11:00 P.M., with a daytime line-up aimed primarily at housewives (chiefly cooking and fashion shows). This caused Jack Gould, television critic for the *New York Times,* to quip:

    . . . the idea of a nation of housewives sitting mute before the video machine when they should be tidying up the premises or preparing the formula is not something to be grasped hurriedly. Obviously it is a matter frought with peril of the darkest sort.

The nation was saved for a while because DuMont's daytime schedule was a colossal failure and served to give daytime television a bad name for years.

In January, 1949, NBC unveiled television's first daytime soap opera, *These Are My Children,* which used blackboards as cue cards, giving the performers a far-away look in their eyes as they strained to read their lines.

In March, ABC brought the violent cheesecake of Roller Derby contests to the air. This gimmick sport consisted of teams of women on roller skates going around and around a roller rink shoving and punching each other trying to score game points. It had been around (and around) since 1935, but attracted very little popular attention until the summer of 1946, when WNBT in New York City used some live telecasts to fill out its local schedule. ABC looked at DuMont's success with theatrical-style wrestling matches and decided to try the same stunt with Roller Derby. The sport was the same sort of constant mindless theatrical action. Even though there were complicated rules, everyone virtually ignored them. ABC's Ken Nydell did the skate-by-skate description and Joe Hasel did the color, as such healthy young women as Midge "Toughy" Brashun and Ann "Red" Jensen threw football- and wrestling-style blocks and punches against their opponents. ABC's strategy succeeded and Roller Derby became a national fad.

When summer arrived, the networks were further pressed. Summer was traditionally the time when the top performers took vacations, along with much of the home audience. With very few films and no reruns available, the networks used the period to experiment. Hollywood's boycott of television prevented most American movies from reaching the air, so CBS dug up somewhat dated British product for *The CBS Film Theater of the Air.* This was the first of many early network movie series that relied on obscure foreign or cheap domestic films to fill out holes in the broadcast day. DuMont used *Program Playhouse* to test pilots for possible series, and "Hands of Murder" earned a spot in the fall 1949 lineup. NBC's *Theater of the Mind* anthology featured psychological drama, while ABC's *Stop the Music* game show (with Bert Parks) tried to duplicate its radio success.

Yet summer proved to be a rich viewing time for those who stayed indoors and sorted through the filler. In addition to *Mama* and *Cavalcade of Stars,* there were off-beat new programs for both children and adults.

Worthington Miner was the producer of *Mr. I Magination* on CBS, which starred Paul Tripp as a magical engineer who took ideas from children's letters and staged them as skits in which the suggestions came true. DuMont's *Captain Video* series, featuring the "guardian of the safety of the world," brought to life Flash Gordon and Buck Rogers style adventures on an absurdly minuscule budget. Despite the constraints, the series worked and became a hit as children realized that Saturday afternoon movie adventure serials were available five nights a week at home. Young viewers also eagerly tuned to NBC to see decade-old Hopalong Cassidy movies starring William Boyd as the virtuous Western cowboy. Perhaps the most unusual and innovative show of the summer

was NBC's unsponsored *Garroway at Large,* placed in a bleak Saturday slot (10:00 P.M.), then still considered television's Siberia. Dave Garroway ran the program as a variety show, only it did not look like one. He had no studio audience or elaborate backdrops. Instead, he calmly meandered about the studio, working with his guests and talented family of regulars, including Jack Haskell, Cliff Norton, and Connie Russell. They sang, told stories, and performed in short skits, always at a very casual pace and usually with the cameras, mikes, and cables in sight. In one sequence, Garroway and Jack Haskell walked onto a simple outdoor set consisting of a few fake trees, some tools, a shovel, and a bucket. As they discussed the song Haskell was about to sing, the studio crew walked on camera and took the props away, one by one, leaving the set bare as he began his song. Another time, the show went for two minutes without any words or music. First, the camera panned the studio, following Cliff Norton as he hid behind boxes and trunks, occasionally mugging to the camera. Connie Russell joined him and silently the two sneaked into a room with a printing press that was turning out counterfeit money. All this served as the lead-in to the duo's rendition of a popular hit tune, "Counterfeit Love."

More than any other variety host then on TV, Garroway understood how important visual imagery was to the new video art. Even with a bare-bones budget, he realized that a few simple actions in the intimate medium of television could produce a program that was visually entertaining to the home viewer. Reviewers were not quite sure exactly what Garroway had in mind, but they liked it, seeing him as NBC's equivalent to the casual Arthur Godfrey.

The key to Garroway's program was its location, Chicago. Television shows from Chicago always had much less money than those in New York and therefore the people working there had to innovate. They were also generally outside the rigid traditions of network radio and Broadway, the two cultures that dominated New York TV, and so were more inclined to take a fresh approach in a production. For instance, instead of staging a big finale, Garroway would smile and say "Peace," adding some unusual description of Chicago as his closing line—such as, "This program came to you from Chicago, where even pigs can whistle."

In spite of all the progress in television, it was still losing money. In 1948, the entire TV industry lost $15 million. None of the networks, and none of their O&Os, made money. The profits in network radio kept television afloat. Yet, sponsors could barely contain their attraction to the glowing tube. By the summer of 1949, they had begun to shift their attention toward television and, wherever possible, they began cutting back the radio budgets to more "cost effective" programs. Even with the freeze in effect, television was demonstrating its ability to produce popular entertainment in the best radio tradition. Besides, the cheaply produced quiz shows on radio offered a perfect alternative to the high-budgeted, high class radio series. No matter how good the ratings were for prestige comedy, variety, and drama programs, those shows could not match the commercial value of radio quizzes, which attracted a large audience at only a fraction of the price.

As radio and television approached a fateful head-to-head battle for audience support, radio was losing its best weapon—a high level of program quality. And that just drove move people into the arms of the waiting television set salesman.

9. Behind the Ion Curtain

WHILE giveaway quiz shows dominated network radio in 1949, it was generally assumed that the bulk of these programs would fade away just like any other format craze, with a few of the better ones hanging on to become stable hits as the next gimmick appeared. During the summer of 1949, however, the FCC decided that it did not want to wait.

On August 19, 1949, the FCC ruled that giveaway quiz shows such as *Stop the Music* violated the U.S. Criminal Code on lotteries and that stations which carried the programs after October 1 would not have their licenses renewed. The commission claimed that the shows met the legal definition of a lottery because they required radio listeners to expend something of value (the time it took to listen to a program) in order to be able to win if called at home. Technically, the FCC's rule applied only to shows that telephoned people (such as *Break the Bank, Winner Take All,* and *Stop the Music*), but the point was clear: The FCC wanted to rid the airwaves of quiz shows.

The networks took the issue to court saying that the FCC had no business sticking its nose into programming decisions. They might not like the quiz shows themselves, but the sponsors wanted them and so did the audience, according to the ratings. In court, the networks managed to block the FCC's October 1 rule from going into effect while the case dragged on. During the court presentations, it became increasingly clear that the FCC was on very shaky legal footing because its charter specifically prohibited program censorship. Even if the giveaways were illegal, the issue was probably outside the commission's jurisdiction. In 1954, the Supreme Court knocked down the FCC ruling, but by then most of the giveaway shows had been taken off the air. The FCC's charge had given the giveaway shows a taint of illegality which drove away listeners and scared off sponsors. By November, 1949, ABC's *Stop the Music* had lost one-half of its radio audience and CBS radio had taken four quiz shows off the air. Nonetheless, producers felt games and quizzes were still viable, so they temporarily turned away from the brash come-ons of the big money giveaways and focused on more restrained formats such as celebrity panels.

Most of the new television quiz shows in the 1949–50 season followed a similar strategy, emphasizing guest celebrities *(What's My Line?),* funny antics *(Beat the Clock* and *Pantomime Quiz),* and revamped parlor games *(Twenty Questions).* Still giveaway shows did not completely disappear. *Stop the Music* continued to run on both television and radio until 1952 and, just weeks after the FCC's August, 1949, quiz ruling, ABC came out with one of the most blatantly exploitative television giveaways yet, *Auction-Aire.* Libby foods sponsored this weekly live auction in which contestants both at home and in the studio bid on merchandise—not with cash but with labels from Libby products. On the second week's show, bidding had reached the astounding level of 20,000 labels when an anonymous viewer called and said, "I'll give you 30,000 labels if you take this show off the air." The generous offer was refused but it raised an obvious question: What sort of person would have 30,000 Libby labels lying about the house? Whatever the explanation, it was clear that the something-for-nothing illusion of the giveaway shows struck a responsive nerve within many Americans and a campaign by the FCC would not kill this interest.

In some ways, the FCC's heavy-handed attempt to purge the airwaves of giveaway shows merely reflected its frustration over the proliferation of what it viewed as a particularly "crass" format. Since the 1920s, culture-minded citizens and profit-oriented businessmen had fought over the content and effects of the new forms of popular entertainment: movies and radio. Businessmen produced what sold, explaining that they were giving the public what it wanted. At the same time, special interest groups worked to remove what they viewed as dangerous and offensive material (no matter how popular) and tried to promote uplifting high quality culture instead. However, not everybody agreed on what was uplifting, proper, or offensive, so the battle never ended and the self-appointed guardians of the public morality remained ever alert for new dangers.

Just as the FCC's crusade against giveaway shows was driving most of the big radio quizzes off the air, television began to supplant radio as the focus for popular entertainment trends. During 1950, television viewing matched radio listening in New York and other major cities and, in this first year of real head-to-head competition, radio rating plummeted. Though network radio continued to make money (in 1949 radio made $56 million while television lost $25 million), it was clear that, once the FCC freeze on television growth was lifted to end radio's monopoly in many markets, the older medium could not match the allure of television. The radio networks joined advertisers in adapting radio to a new marketplace. Instead of high program ratings (which, relative to television, were increasingly irrelevant) they began to emphasize sales effectiveness (the cost-per-listener). To this end, the networks turned to less expensive musical disk jockey shows (using prerecorded music). By the summer of 1950, almost all of radio's superstars decided

MONDAY

Network	7:00	7:30	8:00	8:30	9:00	9:30	10:00	10:30
ABC	local	Author Meets The Critics	local	Science Circus	ABC Barn Dance	MR. BLACK	Roller Derby	
CBS	Roar Of The Rails / PAUL ARNOLD	CBS News / Sonny Kendis	SILVER THEATER	Arthur Godfrey's Talent Scouts	Candid Camera	The Goldbergs	Studio One	
DUMONT	Captain Video	Manhat. Spotlight / Vincent Lopez	Newsweek Views The News	AL MORGAN SHOW	And Everything Nice	Wrestling From Sunnyside Arena With Dennis James		
NBC	Kukla, Fran And Ollie	Morton Downey / Camel News	Chevrolet Tele-Theater	VOICE OF FIRESTONE	Lights Out	BAND OF AMERICA	Quiz Kids	local

TUESDAY

Network	7:00	7:30	8:00	8:30	9:00	9:30	10:00	10:30
ABC	local	On Trial	local				Tomorrow's Champions [to 12 Midnite]	
CBS	PRIZE PARTY	CBS News / Sonny Kendis	CBS Film Theater Of The Air		Actor's Studio	Suspense	THIS WEEK IN SPORTS / Blues By Bargy	PANTOMIME QUIZ
DUMONT	Captain Video	Manhat. Spotlight / Vincent Lopez	Court of Current Issues		THE O'NEILLS	FEATURE THEATER		local
NBC	Kukla, Fran And Ollie	Roberta Quinlan / Camel News	Texaco Star Theater		Fireside Theater	THE LIFE OF RILEY	Original Amateur Hour	

WEDNESDAY

Network	7:00	7:30	8:00	8:30	9:00	9:30	10:00	10:30
ABC	local		Wendy Barrie Show	PHOTO CRIME	YOUR WITNESS	Wrestling From The Rainbo In Chicago		
CBS	KIRBY ST. QUINTET / PAUL ARNOLD	CBS News / AT HOME SHOW	Arthur Godfrey And His Friends		Dunninger & Winchell Bigelow Show	Tournament Of Champions		
DUMONT	Captain Video	Manhat. Spotlight / Vincent Lopez	Flight To Rhythm	local	THE PLAINCLOTHESMAN	Famous Jury Trials	local	
NBC	Kukla, Fran And Ollie	Morton Downey / Camel News	CRISIS	The Clock	Kraft Television Theater		Break The Bank	local

THURSDAY

Network	7:00	7:30	8:00	8:30	9:00	9:30	10:00	10:30
ABC	local	THE LONE RANGER	Stop The Music		STARRING BORIS KARLOFF	THE RUGGLES	Roller Derby [to 12 Midnite]	
CBS	Dione Lucas On Cooking	CBS News / Sonny Kendis	FRONT PAGE	INSIDE U.S.A. THEATER OF ROM.	ED WYNN SHOW	local	Blues By Bargy	local
DUMONT	Captain Video	Manhat. Spotlight / Vincent Lopez	MYSTERY THEATER		Morey Amsterdam Show	Boxing From Sunnyside Arena With Dennis James		
NBC	Kukla, Fran And Ollie	Roberta Quinlan / Camel News	HOLLYWOOD PREMIERE	Mary Kay And Johnny	Fireball Fun-For-All		MARTIN KANE, PRIVATE EYE	local

FRIDAY

Network	7:00	7:30	8:00	8:30	9:00	9:30	10:00	10:30
ABC	local	TOUCHDOWN	MAJORITY RULES	Blind Date	AUCTION-AIRE	Fun For The Money	A COUPLE OF JOES	
CBS	KIRBY ST. QUINTET / PAUL ARNOLD	CBS News / AMAZ. POLGAR	Mama	MAN AGAINST CRIME	54th Street Revue @Ford Television Theater Hour		People's Platform	CAPITOL CLOAKROOM
DUMONT	Captain Video	Manhat. Spotlight / Vincent Lopez	HANDS OF MURDER	Broadway To Hollywood Headline Clues	FISHING AND HUNTING CLUB	Program Playhouse	AMATEUR BOXING FROM CHICAGO	
NBC	Kukla, Fran And Ollie	Morton Downey / Camel News	ONE MAN'S FAMILY	We, The People	VERSATILE VARIETIES	BIG STORY / Believe It Or Not!	Gillette Cavalcade of Sports	Great Fights

SATURDAY

Network	7:00	7:30	8:00	8:30	9:00	9:30	10:00	10:30
ABC	local	Hollywood Screen Test	Paul Whiteman's TV Teen Club		Roller Derby			
CBS	Lucky Pup / local	Quincy Howe / Blues By Bargy	Winner Take All	local	Premiere Playhouse		local	
DUMONT	local		Spin The Picture		Cavalcade Of Stars		WRESTLING FROM THE MARIGOLD IN CHICAGO	
NBC	local	Nature of Things / Leon Pearson	TWENTY QUESTIONS	SESSIONS / STUD'S PLACE	Who Said That	Meet The Press	The Black Robe	local

SUNDAY

Network	7:00	7:30	8:00	8:30	9:00	9:30	10:00	10:30
ABC	PAUL WHITEMAN'S GOODYEAR REVUE	COMEDY THEATER	Think Fast	THE LITTLE REVUE	LET THERE BE STARS		Celebrity Game	Bowling Headliners
CBS	Tonight On Broadway	This Is Show Business	Toast Of The Town		Fred Waring Show		Week In Review	local
DUMONT	Front Row Center		CHICAGOLAND MYSTERY PLAYERS	CINEMA VARIETIES	CROSS QUESTION		local	
NBC	Leave It To The Girls	ALDRICH FAMILY	Supper Club	Colgate Theater	Philco Television Playhouse		Garroway-At-Large	HANK McCUNE SHOW

it was time to jump ship and they made plans to switch to television by the fall. Advertising agencies, which had been easing out of the more expensive radio programs whenever possible for over a year, eyed the expansive postwar baby boom and marked their calendars for 1955—when these offspring would become new TV consumers. Television was the marketplace for the future.

During the 1949–50 season, television also became the new scapegoat for the ills of society. With seventy new TV stations on the air (approved before the FCC freeze went into effect), there were sixty-five cities in the country with at least one television station. More and more people had sets, making television an established part of society. Some saw the tube as the ultimate way to reach out and touch people, while others considered it a disruptive force which was already getting out of control.

Throughout the country, ad-hoc commissions sprang up to study the problem of television, focusing on what they saw as instances of excessive and unnecessary sex and violence. Some blamed televi-

sion programs for an increase in juvenile delinquency, pointing to the violence on TV cop shows as a bad influence on children. Dr. Daniel L. Marsh, president of Boston University, told his 1950 graduating class: "If the television craze continues with the present level of programs, we are destined to have a nation of morons."

Others warned of the potential danger to unstable adults lured by the urge to "make a big splash" on television. One such offbeat act of television violence took place in Texas where, on June 11, 1950, Sanford B. Twente boasted to a waitress, ". . . just watch me at the end of the fifth inning." Later that day, he barged into the announcing booth during the telecast of a Houston versus Dallas minor league baseball game. Viewers heard Twente exclaim, "I've got something to tell you—!" Announcer Dick Gottlieb replied, "Not now, this mike is live." Seconds later, there was the sound of a gunshot. The camera focused on the players and fans turning to stare at the announcing booth; then the cameraman swung around to show the inside of the booth and Twente, slumped dead, in the arms of an engineer. Coroner Tom Mays, who happened to be watching the game at home, turned in his verdict of suicide without ever going to the hospital. The game continued after a short break.

Protests over sex settled on more symbolic connections and issues because there was not any sex, per se, on television in 1950. Instead, people focused on actions that seemed to suggest an erosion in moral attitudes and the encouragement of irresponsible behavior. Two of the first symbols were women's necklines and Arthur Godfrey's tongue.

Arthur Godfrey's natural broadcasting style occasionally resulted in a few bawdy stories and suggestive "blue" jokes, which went over the air uncensored. What upset some people even more than the jokes themselves, however, was the fact that Godfrey was never reprimanded by CBS. It appeared that nobody at the network felt capable of telling him to "clean up his act" because he was too important and powerful. Godfrey was practically a one-man network on CBS, doing eight hours and forty-five minutes of radio and TV broadcasting per week. His two TV programs never left the top ten that season and he was directly responsible for thousands of dollars' worth of advertising. Wayne Coy, chairman of the FCC, drew attention to this turnaround in authority:

> . . . when a comedian gets so big that his network can no longer handle him, then I think we have a case of the tail wagging the dog . . . it seems to me, that the question of just how bad poor taste can get before it merges over into downright obscenity or indecency may be settled one of these days . . .

Performers such as Faye Emerson and Ilka Chase upset some people in a different way. They were attractive women who frequently wore lowcut gowns as part of their image as popular television "glamour girls." For years, such beautiful women had appeared on TV wearing mildly suggestive costumes, usually in background roles on "sophisticated" nightclub formats. Emerson and Chase merely stepped to the forefront as individual stars who dressed in slightly more daring outfits as part of their overall promotion strategy, and they were quite successful at it. Emerson was a regular on three different panel shows and in April, 1950, won her own prime time variety program on NBC. Chase appeared in her own interview show for CBS in February, *Glamour-Go-Round* (with Durward Kirby). Both Emerson and Chase capitalized on creating the impression of introducing viewers to the ultimate in witty, sophisticated society.

As women such as Ilka Chase and Faye Emerson became popular stars, they attracted both approving stares and outraged criticism. In doing so, they sparked animated discussions on the proper attire for women in public and the issue soon became a national *cause célèbre*. Most viewers did not care one way or the other about such supposedly scandalous behavior, though, and merely used the controversy as an excuse to look at beautiful women and to talk about looking at beautiful women. The issue served as a perfect springboard for routines and one-liners by television comedians and punsters. On the humorous panel show *This Is Show Business*, which featured Clifton Fadiman, George S. Kaufman, and Abe Burrows as "problem consultants" to famous celebrity guests, French actress Denise Darcel asked if her sisters should come and work in the United States amid the lowcut controversy. Abe Burrows quickly said "Yes!" suggesting that "LS/MFT," the slogan of the show's sponsor, Lucky Strike cigarettes, really meant: "Let's See More French Tomatoes."

The most important aspect of the interest in sex and violence on television in 1950 was that it vividly demonstrated the medium's

tremendous growth. All of the networks were expanding, but NBC, as the number one network, expanded the most. NBC was reaping the rewards of being the first to begin network television broadcasting. It had the longest association with the older, established TV stations, giving it the best collection of network affiliates and the best showcases for its network programming. By early 1950, NBC had sold out almost all of its available commercial slots in the popular evening hours, or "prime time" (approximately 8:00–11:00 P.M.), so it began looking for new periods to sell. In studying viewer habits, the network noticed a shift from the patterns of radio. Previously, people had listened to their favorite radio shows between 7:00 P.M. and 10:00 P.M., then turned off the set and read the paper or cleaned the dishes. With television, families finished the housework first, tuned in about 8:00 P.M., and watched until it was time for bed. NBC concluded that they might be induced to stick around another hour (11:00 P.M. until midnight) with just the right program. After a very careful search, the network selected twenty-six-year-old Los Angeles comic Don "Creesh" Hornsby to host *Broadway Open House*, a casual mixture of comedy-variety and talk. The day of the scheduled May 22, 1950, premiere, Hornsby died of a sudden attack of polio.

NBC delayed the show for a week, then filled in with guest hosts, including Tex and Jinx, Pat Harrington, and Dean Martin and Jerry Lewis. By June, a new format was ready. The *Broadway Open House* slot was split between two performers: Morey Amsterdam handled Monday and Wednesday, while Jerry Lester took Tuesday, Thursday, and Friday. Amsterdam was a borscht-belt

The Lone Ranger was one of the first important filmed TV series: (from *r.*) Clayton Moore as the Lone Ranger, his horse Silver, and Jay Silverheels as Tonto. *(The Lone Ranger and Tonto are trademarks of Lone Ranger Television, Inc.)*

September 5, 1949
Pat Weaver becomes NBC's programming chief.

October 10, 1949
RCA at last unveils a totally compatible color television system.

October 24, 1949
"Battleship Bismark" plays on *Studio One* and provides young Charlton Heston his first starring role. He portrays a conscience-troubled Jewish gunnery officer on a large Nazi ship.

November 11, 1949
John Daly leaves CBS News for ABC.

November 26, 1949
Stud's Place. (NBC). Another off-beat high-quality (rarely sponsored) television series from Chicago. Writer-philosopher Studs Terkel acts as barkeep, sharing stories and songs with his "regulars," including a folk singer and a jazz pianist. The show is relaxed and loose, with a blue and lonesome tone.

January 1, 1950
Mark Woods, ABC's first president, becomes vice-chairman of the board. Forty-year-old Robert Kinter moves up to become the youngest network president in television.

January 30, 1950
Robert Montgomery Presents. (NBC). The first major defection from Hollywood's closed ranks. Montgomery directs and occasionally stars in this fancy, top-class drama showcase.

April 9, 1950
"Star Spangled Revue." (NBC). Max Liebman produces one of the vanguard big-budget television specials. Host Bob Hope makes his first major television appearance and is the first important radio comic to take the plunge into video.

vaudeville comic who was already a TV veteran from his own prime time series and a string of guest spots on panel shows. Lester had spent a few months hosting DuMont's *Cavalcade of Stars,* replacing Jack Carter. In the new form, the late night program quickly became a hit. The number of TV sets in use after 11:00 P.M. increased dramatically and the show registered ratings as high as many prime time shows.

Broadway Open House was loose and had no formal script. There was light chatter, strains of comedy and variety, a family of regulars, and some guests. Above all, the program ran on the personality of its hosts. Though Amsterdam did a good show, Lester quickly attracted the more devoted following. He was described as "a middle-aged Mickey Rooney, a walking seltzer bottle who never runs out of fizz." Lester cultivated the image of *Broadway Open House* as a late night private party and viewers picked up the spirit, latching onto his catch phrases and in-jokes. A detractor once labeled him a bean bag, so Lester immediately formed the fictitious Bean Bag Club of America, naming himself as president. Seventy thousand people wrote in to join.

In addition to his own off-beat humor, Lester used a family of regulars including dancer Ray Malone, the Milton Delugg Orchestra, and Dagmar. Jennie Lewis (Dagmar) was a tall, buxom blonde who delivered dry spicy one-liners, somewhat in the style of Mae West. Her deft, often suggestive, comments frequently stole the show, though some sensitive viewers described Dagmar as "nothing more than a walking pin-up picture," apparently even more dangerous than Faye Emerson and Ilka Chase. Nonetheless, Dagmar's

wit and figure made her the most popular member of Lester's supporting crew.

Broadway Open House lasted only one year as first Amsterdam, then Lester, left the program. Lester tried to bring his style of late night zaniness to prime time but his off-beat personality worked against him there as the much larger and more diverse evening audience found his oddities harder to accept. Dagmar hosted a brief late night show of her own, *Dagmar's Canteen,* but it folded after only four months. NBC used a few other hosts for *Broadway Open House,* but none seemed to have a similar rapport with the home viewers. Reluctantly, the network turned the time slot back to the local affiliates. NBC had demonstrated the viability of late night TV, but had also discovered the importance of finding just the right personality for the slot.

Broadway Open House was only one of NBC's television innovations in 1950. Though the network had lost some of its top radio comedy talent to CBS in the Paley's Comet raids of 1948, NBC was determined to maintain its momentum in television. It pressed to develop not only new time periods but new programs and formats uniquely suited to TV. In August, 1949, NBC hired Sylvester "Pat" Weaver, who had been vice president for radio and television at the powerful Young & Rubicam ad agency. Weaver became chief of programming and almost immediately began testing creative new ideas.

Weaver's first project was a two-and-one-half-hour concept he called *Saturday Night Revue.* The previous season, DuMont's *Cavalcade of Stars* had demonstrated that viewers were willing to stay home on Saturday night to watch television, so Weaver planned a full night of special entertainment that could realistically compete with feature films and live theater. As first conceived, *Saturday Night Revue* consisted of an hour-long film or play done especially for television, followed by an hour of Broadway revue material, and ending with a thirty-minute nightclub variety segment. Weaver's grandiose plan faced staggering financial and casting problems, as well as strong opposition by the other networks.

In early 1950, AT&T still had only a few coaxial cable links connecting TV stations in the East and Midwest, and the networks fought with each other for use of these cables on a show-by-show basis. NBC, with the largest number of popular shows and the most affiliates, consistently grabbed the choice slots on the cable. ABC, CBS, and DuMont quickly realized that the proposed *Saturday Night Revue* would tie up the East-to-West cable all night and, in effect, prevent any of their Saturday night programming from being aired in the Midwest. DuMont was particularly incensed because the NBC show would directly affect its *Cavalcade of Stars,* which had broken the ground for Saturday night broadcasting. DuMont complained to the FCC, which, after complicated legal maneuvering, forced NBC to make two concessions: The first hour of the *Saturday Night Revue* would originate in Chicago (thereby freeing one of the East-to-West cable lines), and NBC was forbidden to insist that stations take the entire two and one-half hours as a package. Instead, the show was to be offered in thirty-minute blocks so that local programmers—especially in those crucial one-station markets—could run fare from other networks as well.

Ironically, the forced partitioning of *Saturday Night Revue* made the entire project economically feasible by allowing NBC to institute a revolution in sponsorship. Previously, there had been three ways to sponsor a show: sustained (paid for by the network), co-op (no national advertising, but local stations inserted commercials from local sponsors), or, the most common form, direct sponsorship (one sponsor paid for an entire program). Weaver conceived a new form, participating sponsorship, which allowed a number of national sponsors to carve a program into separate blocks of time, each considered its own segment. With the costs of television rising rapidly, such a move was inevitable because there were few sponsors that could continue to bankroll an entire program alone. *Saturday Night Revue,* for example, cost $50,000 a week to produce.

Besides devising a method to encourage sponsorship for the expensive new show, Weaver also revised its structure. He dropped the costly idea of an original film or play every week and broke *Saturday Night Revue* into just two programs: *The Jack Carter Show* (one hour of standard vaudeo from Chicago) and *Your Show of Shows* (ninety minutes of comedy-variety from New York). Nonetheless, Madison Avenue agencies played it cozy, waiting to see if NBC could make the two and one-half hour format work. Consequently, when the two shows premiered at the end of February, 1950, not one of their fifteen commercial slots was sold.

The Jack Carter Show was fairly funny, but nothing special. Carter had recently departed from DuMont's *Cavalcade of Stars* and did not change his act much for the new program. In contrast, *Your Show of Shows* marked a major improvement by producer Max Liebman and headliners Sid Caesar and Imogene Coca over their previous series, *Admiral Broadway Revue.* This time, their

television comedy-variety act worked perfectly. Part of the improvement was a reflection of more polished writing. At the same time, the Broadway-based Liebman adjusted his techniques to meet television's demand for intimacy, bringing the camera "up on stage," which managed to convey to the viewers at home the humor and excitement of the wide-open production. Above all, Caesar blossomed. His frequent coughing and throat-clearing, which had marred his *Admiral Broadway Revue* performances, were gone. He was cooler, more controlled, and better suited to carry a wide range of skits with Coca. Though *Your Show of Shows* included fine supporting crews of singers and dancers, as well as a weekly guest star host (Burgess Meredith the first two weeks), the comedy sketches featuring Caesar and Coca transformed the show into truly exceptional entertainment.

The most obvious vehicles for the two were man and woman settings, and these ranged from starry-eyed lovers on a first date to an unhappy couple trying to put some romance back into their tired marriage. In these sketches, Caesar and Coca conveyed the humor and drama of everyday life, yet they functioned just as well in more abstract settings such as a pair of lions looking out at the visitors to the zoo. Both could also handle solo spots. Coca

On June 25, 1950, Communist forces invaded South Korea, and the U.S. was drawn into war. *(U.S. Army.)*

excelled in comic dance and singing while Caesar demonstrated remarkable versatility in monologues, pantomime, and crazy dialects. They were soon joined by sidemen Carl Reiner and Howard Morris, and the ensemble of four was able to tackle virtually any comedy routine concocted by the writers (including then-unknowns Neil Simon and Mel Brooks). They reached heights of gleeful frenzy in the parodies of movies and television, including *This Is Your Life*, "Shane," "The Mark of Zorro," and "From Here to Eternity." With such a strong basic cast, *Your Show of Shows* became a long-lasting hit and it quickly sold all of its ad slots.

Your Show of Shows was better than almost anything else then on TV, so Jack Carter's merely adequate program suffered in comparison. Yet Carter's presence infuriated the Chicago television community, which felt that the town's reputation for innovation was being hurt. Instead of drawing on the still unsponsored home-grown talents such as Dave Garroway and Studs Terkel, NBC had used a New York flavored, New York run program for its required telecast from Chicago. The network seemed to consider Chicago's own creative talent irrelevant, while national sponsors treated the city like a cowtown that did not warrant a business trip.

Chicago received such cavalier treatment because ultimately the city was not important to the networks' future expansion plans. It was merely an O&O city that, by circumstance (the route of the coaxial cable construction), became a convenient location for some stopgap TV production. Once the coast-to-coast cable was completed, Chicago programs would become largely expendable. Television, like radio and the movies, would operate from the two coasts.

New York and California had been battling for control of American popular culture since the early 1900s, when Hollywood replaced Long Island as the nation's movie capital. In the late 1930s, Los Angeles had supplanted New York as the main locale of network radio programming. New York TV people prepared for another conflict as the theater oriented East Coast and the Hollywood based West Coast faced off over television production. Network television was oriented toward live performances, so the technical limitations facing Los Angeles in 1950 gave New York City the upper hand for the moment. The West Coast was not connected to the coaxial cable and, going into the 1949–50 season, the networks carried very few filmed series. Some Hollywood production was inevitable, though. New York studio space was already tight and the network schedules were still expanding. CBS bought land out in Los Angeles for a future television city and also launched the first important use of Los Angeles-made kines, *The Ed Wynn Show*.

Kinescope recordings were films of live shows shot directly off a picture tube monitor as they played. They were grainy, lacked definition, and were generally a poor substitute for live television. Viewers in cities not connected to the East Coast coaxial cable watched them because there was no other way to receive the New York-based network shows. *The Ed Wynn Show* reversed the process and originated live in Los Angeles, sending kines to the East Coast. Wynn staged a revue show, mixing variety, comedy, and his own lowkey mimicry and whimsy. He drew on the talent based in Hollywood for guest spots. In December, he sang a duet with Buster Keaton and, in January, did a great pantomime bit with Lucille Ball, who was making her television debut. Viewers out East liked the program, but they hated the kines. Accustomed to high-definition live telecasts, they were appalled by the gray grainy quality of the picture and the poor sound reproduction. Although other series such as *The Alan Young Show* (another comedy revue)

and *The Ruggles* (a sitcom) were staged lived in Los Angeles and shipped out as kines, negative viewer reaction made it obvious that live West Coast productions would have to wait for the cable connection.

Film was an obvious way around the cable problem and, in the 1949–50 season, the concept of filming shows for television received important boosts. At the time, the networks generally regarded film as inferior to live presentations and most filmed efforts seemed designed to prove the point. The *Fireside Theater* drama anthology, produced by the Hal Roach studios, consisted of low budget episodes churned out in just a few days each. Both *The Life of Riley* (starring Jackie Gleason) and *The Hank McCune Show*, two filmed sitcoms, were stilted and cheaply produced. Ed Wynn quipped:

In the beginning a television set cost hundreds of dollars and you could see a few bad shows. In a couple of years, you'll be able to buy a television set for a few dollars and see hundreds of bad shows.

Apart from these, there was a dramatic exception in the fall of 1949, the wide open Western adventures of *The Lone Ranger*.

In looking at the TV success of Hopalong Cassidy, the struggling ABC saw that Saturday matinee-style heroics on television were very popular with children. The network was searching for any sort of hit, so it decided to take a chance on brand new filmed-for-television adventures of a popular radio cowboy hero, the Lone Ranger. The TV series was pure pulp adventure, following the radio legend of a daring masked lawman (Clayton Moore) and his faithful Indian companion, Tonto (Jay Silverheels), who fought for law and order in the amorphous old West of the 1870s. The Lone Ranger helped anyone in need, never accepted payment for his services, and always defeated the bad guys. Unlike previous filmed series, *The Lone Ranger* was treated like a medium-budget adventure movie and the first season's fifty-two episodes (there were no reruns) cost $1 million to produce. The money was well spent—kids found the outdoor action and scenery a thrilling release from the "cooped up" New York studio productions and they made *The Lone Ranger* one of ABC's first TV hits.

Several months after the masked man appeared, TV film pioneer Jerry Fairbanks unveiled a cheaper but more efficient way to produce filmed TV series, the multi-cam system. In February, 1950, the previously live New York based *Silver Theater* moved out West and became the first to use the multi-cam process, which was designed to combine the feel of live TV with the perfectability and permanence of film—without a large increase in budget. Three film cameras with thirty minutes of film in each were positioned in the studio and used like regular TV cameras. All three operated continuously and the director could monitor what they were shooting. Like live shows, a program could be done in one smooth take, from start to finish. Like filmed shows, the action could be stopped to correct mistakes or to change lighting, then resumed. When editing time was added, an average half-hour show took three days to complete, while its live equivalent took five, including rehearsals. The multi-cam made West Coast filmed series a viable alternative to live shows from New York City, and the focus of East Coast objections shifted from technical limitations to the programs themselves.

The New York branch of the TV industry had seen Hollywood assume control of movies and radio, and some executives feared that if the same happened with television the medium would soon be reduced to mindless fluff. They criticized California productions in general as flashy, light, and empty, and pointed to the first wave of West Coast filmed TV sitcoms as confirming their worst apprehensions. *The Hank McCune Show,* for instance, was just like Hollywood's theatrical "screwball" comedies that featured empty-headed adventures of lovable, inoffensive bumblers. The series even "faked" its laughter by dubbing the sound of an audience onto the audio track of the film (creating a "laugh track"), though no audience had been present at the filming. Another program, *The Life of Riley,* was an all-around loser with terrible scripts, cheap sets, and a weak supporting cast. However, the show did have one saving grace: Jackie Gleason in the lead role of Chester A. Riley.

For six years on radio, William Bendix had played Chester Riley as yet another simple-minded, lovable middle class bumbler who could turn the most innocent task into a silly crisis. Though Riley would frequently sputter and moan "What a revoltin' development this is!"—it was all show. He was really a pushover and the problems, which were inevitably just simple misunderstandings, melted away every week. Under Bendix, Riley never really got angry and his chief appeal was a predictable soft heart and forgiving nature.

In 1949, William Bendix was under an exclusive film contract which prevented him from continuing the role on TV, and Jackie Gleason got the job instead. Gleason played Riley a bit differently from the image Bendix had cultivated on the radio. Though Gleason's Riley was also a simple man with a soft heart, his anger was more threatening and he seemed capable of really popping off in a situation. This made the moments of forgiveness and resolution more believable, but Gleason's expressive interpretation went against the public's image of Riley and there was some resistance to it. Gleason was good, but he was not Chester A. Riley! More importantly, the writing and production on the show were exceptionally bad so Gleason did not have the support to build a following for his version of Riley. After six months, the program was off the air.

Though a failure itself, *The Life of Riley* provided Gleason with important television exposure as he demonstrated his ability to shine in a show despite weak writing and production. When Jerry

Lester left DuMont's *Cavalcade of Stars* to do *Broadway Open House,* the network signed Gleason as the new host, beginning in July, 1950. Under Gleason, *Cavalcade of Stars* came closest to DuMont's dream of a hit comedy-variety show and, in September, the network helped it along by moving the program to Friday night, against NBC's boxing matches and away from *Your Show of Shows.*

Though Gleason was surrounded by the usual variety trappings of music (the Sammy Spear Orchestra) and dancing (the June Taylor Dancers), the revamped program worked because of Gleason's energy and versatility. His characters ranged from a down-and-out bum to an arrogant playboy, and his facial expressions could carry a scene without a word of dialogue (only Sid Caesar could top Gleason's contortions of pain). For his sidekick Gleason chose Art Carney and the two developed into smooth comic foils. Carney served as an especially effective balance to Gleason's more boisterous characters, playing a stern father to haughty Reginald Van Gleason III or the prim but caustic Clem Finch to loudmouth Charlie Bratten. In 1951, they introduced what soon became their most popular character sketch, "The Honeymooners," featuring Gleason as a blustery Brooklyn bus driver, Ralph Kramden; series regular Pert Kelton as Kramden's wife, Alice; and Carney as Ed Norton, an obliging sewer worker who was Kramden's best friend. By 1952, Gleason had blossomed into a first rate television star and, in the fall, he jumped to CBS—taking Carney and the June Taylor Dancers with him. As always, DuMont's *Cavalcade of Stars* had been merely a stepping stone to a better salary and a bigger budget.

At the same time that Jackie Gleason was toiling on the ill-fated *Life of Riley,* other stars-to-be were working in the hinterlands of broadcasting, also in search of their lucky break. Future talk show host Mike Douglas was a singer on Kay Kyser's *Kollege of Musical Knowledge* (a musical quiz show); Jim McKay, later a renowned sportscaster, arrived in New York to host *The Real McKay* (a local chit-chat variety show set on his patio); and actor Jack Lemmon played "a brash young lad from Kalamazoo" who was trying to break into show business by serving as houseboy to a famous drama critic (played by Neil Hamilton) on ABC's *That Wonderful Guy.* At the New Jersey state fair, Trenton disk jockey Ernie Kovacs failed in his effort to break the marathon radio broadcasting record of one week, while in nearby Camden, Ed McMahon played a red-nosed circus clown on CBS's *Big Top.*

Despite the many successful new programs and emerging stars, television was still losing money at a disturbing rate. ABC's president Mark Woods explained that his network had expanded too fast to meet expenses and announced major cost-cutting moves: ABC cut 20% from its TV budget in the winter of 1950 and canceled all of its Monday and Tuesday programming. These actions saved the network from total collapse. By the fall of 1950, ABC's five O&Os were nearing the black, but in the tight freeze market the network still had serious problems attracting viewers and selling its shows to sponsors. Even number one NBC was beginning to feel the squeeze. Though it was actually selling more commercial time than ever, costs for programs had shot up. More importantly, the networks could not yet charge advertisers premium rates because the FCC freeze limited television coverage across the country. Established markets might reach a higher saturation of TV sets, but there were still millions of people who had never seen a television program. The nation had settled into a peculiar social division: One half of the country was going TV crazy while the other half, "behind the ion curtain," had to imagine what everybody else was talking about. Though the FCC had instigated the freeze in 1948 merely to investigate signal interference and channel separation, the commission soon found the issue mired in the more complicated questions of UHF frequencies and color. The promised six month halt in processing new station applications had already extended for one and one-half years, and there was no sign that the freeze would be ended in the foreseeable future.

Apart from the stagnation of the freeze, darker shadows tainted American television that season. Since World War II, Americans had become increasingly concerned about the safety of the United States as Communist forces seized control of governments in both Europe and Asia. Congressional committees such as HUAC and private organizations such as *Counterattack* had assumed the task of identifying Communists, Communist sympathizers, and so-called fellow-travelers throughout American society. In response, the Hollywood film industry had begun blacklisting writers and actors charged with having suspicious ties to leftist organizations—usually without ever corroborating the accusations. By 1948, blacklisting had become an established but rarely discussed practice in network radio as well. After examining the programming and the personnel files of the four radio networks, *Counterattack* evaluated each one, concluding:

> NBC and Mutual are the least satisfactory to the Communists . . . ABC is about halfway between most satisfactory and least satisfactory, and CBS is the most satisfying network to the Communists.

At first, television had been dismissed as unimportant, but, as the medium grew, so did concern over its potential for misuse by Communist subversives. Through 1949, television sponsors and network executives also quietly adopted the practice of blacklisting as protection against charges of helping the Communist cause.

Blacklisting was a vague process—there were no lists as such, only individual campaigns and reports published by self-proclaimed Communist investigators who would tout every rumor and innuendo as fact. A brave network or sponsor could decide to ignore such accusations and hire the "suspicious" talent anyway. Ed Sullivan chose to do just that by scheduling dancer Paul Draper for an appearance on *Toast of the Town* in January, 1950. Reluctantly, the network and sponsor went along, even though Draper had been blacklisted from network television for more than a year.

On Sullivan's show Draper danced to, of all things, "Yankee Doodle Dandy." Benson Ford, of the Detroit Ford family (who owned Sullivan's sponsor, Lincoln Mercury) happened to be in the audience that night and was shown clapping when Draper finished. In spite of this apparent corporate approval, a concerted letter writing and phone campaign produced hundreds of complaints about Draper's appearance. At first Sullivan defended his decision to have Draper on the show, but after intense pressure from the American Legion, the Catholic War Veterans, and banner

headlines in the *New York Journal American,* Sullivan backed down, agreed to clip Draper from the kine being sent to the nonconnected stations, and issued a public apology, saying he was opposed to "having the program being used as a political forum, directly or indirectly." Draper's dismissal was the first public acknowledgement that television had begun blacklisting writers and performers. A network talent chief candidly complained:

> Now we spend our time trying to satisfy our top brass that the actors have never been on the left side of the fence. If one of them has even had his picture taken with a known Communist, even if it was several years ago, he's a dead duck as far as we're concerned.

Two weeks after the Draper incident, an obscure senator from Wisconsin, Joseph McCarthy, gave a speech in Wheeling, West Virginia, in which he stated:

> I have here in my hand a list of 205 [State Department employees] that were known to the Secretary of State as being members of the Communist party and are still working and shaping the policy of the State Department.

McCarthy, in fact, did not have any such list, but his bold accusations brought him national attention. Within weeks, McCarthy had been embraced by crusaders against communism as the popular new leader of the movement. Others had said much the same thing, but McCarthy served as a dramatic and crafty individual who did not bother with corroboration or offer the opportunity for rebuttal. He knew how to appeal to people's gut feelings and fears. Adopting the theory that nobody was too high to accuse, McCarthy offered the public reasons for the rise of communism—American traitors. Russia had the atomic bomb and some American scientists confessed to passing secrets to the Russians. If the scientific world was rife with traitors, why not the world of government, the military, or, for that matter, the world of broadcasting?

On June 22, the publishers of *Counterattack* issued a special pamphlet, *Red Channels* ("The Report of Communist Influence in Radio and Television"), which was designed as a handy reference source for blacklist-minded networks and sponsors. It contained the names of 151 entertainment personalities said to have ties with the Communist party. Among those listed were Leonard Bernstein, Lee J. Cobb, Ben Grauer, Pert Kelton, Gypsy Rose Lee, Philip Loeb, Burgess Meredith, Arthur Miller, Zero Mostel, Pete Seeger, Howard K. Smith, and Orson Welles. Like previous efforts by *Counterattack,* the listings were based on rumor and hearsay information. In less paranoid times, the audacity of such sweeping accusations without substantiation might have been dismissed outright.

Instead, three days later, the eternal vigilance called for by *Red Channels* seemed completely vindicated as Communist forces invaded South Korea.

10. What's My Crime?

THE KOREAN war was not a television war. Film cameras were too bulky to allow the extensive on-the-spot battlefield reporting that would mark the networks' coverage of the Vietnam war more than a decade later. In 1950, TV news crews barely covered events at home, so there was no reason to expect them to turn up in Korea. More importantly, the networks saw no need to supplant the official information supplied by the government. A month after the invasion of South Korea by the Communist forces from the north, NBC was the only TV network there with a technical crew—which consisted of three cameramen and one reporter. Consequently, most of the television coverage of the Korean war consisted of live pick ups of debates at the United Nations and frequent one-minute battle summaries. The little film footage shown at home came largely from the U.S. Signal Corps.

The idea that television news could be an independent force, like the newspapers, had not occurred to most people. Both the government and the networks regarded television as an entertainment medium which, in special cases, could be used by officials to communicate directly with the voters. In this spirit, NBC created a weekly series, *Battle Report Washington,* which was designed for administration spokesmen who wished to address the nation on war-related questions. The government controlled the show and said whatever it wished, without any second-guessing or cross-examination from NBC reporters. To debunk propaganda emanating from Moscow and Peking, DuMont contributed *Our Secret Weapon—The Truth,* a weekly panel show produced by Freedom House. CBS, in its part to promote civil defense, aired a timely forty-five minute documentary in September, "What To Do During an A-Bomb Attack," hosted by a thirty-three-year-old reporter the network had just picked up from United Press International, Walter Cronkite.

The news from the battlefront was rather grim during the summer of 1950. By the end of August, the North Koreans controlled most of the peninsula; the U.N., American, and South Korean forces held only a small enclave in the south near Pusan. At home, the question of Communist influence in America was no longer restricted to the theoretical level—the nation was at war. With American boys being felled by Red bullets, no sponsor wanted to be charged with satisfying the Communists by putting one of their fellow-travelers on national television. Publications such as *Red Channels* became unofficial Madison Avenue bibles on performers with alleged Communist connections and soon the practice of blacklisting again broke out into the open.

At noon on August 27, 1950, the cast of *The Aldrich Family* (a frothy TV situation comedy that had been transferred from radio a year earlier) assembled in NBC's New York studios for a final rehearsal for that night's season premiere. The only news expected to come from the day's broadcast was the response to the performances of two new members of the cast: Richard Tyler who replaced Bob Casey as Henry, and Jean Muir who replaced Lois Wilson as Henry's mother, Alice. The rehearsal never took place. A spokesman from the Young & Rubicam ad agency announced that Jean Muir was being temporarily suspended from the program because of protests the agency had received about her background. Muir, it was learned, had been listed in *Red Channels.* She was cited as one of twenty actors named in grand jury testimony in August, 1940, as a member of the Communist party (an association she denied and an association never proved). She was also said to have been a member of such leftist groups as the Artists' Front to Win the War and the Congress of American Women. She even subscribed to *Negro Quarterly.* Muir denied knowing about many of the groups and publications, but it did her no good. On August 29, the show's sponsor, General Foods, dropped Muir permanently from *The Aldrich Family* cast, saying that it made no difference whether she was guilty or not: Muir had become too controversial and her presence on the program could hurt sales. This reasoning by General Foods became a model for other blacklisting cases. It did not matter how truthful the charges of Red tainting were. The very fact that somebody had been accused at all made them guilty of being too controversial. Muir, like most blacklisted people, spent her energies trying to disprove the charges without realizing that it was already too late.

The extensive news coverage given to Muir's firing combined with the bad battle news from Korea to produce a sharp upswing in the number of sponsors who agreed to let publications such as *Red Channels* be the final arbiter of TV employment. Before the Muir case, a few well-known broadcasting figures had withstood the pressure from the blacklist lobby and defended the rights of their associates. Robert Kinter, the new president of ABC, had rejected demands that he fire Gypsy Rose Lee (a *Red Channels* target), who hosted an ABC radio show, *What Makes You Tick.* Gertrude Berg had persuaded General Foods to allow Philip Loeb (who was also listed in *Red Channels*) to continue to appear as Molly Goldberg's husband on *The Goldbergs.* After the Muir firing, even having a friend "upstairs" meant nothing for all but the most popular celebrities.

FALL 1950 SCHEDULE

MONDAY

7:00	7:30	8:00	8:30	9:00	9:30	10:00	10:30	
Club Seven	Hollywood Screen Test	Treasury Men In Action	Dick Tracy	College Bowl	On Trial	ABC Feature Film		ABC
Stork Club	CBS News / Perry Como	Lux Video Theater	Arthur Godfrey's Talent Scouts	Horace Heidt Show	The Goldbergs	Studio One		CBS
Captain Video	local / Hazel Scott	Visit With The Armed Forces	Al Morgan Show	Wrestling From Columbia Park With Dennis James				DUMONT
Kukla, Fran And Ollie	Roberta Quinlan / Camel News	THE SPEIDEL SHOW W/ PAUL WINCHELL	Voice of Firestone	Lights Out	Robert Montgomery Presents MUSICAL COMEDY TIME		Who Said That	NBC

TUESDAY

7:00	7:30	8:00	8:30	9:00	9:30	10:00	10:30	
Club Seven	BEULAH	ALL-AMERICAN FOOTBALL GAME	Buck Rogers	BILLY ROSE'S PLAYBILL	CAN YOU TOP THIS?	Life Begins At 80	Roller Derby	ABC
Stork Club	CBS News / Faye Emerson	PRUDENTIAL FAMILY THEATER Sure As Fate		VAUGHN MONROE SHOW	Suspense	DANGER	We Take Your Word	CBS
Captain Video	local / JOAN EDWARDS	Court of Current Issues	Johns Hopkins Science Review	Cavalcade Of Bands		STAR TIME		DUMONT
Kukla, Fran And Ollie	Little Show / Camel News	Texaco Star Theater		Fireside Theater	Armstrong Circle Theater	The Original Amateur Hour		NBC

WEDNESDAY

7:00	7:30	8:00	8:30	9:00	9:30	10:00	10:30	
Club Seven	CHANCE OF A LIFETIME	FIRST NIGHTER		DON McNEILL'S TV CLUB		Wrestling From The Rainbo In Chicago [To 12 Midnite]		ABC
Stork Club	CBS News / PERRY COMO	Arthur Godfrey And His Friends		TELLER OF TALES	The Web	Blue Ribbon Bouts	SPORTS SPOT	CBS
Captain Video	Manhattan Spotlight / HAZEL SCOTT	local		Famous Jury Trials	The Plainclothesman	Broadway To Hollywood Headline Clues	local	DUMONT
Kukla, Fran And Ollie	Roberta Quinlan / Camel News	FOUR STAR REVUE		Kraft Television Theater		Break The Bank	STARS OVER HOLLYWOOD	NBC

THURSDAY

7:00	7:30	8:00	8:30	9:00	9:30	10:00	10:30	
Club Seven	The Lone Ranger	Stop The Music		Holiday Hotel	Blind Date	I COVER TIMES SQUARE	Roller Derby [to 11:15]	ABC
Stork Club	CBS News / Faye Emerson	BURNS AND ALLEN	The Show Goes On	Alan Young Show	BIG TOWN	TRUTH OR CONSEQUENCES	NASH AIRFLYTE THEATER	CBS
Captain Video	Manhattan Spotlight / JOAN EDWARDS	local		ADVENTURES OF ELLERY QUEEN	Boxing From Eastern Parkway With Dennis James			DUMONT
Kukla, Fran And Ollie	Little Show / Camel News	YOU BET YOUR LIFE	Hawkins Falls	Kay Kyser's Kollege Of Music Knowledge		Martin Kane, Private Eye	WAYNE KING SHOW	NBC

FRIDAY

7:00	7:30	8:00	8:30	9:00	9:30	10:00	10:30	
Club Seven	LIFE WITH LINKLETTER	Twenty Questions	N.Y. GIANTS FOOTBALL HUDDLE	PULITZER PRIZE PLAYHOUSE		PENTHOUSE PARTY	Stud's Place	ABC
Stork Club	CBS News / PERRY COMO	Mama	Man Against Crime	Ford Television Theater Hour / MAGNAVOX THEATER		STAR OF THE FAMILY	Beat The Clock	CBS
Captain Video	Manhattan Spotlight / SUSAN RAYE	local	HOLD THAT CAMERA	Hands Of Mystery	Roscoe Karns, Inside Detective	Cavalcade Of Stars		DUMONT
Kukla, Fran And Ollie	Roberta Quinlan / Camel News	Quiz Kids	We, The People	Versatile Varieties	The Big Story / The Clock	Gillette Cavalcade Of Sports	Great Fights	NBC

SATURDAY

7:00	7:30	8:00	8:30	9:00	9:30	10:00	10:30	
SANDY DREAMS	LIFE WITH THE ERWINS	Paul Whiteman's TV Teen Club		Roller Derby				ABC
Big Top [from 6:30]	Week In Review / Faye Emerson	Ken Murray Show		FRANK SINATRA SHOW		SING IT AGAIN		CBS
Captain Video	Country Style			SATURDAY NIGHT AT MADISON SQUARE GARDEN				DUMONT
Hank McCune	One Man's Family	Jack Carter Show		Your Show Of Shows			Your Hit Parade	NBC

SUNDAY

7:00	7:30	8:00	8:30	9:00	9:30	10:00	10:30	
Paul Whiteman's Goodyear Revue	SHOWTIME U.S.A.	HOLLYWOOD PREMIERE THEATER	SIT OR MISS	Marshall Plan In Action	Faith For Today	OLD FASHIONED REVIVAL HOUR	Youth On The March	ABC
Gene Autry Show	This Is Show Business	Toast Of The Town		Fred Waring Show		Celebrity Time	What's My Line	CBS
Starlit Time		RHYTHM RODEO		Arthur Murray Show		They Stand Accused		DUMONT
Leave It To The Girls	The Aldrich Family	COLGATE COMEDY HOUR		Philco Television Playhouse		Garroway-At-Large	TAKE A CHANCE	NBC

In the wartime atmosphere of Communist expansion into Korea, sponsors and networks were determined to avoid controversial performers at any cost. In December, 1950, CBS, still stinging from the charge of being "the most satisfying network to the Communists," went so far as to announce that it would require all 2,500 of its employees to take a loyalty oath. In May, 1951, General Foods dropped *The Goldbergs* because of the continued presence of Philip Loeb, even though the program had increased the sales of Sanka coffee an amazing 57% among TV viewers and had occasionally been a top ten TV show. No other sponsor stepped forward and CBS soon took the popular series off the air. NBC picked up options to the program, but also could not find a sponsor willing to accept the show with Loeb. In January, 1952, Mrs. Berg gave in and agreed to dismiss Loeb (who was unable to find work elsewhere and later committed suicide). Within a month the show was back on—with Harold J. Stone as Papa—but it never recaptured the following or feeling of its CBS run. The united front put up by sponsors in forcing Loeb off *The Goldbergs* was dramatic proof that blacklisting had become firmly established as an unofficial but iron-clad rule that advertisers, networks, and performers had to accept as part of the broadcasting business.

Networks and ad agencies established elaborate procedures for checking the acceptability of individuals under consideration as writers, directors, and performers. They funneled the names of all prospective talent through a company executive in charge of personnel "security," who would, in turn, consult self-appointed authorities on Communist subversion such as Vincent Hartnett, who had helped write *Red Channels*.

Using as a base the single issue of *Red Channels* (published in June, 1950), such consultants provided up-to-date information on further charges of Communist infiltration. The clearance procedure on talent was usually conducted by phone and consisted of little more than the agency or network security chief ticking off a list of names and being told "Yes" or "No" by the consultant after each one. Just as in *Red Channels,* the consultants relied on hearsay evidence as well as words and actions twisted out of context.

The blacklisting process was well insulated from criticism and rebuttal because the people identified as suspicious were never confronted with the charges. Instead, they were merely told that they were "not right" for the job (too tall, too short, and so forth). It was only after being consistently turned down that individuals realized they had probably been blacklisted, but they faced a nearly impossible situation. There were no formal charges to dispute and no accusers to face. As a result, dozens of people were added to blacklists and effectively denied employment without a word of explanation or formal accusation. The networks viewed this system as a distasteful, but necessary, procedure forced upon them by the sponsors and by the paranoid state of the country. Blacklisting was seen as the networks' way of policing themselves in a wartime situation—when it was wise to be extra cautious anyway.

Though the practice of blacklisting proved to be a traumatic experience for those affected, the viewing public found it only vaguely disturbing. Only a few incidents, such as the Philip Loeb firing, ever made the papers and most Americans could not believe that people would be accused of Communist connections unless there was some truth to the charges. Because blacklisting usually only affected second-level TV personalities (the superstars were generally left alone), average Americans found the situation easy to ignore. Viewers turned to television for entertainment, not disturbing news, and blacklisting remained a behind-the-scenes internal problem that would have to be resolved by the people within the industry. Even the news of the Jean Muir firing in August, 1950, was soon superseded in the public's mind by the glittering events of the new season premieres.

In September, viewers were treated to the most exciting fall season since Milton Berle's first appearance, as the nation's most popular radio stars made the plunge into video. With a great deal of advance publicity, NBC unveiled *The Colgate Comedy Hour* and *Four Star Revue,* two lavishly furnished comedy-variety hours staged live, in huge New York theaters, with flashy sets, music, dancing, and skits. The two shows were the network's vehicles for bringing to TV nine of its top comedy acts: Eddie Cantor, Dean Martin and Jerry Lewis, Fred Allen, Bob Hope, and Bobby Clark on *The Colgate Comedy Hour,* and Jimmy Durante, Ed Wynn, Danny Thomas, and Jack Carson on *Four Star Revue.* In order to avoid the wear and tear of a week-in, week-out routine, each of the nine had a separate production staff and was scheduled to appear as host only about once a month, rotating the chores with the other headliners. This was thought to be the perfect solution to the pressures that frequently faced such performers as Sid Caesar and Milton Berle, whose writers had to come up with material for an entire program every week. Even though the rotating procedure was very expensive ($50,000 a week), NBC felt this was the best way to produce comedy blockbusters and the network confidently slotted the programs against the two most popular shows on CBS: *The Colgate Comedy Hour* aired on Sunday versus the number three rated *Toast of the Town,* while *Four Star Revue* took on the number two ranked *Arthur Godfrey and Friends* on Wednesday.

In September and October, as the stars each made their first appearances, ratings were high and reviewers were ecstatic in their praise of the two shows. It looked as if NBC had pulled off a minor miracle. Though the network had lost a slew of big comedy names to CBS radio in 1948, NBC appeared to be on the verge of locking up the field of TV comedy. Week after week, viewers saw top-notch material that had taken the stars years to polish and perfect.

Eddie Cantor's first program showcased a marvelous "Cavalcade of Cantor"—a reprise of his many hits—ending with Cantor in

blackface singing "Ain't She Sweet" and "Ma, He's Making Eyes at Me." Cantor made it a point to give exposure to new talent and during the season he featured the TV debuts of Eddie Fisher and sixteen-year-old Joel Grey, son of veteran borscht-belt comedian Mickey Katz. Dean Martin and Jerry Lewis, who had become big radio and film stars by 1950, brought back to television their highly polished combination of Martin's romantic "paisano" crooning and Lewis's zany "swell nonsense." Comedy newcomer Norman Lear usually wrote many of their segments. Ed Wynn came in from the West Coast and used the cavernous Center Theater in New York as a TV playground, staging such show-stopping routines as bicycling French singer Edith Piaf around on top of a movable piano. Bob Hope added hilarious visual double takes to his radio style of sharp one-liners and clever skits, while Jimmy Durante drew on his electric personality and unbeatable charm with lady guests.

There were some problems. Danny Thomas, one of the youngest of the nine, did not click at first. Though his opening monologues were good—Thomas assumed the pose of belligerent underdog—the rest of the show emerged as static and bland. Instead of projecting his personality to the folks at home, Thomas began to play to the studio audience (he frequently lapsed into wartime flag-waving that came over only as bad corn). By March, though, Thomas gained more confidence and the show improved tremendously. He was helped by better writing and the adoption of the more cohesive "book show" style. In this process, an hour-long comedy-variety show tied together its sketches and music with a thin continuing thread, such as Thomas and his crew taking a train ride to Miami.

The three other stars had more serious problems. Los Angeles

From 1949 to 1954, Ralph Bellamy played private eye Mike Barnett (a sleuth who never carried a gun). (*From* Man Against Crime. *Courtesy of MCA Television Limited*)

September 7, 1950
Truth or Consequences. (CBS). After ten years on radio, Ralph Edwards brings his popular audience participation show to television, intact. "Consequences" on the first video episode include a wife throwing trick knives at her husband, and the sentimental reunion of a wounded G.I. and his mother (after a thirty-one month separation).

September 18, 1950
NBC Comics. (NBC). Animated cartoons come to network television in a fifteen-minute late afternoon weekday program made up of four three-minute cartoon series: "Danny Match" (a young private eye), "Space Barton" (interplanetary adventures), "Johnny and Mr. Do-Right" (a school boy and his dog), and "Kid Champion" (a young boxer).

September 25, 1950
The Kate Smith Show. (NBC). NBC succeeds with the first major venture in afternoon network television: an hour of music and variety.

October 6, 1950
Pulitzer Prize Playhouse. (ABC). Alex Segal directs ABC's first major dramatic series. The acting and writing are top-notch, with scripts from a number of Pulitzer Prize winning authors such as Maxwell Anderson, Thornton Wilder, and James Michener.

October 16, 1950
Following the lead of NBC and Kate Smith, CBS jumps into afternoon television with two hour-long variety shows. Garry Moore and Robert Q. Lewis are the hosts.

December 15, 1950
Hear It Now. (CBS Radio). Ed Murrow is reunited with Fred Friendly (recently signed to CBS) and together they create "a document for the ear."

December 25, 1950
The Steve Allen Show. (CBS). "Steverino" shifts to television (weekday evenings) with a simple format that will serve him well for years: He plays the piano, interviews guests, and talks to the audience. The following May, Allen is moved to noontime and his show expands to an hour.

comic Jack Carson's shows were replete with bad timing and insufficient planning. Bobby Clark, whose appearances were produced by famed showman Mike Todd, was lost amid a bevy of beautiful legs (a Todd trademark), sloppy slapstick routines, and erratic production work. The big failure, though, was Fred Allen. After being away from audiences for a year (following his radio banishment by *Stop the Music*), Allen seemed rusty, spiteful, and uncomfortable in the role of emcee. He had not performed on the open stage for eighteen years, yet NBC placed him, like the others, in a huge Manhattan theater that often swallowed up guests and hosts that did not come on brash and brassy. Allen was a humorist used to the close, relaxed atmosphere of a radio studio and he never hid his disdain for television, which added an unwanted Scrooge-like element to his already acerbic character. For Allen's long-time radio fans, one of the big letdowns in the television show was the treatment of Allen's Alley. Instead of using talented character actors to flesh out the residents of the famed fictional street, the program presented Ajax Cassidy, Titus Moody, Mrs. Nussbaum, and Senator Claghorn as puppet characters, turning the program into some bizarre sort of Kukla, Fred, and Ollie show.

Of the September array of NBC comedy celebrities, Allen was the first to fall. He left the show in December, citing high blood pressure and issuing a parting blast at the network, which he said had forced the revue format on him. "I'm through with this kind of television," Allen said, adding that if he returned it would be in a lowkey thirty-minute format closer to the style used by Chicago's Dave Garroway.

CBS also brought a number of radio stars to TV in the 1950–51 season, including some that had been lured to the network in the Paley's Comet talent raids of 1948. Edgar Bergen, Jack Benny, and Bing Crosby did occasional specials, while Frank Sinatra had a weekly series running against *Your Show of Shows*. Despite the big budget variety shows in its schedule, though, CBS felt that situation comedy was actually a more stable television form that would be easier to exploit in the long run. The network felt such programs could overcome some of the weaknesses of the variety format by presenting viewers with continuing characters, settings, and stories, rather than week after week of unrelated skits, which often looked like sixty minutes of random activity. Consequently, CBS, as it had previously done in radio, concentrated on sitcoms, trying to give its programming a different "feel" from NBC and hoping to develop a blockbuster hit that could push it ahead of NBC in the TV ratings race. In the fall of 1950, however, the network had only one new sitcom ready, *The George Burns and Gracie Allen Show*—and even that aired only on alternate Thursdays, live from New York.

George Burns and Gracie Allen performed an effortless transition into television, bringing to the new medium the characters they had developed through twenty-five years in vaudeville and on radio. They were a real life husband and wife comedy team and they played themselves in a domestic setting. George was the long-suffering straightman and Gracie was the mistress of malapropism who seemingly was on a different plane of reality from the rest of the world. The structure of the series was simple: Using a very thin plot line to hold each episode together, George and Gracie interacted with each other and various members of the supporting cast, in effect staging their familiar comedy routines throughout the program. George described the show as having "more plot than a variety show and not as much as a wrestling match."

The Burns and Allen Show drew elements from both Jack Benny and Ozzie and Harriet. Like Benny, George and Gracie portrayed performers who put on a weekly comedy show, but while they often talked about their fictional television program, they never got near the studio. Instead, like Ozzie and Harriet, they used their showbiz identities as a springboard for behind-the-scenes homelife escapades. In these, George and Gracie were joined by their announcer, Harry Von Zell, and their next door neighbors, Blanche Morton (Bea Benaderet) and her straight-laced C.P.A. husband, Harry (played by a succession of actors: Hal March, John Brown, Fred Clark, and Larry Keating). Each week's complications were very simple, inevitably the result of some household or showbiz misunderstanding by Gracie. Though in some ways the program's plots were very much like Hollywood's "screwball" theatrical comedies and the first wave of West Coast filmed TV sitcoms, the excellent writing and emphasis on the comic characters and routines raised the show far above such routine fare. In fact, even when the program became a weekly series in 1952, moving out West and onto film, it retained its high quality production and unique point of view. Gracie Allen was not a dumb blonde or a two-faced schemer—she merely followed her own illogical logic to its nonsense conclusions, leaving everyone who crossed

George Burns and Gracie Allen, successful radio stars from 1932, made an effortless transition to CBS television in 1950. *(Courtesy George Burns)*

it felt would usher in the age of sitcom supremacy on television: *Amos and Andy*.

Since May, 1949, CBS had been scouring the country in search of an all-black cast for the TV version of radio's *Amos and Andy*, building as much interest and anticipation as possible for the show. With its proven history of success and viewer loyalty on radio, the series seemed a good choice by CBS for a possible breakthrough in television situation comedy. Created by Freeman Gosden and Charles Correll, two white men, *Amos and Andy* had been one of radio's first nationwide sensations, becoming a national obsession soon after arriving on the NBC network in 1929. People planned their lives around the 7:00-7:15 p.m. weekday radio broadcasts. Movie theaters altered showtimes and some even piped in the program for patrons.

Amos and Andy began as the humorous adventures of two black men, focusing on their home lives, friends, and the funny situations they got themselves into. Amos Jones (portrayed by Gosden) was the respectable straightman—a hard-working, church-going solid citizen, happily married with two children. Andy Brown (Correll) was the good natured comic foil—a pudgy addlebrained bachelor. They lived in the Harlem area of New York City and operated the "Fresh Air Taxi Cab Company, Incorpulated"—consisting of one run down old car that did not even have a windshield. Amos did most of the work while Andy loafed or chased women. They both socialized with George Stevens—nicknamed the Kingfish—who was the head of the Mystic Knights of the Sea Lodge and a fast talking conniver. The Kingfish (also played by Gosden) was always ready to fleece Andy with some new get-rich-quick scheme and, as the series evolved in the 1930s, he began to supplant Amos, whose character was a bit too straight for many comic situations and misunderstandings. Governor Huey Long of Louisiana, a great fan of the show, even adopted the nickname Kingfish for himself.

Though the Kingfish put on a boastful front as a big-time operator, his schemes were generally penny ante manipulations and he

her path totally confused. "If she made sense," George quipped, "I'd still be selling ties."

While Gracie was the comic center of the program, George's special outlook added extra flavor. Going beyond the simple role of straightman to Gracie, George took mischievous delight in confusing people himself because, of all the characters in the show, George alone acknowledged that they were all doing a comedy program and that ultimately none of the complications were meant to be taken seriously. Looking directly into the camera, he made frequent witty asides to the audience, delivering both comic monologues and comments on the story. George usually knew what everybody else in the show was doing, occasionally getting this information just as the home viewer did, by watching the program on TV while it was still in progress. He became a special confidant to the audience at home, acting as both a character and an omniscient observer. As a result, *The Burns and Allen Show* emerged as a relaxed, leisurely visit with some very funny people.

Though the show did well in its time slot against tough competition, the program was not a runaway hit in its early years. CBS's sitcom strategy had yet to be proved for television. In fact, by January, 1951, there was not one sitcom listed among TV's top ten rated shows. According to the A.C. Nielsen Company (which had taken over the Hooper ratings service in early 1950), NBC dominated the television ratings chart with comedy-variety hours, drama anthologies, and Friday night boxing. CBS was represented at the top of "the Nielsens" with a few of its own variety, drama, and sports shows, but the network continued to bank on sitcoms for the future. In the summer of 1951, when most of the comedy-variety stars were on vacation, CBS presented a new show that

December 25, 1950
"One Hour In Disneyland." (NBC). Walt Disney's first television special. He quickly displays a great blend of television showmanship and commercialism, incorporating plugs for upcoming Disney films in a "best of Disney" retrospective.

January 20, 1951
The Cisco Kid. Duncan Rinaldo plays a Mexican equivalent to the Lone Ranger in a syndicated adventure series distributed to the local stations by Ziv. Just to be prepared, the episodes are filmed in color.

April 23, 1951
Ed Thorgensen and the News. (DuMont). The second of DuMont's three attempts at its own nightly news show. This version uses a top newsreel announcer, but settles for a very cheap set (even by DuMont's standards). One month later, the program is gone.

May 14, 1951
Time for Ernie. (NBC). Ernie Kovacs makes it to network television in a brief afternoon series. In July, he is moved into Kukla, Fran, and Ollie's time period.

August 24, 1951
After two months under the leadership of Jack E. Leonard, *Broadway Open House* is closed, ending (for the moment) NBC's experiment in late night television.

Senator Estes Kefauver (seated, *l.*) campaigning in the 1952 New Hampshire presidential primary. He used notoriety gained from televised crime hearings in 1951 to mount a serious bid for the Democratic nomination. *(National Archives)*

was caught as the fall guy almost as often as Andy. Over the years, the Kingfish became the main character of the series, with more and more attention given to his home life. There the Kingfish was just a hen-pecked husband, dominated by his wife, Sapphire (Ernestine Wade), and hounded by his sour mother-in-law (Amanda Randolph). As a result, the Kingfish emerged as an earthy, uneducated, but lovable conniver rather than as a cruel and malicious schemer. The only chance he ever had to show off was down at the lodge where he could always talk Andy into another hair-brained venture or berate Lightnin', the lodge's shuffling dim-witted janitor.

Like all radio comedies of the era, *Amos and Andy* had its share of stock phrases. During the program's heyday in the 1930s, many of these became part of the nation's vocabulary, including "I'se regusted!" "Ow-wah, ow-wah, ow-wah!" "Now ain't that sumpin'!" and "Holy mackerel, Andy!" Even into the 1940s when it became a half-hour weekly series, *Amos and Andy* was still a top ten radio show with a strong following. The program was a logical first choice for CBS's famed Paley's Comet talent raids of 1948 and the network had high hopes that a TV version of *Amos and Andy* would be just as successful and long-lasting as the radio show. Freeman Gosden and Charles Correll, who did their radio show from Los Angeles, personally supervised the long casting process and they produced the series' TV pilot film, on the West Coast, at the then expansive cost of $40,000.

Amos and Andy was the first important television situation comedy filmed in Los Angeles, and it used a program formula that was identical to the vanguard West Coast filmed sitcoms of the previous season, only with a bigger budget and better overall production. These filmed series were just like Hollywood's theatrical "screwball" comedy films, which relied on simple cardboard characters placed in silly situations that could be easily repeated

and endlessly exploited. In this form of comedy, the situation became all important. The stereotyped characters ran through the paces of the plot as if it were an obstacle course, serving as mouthpieces for one-liners as they reacted to the absurd events. This formula had worked well for movie and radio comedies and CBS thought that *Amos and Andy* could produce television's first smash hit sitcom with this style.

Like the formula screwball comedies, the TV series relied on misunderstood situations, a ploy which allowed even the most trivial actions to become the basis for an outlandish story. In one episode, Andy (Spencer Williams) and the Kingfish (Tim Moore) mistook an atomic testing plant for a fancy clock factory and they brought in their broken clock to exchange for another. At first, the two were mistaken for experimental scientists but, when Andy and the Kingfish walked off with the super secret atomic clock they were assigned to test, they found themselves pursued as enemy spies. Another week, the overage Kingfish received a draft notice intended for another, much younger, George Stevens. He felt honored to prove his manhood at middle age and proudly reported for the Army physical. When the Army turned him down, the Kingfish felt ashamed and had Andy hide him at the lodge, where he wrote postcards "from training camp" and sent them to Sapphire. Inevitably, a few words of explanation cleared up such misunderstandings, and the characters were ready to do it all again the following week. These simple stories were silly but funny, and the actors were good in their comic roles (Ernestine Wade as Sapphire and Amanda Randolph as Sapphire's Mama even came directly from the radio version.) However, instead of giving CBS its first important sitcom success, *Amos and Andy* created nothing but problems once it hit the air.

Because *Amos and Andy* was the first major television sitcom series from Los Angeles, the inherent weaknesses of the style were painfully evident. Characters in West Coast comedies were exaggerated comic caricatures living in a fantasy world of formula humor. Even though *Amos and Andy* was done much better than such dismal TV vehicles as *The Hank McCune Show,* East Coast critics still had serious reservations about the form. *Amos and Andy* faced an additional problem. Because the series was also the first television program to deal exclusively with blacks, the underlying silliness of the characters was interpreted by some as a putdown directed specifically against blacks. Protests began almost immediately after the program premiered. The National Association for the Advancement of Colored People (NAACP) blasted the series:

> [*Amos and Andy*] depicts the Negro in a stereotyped and derogatory manner . . . it strengthens the conclusion among uninformed or prejudiced people that Negroes and other minorities are inferior, lazy, dumb, and dishonest.

Though there had been a great deal of ballyhoo over the search for an all-black cast for *Amos and Andy,* the fact that the performers were black was secondary. The characters and plots were totally interchangeable with scores of "white" sitcoms that both preceded and postdated *Amos and Andy.* Gosden and Correll had never used the incongruity of white men playing black roles as a source of laughs, and the approach in the television version also avoided situations that might have been staged as cheap racial putdowns. *Amos and Andy* was set up in an essentially all-black world, where whites were rarely seen. If the Kingfish was outsmarted, it was by a black con artist, not a white one. There were black lawyers and black doctors to balance off black stooges. As in any screwball comedy, the stories depended on misunderstandings and crazy antics by such tried and true stereotypes as a money-hungry bumbler, a slow-witted second banana, a shrewish wife, and a battleaxe mother-in-law. In *Amos and Andy,* these familiar comic caricatures just happened to be black. Nonetheless, the NAACP was outraged that the first major television program to feature blacks prominently was a screwball situation comedy, a form which included as a matter of course comic caricatures that the organization was particularly sensitive to seeing identified with blacks. For example, the minor supporting character of Lightnin' (Horace Stewart), the janitor at the lodge, was shiftless, lazy, and dumb. Worse yet, he spoke with a high-pitched drawl ("Yazzah") and walked with a lazy shuffle.

Reacting to the characters and the stories, the NAACP urged a boycott of the show's sponsor, Blatz beer. The boycott never caught on, but then again neither did the show. Television's *Amos and Andy* never attracted anywhere near the loyalty and support of the radio version, and for CBS it was an expensive disappointment. Instead of dethroning Milton Berle and comedy-variety, *Amos and Andy* secured only marginal ratings and, after two years, the show was taken off the air. Fifteen years later, in response to protests over the program's racial tone, CBS even withdrew *Amos and Andy* from circulation as an off-network rerun.

In a way, *Amos and Andy* was kicked off the air for the wrong reason. Though its black stereotyped characters were gone, the underlying assumptions for West Coast screwball sitcoms remained. For more than a decade similar series flourished featuring white performers. In that light, *Amos and Andy* was merely the harbinger of a successful trend, with its black characters no more or less demeaning than their white equivalents.

Lost amid the controversy over *Amos and Andy* was another West Coast filmed sitcom that focused on blacks, ABC's *Beulah.* Arriving six months earlier than *Amos and Andy* and receiving much less attention, *Beulah* more justifiably deserved harsh criticism. While *Amos and Andy* presented an essentially all black world that rarely even alluded to the presence of whites, *Beulah* cast blacks exclusively as servants in a simplistic update of the antebellum "Gone With the Wind" setting.

Beulah (Ethel Waters) was the much put-upon "Mammy" for a suburban white middle class family, running their day-to-day domestic lives as "queen of the kitchen." Though a sharp woman who often rescued her "masters" from their own household incompetence, Beulah was still just hired help. Unlike *Amos and Andy,* there were no respectable black professionals in the supporting cast; instead, Beulah had a shiftless boyfriend, Bill (Percy Harris), and a scatterbrained girlfriend, Oriole (Butterfly McQueen).

Beulah's taint of racial deprecation had begun on radio. The character of Beulah was created by a white man, Marlin Hurt, and had first appeared in 1944 as part of *The Fibber McGee and Molly Show.* In 1945, ABC radio gave Beulah "her" own show, with Hurt continuing the character in the new series. Each week, he got his first big laugh by exploiting the incongruity between his radio character and his physical appearance. After an introduction by the studio announcer leading up to Beulah's first appearance, Hurt, previously unseen by the studio audience, jumped into place and yelled, in character, "Somebody bawl for Beulah?" The sight of a small white man with the voice of a large black woman never failed to touch off a roar of laughter from the studio audience. When Beulah shifted to CBS radio in 1947, a real black woman (Hattie McDaniel) took the title role, but the program never lost its condescending attitude, even in the transfer to television.

The Los Angeles-produced filmed sitcoms introduced in the 1950–51 season were, at best, only marginally successful. Yet there would be more. As the coast-to-coast coaxial cable neared completion, television executives prepared to link the operations of the two centers of popular entertainment in America, New York and Los Angeles. Increased Hollywood production was inevitable as the East and West branches of television moved into a new phase of their battle for dominance in the medium.

With the final hookup of the East-West cable targeted for the fall of 1951, the networks eliminated practically all of their remaining Chicago-based productions. Executives found that it made more sense to draw on the resources of the two coasts instead. New York-based producers had tremendous expertise with complicated in-studio productions, especially live drama, plus a rich stock of Broadway performers to draw from. Los Angeles had talent proficient in filmed productions and was also the home of the top stars in radio comedy and variety (many of whom had temporarily relocated out East for the move to television). Chicago programming was totally expendable. Throughout the season, most of the Chicago-based variety programs—usually unsponsored anyway—were replaced by more easily sold programs live from New York or on film from Los Angeles. Even *Garroway at Large,* the most popular of the Chicago television stable, found itself without a sponsor at the end of the season.

One of the last successful network programs to come out of Chicago was a lowkey new game show, DuMont's *Down You Go,* hosted by a professor of English from Northwestern University, Bergen Evans. Even though it was created by Louis G. Cowan, who had conceived such flashy vehicles as *Stop the Music, Down You Go* had a distinctively different flavor from other network programs, chiefly because of its Chicago-based production. Using fresh, unknown talent rather than a panel of familiar big name celebrities, *Down You Go* emerged as one of the wittiest, most relaxed game shows on television. The mechanics of the game were simple: Using clues provided by Evans, the four panelists had to guess a slogan, sentence, word, or phrase, filling in each word, letter by letter. For "I don't want to set the world on fire," Evans suggested that this was "the usual excuse for those who have no burning ambition." Evans and the panel members obviously enjoyed working with each other and their personal charm and effortless good humor consistently came through to the home audience. The program stood out favorably against the competition and ran on DuMont for four years, subsequently appearing briefly on each of the other three networks as well.

Though the top rated programs in the 1950–51 season were variety shows, drama anthologies, and sports contests, the networks usually selected a game, panel, or quiz show format to fill holes in their schedules. Such programs were easy to stage, inexpensive, and practically interchangeable. Only a few ever stood out. Besides *Down You Go*, there were two other distinctive game shows that season, *You Bet Your Life* and *Strike It Rich*.

Strike It Rich began on television as a CBS daytime offering and was soon added to the network's nighttime schedule as well. Hosted by Warren Hull and occasionally by Monty Hall, *Strike It Rich* described itself as "the quiz show with a heart," though critics claimed it merely exploited the weaknesses of contestants in order to garner high ratings. The program featured people in need, including such unfortunates as someone who needed money for an expensive operation, a childless couple looking for an orphan to adopt, and a widow needing funds to start a new life. After answering a few simple qualifying questions, the contestants had to stand in front of the audience, tell their stories, and plead for assistance. The loudness of the applause by the audience in response to their presentations determined who received the most money. Afterward, home viewers were invited to phone in pledges for those who still needed additional help.

Strike It Rich regularly crossed the line between entertainment and exploitation. Reacting to the absurd mechanics of the program, humorist Al Capp proposed that the show use a Misery Meter which would measure the strength of each tale of woe. The scale began with "sad," and worked its way through "depressing," "heartbreaking," "sickening," and "sickeningly heartbreaking" before reaching the ultimate: "unbearably tragic." The program was regularly criticized for its maudlin tone, but the most dramatic expression of outrage took place in the studio control room when the show's director was ordered to broadcast a tight closeup of the legs of a cripple trying to walk. Instead, the director silently stood up, walked out of the control room, and never returned.

You Bet Your Life, the season's most successful new game show, was far more tasteful. The program had begun on radio as a vehicle for the ad-lib wit of Groucho Marx, and continued unchanged in the move to television. Prior to *You Bet Your Life*, Groucho had been a flop on radio in four short-lived scripted programs. In 1947, John Guedel, the creator of Art Linkletter's audience participation shows *People Are Funny* and *House Party*, talked Groucho into trying the quiz show format. At first Groucho resisted, feeling that the role of quizmaster was beneath his professional dignity. Once the program started rolling, it quickly became apparent that Guedel had found the perfect setting for Groucho's wit. The quiz portion of *You Bet Your Life* was unimportant; it served as the excuse to have pairs of contestants brought out to be interviewed by Groucho before "playing the game." Groucho did not see the contestants before they were introduced by announcer George Fenneman, so all of Groucho's comments were spontaneous.

In order to assume control over such a potentially volatile format, the show's producers carefully selected the contestants, looking for people that could play well against Groucho. For further control, one hour of material was taped live before a studio audience,

then edited down to thirty minutes. This allowed the producers to assemble a tight package and to discard unsuccessful exchanges and exceptionally risque comments. The format clicked and *You Bet Your Life* became a top ten radio show for NBC. When the program came to television, the producers merely added a camera. Television viewers could then see Groucho's leering eyes whenever a beautiful woman appeared, and the flustered attempts at composure by any contestant whom fate had saddled with a funny-sounding name—a favorite target of Groucho's tongue. *You Bet Your Life* continued on television virtually unchanged until the early 1960s, a monument to Groucho's creativity and Guedel's insight.

While *You Bet Your Life* shot into the top ten for NBC, Groucho's brother, Chico Marx, bombed in *The College Bowl*, an odd musical comedy on ABC. Cast as the owner of a campus malt shop, Chico played essentially the same character as he did in the successful Marx Brothers feature films, singing nonsense songs at the piano and cracking horrible puns in Italian dialect. He was surrounded by a crew of young singers and dancers (including eighteen-year-old Andy Williams) who played the local "campus types" that hung around the malt shop. There was constant singing, dancing, and light humor, but the scripts were terrible, the staging lackluster, and the program never caught fire.

Another major disappointment for ABC was the performance of a TV film version of Chester Gould's comic strip crimefighter, Dick Tracy. The show was unable to duplicate the success of ABC's only big hit, *The Lone Ranger*, even though it possessed many of the same pulp adventure elements in an urban crime setting. From its beginning in 1931, the Dick Tracy comic strip presented a violent world of clearcut good guys, bad guys, crime, and punishment. Tracy joined the police force as a plainclothes detective following the murder of his financee's father, and his pursuit of off-beat criminals such as Flattop, Prune Face, and Pouch inevitably included a graphic, fatal shoot-out. Through the 1930s and 1940s, the comic strip inspired a successful radio show and a series of theatrical films starring Ralph Byrd. Yet the television series, which even had Byrd repeating the title role, never took off.

One unexpected problem the producers faced was that when the series began filming in early 1950, Congress was going through one of its first seizures against television violence. Word was flashed to Los Angeles to tone down Tracy's escapades. Consequently, the first two episodes of *Dick Tracy* shown in September were very mild. The third and fourth episodes, filmed after the congressional heat had cooled, brought Tracy back to his more familiar tough guy stature. The fifth show featured two murders, a gun fight, and a fist fight. The sixth show opened with a hanging. Even so, the program failed to make a dent in Arthur Godfrey's Monday night audience.

ABC's poor showing in the fall served to compound the network's shaky financial position. While NBC and CBS battled for ratings points at the top, ABC was fighting for its life. The network had saved some money the previous season by substantially cutting back its schedule, but when ABC resumed seven-day-a-week programming, it found the money and ratings problems worse than ever. Though ABC had a few hits such as *The Lone Ranger* and *Stop the Music*, the rest of its programs were regularly trounced by the other networks. Worse yet, all through 1950, TV production costs multiplied at a staggering rate and, for the first time, the networks' television budgets surpassed their radio budgets. All the other networks pumped money into TV broadcasting from other, more profitable, parts of their corporate setup. NBC was part of RCA, CBS owned Columbia Records, and DuMont made TV sets. ABC had to sink or swim with its radio and TV operations alone.

ABC saw no hope for a quick upswing in either the number

of viewers or the number of affiliates. The outbreak of the Korean war had forced a sharp reduction in TV set production, and the FCC's unending freeze on new TV station construction had halted such expansion. ABC decided that if a new source of income was not found, the network would not be able to continue. In May, 1951, after flirting with a merger offer from CBS, ABC announced plans to merge with United Paramount Theaters. United Paramount had been formed when Paramount Pictures was ordered by the Supreme Court to divest itself of the ownership of movie theaters while the studio continued to produce films. Besides offering ABC much-needed cash, United Paramount had a number of officials steeped in Hollywood techniques and tradition. It was felt that such an influx of West Coast showmanship could give the young and struggling ABC a distinctive flair, contrasting with the New York orientation of the other three networks.

The parties asked the FCC to approve the merger before September to allow ABC to begin the next season on a new footing. Perhaps they should have specified which September they intended, because two seasons slipped by while the FCC sat on the merger request. The FCC was still struggling with the comparatively simple decision of whether to accept the Paramount Pictures-United Paramount split. Because the FCC repeatedly had contended that Paramount Pictures controlled DuMont, the ABC request would go nowhere until the FCC decided whether to accept United Paramount as a separate entity. Only then would the commission get into the question of whether a theater chain should own a television network. As the bureaucrats at the FCC chewed on these questions, ABC watched its financial reserve sink lower and lower.

Though the FCC postponed a decision on ABC's merger request, during the 1950–51 season the commission ended, for the moment, ten years of deliberation on another topic: color. In October, 1950, the FCC voted to approve CBS's mechanical noncompatible process as the country's official color television system. The Korean war and the freeze on station construction had temporarily halted the growth in TV set sales but, even so, when the decision was announced there were nine million black and white sets in use that would have to be scrapped and replaced by new color models. Even though RCA had produced a working, compatible color system, the FCC justified its decision by pointing out that CBS's was better in quality and ready at the moment. The RCA system appeared to be a few more years from commercial viability.

RCA appealed the FCC decision, taking the battle all the way to the Supreme Court. The legal wrangling delayed CBS's commercial color debut for more than seven months and, during that time, RCA decided to carry the fight into the public sector. In December, 1950, RCA called in television critics from the major newspapers for a demonstration of its compatible color system. The improvement from the previous RCA public exhibitions was substantial and the critics noted that there was only a slight difference in quality between the CBS and RCA systems. This effectively changed the nature of the color debate. Some people observed that the FCC had chosen noncompatible color just as a compatible color system was nearing completion. They questioned the wisdom of asking the nation's viewers either to invest in expensive new color sets or to miss out on important chunks of color TV programming that could not be picked up by black and white models. In May of 1951, however, the Supreme Court turned down RCA's legal appeal and it appeared that CBS had won. Most TV set manufacturers said they would go along with the decision and produce the new color sets when there was an evident public demand for them.

At 4:30 P.M. Monday, June 25, 1951, Arthur Godfrey walked onto the stage of CBS's Grand Central Station studios and was seen in lovely, spinning disk, noncompatible color by the 400 guests watching on eight color sets at CBS, and by other viewers gathered around the thirty color receivers then available in the New York City area. The program was broadcast in color to Boston, Philadelphia, Baltimore, and Washington, though it is doubtful that anyone outside the control rooms of those CBS affiliates saw anything but jumbled static. Sixteen sponsors (such as the makers of multi-tinted automobiles and vibrantly colored lipsticks) paid $10,000 for the privilege of being seen by a handful of people. CBS felt color would follow the progression of black and white television the previous decade: Early test programs would be seen by next to nobody, a few brave sponsors would stake out some turf in this goldmine of the future, and eventually a few hit shows would lure the reluctant public into the color TV showrooms.

Following the opening day special, no hit shows turned up. No brave sponsors presented themselves. The war-conscious public refused to give up its old black and white sets. In fact, the public showed complete apathy toward color television. CBS soon realized that the FCC approval had come too late. The network had a multi-million dollar lemon on its hands that it needed to unload. In October, 1951, National Production Authority chairman Charles Wilson (whose top aide was CBS chairman William Paley) politely asked CBS to cease all color television operations for the duration of the national emergency resulting from the war in Korea. Before the print was dry on Wilson's request, CBS graciously agreed to this virtual death sentence for the government-ordered monopoly it had fought so long for. Everybody said publicly that the halt in color operations was just temporary and the FCC continued to limit tests of compatible color to outside regular broadcast hours. Within the television industry, however, it was felt that noncompatible color was dead.

The public's indifference to color television had nothing to do with its feelings toward TV in general. Viewing levels were greater than ever. In fact, three months before color's inauspicious debut, interest in a new television programming event swept the country. Alternately labeled "What's My Crime" and "Underworld Talent Scouts," this program had everything a hit TV show needed: a cast Hollywood could not beat, an ad-libbed script better than any drama, and free publicity from the morning papers. There was suspense, personality conflict, suspicious motivation, and real life human drama. The program was the traveling road show staged by the Senate Crime Committee, Senator Estes Kefauver, chairman.

The committee's investigation into organized crime began to attract attention in early February, 1951, when local Detroit TV coverage of the proceedings pulled in top ratings. The story broke into the headlines later that month in St. Louis when nationally known betting expert James J. Carroll refused to testify if television cameras were present. Carroll's lawyer called such television coverage "an invasion of privacy," and observed that his client, "may be ridiculed and embarrassed as a result." When the hearings moved to New York City in mid-March, all the TV networks decided to run them live, during their nearly empty daytime hours. Over the course of the broadcasts, daytime viewing reached twenty times its usual level. TV viewing parties sprang up and people suddenly became aware of the previously untapped power that television had for conveying and even creating events.

Committee Counsel Rudolph Halley and Senator Kefauver became instant celebrities as they probed into the shady activities of such underworld bigwigs as Frank Erickson, Frank Costello, and Joe Adonis before millions of television viewers. One of the most dramatic and damaging of the sessions took place when Frank Costello, like James Carroll, said that he would not testify with television cameras present. Unlike Carroll, Costello then modified his stance and agreed to a compromise—the network cameramen could show only his hands during the testimony. In a weird way, this arrangement backfired for Costello because it attracted much more attention than if his face had been routinely shown like the others. Instead, viewers were given an eerie contrast between a calm voice seeking exoneration and the fidgeting hands of a clearly nervous man. After hours of intense questioning under the hot TV lights, Costello said, "I am not going to answer another question!" and walked out of the committee room. Thirty million viewers saw him leave and the committee cited Costello for contempt.

In spite of the publicity and increased daytime viewing from the hearings, the networks were happy when they came to an end. Extended broadcasting without commercial sponsors meant losing money. In fact, when a night session was held, NBC and CBS stuck with their regular programming and only ABC and DuMont, both with few sponsored shows, continued the broadcasts.

Television's coverage of the Kefauver hearings was called the advent of electronic journalism. Had the hearings been reported only in the newspapers and on the brief nightly TV news shows, they would not have received such wide public attention. Instead, the issues and personalities involved became household topics simply because they had been on live TV. One reviewer marveled that "[Television] has shown that it can arouse public interest to a degree which virtually beggars immediate description." With a presidential election little more than a year away, politicians with foresight realized that television could be something more than a mute conveyor of convention hoopla.

The Kefauver hearings had other peculiar forms of fallout. The networks saw that there was a tremendous audience waiting for daytime broadcasting and they prepared to exploit it. They also increased the number of crime dramas about the mob throughout the prime time schedule. Senator Kefauver decided to use his newly acquired national celebrity status to run for the Democratic presidential nomination the following year. Though he lost that bid, Kefauver was a serious contender right up to the party's nominating convention.

Perhaps the man who made the best use of his exposure was Halley, the committee counsel. In September he became host of a network crime show called *Crime Syndicated*. Even though he only appeared at the beginning and end of the program, laboriously reading cue cards, the exposure was enough to help secure his election as president of the New York City Council in November. Now, *this* was a facet of television politicians could really understand.

11. The Thaw

AT 10:30 P.M. (Eastern time), September 4, 1951, coast-to-coast network television became a reality. In the fifty-two cities joined by the coaxial cable, ninety-four of the 107 American television stations then on the air broadcast the same event: President Harry Truman's address to the opening session of the Japanese Peace Treaty Conference at San Francisco's Opera House.

Before the completion of the Western cable hookup, only 45% of the American homes with a television could be reached by live network TV. Afterward, 95% of the TV homes, from Atlanta north to Boston, west to San Francisco, and south to San Diego, could all watch the same thing at the same time. By the opening of the political conventions in the summer of 1952, only one TV station—KOB in Albuquerque, New Mexico—was not hooked in with the national networks.

All four television networks carried President Truman's speech from the West Coast and, at the end of September, regular commercial coast-to-coast programming began with a string of star-studded variety hours from Hollywood. Still, the most effective demonstration of the electronic magic of transcontinental sight did not take place until Sunday afternoon, November 18, on the premiere broadcast of CBS's *See It Now* (a television version of Edward R. Murrow's respected *Hear It Now* radio news documentary series). On that first show, Murrow sat before two television monitors in CBS's New York City Studio 41 and asked director Don Hewitt to punch up a live signal from the West Coast on one monitor, while showing a scene from New York City on the other. Instantly, a panorama of the Golden Gate Bridge, Alcatraz, and the San Francisco skyline appeared alongside the view of the Brooklyn Bridge, Manhattan, and New York Bay. For the first time, Americans could see both coasts of their vast continent at once, live and instantaneously. Murrow, a man not easily moved, said he was "very impressed" with this technical miracle, and that he expected a lot from TV.

The biggest change in programming caused by the coast-to-coast link was the immediate availability of Los Angeles as a live origination point. Performers who had moved East to host the top variety shows on NBC and CBS immediately transferred back to the West Coast, where their film and radio careers had long been centered. Television was at last ready for coast-to-coast operation. More big money sponsors began to buy television commercial time because there were, via cable, enough markets capable of receiving the networks' signals to justify the investment. With more people tuning in and more sponsors interested in purchasing spots, the

cost of advertising on a prime time show shot up. On NBC and CBS, the two most successful networks, prime time was soon filled with sponsors and, by the end of 1951, their network TV profits exceeded those of their network radio operations for the first time. Television also registered an overall profit in 1951, with ninety-three of the 108 TV stations on the air finishing in the black.

Yet even amid this expansion there was disappointment. Though DuMont and ABC also saw their network television incomes increase, they were far behind CBS and NBC. The continuing FCC freeze on new stations still kept many cities without television at all, or limited to just a few stations. Pacific residents, who for years had endured the low quality kines of live East Coast fare, found themselves inconvenienced even with the live cable connection. Due to the difference in the time zones, the top live prime time hits began at 5:00 P.M. out West so that the East Coast viewers could see the shows at 8:00 P.M.

The biggest disappointment voiced by many viewers was that, aside from the technical magic of bridging the cross-country chasm, there was very little excitement over the approach of the 1951–52 season. For the first time since the arrival of Milton Berle more than three years before, the networks' fall line-ups consisted primarily of familiar shows returning for another season. Compared to the avalanche of superstar talent that had descended upon TV for the first time during the 1950–51 season, the upcoming season seemed very dull. With most of radio's top talent on television, the period of continuous innovation and expansion appeared to have come to an end.

Television reviewers, bemoaning the absence of any exciting new headliners on the horizon, pointed out that prime time had become too valuable for experimentation, especially at NBC and CBS. The problem was that television had automatically adopted radio's rigid approach to the time period. Programmers assumed that the best way to keep an audience was with the same format, week-in and week-out. With ad slots in the evening sold out, they saw no reason to risk upsetting this rhythm with out-of-the-ordinary fare. As a result, newcomers went through try-outs as second bananas, in fringe hours, and, ironically, on network radio. In these settings, new and different personalities could try to carve out a niche for themselves and spring into prime time as headliners.

In 1951, there were many such stars-to-be still toiling in relative obscurity, waiting for their lucky break. Steve Allen was host of a ninety-minute daytime TV variety talk show on CBS, and also served as one of the network's favorite panel show substitutes.

FALL 1951 SCHEDULE

MONDAY

	7:00	7:30	8:00	8:30	9:00	9:30	10:00	10:30	
ABC	local	Hollywood Screen Test	MR. D.A. AM. MR. MALONE	Life Begins At 80	CURTAIN UP!		Bill Gwinn Show	Stud's Place	ABC
CBS	local	CBS News / Perry Como	Lux Video Theater	Arthur Godfrey's Talents Scouts	I LOVE LUCY	It's News To Me	Studio One		CBS
DUMONT	Captain Video	local	Stage Entrance	Johns Hopkins Science Review	Wrestling From Columbia Park With Dennis James				DUMONT
NBC	Kukla, Fran And Ollie	Roberta Quinlan / Camel News	Paul Winchell And Jerry Mahoney Show	Voice Of Firestone	Lights Out	Robert Montgomery Presents / Somerset Maugham Theater		Who Said That	NBC

TUESDAY

	7:00	7:30	8:00	8:30	9:00	9:30	10:00	10:30	
ABC	local	Beulah	Charlie Wild, Private Detective	HOW DID THEY GET THAT WAY?	Q.E.D.	On Trial	CRUSADE IN THE PACIFIC	CHI. SYMPHONY CHAMBER ORCH.	ABC
CBS	local	CBS News / Stork Club	Frank Sinatra Show		CRIME SYNDICATED	Suspense	Danger	local	CBS
DUMONT	Captain Video	local	What's The Story	KEEP POSTED	COSMOPOLITAN THEATER		Hands Of Destiny	local	DUMONT
NBC	Kukla, Fran And Ollie	Little Show / Camel News	Texaco Star Theater		Fireside Theater	Armstrong Circle Theater	The Original Amateur Hour		NBC

WEDNESDAY

	7:00	7:30	8:00	8:30	9:00	9:30	10:00	10:30	
ABC	local	Chance Of A Lifetime	Paul Dixon Show I		Don McNeill Arthur Murray Party	The Clock	CELANESE THEATER KING'S CROSSROADS		ABC
CBS	local	CBS News / Perry Como	Arthur Godfrey And His Friends		Strike It Rich	The Web	Blue Ribbon Bouts	Sports Spot	CBS
DUMONT	Captain Video	local			GALLERY OF MME. LIU-TSONG	Shadow Of The Cloak	local		DUMONT
NBC	Kukla, Fran And Ollie	Roberta Quinlan / Camel News	KATE SMITH EVENING SHOW		Kraft Television Theater		Break The Bank	Freddy Martin Show	NBC

THURSDAY

	7:00	7:30	8:00	8:30	9:00	9:30	10:00	10:30	
ABC	local	The Lone Ranger	Stop The Music		HERB SHRINER TIME	GRUEN GUILD THEATER	Paul Dixon Show II	At Home Show / Red Grange	ABC
CBS	local	CBS News / Stork Club	Burns And Allen GARRY MOORE	Amos And Andy	Alan Young Show	Big Town	Racket Squad	Crime Photographer	CBS
DUMONT	Captain Video	local	Georgetown University Forum	Broadway To Hollywood Headline Clues	Adventures of Ellery Queen	local	Bigelow Theater	local / FOOTBALL THIS WEEK	DUMONT
NBC	Kukla, Fran And Ollie	Little Show / Camel News	You Bet Your Life	Treasury Men In Action	Ford Festival		Martin Kane, Private Eye	Wayne King Show	NBC

FRIDAY

	7:00	7:30	8:00	8:30	9:00	9:30	10:00	10:30	
ABC	local	Life With Linkletter / Say It With Acting	MARK SABER MYSTERY THEATER	Stu Erwin Show	CRIME WITH FATHER	Tales Of Tomorrow / Versatile Varieties	DELL O'DELL SHOW	INDUSTRIES FOR AMERICA	ABC
CBS	local	CBS News / Perry Como	Mama	Man Against Crime	SCHLITZ PLAYHOUSE OF STARS		Live Like A Millionaire	Hollywood Opening Night	CBS
DUMONT	Captain Video	local	Twenty Questions	You Asked For It	Down You Go	Front Page Detective	Cavalcade Of Stars		DUMONT
NBC	Kukla, Fran And Ollie	Roberta Quinlan / Camel News	Quiz Kids	We, The People	The Big Story	The Aldrich Family	Gillette Cavalcade Of Sports	Great Fights	NBC

SATURDAY

	7:00	7:30	8:00	8:30	9:00	9:30	10:00	10:30	
ABC	The Ruggles	Jerry Colona Show	Paul Whiteman's TV Teen Club		LESSON IN SAFETY	HARNESS RACING			ABC
CBS	Sammy Kaye Show	Beat The Clock	Ken Murray Show		Faye Emerson's Wonderful Town	The Show Goes On	Songs For Sale		CBS
DUMONT	local	THE PET SHOP	local			Wrestling From The Marigold In Chicago With Jack Brickhouse			DUMONT
NBC	ASSEMBLY VI	One Man's Family	All Star Revue		Your Show Of Shows			Your Hit Parade	NBC

SUNDAY

	7:00	7:30	8:00	8:30	9:00	9:30	10:00	10:30	
ABC	Paul Whiteman's Goodyear Revue	BY-LINE	Admission Free		In Our Time	Marshall Plan In Action	BILLY GRAHAM'S HOUR OF DECISION	Youth On The March	ABC
CBS	Gene Autry Show	This Is Show Business @ Jack Benny Program	Toast Of The Town		Fred Waring Show		Celebrity Time	What's My Line	CBS
DUMONT	local			Pentagon-Washington	Rocky King, Inside Detective	The Plainclothesman	They Stand Accused		DUMONT
NBC	SOUND-OFF TIME	YOUNG MR. BOBBIN	Colgate Comedy Hour		Goodyear/Philco Television Playhouse		RED SKELTON SHOW	Leave It To The Girls	NBC

Jack Paar, who had starred in a few unsuccessful comedy series on network radio, was host of the NBC radio quiz, *The $64 Question.* Even in this simple setting, his fiery personality proved unnerving to network executives. When the quiz show's sponsor pulled out and NBC asked all involved to accept a pay cut, Paar promptly walked off the show (a dramatic action that became a Paar trademark). Buff Cobb and her husband, Myron (Mike) Wallace, were brought by CBS from Chicago to New York, where they became hosts of an endless series of afternoon TV chit-chat shows, some of which aired during CBS's brief and unreceivable color run. Merv Griffin was a lead vocalist on *The Freddy Martin Show,* one of the numerous unsuccessful attempts to bring the big band sound to TV. Soon thereafter Griffin had a solo hit record, "I've Got a Lovely Bunch of Coconuts," and he began to appear as a TV guest on his own.

Going into the 1951–52 season, the few new prime time series that evoked any anticipation featured as headliners performers who had served similar warm-up stints in previous late night or afternoon programs. Industry insiders watched to see whether stars such as Kate Smith, Jerry Lester, and Garry Moore would be able to transfer their magic to prime time competition. Yet, what would prove to be the most popular and important new show of the season was barely considered in the preseason projections. Critics did not expect anything more than run-of-the-mill Hollywood TV production from a new filmed series, *I Love Lucy.*

Through the 1940s, Lucille Ball had pursued a career as a Hollywood film star, but never had any big hits. In 1948, she began a more successful venture, playing the part of a scatterbrained suburban housewife on the CBS radio sitcom, *My Favorite Husband.* That series ended in 1951 just as her real favorite husband, Cuban band leader Desi Arnaz, was involved in his own radio show for CBS, *Your Tropical Trip.* Each week, Arnaz mixed his bouncy, infectious Latin "babaloo" rhythms with a hokey giveaway segment—for instance, a contestant who could guess how many bags of coffee Brazil produced the previous year would win a trip to South America. The program was a disaster and vanished in April, 1951, after only a three-month run.

The two were then able to try their hands at a television comedy vehicle and CBS, still eager to develop the TV sitcom form, encouraged them. Lucy and Desi had made several competent guest appearances together on TV variety shows and, with Lucy's radio mentor, Jess Oppenheimer, serving as producer and writer, they developed a domestic sitcom premise and submitted it to the network. Immediately, several points of disagreement arose. CBS wanted to do the show live from New York, like *The George Burns and Gracie Allen Show*. Lucy wanted to do it from Los Angeles, on film, so she could be at home with her husband. CBS also balked at the suggestion that Desi Arnaz play the part of the husband in the series. Network brass doubted that he could carry the acting for the comic role. Though a competent band leader and talented song and dance man, Desi was also a foreigner with a heavy accent. Lucy held firm on both points, which CBS agreed to only after some horse trading. CBS demanded that Lucy and Desi take a pay cut, to help make up for the added expense of film production. The couple went along with the cut, as long as CBS allowed them to retain total production control over the series. After both sides approved the arrangement, Lucy and Desi formed their own TV film production company, Desilu, which would produce the show, and they set about assembling a cast and turning out the first filmed episodes.

At the time, Los Angeles TV films were usually produced by small independent filmmakers because the big studios still refused to become involved with television production. Most of these filmed series adhered to a predictable formula and suffered from inadequate scripts, cheap sets, and weak acting. Though there were a few good Los Angeles productions under way, most were considered inferior to live East Coast shows. In their series, Lucy and

Desi also followed a basic screwball comedy formula, but unlike the others they carefully fashioned it into a delicate balance of exaggerated domestic farce and believable comic characters.

The setup for *I Love Lucy* was an intriguing variation of the "I Me Mine" formula successfully used by Jack Benny and Ozzie and Harriet for years on radio, focusing on both professional and domestic situations. Desi Arnaz played Ricky Ricardo, a Cuban band leader who worked in a Manhattan nightclub, the Tropicana. Lucille Ball played his showbiz-starved wife, Lucy. This combination allowed Arnaz to, in effect, play himself while Ball took off as the comic center for the show, using her talents for slapstick and comic timing that were matched only by Sid Caesar and Jack Benny.

Though the series was filmed in Hollywood, the action was set in New York City, and—in an important break from many previous filmed comedies and radio sitcoms—the two stars were not presented as an already successful suburban couple. Instead, Ricky Ricardo was an up-and-coming, but still struggling, nightclub performer who lived in a middle class Manhattan brownstone within a comfortable but not extravagant family budget. The characters of Lucy and Ricky were especially believable because they resembled the real life Lucy and Desi in a setting that viewers found easy to relate to and accept. The apartment building itself was owned by a down-to-earth middle-aged couple, Fred and Ethel Mertz (William Frawley and Vivian Vance), who were the landlords, upstairs neighbors, and best friends to Lucy and Ricky.

I Love Lucy was set in this essentially real world with three normal characters and one zany but lovable madcap—Lucy. This effectively combined the best of two strains of comedy. From the warm and natural style championed by *The Goldbergs* came a concentration on character interaction. From the Hollywood screwball comedy style exemplified by *Amos and Andy* came absurd coincidences and misunderstandings as the basis for the plots. Ball

Coast-to-coast network television becomes a reality. President Truman addresses the opening session of the Japanese Peace Treaty Conference. *(Reproduced with permission of AT&T Co.)*

played the Lucy character as a sharp but scatterbrained housewife who inevitably misunderstood conversations and events, turning everyday complications into comic disasters. The other three reacted as basically normal people caught up in a screwball situation. Together they formed a strong performing ensemble that could handle practically any comedy situation.

In one of the first episodes of the series, Lucy—engrossed in a lurid murder novel—overheard Ricky talking on the telephone and became convinced that he was trying to kill her. She asked Ethel to help her avoid Ricky's clutches while a confused Ricky turned to Fred for suggestions on what could possibly be wrong with Lucy. Like any misunderstood situation, the mix-up took only a few words of explanation to clear up at the end, but the sharp script and strong performances by each character turned such silly fluff into engaging comedy.

Other stories focused on deliberate schemes by Lucy, especially as she tried to follow Ricky into the glamorous world of show business. Ricky always insisted that Lucy stay home as a loving wife, but she used any outlandish disguise and complicated lie to get on stage or even just meet famous stars and directors. Ethel inevitably acted as Lucy's accomplice, slightly scared of Lucy's schemes but eager underneath to give them a try. Usually, Lucy's hard-fought-for tryouts turned into hilarious failures.

Often, the program avoided show business completely and focused on domestic complications. Sometimes the Ricardos argued with the Mertzes. Other times, the wives and husbands teamed up against each other. In other situations, all four neighbors took on a common problem. Through all the settings, the energy between the Ricardos and the Mertzes served as the driving force behind the show. They faced situations together as believable, humorous

people. Even with Lucy's zany schemes, the farce never completely overshadowed the characters and the characters never got in the way of the humorous situations. As a result, *I Love Lucy* emerged as a perfect combination of sharp comic writing and acting.

The production style used in filming *I Love Lucy* also represented a careful mix of techniques, combining the best traits of both Hollywood films and live TV staging. As in a theatrical film, there was full screen action, effective editing, and well-planned direction. As in live sitcoms, character movement was generally continuous and compact, staying within a few basic sets: the Ricardo apartment, Ricky's nightclub, and one or two special "location" scenes. There was also a studio audience present for the filming, so the comedy was staged for real people responding to the energy of the players.

I Love Lucy premiered on CBS on October 15, 1951, in a choice time slot—Monday night, following the number two rated *Arthur Godfrey's Talent Scouts.* Reviewers marvelled at how well the Ricardos and Mertzes walked the tightrope between character and caricature, and how well producer-writer Jess Oppenheimer had made use of the standard screwball elements. Within four months, *I Love Lucy* deposed Milton Berle's *Texaco Star Theater* as the top-rated show on TV, and *Lucy* stayed on top for the next four years. In the process, the Ricardos became the first TV family to be taken to heart by the entire nation, becoming just as real and alive as the characters of radio's *Amos and Andy* had been to a previous generation.

For CBS, *I Love Lucy* accomplished what the network had hoped television's *Amos and Andy* would do. It proved the strength and acceptability of TV sitcoms, giving the network a strong weapon against NBC's flashy comedy-variety hours. Sitcoms presented viewers with continuing characters, settings, and stories, rather than a mixed bag of skits, and CBS planned to bring others to the schedule as soon as possible.

It quickly became evident that many of the new sitcoms would be quite a letdown from the careful craftsmanship of *I Love Lucy.* Radio's *My Friend Irma* began a live TV version in January, 1952, featuring Marie Wilson as a female even more scatterbrained than Lucy Ricardo. (Irma was once convinced that her cat was a missing friend, reincarnated.) Though adequate, the series had nowhere near the energy of *I Love Lucy. My Little Margie,* the summer replacement for *I Love Lucy,* had terrible scripts and a cast of characters that seemed designed to embody as many offensive Hollywood stereotypes as possible. Produced by the Hal Roach studios, *My Little Margie* featured: Gale Storm in the title role of a bratty, know-it-all young girl; Charles Farrell as her dad, Vernon Albright, an emasculated, mushy widower; Clarence Kolb as George Honeywell, Albright's boss, a stuffed-shirt, blustery capitalist; Gertrude Hoffman as the eighty-three-year-old Mrs. Odettes, who gave senility a bad name; and Willie Best as Charlie, the black elevator operator, who made *Amos and Andy*'s Lightnin' look like a Rhodes scholar. Yet even this series became a big enough summer hit to be picked up as a winter replacement the following season. It was clear that while there might be many successful *I Love Lucy-*inspired sitcoms, few would match the quality of the original.

A summer sitcom that achieved success with a radically different style was *Mr. Peepers,* a lowkey live NBC series produced by Fred Coe. Wally Cox portrayed Robinson J. Peepers, a quiet slow-tempered high school biology teacher in the small Midwestern town of Jefferson City. Unlike the screwball sitcoms, the humor in *Mr. Peepers* developed from just slightly exaggerated situations that the soft spoken Peepers encountered. His friend, Harvey Weskit, a brash history teacher (Tony Randall), and Mrs. Gurney, a befuddled English teacher (Marion Lorne), served as excellent comic

The first TV sitcom superstars: (from *l.*) Lucille Ball, Vivian Vance, Desi Arnaz, William Frawley. *(Photo by Viacom, Hollywood)*

foils to his mild manner, and the stories emerged as whimsical visits with friendly, good-natured people. The show was originally scheduled for just a summer run, but viewer response was so strong that NBC used it early in the 1952–53 season as a replacement series. The program ran until 1955 and, at the end of the second full season, the mild mannered Peepers summoned the courage to ask Nancy Remington (Patricia Benoit), the school nurse, to marry him.

One of NBC's first major experiments in filmed TV series was not a sitcom but a crime show, *Dragnet,* which the network brought in as a winter replacement in early 1952. Under the direction of producer-narrator-star Jack Webb, *Dragnet* had begun in the summer of 1949 on radio, featuring Webb as Sergeant Joe Friday of the Los Angeles police department and Barton Yarborough as his partner, Sergeant Ben Romero. The series broke from radio's romanticized image of crime fighting and emphasized instead the mundane legwork necessary for success by real policemen. Stories were based on "actual cases" from the Los Angeles police department and each week, following the opening theme ("Dum-De-Dum-Dum"), the announcer reminded the audience, "The story you are about to hear is true. Only the names have been changed to protect the innocent." Webb's clipped narration described each case step by step, introducing to the general public the jargon and methodology of police work as well as his own catch phrases such as "Just the facts, ma'am." Listeners, who did not know any more about the cases than Friday and Romero did, followed the painstaking investigations clue by clue and became caught up in the excitement of piecing together the solutions to real life urban crimes. Each show tied everything together at the conclusion with a crisp report on the trial and punishment given to the apprehended criminal. Without resorting to excessive blood and violence, *Dragnet* turned investigative police work into exciting and popular entertainment.

The television version of *Dragnet* continued the methodical style

December 24, 1951
"Amahl and the Night Visitors." (NBC). Gian-Carlo Menotti presents the first written-for-television opera, a gentle Christmas fantasy of a twelve-year-old boy who befriends the three kings searching for Jesus. The opera becomes an annual Yuletime tradition on NBC.

January 6, 1952
Hallmark Hall of Fame. (NBC). Actress Sarah Churchill (daughter of Winston) serves as host of a Sunday afternoon drama anthology. Later, as a series of floating specials, the *Hall of Fame* productions serve as one of television's classiest series.

January 7, 1952
Arthur Godfrey Time. (CBS). A television simulcast of Godfrey's morning radio variety show pushes CBS-TV up to a 10:00 A.M. starting time.

April 26, 1952
Gunsmoke. (CBS Radio). William Conrad plays marshal Matt Dillon in a Western that takes dead aim at adults.

June 19, 1952
I've Got a Secret. (CBS). Garry Moore runs another Mark Goodson-Bill Todman celebrity panel quiz show, emphasizing the sharp banter of its regulars. The format is simple: Each contestant has a secret which the panel attempts to guess.

June 30, 1952
The Guiding Light. (CBS). CBS adds this veteran fifteen-year-old radio soap opera to its afternoon television line-up. By the 1970s, *The Guiding Light* will be the longest running network entertainment show in American broadcasting.

July 7, 1952
The Republican National Convention opens in Chicago. CBS has a new anchor, Walter Cronkite.

of the radio show and its dedicated support for the average cop on the beat. *Dragnet* first appeared at Christmastime in a special "preview" episode featuring Webb, Yarborough, and guest Raymond Burr as a deputy police chief. Yarborough died on December 19, so when the show came to the regular NBC television schedule in January, 1952, Webb tried out a few new assistants, eventually choosing Ben Alexander as his new partner, officer Frank Smith. Like the radio version three years before, TV's *Dragnet* marked a major change from the standard crime shows proliferating on television. In series such as *Martin Kane, Private Eye,* the hero was a loner detective so the police were presented as fumbling fools who would probably trip over a dead body before they realized that a crime had been committed. Series such as *Dick Tracy, Mr. District Attorney,* and *Racket Squad* consisted entirely of character stereotypes. The bad guys wore slouch hats and needed a shave while the smooth know-it-all heroes relied on third-degree grillings and coincidence to break a case. *Dragnet,* on the other hand, pictured police neither as boobs nor glamour boys, but as dedicated human beings who solved crimes by careful deduction, using brains rather than brawn.

Dragnet was a tremendous success and, like *I Love Lucy,* set a program style that would be imitated for years. Both shows also made filmed television series respectable. While most of the programs emanating from Los Angeles were still live, the television networks ceased considering filmed series as simply filler. The major Hollywood studios continued to treat television as a leper, but smaller, independent studios were more than happy to fill the new demand for filmed product.

The *I Love Lucy*-inspired boom in sitcom development served as a direct challenge to NBC's emphasis on comedy-variety giants. Even Milton Berle, the network's biggest star, felt the pressure. Though he began the season by knocking off his first serious Tuesday night competition in years (CBS's *Frank Sinatra Show*), Berle dropped as *I Love Lucy* climbed. After being dethroned by *Lucy,* Berle began changing his program's tone, aiming the show more and more toward the kiddies, adopting a new cognomen, Uncle Miltie. In mid-season, large numbers of adults began to turn from the *Texaco Star Theater* to a new, unexpected source of competition: God. DuMont, which prided itself—out of financial necessity—on producing "sensibly priced" entertainment, threw up against Berle a concept considered too ridiculously simple for the other networks to take seriously: a sermon. For thirty minutes each week on *Life Is Worth Living,* Roman Catholic Bishop Fulton J. Sheen delivered a strong but sensitive religious presentation. He was not plugging a particular doctrine, but rather was discussing everyday problems and the help a faith in God could bring. He even had a sense of humor, often joking about his competition with Berle. One quip had it that both worked for the same boss, Sky Chief.

Even with the challenges to Berle, NBC stuck with its big name variety shows—highlighted by *The Colgate Comedy Hour* and *All Star Revue* (the renamed *Four Star Revue*)—because overall they were still producing top ratings. Throughout the 1950–51 season, *The Colgate Comedy Hour* had regularly defeated its Sunday night competition, Ed Sullivan's *Toast of the Town,* and for the new season NBC came up with another TV winner, Red Skelton.

Red Skelton's television act centered on little hats, big grins, his rubber face, and a ready-made roster of already familiar characters from radio including Clem Kadiddlehopper, Willie Lump-Lump, Bolivar Shagnasty, and the infamous Mean Widdle Kid. Each week, Skelton merely stepped on stage in front of a curtain and performed, vaudeville style. His decade-long success on radio

carried over to television and he shot straight into TV's top ten.

NBC also tried to expand comedy-variety into a new, earlier time period that season, in an attempt to duplicate the early-evening radio success of Jack Benny. For years, Benny had led off CBS's Sunday night radio line-up with his top-rated 7:00–7:30 P.M. program, so NBC slotted *Chesterfield Sound Off Time* for the same period, which was unusually early for TV variety. Once again, there was a rotating format, with Bob Hope, Fred Allen, and Jerry Lester taking turns as the show's host. Hope was just as good as always; Lester, who had quit the late night *Broadway Open House* in May, failed with a mix of bland scripts and racy ad-libbed humor; and Allen was once again saddled with hosting a vaudeville show, a task unsuited to his nature. *Sound Off Time* vanished by Christmas, only to be replaced by another variety show, *Royal Showcase.* This was also unable to snare a large audience, though it did feature Fred Allen's best TV performances ever. Appearing as a guest two times in the spring, Allen at last brought to life the characters of his famed Allen's Alley. If this had been done a year and one-half earlier, Allen might have become the TV star everyone expected him to be, using his familiar stock of characters in much the same way as Red Skelton.

NBC's experiment with early evening variety achieved only occasional success. However, there was a much more serious problem beginning to show in the network's comedy-variety showpieces, *The Colgate Comedy Hour* and *All Star Revue.* Nightclub and film commitments of the original regulars disrupted the smoothly balanced rotating schedule that had been set up for the two shows and, as the major headliners decreased the number of their appearances, NBC was forced to rely increasingly on less popular substitute hosts. These included Donald O'Connor, Martha Raye, Ezio Pinza, Ben Blue, Tony Martin, the Ritz Brothers, Jack Paar, Spike Jones, Abbott and Costello, and Jerry Lester. Colgate was sinking $100,000 per week into its show (which totaled $3 million per year, then the highest budget in television) and desperately wanted only the familiar big names as headliners. But the top stars were getting tired of the routine. They found their backlog of material used up very quickly and were forced to fall back on writers who could turn out only so much greatness on a week-to-week basis. At the end of the season, Danny Thomas quit the grind, exploding:

> TV is for idiots! I don't like it . . . it has lowered the standards of the entertainment industry considerably. You . . . work years building routines, do them once on TV, and they're finished. Next thing you know, you are, too. . . . When and if I ever do my own TV show, I'd like it to be a half-hour on film.

Eventually most of the other major headliners echoed the criticisms of both Danny Thomas and the previously departed Fred Allen. Television comedy-variety used up routines at an incredible rate and performers quickly had to settle for presentations that were just average, frustrating themselves and disappointing viewers. Their shows began to look the same, with the same guests, the same format, and the same material.

As *The Colgate Comedy Hour* turned more frequently to lesser light substitute hosts, Ed Sullivan's show began to nibble away at NBC's hold over the Sunday at 8:00 P.M. slot. After being consistently beaten in the 1950–51 season, Sullivan had decided to give his show a new wrinkle in the hope of drawing even with the celebrity-studded variety hour on NBC. In September, 1951, the budget for *Toast of the Town* was increased and Sullivan began doing elaborate special tribute shows. Throughout the season, entire programs were turned over to salutes to Oscar Hammerstein, Helen Hayes, Bea Lillie, Cole Porter, and Richard Rodgers, with the

The center camera stand at the 1952 Democratic Convention gave home viewers the best seats in the house. *(National Archives)*

featured artist as headliner and well-known friends as the supporting cast. These tribute shows were, in effect, floating specials that aired within the *Toast of the Town* framework. When stars such as Dean Martin and Jerry Lewis were on *The Colgate Comedy Hour,* NBC still came out on top. However, when viewers were faced with headliners such as Spike Jones or Abbott and Costello, Sullivan's specials provided an attractive alternative on CBS.

NBC's programming chief, Pat Weaver, learned a lesson from Ed Sullivan's success against *The Colgate Comedy Hour* and, late in the fall of 1951, he proposed that NBC adopt the idea of regularly scheduled specials as part of its network strategy. Weaver felt such programs—which he dubbed "spectaculars"—could be used to keep NBC's TV schedule vibrant by breaking the weekly routine that too many shows had fallen into. He suggested that a two-hour spectacular could be scheduled to appear about once a month, financed by the regular sponsor of the time slot. Television's big advertisers, as well as NBC itself, were not receptive to this idea. They believed that week-in, week-out regularity in programming was the best way to keep an audience, with Christmas specials such as "Amahl and the Night Visitors" the only exception. Weaver pressed the spectacular idea but was soon "kicked upstairs" to a largely meaningless corporate post before he could develop it fur-

ther. However, another of Weaver's pet projects did get on the air while he was still in charge of programming—*Today,* a two-hour news and information series broadcast in the early morning.

At the start of 1952, daytime TV programming was still exceedingly sparse. A few stations signed on at about 10:00 A.M., but nothing of any importance took place until about 4:00 P.M. One exception was WPTZ in Philadelphia which, each weekday morning from 7:00 A.M. to 9:00 A.M., ran *Three to Get Ready,* a loose show led by former radio disk jockey Ernie Kovacs. The program had begun in late November, 1950, and featured some live music, records, time and weather checks, and great doses of Kovacs's own peculiar television insanity. He read fan letters on the air, performed skits he had written himself, shot off toy guns after puns, picked his teeth, and even held an audition for goats. Oddly enough, *Three to Get Ready* did very well in the local ratings and the success of Kovacs apparently convinced NBC that Weaver's idea for an early morning show might attract network viewers as well.

Chicago's Dave Garroway, who had been without a show for a few months, was chosen as the lowkey host for the new program—originally called *Rise and Shine* but retitled *Today* before its premiere. NBC budgeted the concept at $40,000 per week and took out full page ads in trade magazines declaring the show to be "a revolution in television," and that, via *Today,* "the studio becomes the nerve center of the planet." When the program began in January, 1952, though, such proclamations could only be regarded as promises for the future. Skeptical advertisers withheld support and there was only one sponsor for the premiere.

On the home screens the first *Today* broadcast appeared as an almost meaningless hodge-podge. The cast and crew were squeezed into a tiny street-front New York City studio that had originally been a public display showroom for RCA TV sets, and viewers could see: three teletype machines, weather maps, wirephoto displays, clocks set to the times of various world cities, record players, newspapers, the crowd outside the studio, and, oh yes, the show's regular cast of Dave Garroway, Jim Fleming, and Jack Lescoulie. Throughout the program there were frequent cuts to live reports from the Pentagon, Grand Central Station, and the corner of Michigan Avenue and Randolph Street in Chicago, as well as live phone reports describing the weather in London, England and Frankfurt, Germany. Viewers were bombarded with data and the first reactions to *Today* were confusion and indifference. *Today* did not seem to have any point other than to show off fancy gadgets. Before long, NBC toned down the video tricks and adopted a news, reviews, features, and interviews format more suited to Garroway's relaxed nature. By May, the show was in the black.

Today was so successful that WPTZ, in order to carry it, was forced to shift the Ernie Kovacs *Three to Get Ready* program to noon, a move soon followed by his departure to New York City. There, Kovacs did a few daytime network shows for NBC, but soon found himself on the CBS local New York affiliate doing a morning show against his old nemesis, *Today.* His new show continued the loose off-beat style of *Three to Get Ready,* with such features as Tondelayo, an "invisible" cat that was visible to everybody, and Yoo-Hoo Time. Kovacs noticed that most members of a studio audience began waving as soon as a camera was pointed in their direction, so he generously set aside Yoo-Hoo Time for just such activity. A display card showed the name of a person in the audience who was invited to stand up and wave to his heart's content, egged on by Kovacs. Actor Peter Boyle also made guest appearances, often appearing as either a rotund Irish cop on the beat or a rotund uncle-figure who urged the kiddies to "Eat up like Uncle Pete!" When the makers of Serutan ("Natures spelled backwards") took over five minutes of his morning slot, Kovacs insisted for weeks on referring to himself as Ernie Scavok. Above all, Kovacs constantly ribbed the effusive wall gadgets and world-wide air of the competing *Today* show. He hung up signs on his set with such helpful descriptions as: "London," "Cloudy," "Frown," and "Trenton."

On the other side of the broadcast day, the networks were experimenting with new late night telecasts, but these were far less successful than the early morning *Today.* One of the worst shows was CBS's gauche attempt at sophistication, *The Continental,* which aired Tuesday and Thursday nights, 11:15 P.M. to 11:30 P.M. Renzo Cesana played a TV gigolo who sat in an apartment setting, trying to look like a swank European melange of Charles Boyer and Ezio Pinza. Cesana sipped fancy drinks, puffed expensive cigarettes, sang, and pitched woo to the presumably palpitating housewives at home. The camera was supposed to be their eyes and ears, so Cesana acted as if the viewers were really in the room with him. He handed cigarettes and drinks to the camera, gushing sweet nothings such as "Don't be afraid, darling, you're in a *man*'s apartment!" Trying to tickle romantic fantasies, Cesana went on and on that he loved the marvels of a woman's smile, that he valued

champagne that did not tickle your nose, and that his ladies looked great in Cameo stockings. Inevitably this led to a plug for women's stockings, revealing the great lover as a pitchman in a rented tuxedo. One critic labeled this extended commercial "the most needless program on television."

The expansion by the television networks into the fringe operating hours reflected the increasing growth in the country's economy, despite the fighting in Korea. The war had settled into a peculiar state in July, 1951, as cease-fire and armistice talks began. Though these dragged on for two more years while thousands of American soldiers remained in Korea, the level of fighting toned down sufficiently for domestic production facilities to be returned to civilian use. Manufacturing and consumer buying picked up and it was against this background that television programming and sponsor support took off with the coast-to-coast cable connection and the success of shows such as *I Love Lucy.* Though the FCC freeze still prevented television from touching many areas, viewer interest in television cities was greater than ever. Competing magazines listing the week's TV fare hit the stands, giving the home viewer a choice of *TV Preview, TV Review, TV News, TV Views, TV Forecast, TV Digest, TV Today,* and an early version of *TV Guide.* Besides the program listings, these magazines usually featured short puff piece articles on individual shows, star biographies, and ads. The program listings sometimes served as plugs themselves with the sponsor's name as part of the title in such shows as *Texaco Star Theater, Pabst Blue Ribbon Bouts,* and *Chesterfield Sound Off Time.* Most TV magazines and newspapers drew the line, though, at an ABC Sunday night adventure show whose official title was *Your Kaiser-Frazer Dealer Presents "Kaiser-Frazer Adventures in Mystery" Starring Betty Furness in "By-Line."* Despite the sponsor's determined effort to squeeze in an extra plug while taking as much column space as possible, the title in print was inevitably shortened to *By-Line.*

As television became more and more popular, those concerned about the medium's persuasive effects on others became increasingly vocal. Aspiring politicians discovered that they could catapult themselves into the headlines by claiming that sex and violence on television was corrupting the nation and that such programming should be halted by federal fiat. Those who wanted to clamp down on television pointed to seemingly ominous incidents such as one that took place in Detroit. There, John R. Sikron, a forty-six-year-old deputy sheriff in Macomb County, had been arguing with his wife over whether the family should watch CBS's thriller series, *Suspense,* claiming that the show was too violent for her and their six children to see. During the argument, Sikron's fifteen-year-old son, Jerry—who later explained that he could not stand to see his father push his mother around—picked up his father's shotgun and shot his dad through the back, killing him.

In the early days of motion pictures, there had been similar charges that violence on the silver screen translated into violence in real life. When governmental intervention appeared imminent in the 1920s, the major studios called in a respected former postmaster general, Will Hays, to help draw up a morality code which would govern the content of all Hollywood films. With a self-regulating code in effect, the demand for federal censorship abated. In 1951, the self-appointed guardians of the public morality began looking askance at examples of television sex and violence, such as Dagmar's cleavage and Dick Tracy's mayhem, and TV moguls decided to adopt a Hollywood-style code of ethics. The networks hoped that their declaration of support for such industry self-regulation would assuage the vocal critics, prevent federal intervention, and prove that television was doing its part to keep Americans square with God. There were four basic rules laid down to guide all producers of television programs:

1. Shows will not sympathize with evil.
2. Shows will not degrade honesty, goodness, and innocence.
3. Figures exercising lawful authority should not be ridiculed.
4. Law breakers must not go unpunished.

In October, the proposed television code was adopted by the National Association of Broadcasters (NAB), which asked its members to voluntarily agree to abide by it. On the day the code went into effect, March 1, 1952, television industry publications proudly proclaimed that seventy-seven of the 108 American television stations had taken the pledge. The airwaves had been cleansed and the nation could sleep in peace.

That may have been enough for the television industry, but it was not enough for U.S. Representative Ezekiel C. Gothings, a Democrat from Arkansas. He induced the House Interstate Commerce Committee to hold public hearings on the morality of TV programs. One witness, conservative radio commentator Paul Harvey, complained that television had become an outlet for comics schooled in the "bawdy night life" of New York City, who were disseminating their "purple" jokes to the nation, thereby imposing "their distorted views on the rest of the forty-seven states." Representative Gothings himself presented the committee with a more specific bill of particulars. One night, he announced, he had viewed a network variety show in which ". . . a grass-skirted young lady and a thinly-clad young gentleman were dancing the hoochie-koochie to a lively tune and shaking the shimmy!"

In spite of such shocking observations, the committee at large accepted the explanations and assurances of the network presidents who testified at the hearings. The TV executives admitted that much of what was on television was bad, but quickly pointed out that many books and many plays were also bad. Television was just another mass medium which was trying to appeal to a mass audience. Some banality had to be expected with so many hours to fill. Besides, they concluded, the public was not forced to watch everything on television and, in fact, if a viewer chose carefully, there were many good shows throughout the schedule. In its final report, the committee stated that there was too much crime and suggestiveness on television, but government control would be worse than the moments of poor taste. The committee also commended intra-industry self-regulatory measures, such as the NAB code, which, it pointed out, was already having a beneficial effect— Dagmar's neckline had gone up.

Interest in the effects of television on the public became more intense during 1952 because, in April, the FCC at last ended its freeze on processing station applications and cleared the way for television to eventually reach nearly every home in America. The commission had first ordered the freeze in 1948 to study and revise frequency allocations in order to solve problems of cross-station interference. After three and one-half years of deliberation, the FCC announced a comprehensive new set of rules. First, the commission squeezed 220 additional stations into the VHF band, raising that system from its previous maximum of 400 to a new level of 620. It also opened seventy channels (14 to 83) on the UHF spectrum for television broadcasting, making 1,400 new UHF stations available nationwide. Both systems combined permitted more than 2,000 TV stations in 1,291 cities. This meant that, theoretically, television at last had enough channels to allow operations by four (or more) national TV networks. In a bold step, the FCC also reserved 242 channels (mostly in the UHF spectrum) for independent noncommercial educational stations. By July, less than three months after "the thaw" took place, almost 600 station applications had been received by the FCC, many for the new UHF band.

The chief flaws in the new television status quo were in the setups for both the UHF system and the noncommercial stations. None of the eighteen million TV sets in use in 1952 were able to receive the UHF frequencies, and set manufacturers saw no reason to spend extra money to include the feature unless their customers demanded it. With plenty of entertainment available on VHF, the public ignored the new system. Few people purchased UHF converters for existing sets or asked for UHF capabilities on new sets. Almost immediately, fierce battles began over the more accessible VHF frequencies as applicants realized their competitive value. In launching the new system, the FCC might have unofficially declared certain cities as all-UHF, giving manufacturers a captive audience for UHF sets, but this did not occur. Instead, the commission decided to let the subtle pressures of supply and demand solve the UHF problem.

Most of the newly created noncommercial channels were on the UHF band, so their future hinged on the success of the new system. Yet, they also faced an additional, fundamental problem of their own: funding. The FCC had left this important aspect of noncommercial television unsettled—it was not clear where the money was to come from if the stations were to be both noncommercial and independent of the government. San Francisco's KQED (one of the few educational stations on the VHF band) soon hit upon the concept of a yearly on-air auction to raise operating funds, but the UHF stations, with far fewer potential viewers, could not do even that. The only major source of revenue for noncommercial TV came from the Ford Foundation, which donated $1½ million to establish the Educational Television and Radio Center (forerunner of the National Educational Television Network) to produce and distribute educational programs. However, through poor organization and faulty funding, both of the major TV cities, New York and Los Angeles, did not have an educational station at all. Without them, noncommercial television remained, for all practical purposes, a very expensive television laboratory.

The failure of UHF and the lack of major market outlets for educational TV prevented the noncommercial system from having any influence on American TV programming for more than a decade. Commercial television experienced no such delay. At the time of the thaw, there were only 108 stations (all VHF) on the air in sixty-three cities, and thirty-seven of those cities—places such as St. Louis, Pittsburgh, Buffalo, New Orleans, Houston, and Indianapolis—still had only one TV station each. Within a year, the number of TV stations on the air increased from 108 to 200, and another 200 were in the process of construction.

The birth of live coast-to-coast television and the surge in TV station growth assured by the thaw made television a much more important factor in the 1952 presidential campaign. The politicians remembered the amazing effects of television during the 1951 Kefauver hearings and prepared to exploit it. At the same time, CBS and NBC decided to build some much-needed television news respectability with early and extensive coverage of the 1952 electoral process.

In March, for the first time, CBS and NBC film crews descended upon New Hampshire, forever turning the state's previously unimportant presidential primary into a vital national bellwether. Among the Republicans, General Dwight Eisenhower scored a surprise write-in victory and the wide play this received on TV made "Ike" a credible candidate. The quality and depth of the two networks' coverage of New Hampshire showed that television could cover news on its own, independent of radio and newsreels. Candidates soon discovered that they had to augment their speech-writing staffs to have new catchy phrases ready for the ever-present TV cameras. As with the comedy-variety shows, television used up political speech material very quickly. Without new lines, candidates ran the risk of turning off the public with "the same old stuff."

The most important breakthrough in television's news stature came in June when Eisenhower held his first big campaign press conference. Though the event marked the beginning of his active run for the Republican nomination (after leaving the Army), Eisenhower's press aides—in collusion with the newspaper and newsreel reporters—announced that television crews would be barred from covering the press conference. This practice was not at all unusual in those days, but CBS's William Paley decided to take a stand. He boldly announced that CBS was sending a camera crew anyway and Eisenhower would have to throw it out. Fearing bad publicity, Eisenhower's people let CBS (and the late-coming NBC) into the conference, and a milestone in TV journalism had been reached. For the first time, TV news had stood up for itself, and won.

At the Republican National Convention in July, the Eisenhower aides showed that they had learned their lessons well. When the forces of Eisenhower's chief rival, Robert Taft (who controlled the convention machinery), tried to sneak through an important delegation challenge out of sight of the cameras, Eisenhower's people suddenly appeared all over television talking about "convention rigging," "the big steal," "smoke-filled rooms," and "steam-rollered conventions." Incensed viewers sent telegrams to the convention and the public outcry that resulted from the charges on television swayed enough delegates to put Eisenhower over the top. Television news coverage had been proved even more powerful than many people had imagined. TV had not only come of age, it was also affecting who was chosen to lead the country.

12. Grade-B TV

IN SPITE of the great strides made in television coverage of politics in the spring and summer of 1952, the real beginning of political television took place at 9:30 P.M., September 23, 1952, when, live from NBC's El Capitan studio, Senator Richard M. Nixon faced the nation, and won. Nixon had made a name for himself as a congressman a few years before by "getting" Alger Hiss, an accused Soviet spy in the State Department, and, in 1952, Republican presidential nominee Dwight Eisenhower chose Nixon as his running mate. Soon thereafter, stories began circulating that a group of California businessmen were supplying Nixon with a secret slush fund. Republican leaders, primarily concerned with ensuring Eisenhower's election, urged him to drop the young senator from the ticket, but Eisenhower gave Nixon a few days to clear himself. Nixon talked the Republican National Committee into buying a half-hour of radio and television time so that he could explain his side of the story. With pressure mounting for Nixon's ouster, tension on the day of the broadcast was quite high, because nobody knew what Nixon was going to say.

Nixon's presentation that night demonstrated that he was one of the first major politicians to grasp fully the impact and nature of television as a political tool. His performance was a playwright's dream. The young star (with his devoted wife Pat at his side) faced the allegations on his own, trying to save his honor in a world turned cruel and hard. The charges concerning the $18,235 in a supplementary expenditures fund were quickly dismissed. Yes, Nixon admitted, he received the money, but he denied any sinister or illegal motives. It was not an under-the-table gift, Nixon said, but merely a fund to help him better serve his constituents. Then almost immediately, Nixon left the original topic behind and launched into a brilliant "Just Plain Bill" portrait of himself as simple, downhome folk. He told a tear-jerker story of his impoverished background and minimal current financial holdings. He described his war record, the two-year-old car he drove, the mortgage on his home, and his repayments of loans, with interest, to his parents.

The Horatio Nixon story culminated in the ultimate heart-tug, a little dog. He had used such sure-fire gambits as mom, the family hearth, the poor-boy-makes-good, and the story of a struggling young couple, so all that remained were cute little puppies and young children. Near the end of the speech, Nixon disclosed that, yes, he had received a gift from a supporter after all:

One other thing I probably should tell you, because if I don't, they'll probably be saying this about me too. We did

get something—a gift. . . . A man down in Texas heard Pat on the radio mention the fact that our two youngsters would like to have a dog and, believe it or not, the day before we left on this campaign trip, we got a message from Union Station, saying they had a package for us. We went down to get it, and you know what it was? It was a little cocker spaniel dog in a crate that he sent all the way from Texas. [It was] black and white and spotted, and our little girl—Trisha, the six-year-old—named it Checkers, and you know, the kids love the dog, and I just want to say this right now, that regardless of what they say about it, we're gonna keep it.

What a scenario! All it needed was some organ music underneath and the nation would have been awash in bathos. Who could resist such a presentation? Nixon correctly assumed that television (which everyone had said was an intimate medium) was the perfect way to get to people's hearts for an emotional response. The "little people" came to Nixon's defense and flooded the Eisenhower campaign headquarters with telegrams urging the retention of Nixon. Television industry people, while admiring the showmanship in Nixon's presentation, were vaguely disturbed by its implications. It was an implied declaration that a clever politician could, via television's immediacy, reduce politics to personalities, issues to emotions, and complexities to simplifications. Certainly this was not a new trend in politics—Franklin Roosevelt's references to "my little dog Fala" on radio was close to Checkers in such intent— but TV had elevated it to a much higher level of effectiveness.

The rest of the campaign was dull by comparison. Eisenhower, always uncomfortable in front of television cameras, relied chiefly on ad agency-produced short spots, many of which featured cartoon marching bands endlessly repeating "I Like Ike! You Like Ike! Everybody Likes Ike!" Adlai Stevenson, the Democratic nominee, stuck to the more traditional half-hour speech format.

Election night itself was not all that dramatic, either. It was evident early on that Eisenhower and Nixon would win, and NBC and CBS's much-touted Univac computers made little difference in the speed of calling the races. The only news about the news coverage was the surge in popularity of CBS, which decided to stick with its successful new convention anchor man, Walter Cronkite. The CBS sponsor, Westinghouse, also stuck with its anchor, commercial spokeswoman Betty Furness.

In December, fulfilling a campaign promise, Eisenhower flew to Korea. TV news, still flexing its muscles, was able to force

MONDAY

	7:00	7:30	8:00	8:30	9:00	9:30	10:00	10:30	
	local	Hollywood Screen Test	Mark Saber – Homicide Squad	United – Or Not	ABC ALL STAR NEWS		local		ABC
	CBS News	Perry Como	Lux Video Theater	Arthur Godfrey's Talent Scouts	I Love Lucy	LIFE WITH LUIGI	Studio One		CBS
	Captain Video	local	Pentagon-Washington	Johns Hopkins Science Review	Guide Right	FOOTBALL FAMOUS SIDELINES FIGHTS	Boxing From Eastern Parkway With Ted Husing	Ringside Interview	DUMONT
	local	Those Two	Camel News	Paul Winchell – Jerry Mahoney Show	Voice Of Firestone	Hollywood Opening Night	Robert Montgomery Presents	Who Said That?	NBC

TUESDAY

	7:00	7:30	8:00	8:30	9:00	9:30	10:00	10:30	
	local	Beulah		local					ABC
	local	CBS News	HEAVEN FOR BETSY	LEAVE IT TO LARRY	RED BUTTONS SHOW	Crime Syndicated City Hospital	Suspense	Danger	local	CBS
	Captain Video	local	Life Is Worth Living	Keep Posted	WHERE WAS I?	Quick On The Draw	Meet The Boss	local	DUMONT
	local	SHORT ST. DRAMA	Dinah Shore	Camel News	Texaco Star Theater @BUICK CIRCUS HOUR	Fireside Theater	Armstrong Circle Theater	TWO FOR THE MONEY	CLUB TIME	Bob Considine	NBC

WEDNESDAY

	7:00	7:30	8:00	8:30	9:00	9:30	10:00	10:30	
	local	The Name's The Same	ABC ALL STAR NEWS		Adventures Of Ellery Queen	Wrestling From The Rainbo In Chicago [to 12 Midnite]			ABC
	local	CBS News	Perry Como	Arthur Godfrey And His Friends	Strike It Rich	Man Against Crime	Blue Ribbon Bouts	Sports Spot	CBS
	Captain Video	N.Y. Giants Quarterback Huddle	local		STAGE A NUMBER		local		DUMONT
	local	Those Two	Camel News	I MARRIED JOAN	Scott Music Hall CAVAL. OF AMER.	Kraft Television Theater	THIS IS YOUR LIFE	local	NBC

THURSDAY

	7:00	7:30	8:00	8:30	9:00	9:30	10:00	10:30	
	local	The Lone Ranger	ABC ALL STAR NEWS	Chance Of A Lifetime	PERSPECTIVE	POLITICS ON TRIAL	NFL FOOTBALL HIGHLIGHTS	local	ABC
	local	CBS News	HEAVEN FOR BETSY	Burns And Allen Show	Amos And Andy 4 STAR PLAYHOUSE	BIFF BAKER, U.S.A.	Big Town	Racket Squad	I've Got A Secret	CBS
	Captain Video	local		Broadway To Hollywood Headline Clues	TRASH OR TREASURE	What's The Story	Author Meets The Critics	local	DUMONT
	local	SHORT ST. DRAMA	Dinah Shore	Camel News	You Bet Your Life	Treasury Men In Action	Dragnet Gangbusters	FORD THEATER	Martin Kane, Private Eye	Ask Me Another	NBC

FRIDAY

	7:00	7:30	8:00	8:30	9:00	9:30	10:00	10:30	
	local	Stu Erwin Show	OZZIE AND HARRIET	ABC ALL STAR NEWS		Tales Of Tomorrow	local		ABC
	local	CBS News	Perry Como	Mama	My Friend Irma	Schlitz Playhouse Of Stars	OUR MISS BROOKS	MR. AND MRS. NORTH	local	CBS
	Captain Video	local	HOLLYWOOD OFF-BEAT	Rebound DARK OF NIGHT	Life Begins At 80	local	Twenty Questions	Down You Go	DUMONT
	HERMAN HICKMAN	local	Those Two	Camel News	RCA Victor Show	GULF PLAYHOUSE	The Big Story	The Aldrich Family	Gillette Cavalcade Of Sports	Great Fights	NBC

SATURDAY

	7:00	7:30	8:00	8:30	9:00	9:30	10:00	10:30	
	Paul Whiteman's TV Teen Club	Live Like A Millionaire	Feature Playhouse					local	ABC
	Stork Club	Beat The Clock	JACKIE GLEASON SHOW	U.S.A. CANTEEN	MEET MILLIE	BALANCE YOUR BUDGET	Battle Of The Ages		CBS
	local	The Pet Shop	local		Wrestling From The Marigold In Chicago With Jack Brickhouse				DUMONT
	Mr. Wizard	MY HERO	All Star Revue		Your Show Of Shows			Your Hit Parade	NBC

SUNDAY

	7:00	7:30	8:00	8:30	9:00	9:30	10:00	10:30	
	You Asked For It	The Hot Seat	ABC ALL STAR NEWS		PLAYHOUSE ONE	THIS IS THE LIFE	Billy Graham's Hour Of Decision	ANYWHERE U.S.A.	ABC
	Gene Autry Show	This Is Show Business @Jack Benny Program	Toast Of The Town		Fred Waring Show	Break The Bank	The Web	What's My Line	CBS
	Georgetown University Forum	local		Rocky King, Inside Detective	The Plainclothesman	Arthur Murray Party	Youth On The March	DUMONT
	Red Skelton Show	DOC CORKLE	Colgate Comedy Hour		Goodyear/Philco Television Playhouse		THE DOCTOR	local	NBC

the Eisenhower staff into allowing a TV camera crew to join the print, radio, and newsreel members of the press pool. The heavily advertised Korean trip turned out to be something of a "news snooze." Even as President-elect, Eisenhower was unable to produce any significant progress in the stalled peace talks, and there was little exciting footage relayed to the folks back home. It remained for CBS and Ed Murrow, just a few days after Eisenhower's return, to bring the Korean war into the living room.

For two and one-half years, most of the day-to-day television coverage of the Korean war had consisted of Washington-based battle reports, or mild combat footage, often supplied by the government itself. Just before Christmas, Murrow's *See It Now* crew filmed soldiers at the front. The film was hastily returned to New York where it was quickly edited for presentation on December 28, an amazing turnaround time for a one-hour documentary. The program ignored the usual topics of why the war was being fought, how the fighting was going, and what political games of one-upmanship were transpiring at the truce talks. Murrow focused instead on average people and how they reacted under the intense pressure of a stalemated war. One reviewer called the program "a visual poem" because some of the show's best moments contained very little dialogue. These included a native girl in a South Korean military uniform singing "Silent Night" in a plane flying over enemy territory, a French officer who kept shrugging his shoulders as he noted that nobody really knew how to end the war, and a weary patrol being given its orders and then trudging off to face the enemy. Such scenes gave the show a feel for detail unrivaled at the time. Seeing the war portrayed in such human terms came as almost a shock to viewers at home, and they were deeply moved by the show. Seven months later, an armistice was signed, officially ending the three years of fighting in Korea. For many, Ed Murrow's Christmas documentary served as their only real glimpse of the confusion, frustration, and personal dedication of the forces stationed halfway around the world.

Television news was becoming increasingly important to American life. Network coverage of the 1952 presidential campaign, as well as the use of television by the Eisenhower-Nixon ticket, had proved to be decisive factors in the outcome of the race. Prominent newsmakers were beginning to treat television with more respect. Yet television remained, above all, a popular entertainment medium. Though millions saw the broadcast of Eisenhower's presidential inauguration—the first to be shown live, coast-to-coast—far more watched *I Love Lucy* as a matter of course every week. In fact, on January 19, 1953, the night before the inauguration, a record number of viewers tuned in the program to see a special event: the birth of Lucy and Ricky Ricardo's first child.

At the time, pregnancy was considered a fairly taboo topic for broadcast, especially in a comedy format. Desi Arnaz and Lucille Ball were sticking their necks out a bit by devoting so much attention in that season's episodes to Lucy's pregnancy, but because Lucy was pregnant in real life, it would have been harder to avoid it. Production of the 1952–53 *I Love Lucy* episodes began a few months earlier than usual. In June, 1952, five post-birth shows were filmed while Lucy showed no growth. In August, as she grew larger, the pre-baby shows were filmed. To ensure the acceptability of the treatment of so delicate a subject, a priest, a rabbi, and a minister were present at these filmings to lend divine approval. The nation, which had already come to accept the Ricardos as real, became caught up in this latest development. What could make more sense in this natural show than for the couple to have a baby, certainly a common enough occurrence. As the new year approached, the big event drew closer. Lucy began having cravings for papaya milk shakes, and Ricky experienced sympathetic morning sickness. In an event that was a press agent's utopia, the real baby and the celluloid baby arrived within hours of each other, almost overshadowing the Eisenhower inauguration the next day.

More than 70% of America's TV sets were tuned to *I Love Lucy* that night, and this tremendous ratings performance boosted CBS past NBC in that week's Nielsen ratings. Occasionally, CBS had topped NBC before, but this was the first of a string of weekly CBS victories that, by spring, put the network ahead of NBC in the season's average. For more than a year after that, NBC insisted—through some fancy juggling of figures—that it was still number one, but by 1954 CBS's lead had widened and NBC had to concede that it had become number two. CBS's sitcom strategy had paid off. After twenty-five years, CBS had displaced NBC as America's number one network.

Besides boosting CBS to the top, *I Love Lucy* also touched off a stampede toward West Coast films, the first wave of which arrived for the 1952–53 season. Between 1951 and 1952, the number of filmed TV series almost doubled, going from twenty-five to forty-six. There were new crime, adventure, and drama anthology series, though sitcoms were regarded as the most important ventures as everyone hoped to duplicate the instant success of *I Love Lucy*. A large number of new shows began on film while some series that had been previously done live such as *The George Burns and Gracie Allen Show* transferred to celluloid.

One of the important advantages of a filmed series was that it could be rerun. This lowered the overall cost for the season by allowing a thirteen-week summer rerun cycle consisting of selected episodes from the previous thirty-nine weeks. Reruns also helped the networks to fill the summer programming gaps that opened when many top stars were on vacation. The rerun value of filmed series, however, went beyond summer filler and opened a whole new market not possible with live network shows. Once a popular network filmed series completed its prime time network run, the films could be sold to individual stations for local broadcast and, conceivably, even to other countries.

Interest in film, and its rerun value, was inevitable as television continued to grow. The need to fill so many hours of broadcasting each day put both the networks and local programmers into the same position that Hollywood had been in years before with its theatrical features. In order to keep the public occupied in between big name features and large budget spectaculars, the studios regularly churned out screwball comedies, soap opera-ish romances ("women's films"), kiddie Westerns, and pulp adventure sagas—all labeled "grade-B" movies. As television expanded, the appearance of TV equivalents to grade-B films was almost unavoidable.

Through the late 1940s, West Coast filmmakers such as Jerry Fairbanks worked to develop such filmed television series, but most of these vanguard efforts were terrible. They were also not considered very important to the networks' schedules, which were oriented toward live productions from New York, especially variety and drama vehicles. However, local stations desperately needed material to use when there was no network program, especially before completion of the coast-to-coast coaxial cable. In 1948, Frederick Ziv, radio's top program syndicator, set up a television branch to produce and distribute TV films to local stations. By the 1950s, Ziv was the most important independent syndicator in television, with material aimed chiefly at the 7:00 P.M. and 10:30 P.M. periods, when the networks often did not offer any shows to their affiliates. Besides Ziv, the Hal Roach studios, Screen Gems, and Revue also produced such TV films. In aiming programs at the syndication market, the Hollywood-based producers devised virtual carbon copies of Hollywood's grade-B theatrical films because their interchangeable plots and characters made them practically timeless.

The success of *I Love Lucy* prompted NBC to try some filmed sitcoms in the fall of 1952. This strategy got off to a disastrous start, though, with what was generally regarded as the worst new sitcom of the new season, *Doc Corkle,* a highly-touted series starring Eddie Mayehoff as a screwball neighborhood dentist. The show was panned by critics, shunned by viewers, and abandoned by its sponsor. After three weeks, NBC replaced the program with its surprise success of the previous summer, *Mr. Peepers.* NBC's other new filmed sitcom entries for the fall were *I Married Joan* and *My Hero. I Married Joan,* starring Joan Davis and Jim Backus, was a competent copy of *I Love Lucy.* Backus played a believable judge who handled other people's domestic problems in court while facing complications at home from his own scatterbrained wife, Joan. *My Hero,* on the other hand, was a weak slapstick vehicle for Bob Cummings, who not only starred in the show but was its co-writer, co-executive producer, and part owner. He played a dopey California real estate salesman and, said one critic, brought a "magnificent terribleness" to his role.

Another unsuccessful NBC filmed comedy was the previously live *Red Skelton Show.* For the fall of 1952, Skelton changed to film production while NBC moved him to the Sunday at 7:00 P.M. period, hoping that his established success could turn the early evening slot into a strong lead-in for the entire evening. Instead, the filmed series fell badly in the ratings. Skelton continued to rely almost entirely on the bare-bones vaudeville setting of acts performing on a simple stage, and these appeared stale and cheap compared to even simple filmed sitcom stories. In March, when Skelton was ill, it was decided to take advantage of having the shows on film, and instead of using a substitute host, reruns of very recent shows were inserted to fill the time. This strategy backfired and Skelton's ratings fell further. At this point, NBC let Skelton escape to CBS, where he returned, live, in the fall of 1953

The inauguration of Dwight Eisenhower was covered live on all networks. (National Archives)

with a much more rounded variety format (and a larger budget) that lasted seventeen years.

Even with the failure of Red Skelton on film and the proliferation of weak sitcoms, the continued high quality and success of *I Love Lucy* and the transplanted *Burns and Allen Show* demonstrated that filmed comedy series could be both well done and popular. While rejecting terrible shows such as *Doc Corkle,* viewers continued to show their willingness to accept and support the TV film format, and both CBS and ABC came up with a successful new filmed sticom each for the fall, *Our Miss Brooks* and *The Adventures of Ozzie and Harriet.*

Our Miss Brooks, on CBS, was a Desilu production that featured Eve Arden as Connie Brooks, an English teacher at Madison High School. The show had begun on CBS radio in July, 1948—just two weeks after Lucille Ball's *My Favorite Husband* premiered— and was still a hit when the TV filmed version began. Arden played Brooks as a wise-cracking tough gal with a heart of gold who was both human and humorous in facing the daily grind of a high school teacher. She was constantly at odds with the school's blustery, authoritarian principal, Osgood Conklin (Gale Gordon), while trying to control her pupils, especially her main classroom problem, the squeaky-voiced Walter Denton (Richard Crenna). Perhaps her biggest problem was Philip Boynton (Robert Rockwell), a handsome biology teacher, who was too shy to respond to her advances and suggestions of marriage. At home, her elderly landlady, Mrs. Davis (Jane Morgan), constantly offered words of advice on every situation: how to handle the principal, how to control the students, and how to snare Philip Boynton.

Our Miss Brooks reflected the same care and craftsmanship that went into *I Love Lucy,* with an effective reversal of the setup in that show: Connie Brooks was presented as a level-headed person surrounded by exaggerated but generally realistic characters. The cast was especially effective together (Gordon, Crenna, and Morgan

all came over with Arden from the radio version) and the stories evolved from their comic misunderstandings and interaction.

The strong, independent personality of Connie Brooks set her apart from other female sitcom characters in the 1950s. Yet, in keeping with the prevailing social philosophy of the era, she was also presented as just waiting for her wedding day so she could retire from teaching and become a good wife. Until that day, Miss Brooks led a Victorian social life—never going beyond a discussion of the reproduction of horned toads with Mr. Boynton. There was, however, a happy ending. Though shyly avoiding romance with Miss Brooks for eight years on radio and television, in a movie adaptation of the series, Mr. Boynton finally popped the question.

ABC's *Adventures of Ozzie and Harriet,* like *Our Miss Brooks,* had begun on radio in the 1940s. There, Ozzie and Harriet Nelson had pioneered the "I Me Mine" style of domestic comedy in which they essentially played themselves: a happily married showbiz couple with two sons, David and Ricky. The only change made for television was that Ozzie and Harriet dropped all references to their show business careers and instead played solid middle-aged parents raising their family full time in a classy Los Angeles suburb. When the program came to television, David was fifteen and Ricky was twelve, and, over the next fourteen years, the main focus of the series was on their lives, from the teen years to young adulthood.

The Adventures of Ozzie and Harriet was not a screwball sitcom, but rather a continuing story about growing up in suburban America. The Nelsons were relaxed and natural people and the humor on the show developed from everyday problems and simple misunderstandings that the family and their friends and neighbors faced. Though the setting was an idealized household and the complications were as simple and noncontroversial as needing money for a date, the program was very much in the spirit of radio's epic family series, *One Man's Family,* and was very effective in presenting the growing pains and daily lives of a very likable TV family.

Even Ricky's moment as a heart-throb rock'n'roller was incorporated. As Ozzie and Harriet proudly looked on, Ricky played his songs to screaming teenage fans on the show—and then he did the same in real-life concerts. From 1957 to 1964, he had more than a dozen top ten hits, including "Teenager's Romance," "Travelin' Man," "Poor Little Fool," and "Hello Mary Lou." In time, first David, then Ricky, got married. Even then, they never lost touch with the folks back home and, by the early Sixties, all three couples—Ozzie and Harriet, David and June, Rick and Kris—were introduced at the beginning of each episode as part of "America's favorite family."

On radio, the Nelsons had been one of many families that listeners followed with affection and interest, including the strong ethnic characters on programs such as *Life with Luigi* (Italians in Chicago) and *The Goldbergs* (Jews in New York). While Ozzie and Harriet thrived on television, however, the ethnic TV shows were in retreat. During the 1952–53 season a television version of *Life with Luigi* ran only three months, NBC's revival of *The Goldbergs* flopped, and CBS canceled *Amos and Andy*. Unlike their radio counterparts, ethnic TV shows touched off embarrassing criticism and controversy for the networks. Even though *Life with Luigi* came to television virtually unchanged from radio—including many performers from the radio cast—it was criticized for ethnic stereotyping. Despite the all-black cast for TV's *Amos and Andy,* black groups such as the NAACP urged a boycott of the program's sponsor. At the same time, the ethnic shows were not runaway big hits in the TV ratings. The networks decided that they were just not worth the trouble. As a result, programmers turned increasingly to comedies that avoided obvious ethnic slants while focusing on nondescript white middle class life, usually in safe, homogeneous suburbs. This dovetailed perfectly with the settings of many Los Angeles filmed sitcoms which were generally set in faceless California suburbs. *The Goldbergs* even tried to adapt to this new style in its final revival attempt in 1955. After twenty-six years of city living, the family moved to the suburbs, but this approach was an even worse failure. Not only were the Goldbergs visibly ethnic, they were *right next door!*

The increasing interest in noncontroversial settings and characters removed an important edge from the television sitcom form. Through the remainder of the decade, only a handful of new shows would have the touch of reality found in *I Love Lucy* or the expressive ethnic characters found in *Amos and Andy*. Even with well written, funny scripts, most of the new series would be trapped in a bland never-neverland beneath the ever-present California sun. A perfect example of this approach was NBC's revival of *The Life of Riley,* a winter replacement series that began in January, 1953.

Chester A. Riley (William Bendix) was a lovable bumbler who lived in a quiet nondescript Los Angeles suburb that was never disturbed by anything more than a harmless misunderstanding—it never even got cold there. His wife, Peg (Marjorie Reynolds), faithfully stood by him in any situation and was interested only in housework and raising the children. Their children, Babs (Lugene Sanders) and "Junior" (Wesley Morgan), were perfect kids—always in some lovable mixup but at heart never selfish or malicious. Occasionally, the Rileys had friendly spats with their next-door neighbors, Jim and Honeybee Gillis (Tom D'Andrea and Gloria Blondell), but afterward they always remained good friends. Riley was presented as the comic focus of the series, and his simple-minded bumbling and misunderstandings touched off the weekly complications with his family and neighbors.

This setup had already failed in the 1949–50 season with a completely different cast, including Jackie Gleason as Riley. *The Life of Riley* had been one of the first network radio sitcoms to transfer to television as a filmed series, but that version had a weak supporting cast for Gleason, terrible scripts, and cheap sets. Though the revival with Bendix—who had played Riley in the radio show—reflected better overall production and writing, several problems remained. The supporting characters were still lifeless stereotypes, overshadowed by the silly situations and reduced to mouthpieces for one-liners. More importantly, Bendix's Riley was too predictably powerless to carry the series. Jackie Gleason's Riley had at least seemed capable of blowing his stack, bringing a strong comic tension to the character. With Bendix, it was a foregone conclusion that Riley would forgive and forget because he was as bland as everyone else. Yet despite all its shortcomings, the revived *Life of Riley* caught on and ran until 1958, a sure sign of the growing popularity of such noncontroversial sitcoms.

The failure of the ethnic comedies along with the success of *The Life of Riley* also reflected a subtle change in social attitudes across the country. In the expanding postwar economy of the early 1950s, more and more blue-collar Americans (like Chester A. Riley) were achieving their personal dream of joining the middle class and moving to the clean, homogeneous suburbs. They wanted to leave behind the distinctive problems of urban life, and television programs with obvious ethnic or racial settings were disturbing, especially as comedies. Such stories served as reminders to people of both where their family had probably been some twenty years earlier and where other families still lived. It was much more reassuring to follow "nice" American families such as the Nelsons and the Rileys.

September 20, 1952
The Jackie Gleason Show. (CBS). The "Great One" comes to CBS from DuMont, bringing along Art Carney, the June Taylor dancers, Joe the Bartender, the Poor Soul, and The Honeymooners. Pert Kelton is left behind, though, as Audrey Meadows becomes Alice Kramden number two.

October 3, 1952
Death Valley Days. Stanley Andrews is "the old Ranger," host and narrator to this popular syndicated Western anthology. Already a twenty-two-year radio veteran, this show runs another twenty years on television without ever receiving a network slot.

October 9, 1952
ABC All-Star News. (ABC). ABC reenters television news with a five-night-a-week prime time combination of straight news, man-on-the-street interviews, and filmed reports. Against the standard entertainment fare of the competition, the program dies by Christmas.

October 26, 1952
Victory at Sea. (NBC). A twenty-six-week Sunday afternoon documentary series on the naval battles of World War II, using film from ten countries and an original musical score by Richard Rodgers.

December 30, 1952
The Ernie Kovacs Show. (CBS). CBS gives Kovacs a four-week tryout opposite NBC's Milton Berle.

January 15, 1953
Rod Serling's "Ward Eight" wins the $1,000 first prize in a TV script contest held by WTVN in Cincinnati.

February 1, 1953

You Are There. (CBS). Up-and-coming CBS newsman Walter Cronkite gets his own Sunday evening show on which he serves as anchor for a simulated news report covering an important event from history. Actors portray the historical figures while actual CBS reporters tell the story "from the scene."

March 1, 1953

WJZ becomes WABC in New York City.

March 19, 1953

NBC presents the first national telecast of Hollywood's Academy Awards ceremony. Bob Hope is emcee and Gary Cooper wins the "Best Actor" Oscar for his role in "High Noon."

April 1, 1953

The Adventures of Superman. One of the great syndicated television series of the 1950s brings Krypton's man of steel to life in the person of George Reeves. The program adheres faithfully to the straight-laced spirit of the Superman comic books, promoting "truth, justice, and the American way." And, of course, no one ever seems to notice the obvious resemblance between mild-mannered reporter Clark Kent and his famous alter ego.

April 18, 1953

Rod Brown of the Rocket Rangers. (CBS). Future *Batman* major domo William Dozier produces a Saturday morning kiddie space opera. Cliff Robertson stars as the clean cut Rod Brown and Jack Weston plays his bumbling sidekick, "Wormsey."

May 30, 1953

ABC brings major league baseball to network television with Saturday afternoon "game of the week" broadcasts. For the first contest, Dizzy Dean and Buddy Blattner report the play-by-play as the Cleveland Indians beat the home team Chicago White Sox, 7 to 2.

The move toward a lighter approach to entertainment on TV reflected the growing influence of the Hollywood branch of the industry, as the medium shifted its operations westward. West Coast TV production received tremendous boosts from the opening of the coast-to-coast coaxial cable and the ratings success of filmed series such as *I Love Lucy* and *Dragnet*. In late 1952, both CBS and NBC opened new "television city" studio production facilities in California (CBS near Hollywood; NBC in Burbank), so that, for the first time, New York and Los Angeles were competing on an equal footing. The preference for one or the other location more and more reflected a choice in program philosophy. As with radio, the West Coast TV producers worked well in light comedy, adventure, and variety formats done Hollywood style. Applying their approach to drama, however, tended to eliminate serious or controversial productions, especially in the filmed drama anthology series.

Radio producers had faced a similar philosophical choice during the 1930s. In 1936, when the producers of the New York based *Lux Radio Theater* needed to boost sagging ratings, they moved out West. Once in California, they quickly adopted the West Coast emphasis on flashy stars over the weekly stories as the main attraction for listeners. In 1953, *The Lux Video Theater* made the complementary change for television, becoming one of the first TV drama series to originate from CBS's new television city.

Much of the difference in the approach to drama between the two coasts came from the dissimilar philosophies behind New York and Los Angeles entertainment productions. The East Coast,

Broadway-based live TV plays were, by their very nature, imperfect. Like any individual performance on Broadway, mistakes were bound to occur and often did. Even the best performances were usually gone after one broadcast because few were kept on kines. Yet these limitations were a source of strength. Producers were more willing to experiment with new ideas and challenging themes because the plays were one-shot affairs. If they did not work, there was always next week.

The fluffy West Coast Hollywood-influenced filmed dramas, on the other hand, were designed, like filmed sitcoms, to play for years, especially in post-network syndication runs. As a result, they took fewer chances. One of the first West Coast TV producers explained:

> Most of us are from the motion picture business, where we worked under a code for a long time, so we automatically observe good taste in programs. We must also consider the rerun value of a film, which would be impaired if we injected controversial material. You don't have this on live television.

As the Hollywood branch of TV asserted more influence on television production, this more restrictive attitude sometimes spilled over into the networks' overall approach to drama so that, given a choice, some executives would opt for the more cautious route in programming. The most obvious instances of this took place in the TV drama scripts that were adaptations from other sources, some of which were changed to seem "nicer" for television. Sometimes the changes were humorous and trivial, as when General Electric discovered that the episode it was sponsoring on *Studio One Summer Theater* was Rudyard Kipling's "The Light That Failed." GE forced CBS to change the title to "The Gathering Night." Other revisions went further, completely changing the thrust of a story.

Though *Schlitz Playhouse* proudly proclaimed that it was presenting the first Ernest Hemingway play to appear on television, "Fifty Grand," it did not point out the major alterations made to the story. In Hemingway's original plot, the central character, a boxer, bet against himself and deliberately threw a fight in order to win some money. The modified story had the boxer bet on himself to win, and then be beaten. By losing the fight, he learned the evils of gambling, gave up the habit, and went back home to his wife. In much the same vein, *The Lux Video Theater* performed a frontal lobotomy on "The Brooch," the first work by William Faulkner to be presented on television. The original story featured a mama's boy who permitted his mother to rule over his wife (described as "the trampy type"). When his wife left him, the boy realized his unending dependence on his mother, and killed himself. The television version presented him as a nice young kid who married the sweet young thing from next door. The mother tried to interfere in their lives, but the husband stood up to her, the mother gave in, and they all lived happily ever after. The producers said that the new self-regulating TV code forbade presenting suicide as a possible solution for someone's problems, but clearly the people at *Lux* could have eliminated the suicide while keeping the point and tenor of the play. The reasoning behind such alterations was best described by Frank Wizbar, director of the Hollywood-based filmed drama series, *Fireside Theater:* "We sell little pieces of soap, so our approach must be the broadest possible . . . we never take a depressing story."

There were people, chiefly on the East Coast, who were fighting this attitude toward television drama. They took their productions in the opposite direction, venturing into areas theretofore thought too topical for television. In early 1952, Fred Coe made an important change in his NBC drama showcase—he decided to stop relying so much on adaptations and start cultivating writers who could turn out original works. Previously, some thirty-minute drama anthology series had turned to original scripts, but most of them were slapdash, hackneyed, and meant just to fill time. With his original stories, Coe hoped to substantially upgrade *The Philco/ Goodyear Television Playhouse* (the program had taken on Goodyear as an alternate sponsor in 1951). Throughout 1952, Coe tried out plays by young unknown writers who were not shackled by years of experience on Broadway or in Hollywood and seemed better able to create works that were specifically tailored for the small screen. Most of the new plays tended to be extended character sketches, taking one or two people and placing them in engrossing lifelike situations. One of Coe's first finds was a Texan, Horton Foote, who came up with "The Travelers," a mildly amusing look at two Texas women who were husband hunting in New York City.

By 1953, other hour-long drama shows began seeking new writers, and original television dramas began attracting critical acclaim. *Kraft Television Theater* presented two compelling originals by Robert Howard Lindsay, "The Chess Game" and "One Left Over." The first depicted an atheist alcoholic who, after discussing the idea with a priest, confessed to a murder he did not commit in order to save a young man he knew was being framed. The second portrayed the struggles of a young husband who lost his wife and two of his children in a car crash. The man had to overcome his grief and carry on life with his remaining daughter. Both plays were out of the ordinary for that era: alcoholics were seldom acknowledged, much less portrayed with dignity; and death and its consequences were rarely discussed at all. Though dealing with highly emotional subjects, both plays avoided easy, maudlin clichés.

Fred Coe's year-long search for good, original material at last paid off on May 24, 1953, when he presented Paddy Chayefsky's "Marty," starring Rod Steiger. "Marty" was well-suited for television in that it concerned the close, cramped life of simple people. Unlike most of its contemporaries (theater and tube), "Marty" did not concern itself with prominent people doing momentous things or beautiful people doing remarkable things. Instead, it focused on common people doing common things. Marty, as played by Steiger, was a not-so-young local butcher who still lived with his mother. She wished he would get married (to almost anybody) because she felt it was not right for anyone not to be married. Marty, who knew his looks were, at best, average, had tried and failed at meeting girls and had no desire to endure the pain of rejection again. After persistent nudging from his mother and his friends, Marty attended a weekly neighborhood ballroom dance where he met and fell in love with an equally lonely young woman (who was no beauty herself). It was a simple story, told well, that used television's close quarters to its advantage.

The importance of "Marty" to the TV industry was that, for the first time, serious filmmakers in Hollywood showed some interest in a production done for television. "Marty" received next to no publicity from NBC before its airing, and afterward the play was not even reviewed by many leading television critics. It was Hollywood that declared "Marty" worthy of merit by making a movie version (starring Ernest Borgnine). The word was out that television drama could be a source of high quality, commercial material. Established playwrights began taking television more seriously, while unknown writers and actors saw the opportunity for exposure they had been looking for. Viewers, too, were struck by the increased respect for television drama. Previously, important theatrical films had been based on novels, short stories, and Broadway plays, but never on television scripts. Hollywood was, in effect,

saying that original television drama could be just as good as live theater and popular literature. If there was such a thing as television's golden age, this marked the beginning of it.

Yet just as television drama was coming of age, Worthington Miner, one of TV drama's founding fathers, found himself without a job. After four years with *Studio One,* Miner had switched to NBC in the spring of 1952. He produced a brief summer series, *Curtain Call,* as a warm-up for a projected hour-long program in the fall (labeled "Studio Miner" because it had no real title). However, NBC was unable to sell this show and instead of "Studio Miner" the network presented *I Married Joan* and *The Scott Music Hall* with Patti Page. Throughout 1952 and 1953, Miner sat idle while NBC searched for a time slot. A new hour-long series (this one had a title, *Gallery*) was scheduled to start alternating with the new *Hallmark Hall of Fame* on Sunday afternoons, but the Hallmark company had no desire to cut back. It was enjoying great success featuring Sarah Churchill and Maurice Evans in Shakespeare classics. As a result, Miner found himself out in the cold.

The difficulty that even a veteran of Miner's stature faced in securing a new slot demonstrated the increasing competition for advertising dollars. With prime time filling up with filmed series, the non-prime time hours were becoming increasingly important to the networks as a repository for experimental "class" programming. Such material might be brought to prime time as a special prestige hit, but only after it had proved itself in the less critical time period. NBC placed *The Hallmark Hall of Fame* on Sunday afternoons and CBS did the same with Edward R. Murrow's *See It Now* news program. In November, 1952, CBS added *Omnibus,* a ninety-minute production by the Ford Foundation's Radio and TV Workshop, directed by Alex Segal and hosted by Alistair Cooke.

Alan Hale, Jr., and Randy Stuart played an American husband and wife undercover spy duo. (*From* Biff Baker, U.S.A. *Courtesy of MCA Television Limited*)

Cooke described the series as a "vaudeville show of the arts and skills of man," though some reviewers saw it as being closer to a long-haired *Toast of the Town* with some *Studio One* on the side. The first episode featured excerpts from "The Mikado," "Tales of Anne Boleyn," and a William Saroyan original (with Sidney Poitier in a bit part). One of the highlights of the new series was a patient explanation of the great works of Beethoven by young conductor Leonard Bernstein. With its "mixed bag" approach, *Omnibus* constantly experimented in a generally unexplored field: adapting different forms of classical culture to popular tastes. Occasionally the program fell into the habit of repetition and condescension, but, as Cooke observed, "If you aim at the stars you sometimes land on the roof."

It was this willingness to try new ideas that might even fail that gave the so-called golden age of TV its life. Vehicles such as *Omnibus* as well as the top of the line prime time drama showcases treated television drama as an exciting challenge. But this uninhibited spirit was soon doomed by technological progress. In 1953, technicians were already demonstrating early versions of video tape recorders, which would eventually sound the death knell for live television by providing an easy way to prerecord and preserve any show. What's more, the move to film and Los Angeles-style production continued to pick up steam.

The network that was leading the way in the marriage of television and Hollywood was granted salvation in 1953. On February 9, the FCC approved the merger of ABC and United Paramount Theaters—having decided that United Paramount was not connected to the Paramount Pictures-DuMont "cartel." ABC, which lost $141,000 in 1952 and owed $12 million, received an influx of $30 million with its marriage to United Paramount. The network felt that it could at last compete with NBC and CBS as an equal. Within one month, ABC's radio and TV O&Os signed up $4 million of new business. By the summer, George Jessel, Ray Bolger, Paul Hartman, Cesar Romero, Danny Thomas, Sammy Davis, Jr., and Joel Grey were signed to headline shows (though the last two never made it to the air). U.S. Steel, which had sponsored *Theater Guild of the Air* on radio since 1945, agreed to come to television on ABC, rather than NBC, which had the radio show. ABC even moved out of the RCA building.

ABC was not the only innovative force busy in television. Steve Allen reactivated the concept of a late night variety-talk show (on New York's WNBT), while KNXT in Los Angeles featured *Carson's Cellar*, a Friday night comedy-variety show starring Johnny Carson, who listed as his co-writer a fellow named Joe Twerp. Canada's top TV news commentator, Lorne Greene, came to New York to plug his stopwatch invention. Paul Newman portrayed Nathan Hale on CBS's historical dramatization series, *You Are There*, while newcomer James Dean "stole the show" from Walter Hampton in "Death Is My Neighbor" on the *Danger* drama anthology. Dean played a young psychotic who nearly killed someone, a role he soon mastered on the movie screen. While all this was going on, young Philadelphians were watching WFIL-TV where, five days a week, radio disk jockeys Bob Horn and Lee Stewart presented *Bandstand*, a program later taken over by Dick Clark. In 1952, the kids were "gone" over Johnny Ray.

ABC did manage one humorous triumph over its competition to start the summer of 1953. With NBC and CBS neck and neck in the ratings, practically any event became an opportunity for one-upmanship. As a result, the two turned the June 2nd coronation of Queen Elizabeth into a childish race to be the first on the air with film from England of the ceremony—pompously dubbed "the birth of world TV." Both CBS and NBC hired speed pilots to fly in the films when they arrived in Canada. Appropriately, the two speed demons were late and NBC had to go crawling to ABC, which calmly beat them both simply by arranging to pick up a Canadian television feed from Montreal.

Earlier in the day, NBC had faced other embarrassing technical problems when wire photo and live phone reports from London during *Today* were interrupted by ads from General Motors brazenly touting cars described as "queen of the road" and "royal carriages." British egos were also offended by J. Fred Muggs, a baby chimp that had become *Today*'s on-air mascot in February. He was shown bouncing about the studio making chimp noises in between reports on the coronation. People felt that his antics degraded a solemn occasion by injecting a circus atmosphere. Though NBC eventually issued a semi-apology, at the so-called "birth of world TV" American television had put its worst foot forward, pairing the queen of England with a monkey.

13. Point of Order

ON MARCH 25, 1953, the seemingly endless battle over the development of color television technology reached a dramatic climax with the collapse of the CBS forces. The erosion of CBS's strength had begun in 1951, despite the government-ordered monopoly status granted to the CBS noncompatible color system in June of that year. Within months, CBS had discovered that few television set owners had any desire to discard black and white sets in favor of expensive color models, and by October the network had "temporarily" suspended its color broadcasts under the guise of complying with wartime production cutbacks. For longer than a year, CBS allowed the losing venture of noncompatible color television to lie dormant, while RCA's ever-improving compatible color process was limited to off-hour experimental broadcasts. Eighteen months after the much ballyhooed inauguration of CBS color, the viewing public found itself effectively denied any color broadcasts at all. In March, 1953, the House Committee on Interstate and Foreign Commerce began hearings on the color question, trying to determine whether color TV was ready for the public or not.

RCA sensed the mood of the committee and saw the opportunity for victory. The company carefully modified its approach by presenting the RCA color process under the umbrella of the National Television Systems Committee, an industry-wide group of twenty top television set manufacturers. As the NTSC color process, the proposal offered CBS a face-saving opportunity to terminate its noncompatible system officially. Rather than surrender to RCA, its hated rival, CBS could adopt a conciliatory stance and step aside in favor of a "new" color system with broad-based industry support. Following an RCA-NTSC demonstration that was almost identical to many previous RCA presentations, CBS president Frank Stanton announced, on March 25, that CBS had "reluctantly but realistically" recognized that it would be "economically foolish" to attempt to persuade the public to discard twenty-three million black and white television sets to institute CBS color. Without specifically endorsing RCA, Stanton ended the decade-old battle with the almost weary admission, "perhaps this time it is different, perhaps this time they have found the answer."

Others were more enthusiastic. Committee chairman Charles A. Wolverton said he was "astounded" by the quality of RCA-NTSC color, and his committee urged the FCC to approve the system forthwith. Wolverton said, "Color TV is ready for the public; there is no reason for more delay." RCA submitted its petition to the FCC in June, and the commission took a few months to ruminate. On December 17, 1953, in one of the few instances in which the FCC publicly admitted a change of heart, the commission reversed its October, 1950, decision favoring CBS color and approved the RCA-NTSC system. Immediately, NBC scheduled several color holiday specials, including the perennial "Amahl and the Night Visitors," the traditional *Dragnet* Christmas story, and the New Year's Tournament of Roses parade. By this time, the Korean armistice had been signed and the remaining limits on domestic production had been lifted, so NBC expected color TV set sales to skyrocket over the next twelve months.

NBC pursued color broadcasting with more vigor than the other networks in 1954. Realizing that its technicians still needed a good deal of practical experience, the network set up a rotating color broadcast schedule in the first part of the year. NBC broadcast, on the average, ten color programs each week, selecting different shows each week for treatment in color. By March virtually every NBC program had been telecast in color at least once.

The addition of color to some programs such as quiz, discussion, and children's shows did not seem to add much. The same held true for news. The only new information conveyed in the February 16 color telecast of the *Camel News Caravan* was the color of the bathing suits in the cheesecake feature footage (shot in Florida) and the color of John Cameron Swayze's ever-present carnation (red that day). However, women's programs—with those colorful fashions and taste-tempting food tips—were enhanced by color. The process was also an enormous aid to musical productions in programs such as "Amahl and the Night Visitors" and *Your Hit Parade,* so NBC began staging lavish musical-variety specials as sure-fire promotions for color. Advertisers, too, found color a welcome bonanza. Kraft was nearly apoplectic over the vibrant yellow luster of products like Velveeta, which provided a rich complement to the sincere voice of Ed Herlihy (". . . then smother it with thick Velveeta cream sauce . . ."). Car manufacturers emphasized their two-tone autobehemoths while cigarette companies presented their brands in bright, decorative packs. CBS went a little more slowly, restricting its color tryouts to a Friday afternoon variety show called *The New Revue,* with Mike Wallace and his wife, Buff, as hosts. ABC decided to postpone color broadcasting until the public demanded it.

There was no public demand for color TV. Only 8,000 of the expensive color sets were produced in the first six months of 1954 and manufacturers discovered that they were very hard to sell.

MONDAY

Network	7:00	7:30	8:00	8:30	9:00	9:30	10:00	10:30
ABC	local	JOHN DALY	JAMIE	Sky King	OF MANY THINGS	Junior Press Conference	THE BIG PICTURE	This Is The Life / local
CBS	local	CBS News / Perry Como	Burns And Allen Show	Arthur Godfrey's Talent Scouts	I Love Lucy	Red Buttons Show	Studio One	
DUMONT	Captain Video	MARGE AND JEFF / local	Twenty Questions	The Big Issue	Boxing From Eastern Parkway With Chris Schenkel			Ringside Interview
NBC	local	Arthur Murray / Camel News	Name That Tune	Voice Of Firestone	RCA Victor Show	Robert Montgomery Presents		Who Said That

TUESDAY

Network	7:00	7:30	8:00	8:30	9:00	9:30	10:00	10:30
ABC	local	JOHN DALY	Cavalcade Of America	local	MAKE ROOM FOR DADDY	U.S. STEEL HOUR / THE TV HOUR		The Name's The Same
CBS	local	CBS News / Jane Froman	Gene Autry Show	Red Skelton Show	This Is Show Business	Suspense	Danger	See It Now
DUMONT	Captain Video	MARGE AND JEFF / local	Life Is Worth Living	Pantomime Quiz	local			
NBC	local	Dinah Shore / Camel News	Buick Berle Show @BOB HOPE SHOW		Fireside Theater	Armstrong Circle Theater	JUDGE FOR YOURSELF	Bob Considine / It Happ. In Sports

WEDNESDAY

Network	7:00	7:30	8:00	8:30	9:00	9:30	10:00	10:30
ABC	local	JOHN DALY	Mark Saber – Homicide Squad	At Issue / THR. THE CURTAIN	ANSWERS FOR AMERICANS	TAKE IT FROM ME	DR. I.Q.	Wrestling From The Rainbo In Chicago [to 12 Midnite]
CBS	local	CBS News / Perry Como	Arthur Godfrey And His Friends		Strike It Rich	I've Got A Secret	Blue Ribbon Bouts	Sports Spot
DUMONT	Captain Video	MARGE AND JEFF / local	Johns Hopkins Science Review	JOS. SCHILDKRAUT THEATER	COL. HUMPHREY FLACK	ON YOUR WAY	STARS ON PARADE	The Music Show
NBC	local	Eddie Fisher / Camel News	I Married Joan	My Little Margie	Kraft Television Theater I		This Is Your Life	local

THURSDAY

Network	7:00	7:30	8:00	8:30	9:00	9:30	10:00	10:30
ABC	local	JOHN DALY	The Lone Ranger	Quick As A Flash	WHERE'S RAYMOND	BACK THAT FACT	Kraft Television Theater II	local
CBS	local	CBS News / Jane Froman	MEET MR. McNUTLEY	Four Star Playhouse	Lux Video Theater	Big Town	PHILIP MORRIS PLAYHOUSE	City Hospital / Place The Face
DUMONT	Captain Video	MARGE AND JEFF / local	N.Y. Giants Quarterback Huddle	Broadway To Hollywood Headline Clues	What's The Story	Author Meets The Critics	The Big Idea	local
NBC	local	Dinah Shore / Camel News	You Bet Your Life	Treasury Man In Action	Dragnet	Ford Theater	New Adventures Of Martin Kane	local

FRIDAY

Network	7:00	7:30	8:00	8:30	9:00	9:30	10:00	10:30
ABC	local	JOHN DALY	Stu Erwin Show	Ozzie And Harriet	PEPSI COLA PLAYHOUSE	PRIDE OF THE FAMILY	THE COMEBACK STORY	SHOWCASE THEATER / local
CBS	local	CBS News / Perry Como	Mama	TOPPER	Schlitz Playhouse Of Stars	Our Miss Brooks	My Friend Irma	PERSON TO PERSON
DUMONT	Captain Video	MARGE AND JEFF / local	Front Page Detective	MELODY STREET	Life Begins At 80	NINE THIRTY CURTAIN	Chance Of A Lifetime	Down You Go
NBC	local	Eddie Fisher / Camel News	DAVE GARROWAY SHOW	The Life Of Riley	The Big Story	Campbell TV Soundstage	Gillette Cavalcade Of Sports	Great Fights

SATURDAY

Network	7:00	7:30	8:00	8:30	9:00	9:30	10:00	10:30
ABC	Paul Whiteman's TV Teen Club	Leave It To The Girls	Talent Patrol	Music From Meadowbrook	Saturday Night Fights	Fight Talk	MADISON SQUARE GARDEN HILIGHTS	local
CBS	Meet Millie	Beat The Clock	Jackie Gleason Show		Two For The Money	MY FAVORITE HUSBAND	Medallion Theater	Revlon Mirror Theater
DUMONT	local		NATIONAL FOOTBALL LEAGUE PRO FOOTBALL					
NBC	Mr. Wizard	Ethel And Albert	BONINO	The Original Amateur Hour	Your Show Of Shows @All Star Revue			Your Hit Parade

SUNDAY

Network	7:00	7:30	8:00	8:30	9:00	9:30	10:00	10:30
ABC	You Asked For It	FRANK LEAHY	NOTRE DAME FOOTBALL		Walter Winchell / Orchid Award	JUKE BOX JURY		Billy Graham's Hour Of Decision
CBS	LIFE WITH FATHER	Private Secretary @Jack Benny Prog.	Toast Of The Town		Fred Waring Show	MAN BEHIND THE BADGE	The Web	What's My Line
DUMONT	local	OPERA CAMEOS	local		Rocky King, Inside Detective	The Plainclothesman	DOLLAR A SECOND	Man Against Crime
NBC	Paul Winchell Show	Mr. Peepers	Colgate Comedy Hour		Goodyear/Philco Television Playhouse		LETTER TO LORETTA	Man Against Crime

Westinghouse staged a big color push and found after one month that it had sold only thirty sets, nationwide. On one of the variety specials NBC held to promote color, emcee Bob Hope quipped that there was a "tremendous" audience watching in color—"General Sarnoff and his wife."

ABC was more than willing to let NBC occupy itself with color. Entering its first full season with the financial backing of United Paramount, ABC was hoping to win over the television audience with fancy new black and white programming and catapult itself into direct competition with CBS and NBC. Such a leap would have been astounding, because when the merger with United Paramount was approved, ABC's status was much closer to that of the ailing DuMont system.

As the new season commenced, ABC presented a seemingly impressive line-up of new shows, highlighted by drama and situation comedy. The two showcases for drama represented a tentative vote of confidence in the struggling network by two major sponsors, United States Steel and Kraft Foods. Kraft had decided to launch a second weekly hour-long drama series, not on NBC (home of its Wednesday night series) but on ABC. U.S. Steel, too, had passed over NBC (home of its radio series) and scheduled *The U.S. Steel Hour* for ABC. While such support was gratifying and impressive, the network was banking on comedy as its chief ratings weapon.

ABC expected quick success with its new roster of veteran comics (George Jessel, Paul Hartman, Ray Bolger, and Danny Thomas) while holding high hopes for a new sitcom, *Jamie*. The list of newly acquired talent was formidable, but none of the shows became hits and ABC was unable to place a series in the top ten. The network was doing better in the ratings overall, winning some time slots and coming in number two in a few more, but the hoped-for leap to respectability did not take place. The chief stumbling block was one that would plague ABC for the rest of the decade: affiliates. Because station investment and construction was just gearing up after the freeze and Korean war, many large and medium-size cities still had only one or two channels operating. As a result, ABC had fewer affiliates than either NBC or CBS. In addition, many of ABC's affiliates were UHF stations and, because most home sets lacked UHF converter attachments, the network's programs, no matter how good, could not be picked up by large numbers of Americans. Until its affiliate situation improved, ABC would remain far behind the two television leaders.

Though its potential success was severely limited, ABC approached the season aggressively, out to score substantial gains despite the affiliate handicap. The network's emphasis on comedy vehicles was a sound strategy, building on a proven formula that had taken CBS to the top. ABC won warm critical praise for two of its new shows, though there were some disappointments.

The much-touted *Jamie* series proved to be the biggest letdown. Eleven-year-old Brandon De Wilde played Jamie, a young orphan living with his aunt. There, he became best friends with Grandpa (played by sixty-three-year-old Ernest Truex), who understood Jamie's loneliness and frustration at being an extra burden to an unwilling relative. Despite the age difference, the two constantly shared adventures and experiences together, often just sitting and gazing thoughtfully at the sky—perhaps searching for a brighter tomorrow. Though the pilot for the program had won rave reviews the previous season on the network's anthology series, *ABC Album*, the sentimentality dished out on the weekly series frequently overshadowed both the plots and the characters.

Veteran George Jessel was also lost in a great gush of tears and sentiment. He began the season as host of two programs, *The Comeback Story* and *George Jessel's Show Business*. The *Show Business* variety program included music and monologues and featured Jessel in his favorite, familiar role of toastmaster general of the United States, leading combination toast-roasts of celebrities. This show was squirreled away Sunday at 6:30 P.M., just before *You Asked For It,* while *The Comeback Story* received a Friday night prime time slot. As host to this maudlin copy of *This Is Your Life,* Jessel presented each week the tear-filled life story of a once famous celebrity who had fallen from grace but was battling back. Doing both shows proved too much for Jessel and in December Arlene Francis took over *The Comeback Story* while Jessel continued the Sunday variety series. In its terrible time slot, though, this barely lasted the season.

Pride of the Family, Paul Hartman's vehicle, turned out to be just an average Los Angeles filmed sitcom. Though Hartman was a talented dancer and satirist, he appeared as a bumbling father who, like Chester A. Riley, had a loving, faithful wife (played by King Kong's former flame, Fay Wray) and two bland teenage children, Junior (Bobby Hyatt) and Ann (Natalie Wood). Apart from these drab disappointments, ABC's new sitcom schedule contained two jewels, *Where's Raymond?* and *Make Room for Daddy,* which both featured stars essentially playing themselves.

Where's Raymond? cast Ray Bolger as Ray Wallace, a professional song and dance man who had a habit of arriving at the theater only minutes before he was to step on stage—causing the supporting crew to wonder constantly: "Where's Raymond?" Once he began performing, everyone forgot the frustrations and watched the charming, whimsical star. The show was less a sitcom and more a loose musical comedy tied together by a slim thread of situation—Bolger's stage act was the focus of the series. Each week's musical numbers often incorporated his character bits from Broadway and feature films (such as the Scarecrow in "The Wizard of Oz"), and the show was greatly admired by critics as one of the more imaginative filmed series to come from Los Angeles. With ABC's affiliate problem, though, *Where's Raymond?* never

developed a large following and ran only two seasons.

In *Make Room for Daddy,* Danny Thomas—who apparently had concluded that television was no longer "just for idiots"— portrayed a show business father and, in effect, himself. The character of nightclub comedian Danny Williams was almost identical to the character Danny Thomas had been projecting for years in his own nightclub act and on television comedy-variety shows. In the sitcom setting, Thomas was given a strong TV family for support, consisting of Jean Hagen as his wife, Margaret; eleven-year-old Sherry Jackson as his daughter, Terry; and six-year-old Rusty Hamer as his son, Rusty. The concept was perfect for Thomas, resolving the many objections that had driven him from television variety the previous year. Unlike the random skits of a comedy-variety show, *Make Room for Daddy* provided a workable setting that allowed stories to be built around both domestic and show business complications.

Make Room for Daddy was filmed at Desilu and, like *I Love Lucy* and *Our Miss Brooks,* reflected important touches of real life. The Williams family lived in a New York City apartment, rather than a Los Angeles suburb. Danny was not a bumbler or a dummy, but an intelligent, principled, often stubborn, father and husband. Margaret was a loving but creditable wife, and the children were cute, though pushy and conniving often enough to seem real. More importantly, Danny Williams actually worked. His nightclub act was sometimes incorporated into the show and he even had to "go on the road" to perform. This served as an important basis of the humor at home because his absences caused family

Make Room for Daddy did not become a hit until it moved from ABC to CBS in 1957. After the switch, the cast included: (from l.) Marjorie Lord, Sherry Jackson, Angela Cartwright, Danny Thomas, Rusty Hamer. *(Courtesy Danny Thomas Productions)*

problems, especially when he tried to compensate upon returning. The kids shamelessly exploited him to cover their mischief—until Danny caught on. Then, he exploded. When Thomas bellowed, the show crackled with energy. The moments of forgiveness and reconciliation that followed were especially effective because they showed that, underneath, he had a heart of gold and really loved his family.

Make Room for Daddy demonstrated that a believable father could serve as an effective comic focus for a series. Critics were effusive in praising the program, but the ratings were disappointing. Sixty stations carried the premiere episode (a good figure for ABC) and by November the show was on 112 stations—the largest number of any ABC program. Yet this could not match coverage by NBC and CBS, so *Make Room for Daddy* remained rather a cult program for three years. It became a big hit only when it moved to CBS in 1957.

Even with ABC's strong new line-up, NBC and CBS again dominated television. Like ABC, they also included a healthy dose of comedy, though NBC continued to emphasize both filmed sitcoms and live comedy-variety hours. In fact, the network introduced only one new sitcom in the fall, *Bonino,* while bringing *My Little Margie* over from CBS.

Bonino was NBC's own "daddy" TV show, a live production by Fred Coe featuring one of the network's favorite "paisano" guest stars, singer Ezio Pinza, as a concert singer whose career conflicted with his family life. Though the premise of *Bonino* resembled that of *Make Room for Daddy,* Coe took it the opposite direction. Unlike Danny Williams, Babbo Bonino was established as a widower who gave up his far-flung touring schedule in order to return home and raise his six children (one of whom was played

by Van Dyke Parks, who later became a rock musician and wrote music for TV commercials). The series was strongly ethnic and the children were considerably more independent than Terry and Rusty Williams, but the stories lacked the driving force of a personality like Danny Thomas. The program never took off, even though making Bonino a widower opened up a wide range of possibilities. Such a character offered the best of two comedy worlds: children to add a family touch, and girlfriends for sex appeal. Though not much happened in this series—which ended after just three months—many TV widowers followed Bonino and they exploited both angles extensively.

Prior to his stint on *Bonino,* Ezio Pinza had alternated with singer Dennis Day on *The RCA Victor Show* during the 1951–52 season. In the fall of 1952, Day became the sole star of the program and in the 1953–54 season the show went to film and its title was officially changed to *The Dennis Day Show.* Through each permutation, Dennis Day played himself, Dennis Day, an often naive but determined young bachelor-vocalist living in Hollywood and trying to get ahead in show business. His character had been developed on Jack Benny's radio show during the 1940s and came virtually unchanged to television (he also continued on Benny's program). Cliff Arquette, who had appeared occasionally on Benny's radio series himself—playing Jack Benny's father—brought his Charlie Weaver character to television as the janitor for Day's apartment building. NBC seemed to consider the filmed series to be either a sleeper hit or doomed from the start because the network threw it to the wolves by placing it against *I Love Lucy* on Monday night.

Jack Benny, who had perfected the "I Me Mine" style of comedians playing themselves two decades earlier on radio, continued his own steady expansion into television that season. Beginning in the fall of 1950, Benny had done occasional floating specials on CBS television, while maintaining his successful Sunday night CBS radio show. By 1951, he settled on 7:30–8:00 P.M. Sunday as a good television slot, appearing there about once a month. By slowly increasing his television work, he developed an excellent feel for the medium before attempting more frequent exposure. He had seen too many comedians burn themselves out trying to do too much on a weekly basis. In the fall of 1953, Benny's TV show appeared every third week and the following season he agreed to an every-other-week schedule.

The Jack Benny radio show combined the variety and situation comedy formats by presenting Benny as the lowkey star of a comedy-variety show about trying to put on a comedy-variety show. The show-within-a-show setup allowed Benny to act in a very relaxed, natural manner and gave him the option of shifting back and forth from variety to sitcom. Sometimes the comedy-variety show was presented intact, with guests, songs, and sketches. Other times, the show would never start at all as the action focused on backstage complications and Benny's home life. For television, he continued this winning format intact.

What separated Jack Benny's show from others that used a similar formula was Benny's uncanny sense of comic timing and delivery, combined with his strong supporting cast. The familiar characters that had surrounded him for years on radio made the transition to television almost as easily as he did, drawing on their own well-established personalities. Portly Don Wilson the announcer portrayed Don Wilson the announcer; Eddie Anderson continued as Benny's valet, Rochester; and Dennis Day the vocalist played Dennis Day the vocalist (a role he obviously relished). Mel Blanc (the voice of Bugs Bunny, Daffy Duck, and other cartoon zanies) appeared as an assortment of crazy characters including

When Jack Benny *(r.)* moved to television, he brought along his entire radio "family," including his valet, Rochester (Eddie Anderson). (*From* The Jack Benny Program. *Courtesy of MCA Television Limited*)

Professor Le Blanc, Benny's frustrated violin teacher; Sy, a very concise Mexican who spoke in one word sentences; and the sputtering personality of Benny's limousine, a misfiring old Maxwell.

At the center of the show was the easily identifiable character of Jack Benny, the vain miser. Benny employed an excellent crew of writers who came up with continuing routines that fit the character: he had a pay phone in his house, kept his money in a subterranean bank vault, and filled his Maxwell with gasoline one gallon at a time. As a master of delivery and timing, Benny used such material for years. Though Fred Allen once said that Jack Benny couldn't ad-lib a belch after a Hungarian dinner, it was obvious that he did not have to. Benny's elongated double-takes and phrases such as "Well!" "Now cut that out!" and "Wait a minute!" became legendary. He could milk a bit better than anyone. Benny once carried the audience through five minutes of sustained laughter with a staged telephone call to his sponsor in which he asked about a raise supposedly promised to him. The sponsor was never heard. All the viewer saw was Benny on the phone saying "but—" over and over again, with different intonations and pauses.

Jack Benny's television show, like his radio program, became a top ten hit. Even with this success, Benny did not drop his weekly radio show until 1955 (he was one of the last of the big name comics to do so) and he did not begin doing his television show on a weekly basis until the fall of 1960.

With the strong showing by Jack Benny and the continued top ratings by veteran filmed sitcoms such as *I Love Lucy* and *Our Miss Brooks,* CBS held its lead as the number one television network. The strength of its sitcoms in the 1953–54 season contrasted

sharply with the downturn in NBC's comedy-variety vehicles. Both of the network's top of the line showcases, *All Star Revue* and *The Colgate Comedy Hour,* were in serious trouble—in artistic quality as well as in ratings strength.

In the fall, NBC reduced *All Star Revue* to a once-a-month offering placed in the *Your Show of Shows* time slot and, by December, after Martha Raye had often been called upon to act as host, the title was changed to *The Martha Raye Show.* The remaining headliners from *All Star Revue* were merged into *The Colgate Comedy Hour* rotation so that the Sunday night show was divided almost evenly (but erratically) among Dean Martin and Jerry Lewis, Jimmy Durante, Eddie Cantor, Donald O'Connor, and Bud Abbott and Lou Costello. Ed Sullivan's show regularly topped this line-up in the ratings and, at a yearly budget of $6 million, the Colgate program was turning into a growing disappointment. Colgate's producers seemed unable to find fresh new talent to act as hosts, and the old timers, who often repeated their old routines over and over again, began to irritate many home viewers. During one of the frequent appearances by Abbott and Costello, a frustrated viewer, Frank Walsh of West Hampstead, Long Island, took out his gun and shot his television set. He later told police he thought the show was too loud. Naturally, such a cult figure could not be ignored by the medium he wished to destroy. Less than a week later, Frank Walsh of West Hampstead, Long Island, appeared on *Strike It Rich* ("the program with a heart") and won—what else—a new television set.

The erosion of the comedy-variety format during the 1953–54 season was not limited to NBC's *Colgate Comedy Hour;* stars throughout the networks' schedules were suffering from escalating costs and format fatigue. The grueling weekly TV schedule that

November 13, 1953
The Jack Paar Show. (CBS). Paar hosts an easy-paced daytime variety show, assisted by a family of regulars that includes Edie Adams and Jose Melis.

December 4, 1953
Sylvester "Pat" Weaver becomes president of NBC-TV.

December 30, 1953
The first compatible color TV sets, built by the Admiral corporation, go on sale. Price: $1,175.

January 3, 1954
"The Bing Crosby Show." (CBS). Even more hesitant toward television than Jack Benny, "Der Bingle" headlines his first television show. He will continue to do a few specials each season, resisting a weekly series for nearly a decade.

February 22, 1954
Breakfast Club. (ABC). ABC returns to the daytime television battles with a video version of Don McNeill's veteran radio variety hour. Though the program is sold out on radio, the network cannot *give* away ads for the television series, which is carried by only a few stations.

May 23, 1954
Earn Your Vacation. (CBS). Johnny Carson debuts on network television as host of a short-lived game show.

July 9, 1954
It's News To Me returns to the air on CBS with a new quizmaster, the ubiquitous Walter Cronkite. John Henry Faulk remains a regular panelist.

Jack Benny so carefully avoided was taking its toll. Even Godfrey stumbled.

As a virtual one-man network for CBS radio and television, Arthur Godfrey appeared invulnerable. With his consistently high ratings, Godfrey was responsible for millions of dollars' worth of advertising and stood practically beyond network criticism. If he decided to tell a slightly risque story or to change around the format of one of his programs, sponsors and network executives accepted it. Over the years, he had built his own strong organization to handle the multi-million-dollar enterprise, taking care of booking and paying guests, as well as managing his own cast of regulars. Godfrey treated his shows as both a business and family affair, acting like a benevolent father who was determined to take care of his performing family.

Since 1951, Godfrey's "family" had included young singer Julius La Rosa. Over just eighteen months, La Rosa became the most popular member of the supporting cast, with his fresh, modest personality generating a tremendous following, second only to Godfrey himself. In the fall of 1953, as his career continued to expand, La Rosa violated an unwritten rule of Godfrey's organization—he arranged his own business deals, hiring an agent and signing an independent recording contract. Godfrey's response came a short time later.

On Monday, October 19, as Godfrey was nearing the conclusion of his morning radio-television simulcast program, he brought La Rosa to the microphone and began a fatherly reminiscence of how he had brought the young singer so far so fast. La Rosa, he noted, seemed to be on the verge of stardom on his own. He had signed an independent recording deal and was going to become "a great big name." Godfrey asked La Rosa to sing "I'll Take Manhattan" (which he sang). Then, as the show was ending, Godfrey said: "Thanks ever so much, Julie. That was Julie's swan song with us; he goes now out on his own, as his own star . . ."

What this meant was that Julius La Rosa had been fired.

At a press conference the next day, Godfrey was pressed to explain why he so suddenly dismissed one of his protégés. Godfrey responded that La Rosa did not understand that on his show "we have no stars . . . we're all one family." By trying to venture into independent recording, La Rosa had "lacked humility"—two words that Godfrey would regret. To the public, it appeared just the opposite. It was Godfrey who seemed to lack humility, firing an aide who had become very popular on his show.

Immediately after the firing, La Rosa became an instant *cause célèbre*. He was signed to appear on a number of Ed Sullivan's programs where he acted very humble, but was lost in some silly production numbers. Later, La Rosa was host of a few TV summer replacement musical series, but he never really made it big on his own. But something did happen to Godfrey. He began losing his audience. For a decade, the Old Redhead had been Mr. Nice Guy, Mr. Natural. After his firing of La Rosa, he appeared instead to be an evil taskmaster, jealous of every scrap of publicity. This was clearly a wild over-reaction to the La Rosa incident, but the public's view of Godfrey had become jaundiced. By March, 1954, neither of his two television shows was in the top ten, an unprecedented situation at that time. Though he remained on the tube for another five years, and on radio into the 1970s, Godfrey was never able to regain the stature he had before the October day he gave young La Rosa the kiss of death.

Another television institution, *Your Show of Shows,* ended its successful run in 1954. The program had been one of NBC's first comedy-variety blockbusters, but unlike many others that followed it, *Your Show of Shows* quit while it was still in top form. Performers

Sid Caesar, Imogene Coca, Carl Reiner, and Howard Morris were still sharp and the writers, including Neil Simon and Mel Brooks, were often brilliant. Nonetheless, the program's ratings had dipped a bit in the 1952–53 season, so producer Max Liebman instituted a few changes for the fall of 1953. He dropped the Billy Williams Quartet and the dance team of Bambi Lynn and Rod Alexander, invited more guests, and worked with an increased budget. It soon became apparent that there was a more fundamental problem that could not be solved by such minor tinkering.

Viewers who followed the program show after show, season after season, had come to know the cast and writers inside out and there was little either could do that seemed fresh and new—even very funny skits were somehow familiar and repetitious. The escalating costs of the program applied further pressure. With a budget of $100,000 to $125,000 per week ($4 million per year), the loss of even one sponsor pushed the program into the red. In February, 1954, Caesar, Coca, and Liebman decided that they had done all they could in *Your Show of Shows* and made plans to split up and start fresh as headliners of their own shows in the fall. The last three *Your Show of Shows* programs recapitulated the most popular skits of the series, which had become practically a TV legend while it was still on the air. The tear-filled final program on June 5 featured a guest appearance by Pat Weaver, the man responsible for selling the show's original concept in 1949. All the central figures from *Your Show of Shows* had varying degrees of success in their subsequent series, but none of them was able to assemble such a pool of consistently successful writing, producing, and acting talent again. In 1973, the feature film "Ten from *Your Show of Shows*" brought kines of their hilarious performances back to the screen—many of which had become landmarks in TV comedy—and they were as sharp and fresh as ever.

The appearance of Pat Weaver on the final edition of *Your Show of Shows* reflected his return to power following a year of corporate disfavor. Weaver was brought in from the cold to become the president of NBC just before New Year's, 1954, in order to meet the challenge of CBS's continued strong ratings. At once, he reactivated his concept of regularly scheduled special programs—dubbed spectaculars—which had run into network and sponsor opposition when first proposed in 1951. This time, Weaver presented the spectaculars as the means to catapult NBC back into the TV ratings lead, and he was able to convince the sponsors to try it. Weaver signed Max Liebman to coordinate the project, which was slated to begin in the fall of 1954.

One reason that skeptical sponsors were more receptive to the concept of spectaculars was that another Weaver innovation, *Today,* had turned into the biggest money-making show on television. Even J. Fred Muggs, the program's mascot chimp, had become a celebrity and turned up as a guest on a number of NBC variety shows. Unfortunately, Muggs lacked the sense of camaraderie that usually existed among showbiz folk and he began biting people. After he bit Martha Raye on the elbow in April, Muggs was sent on a worldwide promotional tour. There, he attracted the attention of the Russian newspaper, *Izvestia,* which described J. Fred Muggs as:

A symbol of the American way of life . . . Muggs is necessary in order that the average American should not look into reports on rising taxes and decreasing pay, but rather laugh at the funny mug of a chimpanzee.

In March, 1954, CBS launched *The Morning Show* in an attempt to duplicate NBC's success with *Today.* The new show included a similar mixture of news, interviews, and features, with Charles Collingwood as the news anchor and Walter Cronkite as the genial

In the fall of 1953, after two years of Sunday afternoon broadcasts, *See It Now* with Ed Murrow (foreground) moved into prime time. *(CBS News Photo)*

host. Like *Today, The Morning Show* had its own flashy wall gadgets and animal mascots, though Humphrey the hound dog and Charlamane the lion were puppet characters—from Bil and Cora Baird—and much easier to control than J. Fred Muggs. However, the wall gimmicks were just as confusing and silly as *Today's*. At appropriate moments in the program, Cronkite pointed to an electric weather map that was covered with special effects meant to resemble falling rain, snow, and clouds. On the home screen, it seemed more like a giant pinball machine than a helpful guide to the nation's weather. Cronkite soon tired of his role as entertainer-bon vivant and left *The Morning Show* in August, though the program continued under a cavalcade of successors including Jack Paar, John Henry Faulk, Will Rogers, Jr., and Dick Van Dyke. None of them could boost the program anywhere near *Today's* ratings and, after three years, CBS gave up and canceled the show.

Pat Weaver had more success with NBC's new one-hour features and interview program, the late-morning *Home* show, also begun in March, 1954. Like many other daytime shows, *Home* was aimed at housewives, but Weaver treated them with considerably more respect, assuming that they were intelligent, perceptive viewers. With Arlene Francis and Hugh Downs as hosts, *Home* avoided the glamour chit-chat formula in favor of a more down-to-earth style of dealing with fashion, food, home decorating, leisure activities, home gardening, and children. It was an immediate hit and dominated late morning programming for three and one-half years, before succumbing to the competitive pressures from a line-up of popular soap operas on CBS.

By the summer of 1954, Pat Weaver's amazing programming

abilities and willingness to innovate had generated new excitement at NBC. With Weaver back, three of the four television networks were once again in the position of tremendous growth and expansion, after the slowdown caused by the FCC freeze and the Korean war. CBS was solidifying its newly-won ratings lead, NBC was banking on Weaver's leadership skills, and ABC was drawing on the money and Hollywood experience on United Paramount.

The only network that was slipping was DuMont, which was in both financial and programming distress in early 1954. The FCC continued to prevent DuMont from acquiring any new owned and operated stations, and the failure of UHF meant that there still were not enough TV stations in most major cities to provide strong affiliates for all four networks. DuMont inevitably came up last in the competition. Actually, DuMont did have a brand new project that it hoped would provide a boost in its network prestige and income, a giant new television production facility located in New York. However, instead of serving as DuMont's successful equivalent to the expansion by the other three networks, the five-studio $4 million "telecenter" proved to be a very expensive failure.

Over the years, while the DuMont network had been losing money, the parent DuMont Labs had made enough to keep the overall DuMont operations solvent. In building the New York telecenter (the biggest on the East Coast), DuMont funneled what little company profits there were away from program development and into the future facility. This strategy proved to be a disaster. By the time the telecenter was completed and dedicated on June 14, 1954, television producers interested in expanded facilities were heading west. As a result, while the telecenter remained largely unused, DuMont's programs reflected the painful absence of money.

The network's new offerings for the 1953–54 season were practically doomed from the start by third rate scripts and cheap production. *Love Story* was a simpering romance anthology, *The Stranger* was a stale pulp adventure featuring a mysterious Shadow-like character, and *Melody Street* required the performers to lip sync other people's records. Even a series such as *Colonel Humphrey Flack,* with a moderately good character actor (Alan Mowbray) as lead, could not compensate for DuMont's inadequate budgets. Compared to the flashy variety shows, big name sitcoms, and classy drama programs on the other networks, DuMont's series looked cut rate. Fewer and fewer viewers and local stations bothered to even consider DuMont's offerings. The only large audience DuMont attracted in 1954 tuned in for a show the network itself did not stage—the Army-McCarthy hearings broadcast in April, May, and June.

Senator Joseph McCarthy had been awarded his own committee and staff after the Republicans took control of Congress in the 1952 elections. As a member of the President's party, the majority party in Congress, McCarthy acted as if he had been given a blank check to pursue his far-flung investigations of Communist infiltration into any area of public life he wished. He often used the mass media to rally support and to blunt criticism, bending broadcast rules to suit his needs.

In 1949, the FCC had formally articulated a Fairness Doctrine applying to broadcasters in reporting important public issues. Previously, stations had been obliged to cover issues fairly, but also to refrain from expressing their own editorial views. The commission said in the Fairness Doctrine that stations could editorialize on the air, as long as their overall coverage provided "reasonably balanced presentations" of current issues. McCarthy interpreted this to mean that anytime anyone on television took a stand on a controversial issue, an equal and opposing opinion had to be presented. He sold the public on this view and cajoled the individual stations and networks into accepting it, giving him free access to television for the flimsiest of reasons. In November, 1953, after much huffing and puffing, McCarthy even received "equal time" to reply to a TV speech by former President Harry Truman.

In his speech, Truman had merely used the word "McCarthyism"—as the senator's process of guilt-by-inference had been labeled—while defending himself against charges from the new Republican attorney general, Herbert Brownell. That did not matter to McCarthy, who ignored everything Truman said and used the television time to launch a thinly veiled assault on the Eisenhower administration's brother Republicans for not doing a good enough job weeding out Communists. McCarthy also promised to intensify his latest investigation, which was aimed at finding Red subversives in the U.S. Army. For once, it seemed as if McCarthy had aimed his sights too high. The President and the Republican party leaders felt McCarthy needed to learn who was boss and they waited for an appropriate opportunity to discipline him.

On March 7, 1954, CBS broadcast a speech from Miami by Adlai Stevenson, who blasted the Republican party and Senator McCarthy in particular. Though this program was part of the network's policy of regularly offering air time to major political figures, McCarthy immediately demanded equal time to reply. On March 8, the Republican National Committee pulled an end-run around McCarthy by announcing that Vice President Richard Nixon, not McCarthy, would respond to Stevenson. This was the break the networks had been waiting for, and CBS rejected McCarthy's request. McCarthy fumed: "They will grant me the time, or they will learn what the law is. I will guarantee that."

This threat could not be lightly dismissed, and CBS was quick to point to the Republican party action as the reason for its refusal. Though the networks resented McCarthy's heavy-handed demands, he had successfully intimidated them because they knew he generally had strong support from the public and powerful allies in the government. Executives went along to avoid embarrassing public controversies and, more importantly, threats of trouble from the FCC. McCarthy had effectively handpicked two of Eisenhower's nominees for the FCC and the commission almost routinely followed McCarthy's suggestions to investigate "suspicious" broadcasters. In one case, Edward Lamb, an Ohio station owner who had failed to carry McCarthy's speeches, found himself enmeshed in an FCC plot to deprive him of his stations' licenses because of alleged Communist connections. Lamb aggressively defended himself and placed full-page ads in the *New York Times* and other papers offering $10,000 to anyone who could prove he was a Communist. Three years of expensive, drawn-out hearings ensued, and only the depth of Lamb's financial resources and the eventual fading of McCarthy's influence prevented him from being beaten. The message of the Lamb case had not been lost on other broadcasters: Don't mess with McCarthy.

However, McCarthy's seemingly invulnerable stature was shaken when the Republicans circumvented his request for equal time after Stevenson's Miami speech. The next day, March 9, Senator Ralph Flanders of Vermont followed up the action and became the first Republican to attack McCarthy on the Senate floor. Later that night, CBS's Ed Murrow attacked McCarthy in a much larger forum.

Murrow's *See It Now* had moved into prime time on Tuesday evening in the fall of 1953, after two years of Sunday afternoon broadcasts. In October, the program carried a report on a victim of McCarthy-style guilt by association, Lieutenant Milo Radulo-

vich. In March, Murrow and producer Fred Friendly pieced together film clips and information on McCarthy that their crew had assembled and, on March 9, *See It Now* presented "A Report on Senator Joseph McCarthy."

In the program, Murrow deliberately let the film clips speak for themselves because they vividly illustrated McCarthy's style of using half-truths and vague associations to inflame audiences, badger witnesses before his committee, and embarrass people he had under suspicion. After each film sequence, Murrow came on camera, simply noted the inaccurate statements made by the senator, point by point, and then moved on to the next piece. At the conclusion of the report, Murrow underscored the presentation, taking a very strong editorial position:

> . . . It is necessary to investigate before legislating, but the line between investigation and persecuting is a fine one, and the junior senator from Wisconsin has stepped over it repeatedly. . . . We must remember always that accusation is not proof, and that conviction depends upon evidence and due process of law. . . . This is no time for men who oppose Senator McCarthy's methods to keep silent, or for those who approve. . . . The actions of the junior senator from Wisconsin have caused alarm and dismay amongst our allies abroad and given considerable comfort to our enemies, and whose fault is that? Not really his. He didn't create this situation of fear; he merely exploited it, and rather successfully. . . .

Murrow took this step with great trepidation. To spell out his judgment of McCarthy so clearly and firmly violated a cardinal rule in his style of journalism: Don't tell the viewer what the story is supposed to mean; instead present the facts and let the viewer decide. Murrow felt, however, that the issue of McCarthyism was too important and that, in this case, there should be a temporary suspension of the rules.

This suspension was both good and bad for television news. For one thing, it marked a shining moment in broadcast journalism in which Ed Murrow drew the American people's attention to a grave situation many were not aware of. Other reporters in the early 1950s had tried to expose McCarthy as a tricky operator, but none had Murrow's stature and vast television pulpit. Murrow's *See It Now* show on McCarthy set a standard for bravery and decisiveness that television newsmen would measure themselves by for years.

The day after the Murrow broadcast, CBS was flooded with telegrams supporting the show, and Eisenhower praised Senator Flanders for his Senate speech criticizing McCarthy. The tide had turned. CBS turned down McCarthy's request that William F. Buckley appear in his place to respond to Murrow's program. McCarthy had to appear himself. Though McCarthy had often used television to air charges against other people, he was on foreign turf trying to respond to a well-produced documentary with his blustery style. Because Murrow had used McCarthy's own words throughout the report, McCarthy was put in the position of trying to respond to himself. William F. Buckley might have been able to sidestep this problem with the force of his cultivated, smooth manner, but McCarthy would not. Yet he also could not turn down the air time without losing face.

In his filmed reply, McCarthy assumed his usual approach to television: Take the offensive and use the air time to generate other news. He treated Murrow's broadcast as unimportant and not worthy of a detailed reply, turning instead to the juicier topic of a possibly sinister eighteen-month gap in the development of America's first hydrogen bomb. Six days later, while denying any connection with McCarthy's charges, the Atomic Energy Commission suspended the security clearance of J. Robert Oppenheimer, a top nuclear scientist who had urged delay in constructing the H-bomb. Though McCarthy's response to Murrow's program did stir up another controversy, it failed to blunt the impact of the original presentation. More than ever, McCarthy was open for attack.

Murrow's *See It Now* show on McCarthy demonstrated that the medium of television could serve as a powerful independent force with the ability to affect national politics even beyond a national election. Yet the broadcast also opened a Pandora's box of troubles. For the first time, a television newsman had taken a definite stand on a controversial topic and, naturally, there were many viewers who disagreed with his conclusions. More importantly, they questioned Murrow's decision to use *See It Now* to present his personal viewpoint over the air. "Who elected him?" the cry went. A suspicion began to grow that television could be used as a propaganda mouthpiece to champion unpopular causes.

Some of this suspicion was well founded and even some anti-McCarthy forces, who applauded Murrow's show, expressed reservations about the precedent that the *See It Now* episode had set. What would have happened if the tables were turned? If Morrow could awaken the nation with his thoughtful analysis, what could a clever rabble rouser do? What if McCarthy knew television techniques better than he did, and had responded with a slicker program wounding Murrow? Or what if McCarthy had been a broadcaster in the first place? If the networks allowed newsmen to take stands in their newscasts, what could prevent a sharper, better-looking version of Joseph McCarthy from putting everyone in his pocket? The fear of just such an event spread through CBS and, in later years, Murrow found the opportunity to express such a strong conviction on TV much harder to come by. For some people, Murrow's McCarthy broadcast marked the day the device they had so eagerly brought into their homes turned against them, challenging their pre-established views. Television and, more specifically, television news, would never be seen as the same benign servant it had appeared to be before March 9, 1954.

The attacks against McCarthy continued. On March 11, the Army put McCarthy on the defensive by charging that he and his assistant, Roy Cohn, had threatened to "wreck" the Army and Army Secretary Robert T. Stevens if a recently drafted McCarthy staff member, G. David Schine, was not given preferential treatment. Public hearings were scheduled for April to delve into the complicated Army and McCarthy charges and counter-charges.

The thirty-six days of public testimony at the Army-McCarthy hearings were broadcast live by DuMont and ABC, both of which had little or no daytime programming. NBC and CBS, which did, stuck to late night wrapups of each day's proceedings. At first, with the hearings entangled in procedural wrangling, the size of the viewing audience was less than expected. As the personalities and the issues involved sunk in, the public began to tune in. In May, a Cincinnati housewife wrote to a Democratic member of McCarthy's committee:

> Just when do you think you can stop these hearings? My husband has given up his job, just sits and watches those hearings all day, and doesn't work anymore. Being a Democrat, he has laughed so much that he has become ill, and I don't think he'll be able to go back to work even if it was over.

It was soon apparent that all the parties involved knew that the hearings were being staged chiefly for the public. No decision on either side's contentions would be reached in the hearing room in Washington. Instead, throughout the country, the viewing public would decide which side "came over better." On this level, McCarthy lost. His image as a fearsome warrior who was never defeated collapsed and instead he appeared as a venal, cantankerous, pushy man who displayed no sensitivity for the feelings of other people. His frequent interjections of "Mr. Chairman, Mr. Chairman!" and "Point of order!" became national running gags. Panelists on game shows started using them for sure-fire laughs. There was even a song called "Point of Order, Baby, I Love You." McCarthy the person had been separated in the public's mind from the larger issue of anti-communism. Once he became the butt of humor, McCarthy could never again make the nation cower.

In June the hearings ended. ABC and DuMont absorbed their financial losses and the Senate went on to condemn McCarthy in private. Joseph McCarthy was gone, but many of the other transgressions of the "McCarthy era," such as blacklisting, continued unabated for years.

14. Showbiz in a Hurry

ONCE the Army-McCarthy hearings ended and TV programming returned to normal, the prime topic of discussion in television circles was NBC's upcoming series of spectaculars. These were seen as the biggest programming gamble of the new season because network chief Pat Weaver was risking his reputation on the belief that the American public was willing to disrupt its normal viewing patterns in favor of one-shot programming.

There had already been successful examples of Weaver's basic concept in the previous two seasons. To celebrate its fiftieth year in business, the Ford Motor Company, in 1953, had purchased the same prime time slot on all the networks and replaced the regularly scheduled programming with a lavish variety special, "The Ford Fiftieth Anniversary Show." Produced by Leland Hayward at a cost of $500,000, the program featured big name stars such as Mary Martin, Ethel Merman, and Helen Hayes, and won both critical praise and high ratings. General Foods did a similar show in early 1954 on its corporate anniversary. Both programs had a tremendous built-in advantage, however. Because they were on all the networks at once, there was no competition—their ratings had to be high. Pat Weaver felt that such programming could succeed on a regular basis even carried by only one network, and he presented the spectaculars as the gimmick that would pump new life into the schedule and help NBC to regain its position as the number one network.

Sponsors found the concept of frequently scheduled specials disturbing because it disrupted the usual audience flow from one familiar series to another. After extended negotiations during the winter and spring of 1954, the spectaculars received advertising support—primarily based on Weaver's track record with such hit concepts as *Today* and *Your Show of Shows*. NBC's publicity department then went to work cranking out mountains of notices which created the impression that the entire television world was about to undergo a massive alteration and that NBC would crush its competition with the spectaculars. Once a month, ninety minutes of the network's normal entertainment schedule on Saturday, Sunday, and Monday would be replaced by Weaver's spectaculars: special programs of either variety, drama, comedy, or music.

Max Liebman, the former producer of *Your Show of Shows*, was put in charge of the Saturday and Sunday slots. The Monday night program, called *Producers' Showcase*, was to be a cooperative, supervised by Fred Coe, who had recently left *The Philco/Goodyear Television Playhouse*. Individual guest producers were scheduled

to handle the details of each Monday broadcast, while Coe assumed overall responsibility. Though the exact format of both Liebman and Coe's programs was unclear, sponsors knew that whatever form they took, the shows would be big, expensive, and in color (an added incentive to boost color set sales). The television industry anxiously awaited the night of the first spectacular, Sunday, September 12. It was a disaster.

For ninety minutes live from New York, Max Liebman presented "Satins and Spurs" in four acts, thirteen scenes, in color, at a cost of $300,000. Star Betty Hutton jumped, twirled, sang, and yelled the part of a rodeo performer in New York City who fell for a photographer from *Life* magazine. Critics described the production as loud and annoying, somewhat sophomoric, and certainly not spectacular. Though "Satins and Spurs" had been labeled an original musical comedy, they also noticed a strong resemblance to "Annie Get Your Gun," a Broadway musical comedy that had also starred Betty Hutton.

Worst of all, the ten-city Trendex ratings service (which emphasized speed by focusing on fewer cities than the national Nielsen ratings) indicated that Ed Sullivan's *Toast of the Town* had devastated the first spectacular, registering twice the audience. From the start, the spectaculars were given a black eye. Betty Hutton said she was quitting television. Nervous sponsors began muttering about throwing away their money and sent their lawyers searching for ways to break contracts. Liebman's second show, "Lady in the Dark," a Broadway adaptation starring Ann Southern, barely beat its CBS competition—at a price of $500,000.

In spite of all the advance publicity, the nation's viewers had not joyfully risen to embrace the spectaculars, the competition had not been destroyed, and sales of color television sets were as abysmal as ever. Pat Weaver held firm, saying, "Take my word for it, this is it!" He knew that his spectaculars required a major change in audience habits. It would take time for the public to adjust to the idea of setting aside a familiar program routine for a one-time special. In October, a major psychological break occurred. The season's first national Nielsen ratings (which took almost a month to compile) gave the spectaculars generally higher ratings than the Trendex service had. Sensing that maybe the programs were not as disastrous as they first appeared, the skeptics decided to withhold final judgment for a while.

Despite the reprieve, the spectaculars still faced a tremendous uphill battle. Some of the difficulties were inherent in the format of a one-shot show. Unlike a weekly series, which could draw on its familiar structure, continuing characters, or running gags, the spectaculars had to present something entirely new for every outing. Each program required new scenery, a new story line, and a new line-up of stars. Even one month was not enough time to properly plan, write, and rehearse the productions.

The spectaculars faced an additional problem. Because of the tremendous ballyhoo that preceded them, public expectations were far higher than for any individual segment of a continuing series. Even with the live drama anthologies, which faced many of the same time and rehearsal pressures, there was always next week's production. With a once-a-month big budget spectacular, every presentation was expected to be special. Any Broadway producer could point out the problems of trying to throw together a successful show from scratch every few weeks. Even with adequate preparation and rehearsal, many plays and revues on Broadway flopped. Television compounded the difficulties and underscored failure. Unlike Broadway productions which could open, play awhile, and build an audience—or quietly close after unfavorable reviews—a TV spectacular had one chance. One night, no previews. Worse yet, there were only two or three other stations to choose from so that a failure, or even a mediocre effort, stood out much more on TV than it would on Broadway.

Trying to solve some of these problems, Max Liebman very quickly began to adopt some familiar trappings from regular series, especially on his Sunday spectaculars against Ed Sullivan. In late October he teamed Judy Holliday, Steve Allen, and Dick Shawn to form the central cast for a musical-comedy revue, "Sunday in Town." The team clicked and throughout the remainder of the season they reappeared on a number of Sunday evenings, with different guests but in the same sort of revue. Liebman saved his more unusual shows for Saturday night, when the competition was not as formidable. One of his best productions was a musical version of "Babes in Toyland" starring Jack E. Leonard as the inventor of castor oil, Wally Cox as a toymaker, and Dave Garroway as Santa Claus. By Christmas, spectaculars, while still viewed with deep suspicion, were pulling in decent ratings and were no longer a dirty word. It was Fred Coe, however, who wiped out any remaining doubts about the ratings potential of the spectaculars with his March 7 presentation of the Sir James Barrie fantasy classic, "Peter Pan."

Coe, like Max Liebman, had experienced difficulties at the beginning of the season with his spectacular slot. As a result, *Producers' Showcase* generally downplayed original productions and stuck to less risky adaptations of Broadway chestnuts. Though well done, these did not generate much excitement. They seemed to belie the spectacular buildup by focusing on well-worn material that could have just as easily fit into an average drama anthology program. With "Peter Pan," though, Coe brought a successful Broadway production to television almost intact only nine days after it had finished its theatrical run. Not only was interest in the show high, but the cast and crew were exceptionally sharp. In effect, they had been practicing for months for their TV appearance and the program reflected their confidence and energy.

"Peter Pan" was the story of a magical trip by several turn-of-the-century London children to another world. Working with a $700,000 budget and the excellent cast, Coe and producer Richard Halliday skillfully adapted the elaborate stage choreography for television, retaining both the sense of wonder and the spirit of youthful adventure from the original. Mary Martin as Peter Pan, an impish pixie, flew about the studio aided by nearly invisible wires, guiding the children under the care of the oldest child, Wendy

Darling (Kathy Nolan), to Never-Never Land. There they had a series of adventures, culminating in a fearful battle with the villainous scalawag and pirate, Captain Hook (Cyril Ritchard). In the spirit of the fanciful evening, even the Ford automobile commercials were staged as humorous productions, presented by Ernie Kovacs and Edie Adams.

The public response to "Peter Pan" was extraordinary. One-third to one-half of all Americans saw the program. Twenty-one million TV homes, containing sixty-five million to seventy-five million viewers, tuned in. "Peter Pan" became the highest rated show of television's brief history and served to convince sponsors that spectaculars could live up to Pat Weaver's promises. By the end of the season, all but one of the sponsors for NBC's spectaculars renewed.

Even CBS offered its own "minor spectacular" color programs for the 1954–55 season, though the network's two monthly shows—*Best of Broadway* and *Shower of Stars*—rarely reached the level of NBC's productions. CBS had decided to try such special programming late into the planning for the fall, and the lack of preparation and whole-hearted commitment showed through. *Shower of Stars*, which replaced the Thursday night drama anthology *Climax* once a month, wasted big name stars such as Betty Grable, Harry James, and Mario Lanza in splashy but slapdash variety programs. *Best of Broadway*, the monthly stand-in for CBS's Wednesday night boxing matches, usually stuck to merely adequate one-hour cut-downs of old Broadway classics. Yet even this show scored well when, like "Peter Pan," it used an experienced crew that had worked out the production kinks long before the play was brought to television. In January, 1955, for example, members of the original Broadway cast of "Arsenic and Old Lace" (including Boris Karloff) reunited for a succesful new television production of the macabre murder story.

Despite the recovery by the spectaculars after their disastrous start, programmers, sponsors, and viewers soon came to realize that only a handful of the shows could possibly live up to the tremendous advance hype. This in itself represented an important shift in attitude because it broke the dependence on an unchanging weekly routine that the networks had automatically carried over from radio. Spectaculars proved that, with the right mix, a special program could succeed and provide a temporary, but dramatic, ratings boost for a network.

Pat Weaver's once-a-month spectacular schedule survived on NBC for three seasons, though to meet production deadlines the shows often settled for traditional variety showcases and safe Broadway adaptations in between truly "spectacular" events. By the late Fifties, the monthly frequency of such programming was reduced to a more realistic and manageable level and the term "spectacular" was replaced by the less bombastic description of "special." Nonetheless, even as irregularly scheduled specials, Weaver's concept provided an important opportunity to try something different on television, and they often served as a showcase for the best programming television had to offer.

In the prime time ratings race for the 1954–55 season the spectaculars proved too erratic to deliver consistent blockbuster ratings against CBS's strong weekly series. With full sponsor support after the success of "Peter Pan," though, Pat Weaver looked optimistically toward the following season for the flowering of the spectaculars and the promised return of NBC's supremacy.

Besides the spectaculars, the most important addition to the network's schedule that fall was the late night *Tonight* show. Pat Weaver had been tremendously successful with the early morning *Today* show and the mid-morning *Home* program, so in preparing

MONDAY

Network	7:00	7:30	8:00	8:30	9:00	9:30	10:00	10:30
ABC	Kukla, Fran And Ollie / John Daly & The News	The Name's The Same	COME CLOSER	Voice Of Firestone	College Press Conference	Boxing From Eastern Parkway		Neutral Corner
CBS	local	CBS News / Perry Como	Burns And Allen Show	Arthur Godfrey's Talent Scouts	I Love Lucy	December Bride	Studio One	
DUMONT	Captain Video / MORGAN BEATTY	local	ILONA MASSEY SHOW	local	Monday Night Fights From St. Nicholas Arena With Chris Schenkel			At Ringside
NBC	local	Tony Martin / Camel News	CAESAR'S HOUR @PRODUCER'S SHOWCASE		MEDIC	Robert Montgomery Presents		local

TUESDAY

Network	7:00	7:30	8:00	8:30	9:00	9:30	10:00	10:30
ABC	Kukla, Fran And Ollie / John Daly & The News	Cavalcade Of America	local	Twenty Questions	Make Room For Daddy	U.S. Steel Hour / Elgin Hour		Stop The Music
CBS	local	CBS News / Jo Stafford	Red Skelton Hour	HALLS OF IVY	Meet Millie	Danger	Life With Father	See It Now
DUMONT	Captain Video / MORGAN BEATTY	local	Life Is Worth Living	STUDIO 57	local			
NBC	local	Dinah Shore / Camel News	Milton Berle Show / Martha Raye Show @Bob Hope Show		Fireside Theater	Armstrong Circle Theater	Truth Or Consequences	IT'S A GREAT LIFE

WEDNESDAY

Network	7:00	7:30	8:00	8:30	9:00	9:30	10:00	10:30
ABC	Kukla, Fran And Ollie / John Daly & The News	DISNEYLAND		New Stu Erwin Show	Masquerade Party	Enterprise U.S.A.	local	
CBS	local	CBS News / Perry Como	Arthur Godfrey And His Friends		Strike It Rich	I've Got A Secret	Blue Ribbon Bouts @BEST OF BROADWAY	Sports Spot
DUMONT	Captain Video / MORGAN BEATTY	local			Chicago Symphony Orchestra		Down You Go	GREATEST PRO FOOTBALL PLAYS
NBC	local	Eddie Fisher / Camel News	I Married Joan	My Little Margie	Kraft Television Theater I		This Is Your Life	Big Town

THURSDAY

Network	7:00	7:30	8:00	8:30	9:00	9:30	10:00	10:30
ABC	Kukla, Fran And Ollie / John Daly & The News	The Lone Ranger	THE MAIL STORY	Treasury Men In Action	So You Want To Lead A Band	Kraft Television Theater II		local
CBS	local	CBS News / Jane Froman	Ray Milland Show	CLIMAX @SHOWER OF STARS		Four Star Playhouse	Public Defender	Name That Tune
DUMONT	Captain Video / MORGAN BEATTY	local	They Stand Accused		What's The Story	local		
NBC	local	Dinah Shore / Camel News	You Bet Your Life	Justice	Dragnet	Ford Theater	Lux Video Theater	

FRIDAY

Network	7:00	7:30	8:00	8:30	9:00	9:30	10:00	10:30
ABC	Kukla, Fran And Ollie / John Daly & The News	RIN TIN TIN	Ozzie And Harriet	Ray Bolger Show	Dollar A Second	THE VISE	local	
CBS	local	CBS News / Perry Como	Mama	Topper	Schlitz Playhouse Of Stars	Our Miss Brooks	THE LINEUP	Person To Person
DUMONT	Captain Video / MORGAN BEATTY	local			The Stranger	One Minute Please	Chance Of A Lifetime	TIME WILL TELL
NBC	local	Eddie Fisher / Camel News	Red Buttons Show @JACK CARSON	The Life Of Riley	The Big Story	DEAR PHOEBE	Gillette Cavalcade Of Sports	Moments In Sports

SATURDAY

Network	7:00	7:30	8:00	8:30	9:00	9:30	10:00	10:30
ABC	local	COMPASS	LET'S DANCE		Saturday Night Fights	Fight Talk	Stork Club	local
CBS	Gene Autry Show	Beat The Clock	Jackie Gleason Show		Two For The Money	My Favorite Husband	That's My Boy	WILLY
DUMONT	local		National Football League Pro Football					
NBC	Mr. Wizard	Ethel And Albert	HEY MULLIGAN	Place The Face	IMOGENE COCA / Texaco Star Theater @MAX LIEBMAN PRESENTS I		GEORGE GOBEL	Your Hit Parade

SUNDAY

Network	7:00	7:30	8:00	8:30	9:00	9:30	10:00	10:30
ABC	You Asked For It	Pepsi Cola Playhouse	Flight #7	The Big Picture	Walter Winchell / Martha Wright	Dr. IO	Break The Bank	local
CBS	LASSIE	Private Secretary / Jack Benny Program	Toast Of The Town		G.E. Theater @Fred Waring Show	HONESTLY CELESTE	FATHER KNOWS BEST	What's My Line
DUMONT	local	Opera Cameos	local	Author Meets The Critics	Rocky King, Inside Detective	Life Begins At 80	The Music Show	local
NBC	PEOPLE ARE FUNNY	Mr. Peepers	Colgate Comedy Hour @MAX LIEBMAN PRESENTS II		Goodyear/Philco Television Playhouse		Loretta Young Show	The Hunter

for the 1954–55 season he turned his attention to the period immediately following prime time. In 1950 and 1951, NBC had ventured into the post-prime time slot with a one-hour variety-talk program at 11:00 P.M., *Broadway Open House,* and had discovered that there was a surprisingly large reservoir of late night viewers. When host Jerry Lester left the program, the network was unable to come up with a personality that the affiliates would accept as a replacement, so, reluctantly, NBC turned back the time to the locals. They, in turn, were more than happy to run old movies and sell the lucrative commercial time themselves. Though not ruling out the resumption of network control, the affiliates made it clear that any new late night program would have to be worth more to them than their films.

Eager to reclaim the time, the network floated alternative plans such as a midnight mystery show and live extravaganzas from the streets of New York City, but these were dismissed as unproven and too risky. NBC soon revived the notion of the talk-variety format and began to search for an appropriate host. It was generally agreed that Jerry Lester's distinctive personality had made *Broadway Open House* click and that if the network could find someone with similar strengths the locals would probably buy the show. The major stumbling block to launching such a program from scratch was that any new host—no matter how talented—needed time to build a following.

The solution to the late night problem began to emerge in 1953 when Steve Allen joined NBC. Allen had worked previously as a variety-talk host on a number of programs broadcast at odd hours on CBS and, in July, he was given a forty-minute show (just before midnight) weeknights on NBC's local New York City station. In effect, this slot provided him with a major market showcase for his approach to late night television. He quickly demonstrated that his many years of experience as a television performer on five days a week had taught him the basics for survival in the daily grind. Above all, Allen realized that funny routines were not as important as a positive, identifiable personality:

If the audience likes you, they'll laugh at anything you say. . . . The reason people don't tire of Arthur Godfrey is that he doesn't do anything. Martin and Lewis put on a much better show, but the audience gets tired of them quicker. I have found that people get tired of you on TV nine times faster than they do on radio.

Allen drew on his dry, humorous appreciation for the irrelevant and often overlooked aspects of life to project a casual, distinctive TV personality. He also surrounded himself with a talented family of supporting players, beginning with singers Steve Lawrence and Helen Dixon (who was soon replaced by Eydie Gorme). By the fall of 1954, he had gained enough support from NBC affiliates to move his *Tonight* show onto the network schedule, beginning September 27, 1954. For ninety minutes each weeknight, the program came live to the East and Midwest. Slowly, it began to catch on with the national audience.

By the time *Tonight* began its network run, Allen's supporting family had grown to include former disk jockey Gene Rayburn as his announcer, band leader Skitch Henderson, and singer Andy Williams. Over the years other performers joined the troupe, but Steve Allen always remained the focus of the entertainment. Dubbed "the midnight Godfrey," Allen would stroll through the studio, play the piano, conduct humorous interviews with members of the audience, and ad-lib routines with the regulars. His most popular reoccurring bits were "man-on-the-street" interviews and his "reports to the nation." Though Allen was willing to try virtually any comic stunt (he once took a swim in a huge vat of gelatin), he also occasionally delved into serious non-showbiz topics with his guests. Under Allen, *Tonight* developed into a consistent ratings hit for NBC, reestablishing the network's hold on the slot and providing the model for late night entertainment that would survive for decades.

Just as *Tonight* reached the network schedule, twenty-nine-year-old Los Angeles comic Johnny Carson, a self-effacing, quiet charmer who had hosted a mundane prime time quiz show during the summer of 1954, received his big break on CBS. Red Skelton hurt himself one night in rehearsal for his live comedy-variety show and Carson, who wrote for Skelton, was picked as a last minute stand-in. Carson's on-the-spot cool won him his own prime time summer series on CBS in 1955. In *The Johnny Carson Show*, Carson appeared as emcee to a traditional comedy-variety mix of singers, dancers, guests, skits, and monologues, but it just did not work. After years of developing his "boy down the block" appeal into a strong ad-lib personality, he seemed to be miscast in a heavily scripted prime time format. Though the summer series continued into the fall, by the spring of 1956 Carson was taken out of the evening schedule and slotted into the daytime, where he flourished. He later compared the freedom allowed in daytime television (and, he might have added, late nighttime) with the restrictions imposed in the closely watched prime time shows:

I think that any comic who appears as a personality, week after week [in prime time] has got to lose ground in two or three years . . . in daytime, you can be relaxed and informal, but an easy informal show won't go [in prime time] because people aren't conditioned to it.

While the late night *Tonight* show and the spectaculars eventually caught on, the performance of NBC's comedy-variety showcases, the mainstay of the network's prime time schedule, proved to be disappointing. *Your Show of Shows* star Sid Caesar brought along sidekicks Carl Reiner and Howard Morris to his new vehicle, *Caesar's Hour*, but the program had a shaky takeoff with weak sketches

and a lack of direction. Though the show stabilized by mid-season with the writing and production returning to Caesar's previous levels of quality, *Caesar's Hour* could not overcome CBS's powerful Monday night sitcom line-up. Red Buttons came over from CBS, but was unable to find a format or writers that clicked for him. Every few months he reworked his show, but it died at the end of the season.

On Sunday, the sagging *Colgate Comedy Hour* lost the services of most of the few strong headliners it had left. Dean Martin and Jerry Lewis appeared infrequently; Jimmy Durante and Donald O'Connor moved to a reactivated *Texaco Star Theater* (Texaco had bailed out of Milton Berle's show in 1953, when production costs seemed to be soaring out of sight); and Eddie Cantor jumped ship entirely. Cantor signed with the independent film syndicator, Ziv, to do two years of half-hour variety shows, but the syndicated product seemed cheap in comparison to his previous network offerings. After a half-year of tepid local ratings, Cantor, citing ill health, parted ways with Ziv and retired from regular television work.

After the many defections, *The Colgate Comedy Hour* focused more and more on flashy sets and production numbers rather than the comedy headliners. Singer Gordon MacRae became a semi-regular host and, during the summer of 1955, Paramount Pictures supplied guest stars and clips from upcoming films. The studio treated the TV shows as little more than a chance to plug its new films for free, so programs such as a "behind the scenes peak" at "Pete Kelly's Blues" were really just sixty-minute ads. Yet even with these excesses, Paramount's involvement with a network television show reflected the fact that the long-standing Hollywood-television feud was beginning to cool.

In the early years of television, the major Hollywood studios chose to meet the TV challenge by treating the new medium with

---

September 11, 1954
"Miss America Pageant." (ABC). John Daly and Bess Myerson host the first television coverage of Atlantic City's annual fall rite, as Lee Ann Meriwether (of California) wins the top prize.

September 27, 1954
Morgan Beatty and the News. (DuMont). The third and final try by DuMont at a nightly news show.

October 3, 1954
Father Knows Best. (CBS). Robert Young plays an all-knowing, patient father. Low ratings nearly kill the series in its first season.

October 21, 1954
James Bond comes to the screen for the first time in "Casino Royale" on CBS's *Climax* anthology. All-American Barry Nelson is the urbane secret agent and Peter Lorre plays a Soviet operative.

November 7, 1954
Face the Nation. (CBS). A Sunday afternoon answer to NBC's *Meet the Press.* CBS's Ted Koop is moderator and Senator Joseph McCarthy is the first guest.

January 2, 1955
The Bob Cummings Show. (NBC). A product of the mind of Paul Henning. Bob Cummings plays an oversexed, swinging bachelor photographer. The series (later retitled *Love That Bob*) also has a great line-up of sidekicks: Rosemary DeCamp as Bob's widowed sister, Dwayne Hickman as her son, Chuck, and Ann B. Davis as Bob's assistant, Schultzy.

Fess Parker *(r.)* as Davy Crockett, "King of the Wild Frontier," with Buddy Ebsen as sidekick George Russel. *(Walt Disney Productions)*

disdain. They refused to give it any help or support, pretending that television might fade away if they just ignored it. Network executives, who had seen radio profits in the 1930s diluted by the involvement of West Coast production agencies, were similarly wary of the major West Coast studios. As a result, when the networks began looking for sources of filmed programs, they turned to small independent filmmakers. CBS and NBC, which early on recognized the many practical advantages of West Coast TV production, were able to keep almost complete control over any live and filmed work done for them in Hollywood. By 1954, both had built huge live studios in California and had established working agreements with the smaller filmmakers. As independents such as Desilu prospered, the possibility of the networks and the major studios working together seemed increasingly remote.

If the major studios had not been so determined to ignore the challenge of television in the 1940s, they might have realized from the beginning that the new competitor could also open a new field of production to them, films for television. They, not the small independents, should have led the way in producing TV sitcoms, spy chillers, and adventure yarns. Even following the ruling in the Paramount case of 1948 which forced the major studios to surrender control of their lucrative theater chains, they seriously questioned the viability of TV films and made no moves to court the networks.

There were a few exceptions to Hollywood's "hands off TV" policy, chiefly in efforts by individual film actors and producers. In February, 1950, star Robert Montgomery began producing and often starring in an NBC drama anthology series sponsored by Lucky Strike. The fall of 1952 brought the first major defections to the television market—David Niven, Dick Powell, Charles Boyer, and Ida Lupino, who alternated as the stars of CBS's *Four Star Playhouse,* a thirty-minute filmed anthology. In 1953, Loretta Young began the sudsy *Letters to Loretta,* which staged heart-throb soapy situations described in Young's fan mail and cast her as a Dear Abby-style counselor who offered possible solutions after each story. That same year, matinee idol Ray Milland played the

part of an addlebrained drama professor at a women's college in *Meet Mr. McNutley.* While bringing some big name Hollywood stars to television, these efforts in no way reflected a change of heart by any of the major studios or the networks. Instead, the Hollywood-network feud ended gradually as both sides discovered that they could use each other.

ABC, which was far behind CBS and NBC in the ratings, had made the first serious moves toward Hollywood at the beginning of the decade. More than the others, ABC needed help in producing and developing enough programs to fill its schedule, and the network was one of the first to rely on vanguard filmed series such as *The Lone Ranger.* ABC had also turned to Hollywood for financial help when, in 1953, it merged with United Paramount Theaters for a much-needed influx of cash. As Hollywood became an increasingly important television production center following such successes as *I Love Lucy* and *Dragnet,* ABC decided to take a chance with an established film studio in the hope of finding a blockbuster hit. On April 2, 1954, the network signed an agreement with the Walt Disney studios for a one-hour weekly series beginning in the fall of 1954, *Disneyland.*

ABC's agreement with Disney represented several important changes in television programming philosophy. Though Disney was not one of the eight major Hollywood studios, it was the largest to venture into full scale television production at the time. More importantly, by turning to Disney, ABC was tacitly admitting that unlike CBS and NBC it was willing to rely on outside sources— even established film studios—for major programs, thereby conceding loss of network control. ABC paid a premium price for the Disney series, including funds toward the construction of a "Disneyland" amusement park planned for Anaheim, California. In return, the network received twenty one-hour programs, which were to be rerun to fill out the entire season.

ABC considered *Disneyland* its biggest hope for the 1954–55 season and very quickly sold out the available ad time on the show. The network also decided to use the program for a calculated assault against the programming strategies of the competition and scheduled it to run Wednesdays, from 7:30 P.M. to 8:30 P.M. At the time, CBS and NBC did not begin prime time broadcasting until 8:00 P.M., filling the 7:30–8:00 P.M. period with fifteen minutes of news and fifteen minutes of musical entertainment. (Perry Como, Jo Stafford, and Jane Froman appeared on CBS while Tony Martin, Dinah Shore, and Eddie Fisher sang on NBC.) Only ABC had regularly scheduled half-hour programs in the 7:30 P.M. slot but, aside from *The Lone Ranger,* these had never made a significant difference in the ratings. As a one-hour program, however, *Disneyland* would be in progress when the other networks began their prime time shows, giving ABC a critical edge. Just as important, *Disneyland* would begin early enough to catch the attention of the nation's children by providing an attractive alternative to news and music. ABC was counting on them to raise a ruckus and control the channel selection as family viewing began for the evening. The kids came through.

Disneyland premiered in late October, 1954, to rave reviews. One critic declared: "It's happened and it's wonderful!" Drawing on more than twenty years of theatrical material, as well as new features shot specifically for the television show, *Disneyland* presented a delightful combination of kiddie adventure yarns, travelogues, real-life nature stories, mildly educational documentaries, and classic Disney animation. It was the perfect family show and a resounding ratings success, providing ABC with its first top ten hit in five years.

Until his death in 1966, Walt Disney himself hosted the series, demonstrating how to mix promotion, education, and homespun humor into an enchanting visit to the "magic kingdom." Though in effect many of the shows were actually plugs for one of Disney's new theatrical features or for the Disneyland amusement park, they were always entertaining. Disney the showman never forgot that people, especially children, watched television for pleasure and that they would accept a commercial pitch as well as some basic history and science if it was well done and fun to follow. One episode, meant to coincide with the release of Disney's "20,000 Leagues Under the Sea" (based on the Jules Verne novel), focused on the complex underwater photography techniques used in the production. The program was a perfect promotion for the film (which was a box office smash) yet also a worthwhile documentary (it received an Emmy award). Viewers actually were interested in how the special effects had been staged for that adventure film.

The frequent glimpses of Disney's California amusement park put Anaheim, California, at the top of every child's list of dream vacation spots, but the most dramatic instance of fan support began in December when *Disneyland* touched off a nationwide fad with the first of five programs fantasizing the life of Western hero Davy Crockett. In response to the stories (which starred Fess Parker in the title role and Buddy Ebsen as Crockett's sidekick, George Russel), a Davy Crockett mania swept the nation. It seemed as if every child—along with many adults—owned a "genuine imitation" Davy Crockett coonskin cap. Senator Estes Kefauver wore one through most of his 1956 campaign for the presidency. There were even seventeen recordings of "The Ballad of Davy Crockett" competing for the fans' attention.

By the spring of 1955, the competition on the other networks was reeling. NBC's *I Married Joan* was knocked off the air and Arthur Godfrey saw a huge chunk of his audience carved away. Due to a short production year, *Disneyland* operated on a 20–20–12 schedule its first season, meaning that the twenty episodes were presented, then all twenty were repeated (beginning on March 26), and then twelve selected episodes were run a third time during the summer. This procedure was almost unheard of at the time,

yet the ratings for the Davy Crockett episodes actually increased for the reruns, and the drop off in viewers for the third runs was nowhere near what had been feared. *Disneyland* proved once and for all the viability of reruns as well as the strength of kiddie-related programming. The series kept right on rolling through the mid- and late Fifties, serving as a display window for such Disney classics as "Alice in Wonderland," "Treasure Island," and "The Legend of Sleepy Hollow," as well as endless reels of cartoons featuring such familiar Disney characters as Donald Duck, Mickey Mouse, Goofy, and Pluto. The program moved to NBC in 1961 where it went to color and eventually became the longest running prime time series on television.

The success of *Disneyland* in the 1954–55 season provided a tremendous boost to ABC and convinced executives at both the Hollywood studios and the networks that a potential ratings bonanza lay at their feet. In planning for the fall of 1955, NBC and CBS joined ABC in scheduling programs produced by other major Hollywood studios as the first tentative followups to *Disneyland.* At the same time, number one CBS also made a hasty decision to eliminate its 7:30–8:00 P.M. news and music block in the fall and to fill it instead with kidvid programming. (NBC resisted that temptation for two more years.) The performance of two other early evening kiddie-related series—*Lassie* and *Rin Tin Tin*—underscored the fact that children were increasingly important in program selection, and CBS was determined not to cede the advantage in that market to ABC.

The Adventures of Rin Tin Tin, which led off ABC's Friday night schedule, became the network's second top ten program for the 1954–55 season. The show starred a perspicacious German shepherd, Rin Tin Tin, that barked out orders in a post-Civil War frontier camp, Fort Apache. Surrounding the canine was a set of characters that soon set the standard for kiddie TV action shows: a young child (Lee Aaker as Corporal Rusty, who theoretically owned Rin Tin Tin), his strong clean-cut male guidance figure (James Brown as Lieutenant Rip Masters), and the bumbling comic friend-of-the-hero (Joe Sawyer as Sergeant Biff O'Hara). The venerable quartet of animal, kid, man, and comic fool followed the grade B adventure formula of fights, frantic gunplay, and dramatic chases in a program that was, like *The Lone Ranger,* an effective television equivalent to the Saturday kiddie matinees and radio adventure shows of the Thirties and Forties. Rin Tin Tin, in fact, had first appeared on the silver screen in 1923 and subsequently starred in a successful four-year radio adventure series before turning up at Fort Apache.

The other dog star of the season was CBS's Lassie, a cerebral collie that had also appeared in films and on the radio in the Forties. In contrast to *Rin Tin Tin's* rugged Western adventures, television's *Lassie* adhered to the spirit of the heart-tugging MGM film "Lassie Come Home" and focused on "the world of love and adventure shared by a boy and his dog." Though the program included dramatic animal heroics to keep the children interested, the series was a gentle family show featuring tales of kindly people who were in trouble and received help from Lassie. A pair of young boys, Jeff Miller (Tommy Rettig) and Timmy (Jon Provost), along with a trio of mothers (played by Jan Clayton, Cloris Leachman, and June Lockhart) appeared as Lassie's sidekicks until the 1960s. Then the dog began wandering from the care of such families taking up first with a park ranger and later striking off on her own, sleeping under the stars with itinerant raccoons and squirrels. During her final season in the early 1970s, Lassie even fell in love and gave birth to a litter of puppies.

Kidvid was yet another hit formula that was done best on film in Hollywood, rather than live from New York, and a line of imitations was inevitable. *I Love Lucy* had spawned dozens of screwball sitcoms, and copies of NBC's first important filmed series, *Dragnet,* were already on the air.

By early 1954, *Dragnet* was regularly coming in number two in the ratings, right behind *I Love Lucy,* and each of the networks had planned similar "docudrama" shows for the 1954–55 season. CBS presented the most blatant duplicate, *The Lineup,* a cop show produced in cooperation with the San Francisco police department. Warter Anderson played Lieutenant Ben Guthrie, a slightly more talkative version of *Dragnet's* Sergeant Joe Friday. Like Friday, he fought everyday crime in a generally realistic setting, with stories based on actual cases from the police department's files.

The next step in cashing in on the success of *Dragnet* was to take the docudrama format into another profession. NBC's Worthington Miner produced one of the best of such series, the "authentic medical dramatizations" of *Medic,* starring Richard Boone as Doctor Konrad Styner. Overall, *Medic* did a good job duplicating the manner in which real doctors handled life-or-death cases, as Miner combined in-house jargon—like *Dragnet*—with such innovative touches as intercutting film footage of real-life surgery with close-ups of a white-masked, profusely sweating Richard Boone. Along with doctors there were also lawyers, with Gary Merrill starring in NBC's live *Justice* series. Producer David Susskind drew from the files of the National Legal Aid Society and usually focused on poor people needing legal advice.

ABC also jumped on the docudrama form in the fall of 1954 but, in searching for a suitable new profression to protray, the network came up with a rather silly vehicle, *The Mail Story* (subtitled "Handle With Care"), based on the files of the United States Post Office Department. Herb Nelson played the "relentless" inspector who tracked down the malefactors that used the mails to send subversive explosives, threatening letters, junk mail—anything that could undermine the moral edifice of the nation. The hokey series lasted only three months and disappeared before it could spawn its own logical spinoffs, *Insufficient Postage* and *Overdue Book.*

Even as the networks continued to expand their reliance on Hollywood filmed series, they also maintained their New York-based drama anthologies. These East Coast programs were particularly powerful because, after years of developing plays for television, the producers and writers had come of age. They had learned what worked best within the limitations imposed by live television and consequently turned out an amazing number of high quality original plays.

Aspiring new writers had flocked to the drama anthology programs because they knew that a successful TV production could very well be picked up by Hollywood and turned into a theatrical feature. This had happened in 1953 with Paddy Chayefsky's "Marty" and since then many of the most popular TV plays were selected for film treatment. The writers also came to realize that with so many anthology programs to fill, they had a constant opportunity to experiment and grow. Neither Broadway nor Hollywood offered so many script outlets, and many of the best TV writers used the shows to develop simple mood pieces and slices of life. They sharpened their sense of character interaction and dialogue, developing a needlelike perception of human relationships. Their stories often focused on the difficult personal decisions faced by realistic people and the consequences of their actions. In the process of turning out these intimate, human stories, both the veterans and the newcomers produced a string of outstanding dramatic productions that matched and sometimes even surpassed the best works on stage and in the movies.

January 19, 1955
President Eisenhower allows television crews to film his press conferences for the first time. ABC gives the delayed films a weekly prime time slot.

January 19, 1955
The Millionaire. (CBS). Fabulously wealthy J. Beresford Tipton starts handing out million-dollar checks, through his executive secretary, Michael Anthony (Marvin Miller). Oddly, on the first episode, a woman *refuses* the loot because she does not want to be richer than her fiancé!

March 7, 1955
Steve Allen is emcee for the first nationwide telecast of the Emmy Awards, presented by NBC.

March 15, 1955
"No Time for Sergeants" plays on ABC's *U.S. Steel Hour.* What it was, was Gomer.

April 16, 1955
CBS captures the Saturday afternoon baseball game of the week from ABC. In 1957, NBC gets in on the action by signing away a few teams as a basis for a separate Saturday baseball series.

June 6, 1955
Chet Huntley defects from ABC to NBC.

July 21, 1955
CBS removes *See It Now* from the weekly prime time schedule, slotting it as an hour-long monthly floating special instead.

ABC's often retitled *Elgin Hour,* produced by Herb Brodkin, presented "Crime in the Streets" by Reginald Rose. John Cassavetes starred as the leader of a teenage gang in this perceptive portrayal of the bitterness, loneliness, and violence of slum life that turned natural born leaders into outlaws. *The Elgin Hour* alternated with *The U.S. Steel Hour* (directed by Alex Segal), which had premiered in November, 1953, with a David Davidson original, "P.O.W." Richard Kiley and Brian Keith played former Korean war captives who attempted to defend the ways they handled the pressures while in a prisoner-of-war camp. Gary Merrill was the American psychiatrist who listened intently to their stories.

In subsequent productions, *The U.S. Steel Hour* presented Frank Gilroy's "Last Notch," a serious Western featuring Jeff Morrow as George Temple, a mild mannered man who happened to be the fastest gun in town. Because people were constantly coming to town to challenge him, he found himself repeatedly facing total strangers and killing them. The story was in the spirit of two adult Westerns that had been successful theatrical films, "High Noon" (in 1952) and "Shane" (in 1953). In March, 1955, the program offered a much lighter tale, "No Time for Sergeants," based on the hit book by Mac Hyman. Andy Griffith—who had made a name for himself the year before with a left field hit record, "What It Was, Was Football"—played Will Stockdale, a Georgia farm boy drafted into the Air Force. In uniform, he constantly bedeviled his sergeant (played by Harry Clark) with his unorthodox plowboy logic. The success of the TV play inspired a film, which was a virtual copy of the television production except that Don Knotts was cast as the goggle-eyed camp psychologist. In the 1960s, Andy Griffith used the same format for *Gomer Pyle, U.S.M.C.,* a spinoff from his own successful TV series.

CBS's drama showcase, *Studio One*, produced by Felix Jackson, presented three works by the prolific Reginald Rose that season. "Thunder on Sycamore Street" touched on the sensitive issue of racial prejudice by depicting an analogous situation in which an ugly gathering of suburban neighbors wanted to get rid of an ex-convict that had moved into their town. As the mob grew increasingly hostile, a previously weak and silent neighbor stood up, horrified at his neighbors' actions, and defended the ex-con, causing the crowd to disperse. "The Incredible World of Horace Ford" cast Art Carney as a thirty-five-year-old toymaker on the edge of a nervous breakdown, longing to return to his childhood. In a delightful fantasy ending, his wish came true and he somehow returned to his old home street, set as it was when he was a boy.

The most powerful of Rose's works was "Twelve Angry Men," the story of a jury debating a life and death decision—whether to convict a young boy of murder. The entire play was set inside the cramped jury room as each of the men struggled with his conscience. At the beginning all but one of the jurors voted guilty. The lone holdout (played by Bob Cummings) explained why he felt there was "a reasonable doubt" in the case and he then pressed the others to reexamine the evidence and reconsider their votes. In the heated arguments that followed, personal one-upmanship, peer pressure, and the desire to simply end the long deliberation became just as important as analyzing the case itself. One by one, the jurors changed their votes, shifting the total to eleven not guilty, one guilty. At the dramatic conclusion, the last man, frightened at the prospect of standing alone to defend his guilty decision to the others, agreed to the not guilty verdict.

NBC's top drama producer, Fred Coe, had left the Sunday night *Philco/Goodyear Television Playhouse* at the end of the 1953-54 season to supervise *Producers' Showcase*, but he left his old program in able hands. Under replacement Gordon Duff, Coe's stable of writers, including Paddy Chayefsky and Horton Foote, continued to turn out sensitive original works dealing with such situations as the disintegrating marriage of a man out of work, a woman who refused to be shut away in an old age home, and the inhabitants of a boarding house in a small Texas town. One story was particularly striking, Robert Alan Aurthur's "A Man Is Ten Feet Tall," which cast Sidney Poitier as a black dock worker who encouraged a white GI deserter (played by Don Murray) to straighten out his life and pull himself together. Because blacks rarely had leading roles in TV drama, Poitier's appearance brought a special edge to the production. In May, Gore Vidal's satirical fantasy, "A Visit to a Small Planet," used a light, humorous touch to poke fun at the foibles of modern society, including its elaborate war-game strategies. Cyril Ritchard portrayed Mr. Kreton, an eccentric but superpowered visitor to earth who arrived dressed in Civil War-era fashions, thinking it was 1860, not 1960. Realizing that he could not participate in the war between the states, Kreton decided to direct a modern world war instead because, he observed, that's what mankind seemed to want anyway.

One of the most important dramas of the 1954-55 season was "Patterns," written by Rod Serling. The story appeared on NBC's *Kraft Television Theater* in January, 1955, and received so much acclaim that it was restaged less than a month later. It provided the big break for Serling, who soon became one of television's top dramatic writers.

"Patterns" was set in the high pressure world of big business. An up-and-coming young executive, Frank Staples (Richard Kiley), joined a large New York organization and was assigned to work with one of the experienced old timers, Bill Briggs (Ed Begley). The two became good friends and worked well together, as Staples quickly demonstrated his sharp business acumen. He was shocked to discover, however, that Jim Ramsey (Everett Sloan), the head of the company, was grooming him as a replacement for Briggs.

There was no obvious solution to the situation. Each man had to determine what was important to him, how hard to fight for it, and the consequences of his decision. Staples realized that he wanted and deserved the job, yet was determined to defend and protect his friend. Ramsey felt that Briggs was no longer effective and that, for the good of the company, Staples should replace him. Because Briggs had seniority and a good track record, though, Ramsey could not fire him outright, so he planned to pressure and humiliate him into retiring. Briggs himself had allowed his job to become the most important part of his life and could not conceive of quitting.

Building on these decisions, Serling developed "Patterns" into a highly charged, intensely exciting human debate. The confrontations between Ramsey and Staples were the most powerful because Staples was the only person in the entire company brave enough and strong enough to stand up to the boss—and both knew it. In fact, it was for that very reason that Ramsey was determined to promote Staples, at any cost. Following a public dressing down of Briggs by Ramsey at a board meeting, the humiliated executive collapsed of a heart attack. At first the enraged Staples threatened to resign, but then reconsidered and proposed a more lasting revenge. He agreed to stay with the company as one of its top executives and pledged to constantly criticize and attack Ramsey's every move, until he was toppled. Ramsey agreed. It was an acceptable price to pay for the good of the company.

Such standout works of original television drama provided spectacular moments of entertainment. New York based TV critics, steeped in Broadway tradition, regarded the television anthology programs featuring original drama as the best possible use of the medium and called for more. In doing so, however, they ignored many obvious signs that the form was doomed to a short life cycle.

The nature of television made demands on writers and producers that were suicidal, even compared to the rigorous grind of the theater. On Broadway, there might be fifty major openings in a year, plus a dozen revivals and a number of continuing productions. All of these plays would be presented (or rerun) hundreds of times. At the start of 1955, there were ten regular hour-long drama anthologies on the four TV networks, accounting for thirty-five hours of programming a month. Adding the fourteen thirty-minute drama anthologies, the monthly total rose to sixty-three hours. To expect television to turn out even two good hour-long plays per week, for an entire season, was to expect it to almost double Broadway's normal yearly output. For television to consistently stock all of its anthology programs with good material bordered on the impossible. Yet the most amazing thing about the "golden age of TV drama" was that the writers and producers managed to come up with as many good productions for as long as they did.

One reason the medium performed so well was that fresh talent emerged and eagerly turned out new stories for television. When the initial infusion passed, though, the high percentage of truly exceptional work had to pass as well. With so many anthology programs on the air, the demand for new TV plays began to outdistance the supply of good material, and the overall quality of original TV drama began to drop. Even returning to adaptations of books, films, and old plays (which had been the basis of most TV drama in the 1940s) did not offer much help because it was very hard to squeeze a wide open story line into sixty minutes, especially within the confines of a live television studio.

Writers found it harder and harder to create so many new settings and new characters week after week. Viewers found it harder and harder to get involved in the constantly changing worlds tossed

Bob Cummings played a professional photographer of beautiful models in *The Bob Cummings Show,* later known as *Love That Bob.* (*From* Love That Bob. *Courtesy of MCA Television Limited*)

out before them in the anthology programs. Television producers began to consider seriously alternatives to the highly praised anthology format. Successful series such as *Dragnet* and *Medic* suggested one answer; they provided viewers with a familiar cast and setting, yet still showcased well written stories. Perhaps it would be easier on everyone to work some dramatic themes into weekly drama series with continuing central characters, while saving more ambitious original stories for one-shot specials (such as Pat Weaver's spectaculars) or for a select number of special anthology shows. Such a strategy could reduce some of the production pressure while

allowing the best writers the opportunity to flourish.

There was another very practical reason for considering such changes in television drama—the anthology showcases were becoming less and less popular with the large corporations that had been acting as sponsors since the late Forties. They recognized that, with almost 40 million TV sets in use in the United States in 1955, the average television viewer was no longer part of the elite upper middle class. Instead, there was an increasingly large audience (of both post-World War II "baby boom" youngsters, and working class adults) that considered television to be primarily a source of light entertainment. These viewers preferred following the adventures of their favorite sitcom characters rather than searching out dramas which often posed disquieting questions on the basics of American life.

In August, 1955, Philco pulled out of its alternating sponsorhip of NBC's Sunday *Television Playhouse.* Dealers had complained that customers told them they wanted more "boy meets girl" shows rather than the often complicated realism dispensed by the *Playhouse* writers. Critical acclaim and respectable ratings were no longer enough to guarantee support even for a top flight show.

The networks were also beginning to cast a critical eye at the more limited interest "class" programming in their prime time schedules. With the ratings race more heated than ever, programs that could not beat the competition by attracting the largest possible audience were becoming harder to justify. Original drama anthology programs were expensive to produce, increasingly difficult to sell to sponsors, and often disturbing to viewers.

It was not just drama that was squeezed. News, too, felt the crunch. *See It Now,* carried for years by Alcoa, found itself without a sponsor when Alcoa announced that it would replace Philco as the sponsor for NBC's Sunday night drama (with the assurance that *The Television Playhouse* would "lighten up"). Even without Alcoa, CBS was going to carry *See It Now* in its regular late Tuesday night slot into the fall of 1955, unsponsored if necessary. During the summer, however, a more compelling element entered the equation: *See It Now*'s time slot became too valuable. By September, 1955, every advertiser in the business wanted to place a show on CBS at 10:30 Tuesday night, so it could follow *The $64,000 Question.*

15. The Road to Reruns

IN APRIL, 1954, after five years of legal debate, the Supreme Court ruled that the FCC's 1949 proposal to ban giveaway quiz shows was illegal. The commission had claimed that giveaway shows violated the U.S. Criminal Code on lotteries and should be barred from the airwaves. By definition, participants in a lottery had to expend "something of value" to win, and the FCC had stretched that to include programs such as *Stop the Music,* which required viewers to "spend" time watching the show in order to learn information necessary to win. Even though the Supreme Court agreed that giveaway shows were a complete waste of time, it rejected the commission's attempt to kick them off the air by defining them as lotteries.

During the five-year court battle, giveaway quiz shows had virtually disappeared anyway, with most new quizzers following the more cautious celebrity panel format that emphasized repartee over financial largess. Once the Supreme Court had cleared the good name of the giveaway format, the big money programs were primed for a comeback. In the fall of 1954, *Stop the Music,* which had started the giveaway trend on radio in 1947, returned to ABC-TV. Despite network ballyhoo, the revived program managed to bring in only marginal ratings and could not generate anything near the excitement of its top ten TV run in the late 1940s. Some television programmers pointed to this as proof that the era of the big money quiz shows had passed. Louis G. Cowan, creator of *Stop the Music,* disagreed. He felt the idea was still good, it just needed a new package.

The FCC's actions in 1949 had effectively scuttled the giveaway quiz shows before television developed many strong vehicles that could convey visually the excitement of the contests. In early 1955, Louis Cowan's production company put together a big money quiz package that was specifically tailored to meet the demands of television. The show was based on a simple radio quizzer from the 1940s, *Take It Or Leave It,* which had run for ten years without any fancy frills or expensive gimmicks. On the radio show, contestants were asked to answer a series of increasingly difficult questions in order to earn an increasingly valuable cash prize. Each contestant selected a category of questions from a prepared list and, at any point along the way, could stop—keeping the money already won— or choose to move on to the next question and risk losing it all. The value of the questions doubled at each step: $1, $2, $4, $8, $16, $32, and finally $64. *Take It or Leave It* eventually changed its name to *The $64 Question* because that was what most people came to call the show.

For the transfer to television, Cowan took the basic idea of *The $64 Question* and added mounds of show business hype. Instead of the sixty-four-dollar question, the goal became the sixty-four-*thousand*-dollar question. Upon reaching the $8,000 level, the contestant was placed inside an isolation booth. Ostensibly this was to prevent hearing clues yelled by members of the audience, but it was really done to increase the visual suspense for the home viewers. The contestant stood alone in the isolation booth, ready to face the challenge of the four big money questions: $8,000, $16,000, $32,000, and $64,000. To prolong the suspense, only the $8,000 and $16,000 questions were posed the first week. If these were answered correctly, the contestant was given a week to decide whether to keep the money or go on. If the $32,000 question was answered correctly the next week, the contestant was given another week to decide whether to keep the winnings or to try for the ultimate jackpot. As an added incentive to go for the $64,000 question, the contestant was permitted to bring into the isolation booth an expert in the chosen category for advice. To demonstrate the program's unimpeachable standards of honesty, a grand show was made of having armed guards surround the safety deposit box in which the questions were stored. A bank official regularly appeared on the show to testify that nobody who had any connection with the program had access to the safety deposit box, "except the editors" (an exception mentioned very quickly and, at the time, no one seemed to notice it).

The super-charged big money package, with veteran sitcom sidekick Hal March as emcee, premiered on CBS live from New York on June 7, 1955, as a summer replacement for the *Danger* drama anthology. Within one month, *The $64,000 Question* was the most popular television show on the air. People found it irresistible and became caught up in the hokey but nonetheless real human drama, unfolding live before them. Unlike most previous big money quiz shows, *The $64,000 Question* asked tough, but not tricky, questions, written by Professor Bergen Evans, host of another Louis G. Cowan program, *Down You Go.* Contestants on *The $64,000 Question* were allowed to choose their own category of questions and this encouraged participation by smart but basically average people who happened to have a greal deal of specialized knowledge in one particular topic. This helped the show's popularity enormously because members of the audience could see themselves in the ordinary, run-of-the-mill people competing, and they shared vicariously in the decision to "go for the big dough."

The producers had hoped for an enthusiastic public response

FALL 1955 SCHEDULE

MONDAY

7:00	7:30	8:00	8:30	9:00	9:30	10:00	10:30	
Kukla, Fran And Ollie / John Daly	Topper	TV Reader's Digest	Voice of Firestone	Dotty Mack Show	Medical Horizons	The Big Picture	local	**ABC**
local	ROBIN HOOD	Burns And Allen Show	Arthur Godfrey's Talent Scouts	I Love Lucy	December Bride	Studio One		**CBS**
local				Monday Night Fights From St. Nicholas Arena With Chris Schenkel			At Ringside	**DUMONT**
local	Tony Martin / Camel News	Caesar's Hour @Producer's Showcase		Medic	Robert Montgomery Presents		local	**NBC**

TUESDAY

7:00	7:30	8:00	8:30	9:00	9:30	10:00	10:30	
Kukla, Fran And Ollie / John Daly & The News	WARNER BROTHERS PRESENTS (KING'S ROW, CHEYENNE, CASABLANCA)		WYATT EARP	Make Room For Daddy	Du Pont Cavalcade Theater	Talent Varieties	local	**ABC**
local	Name That Tune	NAVY LOG	YOU'LL NEVER GET RICH	Meet Millie	Red Skelton Show	$64,000 Question	My Favorite Husband	**CBS**
local								**DUMONT**
local	Dinah Shore / Camel News	Milton Berle Show / Martha Raye Show — CHEVY SHOW		Jane Wyman's Fireside Theater	Armstrong Circle Theater — PLAYWRIGHTS '56		Big Town	**NBC**

WEDNESDAY

7:00	7:30	8:00	8:30	9:00	9:30	10:00	10:30	
Kukla, Fran And Ollie / John Daly & The News	Disneyland		M-G-M PARADE	Masquerade Party	Break The Bank	Wednesday Night Fights		**ABC**
local	BRAVE EAGLE	Arthur Godfrey And His Friends		The Millionaire	I've Got A Secret	U.S. Steel Hour / 20TH CENTURY-FOX HOUR		**CBS**
local					What's The Story	local		**DUMONT**
local	Eddie Fisher / Plymouth News	SCREEN DIRECTOR'S PLAYHOUSE	Father Knows Best	Kraft Television Theater		This Is Your Life	Midwestern Hayride	**NBC**

THURSDAY

7:00	7:30	8:00	8:30	9:00	9:30	10:00	10:30	
Kukla, Fran And Ollie / John Daly & The News	The Lone Ranger	Life Is Worth Living	Stop The Music	Star Tonight	Down You Go	OUTSIDE U.S.A.	local	**ABC**
local	SGT. PRESTON OF THE YUKON	Bob Cummings Show	Climax @Shower Of Stars		Four Star Playhouse	Johnny Carson Show	WANTED	**CBS**
local								**DUMONT**
local	Dinah Shore / Camel News	You Bet Your Life	THE PEOPLE'S CHOICE	Dragnet	Ford Theater	Lux Video Theater		**NBC**

FRIDAY

7:00	7:30	8:00	8:30	9:00	9:30	10:00	10:30	
Kukla, Fran And Ollie / John Daly & The News	Rin Tin Tin	Ozzie And Harriet	CROSSROADS	Dollar A Second	The Vise	Ethel And Albert	local	**ABC**
local	ADVENTURES OF CHAMPION	Mama	Our Miss Brooks	THE CRUSADER	Schlitz Playhouse Of Stars	The Lineup	Person To Person	**CBS**
local								**DUMONT**
local	Eddie Fisher / Plymouth News	Truth Or Consequences	The Life Of Riley	The Big Story	STAR STAGE	Gillette Cavalcade Of Sports	Red Barber	**NBC**

SATURDAY

7:00	7:30	8:00	8:30	9:00	9:30	10:00	10:30	
local	Ozark Jubilee @GRAND OLE OPRY			Lawrence Welk Show		Tomorrow's Careers	local	**ABC**
Gene Autry Show	Beat The Clock	Stage Show	THE HONEYMOONERS	Two For The Money	IT'S ALWAYS JAN	GUNSMOKE @FORD STAR JUBILEE	Damon Runyon	**CBS**
local								**DUMONT**
local	BIG SURPRISE	Perry Como Show		People Are Funny	Texaco Star Theater @Max Liebman Presents	George Gobel Show	Your Hit Parade	**NBC**

SUNDAY

7:00	7:30	8:00	8:30	9:00	9:30	10:00	10:30	
You Asked For It	FAMOUS FILM FESTIVAL			Chance Of A Lifetime	The Original Amateur Hour	Life Begins At 80	local	**ABC**
Lassie	Private Secretary / Jack Benny Program	Ed Sullivan Show		General Electric Theater	ALFRED HITCHCOCK PRES.	Appointment With Adventure	What's My Line	**CBS**
local								**DUMONT**
It's A Great Life	FRONTIER	Colgate Variety Hour @Color Spread		Goodyear Television Playhouse / Alcoa Hour		Loretta Young Show	Justice	**NBC**

to the program, but they were pleasantly surprised to receive an unexpected bonus from the nation's major newspapers, which devoted a great deal of space to the trials and tribulations of *The $64,000 Question*'s contestants. The weekly progress of the suddenly famous people was treated as a news item and reported in articles outside the TV page. The day after the first show, large write-ups described the performance of a housewife from Trenton who answered seven questions on the movies, but lost on the eighth. (She received a Cadillac as a consolation prize.) Then, a Staten Island policeman, Redmond O'Hanlon, worked his way through questions on Shakespeare and found himself facing what was soon to become a familiar, agonizing decision: keep the $8,000 or go for more. He went on, but stopped at $16,000, so public attention shifted to Mrs. Catherine E. Kreitzer, a Bible expert who eventually stopped at $32,000. (She did, however, "go on" to read a chapter from the Bible on Ed Sullivan's *Toast of the Town*.) Mrs. Kreitzer was followed by Gino Prato, a Bronx cab driver-opera buff, who reached the $32,000 plateau. All week, New York was abuzz: Would Gino go? A local radio station broadcast a recording of a phone call to Gino from his ninety-two-year-old father, who lived in Italy. Papa Prato urged caution and Gino, ever the dutiful son, took the money and ran. The tension became unbearable. Was there no American strong enough to stand up and challenge the fates on the $64,000 question? Just as the 1955-56 season began such a man appeared. Appropriately, he was a soldier, twenty-eight-year-old Marine Corps Captain Richard S. McCutchen, who decided to try for the $64,000 question and chose his father as the expert to accompany him into the isolation booth. For the final question in the category of food and cooking (his hobby), McCutchen was asked to explain an exotic menu served to the king and queen of England in 1939. He answered correctly. McCutchen's boldness had paid off and his success at winning $64,000 (which, after taxes, came to about $32,000) was reported on page one of the staid gray *New York Times*.

On December 6, a twenty-eight-year-old psychologist, Dr. Joyce Brothers, became the second contestant to go all the way. In her chosen topic, boxing, she identified the caestus as the special gloves worn by gladiators in ancient Rome, and won $64,000. Dr. Brothers received so much publicity from her victory that she went into broadcasting full time, and became a well-known TV and radio personality. Around the time of Dr. Brothers's triumph, some major newspapers reached an unofficial agreement with each other to downplay their treatment of *The $64,000 Question*. There was a feeling that the free publicity generated by reporting the contestants' progress with such gusto had helped foster the program's sudden popularity. Whatever the cause, *The $64,000 Question* had become a television phenomenon by the fall of 1955, and it handily defeated all the returning series, staying the number one rated TV show throughout the 1955-56 season.

Many other programs used the distinctive game show as a hook. Almost every variety show did a take-off, and one of the best was by Dean Martin and Jerry Lewis on *The Colgate Variety Hour*. Martin played Hal April, emcee of *The $64,000,000 Question*. At the $16,000,000 plateau, Lewis, an unwilling contestant, was shoved into taking the next question. Instead of entering an isolation booth, he was pushed under water. Jackie Gleason wrote and starred in a serious play on the topic, "Uncle Ed and Circumstance," which aired on *Studio One*. Using the actual *$64,000 Question* set, Gleason played the family goat who suddenly came into favor by winning $64,000. The triumph on the quiz show provided him with a victory his relations could admire and gave him the inner strength to cut his home ties and go off on his own. He actually did not care about the prize money itself and gave it to his family. Gleason aired another quiz story that season on his regular weekly series. In a humorous Honeymooners tale, Gleason (as Ralph Kramden) went through the agony of mastering music, his chosen topic, only to get stagefright and blank out on the opening question of identifying "Swanee River."

Within the television industry, the sudden success of *The $64,000 Question* over the summer prompted a frantic race by all the networks to come up with copies. One of the first to appear was another Louis G. Cowan product, *The Big Surprise* (hosted by Mike Wallace), which premiered on NBC in October. Though the program increased the winning ante to $100,000, it lacked the raw edge of human emotion symbolized by the isolation booths of CBS's *$64,000 Question*. The first quiz clone that proved a ratings success was *The $64,000 Challenge* created by—who else—Louis G. Cowan as a virtual carbon copy of his established hit. On *The $64,000 Challenge*, winning contestants from *The $64,000 Question* returned to the isolation booths to face new challengers and to try for a top prize of $128,000. Soon after its spring debut on CBS in 1956, *The $64,000 Challenge* joined *The $64,000 Question* in television's top ten list.

The spectacular success of *The $64,000 Question* came as a major surprise to the networks. In just a few months, the rank upstart quizzer had deposed *I Love Lucy* as America's number one show. The preferences of the television audience were obviously changing and the network executives faced the difficult and sometimes puzzling task of trying to analyze them.

One reason that tastes were changing was that the audience was changing. As TV set sales continued to grow, the size and makeup of the audience had turned television into a more broad-based mass medium. In addition, the post-World War II baby boom children were almost ten years old and increasingly influential in setting family viewing patterns. With these important new factors affecting program selection, even previously successful stars, shows,

and formats were on uncertain ground. Throughout the season there were surprise failures and unexpected hits, some of which, like the big money quizzes, had been previously unsuccessful or dismissed as past their prime.

During the summer of 1955, just as *The $64,000 Question* was topping the ratings charts, a less meteoric but equally unexpected hit appeared on ABC: *The Lawrence Welk Show*. Over the previous seven years, band leaders such as Eddie Condon, Vincent Lopez, Sammy Kaye, Wayne King, and Freddy Martin had come and gone on TV with no success. They seemed to violate the cardinal rule of television by presenting a format that emphasized sound rather than visuals. When Lawrence Welk, who had been on TV locally in Los Angeles since 1951, brought his pleasant, unpretentious schmaltz to ABC's summer schedule, he was expected to follow the other band leaders to oblivion. Instead, Welk's Saturday night dance party, featuring his patented champagne music, turned into the sleeper hit of the season.

Welk led a relaxed hour of dance music, featuring a talented crew of supporting players including accordionist Myron Floren, singer-dancer Alice Lon, clarinetist Pete Fountain, and the singing Lennon Sisters. The key to the success of his simple, direct musical format proved to be an elusive enigma. Trying to duplicate the chemistry, a rash of musical hopefuls soon appeared: Guy Lombardo's *Diamond Jubilee* (part music, part giveaway, part *This Is Your Life*), *The Ina Ray Hutton Show* (featuring an all-female orchestra), *The Russ Morgan Show* (like Welk's, presented straight), and *It's Polka Time* (with lively emcee Bruno "Junior" Zielinski, who shouted loud, enthusiastic introductions to each song). None of these attracted a following like Welk, whose natural but cultivated accent and manner made him a popular national figure. (Even his trademark phrase "a vun and a two and a t'ree" became a popular gag line.) Unlike the failed competition, Welk not only continued to thrive on Saturday night, he also launched a successful spinoff series, *Lawrence Welk's Top Tunes and New Talent*, which ran three seasons.

One of the most important changes for the 1955-56 season was the expanded role of Hollywood in network programming. Following the success of *Disneyland* the previous season, ABC, CBS, and NBC had made agreements with several major studios for programs produced specifically for television. The networks hoped for another ratings bonanza and the studios hoped to duplicate Disney's ploy of using a profitable TV show to plug the latest theatrical features. Almost every one of the highly touted film industry productions was a disappointment.

Number one CBS showed the most restraint and selectivity in approaching the major studios, and secured the closest thing to an all-around Hollywood success that season, *The 20th Century-Fox Hour*. Joseph Cotten hosted the bi-weekly series, which presented high quality adaptations of old movies such as "The Ox-Bow Incident" and "Miracle on 34th Street," and occasionally featured a few big name stars not usually seen on television.

NBC talked the Screen Directors Guild into producing a half-hour weekly drama anthology, *Screen Director's Playhouse*. Despite the participation by such distinguished feature film directors as John Ford and Fred Zinnemann, the series was unmitigatingly bland and indistinguishable from every other thirty-minute drama anthology. NBC was also let down by the first world premiere on American television of a major feature length film, the British-made "The Constant Husband." The story was a light farce starring Rex Harrison as an amnesia victim who married several different women, and its November telecast drew universally tepid reviews. This created the impression that NBC had been taken for a ride by the British film studio, paying a great deal of money to show a film that would not have been a hit if released to the theaters.

ABC also turned to Britain for filmed material and purchased fifty features from the J. Arthur Rank studios to launch one of the first network schedulings of feature films in prime time, the Sunday evening *Famous Film Festival* (soon expanded to include *The Afternoon Film Festival*). Most Americans at the time found British drama too stiff and British accents too confusing to follow, so the network's experiment was unable to beat the tough competition of Ed Sullivan's *Toast of the Town.* Acceptance of prime time movies did not come about until NBC acquired the television rights to more recent American films six years later. Though disappointed by the failure of the prime time British films, ABC was much more concerned by the weak performances of its major new Hollywood produced series, *MGM Parade* and *Warner Brothers Presents.*

The network ran the hour-long Warner Brothers adventure series Tuesday from 7:30 P.M. to 8:30 P.M., repeating the early starting time strategy that had worked so well with *Disneyland.* In order to fill the program each week, the studio set up *Warner Brothers Presents* as a showcase for three continuing series that rotated in the slot. Each was a television adaptation of a past Warner Brothers film. The first in the series, *King's Row,* came from a competent but unexciting grade–B film about a small-town psychiatrist. Appropriately, the film inspired a competent but unexciting grade-B adaptation. Second in the series was *Casablanca,* a silly grade-Z yarn based on the grade-A film thriller. The original film had been set in Morocco during World War II and starred Humphrey Bogart

as Rick, an American expatriate who operated a cafe in Casablanca, and Ingrid Bergman as Ilsa, his long-lost love from Paris, who was working underground against the Nazis. For the television adaptation, the setting remained Rick's cafe in Casablanca, but everything else was updated to the 1950s. The town was no longer overrun by Nazis, but by Russian spies on the lookout for nuclear secrets. Charles McGraw and Anita Ekberg took Bogart and Bergman's roles, though in keeping with the updated setting, Ekberg's character was transformed into Trina, a Swedish scientist. The magic of the original premise was smothered in Fifties relevancy. It was a close race, but *King's Row* was judged to be worse than *Casablanca,* and it was the first to be axed, replaced in January by *Conflict,* an undistinguished drama anthology.

The only member of the original Warner Brothers triumvirate to succeed was *Cheyenne,* a better-than-average stock Western starring Clint Walker as Cheyenne Bodie, a half-Indian government scout in the classic "strong silent type" mold. *Cheyenne* attracted a sizeable audience, composed largely of youngsters, that became caught up in the Western setting and adventures. When *King's Row* faded around New Year's, *Cheyenne* was increased to an alternate week frequency, with *Casablanca* and *Conflict* filling out the month.

The real reason for *Warner Brothers Presents* was not left to the imagination. Every week the last fifteen minutes was turned over to Gig Young who hosted "Behind the Camera at Warner Brothers Studios." Plug. Plug. Plug. More fascinating interviews with fascinating stars about their fascinating movies soon to open at a local fascinating movie theater.

The behind the scenes features on *Disneyland* were subtle and entertaining. It was possible for viewers to watch and enjoy that program without ever seeing the theatrical films involved—though it was likely they would attend after being teased by the well done background reports. Warners' features were little more than cheaply produced promotional trailers. The fifteen minutes of plugs, added to the normal commercial allotment, brought the one-hour program dangerously close to a fifty-fifty mix of entertainment and commercials. ABC's other new Hollywood showcase was even worse. *The MGM Parade* was set up as a weekly behind-the-scenes peek at the MGM studios in a half-hour melange of old film clips, new film clips, shots of productions in progress, and a few interviews. The program was poorly paced, lacked cohesion, and played as a blatant plug for the studio.

The public reaction to both programs (with the exception of the *Cheyenne* segment) was largely negative and the ratings were nowhere near the blockbuster success of *Disneyland.* The major Hollywood studios soon realized that television had to be treated as more than a garbage dump for promotional messages. In the spring, MGM upgraded its program and presented several high quality episodes, such as a well researched review of the career of Greta Garbo. By then, however, the show had already been canceled. Warner Brothers scuttled the *Warner Brothers Presents* format at the end of the season, but carried over *Cheyenne* as a series on its own. The success of *Disneyland* and *Cheyenne* pointed to a simple, but effective, strategy. Leave the obvious plugs behind and produce programs that would stand on their own as profitable hits.

Though the major studios fared poorly in the initial attempts to package feature programs for the networks, their failure did little to slow the steady shift in the balance of power in television from New York to Hollywood. Later that season, in fact, the major studios successfully released almost 2,000 pre-1948 theatrical films to television and in the process almost single-handedly killed off live local programming. Stations quickly snapped up the features because running the old films was much cheaper than anything else they could do. Like the networks, the locals were increasingly willing to cede control in return for reliable, popular product.

Throughout the years, Hollywood had consistently displayed a better grasp than New York of how to produce pop culture material that appealed to the average American. In the 1910s, the center of the American film industry had shifted from the East to the West and, in the 1930s, the same thing had taken place in radio. By the 1950s, the ascendancy of Hollywood-based filmed sitcoms, cop shows, and adventure series gave the West Coast the upper hand in the battle for control over television. Even many live variety programs originated from Hollywood because that's where the stars lived. ABC was largely committed to California production and CBS was not far behind. With so much of its new programming originating from Los Angeles, CBS created the position of Manager of West Coast Network Programming. James Aubrey, general manager since 1952 of CBS's Los Angeles station, KNXT, became the first to fill the new post.

The rise of programs such as *Disneyland* and *The Adventures of Rin Tin Tin* in the 1955-56 season had added to prime time another popular format that was easily done on the West Coast, kidvid adventure films. For the fall of 1955, CBS dumped its 7:30-8:00 P.M. news and music programs in favor of kiddie-oriented sagas such as *Sergeant Preston of the Yukon, Brave Eagle, The Adventures of Champion,* and the British-made *Adventures of Robin Hood.* These standard pulp adventure yarns focused on animals, young boys, and stalwart adults in rugged settings ranging from the frozen tundra to the forests of Sherwood. Though none of them produced outstanding ratings, they served their purpose and attracted a large pre-teen audience for advertisers.

CBS also made a bid for children in the early morning, taking one hour from the foundering *Morning Show* news program and installing Bob Keeshan (formerly Clarabell the clown on *Howdy Doody*) as the gentle Captain Kangaroo. ABC took its kidvid strategy to the late afternoon and challenged NBC's *Howdy Doody* with another Disney series, *The Mickey Mouse Club.* For one hour on film each afternoon, host Jimmie Dodd and a dozen young "Mouseketeers" performed in skits, sang songs, and introduced special features such as the Mickey Mouse Newsreel, safety lectures by Jiminy Cricket, nature films, Disney cartoons, and guest performers ranging from circus aerialists to veteran comedian Morey Amsterdam. There were also adventure serials such as "Corky and White Shadow," "Annette," "The Hardy Boys," and "Spin and Marty," usually featuring members of the Mouseketeers in the lead roles. (Annette Funicello was the most popular performer.) Local California children sometimes participated in the show as well, often taking part in studio contests. (In 1957, a youngster named Jerry Brown was a contestant. Seventeen years later, when the series was still being seen in reruns, Brown was elected governor of California and later became a candidate for president.) *The Mickey Mouse Club* proved so successful for ABC that *Howdy Doody* was soon banished to Saturday morning.

One format that had kept preadolescents enthralled long before television emerged was the Western, a popular setting for American adventure tales throughout the twentieth century. During the 1930s, near-mythic hero types such as Wild Bill Hickok, Hopalong Cassidy, Gene Autry, and Roy Rogers had filled countless Saturday morning matinees with hard-riding action interrupted by only a few "boring" love scenes. The stories were simple morality plays, with good and bad clearly defined and justice always triumphant over evil. When television arrived in the late 1940s, the kiddie

Westerns made an easy transfer to the home screen where a new generation of children eagerly snapped them up in both reruns of the old films and new exploits made for television.

In the early Fifties, the assumption that Westerns were "just kid stuff" began to change as theatrical films such as "High Noon" and "Shane" placed more serious plots in Western settings. These stories became known as adult Westerns and did well at the box office. ABC staged a successful adult Western ("Last Notch") on its *U.S. Steel Hour* anthology and, in the 1955-56 season, all three networks made tentative tests of the popularity of the format in a weekly series.

NBC handed Worthington Miner the task of developing a continuing adult Western, and Miner responded with *Frontier,* an anthology based on Western folklore. *Frontier* was an abysmal failure, partly because of its often pretentious plots (liberally sprinkled with heavy-handed psychology), but largely due to the absence of a continuing identifiable Western hero that viewers could latch onto.

ABC's *The Life and Legend of Wyatt Earp* was a half step removed from *Frontier* and considerably more successful. Most of the early episodes were based on allegedly historical events from a biography of frontier lawman Wyatt Earp (who had died in Los Angeles in 1929 at the age of eighty-two). To this base, ABC added a more traditional handsome leading man, Hugh O'Brian, as sheriff Earp. As portrayed by O'Brian, Wyatt Earp was a genuinely interesting character and far beyond the one-dimensional heroic figures such as Hopalong Cassidy. Earp took his job seriously, but compassionately, first in Kansas (Ellsworth and Dodge City) and then in Tombstone, Arizona. The conflict between a previously lawless town and an effective, dedicated sheriff provided a strong

January 3, 1956
    Do You Trust Your Wife? (CBS). Edgar Bergen, like Groucho Marx, hosts a quiz show that emphasizes humorous patter over the actual game.

January 3, 1956
    Queen for a Day. (NBC). "Would *you* like to be queen for a day?" Jack Bailey asks. America's housewives respond in the affirmative, as NBC regains control of the weekday afternoon hours with this successful, heart-tugging audience participation show.

February 20, 1956
    Good Morning. (CBS). A last gasp move to salvage CBS's version of *Today.* Will Rogers, Jr. takes over as host. Ratings rise at first, but *Today* appears to be unbeatable.

April 2, 1956
    CBS presents the first daily thirty-minute television soap operas, *As the World Turns* and *The Edge of Night.*

May 28, 1956
    After a year in prime time, Johnny Carson is demoted to daytime duty on CBS, replacing Robert Q. Lewis. Carson "loosens up" in his new slot, adopting a style similar to Steve Allen's. Nonetheless, CBS cans Carson in September.

August 13, 1956
    The Democratic National Convention opens in Chicago. Along with Bill Henry, NBC adds as co-anchors two new faces: Chet Huntley and David Brinkley.

September 7, 1956
    Pat Weaver quits as chairman of NBC.

On their simple kitchen set, the stars of *The Honeymooners:* (from *l.*) Art Carney, Jackie Gleason, Audrey Meadows. *(Photo by Viacom, Hollywood)*

basis for the weekly plots. The program was well executed and avoided obvious Western film clichés even within the obligatory fights, chases, and shoot-outs. (During a fist fight near the town water reservoir, *nobody* fell in!)

CBS based its adult Western series on its successful radio hit, *Gunsmoke.* The innovative radio Western had premiered in early 1952 (predating the breakthrough film "High Noon") as a finely crafted portrait of the old West as seen through the eyes of a tough but compassionate U.S. marshal, Matt Dillon (played by William Conrad). Dillon lived in a tough, violent West that cheated honest men and sometimes left the heroes frustrated and confused, even after winning a showdown. At the start, CBS radio did not quite know what to make of the show and relegated it to an obscure time slot, where it stayed for one and one-half years before securing a sponsor. By that time, "High Noon" had won an Oscar and *Gunsmoke* was moved to a better time period, where it flourished.

In 1955, when CBS began to search for an adult Western television vehicle, all it had to do was look to its radio branch. For the video version, an entirely new cast was chosen, with the rotund, slightly grumpy William Conrad replaced by the tall, lean figure of James Arness. America's number one traditional Western film star, John Wayne, who had suggested Arness for the lead, introduced the first episode of the series, assuring old-time sagebrush fans by his presence that TV's *Gunsmoke* was worthy of their patronage. The program successfully maintained the tight combina-

tion of effective, inevitable violence and compelling slices of human drama that had worked so well on radio. In one story, Dillon spent most of the program in relentless pursuit of a killer, only to discover—on confronting him—that the man was not so much an evil murderer as a slightly psychotic individual who only wanted to be left alone. Dillon understood the man's desire for solitude, felt compassion, and cursed the circumstances that turned him into a killer—but nonetheless brought him in. It was his painful, necessary duty as marshal.

While NBC's *Frontier* was a flop, CBS's *Gunsmoke* and ABC's *Wyatt Earp* proved quite successful, Neither was a ratings smash in its first season, but both were solid performers, with a slowly but steadily growing legion of regular viewers. The two-out-of-three scorecard for adult Westerns, while not overwhelming, combined with the success of *Cheyenne* to underscore the surprising strength of the Western format. Once again, a durable Hollywood film staple provided yet another network television hit. The growing feeling that Hollywood production represented the best chance for success with the expanding TV audience pushed program activity westward, and it dealt the crippling blow to one of television's pioneers, the DuMont network.

For some time, DuMont had conceded the fact that it was not in the same league as CBS and NBC, preferring instead to bill itself as the reasonably priced network that allowed not-so-large sponsors a crack at television. This proved to be a workable, if limited, strategy that did attract a number of new sponsors to television for the network's few successful low-budget programs: *Calvalcade of Stars, Captain Video, Down You Go, Life Is Worth Living, Rocky King, The Plainclothesman, They Stand Accused, Life Begins at Eighty,* wrestling, and prime time NFL football. In time, however, even these inexpensive programs became impossible to maintain as television costs continued to escalate.

The turning point for DuMont came around New Year's 1955, when the network sold its Pittsburgh O&O, WDTV, to Westinghouse for $9.7 million. WDTV's position as the only television station in Pittsburgh had been the main reason DuMont stayed alive as long as it had, but by the end of 1954, DuMont Labs was in desperate need of cash. The network operation had never been very profitable, but TV set sales had always been great enough for an overall company profit. When the labs began sliding into the red, DuMont was forced to sell the only valuable property it owned, even though WDTV would remain the only commercial VHF station in Pittsburgh for three more years.

The sale of WDTV was an admission that the DuMont television network was a failure. In early 1955, DuMont began cutting its use of the costly coaxial cables, effectively reducing network output to almost nothing. The long-running Monday through Friday *Captain Video* serial ended April 1. *Down You Go, Chance of a Lifetime, Life Begins at Eighty,* and Bishop Sheen's *Life Is Worth Living* moved to ABC. By October, 1955, DuMont maintained only one or two live sporting events.

While effectively out of the television network business, DuMont hoped to stay alive as a source of television programming. With more and more prime time programs on film, DuMont decided to offer its newly built five-studio New York telecenter as a convenient location for East Coast film production. It tried to convince New York producers to stay put and transfer to film without the expense of a cross-country shift, using a new DuMont TV film process, the electronicam. The lure of Hollywood was too hard to buck and, by the fall of 1955, only Jackie Gleason had signed on as a customer.

In the face of such an all-around failure, Paramount Pictures staged a coup d'état in August, 1955, and at last took complete control of DuMont. By teaming up with the investment firm of Loeb & Rhodes (another major DuMont stockholder) Paramount obtained a working majority of stockholders and instituted immediate changes. Dr. Allen DuMont was kicked upstairs to the meaningless position of chairman of the board, and Bernard Goodwin (a Paramount man) was installed as president. Soon thereafter, DuMont announced that it no longer considered itself a national television network.

Paramount's dramatic victory turned out to be a Pyrrhic one. In July, 1957, Paramount was voted out of control when the Loeb & Rhodes faction teamed up with the owners of WNEW, a newly acquired New York City radio station. A year later, the DuMont network was officially put to rest when Paramount sold its remaining shares of stock and Dr. DuMont retired. DuMont Broadcasting, which had failed so miserably as a television network, was renamed Metromedia and, ironically, it ultimately became a very healthy string of independent radio and TV stations, similar to the Westinghouse ("Group W") organization.

DuMont's brief venture in 1955 as an East Coast production outfit did result in one major contribution to American television—the preservation of thirty-nine episodes of Jackie Gleason's *Honeymooners* series. By early 1955, three years after leaving DuMont for CBS, Gleason's Saturday night comedy-variety hour had replaced *Dragnet* as the number two television program in America. Despite the success of his proven format, Gleason decided to gamble and discard the variety part of his show in favor of a thirty-minute filmed situation comedy devoted exclusively to the long-running

Honeymooners characters. CBS was very nervous over Gleason's plan because it practically invited rival NBC to counter with a strong hour-long program in a time slot previously conceded to CBS. After extended negotiations, Gleason got his way, but with some limitations. Though he signed a very generous contract which granted him a hefty percentage of the rerun profits for the filmed series, the deal was limited to one year, to see if it would work.

Despite network misgivings, Gleason's venture seemed to have every reason to succeed. The Honeymooners had been a part of his repertoire for years, originating during Gleason's tenure as host of DuMont's *Calvalcade of Stars*. When he transferred to CBS in the fall of 1952, Gleason brought the Honeymooners along, though at first it remained just another element in his stock of character skits. Soon it became evident that the Honeymooners was the most popular of all and sometimes the entire hour was devoted to a Honeymooners story. A Honeymooners series was the logical next step, lifting the familiar cast and concept, intact, from the variety show. Using the DuMont electronicam process, the episodes were filmed before a live audience which retained the spontaneous energy of the live sketches and helped the program to appear as just a continuation of Gleason's variety show.

The Honeymooners was a working class character piece, built around the chemistry between Jackie Gleason and Art Carney. Over the years the duo had developed superb physical and verbal comic timing together, carrying even weak sketches by the sheer force of their personalities. *The Honeymooners* was a showcase for two of their best characters and some of their most effective interaction. Gleason played Ralph Kramden, a fat, loud-mouthed, but basically warm-hearted Brooklyn bus driver, while Carney was Ed Norton, an uneducated, clumsy, but cheerful and innately perceptive sewer worker. The two were best friends and constantly played off each other. When Ralph was blustery, Norton was befuddled. When Ralph was scheming, Norton was gullible. When Ralph was hurt, Norton was consoling. When Ralph was pompous, Norton was there to prick the balloon. Through it all they remained inveterate dreamers, convinced that just one lucky break could make them wealthy.

Equally important to *The Honeymooners*, however, was the relationship between Ralph and his wife, Alice (played by Audrey Meadows, who replaced Pert Kelton in the role when Gleason moved from DuMont to CBS). Ralph and Alice stood apart from the typical television sitcom couples of the time, which often contained a bland, lovable husband and a flighty, lovable housewife. Ralph Kramden was not a particularly lovable man. He had no patience, was often self-centered, quick tempered, and had an overblown estimate of his own importance. Alice was a bedrock of stability who knew Ralph's faults and still loved him in spite of (perhaps even because of) his occasional bursts of irrationality. Unlike Ralph and Norton, she had long ago accepted their lowly position in life and her realistic, almost fatalistic, personality provided a strong counterbalance to the flights of fancy the "boys" engaged in.

The emphasis on reality distinguished *The Honeymooners* from the mainstream of 1950s television sitcoms. The sets suggested a simple working class neighborhood. There were no split level houses or expensive apartments. The Kramdens did not even own a telephone. In fact, there was very little scenery at all, just the all-too-familiar Kramden kitchen and a few occasional secondary locations. The entire world of *The Honeymooners*—the domestic squabbles, money shortages, the get-rich-quick schemes—took place on the basic set containing a door, a chest of drawers, a table, some chairs, a window, a stove, and an ice box.

The *Mickey Mouse Club:* (from *l.*) Jimmie Dodd, Doreen Tracey, Karen Pendleton, Bobby Burgess, (top); Cubby O'Brien, Annette Funicello, Darlene Gillespie, Roy Williams. *(Walt Disney Productions)*

I Love Lucy also had trappings of reality, but it used the setting as a launching pad for zany situations with a showbiz flavor. (In 1955, the *Lucy* plots revolved chiefly around Ricky's movie career in Hollywood.) *The Honeymooners* accomplished something much more difficult, restricting the focus to average Americans facing everyday problems. In the process, the show brought out the humorous twists in the often mundane workaday world and demonstrated how funny reality could be.

Oddly enough, *The Honeymooners* did not do all that well. As part of the deal with Jackie Gleason, CBS was forced to accept *Stage Show,* a half-hour program from Gleason's production company. This gambit (called "Buy me, buy my show") had been used by other stars in previous years to affect the selection of their summer replacement series. *Those Whiting Girls,* a Desilu production, became *I Love Lucy's* summer sub; *Caesar's Hour* was spelled by the Sid Caesar-produced *Caesar Presents;* and pinch-hitting for George Gobel was *And Here's the Show,* a product of Gobel's Gomalco Enterprises. However, unlike these short lived summer series, *Stage Show* (which had already *failed* as Gleason's summer replacement in 1954) was included in CBS's 1955 fall line-up, leading off the vital 8:00-9:00 P.M. Saturday night slot (preceding *The Honeymooners*). As feared, the program turned into a ratings disaster, driving viewers to the new Perry Como variety hour on NBC and away from *The Honeymooners.*

Stage Show was a straight vaudeville style vehicle, hosted by the musical Dorsey Brothers (Tommy on trombone, Jimmy on sax). Just like the "good old days," one performer after another appeared on stage, while the Dorsey Brothers and their orchestra filled the moments in between acts with a few musical numbers. The only exception to this predictable routine was the network television debut of "young hillbilly singer" Elvis Presley on January 28, 1956 (with his hip-churning renditions of "Blue Suede Shoes" and "Heartbreak Hotel"). At the start of 1956, CBS convinced Gleason to, at least, swap times with *Stage Show* so that the much stronger *Honeymooners* would lead off the 8:00 hour. Even after this move, though, Gleason could not regain the control of Saturday night he had previously enjoyed. In the spring of 1956, he decided to suspend the filmed *Honeymooners* series and in the fall return to his live hour-long variety format, which would occasionally contain some Honeymooners sketches. This was not only a mortal blow to DuMont's electronicam system (Gleason was its only customer) but also a loss to viewers of the future because there would exist only thirty-nine filmed episodes of *The Honeymooners.* Strangely enough, the series (which went into syndication one year later) garnered much better ratings as an off-network rerun than as part of the CBS schedule. The far-sighted Gleason raked in year after year of rerun profits as a result, while he had only varying success with his restablished variety format.

Another classic sitcom made its debut on CBS during the 1955-56 season, *You'll Never Get Rich* (later retitled *The Phil Silvers Show,* but popularly known as *Sgt. Bilko*). Phil Silvers had worked briefly as a TV variety show host during the late 1940s, and subsequently proved more popular as a variety show guest star. He usually played an underhanded type of fellow and the networks said he was not "warm" enough for a regular series. Nat Hiken, a former writer for Martha Raye, disagreed. He analyzed Silvers's acerbic characters and devised what he saw as the perfect setting: the United States Army.

With Hiken as director, Silvers portrayed Master Sergeant Ernest Bilko, a sly conman who served in the peacetime Army on a base filled with men who had nothing to do but eat, sleep, and gamble. This very workable situation gave Silvers a setting for a double

dealing character that could launch numerous money making schemes and deceptions without really hurting anyone. In civilian life his actions would have appeared cruel and selfish. As a soldier, he was helping the GIs to pass away the time at an otherwise boring military base in Kansas—while lining his own pockets in the process. Best of all, Bilko did not have to worry about going to jail—he was already in the Army.

There was little chance of Bilko ever being caught because Hiken surrounded him with the most inept, disheveled Army outfit ever conceived. No commanding officer would ever be as blind and addlebrained as Colonel Hall (Paul Ford). No tub-of-flesh like Private Doberman (Maurice Gosfield) would be allowed in this or any other Army. The other borscht-belt confederates (Herbie Faye, Harvey Lembeck, Alan Melvin, and Joe E. Ross) seemed more appropriate in Broadway's Palace Theater than on Fort Baxter's parade ground. In effect it was vaudeville burlesque, complete with ridiculous outfits, breezy plots, and cardboard characters. But when had vaudeville ever been done so well on television? The scripts and supporting cast were excellent and the weekly schemes sheer magic. A setup took place in the first few minutes and, once again, Bilko would be off.

The entertaining joy of a Bilko con was its execution. He had an ear-to-ear grin that told everyone except the unknowing target that the master was at work. Bilko manipulated his boys and other military personnel like a Chicago ward heeler, buttering up bigwigs, choosing the perfect flunkies, and twisting every Army regulation to suit his needs. Though he was never allowed to get away with any really big sting, Bilko won most of the little battles with the Army bureaucracy, earning the undying gradfitude of an entire generation of former GIs.

Like *The Honeymooners, You'll Never Get Rich* began in a bad time slot. The program started halfway through the Tuesday night NBC comedy-variety rotation and followed a weak CBS adventure saga, *Navy Log.* At mid-season, *Bilko* swapped slots with its lead-in, the ratings went up, and a pattern developed. When *Cheyenne* appeared on ABC's *Warner Brothers Presents,* the Western was the top show of the evening; when Bob Hope was on NBC, he was number one; and when neither of these two were present, Bilko, the old standby, came out ahead. The Bilko saga lasted for four years and, like *The Honeymooners,* has been in syndicated reruns since, holding up as well as Gleason's show.

As CBS almost routinely developed its sitcom hits, NBC's "old guard" comedy-variety showcases continued to fade. Bob Hope was the only consistent winner but he appeared infrequently, alternating with Dinah Shore as host to *The Chevy Show.* That program shared the Tuesday-at-eight slot, on a rotating basis, with Martha Raye and Milton Berle. For the first time in eight years, Berle did not win his time slot—in fact, he lost big to Phil Silvers who sometimes doubled Berle's ratings. Berle tried getting more serious and arty, expanded the scope of his guest list (one show opened with Elvis Presley singing "Hound Dog"), but it did no good. At the end of the season, NBC canceled the Tuesday night comedy hour and Milton Berle found himself without a show.

Another veteran NBC comedy show was also axed during the 1955-56 season, Colgate's Sunday comedy-variety hour. At the start of 1956, NBC took control of the show and renamed it *The NBC Comedy Hour,* inaugurating a new format with Leo Durocher as emcee for the first three programs. The ratings for *The NBC Comedy Hour* were so bad that, by the spring, the old British films running on ABC outscored it. A final, frantic fix-up provided the show with a decent burial that summer. Satirist Stan Freberg was signed on (he conducted humorous dialogues with his hand

While he rarely had a hand in any of the actual stories on his suspense anthology, veteran director Alfred Hitchcock was the undisputed star of the program. He offered deadpan musings to open and close each show, delivering them from a variety of macabre settings. (*From* Alfred Hitchcock Presents. *Courtesy of MCA Television Limited*)

puppet, Grover) and one-half of the writing staff was replaced by new writers shipped to the West Coast from New York (including nineteen-year-old Woody Allen, whose mother had to sign his contract because he was underage). In late June, the *Comedy Hour* expired and NBC brought in Steve Allen from the successful *Tonight* show in an attempt to salvage Sunday night.

The Pat Weaver-inspired big-budget spectaculars, which NBC was counting on to provide the winning edge in the ratings competition, also lost ground by the end of the season. Going into the fall, they began strong, still in the glow of "Peter Pan's" phenomenal success. Even CBS jumped whole hog into the field with *Ford Star Jubilee*, which presented an excellent adaptation of the Broadway hit, "Caine Mutiny Court Martial," as well as the television debuts of Judy Garland and Noel Coward. NBC's *Producers' Showcase* restaged "Peter Pan," presented some excellent "long hair" variety from impresario Sol Hurok, and revived and musicalized Thornton Wilder's "Our Town" (with Eva Marie Saint, Paul Newman, and the surprisingly nimble Frank Sinatra, who introduced the hit tune, "Love and Marriage").

In spite of these successes, the ultra-high-budgeted, regularly scheduled spectaculars were in serious trouble by the end of the season. Ratings dropped to a generally disappointing level for such an expensive operation. Highly touted productions such as CBS's filmed musical fantasy "High Tor" (with Bing Crosby and Julie Andrews) and Max Liebman's Maurice Chevalier variety shows on NBC, bombed in the ratings. When such simple productions as "Inside Beverly Hills" (puff interviews with film stars in their homes, hosted by Art Linkletter) registered the top ratings for spectaculars, the need to produce anything very elaborate and complicated was increasingly difficult to justify. When an economic recession settled in, it became almost impossible.

Spectaculars had always been extremely expensive to stage and wildly unpredictable in the ratings. Only the largest sponsors had been able to cover the costs, and the 1956 recession forced even these bankrollers, chiefly auto companies such as Ford, to withdraw from the market. They preferred safer and cheaper programs—which, increasingly, meant West Coast filmed series. The other major programming type still emanating from New York, live drama, also felt the squeeze.

Though the New York based drama series attracted all the critical attention, the more popular-oriented Los Angeles dramas attracted more viewers. CBS had three of the top shows: *Alfred*

Hitchcock Presents (with the master of suspense supplying pithy remarks before and after short plays of suspense); *Climax* (which successfully mixed New York style production with Los Angeles style stories and stars); and *General Electric Theater* (which became the top-rated drama show on television by showcasing its host, Ronald Reagan, as well as other top Hollywood names). In addition, Westerns such as *Gunsmoke* and ABC's *Wyatt Earp* presented well written drama with a familiar cast of characters and plenty of action.

The networks did not abandon live New York drama. They were just being more careful with it, limiting the number of showcases and trying to avoid upsetting sponsors and viewers. As a result, while there were still outstanding plays staged, the behind the scenes efforts required to turn them out added a further strain to the already high pressure production schedules. CBS, which had spirited *The U.S. Steel Hour* from ABC, managed to present several striking and memorable plays that season, including a strident Rod Serling original, "Incident in an Alley," which portrayed a policeman's guilt after killing a young boy. Another Serling play, "Noon on Doomsday," faced strong sponsor and network pressure and had to be rewritten before airing. Originally it concerned the highly publicized murder of a Southern black, Emmett Till; in the new version the locale was shifted to New England (where everyone *knew* there was no racial prejudice) and the victim became a white foreigner.

At NBC, Fred Coe at last won a program slot specifically devoted to producing plays written by his troupe of writers from the Sunday night *Television Playhouse. Playwrights '56*, sponsored by Pontiac, began with a David Davidson original, "The Answer," but the long-fought-for series was overshadowed by its strong competition on CBS, *The Red Skelton Show* and *The $64,000 Question.* In an almost eerie juxtaposition of events in the spring of 1956, NBC loudly celebrated Fred Coe's tenth anniversary with the network, then axed his show.

The biggest loser in the shifting fortunes of television in the 1955-56 season was Pat Weaver. The driving force behind *Your Show of Shows, Today, Home, Tonight,* and the spectacular quickly became the scapegoat for NBC's sinking fortunes. Throughout his career at NBC, Weaver had served as a seemingly bottomless well of innovative programming concepts, most of which were highly praised by the nation's television critics and popular with viewers. The fact remained, however, that NBC had fallen from first place and he had failed to bring it back to the top.

In December, 1955, Pat Weaver was, once again, kicked upstairs—this time to the position of chairman of the NBC board—but, unlike his previous "promotion," there was no hope for return. Robert Sarnoff, son and heir apparent to "General" Sarnoff, succeeded Weaver as president. Weaver remained at his figurehead post for a few months and then quietly and politely retired from NBC. Many of Weaver's programming concepts, in fact many of his specific programs, continued successfully long after he was out of power. At the start of 1956, though, the feeling at NBC, and throughout the television industry, was that a new era in television was at hand and that the old generation of executives had to make way for the new.

16. It's Been a Tremendous Strain

CONFUSION and uneasiness gripped the television industry in the fall of 1956. Prime time programming was in flux, the economy was sluggish, and big advertisers were reducing their television budgets. There was pressure from Washington in a new set of congressional hearings that called for a sharp reduction in network control over program production. NBC faced a Department of Justice lawsuit charging that the network had used "undue force" in pressuring Westinghouse to sell its Philadelphia station to NBC. On top of all this, the long smoldering issue of blacklisting had erupted once again, focusing embarrassing national attention and public debate on what was still a common network practice.

The networks themselves had not been directly involved at first in the new blacklisting tempest. It developed in 1955 from an internecine power struggle within television's largest actors' union, the American Federation of Television and Radio Artists (AFTRA). One faction of AFTRA allied itself with Aware, Inc., an anti-Communist *Red Channels* inspired organization. The New York local of AFTRA took the opposite position and issued well-publicized condemnations of Aware's smear tactics and blacklist procedures.

Aware had been founded in December, 1953, by Laurence Johnson, a Syracuse supermarket owner, and Vincent W. Hartnett, a self-appointed authority on Communist subversion who had helped write *Red Channels*. The organization continued, on a day-to-day basis, the crusade begun in the one issue of *Red Channels* published in 1950. Aware informed networks, sponsors, and agencies of supposed leftist tendencies of prospective actors, writers, and directors. It was a clearing house of blacklist information.

The New York local of AFTRA not only blasted Aware's tactics, it also singled out and criticized specific AFTRA members who belonged to Aware and who were cooperating with the Red-baiting House Un-American Activities Committee. The committee used their inside information to subpoena anti-Aware AFTRA members and to pressure them into revealing the names of other entertainers who might have suspicious backgrounds.

In November, 1955, an independent anti-Aware slate, headed by CBS news correspondent Charles Collingwood, campaigned on an anti-Aware, anti-blacklisting platform and was elected to head the New York branch of AFTRA. Almost immediately, Aware launched an extensive smear campaign against these newly elected AFTRA leaders, focusing its attack on comic-personality Orson Bean and local WCBS radio raconteur-humorist John Henry Faulk. Collingwood was too well known and respected by viewers as a credible newsman for a smear campaign to work against him. Bean and Faulk, on the other hand, were second level performers that people vaguely knew but not well enough to assume innocence. Though the two had never been previously linked with left-wing causes, stories suddenly began to spread calling into doubt their patriotic fervor. Some of Bean's personal appearances were canceled with little or no warning, and Faulk lost some of his sponsors. Collingwood held press conferences to denounce Aware's actions, but these had almost no effect. Even the courts seemed to offer no redress.

Lawyers for blacklisted entertainers had repeatedly found themselves trying to grapple with an elusive enemy. In filing personal damage suits, they had to prove that being blacklisted had caused their clients to suffer a personal injury. This was far from easy because no one ever admitted that the blacklisting process even existed, despite its pervasive influence. The publishers of *Red Channels,* the people usually cited in anti-blacklisting cases, stood on solid legal ground and said that *they* had nothing to do with an actor losing a job. They were simply pointing out, to whomever was interested, alleged connections between performers and certain subversive groups. It was the networks and sponsors, they said, that may have made improper use of their publications. The networks, sponsors, and agencies always insisted that they failed to hire particular defendants either because they were "just not right for the part" or because they were "too controversial."

This stance put the blacklisted actors on the defensive, trying to prove a non-event: that they were not hired because of the influence of a list they could not produce. The fact that everyone in the entertainment industry knew an informal blacklist existed did not matter; until someone could present an actual list of names to a court, and document how it was used to damage a career, judges would not accept as proven the very cornerstone of an anti-blacklisting case. It was a perfect "Catch-22" situation. There seemed to be no way to blame anyone, legally, for blacklisting. As a result, anti-blacklisting suits over the years were consistently turned aside.

In spite of the previous failures, John Henry Faulk decided to

FALL 1956 SCHEDULE

MONDAY

7:00	7:30	8:00	8:30	9:00	9:30	10:00	10:30	
Kukla Fran And Ollie / John Daly &The News	Bold Journey	Danny Thomas Show	Voice Of Firestone	Life Is Worth Living	LAWRENCE WELK'S TOP TUNES AND NEW TALENT		local	ABC
local	Robin Hood	Burns And Allen Show	Arthur Godfrey's Talent Scouts	I Love Lucy	December Bride	Studio One		CBS
local	NAT KING COLE / Huntley-Brinkley	SIR LANCELOT	STANLEY @Producer's Showcase	CAN DO		Robert Montgomery Presents	local	NBC

TUESDAY

7:00	7:30	8:00	8:30	9:00	9:30	10:00	10:30	
Kukla Fran And Ollie / John Daly &The News	Cheyenne / Conflict		Life And Legend Of Wyatt Earp	BROKEN ARROW	Du Pont Cavalcade Theater	It's Polka Time	local	ABC
local	Name That Tune	Phil Silvers Show	THE BROTHERS	HERB SHRINER SHOW	Red Skelton Show	The $64,000 Question	Do You Trust Your Wife	CBS
local	JONATHAN WINTERS / Huntley-Brinkley	Big Surprise	NOAH'S ARK	Jane Wyman Show	Kaiser Aluminum Hour / Armstrong Circle Theater		Break The $250,000 Bank	NBC

WEDNESDAY

7:00	7:30	8:00	8:30	9:00	9:30	10:00	10:30	
Kukla Fran And Ollie / John Daly &The News	Disneyland		Navy Log	The Adventures Of Ozzie And Harriet	Ford Theater	Wednesday Night Fights		ABC
local	GIANT STEP	Arthur Godfrey Show		The Millionaire	I've Got A Secret	U.S. Steel Hour / 20th Century-Fox Hour		CBS
local	Eddie Fisher / Huntley-Brinkley	ADVENTURES OF HIRAM HOLIDAY	Father Knows Best	Kraft Television Theater		This Is Your Life	TWENTY-ONE	NBC

THURSDAY

7:00	7:30	8:00	8:30	9:00	9:30	10:00	10:30	
Kukla Fran And Ollie / John Daly &The News	The Lone Ranger	CIRCUS TIME		WIRE SERVICE		Ozark Jubilee		ABC
local	Sgt. Preston Of The Yukon	Bob Cummings Show	Climax @Shower Of Stars		PLAYHOUSE 90			CBS
local	Dinah Shore / Huntley-Brinkley	You Bet Your Life	Dragnet	The People's Choice	TENNESSEE ERNIE FORD SHOW	Lux Video Theater		NBC

FRIDAY

7:00	7:30	8:00	8:30	9:00	9:30	10:00	10:30	
Kukla Fran And Ollie / John Daly &The News	Rin Tin Tin	JIM BOWIE	Crossroads	Treasure Hunt	The Vise	RAY ANTHONY SHOW		ABC
local	My Friend Flicka	WEST POINT	ZANE GREY THEATER	The Crusader	Schlitz Playhouse Of Stars	The Lineup	Person To Person	CBS
local	Eddie Fisher / Huntley-Brinkley	The Life Of Riley	WALTER WINCHELL SHOW	ON TRIAL @Chevy Show I	The Big Story	Gillette Cavalcade Of Sports	Red Barber	NBC

SATURDAY

7:00	7:30	8:00	8:30	9:00	9:30	10:00	10:30	
local	Famous Film Festival			Lawrence Welk's Dodge Dancing Party		Masquerade Party	local	ABC
Beat The Clock	THE BUCCANEERS	Jackie Gleason Show		OH, SUSANNA	HEY, JEANNIE @Ford Star Jubilee	Gunsmoke	High Finance	CBS
local	People Are Funny	Perry Como Show		Caesar's Hour @Saturday Color Carnival		George Gobel Show	Your Hit Parade	NBC

SUNDAY

7:00	7:30	8:00	8:30	9:00	9:30	10:00	10:30	
You Asked For It	The Original Amateur Hour		Press Conference	Omnibus			local	ABC
Lassie	Private Secretary / Jack Benny Program	Ed Sullivan Show		General Electric Theater	Alfred Hitchcock Presents	$64,000 Challenge	What's My Line	CBS
TALES OF THE 77TH BENGAL LANCERS	CIRCUS BOY	Steve Allen Show @Hallmark Hall Of Fame		Goodyear Television Playhouse / Alcoa Hour @Chevy Show II		Loretta Young Show	National Bowling Champions	NBC

try again and hired nationally known lawyer Louis Nizer. In June, 1956, he filed a $500,000 libel suit against Aware, Inc., Laurence Johnson, and Vincent Hartnett. Faulk contended that they had conspired to destroy his income, livelihood, and reputation by the publication of false accusations linking him with Communist infiltration and Communist front organizations. The suit also said that these actions were a patently "sour grapes" response to the defeat of Aware-backed candidates in the 1955 AFTRA elections. Faulk contended that the Aware attacks had effectively kept him off television and had caused him to lose nineteen sponsors for his Monday-through-Friday WCBS radio show. The case immediately became bogged down in tedious legal wrangling that prevented the trial from commencing for years. Faulk managed to retain his WCBS program longer than a year, but the station at last gave in to pressure and fired him. In the process, Faulk's yearly salary dropped from $35,000 to $2,000. Lawyer Nizer said that Aware's actions had cut off Faulk's career "like a knife."

Faulk did not get his day in court until April, 1962. It was only then, with cold war hysteria abated, that the very existence of a blacklist was corroborated by witnesses of considerable stature within the industry. Drama producer David Susskind and quiz show whiz Mark Goodson testified that groups such as Aware were used religiously by networks and sponsors to determine who was hired and who was fired. Susskind and Goodson explained that, as producers, they had to regularly submit names to agencies for "clearance." After a nine-week trial, the jury found Aware guilty and ordered it to pay Faulk $3.5 million in damages, even more than Nizer had asked for. Further appeals (and the death of defendant Johnson) brought the amount of the settlement down, but money was never the central issue in the case. The important point was that, after fifteen years, an American jury at last declared blacklisting to be illegal. Until then, even through the long legal process, blacklisting continued.

The start of the Faulk case in the summer of 1956 was merely the topping on the mound of upsetting problems for the television industry. Though the legal and governmental headaches were disturbing, they had to take a back seat to the more immediate problem of trying to make sense out of the era's vast changes in programming, ushered in by the rise of *The $64,000 Question*. There was no doubt that change was in progress, but what made the networks very nervous was that nobody could be sure just what the emerging new TV status quo would be. Throughout the season, superstar performers who had been top ten material just a few years before found their drawing power fading. Some of the veterans decided to leave the television grind for a while; many more were canceled.

Of the three networks, NBC seemed the most willing to tear up old patterns and start from scratch because, despite its best efforts over the previous few years, the network's programming philosophy had left it still playing number two to CBS. As upstart ABC showed signs of a concerted drive toward equality with NBC and CBS, even that position seemed in jeopardy. NBC's programming was in decline throughout the day. The Pat Weaver-inspired staples of prime time—spectaculars, hour-long dramas, and rotating big name comedy-variety shows—failed to deliver consistently. NBC news veteran John Cameron Swayze was losing the nightly news race. In daytime, CBS's soap operas had a firm lock on the audience.

All through 1956 there was a complete shakeup in NBC executive personnel, reshaping the network's programming philosophy. Flashy, easy to produce quiz and game shows such as *Tic Tac Dough, The Price Is Right,* and *Queen For a Day* began to dominate NBC's daytime line-up. On the nightly news, Chet Huntley and David Brinkley—the two surprise stars of NBC's coverage of the summer's political conventions—deposed anchor John Cameron Swayze.

With Pat Weaver gone, Robert Sarnoff, the new president of the network, named Robert Kinter as NBC's new programming boss. Previously, Kinter had been the president of ABC and he brought with him the policy of filling prime time with programming produced almost exclusively by outsiders. Such a policy had made sense at ABC, which from the beginning of its network operations had neither the background nor the finances to establish a comprehensive, in-house production unit. It seemed an unusual strategy for financially stable NBC because from the very early days of television both NBC and CBS had fought to retain control of programming either by producing most of their prime time shows themselves or by buying into the programs they purchased from independent producers. This policy had obvious economic benefits and gave the two networks a major role in deciding the direction and tone of programs being aired. Even though Kinter's policy surrendered such control to outsiders, he hoped to shake some life into his new network's ratings by adopting the policy that had provided ABC with its few major hits.

There was a sound political reason for Kinter's strategy as well. With NBC fighting a Department of Justice lawsuit in the Westinghouse-Philadelphia case, and Congress vowing to break up the networks' control of programming, Kinter's "outsiders" policy helped deflate public criticism of the networks. In doing so, it helped to hold off any governmental action that might radically alter the fundamental rules of television, causing the networks far greater losses in profits and control.

NBC had begun its major overhaul in prime time programming a few months before Kinter came on board. One of the most important changes took place on Sunday night during the summer of 1956 when late night personality Steve Allen came in to compete with Ed Sullivan. CBS used Sullivan, whose show was number two in the overall ratings, as the pivot in its successful Sunday night strategy. Sullivan's show was popular enough to boost the ratings of the programs on both before and after his; as a result, CBS had a chain of hits to begin the evening. In order to improve its own ratings on the most popular night for TV viewing, NBC had to break up the solid CBS line-up—and that meant beating Ed Sullivan.

Steve Allen took to the air in the summer to get a jump on the fall competition. He took the straight vaudeville style Sullivan

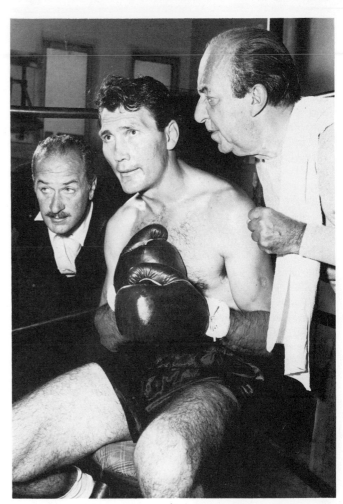

The second production of CBS's live drama series, *Playhouse 90,* was Rod Serling's "Requiem for a Heavyweight," starring: (from *l.*) Keenan Wynn, Jack Palance, Ed Wynn. *(CBS, Inc.)*

used and added to it the popular sketches and the family of supporting characters he had built on the *Tonight* show. Transplanted virtually intact from Allen's late night format were his "man-on-the-street" feature and mock "report to the nation," as well as his increasingly popular band of regulars, including Don Knotts, Louis Nye, Tom Poston, Pat Harrington, Jr., and Bill (Jose Jimenez) Dana.

The Steve Allen-Ed Sullivan face-off became the biggest ratings battle of the 1956–57 season, and the pattern of combat soon emerged: it was a war of guest stars. Allen's June premiere featured Jerry Lewis, Bob Hope, and Sammy Davis, Jr., while Sullivan countered with an eighth anniversary show featuring Lucille Ball, Phil Silvers, and Marlon Brando. On his second show, Allen retaliated with the current teenage phenomenon in music, Elvis Presley. In contrast to his hip-swinging Dorsey Brothers and Milton Berle appearances, Elvis presented a "new Presley," more subdued and in more formal attire. His presence boosted Allen's ratings far above Sullivan's. Undaunted, Sullivan imperiously stated that despite the ratings, he would *never* have Mr. Presley on because he hosted a *family* show. Within two weeks, Sullivan signed Presley to do three shows for $50,000, the most he had ever paid a performer.

On September 9, at the start of the new season, Elvis Presley appeared live, from Los Angeles, on the Sullivan show, performing four songs—"Don't Be Cruel," "Love Me Tender," "Ready Teddy," and "Hound Dog"—in the more familiar "Elvis the Pelvis" style (to the delight of screaming fans in the studio). Once again, Presley meant instant ratings success, as Sullivan's show grabbed more than 80% of the audience that night. Presley's second appearance (in October) did just as well. After this incredible success, CBS grew nervous over the then-current wave of Presley detractors and when the singer returned in January for his third and final Sullivan show, the cameramen were instructed to show Elvis only from the waist up. This truncating of Presley inflamed proponents of the new rock'n'roll craze who felt their hero was being unfairly treated. After a particularly bouncy appearance by Jayne Mansfield on *Shower of Stars,* one Presley fan wrote to CBS, "If you can't show Elvis Presley from the waist down, don't show Jayne Mansfield from the waist up."

The wild competition for stars sometimes seemed humorous, but the stakes were high. At the start of the 1956–57 season, Sullivan maintained a healthy lead over Allen, but as the year wore on Allen whittled down the advantage until the race was a virtual tie. This was a tremendous improvement for NBC, which for several seasons had been decimated on Sunday night running its moribund comedy-variety hour.

Steve Allen was also still in charge of the *Tonight* show. In the fall of 1956, his only concession to the added responsibilities of the Sunday night program was handing over the Monday and Tuesday night *Tonight* slots to perennial fill-in, Ernie Kovacs (who brought his increasingly abstract and inventive style of television

---

September 30, 1956

Following the demise of DuMont, CBS picks up the Sunday afternoon National Football League contests. With this new larger forum, NFL professional football begins a sharp growth in popularity among America's gridiron fans.

October 29, 1956

NBC News. (NBC). The two hits of NBC's convention coverage, Chet Huntley and David Brinkley, take over NBC's nightly news. Brinkley reports from Washington, Huntley from New York. By 1958, the show is known as *The Huntley-Brinkley Report,* and their sign-off exchange of "Goodnight, Chet" and "Goodnight, David" becomes a familiar program trademark.

November 3, 1956

Hollywood's 1939 feature film classic, "The Wizard of Oz," appears for the first time on television (as the final presentation of CBS's *Ford Star Jubilee*). The annual airing of the movie becomes a TV family ritual.

November 26, 1956

The Price Is Right. (NBC). Bill Cullen hosts a daytime quizzer in which contestants try to win shiny new merchandise by guessing the actual retail price (without going over).

December 17, 1956

CBS's James Aubrey temporarily defects, becoming ABC's chief programmer.

December 18, 1956

To Tell the Truth. (CBS). Bud Collyer, the radio voice of Superman, hosts another Mark Goodson-Bill Todman television quiz hit. Three contestants each claim to be the same person and a panel of celebrities tries to separate the bona-fide oddball from the two charlatans.

---

humor to perhaps the largest audience he ever had). By January, however, Allen felt that he was working himself too hard and left the late night slot altogether to devote his full attention to the prime time series. NBC found itself in the same position it had been in when Jerry Lester quit *Broadway Open House* in 1951. The network had to carry on a program based on a familiar character who had departed. NBC had failed miserably in its search for a successor to Lester and it very nearly did the same in 1957 with the poorly planned *Tonight! America After Dark.*

Instead of finding one successor to Allen, NBC set up *America After Dark* as a show with multiple hosts performing in four cities (New York, Chicago, Los Angeles, and a wild card city such as Miami or Las Vegas)—making it a bulky, unwieldy sort of late-night wide, wide world of entertainment. The format called for live remote broadcasts of top performing talent at nightclubs, cafes, and restaurants, as well as light features, hard news, and a few sports figures. The network chose newspaper columnists Hy Gardner, Earl Wilson, Bob Considine, and Irv Kupcinet for emcees, with *Today* show regular Jack Lescoulie as the only television veteran in sight. The columnists may have known their stars but they did not know how to act relaxed before the camera, appearing uncomfortable and spiritless.

Reviewers watching the first week's shows concluded that NBC was committing hara-kiri and seemed determined to kill off its late night programming. The live remotes from the nightclubs proved a disaster of bad timing, and the live feature pickups floundered in the clichés of on-the-spot television ("we're visiting the night shift at a nuclear reactor . . ."). There was a good deal of name dropping and very little entertainment. Though the loose format of *America After Dark* had been set up to create a feeling of spontaneity—the strength of Allen's show—the program emerged instead as a jumble of unconnected, erratic, poorly timed ad-libs. Ratings took a nose dive and affiliates in major cities defected to the more stable format of airing old movies. It appeared as if NBC had once again botched its fragile hold on late night television. In June, 1957, the network decided to make a last ditch attempt to save the slot by scrapping *America After Dark* and reverting to the more familiar desk and sofa talk show style. The new host, Jack Paar, was given an ultimatum: Register good ratings by Christmas or face extinction.

Premiering at the end of July, Paar's show faced a difficult challenge. Viewers in cities such as Houston, Cleveland, St. Louis, Nashville, Pittsburgh, and Boston were unable to see the program because the local NBC affiliates there kept showing old films, having decided that the new format was doomed and useless. Additionally, Paar seemed to lack "warmth," an attribute felt necessary for late night hosts. In spite of these shortcomings, Paar not only managed to keep the show afloat, he made it a hit again. To support his own personality, Paar favored frequent appearances by guest performers over a family of regulars (only announcer Hugh Downs joined Paar each night). Among the many performers that often dropped by were Dody Goodman, a daffy blonde with a sharp tongue for intentional malapropisms; Cliff Arquette as Charlie Weaver, the country philosopher who read humorous and fictitious letters from his mother; and controversial social gadfly Elsa Maxwell, who constantly got Paar into trouble with her outrageous charges about well-known celebrities (such as calling Walter Winchell a "phony patriot" who never voted). Maxwell's slightly ribald and risque style rubbed off on Paar, whose double-entendre jokes soon captured a national audience, thereby saving the show while bedeviling NBC's censors.

The *Tonight* show weathered a difficult transition before becoming a success again under Jack Paar. In prime time, other formats and performers did not fare as well, with spectaculars, comedy-variety, and hour-long drama anthologies suffering major casualties. NBC's monthly Monday and Saturday spectaculars limped along until the end of the season, while CBS's *Ford Star Jubilee* did not even last until Christmas. The Ford show went out on a high note, though, presenting the television premiere of "The Wizard of Oz," the first major Hollywood film to appear on television.

In comedy-variety, several titans were laid low. Even before the season began, NBC had divided Milton Berle's traditional Tuesday night slot between two half-hour shows, a Jack Webb medical drama (*Noah's Ark*) and a Louis G. Cowan quiz program (*The Big Surprise*). As a result, for the first time in eight years, Berle did not have a show. On CBS, Jackie Gleason made a well-publicized return to a live comedy-variety hour after his experiment with a weekly *Honeymooners* series the previous season, but found his reception less than triumphant. His familiar format of glamour girls, dancers, and character skits had become a fond memory in its year-long absence, yet seemed repetitiously familiar when it reappeared. Worse yet, the Honeymooners segment was rarely presented, leaving the show almost devoid of its strongest element. NBC's slow and steady *Perry Como Show* soon garnered double Gleason's ratings. At the end of the season, Gleason temporarily retired from television after seven years of weekly shows.

Veteran Sid Caesar, whose program had been moved to Saturday in the fall to follow the successful *Perry Como Show,* could not carry over the audience from the strong lead-in show. Instead, *Caesar's Hour* was regularly defeated by ABC's Lawrence Welk. Viewing Caesar's enormous budget and low ratings, NBC tried to convince him to leave weekly television and to concentrate on occasional specials. Caesar balked at the idea and, after a brief fight, NBC canceled his show. Sid Caesar was generally considered one of the best comics on television, so his forced departure came as an especially upsetting blow to other TV comedians.

Even the king and queen of television sitcoms—Desi Arnaz and Lucille Ball—ended their weekly series at the end of the season, though they chose to quit while on top. *I Love Lucy,* in fact had regained the number one spot for a time during the season and was still a Monday night blockbuster for CBS. The staff felt, however, that after six years they had done all they could with the half-hour program. The Ricardos and the Mertzes had gone through dozens of domestic plots, traveled to Hollywood, toured Europe, and, in the 1956–57 season, set up housekeeping in a Connecticut suburb. After some wrangling with CBS, which did not want to lose a winner, it was agreed that, after 179 episodes, *I Love Lucy* would cease weekly production at the end of the season. Beginning in the fall of 1957, though, the *Lucy* format would be continued in occasional one-hour specials for the network. At the same time, CBS would move the successful reruns of the older *I Love Lucy* episodes from early Saturday evening to prime time on Wednesday night.

The hour-long drama anthologies, once a pillar of network television programming, also lost considerable ground during the 1956–57 season. *The Lux Video Theater, The Alcoa/Goodyear Television Playhouse,* and *Robert Montgomery Presents,* three old-time stalwarts, were canceled. A more important setback, though, was the treatment of a promising new NBC series, *The Kaiser Aluminum Hour,* Worthington Miner's equivalent to Fred Coe's *Playwrights '56.*

Miner, who had been mostly inactive following his defection

Jack Barry, co-producer of *Tic-Tac-Dough,* hosted the daytime version of the show, which premiered in July 1956. *(Courtesy Barry-Enright Productions)*

to NBC in 1952, formed a production arm called Unit 4 to produce the Kaiser show. He held the post of executive producer, while three others, Franklin Schaffner (a former director at *Studio One*), Fielder Cook, and George Roy Hill (both former directors of *The Kraft Television Theater*), rotated the weekly production and direction chores. From the start, Unit 4 turned out exciting, unique television drama, reminiscent of Miner's glory days at *Studio One.* Early successes included "The Army Game," with Paul Newman (who had become a movie star with "Somebody Up There Likes Me") as a wise-guy draftee with psychological problems, and a bold and exciting adaptation of the Sophocles classic "Antigone" with Claude Rains. Like Coe's *Playwrights '56, The Kaiser Aluminum Hour* was placed in one of the toughest slots possible (against *The $64,000 Question* and the ever-resilient *Red Skelton Show*), yet the program maintained respectable ratings. The problems facing the show came from the Young & Rubicam production agency, which controlled the program, and Henry Kaiser himself.

In November, Miner quit, after two projects were vetoed as being too controversial (an old John Galsworthy play on anti-Semitism in Britain and a new play on the Polish Poznan trials that followed the 1956 anti-Soviet riots). With Miner gone, the sponsor and agency began exerting their veto power more frequently and within three months they rejected: Robert Alan Aurthur's "Memphis by Morning" (on a tense racial situation), Loring Mandel's "The Healer" (on a faith healer who lost, then regained, his faith), and Reginald Rose's "The Gathering" (a sensitive portrait of a family under stress during an air raid, revealed at the end to be

Russians living in Moscow). Repeated crisis sessions were held between the three remaining Unit 4 members and the agency. In February, Henry Kaiser personally appeared to inform the members of Unit 4 that they were fired. He said that they refused to produce the plays Kaiser wanted, those that were noncontroversial and more "Americana-oriented." There were too many people, Kaiser said, who tuned out their more realistic but more depressing plays. Franklin Schaffner of the Unit 4 group responded, "To offend no one is to stimulate no one."

As the era of original television drama anthologies approached its almost inevitable conclusion, CBS presented one last gasp of greatness, *Playhouse 90*, the last major attempt by a network to produce weekly high class drama. Produced by Martin Manulis, the new show represented a double risk for CBS: It marked the first attempt to produce live ninety-minute drama on a weekly basis (to ease the production schedule, however, a Screen Gems-produced filmed play filled the slot once a month) and it was scheduled on Thursday night, following *Climax*. This resulted in two and one-half hours of continuous drama on CBS, a line-up many assumed put too much faith in the attention span of the American public. CBS pressed on and, after faltering a bit with a weak first show, produced in *Playhouse 90* some of the best drama seen on television.

In October, on only its second show, *Playhouse 90* presented perhaps its best play, Rod Serling's "Requiem for a Heavyweight." It was a fabulous character study starring Jack Palance as a washed-up, confused, dumb but honest boxer; Ed Wynn (in his dramatic debut) as the honest and faithful trainer, and his son Keenan Wynn as Palance's manager, who was torn between a desire to help his

fighter and an urge to misuse him in order to make money. The masterful production seemed to defy the inherent time and space limitations of live television by using ingenious and complicated camera work. "It was so good," one critic noted, "it was hard to believe it was live."

In February, *Playhouse 90* presented another powerful original, "The Miracle Worker," the story of blind and deaf Helen Keller, starring Patty McCormack as Keller at age seven, Burl Ives as her father, and Teresa Wright as Helen's teacher, Anne Sullivan. The final dramatic scene, in which Sullivan broke through and communicated with Helen, combined the best in dramatic tension and honest sentimentality (a major factor in Hollywood's decision to turn it into a movie, starring Patty Duke).

In spite of CBS's valiant efforts with *Playhouse 90*, television's commitment to drama continued to move away from live New York anthologies and toward Hollywood filmed adventures. During the summer of 1956, when some of television's big stars were on vacation, *Gunsmoke* had surprisingly popped into the top ten, further encouraging the expansion of Westerns. For the 1956–57 season, the network schedules were stocked with such sagebrush sagas as *Broken Arrow, Tales of Wells Fargo,* and *Dick Powell's Zane Grey Theater.* These joined such grade-B adventure yarns as *Tales of the 77th Bengal Lancers, Wire Service,* and *Circus Boy* (which starred twelve-year-old Mickey Braddock who, a decade later as Micky Dolenz, appeared in another kiddie adventure show, *The Monkees*). CBS even ran *The West Point Story,* a filmed series from Ziv, a TV film syndicator that had been locked out of prime time by the networks for years. Though none of these new programs were runaway hits, they provided clear evidence of the drift in television drama. The most exciting and successful drama of the season, however, did not appear on any of the networks' anthologies, Westerns, or adventure series. It took place on a new quiz show.

After the initial spurt in popularity by *The $64,000 Question*, viewer interest in quiz shows had leveled off. The programs were easy to produce, though, and anxious sponsors—eager for cheap television time—insisted that the shows continue. In a time of economic slowdown, the sponsor's word carried added weight with the networks so they continued to slot new quiz programs, despite the amazingly rapid turnover of the shows throughout the season. Nobody seemed able to single out exactly what elements were needed to ensure success; consequently, endless variations of the same thing developed, with one aspect exaggerated. Many programs, such as *Break the $250,000 Bank* (with Bert Parks), inflated the potential jackpot well beyond a paltry $64,000. Others featured face-offs by celebrity contestants. *Can Do,* hosted by actor Robert Alda (father of Alan Alda) presented guest celebrities who attempted inane stunts while contestants from the audience tried to guess whether the stars "can do" or "no can do." The show itself was a "no can do" and became one of the first of many quiz shows to bite the dust that season.

In place of *Can Do,* NBC moved in *Twenty-One.* Hosted by Jack Barry, *Twenty-One* featured contestants who tried to accumulate twenty-one points by answering increasingly difficult questions. Like *The $64,000 Question, Twenty-One* made use of that deliciously symbolic tool, the isolation booth. In shifting from late Wednesday to Monday night, though, the program seemed destined to meet the bleak fate of most of the other new quiz shows because it was placed opposite *I Love Lucy.* Instead, *Twenty-One* became *the* show that clicked. It came up with what every quiz show producer dreamed of: a contestant who caught the public's fancy.

April 7, 1957
Hollywood Film Theater. (ABC). ABC presents old RKO features, beginning with "Rachel and the Stranger," in another unsuccessful attempt to bring movies to prime time.

April 8, 1957
The Jimmy Dean Show. (CBS). CBS gives up trying to beat *Today* at its own game and opts to fill the early morning slot with a country-style variety show.

April 28, 1957
Mike Wallace Interviews. (ABC). After five months as host of a "no holds barred" late night interview show in New York City, Wallace goes network. His technique of pressing for candid, controversial statements is dubbed "hot interviewing."

June 3, 1957
Sports Focus. (ABC). Up and coming sports commentator Howard Cosell gets his first regular network television show, a daily wrapup of the sporting world.

August 30, 1957
More vets fade from view. Kukla, Fran, and Ollie are laid to rest by ABC.

September 13, 1957
WCBS radio gives in to blacklist pressure and fires John Henry Faulk.

September 29, 1957
After twelve years of Sunday night drama, NBC retires the *Television Playhouse* to make room for musical-variety with Dinah Shore.

The contestant was thirty-year-old Charles Van Doren, a Columbia University English instructor and son of the well-known poet, Mark Van Doren.

Charles Van Doren had first appeared on *Twenty-One* on November 28 and overtook the reigning champion, Herbert Stempel, one week later. By January Van Doren had reached a new high in quiz earnings ($122,000) while leading *Twenty-One* to a new high against *I Love Lucy* (only four rating points behind). As he increased his winnings, Van Doren became a widely discussed national figure. He was treated as a shining example of American intellect and youth, someone parents wanted their children to look up to. Unlike contestants on *The $64,000 Question,* those on *Twenty-One* were not able to choose the topic they wished to be queried on. Instead, they were subjected to an all-around interrogation, something that called for not just a sports fanatic or a drama enthusiast, but an all-around educated American. Van Doren certainly seemed to fit that bill. Without blushing, he quickly identified the Polish volunteer who became Washington's aide in the Revolutionary War (Kosciuszko); with a mere furrow of the brow he identified "caries" as another name for dental cavities, after nervously chewing his lip he correctly identified the "patellar reflex" as the reaction that occurs when a knee is tapped; and after a worried mop of his forehead, he identified which church in which city contained Leonardo da Vinci's fresco "The Last Supper" (Santa María delle Gràzie, in Milan).

The nation was entranced. Charles Van Doren was said to have "gained the affection and esteem of millions throughtout the nation." Viewers found Van Doren the one new television personality that they could become involved with. Millions tuned in *Twenty-One* just to follow the newly-anointed symbol of the state in his weekly battle of wits. His success was their success. His failure would be their failure.

Early in February, a few days after he staged a dramatic come-from-behind victory, Van Doren was on the cover of *Time.* After his February 11 performance, he was offered a $50,000 movie contract. By the February 18 show, the tension was unbearable. Van Doren reached the unbelievable level of $143,000 in earnings but, at the end of the program, was tied with Mrs. Vivienne Nearing, a New York lawyer. When the ratings for the February 18 program came in, they showed that *Twenty-One* had become the first regular series to beat *I Love Lucy* in its time slot. On February 25, newspaper ads posed the question: "Will the Lady Lawyer beat him?" Amazingly, they tied again (think of it—two ties in a row). That night, *Twenty-One* was six points *ahead* of *Lucy,* and the producers were ecstatic. They were immediately frustrated, however, to discover that round two of their sudden-death contest would be delayed a week. As part of NBC's remaining regularly scheduled specials, *Producers' Showcase* was slated for its monthly appearance on March 4, pre-empting *Twenty-One* to present "Romeo and Juliet." A howl went up, demanding that the Bard be postponed so that the nation could see the latest act in a real-life drama. Despite the pressure, "Romeo and Juliet" performed instead, and the nation had to wait until March 11 to learn the answer to the question posed by that week's *Twenty-One* newspaper ad, which showed large photos of both Van Doren and Nearing with the simple caption: "Which one?"

After all the buildup, Van Doren was eliminated on the very first question, being unable to give the name of the king of Belgium (Baudouin). The boy genius had been deposed in a bloodless joust and *Twenty-One* had to face its real test: Could it survive without Charles Van Doren, America's favorite egghead?

For a loser, Van Doren left *Twenty-One* in pretty good shape. He received $129,000 and accepted a job as a regular panelist on NBC radio's *Conversation,* discussing such questions as "What is an educated man?" Nonetheless, on leaving he confided to anxious reporters, "It's been a tremendous strain." Soon thereafter, Van Doren signed an exclusive pact with NBC for five years at $50,000 per year.

Following Van Doren's departure, *Twenty-One* immediately dropped seventeen points in the ratings (from 8½ ahead of *I Love Lucy* on Van Doren's last week to nine behind only seven days later). While no longer in television's top ten list, *Twenty-One* had become a consistently top-rated show and quiz show producers were again given proof that quiz shows could lead to instant success, if only the right gimmick or the right character could be found. Perhaps the two elements were really one and the same thing.

Just a few months after Van Doren's triumph, the television industry, which had been sniffing all season to unearth the prophesied new trend in programming, was surprised to discover that *Gunsmoke* had slowly climbed into the number one position with practically no advance ballyhoo. It had quietly and unobtrusively advanced up the popularity lists while its other Western brethren held to steady, if not standout, ratings.

This meant that, in a season of flux, the only two formats to show a marked improvement were Westerns and quizzes. After two full seasons of vainly searching for what would attract the support of the expanding television audience, the networks concluded that the viewers had cast their votes for the old sage and the isolation booths. If that was what the public wanted, then Westerns and quizzes would be what it would get. In abundance.

17. Oh, Dem Oaters

THOUGH the networks hailed Westerns as a "sure thing" for the new season, there was a sense of caution among the advertisers. The cowboy programs (nicknamed "oaters") would still have to prove themselves in head-to-head competition with television's superstars. Kaiser Aluminum, sponsor of one half of a new ABC Western, *Maverick,* even delivered an ultimatum to the network: Kaiser would guarantee sponsorship only until Christmas; if *Maverick* failed to deliver good ratings by then, Kaiser would pull out.

Maverick (produced by the Warner Brothers studios) was placed in a difficult time slot, Sunday night against the variety blockbusters of Ed Sullivan and Steve Allen. To gain some advantage over the competition, ABC duplicated a strategy that had worked well for *Disneyland,* and started *Maverick* one half hour before the two giants began, hoping to hook the audience before it fell into its usual viewing habits. The first ratings report, released in October, showed *Maverick* surprisingly strong in the tough slot, and ABC easily found a sponsor for the other half of the show. By Thanksgiving, the program had topped Steve Allen and in the spring it even beat Ed Sullivan. Only then was Kaiser, and other sponsors, convinced that Westerns could perform very well and might indeed be the "safest bet" in programming.

Though *Maverick* contained many facets of the traditional adult Western, it was actually the leader of a revisionist new wave that introduced a different brand of hero to television, the maverick, also known as the anti-hero. Television's first wave of cowboys such as the Lone Ranger and Hopalong Cassidy had merely carried on the standard stalwart stances of classic movie heroes. The second wave had focused on grimly realistic characters such as Matt Dillon, who found no joy in violent shoot-outs, but who accepted their necessity. The new breed of hero emerging in Westerns such as *Maverick* not only accepted violence but frankly sought it out for enjoyment (albeit on the side of justice). The maverick devoted his energies to aiding people in need, just as his familiar Western colleagues did, but was guided by his own good-hearted nature and self-interest, rather than by a mythical "code of the West." Additionally, *Maverick* refused to take itself too seriously, injecting into the series elements of humor, a quality notably absent in most Westerns.

The Maverick brothers, (James Garner as Bret and Jack Kelly as Bart) roamed the West not as determined law enforcement agents, but as drifting playboys. They supported their gambling habits and expensive tastes with clever schemes and con games, though they usually saved their most outlandish exploits for overblown figures of authority, especially in defense of hopeless causes and mistreated underdogs. Bret and Bart occasionally worked as a team, but usually went their separate ways in search of high stakes and beautiful women (with Garner and Kelly alternating each week in the lead role). Garner was especially effective as the good-hearted slightly dishonest hero, and his roles in subsequent theatrical features and television series (such as "Support Your Local Sheriff" and *The Rockford Files*) often seemed to be merely Maverick in a different setting. *Maverick's* writers also made a determined effort to avoid the usual Western plots, sometimes even adapting stories from classic literature. In fact, *Maverick* departed so often from the usual Western types that, in many ways, it really was not a Western at all. "We've done three shows in a row without so much as a gun or a horse," *Maverick's* producer said during the program's second season, explaining:

> What we set out to do was create a character that deliberately broke all the rules of the traditional Western hero. He's a little bit of a coward, he's not solemn, he's greedy, and not above cheating a little. He's indifferent to the problems of other people. He's something of a gentle grafter.

Another new wave Warner Brothers cowboy series on ABC that departed from the traditional image of the Western hero was *Sugarfoot,* which featured an anti-hero of a different sort. Tom Brewster, the Sugarfoot (played by Will Hutchins) was a young drifting wanderer who could not shoot (he abhorred guns), was shy, and was even studying to become a lawyer (through a correspondence course). Though he became entangled in other people's problems week after week, he tried to solve them with as little violence as possible, relying on his boyish charm instead of his biceps to overcome evil. This emphasis on talk proved so unnerving that in the first episode the frustrated bad guy (played by Dennis Hopper) asked Sugarfoot, "Whaddya tryin' ta do, talk me to death?"

CBS broke from the standard Western mold that fall with *Have Gun Will Travel,* presenting Richard Boone as a hired gun (Paladin) who operated on the blasphemous premise that he should be paid for protecting people in trouble. Of course, Matt Dillon was paid for being marshal of Dodge City, but the stories left the impression that he would have done it all for free anyway, motivated by principle and a sense of justice. Paladin, however, was little better than a mob hit man who spent his off hours lounging at his San Francisco hotel playing cards and entertaining women (of questionable virtue), while being attended to by two servants he addressed as "Hey Boy" and "Hey Girl." He was motivated entirely by his own self-interest, and cared little for the code of the West or for aiding people for the fun of it. Occasionally, when he detected that someone was trying to manipulate him, Paladin sacrificed payment and confronted his own employer, but only to protect his professional reputation. Usually, though, he was commissioned by "good" people who were simply unable to defend themselves.

Have Gun Will Travel incorporated many of the standard routines of the classic Western heroes, but gave them a diabolic twist in the character of Paladin. Though he was the hero of the series, Paladin always wore black (even in the desert heat), giving him an image as the Angel of Death. Appropriately, the death sequences in the show were the dramatic high point of each episode and choreographed as carefully as a ballet. At the inevitable final confrontation, Paladin and his foe respectfully squared off for what both knew would be a fatal shoot-out. Like Death itself, the dark-robed Paladin seemed to offer a chance to beat the fates with the draw of guns, but he always won. Afterward, though pleased at another victory, out of professional respect Paladin often leaned over to offer his dying adversary a final word of consolation. In many ways Paladin had more in common with his foes than with those who hired him, and this was an important key to one of the great strengths of the best adult Westerns and the anti-hero series. The characters in these stories turned a simple, traditional television morality play into a far more complex conflict.

Generally, all Western adventures took place after the devisive national politics of the Civil War and before the American frontier ended, in a West largely untouched by Eastern civilization. Within the twenty-year period between 1870 and 1890 (the date American historian Frederick Jackson Turner declared as marking the closing of the frontier), virtually the entire American West lost its free-wheeling spirit, as town after town was cleaned up and readied for civilization and business expansion. Setting the stories in this very short period emphasized the theme of inevitable, necessary, but uncertain progress and gave an air of dramatic fatality to all the Westerns.

With civilization always just around the corner, Western heroes faced the same inescapable fate as the villains because both the good guys and bad guys were part of a vanishing breed. By 1890, when the outlaws were gone, the gun-toting marshals also became unnecessary. Traditional kiddie Westerns generally ignored this important conflict with change, but the new breed of Westerns used it to increase dramatic tension and develop the cowboy heroes into characters very similar to a classic private eye type, the inside-outsider.

For years crime buffs had followed such inside-outsiders, usually coarse and surly private eyes typified by Humphrey Bogart's interpretation of Sam Spade in "The Maltese Falcon." These characters were strong-willed independents who refused to abide by the rules of behavior for normal society and often broke the letter of the law themselves in the pursuit of a personal code of justice. The best anti-hero and adult Westerns featured strong characters that embodied the traits of these reluctant heroes, from barely legal gunmen such as the Maverick brothers and Paladin to sensitive souls such as Matt Dillon and Sugarfoot. They all were, in effect, outlaws yet, through the vagaries of fate, they worked with the system if not always actually within it.

Of course, all television Westerns did not feature inside-outsiders and, despite the dramatic strength of the Western setting, there was no denying that many Western series used an inordinate number of clichéd characters and hastily written, weak scripts. NBC,

A heart-to-heart father and son talk between Ward Cleaver (Hugh Beaumont) and the Beaver (Jerry Mathers). (*From* Leave It To Beaver. *Courtesy of MCA Television Limited*)

the last network to commit itself to developing a new slew of cowboy dramas for the fall, had two of the season's more conventional programs. *Restless Gun* featured tight-lipped determination by strong silent type cowboys, while *The Californians* presented lawless San Francisco at the height of the Gold Rush. (Nonetheless, one NBC flak insisted, "[*The Californians*] is not a Western; it's about California in the 1850s!") However, the network also came up with an hour-long epic oater, *Wagon Train,* an adult Western that successfully combined elements of a drama anthology series with a stable cast of regulars. Each week, a new group of frontiersmen (the guest stars) joined the wagon train on its regular run from St. Joseph, Missouri, across a treacherous expanse of Western territory, to California. Ward Bond played the wagon master, Terry Wilson was his assistant, and Robert Horton served as the frontier scout. Though they acted as both protectors and counselors to the traveling party (fighting outlaws and hostile Indians), they often stepped aside in the stories and let the traumas and complications of the passengers carry the episodes. This scripting strategy not only saved wear and tear on the central cast, it also allowed a wide range of character study plots. *Wagon Train* managed to keep rolling with this workable format for eight seasons, setting the pattern later followed by *Bonanza* and *The Virginian.*

The general swing toward Westerns also meshed perfectly with the networks' increasing emphasis on kiddie-oriented adventure tales for early prime time. The ABC-Walt Disney combination came up with *Zorro,* a direct descendant of the old-fashioned Saturday matinee serials, to satisfy the children's desire for less complicated Western adventure. Zorro, the alias of wealthy Spanish

MONDAY

Network	7:00	7:30	8:00	8:30	9:00	9:30	10:00	10:30
ABC	SPORTS FOCUS / John Daly &The News	AMERICAN BANDSTAND	GUY MITCHELL SHOW	Bold Journey	Voice Of Firestone	Lawrence Welk's Top Tunes And New Talent		local
CBS	local	Robin Hood	Burns And Allen Show	Arthur Godfrey's Talent Scouts	Danny Thomas Show	December Bride	Studio One	
NBC	local	THE PRICE IS RIGHT	RESTLESS GUN	Tales Of Wells Fargo	Twenty-One	TURN OF FATE	SUSPICION	

TUESDAY

Network	7:00	7:30	8:00	8:30	9:00	9:30	10:00	10:30
ABC	SPORTS FOCUS / John Daly &The News	Cheyenne / SUGARFOOT		Life And Legend Of Wyatt Earp	Broken Arrow	Telephone Time	West Point	local
CBS	local	Name That Tune	Phil Silvers Show	EVE ARDEN SHOW	To Tell The Truth	Red Skelton Show	The $64,000 Question	ASSIGNMENT: FOREIGN LEGION
NBC	local	Nat King Cole Show	George Gobel Show / Eddie Fisher Show		Meet McGraw	Bob Cummings Show	THE CALIFORNIANS	local

WEDNESDAY

Network	7:00	7:30	8:00	8:30	9:00	9:30	10:00	10:30
ABC	SPORTS FOCUS / John Daly &The News	Disneyland		TOMBSTONE TERRITORY	The Adventures Of Ozzie And Harriet	WALTER WINCHELL FILE	Wednesday Night Fights	
CBS	local	I Love Lucy	BIG RECORD		The Millionaire	I've Got A Secret	U.S. Steel Hour / Armstrong Circle Theater	
NBC	local	WAGON TRAIN		Father Knows Best	Kraft Television Theater		This Is Your Life	local

THURSDAY

Network	7:00	7:30	8:00	8:30	9:00	9:30	10:00	10:30
ABC	SPORTS FOCUS / John Daly &The News	Circus Boy	ZORRO	THE REAL McCOYS	PAT BOONE CHEVY SHOWROOM	O.S.S.	Navy Log	local
CBS	local	Sqt. Preston Of The Yukon	HARBOURMASTER	Climax / @Shower Of Stars		Playhouse 90		
NBC	local	TIC TAC DOUGH	You Bet Your Life	Dragnet	The People's Choice	Tennessee Ernie Ford Show	THE LUX SHOW WITH ROSEMARY CLOONEY	Jane Wyman Show

FRIDAY

Network	7:00	7:30	8:00	8:30	9:00	9:30	10:00	10:30
ABC	SPORTS FOCUS / John Daly &The News	Rin Tin Tin	Jim Bowie	PATRICE MUNSEL SHOW	FRANK SINATRA SHOW	Date With The Angels	COLT .45	local
CBS	local	LEAVE IT TO BEAVER	TRACKDOWN	Dick Powell's Zane Grey Theater	Mr. Adams And Eve	Schlitz Playhouse Of Stars	The Lineup	Person To Person
NBC	local	SABER OF LONDON	COURT OF LAST RESORT	The Life Of Riley	M SQUAD	THE THIN MAN	Gillette Cavalcade Of Sports	Red Barber

SATURDAY

Network	7:00	7:30	8:00	8:30	9:00	9:30	10:00	10:30
ABC	local	KEEP IT IN THE FAMILY	Country Music Jubilee		Lawrence Welk's Dodge Dancing Party		Mike Wallace Interviews	local
CBS	local	PERRY MASON		DICK AND THE DUCHESS	Oh, Susanna	HAVE GUN, WILL TRAVEL	Gunsmoke	local
NBC	local	People Are Funny	Perry Como Show		CLUB OASIS / POLLY BERGEN	GISELE MacKENZIE SHOW	WHAT'S IT FOR	Your Hit Parade

SUNDAY

Network	7:00	7:30	8:00	8:30	9:00	9:30	10:00	10:30
ABC	You Asked For It	MAVERICK		BOWLING STARS	Open Hearing	COLLEGE FOOTBALL GAME OF THE WEEK	SCOTLAND YARD	local
CBS	Lassie	BACHELOR FATHER / Jack Benny Program	Ed Sullivan Show		General Electric Theater	Alfred Hitchcock Presents	$64,000 Challenge	What's My Line
NBC	The Original Amateur Hour	SALLY	Steve Allen Show		Dinah Shore Chevy Show		Loretta Young Show	local

playboy Don Diego (Guy Williams), acted as a latter-day Robin Hood in nineteenth-century Spanish California, defending the town of Monterey from its evil ruler, Captain Monastario (Britt Lomond). Diego's transparent disguise should have fooled no one but, as in the adventures of Superman, the characters in the series were perpetually dumbfounded, particularly the portly Sergeant Garcia (Henry Calvin). *Zorro* provided two years of swashbuckling comic book-style exploits, and even became a minor fad, as thousands of urchins donned cheap plastic "Zorro" robes and brandished rubber-tipped swords.

The upsurge in Westerns of every type on the fall schedule (there were ten new oaters in September) was viewed with alarm by TV's comics, who saw this trend as a direct challenge to them. Though comedy had been a staple of television for years, over the previous few seasons some of television's most successful comics, including Milton Berle, Jackie Gleason, and Sid Caesar, had faded from the screen. Those that remained (such as Red Skelton, Jack Benny, George Burns, and Bob Hope) vowed to "laugh the Westerns off the air" by mercilessly satirizing them at the start of the new season. For example, George Burns poked fun at the sometimes absurd distinctions made among the dozens of cowboy stories by insisting that *his* skit be classified as an adult Western because "every Indian in that scene is over twenty-one." By January, how-

ever, it was clear that the cowboys were having the last laugh, as Westerns occupied seven of the top ten positions in the ratings. Sid Caesar and Imogene Coca tried a reunion on ABC in late January, but their new show bombed. The only comedy successes that season were in the field of sitcoms, which produced one belated hit and three successful sleepers.

For three seasons, *Make Room For Daddy* had suffered from ABC's most vexing problem, a lack of reliable affiliates. In 1956, only eight-three stations carried the program, and fifty of these aired it on delay. Though Danny Thomas had a viable format and a strong cast, the technical limitations of the ABC network had, in effect, reduced his program to a cult show, seen at odd times by a small corps of followers. Thomas shifted the series (renamed *The Danny Thomas Show*) to CBS beginning in the fall of 1957, and the network placed it in the prestigious Monday night slot vacated by *I Love Lucy* (which was seen only in reruns on Wednesday night). At the start of the season, Thomas talked hopefully of attracting at least half of *Lucy's* old audience, and he brought in new characters and situations to help relaunch his show on its new network. During his final season at ABC, Danny had become a widower (Jean Hagen, who played his wife Margaret, had left the series, so her character was quietly killed), and had met a beautiful nurse (Kathy Daly, played by Marjorie Lord) who was, conveniently, a widow with a young daughter (played by Angela Cartwright). Danny began his residency at CBS by marrying Kathy and bringing the daughter into his own family, making *The Danny Thomas Show* seem almost brand-new, at a time when most situation comedies were running short of situations. With a fresh cast, new situations, and a better network (CBS carried the program on 195 stations), the show quickly passed its competition (NBC's quizzer, *Twenty-One*) and became a consistent member of television's top ten.

The only new situation comedies to survive the season were all slow starters: *Bachelor Father, The Real McCoys,* and *Leave It To Beaver. Bachelor Father* was simply another in a long line of television dads trying to raise a family without a wife. John Forsythe played a supposedly swinging Beverly Hills bachelor who found himself saddled with the responsibility of raising his thirteen-year-old niece, Kelly, after her parents were killed in a car crash. The series was slotted against *Maverick* and alternated with Jack Benny, so it did not have the opportunity to strike out on its own and become a hit until it defected to NBC in the summer of 1958. While *Bachelor Father* was a passible but generally uninspired show, the other two sitcom sleepers were exceptional comedies of the decade, with strong characters and genuinely funny situations.

The Real McCoys blazed a trail from the mountains of "West Virginny" to the farms of California's San Fernando valley, turning rural humor into top-rated TV for ABC. Presiding head of this hillbilly clan was veteran sidekick Walter Brennan who, even though growing up fifteen miles north of Boston, was completely believable as the crusty, cantankerous, dyed-in-the-cornpone Grandpa Amos. Grandpa provided most of the humor in the series, usually outwitting everyone else (especially the city slickers) in spite of (or often because of) his backwoods naivete and adherence to proven downhome aphorisms. Richard Crenna and Kathleen Nolan (as grandson Luke and his wife, Kate) played their characters rather straight, though inevitably everyone in the McCoy clan had to face the sputtering wrath of Grandpa. The family's Mexican-American hired hand, Pepino (Tony Martinez) served as the most frequent and convenient target for Grandpa's volatile temper.

The Real McCoys was pure comic fluff and seemed the perfect answer for ABC to CBS's reliance on sitcom superstars such as Lucille Ball, Jack Benny, Phil Silvers, and Danny Thomas. Though the program was practically ignored at the start of the season, by New Year's it had begun a slow and continuous rise in popularity. By early 1959, *The Real McCoys* became the first ABC sitcom to reach the top ten, winning both urban and rural support. Urban viewers laughed at the out-of-place hillbilly ways of the McCoys while rural viewers were amused by the clan's constant triumphs over the absurd, overly sophisticated city folk. (One of the program's writers, Paul Henning, used the same premise five years later and produced the even more successful *Beverly Hillbillies.*)

ABC also became the launching pad for another sleeper sitcom success, *Leave It To Beaver.* The program began in 1957 with an undistinguished season on CBS, losing against *Rin Tin Tin* and then *Disneyland.* In the fall of 1958, *Leave It To Beaver* moved to ABC as a lead-in to *Zorro* and its fortunes began to rise immediately.

Leave It To Beaver was the most effective of the decade's "warm family" strain of sitcom, even outshining the Anderson family of the already popular *Father Knows Best.* Both series presented small, close-knit families living in the vast expanse of television's interchangeable suburbs, but there were important differences between them. Though the Andersons rarely faced the ridiculous misunder-

THE ZANY EXPERIENCES OF A LADY COMIC see page 20 LOCAL LISTINGS · JUNE 11-17

NOREEN CORCORAN, JOHN FORSYTHE, SAMMEE TONG OF 'BACHELOR FATHER'

The cast of *Bachelor Father* did not make the cover of *TV Guide* until 1960. (*From* Bachelor Father. *Courtesy of MCA Television Limited*)

standings that usually occupied TV sitcom families (such as in *The Life of Riley*), the blandness of their characters ultimately undercut the attempts to introduce moderately realistic situations into the story lines. The Anderson children were especially disconcerting. Betty (Elinor Donahue), Bud (Billy Gray), and Kathy (Lauren Chapin) experienced the usual adolescent crises (allowance, school grades, dates), but everything seemed to happen *to* them—they were too nice and aseptically clean to ever get into trouble themselves. The Anderson kids were an adult's view of perfect children: They were never greedy, stupid, or mischievous, just unlucky or unwise. With the vital core of a warm family situation (the children) lacking credibility even for television reality, the frequent heart-to-heart talks in the den with their patient and understanding father (played by Robert Young) and their nervous reactions to minor crises (such as a misfired blind date) seemed hollow and phony.

Leave It To Beaver also contained its share of bland Fifties sitcom stereotypes. The Cleaver family lived in a typical television suburban home in a quiet neighborhood with shady trees and a nice front yard. Like nearly every TV father at the time, Ward (Hugh Beaumont) disappeared between 9:00 A.M. and 5:00 P.M. five days a week to an unknown job, though his real life's work seemed to be mowing the lawn and having weekly heart-to-heart talks with his sons (an annual event, at best, in real families). His wife, June (Barbara Billingsley), was a perfect TV mommie who wanted nothing more out of life than a clean carpet, whiter-than-white laundry,

September 29, 1957

DuPont Show of the Month. (CBS). CBS and David Susskind begin a series of irregularly slotted monthly dramas that pop up all over the schedule.

September 30, 1957

Do You Trust Your Wife? switches to weekday afternoons on ABC and features a new host: CBS reject Johnny Carson (assisted by sidekick Ed McMahon). In July, 1958, the title of the show is changed to *Who Do You Trust?*

October 17, 1957

ABC's *Navy Log* dramatizes John F. Kennedy's wartime naval exploits aboard the PT 109. At the end of the episode, the junior senator from Massachusetts appears to chat about the events.

November 6, 1957

The Lucille Ball and Desi Arnaz Show. (CBS). Television's #1 sitcom couple begin a series of irregularly scheduled monthly specials. First up: a "flashback" on how Lucy and Ricky first met in Havana in 1940.

December 13, 1957

CBS axes *The Jimmy Dean Show* because of continued sponsor indifference—even though it is *ahead* of *Today* in the ratings.

January 6, 1958

Dotto. (CBS). Colgate drops sponsorship of *Strike It Rich* in the CBS daytime schedule and picks up a new game show for the slot.

January 11, 1958

Sea Hunt. Ziv brings local stations a diver-as-cop adventure series, produced by Ivan Tors and starring Lloyd Bridges.

---

and a well-done roast. She was a professional mother who always wore a semi-formal dress, even while doing the housework or baking cookies. (Billingsley received her basic training for this task by serving as the mother in the short-lived 1955 sitcom *Professional Father.*) Ward and June both stuck to the standard Hollywood image of adults, as did the other grownups in the series, such as stuffed-shirt Fred Rutherford (Richard Deacon), over-protective Mrs. Mondello (Madge Blake), and Miss Landers (Sue Randall), the pure and patient schoolteacher. The children in *Leave It To Beaver,* though, provided the crucial difference. More than any other kids on TV, they were real.

The star ("Jerry Mathers as the Beaver") was a young boy, nearly ten years old, with an all-trusting Alfred E. Neuman-ish grin and an appropriate set of dimples. Despite his adorable appearance, the Beaver had very little of the "goodie two-shoes" qualities heaped upon most of television's kids, and he actually engaged in normal, healthy preteen mischief. At the same time, he was honestly trying to decipher the way the world worked, and trying to understand whether people could be trusted or not. He often turned to his older brother Wally (Tony Dow) for help, and his brother responded with genuine concern tempered by total exasperation at the Beaver's frequent ineptitude (summed up in his often repeated phrase, "Aww, Beav'!"). Wally faced his own awkward problem: He was old enough to be interested in girls but too young to do anything about it. He tried to assert himself and create a good impression, even adopting a touch of Fifties teenage cool (closer to Ricky Nelson's somnambulism than the artificial jive of the Fonz in the 1970s sitcom *Happy Days*), but Wally often ran into just as many problems as the Beaver. Even their friends

were touched, to a lesser degree, by this more realistic portrayal of a kid's world. Straight-talking Whitey (Stanley Fafara), fat and selfish Larry Mondello (Rusty Stevens), perpetually flunking Lumpy (Frank Bank), and the brazenly two-faced Eddie Haskell (Ken Osmond) were a fair cross-section of suburban youth.

Leave It To Beaver managed to bridge the chasm between television's caricatures and the real world by keeping one part of the family equation close to reality. Though the adults were cardboard characters, the children in *Leave It To Beaver* were just like real kids: flawed and confused, usually good, but not above some exciting petty-larceny. As a result, *Leave It To Beaver* emerged as a warm family show that offered normal American kids the opportunity to actually identify with children portrayed in a television series. More than any other sitcom at the time, it captured the essence of a child's everyday life in the late Fifties, building a strong and loyal following that watched the Beaver and Wally mature from mischievous kids to spirited teens.

ABC's early evening kidvid strategy had led both CBS and NBC to place similar fare in the 7:30–8:00 P.M. slot, pushing out both the fifteen-minute news and fifteen-minute music shows that had filled this period. NBC's success the previous few seasons with laid-back hour-long series featuring Perry Como and Dinah Shore suggested a new avenue of exposure for the displaced singers: a revival of the thirty- and sixty-minute musical-variety form, which had flourished in the early 1950s. For the fall of 1957 there were new musical-variety showcases for TV veterans Dean Martin, Nat King Cole, Patti Page, Eddie Fisher, and Frank Sinatra, as well as for new headliners Polly Bergen (from Pepsi-Cola ads and panel shows), Rosemary Clooney (from local television syndication), Pat Boone (from *The Arthur Godfrey Show*), Guy Mitchell (from the hit "Singin' the Blues"), Gisele MacKenzie (from *Your Hit Parade*), and Patrice Munsel (from the world of classical music). Only Pat Boone and Eddie Fisher survived to join Dinah Shore and Perry Como in returning the following fall.

Most of the new shows failed for lack of a very important element in a musical-variety program, variety. All the new programs seemed the same, sharing the same guests and staging the same production numbers over and over. Though a popular singer could easily carry a fifteen-minute show with a few lively numbers, much more was needed to fill the longer programs. The hosts were unable to tie together the individual segments of their new shows, frequently falling into stilted, artificial chit-chat as transition. Often, the same writers that had worked on the recently flopped comedy-variety hours supplied the interscene patter, repeating well-worn routines that had eventually strangled the big name comics. Against these odds, the battle for respectable ratings proved frustrating to both the musical stars and the networks.

Frank Sinatra, in his second attempt at a weekly television series, proved a major disappointment for ABC. He just never seemed to devoted all his energies to his much-touted new program, alternating between live and film presentations and changing producers almost weekly. CBS was frustrated at the failure of Patti Page's *The Big Record,* which the network had hoped to use to dominate Wednesday nights. The program was modeled after NBC's familiar *Your Hit Parade,* which used a cast of regulars to sing "cover" versions of the top tunes. *The Big Record* brought in the hit artists themselves to sing their own songs, live, but from the opening show everything seemed to go wrong. A trick piano for Hoagy Carmichael did not work properly. Eddie Cantor, who was miming a song, had to begin singing when somebody stopped the record. While Billy Ward's Dominoes were performing, stagehands had to restrain two policemen that barged into the New York studio with an arrest warrant for a member of the band. More importantly, the program failed in its attempt to appeal to both teenagers and adults by including sharply conflicting styles of music: rock'n'roll and mainstream pop. Instead of attracting both audiences, it alienated them.

Nat King Cole, the first black to host a full-length network television variety show, faced a more serious problem. Cole had been a success with both black and white audiences as host of one of NBC's fifteen-minute musical spots during the 1956–57 season, so when these were eliminated in the summer of 1957, he received a thirty-minute summer slot that the network hoped would catch on and carry over into the fall. Throughout the summer, some of the top names in show business (such as Harry Belafonte, Peggy Lee, Tony Martin, and Ella Fitzgerald) appeared on his show for next to nothing, and Cole started to register very good ratings, coming within a few points of overtaking CBS's *$64,000 Question*. Despite such a strong performance, no sponsor offered to pick up the show, fearing the antipathy of Southern viewers toward seeing blacks on television. Defying the traditional handling of unsponsored programs, NBC bravely invested $17,500 each week (still just a fraction of the budget for most sponsored variety shows) to keep Cole on the air, hoping a sponsor would eventually come forward. In September, the network even increased the weekly budget to $20,000 and kept the program on in prime time, but no commercial support ever emerged. When the show finally went off in December, Cole issued a devastating attack on advertisers, saying it was Madison Avenue, not the South, that was keeping blacks off television. He said the ad agencies deliberately refused to sponsor him, fearing that, as a black, he would be bad for product identification.

Strangely enough, while many middle-of-the-road pop singers failed on television in 1957, raucous rock'n'roll music managed to make important inroads into the network schedule, and the genre even registered its first television hit. Alan Freed, one of the men responsible for popularizing rock'n'roll in the Fifties (with his radio programs and traveling stage shows) presented the first network television show devoted to the new sound, *Rock'n'Roll Revue* (soon renamed *The Big Beat*), which premiered in the spring of 1957 on ABC. Each week Freed presented rockers such as the Clovers, the Del-Vikings, and Screaming Jay Hawkins, though as a concession to the TV audience's wide range of tastes, he also included less frenetic artists such as Guy Mitchell, June Valli, and Connie Francis. Despite his mixture of performers, Freed's program did not catch on. Rock'n'Roll was still somewhat limited in appeal and Freed's own rough, unpolished manner—while perfect for his live stage shows—was unsuited to the demands of network television. *The Big Beat* faded at the end of the summer of 1957. What did succeed, though, was the unpretentious *American Bandstand*, which came to the ABC network weekday afternoon line-up on August 5, 1957, after five years as a local Philadelphia program.

For ninety minutes each day on *American Bandstand*, young disk jockey Dick Clark played the latest hit records while some high schoolers danced to the music. Occasionally, there were appearances by guest performers, but they usually only lip-synced their own records instead of singing live. Many reviewers predicted that *American Bandstand* would be a disastrous flop as a network show and they scoffed at the format, pointing out that local stations could easily produce a similar program on their own (at the time, many did). When the ratings arrived, however, they showed *American Bandstand* clobbering the competition from CBS and NBC. Though the concept was simple to stage, local stations found it

much easier to take the network feed rather than to turn out their own versions.

Once *American Bandstand* was an established hit, hordes of sponsors appeared and it was even given a brief run in prime time. In February, 1958, Clark received a more suitable evening show, sponsored by Beechnut gum. The nighttime program closely resembled Freed's *The Big Beat*, only with more polish, as, live from a New York theater, Clark presented the big names of rock'n'roll in a mix of live singing and lip-synced numbers. Though there was no dancing staged in the theater, the exuberant teenage audience gave the show an exciting energy as it cheered such performers as Jerry Lee Lewis, Chuck Berry, Fats Domino, Fabian, Bobby Darin, and Annette Funicello.

Clark succeeded with rock on television while Freed did not for one important reason: Clark was a sharper businessman and packager. Alan Freed often seemed to be too caught up in keeping the frenzied movement of a live rock show intact to consider toning it down for the television cameras to follow. He also favored the raunchy, less familiar black rhythm and blues performers over more mainstream rockers. As a result, to the uninitiated, *The Big Beat* appeared visually confusing and Freed's own supercharged demeanor somewhat threatening.

Though a true rock'n'roll fan, Dick Clark treated the music first and foremost as a special business enterprise that had to be adjusted to meet the unique demands of television. He realized that the nature of a live rock performance did not transfer easily to the small, confining TV screen. While masters at their music, most rock performers were novices at projecting any visual, physical stage presence (beyond shaking) for television. Clark provided

---

February 17, 1958
Oliver Treyz becomes president of ABC-TV.

March 12, 1958
Game showman Louis G. Cowan becomes president of CBS-TV.

April 28, 1958.
James Aubrey returns to CBS as vice-president of creative services.

May 13, 1958
Dr. Allen DuMont resigns as chairman of the board of the DuMont Broadcasting Corporation, which is renamed the Metropolitan Broadcasting Corporation.

July 1, 1958
Colgate brings *Dotto* to prime time on NBC.

July 7, 1958
Death of *See It Now*. Age: 7 years. Cause: CBS's new leaders feel the floating documentary series is expendable.

July 11, 1958
Robert Kinter becomes the president of NBC-TV as Robert Sarnoff assumes the position of NBC's chairman of the board.

August 4, 1958
Monday Night Fights, the final show of the old DuMont network, dies. At the end, it is carried on only five stations, nationwide.

October 1, 1958
Death of *Kraft Television Theater,* the oldest show on television. Final production: H. Julian Fink's "Presumption of Innocence."

Ward Bond leads the *Wagon Train*. (*From* Wagon Train. *Courtesy of MCA Television Limited*)

the necessary stabilizing control and guidance. He also recognized the need to place rock'n'roll in safer, more accessible surroundings for general consumption. On his programs, Clark was always neatly dressed, clean-cut, warm, and articulate. He usually emphasized less threatening personalities such as Fabian, who did toned-down versions of black rhythm and blues hits. With this approach, Clark ran away with the television teen market and soon his *American Bandstand* show was the most important outlet for new rock'n'roll music. (He could make or break a new disk just by deciding to play it on his show.) Clark's Saturday night *Beechnut Show* lasted until 1960, while *American Bandstand* kept right on going, weathering the British invasion, acid rock, and the rise of disco.

Live television drama continued to lose strength during the 1957–58 season as the networks and sponsors nitpicked the form to death while drastically increasing their commitment to filmed productions. Besides providing a boom for Westerns, this resulted in a new batch of police and private eye shows, including several new loner cop series and the revival of an old crime format. Like the Westerns, they offered the public a mixture of familiar characters and dramatic action.

In *M Squad,* Lee Marvin played Chicago police lieutenant Frank Ballinger, a tight-lipped cop on a violent beat. As in Jack Webb's *Dragnet,* there was a deadpan voice-over narration to explain the story, but unlike that show *M Squad* emphasized physical beatings, frequent car chases, and constant gunplay. David Janssen, as *Richard Diamond, Private Detective,* and Frank Lovejoy in *Meet McGraw* were both tight-lipped, long-suffering, know-it-all private eyes who disliked cops and turned to the police force only when necessary. Peter Lawford (*The Thin Man*) and Donald Gray (as a new one-armed British permutation of *Mark Saber*) were both dilettante detectives that exuded sophistication and occasionally even cooperated with the police. The best new crime series of the season, however, took an old, discarded television format and used it as the basis for a well-executed presentation of the systematic pursuit of justice, *Perry Mason.*

Courtroom drama (with its simple, inexpensive sets) had been a programming staple in the early days of television on such shows as DuMont's *They Stand Accused,* but had gone out of style with the move to filmed series that allowed action to take place outside the cramped confines of the studio. *Perry Mason* brought the courtroom saga back into the limelight. The character of Perry Mason had begun life in a series of murder mystery novels by Erle Stanley Gardner and, in the early Forties, Mason moved from print to a radio soap opera series on CBS, which presented him as the playboy type. As portrayed by Raymond Burr for television, Perry Mason was a no-nonsense legal wizard who never lost a case.

Perry Mason was a triumph of technique over format, because every episode in the series was identical: Somebody in trouble came to Mason who then spent the first half of the show investigating the case. Inevitably, a murder would take place, and Mason would shift his attention to defending his client from this charge, farming out the tedious detective work to his flunky, Paul Drake (William Hopper). In court, Mason carefully questioned each witness, undercutting alibis, exposing contradictions, and shifting suspicion from one character to another, while playing a cat and mouse game with the long-suffering state prosecutor, Hamilton Burger (William Talman). At the dramatic showdown, Mason would reveal a vital piece of evidence (brought in at the last minute by Drake), and force the guilty party to stand up and publicly confess.

The series was a straight whodunit, complete with a full range of suspects and clues that allowed the viewer to become an armchair detective. Because it was clear that Mason would win (he lost only one case in the nine year history of the series), the object was to keep one step ahead of him and spot the damaging evidence or false alibi, and zero in on the killer—or at least understand how Perry did. Even though the series followed the same formula each week, it demanded that viewers think and alertly scan the suspicious characters in the episode. Though it seemed that every hack character actor in Hollywood eventually turned up as a suspect in *Perry Mason,* their character types contrasted well with the strong central cast to provide, for most people, a positive and generally believable portrait of the legal profession. Many practicing attorneys were not happy over such an image, however, finding it impossible to live up to the infallible standard Mason set. Salt Lake County attorney Frank Moss (later a United States senator) complained at a convention of prosecutors that:

A good number of jurors have become convinced, through watching television, that the prosecutor is some sort of trick artist, who pulls a rabbit out of his hat in the last reel . . . if he doesn't resort to theatrics, as the TV prosecutors do, they are inclined to bring in an innocent verdict.

As *Perry Mason* began its long run as a top-notch formula drama show, the long battle between New York and Los Angeles for control of America's television culture passed a symbolic turning point. New York lost. *Studio One,* for years one of the premiere showcases for live New York drama, moved to Hollywood and began accentuating big name stars, fancy scenery, and deep-voiced announcers over dramatic content. The trend was irreversible. Video tape came into general use in 1957, dooming live television, and one of the last remaining reasons for the stars and networks to avoid the West Coast evaporated. It was just so much easier out West: there was more room, a greater number of actors, and less red tape. All of the major studios were heavily committed to television production, and all three networks had virtually conceded control of program production to the filmmakers. Though the amount of prime time programming originating on the West Coast had been increasing slowly for years, in 1957 it jumped—from 40% to 71%.

As the first generation of important network programmers passed from the scene, they left behind bitter comments. Former NBC president Pat Weaver, who failed that year in an abortive attempt to start a fourth network, labeled television "a jukebox to put in the corner to keep kids quiet." Fred Coe quit NBC stating, "I just wasn't happy doing nothing." Max Liebman and NBC parted ways. All season, stories about great drama shows being emasculated by fearful sponsors and networks circulated in the press. Rod Serling said he was "giving up" writing television dramas after *Playhouse 90* tampered with two of his plays: "Aftermath" and "Panic Button."

"Aftermath," a story of a black lynching in the modern South (a topic that Serling had run into trouble with a few years earlier), had been scheduled to open the season for *Playhouse 90*, but sponsor protests forced a delay. Even after Serling changed the story to the lynching of Mexicans in the Southwest in the 1880s, it was not put on the air until June, when most people began their vacations and the number of viewers dropped. Retitled "A Town Has Turned to Dust," the play featured Rod Steiger as a cowardly sheriff torn between the law and the mob (led by William Shatner). Serling's "Panic Button" began as the story of a commercial airliner crash and the investigation that followed. Airline pressure forced Serling to change it to a charter plane, but then the charter companies complained. "We'll wind up with a Yellow Cab," an associate producer moaned. "TV has more sacred cows than India."

Playhouse 90 even permitted showman Mike Todd to take over one episode and turn it into a first anniversary party for his film "Around the World in 80 Days" (in which CBS had purchased a 10% interest the previous year). For "Around the World in 90 Minutes," Todd filled Madison Square Garden with 18,000 of his closest friends, and CBS carried the celebration live. Elizabeth Taylor (Todd's wife) passed out slices from an enormous birthday cake as luminaries paraded aimlessly beneath a giant balloon. Two hundred and forty dancers stood by but never danced. Anchormen Walter Cronkite and Jim McKay tried to make sense of the proceedings and the speeches that ranged from tiresome testimonials to an unexpected call for world peace by Senator Hubert Humphrey. The camera work was generally shoddy and the interviews were constantly interrupted by ads. The *New York Times* television critic Jack Gould succinctly described the affair as "an elaborate bore."

The prostitution of a distinguished series like *Playhouse 90* with the airing of Todd's party was a symbol of the declining status of television drama. *Studio One, Climax,* and NBC's daytime *Matinee Theater* were canceled by the end of the season. Even the eleven-year-old *Kraft Television Theater,* the grandaddy of all TV dramas, bit the dust in 1958. Though long a refuge of sensible dramatic entertainment, it was sacrificed in the spring of 1958 to effectuate Milton Berle's return to television the following fall. Even though Berle had been considered "dead" as a television personality only a few years before, he had stolen the show at the April 15 Emmy awards telecast, so Kraft decided to gamble and sign him for the next season. Though it was generally conceded that comedy-variety was in a bad slump, Kraft felt that the chance of success with Berle was better than continuing to support hour-long drama, which it saw as an increasingly moribund form.

In a last-ditch attempt to salvage the Kraft drama program, the J. Walter Thompson production agency withdrew from the show, and turned it over to David Susskind's Talent Associates (which had done a great deal of television drama work for CBS, especially on *Armstrong Circle Theater*). Susskind turned out a fabulous two-part live presentation of Robert Penn Warren's "All the King's Men," but it was too late. Kraft had settled on Berle and slated the oldest show on television for cancellation. Susskind, who was still very active on CBS, took the defeat personally, calling 1958 "the year of the miserable drivel."

Then there were the quiz shows.

18. Dotto Goes Blotto

REGULAR viewers of CBS TV who tuned in the network at 11:30 A.M. on Monday, August 18, 1958, expecting that day's edition of the quiz show *Dotto* instead heard studio announcer Ralph Paul stampede through a quick disclaimer, "*Dotto,* the program formerly presented at this hour, will no longer be seen. In its place, we bring you *Top Dollar.*" Though the disappearance of this morning quizzer was quite sudden, the fact that one quiz show was being replaced with another was not that unusual. All through 1958, various quiz programs had appeared and disappeared with increasing regularity. Since the ratings triumph of *The $64,000 Question* in the summer of 1955, quiz shows had become a network programming staple, turning up throughout the schedule. They were the easiest format to use in quickly filling holes left by flopped programs or to serve as headliners in launching the new season.

Even though another runaway smash hit had not emerged since the spectacular performance by Charles Van Doren on *Twenty-One* in 1957, sponsors were happy to continue to bankroll the quiz programs. The television economy had been in a very weak state since 1956, and expensive, complicated filmed series often were a more risky and less attractive investment. Besides, sponsor identification was judged to be much higher on the quizzes than on sitcoms or Westerns, and without many of the problems. There were no temperamental stars demanding salary increases, and the possibility of sparking any controversy seemed remote. Best of all, quiz shows were very cheap to produce. All that fancy prize money was nothing compared to the usual price tag on a filmed series. It didn't matter that most of the programs were nearly identical and often disappeared after a short run. Another show with a slightly different gimmick would be brought in and there was always the possibility that ratings lightning would strike with the new program. It soon became clear, however, that *Dotto* was not just another quiz show that bit the dust. Instead, it marked the first step in the collapse of the house of cards that was the TV quiz show.

In the time between Charles Van Doren's final appearance on *Twenty-One* (March 1957) and the fall of *Dotto* (August 1958), quiz show producers had become increasingly concerned over the performance of each show and they tried every possible gimmick and format variation in the hope of attracting ratings equal to Van Doren's. Some offered very large amounts of cash or highly unusual prizes. In one extreme case, *Bid'n'Buy* (hosted by Bert

Parks) planned to auction as one of its prizes the sparsely settled Scottish island of Stroma, which producer Robert Stivers had purchased for $23,000, but canceled the proposed stunt at the last minute in response to the plaintive pleas of the British government. Others adopted weird, off-beat formats such as ABC's *ESP* (hosted by Vincent Price), which tested the extra sensory perception of contestants who had to identify unseen playing cards from isolation booths. Christmas, 1957, brought the home participation craze which gave viewers at home the opportunity to win prizes at the same time as the studio contestants. By Easter, 1958, a local New York program, *Bingo at Home* (hosted by Monty Hall), combined the home participation angle with a new wrinkle, bingo. The first network to pursue the bingo fad was CBS's thinly disguised *Wingo* (hosted by Bob Kennedy) which offered prizes of up to $250,000, though the rules were so complicated no one ever got close. NBC soon followed with *Music Bingo* and even old timers such as *The $64,000 Question* added a special bingo-type feature.

Through all these gimmicks, most quizzes earned adequate, if not spectacular, ratings while waiting for the next public hero to appear. No matter how many variations were devised, audience identification with contestants was the most important element for success. *The $64,000 Question* had featured Gino Prato and Dr. Joyce Brothers. *Twenty-One* found gold with Charles Van Doren. *Name That Tune* once featured Marine Major (and future astronaut) John Glenn, who won $15,000 by correctly identifying twenty-five songs, including "Far Away Places." Still, every show had to eventually face the same problem: The most popular contestants did not automatically win and could be knocked out at anytime by a less attractive challenger. Thus, the most important aspect of a quiz show seemed left to blind chance.

In the spring of 1958, however, quiz shows were still accepted by most people as a solid part of the TV culture and one that would continue to grow. CBS had its Louis G. Cowan-inspired *The $64,000 Question* and *The $64,000 Challenge* as well as the independently produced *Top Dollar, Dotto,* and *Name That Tune.* NBC concentrated on programs devised by Jack Barry and Dan Enright (*Twenty-One, Tic Tac Dough, Dough Re Mi,* and *Concentration*) and added other shows such as *The Price Is Right, Haggis Baggis,* and *Win with a Winner.* As the number of quiz shows on the air increased, the number of more serious news and drama shows decreased. Quiz show impresario Louis Cowan became president of the CBS television network in March, 1958, and soon thereafter it was decided that CBS could do without controversial, expensive loss leaders such as *See It Now*—even as an occasional floating special. At the same time, some producers went even further and brazenly claimed that quiz shows were really a true renaissance in live TV and the successors to the live drama productions from New York, which were rapidly fading from prime time. Television executives responded to anguished cries among critics over the apparent passing of the already mythical golden age of television by insisting that they were performing a public service, giving the people what they demanded: quiz shows and Westerns. TV had become a truly mass medium, they pointed out, and could no longer afford to cater to the elitist tastes of a small, over-educated minority.

Even so, there was uneasiness and exceptional pressure in quiz show circles during the spring of 1958. Sponsors were paying increasing attention to the performance of the quiz programs, and the generally acceptable ratings most quizzes had been coasting along on were beginning to be viewed as inadequate. During the summer, no fewer than ten new quiz shows appeared, but the genre's overall performance declined. Loretta Young's anthology series defeated *The $64,000 Challenge*. A mediocre Western, the *Californians,* nosed out *The $64,000 Question*. Ancient reruns of *I Love Lucy* beat new episodes of *Twenty-One*. *Dotto,* a smash hit on CBS in the daytime, flopped in a nighttime version on NBC. Halfway through the summer, even the off-beat *ESP* abandoned the quiz format and became a drama anthology, focusing on real life incidents of extrasensory perception. (At the end of each dramatization, Vincent Price interviewed the real people involved.)

One reason for the ratings decline was overexposure. The public was beginning to tire of the interchangeable formats used in each quiz program. More importantly, the programs were running out of new heroes. Without a consistent stream of heroes, viewer attention focused on the all-too similar formats of each individual show, and the obvious weaknesses were exposed. By the middle of 1958, it became increasingly clear within the TV industry that quizzes were not a solid commodity, but a very unstable structure that needed just a slight push to collapse.

On May 20, 1958, Ed Hilgemeier, a twenty-four-year-old part-time butler and bit actor, was a standby contestant on the daytime version of *Dotto*. Backstage, Hilgemeier found a notebook belonging to a woman who had been the winning contestant on that day's show. The notebook contained answers to the questions she had been asked. Suspecting foul play, Hilgemeier showed the notebook to the woman's opponent and also protested to the show's producers. After receiving a $1,500 payoff, Hilgemeier was ready to forget the whole matter until he discovered that the disgruntled losing contestant had been given $4,000, just what the winning contestant had received. Feeling double-crossed, Hilgemeier filed a complaint on August 7 with the show's sponsor, Colgate. These maneuvers went on behind the scenes and out of the public eye, so the sponsor's public reaction came as a complete surprise. On August 16, Colgate abruptly announced it was terminating both the weekday morning (CBS) and Tuesday evening (NBC) versions of *Dotto*. No reason for the unexpected cancellations was given by either the networks involved or the sponsor. Yet rumors quickly spread that a disgruntled contestant had charged the show with rigging and was taking his story to the D.A. Appropriately, on the morning of August 25, only hours after Teddy Nadler set the all-time quiz show prize record (he won $252,000 on *The $64,000 Challenge*), New York District Attorney Frank Hogan announced that his office was beginning an investigation into the possibly illegal activities of the producers of *Dotto*. What's more, added Hogan (who happened to be the Democratic nominee for the U.S. Senate that year), "If it leads to other shows, we will have to follow them up."

Even though *Dotto* was the only show publicly under suspicion, questions about other quiz shows began surfacing. On August 28, Herbert Stempel charged that the producers of *Twenty-One* had supplied him with answers during his reign as champion and that after he had been on top for four weeks (winning $49,000), they told him to "take a dive" in his match with Charles Van Doren in December, 1956. This dramatic accusation changed the focus of the quiz show investigation from a relatively obscure program to one of America's new folk heroes, who was still a public celebrity. Van Doren happened to be guest-hosting the *Today* show that week and on August 29 he issued an on-the-air denial:

> I'm sad and shocked . . . it's enough to shake your faith in human nature. . . . I myself was never given any answers or told any questions beforehand, and, as far as I know, none of the contestants received any coaching of this sort . . . the television quiz show in this country has become an institution. A quiz show is fundamentally a matching of wits and it is an American tradition to do this. I, for one, think it's a good tradition.

Twenty-One producers Barry and Enright, as well as NBC itself, also issued categorical denials of Stempel's charges, with the network calling them "utterly baseless and untrue."

In September, quiz show contestants and producers began making pilgrimages to Hogan's office, some voluntarily, some involuntarily. Barry and Enright produced a dramatic audio tape of Stempel in which he seemed to be trying to blackmail them by demanding $50,000 or he'd talk. Stempel replied that the tape had been doctored. Barry, who was also host of *Twenty-One,* issued an on-the-air defense of the program on October 8, assuring home viewers that the *Twenty-One* producers had not abused the audience's trust and would not in the future, adding, "The truth will out." Jack Narz, emcee of *Dotto,* said he knew nothing about any rigging, but one *Dotto* contestant who had won $900, Mrs. Regan Leydenfrost, said she had received "indirect help anyone but an idiot could follow." The Reverend Charles E. Jackson said that during the pregame runthrough before his appearance on *The $64,000 Challenge* he had been supplied the correct answers. Another contestant, James E. Snodgrass, announced that he had received the answers in advance during his five appearances on *Twenty-One* but, unlike the others, he had proof. Before his appearances, he had mailed the answers to himself and he presented the district attorney sealed registered letters containing the evidence.

These charges surfaced just as the 1958–59 season began, and soon every quiz show on the air came under suspicion, throwing the networks' schedules into complete chaos. By mid-September, *Dotto, ESP, Haggis Baggis,* and *The $64,000 Challenge* were axed. In mid-October, *Twenty-One,* which had fallen from sixth to thirty-fifth in a matter of months, was kicked off NBC. In early November, *The $64,000 Question* departed, after giving away $2,106,800 and twenty-nine Cadillacs. At Christmas, even the local *Bingo at Home* was removed from the air, even though it was completely free of taint. The networks steadfastly claimed they were canceling the shows because of their bad ratings, and not in response to the many charges being leveled.

In late September a grand jury was impaneled to hear the mounting charges against the quiz shows, but it handed down only one

FALL 1958 SCHEDULE

MONDAY

	7:00	7:30	8:00	8:30	9:00	9:30	10:00	10:30		
	local	ABC News	Polka-Go-Round		Bold Journey	Voice Of Firestone	Anybody Can Play	Traffic Court	John Daly & The News	local	ABC
	local		Name That Tune	THE TEXAN	Father Knows Best	Danny Thomas Show	ANN SOUTHERN SHOW	WESTINGHOUSE DESILU PLAYHOUSE @Lucille Ball-Desi Arnaz Show			CBS
	local		Tic Tac Dough	Restless Gun	Tales Of Wells Fargo	PETER GUNN	Alcoa-Goodyear Theater	Arthur Murray Party		local	NBC

TUESDAY

	7:00	7:30	8:00	8:30	9:00	9:30	10:00	10:30		
	local	ABC News	Cheyenne Sugarfoot		Life And Legend Of Wyatt Earp	THE RIFLEMAN	NAKED CITY	Confession	John Daly & The News	local	ABC
	local		STARS IN ACTION	Keep Talking	To Tell The Truth	Arthur Godfrey Show	Red Skelton Show	GARRY MOORE SHOW			CBS
	local		Dragnet	George Gobel Show Eddie Fisher Show		GEORGE BURNS SHOW	Bob Cummings Show	The Californians		local	NBC

WEDNESDAY

	7:00	7:30	8:00	8:30	9:00	9:30	10:00	10:30		
	local	ABC News	Lawrence Welk's Plymouth Show		The Adventures Of Ozzie And Harriet	DONNA REED SHOW	OLDSMOBILE SHOW WITH PATTI PAGE	Wednesday Night Fights			ABC
	local		Twilight Theater	PURSUIT		The Millionaire	I've Got A Secret	U.S. Steel Hour Armstrong Circle Theater			CBS
	local		Wagon Train		The Price Is Right	KRAFT MUSIC HALL WITH MILTON BERLE	BAT MASTERSON	This Is Your Life		local	NBC

THURSDAY

	7:00	7:30	8:00	8:30	9:00	9:30	10:00	10:30		
	local	ABC News	Leave It To Beaver	Zorro	The Real McCoys	Pat Boone Chevy Showroom	ROUGH RIDERS	This Is Music	John Daly & The News	local	ABC
	local		I Love Lucy	December Bride	YANCY DERRINGER	Dick Powell's Zane Grey Theater	Playhouse 90				CBS
	local		Jefferson Drum	ED WYNN SHOW	Twenty-One	BEHIND CLOSED DOORS	Tennessee Ernie Ford Show	You Bet Your Life	Masquerade Party		NBC

FRIDAY

	7:00	7:30	8:00	8:30	9:00	9:30	10:00	10:30		
	local	ABC News	Rin Tin Tin	Walt Disney Presents		MAN WITH A CAMERA	77 SUNSET STRIP		John Daly & The News	local	ABC
	local		Your Hit Parade	Trackdown	Jackie Gleason Show	Phil Silvers Show	Lux-Schlitz Playhouse	The Lineup	Person To Person		CBS
	local		Buckskin	FURTHER ADVENTURES OF ELLERY QUEEN		M Squad	The Thin Man	Gillette Cavalcade Of Sports	Post-FightBeat		NBC

SATURDAY

	7:00	7:30	8:00	8:30	9:00	9:30	10:00	10:30		
	local		Dick Clark's Beechnut Show	Jubilee U.S.A.		Lawrence Welk's Dodge Dancing Party		MUSIC FROM MANHATTAN	local		ABC
	local		Perry Mason		WANTED: DEAD OR ALIVE	Gale Storm Show	Have Gun, Will Travel	Gunsmoke	local		CBS
	local		People Are Funny	Perry Como Show		STEVE CANYON	CIMARRON CITY		BRAINS AND BRAWN		NBC

SUNDAY

	7:00	7:30	8:00	8:30	9:00	9:30	10:00	10:30		
	You Asked For It		Maverick		LAWMAN	Colt .45	ENCOUNTER		local		ABC
	Lassie	Bachelor Father Jack Benny Program	Ed Sullivan Show		General Electric Theater	Alfred Hitchcock Presents	The $64,000 Question	What's My Line			CBS
	Saber Of London	NORTHWEST PASSAGE	Steve Allen Show		Dinah Shore Chevy Show		Loretta Young Show	local			NBC

indictment that year, charging Albert Freedman, producer of *Twenty-One,* with lying to the grand jury in October when he said that he had never supplied answers to contestants. The grand jury continued to conduct its business in 1959, but behind closed doors, so the issue of the quiz scandal faded from view for almost a year. Most of the quiz shows were off the air and, while there appeared to have been some cheating, nobody familiar to the public seemed to be at fault. Charles Van Doren, with his steadfast denials, seemed to escape the crisis unscathed and was signed on as a regular for *Today.* Van Doren delivered daily five-minute lectures on science, poetry, history, and famous people in what he felt was a marvelous opportunity to interest the nation in "the intellectual life."

NBC and CBS were adamant in their own statements of innocence, pointing out that almost every one of the quiz shows had been, like most programs on television, produced totally by outsiders over whom they had no control. ABC, which, by coincidence, had few quiz shows anyway, eagerly pointed out that it was cleaner-than-clean. "You can't say anything bad about Westerns. That's our format and we're sticking with it."

With quiz shows knocked out of the picture just as the new season began, the networks rushed to replace the format and build a positive image for their other programming. At first, they at-

tempted to portray the season as marking the reappearance of TV's classic comics. Such an approach made sense because one sponsor, Kraft, had already abandoned its long-running dramatic showcase in favor of the much-heralded return of Mr. Television as host of *The Kraft Music Hall* (an umbrella title for comedy and variety shows borrowed from the network radio program Kraft had sponsored over the years). Unfortunately, it was the same old Milton Berle in the same old skits. His only new feature was a spotlight on up-and-coming talent, but even this was canned after a few months, not long before Berle himself was dropped. Jackie Gleason, also attempting yet another comeback, offered his old formula of familiar stock characters, the June Taylor dancers, and a parade of glamour girls, but without the assistance of sidekick Art Carney, who had been replaced by Buddy Hackett. The program was an unqualified disaster and was banished by New Year's. George Burns tried to make it without his long-time partner, Gracie Allen (who had retired from show business), using the remaining characters and the show-within-a-show premise from the *Burns and Allen Show.* He played a former comedian trying to make it as a theatrical producer and variety show host, but found himself outdistanced by syndicated reruns of his old show. By the end of the season, Burns also disappeared. Veteran Ed Wynn, who had achieved some success as an NBC variety host in the early 1950s, attempted to make the transition to situation comedy as a folksy, sentimental figure in the embarrassingly hokey setting of a lonely old widower trying to raise two orphaned granddaughters in a college town. He, too, was gone by New Year's. Despite the network's efforts to breathe new life into television comedy, the format that dominated programming and ratings again this season was the Western.

The networks exploited nearly every possible aspect of the old West and at one point in the season seven of the top ten shows were oaters (*Wagon Train, Gunsmoke, Maverick, Sugarfoot, The Rifleman, Cheyenne,* and *Have Gun Will Travel*), with only Danny Thomas, Perry Como, and Perry Mason breaking the near-monopoly. In order to stand out within this multitude of frontier heroes, some of the new shows emphasized unusual gimmicks that were either a part of the setting or used by the main character. Bat Masterson carried a cane, wore a derby hat, and used a custom built gun. Gene Barry, as Masterson, projected an air of suave sophistication in his portrayal of the dandified yet adept lawman who was usually looking out for himself, in the style of Maverick and Paladin. In *Yancy Derringer* the producers went to a ridiculous extreme and tried combining at least eight saleable gimmicks into one program: The action took place in bawdy post-Civil War New Orleans and focused on the exploits of a former Confederate captain, Yancy Derringer (Jock Mahoney), a roguish riverboat gambler who used tiny pistols and knives instead of guns, and was good at judo besides. Derringer's compatriot and bodyguard was a stone-faced rifle-toting Indian (played by X Brands) who used sign language to communicate.

In opposition to the gimmick school were the Westerns that emphasized strong silent heroes such as Steve McQueen in *Wanted: Dead or Alive,* Eric Fleming and Clint Eastwood in *Rawhide,* John Russell in *Lawman,* George Montgomery in *Cimarron City,* Rory Calhoun in *The Texan,* and Kent Taylor in *The Rough Riders.*

These characters spoke so infrequently that one critic (in a review of *The Rough Riders*) said the best acting was by the Rocky Mountains. Westerns were doing so well that even the loss of the leading man could be overcome by an enterprising producer. When production for the fourth season of *Cheyenne* began, star Clint Walker was out "panning for gold in contract land" (holding out for more money) so a new character, Bronco Lane (played by former Texas A&M football star Ty Hardin) was brought in. The series ran as scheduled, without even changing its name. When Walker returned for the next season, Bronco was given his own slot.

The season's most successful new Western was ABC's *The Rifleman,* starring Chuck Connors as Lucas McCain. On the surface this appeared to be another gimmick Western, emphasizing the hero's use of a rifle in place of the traditional six-shooter, but the program's real attraction was the warm relationship between Lucas and his young son, Mark (Johnny Crawford). Every episode of *The Rifleman* centered on the son's learning something about life, either on his own or from his father. Once the audience accepted both Connors as a tough guy and gentle father and Crawford as a believable kid, the plots lost their significance, the showdowns became just window dressing, and the show became a hit.

Crime shows, though not as prominent as Westerns, also continued their steady growth. Like Westerns, they occasionally provided high quality stories while attempting to snare the audience with off-beat gimmicks and characters. CBS's *Markham* presented Ray Milland as still another rich dilettante detective in the *Thin Man* mold who was in the business just for kicks, though the network insisted that the series was different—Markham was an investigator, not a private eye. *Naked City* touted realism, both in its story line (the day-to-day routine of a police detective, played by James Franciscus) and setting (the series was filmed entirely on location in New York City). *Man with a Camera* featured Charles Bronson as a freelance photo-journalist and virtual Superman who person-

Dotto's announcer Ralph Paul prepares to pick out the name of a lucky home viewer who will be called by emcee Jack Narz and asked to identify the dotted celebrity caricature on the wall. *(CBS, Inc.)*

to reveal the depth of their commitment to a new way of life. Host Jack Wyatt led the degrading process that often originated from the county jail with some criminals appearing under guard as they faced the panel. Clergymen, lawyers, psychologists, psychiatrists, penologists, and sociologists conducted the questioning, which one critic described as a "public dissection."

One series that broke from these formulas, though, was dropped by its sponsor for being too controversial. Herb Brodkin's *Brenner* marked a drastic shift from 1950s TV tradition and presented policemen who were not always right and who sometimes found their actions indistinguishable from the criminals they pursued. Edward Binns (as Lieutenant Roy Brenner) and James Broderick (as his son) portrayed honest but fallible policemen attempting to sort out the differences between justice and the law. Brenner was responsible for keeping the other policemen in line, and his son helped him by working as an undercover agent in the police vice squad. The series, based on a 1958 *Playhouse 90* story, "Blue Men," was both fifteen years ahead of its time (anticipating the Seventies' "Serpico") and also a return to the inside-outsider type in the crime genre. Though Lever Brothers withdrew as sponsor after *Brenner's* brief run in the summer of 1959, CBS felt strongly enough about the series to bring it back the next few summers with well-written new episodes. Despite the quality at every level, *Brenner* never caught the public's fancy.

The season's most successful new private eye show was *Peter Gunn* (starring Craig Stevens), a triumph of style over substance that tred the traditional turf of blackmail, business intrigue, and murder, but peppered the all-too-predictable adventures with fascinating characters and a jazzy theme by Henry Mancini. The music provided a rich backdrop throughout each episode and created a mood that matched the mix of odd characters Gunn encountered. Gunn himself hung out at Mother's, a jazz nightclub run by a tough but understanding woman (played by Hope Emerson). His girlfriend Edie (Lola Albright) sang there, and his contacts, including police Lieutenant Jacoby (Herschel Bernardi), often met him there. Gunn appeared as a grown-up, cynical boy scout who understood human nature but somehow kept hoping for the best anyway, and his character mixed well with his surroundings. The show became a hit for NBC in its first season and lasted for three years, shifting to ABC for its final season after the ratings slipped a bit.

ABC, which for years had been looking for a new hit show or hit format to make it appear respectable, found the answer in 1959 by unlocking the secret of the Westerns. All three networks had frantically tried to determine what made Westerns so appealing to the American public throughout the decade. At first, executives and producers assumed the Western setting itself was the attraction, because it provided a conveniently noncontroversial stage for modern morality plays. Next, they used gimmicks in setting and paraphernalia to make one show stand out from the horde. They constantly overlooked an obvious but nevertheless vital element that lay at the heart of the most popular Westerns: the characters.

In the best Westerns, the heroes were not wooden demi-gods but well rounded and interesting people. Looking at its success in series such as *Maverick, Cheyenne,* and *Sugarfoot,* Warner Brothers made the connection. Stars of its Westerns had not been well-known figures with an already established audience to start with; instead, the characters portrayed by actors such as James Garner, Clint Walker, and Will Hutchins were themselves appealing and consequently they became stars in the intimate medium of television. If viewers liked the central characters and cared about what happened to them, they would keep returning to the series to find

ally took on tough guys and tackled fleeing criminals—just for the opportunity to "get a good picture." The fights were the high point of each program because the series suffered from weak acting in addition to the hackneyed scripts. The first episode wasted the team of Bronson and Billy Jack-to-be Tom Laughlin in an uninspired story of a fighter asked to take a dive.

Traffic Court came to ABC after years on local Los Angeles television. The series took the concept of "dramatizing actual cases from the files of . . ." and brought it to the trivial world of moving violations. Edgar Allan Jones, an assistant law school dean at the University of California, portrayed the austere traffic court judge while amateur actors played the repentent souls who had double parked or let their licenses expire. Such intense legal drama was apparently very popular in Los Angeles for, at the time, L.A. viewers could watch, within the same week: *Traffic Court, Court Martial, Divorce Court, Juvenile Court, Youth Court, Night Court, Municipal Court,* and *Day in Court*.

Confession was another ABC find from the hustings (this time, Dallas). It also focused on the criminal element, though it followed a format that seemed designed to overstep the boundaries of good taste. Convicted criminals who were trying to reform were brought before a panel and subjected to intense public questioning designed out. That same type of appeal had kept viewers interested in such television heroes as Lucy and Ricky and Charles Van Doren and, in that light, Paladin, Matt Dillon, Lucas McCain, and the Maverick brothers were merely the latest entries in a continuing cycle. If that was the appeal of the Westerns, then there was no reason to keep such a winning formula stuck out West in the 1880s. By retaining the appealing characteristics of such heroes as Bret Maverick, along with the frequent incidents of "action" (a television euphemism for fights and violence), the producers at Warner Brothers concluded that a hit show could be set in almost any time and any place. The theory was put to the test in October, 1958, when Warner Brothers combined the nucleus of its hit Westerns with the setting from a not-so-different format, private eyes. The result was *77 Sunset Strip* and the birth of a new program form: action-adventure series.

77 Sunset Strip took action, humor, sex appeal, and a set of characters that jelled, presenting, in effect, a modern day Western. The first episode of the series was actually a ninety-minute movie reject, "Girl on the Run," in which private detective Stuart Bailey (Efrem Zimbalist, Jr.) tracked down and captured a murderer (played by Edward Byrnes) before marrying the pretty girl at the end. Some elements were changed for the television series itself which began the following week. Zimbalist was still private detective Stuart Bailey who operated an investigation business on the swank Sunset Strip, but he was no longer married and no longer alone at work. His business was a partnership with Jeff Spencer (Roger Smith) and they were assisted occasionally by Byrnes, who was no longer a murderer but rather their parking lot attendant, Gerald Lloyd Kookson III—better known as Kookie. Roscoe (Louis Quinn), the firm's junior partner (a former horse player who retained his unmistakable Brooklyn charm even in the aseptic world of Los Angeles), and Suzanne Fabray (Jacqueline Beer),

Zorro provided ABC with two years of swashbuckling Western adventure. (From *l.*): Zorro (Guy Williams) and temporary ally Joe Crane (Jeff York). *(Walt Disney Productions)*

their switchboard operator, provided additional color. The cast had all the necessary elements to make the show a hit. Smith and Zimbalist were the epitome of suave sophistication, both intelligent and quick-witted. Their office repartee was light and breezy, with the putdowns usually directed at Kookie and Roscoe. Naturally they could solve any case without help from the police, and they displayed a fierce independence riding the streets of Los Angeles. Suzanne added the necessary sex appeal for the men and Kookie, an Elvis-cum-Ricky Nelson hipster who was perpetually chewing gum and combing his hair, appealed to the young women. He even released a hit record-paean, "Kookie, Kookie, Lend Me Your Comb." The show started out very slowly but turned into a solid ratings winner by the spring.

The success of *77 Sunset Strip*, along with that of *Maverick, The Rifleman, The Real McCoys,* and *Walt Disney Presents* (the renamed *Disneyland*) gave ABC its best ratings in its history. The network had more shows in the top ten (four) than either CBS or NBC, and by the end of the season ABC found itself a mere fraction of a point out of second place—unparalleled success for the network that was usually buried deep in the cellar. By unlocking the secret of the action-adventure series, Warner Brothers won the undying friendship of the ABC network and its new president, Ollie Treyz. Singing "Kookie, Kookie, lend me your format," ABC turned over to the studio 30% of its prime time schedule to fill for the fall of 1959.

March 8, 1959

   The three Marx Brothers make their final appearance together in "The Incredible Jewel Robbery," a half-hour pantomime-style comedy on CBS's *General Electric Theater*. Harpo and Chico star, but Groucho makes a cameo appearance, delivering the only line of dialogue.

April 1, 1959

   Under the vigorous leadership of a new president, John White, the National Educational Television network (NET) moves its headquarters from Ann Arbor, Michigan, to New York City. His long range goal: turn NET into a respectable alternative to the three commerical networks. The immediate goal: find a home base educational channel to serve New York City.

June 16, 1959

   Death of George Reeves a.k.a. Clark Kent a.k.a. Superman. Age: 45. Cause: Typecasting.

July 16, 1959

   Oh Boy. (ABC). Bad quality kines of Britain's premiere rock'n'roll television show (produced by Jack Good) receive a short summer run in the U.S.

September 25, 1959

   Death of *The Mickey Mouse Club*. Age: 4 years. Cause: Growing up.

19. Adventures in Syndication

AT THE beginning of the 1950s, the television networks and the Hollywood studios viewed each other as mortal enemies and consequently kept their operations separate. The studios saw television as an unwelcome intruder while the two major networks, CBS and NBC, insisted that they would not give up their direct control over TV programming as they had done with radio. As the decade drew to a close, though, a totally altered relationship existed: Warner Brothers, Screen Gems (Columbia Pictures), 20th Century-Fox, and not-so-minor independents such as Desilu, Four Star Productions, Ziv, Talent Associates, and Goodson-Todman produced almost everything on television while all three networks acted as mere conduits, retaining complete control over only sports and news. This shift in power took place as network chieftains who favored in-house production (such as NBC's Pat Weaver) were replaced by people who supported abdication of network control, primarily out of economic self-interest. It was cheaper to let outside agencies take the financial risks necessary in developing programs; network executives could then sit back and pick and choose from the finished products. At the same time, direct and sustained governmental pressure was also at work, and over the years the networks were forced to "voluntarily" relinquish more and more controls.

Though the federal government, through the FCC, was expressly forbidden by law from dealing with program content (unless it was obscene or libelous), there were many ways to get around the rule. The FCC had made the first major attempt to control programming with its unsuccessful ban on big money quiz shows in 1949, but throughout the 1950s it was Congress, rather than the commission, that sought to influence what went over the air. Beginning in 1951, a seemingly endless stream of hearings dealing with the possible detrimental effect of sex and violence on television occupied congressional attention. Despite numerous impassioned outcries at these hearings over the deteriorating morals of the nation, none of the investigators ever uncovered a dramatic outrage that could be pinned on the networks as an example of a blatant abuse of the public's trust. It was all conjecture and no one could explain what level of sex and violence was harmful—if any. So in the mid-Fifties Congress turned instead to the field of anti-trust action and here the potential for success seemed higher.

In the Forties, such governmental pressure had forced NBC to give up its Blue radio network (which then became ABC) and had broken the grip that the eight major studios held over Hollywood. Testing the waters again, the government suggested that television might be helped immeasurably by breaking the control the three networks held over programming and cited some possible benefits. Broadcasters would no longer all have to appeal to the lowest common denominator. Instead, by allowing a greater number of program producers access to the market, the government would encourage specialization similar to what was then occurring in AM radio (stations catered to specific but differing tastes such as rock'n'roll, classical, and middle of the road music) and perhaps even develop additional competing networks. In reaction to the congressional trust-busters breathing down their necks, the networks acted to forestall any such legislation by relinquishing some programming control on their own. As a result, Hollywood took control of television production through the Fifties and the quality of network programming dropped noticeably. These Hollywood firms were even more timid than the networks and they turned away from any innovative programming to produce safe immitations and duplications of the film industry's classic grade-B staples.

The Hollywood studios could not really be blamed for failing to initiate any bold innovations because even the supplier of the greatest amount of network programming for the 1959–60 season, Warner Brothers, produced only seven hours each week. Each program was one-seventh of its total television commitment, and there was little room for shows that were likely to meet viewer resistance by being different. Warner Brothers felt it was taking a big enough risk in the new season by making a major commitment to the one-hour action-adventure format for ABC. Until the previous few seasons, the only successful sixty-minute shows had been variety and drama presentations, and it wasn't until *Maverick* and *Cheyenne* that regular filmed adventure series dared to go this extra length. After the success of *77 Sunset Strip* in 1958–59, ABC was willing to gamble with more of the same, and Warners, with some trepidation, delivered the new product. At first, it appeared as if the network's gamble had failed. Each of the new action-adventure programs opened to blistering critical reviews and low ratings, but ABC held firm. *77 Sunset Strip* had also opened in a weak position, then slowly built its ratings, becoming a hit by spring. The network had learned that a sixty-minute program needed a slightly longer time to prove itself; besides, the public was still getting used to the action-adventure format. ABC's patience paid off, the numerous echoes of *77 Sunset Strip* caught on, and by spring ABC found itself in second place in the network ratings race for the first time.

Warner Brothers' three new action-adventure programs each followed the previous season's winning formula to a tee ("two parts private eye, one part cutie pie"), just as ABC wanted. *Bourbon Street Beat* ("77 Gumbo Strip") presented blackmail, murder, drug smuggling, dames, fights, and wisecracks in the French Quarter of New Orleans through the eyes of suave and sophisticated Cal Calhoun (Andrew Duggan) and Rex Randolph (Richard Long). The two were assisted by Ricky Nelson-cum-Kookie protégé Ken Madison (Van Williams) and their shapely secretary Melody Mercer (Arlene Howell). A supposedly catchy jazz theme ran through each episode, but it did little to punch up the predictable action sequences. *Hawaiian Eye* ("77 Surfboard Strip") presented the usual outbreak of blackmail, murder, pineapple smuggling, fights, and dames with the palm trees, beaches, and tropical sun of the country's newest state as a backdrop. The crew of detectives (played by Anthony Eisley, Grant Williams, and Robert "Kookie" Conrad) went through the paces of solving crimes and admiring the scenery, with assistance from a beautiful nightspot singer (Connie Stevens) and a local-color taxicab driver (Poncie Ponce). It would have been undiplomatic to ignore the country's other new state, so *The Alaskans* ("77 Tundra Strip") presented blackmail, murder, gold prospecting, dames, fights, and wisecracks in the "beautiful but dangerous Ice Palace of the Northland" in the 1890s. A pair of prospectors, Reno McKee (Jeff York), a rugged cowpoke with gold on his mind, and the aptly-named Silky Harris (Roger Moore), teamed up with a beautiful saloon entertainer, Rocky Shaw (Dorothy Provine), in search of gold and adventure, but they never seemed quite right in the lusty Klondike setting. Moore was too much the epitome of British *sang-froid* and Provine appeared far too Victorian for the part of cafe thrush to the earthy miners. Though these new entries pulled in respectable ratings by the end of the season, for the most part they failed to provide any solid foundation to sustain audience interest. In many ways, they were formula television at its worst.

Just because a program followed a predictable, repetitious formula did not automatically mean it was bad. On the contrary, some excellent television entertainment had emerged from such unchanging stalwarts as *Perry Mason, Peter Gunn,* and *Maverick,* but each of those added something special to the formula. *Perry Mason* drew the viewer into an elaborate murder puzzle with a wide range of clues and suspects. *Peter Gunn* filled its routine detective adventures with off-beat characters and a rich musical undercurrent. *Maverick,* probably the best of the Warner Brothers productions, showcased very appealing characters, clever plots, and humor that was neither forced nor overbearing. *77 Sunset Strip* was near the quality of *Maverick,* supporting the action with appealing, witty characters and usually adequate scripts. The new action-adventure series, in contrast, failed at almost every level. The main characters were handsome but weak, the supporting casts wooden and lifeless, and the stories offered nothing to supplement the action. There were no clever puzzles, baffling mysteries, or intriguing situations—just murder, blackmail, smuggling, fights, and dames. Despite all the action, the programs were also generally bland and inoffensive, offering adventures that were so noncontroversial and timeless that they could have come from any of the hundreds of grade-B Hollywood adventure films produced since the Twenties. Perhaps all these weaknesses could have been overlooked if they turned up in only one or two programs, but with ABC devoting so much of its attention in the new season to action-adventure (from Warner Brothers and other studios) and developing more of the same for the future, the genre was being diluted and overextended while it was just beginning. There were too many series, too soon. The only thing that distinguished one from another was

the so-called exotic setting (Alaska, Hawaii, New Orleans). In fact, all the programs seemed virtually indistinguishable from the low-budget offerings of such syndicators as Ziv. Though they were first-run network series, they seemed designed more for future syndication than current network programming.

Devising the perfect show for syndication was a minor artform and Ziv had perfected it over the years. When the networks had maintained more control over programs, Ziv, as an independent production company, had been practically locked out of the network schedules, so it began producing shows that could be sold individually to local stations. Such a strategy required programs that could be repeated indefinitely without appearing dated. Because local stations were even more reticent than the networks to take on a series that smacked of controversy, stories had to be safe and inoffensive as well. Though Ziv and other independent film producers eventually won a toe-hold in the network schedules by the mid-Fifties, a program's potential for syndication remained their paramount concern. Filmed series cost a great deal to produce and, though a prudent producer could usually break even after a few years on the network, the real profit rested in years of local reruns in which the only new cost was duplicating the episodes. When the major studios ventured into network television, the potential profit in this rerun market did not go unnoticed, and in the late 1950s many network-filmed series (especially the sitcoms, Westerns, and action-adventure shows) began to take on the unmistakable look of syndication. The season's ultimate example of this trend was *Adventures in Paradise* from 20th Century-Fox. The series was set in the alluring South Pacific, following the adventures of Adam Troy (Gardner McKay), the handsome, pipe-smoking skipper of the schooner *Tiki,* who cruised the ocean and visited countless island ports. The stories were nonexistent, Troy's character was emotionless and nondescript, and the supporting cast was

---

October 12, 1959

Play of the Week. David Susskind takes the endangered species of drama anthologies to syndication. This weekly two-hour videotaped program is quickly hailed by critics as being as good as, if not better than, the few drama showcases remaining on the networks.

October 26, 1959

CBS Reports. (CBS). To counter the embarrassing quiz scandal, CBS basks in the desperately needed praise and prestige from "Biography of a Missile," the first presentation of its new Ed Murrow-Fred Friendly documentary series.

November 17, 1959

Radio's payola scandal rolls in right behind the quizzes. ABC's Dick Clark is given an ultimatum by congressional investigators: Get rid of outside music interests, or else. Clark divests.

November 20, 1959

Alan Freed is fired from WABC radio, due to his payola problems. Eight days later, he is fired from WNEW-TV.

December 8, 1959

Quiz show casualties reach the top: Louis G. Cowan is out, James Aubrey is in at CBS.

January 3, 1960

Sunday Sports Spectacular. (CBS). A Sunday afternoon experiment: The first attempt to offer a variety of less familiar sporting events, such as rodeo and stock car racing, on a weekly basis.

	7:00	7:30	8:00	8:30	9:00	9:30	10:00	10:30	
MONDAY	local	Cheyenne		BOURBON STREET BEAT		ADVENTURES IN PARADISE		Man With A Camera	**ABC**
	local	Masquerade Party	The Texan	Father Knows Best	Danny Thomas Show	Ann Southern Show	HENNESSEY	DuPONT SHOW W/ JUNE ALLYSON	**CBS**
	local	Richard Diamond, Private Detective	LOVE AND MARRIAGE	Tales Of Wells Fargo	Peter Gunn	Alcoa-Goodyear Theater	Steve Allen Plymouth Show		**NBC**

	7:00	7:30	8:00	8:30	9:00	9:30	10:00	10:30	
TUESDAY	local	Sugarfoot BRONCO		Life And Legend Of Wyatt Earp	The Rifleman	PHILIP MARLOWE	Alcoa Presents: One Step Beyond	Keep Talking	**ABC**
	local	local	DENNIS O'KEEFE SHOW	THE MANY LOVES OF DOBIE GILLIS	TIGHTROPE	Red Skelton Show	Garry Moore Show		**CBS**
	local	LARAMIE		FIBBER McGEE AND MOLLY	Arthur Murray Party	FORD STAR TIME		local	**NBC**

	7:00	7:30	8:00	8:30	9:00	9:30	10:00	10:30	
WEDNESDAY	local	Court Of Last Resort	CHARLIE WEAVER'S HOBBY LOBBY	The Adventures Of Ozzie And Harriet	HAWAIIAN EYE		Wednesday Night Fights		**ABC**
	local	The Lineup		MEN INTO SPACE	The Millionaire	I've Got A Secret	U.S. Steel Hour Armstrong Circle Theater		**CBS**
	local	Wagon Train		The Price Is Right	Perry Como's Kraft Music Hall		This Is Your Life	WICHITA TOWN	**NBC**

	7:00	7:30	8:00	8:30	9:00	9:30	10:00	10:30	
THURSDAY	local	Gale Storm Show	Donna Reed Show	The Real McCoys	Pat Boone Chevy Showroom	THE UNTOUCHABLES		TAKE A GOOD LOOK	**ABC**
	local	To Tell The Truth	BETTY HUTTON SHOW	JOHNNY RINGO	Dick Powell's Zane Grey Theater	Playhouse 90 THE BIG PARTY			**CBS**
	local	LAW OF THE PLAINSMAN	Bat Masterson	JOHNNY STACCATO	Bachelor Father	Tennessee Ernie Ford Show	You Bet Your Life	Lawless Years	**NBC**

	7:00	7:30	8:00	8:30	9:00	9:30	10:00	10:30	
FRIDAY	local	Walt Disney Presents		MAN FROM BLACKHAWK	77 Sunset Strip		ROBERT TAYLOR IN THE DETECTIVES	Black Saddle	**ABC**
	local	Rawhide		HOTEL DePAREE	Westinghouse Desilu Playhouse @Lucille Ball-Desi Arnaz Show		TWILIGHT ZONE	Person To Person	**CBS**
	local	People Are Funny	THE TROUBLESHOOTERS	Bell Telephone Hour NBC SPECIALS		M Squad	Gillette Cavalcade Of Sports	Jackpot Bowling	**NBC**

	7:00	7:30	8:00	8:30	9:00	9:30	10:00	10:30	
SATURDAY	local	Dick Clark Beechnut Show	JOHN GUNTHER'S HIGH ROAD	Leave It To Beaver	Lawrence Welk's Dodge Dancing Party		Jubilee U.S.A.		**ABC**
	local	Perry Mason		Wanted: Dead Or Alive	MR. LUCKY	Have Gun, Will Travel	Gunsmoke	Markham	**CBS**
	local	BONANZA		THE MAN AND THE CHALLENGE	THE DEPUTY	FIVE FINGERS		It Could Be You	**NBC**

	7:00	7:30	8:00	8:30	9:00	9:30	10:00	10:30	
SUNDAY	Colt .45	Maverick		Lawman	THE REBEL	THE ALASKANS		DICK CLARK'S WORLD OF TALENT	**ABC**
	Lassie	DENNIS THE MENACE	Ed Sullivan Show		General Electric Theater	Alfred Hitchcock Presents	George Gobel Show Jack Benny Program	What's My Line	**CBS**
	RIVERBOAT		SUNDAY SHOWCASE		Dinah Shore Chevy Show		Loretta Young Show	local	**NBC**

mediocre and unbelievable. Nonetheless, the series was perfect for syndication since it was really nothing more than a travelogue through a swank tropical paradise. Though it remained on ABC for only three seasons, *Adventures in Paradise* was still being rerun in syndication through the 1970s. Of course, there were also high quality series worthy of continued off-network reruns. One such program was ABC's most successful new action series for 1959–60, *The Untouchables*.

An amazing wave of nostalgia for the prohibition era surfaced in 1959 on television, beginning with the *Playhouse 90* presentation of "Seven Against the Wall" (produced by John Houseman). It was a realistic re-creation of the Al Capone gang's St. Valentine's Day Massacre in Chicago. The realism was accentuated by using a well-known newscaster, Eric Sevareid, as narrator. A few months later, NBC began a short-lived series called *The Lawless Years*, which was based on the real-life exploits of Barney Ruditsky, a New York City plainclothes detective in the Twenties who worked to infiltrate and expose racketeers and bootleggers. The most successful exploitation of the era came in the spring with a two-part story on CBS's *Desilu Playhouse*, "The Untouchables," based on a book written by Eliot Ness, the federal agent who nailed Al Capone. Robert Stack portrayed the no-nonsense lawman, Neville Brand played Capone, and Bruce Gordon was Frank Nitti, Ca-

pone's assistant. Borrowing *Playhouse 90's* realistic touch of using a well-known newscaster to tell the story, Walter Winchell supplied the dramatic narration. The two episodes were favorably received and the concept was developed into a weekly series. In the fall of 1959, *The Untouchables* premiered, surprisingly, on ABC—a concrete example of the network's growing strength and credibility.

The Untouchables, produced by Quinn Martin, was television docudrama at its best, taking real events and real characters and incorporating them into interesting and entertaining stories. It was a good gangster show, depicting a violent era populated by cruel men who often could be overcome only by violence. Occasionally the writers were not completely faithful to history, but the effective presentation of the struggle between the "untouchable" lawmen (led by Eliot Ness) and the Capone mob (led by Frank Nitti) usually rendered the minor inaccuracies unimportant. The program was merely a re-creation of events in a bygone era, not a strict history lecture, and it was necessary to have clearly defined good guys and bad guys as well as a gaggle of innocent and not-so-innocent bystanders.

Nonetheless, *The Untouchables* upset many Italian-Americans because it appeared at a time when revelations about the Mafia were making front page news. They felt the program merely served to confirm a feeling among Americans that all gangsters were Italians and all Italians were gangsters. In reality, the Capone mob was almost completely Italian, so Quinn Martin had given the characters Italian names and used actors who could "look Italian" in these roles. In doing so, he had violated TV's unspoken ban on presenting identifiable ethnic personalities, a volatile topic in American broadcasting since World War II. Industry reluctance to showcase ethnicity had all but eliminated the ethnic school of humor in the early Fifties and ABC was sensitive to criticism of its new show. In response, the network downplayed the Italianness of the gangsters in the show's second season and had Martin add Italian agents to Ness's crew and non-Italian thugs to the Nitti mob (in a prohibition era equivalent of affirmative action). Even with these modifications, the series still retained a strong flavor of the era.

The Untouchables was also criticized for being too violent with its abundance of gang war shoot-outs and ambushes by federal agents. Though frequent and intense, the violence was never gratuitous, rarely gruesome or morbid, and usually necessary to the story. After all, the program was dealing with gangsters in an era when such dramatic confrontations frequently took place. If Martin had sanitized the subject matter, he would have seriously undercut the very premise of the show and left it virtually indistinguishable from every other TV crime series. Instead, *The Untouchables* stood apart with its strong characters, good scripts, and very realistic setting. Though by no means perfect (over time, the nearly hysterical Walter Winchell narration became rather humorous), the series delivered almost everything an action-adventure show was supposed to.

The criticism of the violent tendencies and historical inaccuracies in *The Untouchables* was, in many cases, just fresh ammunition for people convinced that television was somehow responsible for most of the country's ills. In the fall of 1959, such nit-picking became unnecessary as the long percolating quiz show scandal provided them with the long sought "smoking gun" to clinch the argument against television.

The special grand jury investigating the charges against the quiz shows had met in secret throughout the winter and spring of 1959, so the entire matter had slipped out of sight for a while. On June 10, after hearing 150 hours of testimony from 200 witnesses concerning six quiz shows (many of which were, by that time, no longer on the air), the grand jury finished its work and handed over a 12,000 word report to Judge Mitchell D. Schweitzer. The grand jury's findings did not constitute an indictment, but rather a "presentment," that is, a report calling attention to illegal acts without holding specific people responsible. Because no trial would result from the presentment, Judge Schweitzer felt that the document would damage those named in it by not providing an opportunity for them to publicly clear their names, so he promptly sealed and impounded the report. Members of the grand jury pointed out that they had specifically avoided naming individuals and that no harm would occur. Most of the summer was spent arguing whether the report should be made public or not, and in August a compromise was reached. Judge Schweitzer agreed to show the minutes of the grand jury proceedings to Representative Oren D. Harris, the chairman of the House Committee on Interstate and Foreign Commerce, who had announced that his committee would hold public hearings on the quiz show question beginning October 6. Releasing the minutes was almost as good as showing the committee the actual report, so the matter was put to rest (the report never was made public) and attention shifted to Harris's committee.

Harris had bedeviled the broadcast industry for years with anti-trust allegations and inconclusive hearings on sex and violence.

With the quiz show investigation, he felt he had a clear-cut issue to use against television, even though there was doubt that concrete criminal charges could be leveled against anyone. After months of research, lawyers on both sides had been unable to uncover any law that quiz show riggers might have broken, so the committee hearings were merely a maneuver to put the matter before the public. It was felt that outraged viewers would demand changes in the laws regulating broadcasting after learning the depth of the quiz show rigging first hand.

The first witnesses before the committee were former *Twenty-One* contestants James Snodgrass and Herbert Stempel. Snodgrass offered his proof that he had been supplied answers in advance (the sealed registered letters that he had mailed to himself with the information) and Stempel claimed he had been told when to lose to Charles Van Doren (though he offered no hard evidence). A breakthrough occurred on October 9 when Dan Enright (one-half of the team that created *Twenty-One* and other top NBC quizzes) publicly acknowledged that "controls" (his euphemism for rigging) had been "a practice for many many years" on both his quiz shows and those of many others. The nighttime version of *Tic Tac Dough,* he revealed, was rigged 75% of the time. The daytime version was not fixed because it was not as vital to attract a large audience at that hour. "Deception is not necessarily bad," he explained. "It's practiced in everyday life . . . it should be measured in terms of the hurt it inflicted on people." He said that the whole point of rigging was to ensure a dramatic flow of events while making certain that characters who appealed to the public became the returning champions. After Enright's confession, other people involved with other shows came forward to echo

January 21, 1960
CBS cuts *Playhouse 90* loose, lets it float. The series is quietly killed in 1961.

February 11, 1960
Jack Paar walks out on his late night NBC show after a network censor nixes a somewhat randy bathroom joke. After fuming awhile, Paar returns March 7 and levels a searing blast at the newspaper columnists that criticized him about the incident.

April 1, 1960
Television's foremost couple, Lucille Ball and Desi Arnaz, make their final appearance together in "Lucy Meets the Moustache" (with guest Ernie Kovacs). One month later, their divorce becomes final.

April 5, 1960
Worthington Miner, last of NBC, replaces David Susskind as executive producer of *Play of the Week.*

May 12, 1960
Frank Sinatra, in his fourth and final ABC special for the season, presents the return to television of Elvis Presley, who has just completed a stint in the Army. The Voice and the Pelvis duet on "Love Me Tender" and "Witchcraft."

June 24, 1960
Death of *Gillette Cavalcade of Sports.* Age: 16 years. Cause: Bad punches.

September 24, 1960
Death of *Howdy Doody.* Age: 13 years. The decade is over. "Goodbye kids."

the same line. They had coached contestants merely to ensure good ratings. Hal March, emcee of *The $64,000 Question,* said:

It got to the point where there were just too many quiz programs. Ratings began to drop and some producers turned to rigging to make sure the shows kept their audience. They just couldn't afford to lose their sponsors.

Despite the attempts to couch quiz show controls as just a necessary business practice, the admissions of rigging suggested that the situation was much worse and more widespread than had been previously suspected. More importantly, many of the contestants, including Charles Van Doren, had testified under oath that such rigging hadn't taken place, and it appeared that they were guilty of perjury. Van Doren, then a regular *Today* show staff member, had even issued another complete denial at the start of the committee's hearings, then vanished. Harris issued a subpoena for Van Doren, but for days the former quiz kid could not be found. On October 13, he reappeared in New York City, saying that he had been in New England on vacation and had known nothing of the subpoena, but was ready to testify. By then, the quiz show question seemed to be turning itself into a national self-examination in which the country's self-esteem was at stake. Even President Eisenhower announced that he was worried over the disclosures and was instructing Attorney General William Rogers to look into the matter.

On November 2, 1959, Charles Van Doren, the thirty-three-year-old symbol of American ingenuity, confessed he had been living a lie since 1956, saying "I would give almost anything I have to reverse the course of my life in the last three years." From the very beginning, he said, *Twenty-One* producer Albert Freedman had coached him in both answers and demeanor. Freedman had said that the then-current champion, Herbert Stempel, was hurting the show by being too successful and unpopular with the audience. Van Doren's job was to depose him. Van Doren said he asked to compete honestly, but Freedman replied that was impossible. Such things had to be prearranged. Besides, the methods didn't matter. The important thing was that Van Doren would be promoting the image of the intellectual before the nation. Freedman then:

. . . . instructed me how to answer the questions, to pause before certain of the answers, to skip certain parts and return to them, to hesitate to build up suspense, and so forth. . . .
He gave me a script to memorize and before the program he took back the script and rehearsed me in my part.

Van Doren explained that soon after he became champ, and an unexpectedly popular contestant with the public, he asked Freedman many times to let him go; in January, 1957, the producer agreed, but said it would take some time to arrange. In February, Van Doren faced Vivienne Nearing who, he was told, would be his final opponent. So that every possible twist could be milked for the maximum effect, the final contest was arranged to end in a succession of dramatic ties. On February 18, Van Doren and Nearing were tied. On February 25, they were locked in two more ties, and then the program took a one-week break while the nation held its breath. On March 11, Van Doren was told he would lose that night and was not given any of the answers. In a perverse twist of fate, he was honestly stumped by the first question directed to him and couldn't identify the king of Belgium (a relatively simple question).

Van Doren confessed that he had been surprised by the public's warm and enthusiastic response to him, but took advantage of it with the feeling that he was "promoting the intellectual life." When the grand jury called him in on January 14, 1959, he, like the other contestants, lied to protect himself, his new-found friends, and his own professional image. They had even been coached again, this time in their testimony, by their producers. When he saw the stonewall strategy coming apart, he ran to New England for some serious soul searching, and decided to tell the truth when he returned.

As a measure of the high regard Van Doren was held in, Representative Harris and other members of the committee responded to the lengthy testimony with effusive praise for the newly repentant sinner. He was commended for his fortitude and forthrightness of his soul searching statement. Only Representative Steven Derounian of New York faced reality, observing "I don't think an adult of your intelligence should be commended for telling the truth." It was this view that took hold. Columbia University fired Van Doren from his assistant professorship, and NBC fired him from its staff. *New York Times* TV critic Jack Gould observed that "apparently many witnesses felt that going before a grand jury was just another little quiz game to which the answers could be rigged in advance." The anxious public, intensely interested in hearing Van Doren's side of the story, found the details of the preprogram coaching particularly galling. If Van Doren had really wanted to stop the charade, he could have deliberately answered incorrectly at any time. What's more, not only had Van Doren cheated, but all those nervous tics that viewers had identified with as he struggled to victory had been nothing more than acting craft.

Following the Van Doren testimony, a parade of other contestants, many from the Louis G. Cowan-inspired CBS quizzers, came forward and bared their souls. Each one added to the disillusioning revelations about some of America's television heroes. Staff assistants from *The $64,000 Question* revealed that they had ready access (as "editors") to the safe deposit box containing each week's questions, and that they had regularly used the privilege in order to prep contestants. Band leader Xavier Cugat confessed that he had received help in his appearance on *The $64,000 Challenge.* Thirteen-year-old actress Patty Duke, who had gone from successful appearances on *The $64,000 Challenge* to a Broadway role as Helen Keller in "The Miracle Worker," admitted that she had been merely acting on the quiz show as well. To many this seemed the lowest blow of all. Quiz show producers didn't hesitate to exploit an impressionable child. President Eisenhower said he was bewildered and dismayed by the extent of the quiz rigging, but preferred to view it as a latter day equivalent to the 1919 Black Sox World Series scandal, stating, "It doesn't reflect a general debasement of moral standards."

Though the extensive public hearings and revelations disappointed and outraged many, the only crime committed in the entire matter turned out to be lying to the grand jury. Most of the producers cooperated with the district attorney and copped pleas. In October, 1960, twenty contestants from *Twenty-One* and *Tic Tac Dough,* including Charles Van Doren and Vivienne Nearing, were indicted for second degree perjury. For more than a year their cases were dragged through the courts, and nearly half decided to plead guilty. On January 17, 1962, Van Doren and the nine other remaining contestants pleaded guilty before Judge Edward Breslin, who suspended their sentences because "the humiliation was evident in their faces."

To the television industry, however, the revelations came as a major body blow to its prestige. After years of very vocal but disorganized carping, critics, both in and out of government, were handed more than enough ammunition to use in their efforts to alter the laws governing broadcasting. Viewers felt betrayed by the medium they had placed so much trust in. Television programmers had willingly manipulated their emotions and exploited their loyalties in order to pump up ratings and satisfy the sponsors, so there was very little public sympathy for the broadcasters. CBS president Frank Stanton, realizing the need for bold action to forestall any potentially devastating legislation, saved the situation by immediately canceling the only three big money quiz shows left on CBS (*The Big Payoff, Top Dollar,* and *Name that Tune*) while the quiz hearings were still in progress. In the process, he wrote off $15 million per year in ad revenue. Going even beyond that, Stanton told a convention of news directors in New Orleans that, in the future,

> . . . we and we alone will decide not only *what* is to appear on CBS, but how it is to appear. We accept the responsibility for content and quality and for assuring the American people that what they see and hear on CBS is exactly what it purports to be.

Stanton's statement and quick action drew praise from the public, but Albert Freedman, the producer of *Twenty-One,* felt otherwise and argued that there was no reason to treat quiz shows differently from other entertainment programs:

> In the field of TV programming, saturated with murder and violence, it is my opinion that the quiz shows, as entertainment, were a breath of fresh air . . . it is about time the television industry stopped apologizing for its existence and began to fight back. It should insist that programming be recognized and judged as entertainment and entertainment only.

It was only show business, he said, the same as magicians, Hollywood sets, radio sound effects, Western shoot-outs, movie stuntmen, TV lawyers' perfect records, and ghost writers for politicians. All of these did not present reality, but rather an approximation and re-creation of reality. The real crime perpetrated was the attempt to convince the public that the quiz shows were not approximations of reality, but living breathing reality itself. "Our only error was

that we were too successful," he said. "The stakes were too high, and the quiz winners fused themselves into the home life and the hopes and aspirations of the viewers."

Stanton's firm action and brave announcements contrasted favorably with the self-serving statements of innocence that came from NBC and the "you can't blame us" attitude at ABC. By accepting both blame and responsibility, Stanton diffused much of the antipathy felt toward the networks. Legislation was eventually passed in reaction to the quiz scandal, but it was limited to the very narrow area of making it a crime to fix a quiz show. At the same time, CBS began a drive to upgrade the overall image of network television with positive reforms and programs that emphasized the passing of the quiz show era. The network reestablished at least partial control over programming; the old Edward R. Murrow *See It Now* series was reactivated under a new name, *CBS Reports;* and the ailing Louis Cowan, father of the big money quiz shows, was eased out of his position as head of the television network and replaced by James T. Aubrey.

Just as TV executives began the task of restoring their tarnished credibility, charges of industry misconduct in another area surfaced. Radio disk jockeys and music entrepreneurs were accused of accepting payola (bribes) in return for the exposure and promotion of otherwise unknown or inferior recording artists. Once again, the illusion of popular entertainment was tainted by vested interests and personal gain. Investigations into the radio payola charges touched many people but quickly focused on the two titans of rock'n'roll, Dick Clark and Alan Freed, both of whom had far-reaching business interests ranging from radio and television programs to connections with record companies and song promoters. The two were acknowledged to be very influential in directing teen tastes throughout the country and this raised suspicions about their motives. Both were called before congressional committees

Riverboat set its Western adventures aboard the steamwheeler *Enterprise* in the 1840s. Darren McGavin (2nd from *r.*) was the captain and Burt Reynolds *(c.)* played the ship's pilot. (*From* Riverboat. *Courtesy of MCA Television Limited)*

The Many Loves of Dobie Gillis
with: (from *l.*) Frank Faylen as
Herbert T. Gillis, Dwayne
Hickman as his son Dobie, and
Bob Denver as Maynard G.
Krebs. *(Courtesy of Twentieth
Century-Fox)*

to face heavy questioning, and the grilling left Clark shaken but Freed severely wounded. Though he insisted he had done nothing wrong, Freed was fired from his local New York radio and TV slots. (He died a few years later on the West Coast.) Clark quickly divorced himself from his outside business interests in order to remove any possible conflicts and he managed to keep his two ABC television shows. The careers of both men, however, illustrated the chief by-product of both the payola and quiz scandals—a tremendous increase in the level of fear in the broadcasting world. Even the slightest hint of controversy had to be avoided at all costs.

With TV blackened by the quizzes and radio damaged by payola, both tried desperately to win back the public's trust. Safe, reassuring programming became vital. Experimentation was out. Even a television program that was a critical and ratings winner, *Mr. Lucky,* found itself in trouble over its moral tone. The series, which had premiered in the fall, followed the adventures of a suave gambler, Mr. Lucky (John Vivyan), who operated his own casino aboard his yacht, the *Fortuna.* Lucky and his Latin sidekick Andamo (Ross Martin) cruised along the Pacific coast facing an assortment of odd-ball gamblers, corrupt Latin dictators, and enticing females, while accompanied by rich Henry Mancini mood music. When the quiz scandals erupted, the sponsor demanded that Lucky stop gambling. He was corrupting the public morals (that is, he was providing bad product identification for the sponsor). It wasn't enough that the series stressed the personal integrity of Lucky and Andamo while emphasizing their efforts to keep the operation honest. The idea of a leading man running a floating crap game was too much to bear. So Lucky and Andamo transformed the *Fortuna* from a casino to a restaurant. How the sponsor expected dramatic tension to develop in a floating deli was never revealed because *Mr. Lucky* was soon canceled anyway. In this atmosphere of fear, *Mr. Lucky* earned the dubious distinction of being one of the highest rated shows to be axed in years. More and more,

even sizable minorities or mildly esoteric tastes were being ignored in favor of safe, inoffensive formats.

Though tranquility was the new cornerstone of prime time entertainment, the networks also sharply increased the number of news and public affairs shows. They turned to them and hoped that the public would be impressed and forgive the lapses in taste of the quiz show era. This revival of informational programming marked a clear-cut shift of priorities because those same shows had been deliberately cut back by all the networks in favor of cheaper, flashier commercial fare since the middle of the decade.

CBS was the first to act, bringing *CBS Reports* to prime time even before the quiz scandal reached its peak. The floating hour-long documentary series, produced by Ed Murrow and Fred Friendly, presented high quality programs and managed to attract the support of sponsors—who were also interested in projecting a more positive image. Among the reports in the program's first season were: "Biography of a Missile" (the development of a new missile, the Juno 2, from design to launch); "Who Speaks for the South?" (both sides of the integration issue told by the people directly involved); "Trujillo, Portrait of a Dictator" (a look at the controversial Dominican leader who seemed headed for trouble—he was, in fact, assassinated the next year); and "Lippmann on Leadership" (the first television appearance by noted columnist Walter Lippmann).

Shortly after the quiz scandal revelations, NBC also moved to boost the corporate image and offered *World Wide 60* as its public affairs showcase. Hosted by Frank McGee, the program occasionally turned out hard-hitting material such as "The Winds of Change" (an analysis of the changing situation in black Africa) and a look at Cuba, one year after Castro assumed power. Usually, though, it tended toward either well produced travelogue type features (such as visiting scientists at the South Pole) or soft mood pieces such as "The Living End" (on old age). The network's main cultural drive, however, had actually begun in the fall with two of NBC's traditional strengths, class variety and live drama. *Sunday Showcase,* headed by Robert Alan Aurthur, featured dramas such as "What Makes Sammy Run" and "The American" (the story of Ira Hayes, played by Lee Marvin), as well as high class variety presentations such as "Give My Regards to Broadway" with Jimmy Durante and Ray Bolger. Another series, *Ford Star Time,* also mixed drama with its main strength, variety, and produced "Turn of the Screw," "The Jazz Singer" (Jerry Lewis re-creating the 1927 film classic), and a unique television sing-along, led by popular sing-along recording artist Mitch Miller. Despite these noble efforts to upgrade the quality of American television (and the networks' own public image), the 1959–60 season marked a significant, symbolic loss for serious television drama.

In the fall, CBS's *Playhouse 90* was reduced to an every-other-week feature alternating with the insipid *Big Party,* a free swinging (actually scripted) gathering "live from New York City" that was filled with inveterate scene stealers and glittery showbiz folks (such as Rock Hudson, Eva Gabor, Sammy Davis, Jr., Carol Channing) ready to plug their latest song or film. This television travesty was quietly put to sleep in January and, at the same time, *Playhouse 90* lost its regular Thursday night slot and became a floating special.

The era of regularly scheduled, large scale drama anthologies had passed. Even the once heated confrontations over controversial scripts had settled into a well-worn and hollow routine. CBS postponed the production of a Rod Serling play about Warsaw's Jewish ghetto, "In the Presence of Mine Enemies," (originally scheduled for presentation at the beginning of the season) when three sponsors objected, saying simply that the network had promised to get away from such depressing themes. There was not much of a fight and the story eventually aired on May 18 as one of *Playhouse 90*'s irregularly scheduled special broadcasts. Fittingly, the play was superficial, pretentious, and not worth squabbling over. (Its only memorable feature was a performance by Robert Redford as a young, sensitive Nazi.) Serling himself seemed to have written off TV drama showcases as a lost cause anyway, devoting his efforts instead to a new half-hour filmed series that premiered on CBS that fall, *The Twilight Zone.* He explained his transition:

> I'm tired of fighting the frustrated fights, copping pleas, fighting for points . . . in any case, the half-hour form is a fact of life, and as long as we have to live with it, we might as well try and do something meaningful in it. Even if they fail, I think my shows will be better than *My Little Margie.*

Serling acted as executive producer, host, and frequent writer for *The Twilight Zone,* a suspense anthology similar to *Alfred Hitchcock Presents.* Both series presented "stories with a twist," but while Hitchcock's usually followed an O. Henry-ish style of trick ending, Serling's focused on events that often couldn't be explained at all. Many of the tales drew on science fiction themes, a number were genuinely amusing, and a few were actually scary. Though it never became a runaway hit, the series won a few Emmys and continued for five seasons (expanding to a full hour for one), maintaining Serling's high standards for the entire run. Without a doubt, the provocative and engrossing tales were very much better than *My Little Margie.*

Serling's move to a weekly half-hour series was his acknowledgment that, for the most part, the public preferred that form. Occasionally a special might stir viewer interest, but inevitably the audience would return to familiar weekly series. In the 1959–60 season, Westerns continued to dominate this form, though as the season progressed their popularity seemed to be leveling off. At the start of the season, six of television's top ten program were Westerns but, by spring, the number had dropped to four of the

top fifteen. Though there were more new Westerns in September than any other program format, most seemed content to rely on one obvious hook to snare viewers and so broke no new ground. *Tate* was about a one-armed sheriff. *Law of the Plainsman* featured a U.S. marshal who was a Harvard-educated Apache Indian. *The Rebel* was Johnny Yuma (Nick Adams), a troubled wanderer and former Confederate soldier. *Riverboat* was a floating *Wagon Train,* starring Darren McGavin and TV newcomer Burt Reynolds. *The Deputy* featured occasional appearances by Henry Fonda. Only two of the new series lasted more than a few years and they used the most unusual gimmick of all. The heroes in both *Laramie* and *Bonanza* worked on a ranch—something cowboys really did!

Laramie was competent but unexciting, while *Bonanza* was an epic family drama that relied on its four male leads, joined by frequent guest stars, to carry the program's workload. Former Canadian newscaster Lorne Greene played Ben Cartwright, father of three sons by three different wives. This was the reason, apparently, that Adam (Pernell Roberts), Hoss (Dan Blocker), and Little Joe (Michael Landon) had such different personalities and constantly engaged in excessive fraternal scraps. When the chips were down, though, father and sons clung together to protect the family name and family spread, the Ponderosa, from corrupt and thieving outsiders. As owners of one of the largest ranches in the area, the members of the Cartwright clan were required to make frequent business trips to neighboring towns, and to take an intense interest in any local scheme or development that might affect them. Such a wide open format allowed a great range of plots and the opportunity for individual guest stars to shine. It also permitted great expanses of gorgeous full color outdoor scenery, and this had a surprising effect on color TV set sales. NBC (the only network still pushing color) had assumed all along that variety spectaculars (live or on tape) would provide the motivation for the purchase of the expensive color sets, but dealers reported that *Bonanza,* one of the few color filmed series, had brought more people into the stores than years of such live fare. This was the first good news color manufacturers had heard in years, though even with this special attraction *Bonanza* was not a smash hit in its first season. Only after a few years and several time shifts did it build up a loyal audience that followed it for nearly fourteen years.

The most successful new show of the 1959–60 season wasn't a Western, but rather an unpretentious sitcom, *Dennis the Menace.* As in the popular comic strip the series was based on, Dennis perpetually bedeviled both his parents and his neighbor, Mr. Wilson, as he displayed his natural curiosity and affinity for mischief. Six-year-old Jay North played Dennis as a normal, believable kid in the *Leave It to Beaver* tradition, facing a world filled with lunatic adults.

One of the few Fifties sitcoms to deal with teenagers facing a wacky world also premiered in the fall, though unlike *Dennis* the show made no pretense at dealing with real characters. *The Many Loves of Dobie Gillis* was based on caricature and exaggerated situations that were handled with the comic timing and wit of such TV classics as *I Love Lucy.* The characters were funny, the scripts believable (in the context of their own crazy world), and the series emerged as an effective but affectionate lampoon of middle class teenage life in the Fifties, displaying remarkable insight into an era that was still in progress.

Dwayne Hickman played the perpetually heartstruck Dobie Gillis, straight and clean-cut outside, but slightly wacko inside. Dobie had no gripes with society; all he wanted was women and money. He was constantly frustrated in the pursuit of both and, in George Burns-style asides to the audience, he tried to figure out just what had gone wrong with his latest scheme. His best friend and "good buddy," Maynard (Bob Denver), was a sharp contrast to Dobie's own image as a classic straight middle class teen. Maynard was a beatnik. He talked in jive, had a beard, wore old clothes, and didn't seem to want anything out of life, especially a job (the very mention of work made Maynard jump). Besides fulfilling the age-old requirements for a comical leading man's best friend, Maynard G. Krebs (the *G*, he explained, stood for "William") marked the first regular TV appearance of a beatnik as an unconventional but normal and sensitive person beneath his garb and gab. (Before this, beatniks were usually presented as sadistically insane criminals that were subdued by colorless, methodical policemen.) Dobie and Maynard balanced each other perfectly and provided a strong base for their comic world.

The show's supporting cast was equally colorful and lunatic. Herbert T. Gillis (Frank Faylen), Dobie's father, was a self-made man, the owner of the Gillis Grocery Store. He was an acceptably adult businessman who was obviously just off-beat enough to have fathered a boy such as Dobie. Zelda Gilroy (Sheila James) was the short, plain girl in love with Dobie, to no avail, since he was always pining for classic beauties such as Thalia Menninger (Tuesday Weld). Both Zelda and Thalia were much more intelligent than most TV females of the time; both knew what they wanted and what they didn't want. Zelda wanted Dobie and Thalia wanted lots of money. In Dobie's world, there was also someone who had "lots of money," the spoiled Chatsworth Osborne, Jr. (Stephen Franken), whose family fortune represented opulent excess at its best. Neither Chatsworth nor his widowed mother was ashamed of the Osborne fortune (they rather enjoyed it) and though the series ridiculed their elitist manner and ideals (both matriarch and scion spoke in hilariously exaggerated Harvard accents), it never portrayed them as ogres. Rounding out the supporting cast were two minor characters that made occasional, but effective, appearances: Duncan Krebs (Michael J. Pollard) was Maynard's spacey cousin, and Milton Armitage (Warren Beatty) was a stuffy but talented rival for Thalia's attention. In his own way, though, Armitage was as demented as the rest. In a school play he once performed a hilarious take-off of Marlon Brando's interpretation of Stanley Kowalski in "A Streetcar Named Desire." All of these characters served to illustrate the pleasures and the frustrations Dobie faced in trying to grow up as a typical teenager of the Fifties.

In the 1970s, when nostalgia for the 1950s took hold, programs and films such as *Happy Days* and "Grease" tried to re-create the lives and interests of supposedly typical, happy-go-lucky teenagers of the previous decade. These efforts often seemed to be hokey and artificial because they fell into the rut of accepting at face value caricatures from the era. Despite the passage of more than ten years, the Seventies' vehicles failed to provide any new insight or perspective on the period and paled in comparison to the style and humor of *Dobie Gillis*, a genuine artifact of the Fifties.

This decade, which gained such an identifiable (if not always accurate) character in retrospect, didn't end in December, 1959. The moods, trends, and attitudes of the Fifties petered out over the next four years, during the administration of President John F. Kennedy. Nevertheless, three events took place in the 1959–60 season that seemed to symbolically mark a turning point in television culture and its passage into a new decade.

In 1959, George Reeves, who had appeared as the man of steel in all 104 episodes of the six-year-old syndicated classic, *The Adventures of Superman*, killed himself. In writing his obituary, many felt that Reeves had chosen suicide out of frustration at being unable to escape his Superman image and that his epitaph might be that he died of typecasting. To millions of youngsters who heard the news, it brought a sobering realization that television was not reality and that even Superman could die. In March, 1960, Lucille Ball filed for divorce from Desi Arnaz. Lucy and Desi had been seen together only in monthly specials for the past few seasons, but their breakup officially ended, in reality and forever, a marriage whose fictionalized portrayal had been the cornerstone of television culture throughout the decade. Finally, on September 24, 1960, NBC presented the 2,343rd-and-final episode of *Howdy Doody*. Howdy had been there when TV began and kids who watched the earliest episodes had children of their own who watched the last. It was a graceful farewell that rang down the curtain on one of the last remnants of television's infancy. Perhaps there was never a more poignant moment on television than the last moment of that last show when Clarabell the clown, silent through all thirteen years of the program, looked into the camera and quietly spoke, "Goodbye kids."

20. The Vast Wasteland

SEVEN years after merging with United Paramount Theaters, the ABC television network had reached apparent respectability. The network's commitment to the action-adventure format had paid off and, though it was still far behind CBS, ABC had successfully nosed out NBC for the number two slot in the 1959–60 season. Just as the new decade began, ABC was often placing as many programs in the top ten as the other networks, sometimes even more. Ollie Treyz, president of ABC-TV since 1958, noted this improvement with considerable pride but went even further and asserted that ABC was actually number one—citing a special Nielsen ratings survey that measured markets in which all three networks had full time affiliates to back his claim. Despite these pronouncements, ABC was not yet generally considered at parity with its rivals and was still unmistakably the "third network." Though the number and strength of its affiliates had increased, ABC was far weaker than CBS and NBC. Its news, public affairs, sports, and daytime programming were virtually nonexistent. Even its success in prime time had come almost entirely from one program type, action-adventure, with only occasional hits in other genres. If the action-adventure format faded before a viable followup was found, ABC could slip back into oblivion in a very short time.

While it searched for potential new prime time hits, ABC also began to expand both its news and sports coverage in an attempt to increase prestige and build on its momentum. Its first important move in these areas was the surprise acquisition of exclusive television rights to the 1960 winter Olympics in Squaw Valley, California. For the privilege of carrying the first Olympics held in the United States since the advent of television, the network paid $167,000. ABC viewed this investment in the winter games as essentially a losing venture that was valuable only as a bargaining tool in an attempt to acquire the more profitable summer games scheduled for Rome. When it failed to win the rights to the Roman games, ABC canceled plans for coverage of the winter contests, feeling that they would cost too much and not attract sufficient viewer interest. CBS picked up both the winter and summer TV rights and found itself producing all eighteen hours of winter coverage on an unsponsored basis, just as ABC had expected. When the winter games brought in unexpectedly high ratings, both the networks and sponsors were appropriately stunned. Events such as a dramatic down-to-the-wire hockey win by the U.S. over the U.S.S.R. captured the public's attention and revealed a substantial audience for types of sports previously considered of only marginal interest. In August, CBS followed up the success in Squaw Valley with twenty hours of sponsored, well-produced coverage of the events in Rome, featuring sportscaster Jim McKay. The extensive use of video tape made it possible to present events in the United States on the same day they occurred in Italy, giving the games an immediacy and tension that had been noticeably absent in the long-delayed film reports of previous years. For CBS, the winter and summer Olympic games were both an artistic and ratings success. For ABC, they were a valuable lesson.

Though it had lost this contest to CBS, ABC saw that sports events were a natural area for it to pursue. CBS and NBC had not come up with many dramatic sports innovations in the previous half decade and ABC could compete on an equal footing, meet them head-on, and attempt to outbid them for established events—or pick up contests they had dropped or hadn't considered at all. ABC had already become the sole network outlet for one of the first TV sports, boxing, by attrition. CBS abandoned its *Blue Ribbon Bouts* in 1955 as a worn-out remnant of TV's early days, even though the show had maintained a relatively stable audience for seven years. ABC picked it up on the rebound and joined NBC and DuMont in carrying TV pugilistics through the Fifties. By the end of the decade, DuMont had folded and stories of corruption in the boxing profession and well-publicized deaths of boxers shortly after beatings in the ring had given the sport a sinister and subversive tinge that was reflected in lower ratings. In June, 1960, NBC ended its association with boxing, dropped Gillette's *Cavalcade of Sports* matches after sixteen years, and left ABC alone in the field. (It continued to present weekly bouts until 1964.)

As boxing declined during the late Fifties, other sports supplanted it as the chief focus of television athletics, and ABC scanned these for areas of possible expansion. Major league baseball was firmly in the grip of CBS and NBC, which both presented a weekend "game of the week." Beyond that, NBC had exclusive rights to the popular World Series contest. Television coverage of professional football, however, was especially attractive to ABC because it seemed to have elevated a game of rather limited appeal for thirty years into serious contention with baseball as the national pastime. Though NBC controlled college football telecasts while CBS presented the National Football League, which it had inherited from DuMont, the sport seemed ripe for plunder. Interest in the game was growing and there was serious talk about the formation of a new professional football league.

Television helped to develop the expanding interest and apprecia-

FALL 1960 SCHEDULE

MONDAY

	7:00	7:30	8:00	8:30	9:00	9:30	10:00	10:30	
	local	Cheyenne		SURFSIDE SIX		Adventures In Paradise		Peter Gunn	**ABC**
	local	To Tell The Truth	PETE AND GLADYS	BRINGING UP BUDDY	Danny Thomas Show	ANDY GRIFFITH SHOW	Hennessey	PRESIDENTIAL COUNTDOWN	**CBS**
	local	Riverboat		Tales Of Wells Fargo	KLONDIKE	DANTE	BARBARA STANWYCK SHOW	Jackpot Bowling With Milton Berle	**NBC**

TUESDAY

	7:00	7:30	8:00	8:30	9:00	9:30	10:00	10:30	
	EXPEDITION	BUGS BUNNY SHOW	The Rifleman	Life And Legend Of Wyatt Earp	STAGECOACH WEST		Alcoa Presents: One Step Beyond	local	**ABC**
	local	local	Father Knows Best	The Many Loves Of Dobie Gillis	TOM EWELL SHOW	Red Skelton Show	Garry Moore Show		**CBS**
	local	Laramie		Alfred Hitchcock Presents	THRILLER		NBC Specials		**NBC**

WEDNESDAY

	7:00	7:30	8:00	8:30	9:00	9:30	10:00	10:30	
	local	HONG KONG		The Adventures Of Ozzie And Harriet	Hawaiian Eye		Naked City		**ABC**
	local	THE AQUANAUTS		Wanted: Dead Or Alive	MY SISTER EILEEN	I've Got A Secret	U.S. Steel Hour / Armstrong Circle Theater		**CBS**
	local	Wagon Train		The Price Is Right	Perry Como's Kraft Music Hall		PETER LOVES MARY	local	**NBC**

THURSDAY

	7:00	7:30	8:00	8:30	9:00	9:30	10:00	10:30	
	local	GUESTWARD HO	Donna Reed Show	The Real McCoys	MY THREE SONS	The Untouchables		Take A Good Look	**ABC**
	local	THE WITNESS		Dick Powell's Zane Grey Theater	ANGEL	Ann Southern Show	Person To Person	DuPont Show With June Allyson	**CBS**
	local	THE OUTLAWS		Bat Masterson	Bachelor Father	Tennessee Ernie Ford Show	The Groucho Show	local	**NBC**

FRIDAY

	7:00	7:30	8:00	8:30	9:00	9:30	10:00	10:30	
	local	Matty's Funday Funnies	HARRIGAN AND SON	THE FLINTSTONES	77 Sunset Strip		Robert Taylor In The Detectives	THE LAW AND MR. JONES	**ABC**
	local	Rawhide		ROUTE 66		MR. GARLUND	The Twilight Zone	Eyewitness To History	**CBS**
	local	DAN RAVEN		THE WESTERNER	Bell Telephone Hour / NBC Specials		MICHAEL SHAYNE		**NBC**

SATURDAY

	7:00	7:30	8:00	8:30	9:00	9:30	10:00	10:30	
	local	THE ROARING TWENTIES		Leave It To Beaver	Lawrence Welk Show		Fight Of The Week	MAKE THAT SPARE	**ABC**
	local	Perry Mason		CHECKMATE		Have Gun, Will Travel	Gunsmoke	local	**CBS**
	local	Bonanza		THE TALL MAN	The Deputy	THE CAMPAIGN AND THE CANDIDATES		local	**NBC**

SUNDAY

	7:00	7:30	8:00	8:30	9:00	9:30	10:00	10:30	
	Walt Disney Presents [from 6:30]	Maverick		Lawman	The Rebel	THE ISLANDERS		WALTER WINCHELL SHOW	**ABC**
	Lassie	Dennis The Menace	Ed Sullivan Show		General Electric Theater	Jack Benny Program	Candid Camera	What's My Line	**CBS**
	Shirley Temple Show		NATIONAL VELVET	TAB HUNTER SHOW	Dinah Shore Chevy Show		Loretta Young Show	This Is Your Life	**NBC**

tion for football by making the complicated game more comprehensible to the home audience. Video taped "instant replays" (which at first took almost a half-hour to air) provided viewers with the opportunity to see important plays repeated, and they transformed the sport into a contest that was actually better seen on television than at the stadium. As the fans became more sophisticated, football became a frequent topic of discussion on television. Serious programs in the Sunday afternoon egghead slot began to devote their attention to the personalities and psychology of football in such well-produced entries as "The Violent World of Sam Huff" on CBS's *Twentieth Century* (hosted by Walter Cronkite). More importantly, the plans for a new professional league to compete with the NFL for fan attention came through in late 1959. For the fall of 1960, ABC filched the NCAA college games from NBC and signed a TV pact with the brand new American Football League in a two-pronged drive for prominence in football. The NCAA games were a safe, established draw and the upstart AFL was a perfect mate to the upstart ABC. Although the AFL was clearly no match for the NFL in either talent or prestige, like ABC it had nowhere to go but up, and if either partner proved to be a success, the other would benefit.

ABC made its most daring move in the field of TV sports in April, 1961, with the premiere of its Saturday afternoon *Wide World of Sports*. Hosted by former CBS sportscaster Jim McKay, *Wide World of Sports* was the brainchild of Roone Arledge, a sports producer ABC had picked up from NBC along with the NCAA football games. The show turned from the then accepted practice of slotting specific events one at a time in regular time periods to the revolutionary concept of presenting as many different sports as possible, often within the same program. Using both live and pretaped segments, the program resembled coverage of the Olympics as it brought together a diverse selection of contests from different venues. It exposed sports enthusiasts to many unusual events previously considered too limited in appeal for network television including track and field, auto racing, bowling, and tennis. The rapid pacing of the program as it shifted locale gave *Wide World of Sports* a frantic energy that lured viewers into accepting unfamiliar settings and events as part of an exciting afternoon of sports. The program was an unqualified success for ABC and over the years it established the network's reputation as an effective and innovative source for sports. In this area, ABC's expansion plans worked perfectly.

The network faced a more difficult challenge in upgrading its news and public affairs programming to compete with NBC and CBS because in this area it was unquestionably far behind in both experience and prestige. At the birth of network television in the late Forties, ABC had started near the pace of its competition, offering *News and Views* in August, 1948, just as the other networks were beginning nightly news shows. The Monday through Saturday show was structured exactly like a radio news and commentary program: one of the anchors would present the day's headlines and then offer a few minutes of interpretation. The anchor chores were rotated among a number of analysts such as George Hicks, Walter Kiernan, and the first female network news anchor, Pauline Frederick, but *News and Views* disappeared within one year. Although the format worked very well on radio, it was particularly ill-suited to television's voracious demand for visuals. For four years, ABC had no nightly news show and, for all practical purposes, no news department whatsoever. During this interregnum NBC and CBS significantly developed their news resources and styles, while ABC settled for once-a-week commentary programs by individual radio analysts such as Paul Harvey and Walter Winchell.

As a sign of the growing strength and independence in the NBC and CBS news departments, neither allowed outside sources to produce news or news-related programs, keeping the nightly news shows and occasional news specials under direct network control. ABC, on the other hand, was forced to rely totally on outside sources for both film footage and program production, and it aired documentary series such as *Crusade in Europe, Crusade in the Pacific,* and *March of Time through the Years* from Time-Life in lieu of its own news and public affairs programming. Once the ABC-UPT merger of 1953 brought much-needed cash to the network coffers, ABC reactivated its news organization and resumed Monday through Friday newscasts in October, 1953, with veteran newscaster-quiz master John Daly, a refugee from CBS. Under Daly's leadership, ABC news improved substantially, even adopting the CBS-NBC dogma of "no outside documentaries." Unfortunately, due to the comparatively small budget for the ABC news department, this rule translated into no ABC documentaries at all. Most of ABC's affiliates refused to take the network's improved news posture seriously anyway and didn't bother to carry Daly's fifteen-minute news show. In an attempt to remedy this situation, ABC moved the program into prime time (10:30–10:45 P.M.) during the 1958–59 season, but this shift placed it in a hopeless battle with the popular entertainment programs on the opposing networks. Even though ABC had upgraded its treatment of the news by 1960, it still had the weakest of the three network news organizations by far and found itself constantly losing in direct competition with CBS and NBC.

In the months following Charles Van Doren's revelations to Congress, the news departments at all three networks became very important to network prestige as the industry displayed a sudden deep concern for the value of news and public affairs, hoping that such programs could erase the black mark the quiz show scandal had given television. Some television executives saw such a public commitment as a perfect PR device to counter criticism of the industry and possibly even rekindle the notion of television as cultural savior. Because it lacked the resources and manpower, the ABC news department found itself hard pressed to instantly deliver some new documentary series similar to those announced by NBC and CBS, even on an irregular basis. However, ABC did successfully participate in a fortuitously timed event that allowed television to display its best side—the so-called "great debates" staged in the fall of 1960. An act of Congress temporarily suspended the equal time law and allowed the networks to broadcast four debates between John Kennedy and Richard Nixon without being obligated to offer an equal amount of network time to each of the other legitimate, but minor, candidates for the presidency. For the first time in years, people again began talking about the fabulous nature of television and its ability to allow millions of people across the entire country to share an important and historic series of events. The debates provided a windfall of good publicity for the networks, sparked strong voter interest in the election, and probably provided the thin margin of victory for Kennedy, who came across more effectively than Nixon in the vital first debate. For this special event, ABC News held its own, producing two of the four contests.

In the field of in-house documentaries, though, ABC just could not compete with CBS and NBC. The network was anxious to display its own documentary series and it convinced Charles Percy's Bell and Howell company to finance *Bell and Howell Closeup,* a series of floating specials produced by ABC News and similar to *CBS Reports.* The first few productions of the new series (which premiered in September, 1960) were roundly panned so ABC turned again to Time-Life, relinquishing control of the series to the Time-Life film crew headed by Robert Drew. Daly viewed this production deal as a direct violation of his no outsiders policy and quit ABC at the end of 1960. Ironically, the new *Closeup* series was far removed from the industry-controlled public relations fluff Daly had feared and it presented some of the most imaginative television documentary work in years, satisfying ABC's desire for material that could match the work at NBC and CBS. Drew's first program in the series, "Yanki No!" took its cue from Ed Murrow's *See It Now* "Christmas in Korea" show, downplaying the role of the narrator and avoiding the artificial setting of formal interviews. It attempted to capture people and events "as they were" in a

September 18, 1960
Patrick McGoohan portrays secret agent John Drake in a British television series, *Danger Man.* CBS brings the program to the States for a brief summer run beginning in April, 1961.

September 26, 1960
The largest television audience yet—75 million Americans—tunes in the first of four debates between presidential candidates John F. Kennedy and Richard M. Nixon. Howard K. Smith of CBS is moderator of the first (held in Chicago), which focuses on domestic affairs. Though the two are rated about even by radio listeners, television viewers give Nixon poor marks for personal appearance. He appears tired and haggard while Kennedy looks sharp and bright.

November 27, 1960
Issues and Answers. (ABC). The third network at last gets its own Sunday afternoon interview show. First guest: Senator Paul Douglas of Illinois.

December 16, 1960
Bill Shadel takes over ABC's nightly news show following the resignation of John Daly.

January 5, 1961
Mr. Ed. An off-beat syndicated series featuring Alan Young as Wilbur Post, a young architect who one day discovers that his horse, Mr. Ed, can talk. Allan "Rocky" Lane provides the voice for the good-natured palomino. The program is so successful that CBS puts it on network television in October, 1961, where it becomes a national hit.

January 27, 1961
Sing Along with Mitch. (NBC). Goateed maestro Mitch Miller invites everyone to "sing along—loud and strong."

cinéma vérité-style comparison between Cuba under Fidel Castro, who was on the verge of publicly announcing that he was a communist, and South American countries run by right wing dictators. Drew's crew portrayed Latin Americans as generally restive and fearful under the military rulers supported by the United States government, and showed Castro's supporters happy and enthusiastic. Subsequent shows in the series tackled such diverse subject matter as the effect of automation on the U.S. labor force ("Awesome Servant") and the defiant attitude emerging among American blacks ("Walk in My Shoes"). In each of these, the *cinéma vérité* style seductively underplayed a far stronger editorial stance than most network documentaries of the time chose to assume. Though purporting to present things as they were, Drew's crew carefully selected the film clips they used in order to present a very specific viewpoint, without an easily identifiable narrator cast as an advocate of the position. This style was aimed at conveying a strong point about a controversial issue without confronting the viewers with dramatic accusations that might alienate them before the problem could be fully explored. Someone of the stature of Ed Murrow might be able to use the force of his personality and reputation to argue a specific point of view (as he had done in his McCarthy broadcasts) but such figures were the exception. Murrow, in fact, had sometimes found that the instances in which he had taken a strong stand made it that much harder to present other unrelated issues to people who had concluded he was biased and not to be trusted. Because heightened awareness of an issue was all that could ever be expected to result from even the best documentary, it was vital that the audience be willing to give the program a fair hearing. The *cinéma vérité* style in ABC's *Closeup* series allowed the audience such opportunities and gave the network the class documentaries it wanted, though the use of an outside crew merely postponed the necessary development and expansion of ABC's own news department for several more years.

The news department at NBC occasionally followed the *vérité* style in its floating *NBC White Paper* series. The technique was used in such reports as "Sit In" (a personal study of the individuals involved in the sit-in tactics being used to integrate stores in Nashville), but the producers usually stuck to well-made but traditional in-depth overviews of controversial topics, being careful to avoid taking any stand, explicit or implied. The subject matter of these programs ranged from an analysis of the U-2 spy plane affair to an examination of both sides of a rebellion going on almost unnoticed in Portugal's African colony of Angola. Another NBC floating documentary series, *Project 20,* usually avoided such controversy entirely and focused instead on more cultural topics. One typical program, "The Real West," attempted to present a view of the old West more realistic and accurate than the fictional TV Westerns. Narrated by Gary Cooper, the program used old photographs and personal memoirs to portray the events leading to the closing of the frontier and the conquest of the Indian tribes.

Of all the networks, CBS provided the most dramatic documentary of the season, "Harvest of Shame," one of the strongest programs by Ed Murrow since the Army-McCarthy days. On November 25, 1960, in the middle of the Thanksgiving holidays, Murrow brought the living and working conditions of America's migrant farm laborers to the attention of the general public, which knew next to nothing about the topic. As a sort of updated *Grapes of Wrath,* the program depicted the squalid conditions of the migrant workers in sharp contrast to the wealth of their employers, the food growers. The growers' side of the issue was also presented, but Murrow took a firm stand and left no doubt in viewers' minds that he felt something had to be done, such as federal protection

January 28, 1961
   The Avengers. Britain's ABC network presents the spy duo of Dr. David Keel (Ian Hendry) and a mysterious character referred to simply as Steed (Patrick Macnee).

March 2, 1961
   Newton Minow is sworn in as chairman of the FCC.

April 16, 1961
   Death of *Omnibus.* Age: 9 years. In its final season, the show was relegated to a Sunday afternoon slot once a month on NBC.

April 17, 1961
   ABC Final Report. (ABC). The first network attempt at late night news each weeknight (11:00–11:15 P.M.). At first, the program is carried only by ABC's O&O stations, but in October it expands to the entire network.

June 9, 1961
   Worthington Miner's syndicated *Play of the Week* is canceled.

June 12, 1961
   PM East/PM West. Westinghouse gets into late night television, syndicating ninety minutes of talk and variety five days a week. One-half the program comes from New York (with Mike Wallace) the other half from San Francisco (with Terry O'Flaherty). In February, 1962, the West portion is dumped.

July 17, 1961
   John Chancellor takes over NBC's *Today* from Dave Garroway.

for the workers and industry-wide standards to guide the owners. The timing of the program combined with its firm and effective presentation of a strong point of view touched off a bitter national controversy over the issue of migrant farm labor. Growers complained that they were unfairly portrayed, while average citizens expressed their outrage at the situation and echoed Murrow's appeal for some corrective action. Though sixty minutes of film could never change a situation by itself, "Harvest of Shame" made a deep impression on the American public, and it emerged as one of the most incisive documentaries of Murrow's career. It was also his last major production at CBS because a few months later he accepted newly elected President John Kennedy's offer to become the director of the United States Information Agency. Murrow left behind a well-versed group of correspondents and colleagues at CBS who admired and respected him and worked to maintain his journalistic principles. The door to his office even retained his name plate three years after he was gone. When CBS moved its offices into a new building, the "Murrow door" was taken off its hinges and moved as well.

Of course, even with the extra emphasis on public affairs by the networks during the 1960–61 season, such programming accounted for only a tiny fraction of prime time and was usually tucked away in some unprofitable time slot or presented as a floating, irregularly scheduled special. The networks' real concern rested, as usual, with the performance of their regular prime time shows and the possible emergence of any new program fad. For the most part, 1960–61 marked a discernible pause in the industry, with regular prime time programming continuing almost unchanged from the previous season. NBC and CBS presented their usual selection of Westerns and sitcoms while ABC continued to emphasize action-adventure. Both NBC and CBS also launched a few vehicles in the action-adventure format, but they regarded these as part of a still unproven fad and were ready to drop them at the end of the season if they did poorly.

As the viewing habits for the 1960–61 season developed, it became clear that the bread-and-butter staples were holding steady, but the action-adventure format was in serious trouble, especially for ABC. Though *77 Sunset Strip* and *The Untouchables* remained in the top ten, the new crop of third generation action-adventure clones proved to be the worst of all, registering generally poor ratings with only two shows surviving for the 1961–62 season. The new programs contained no original thought or twist, only the same lifeless characters, tired plots, mindless murders, and so-called exotic settings. *The Aquanauts,* produced by Ivan Tors, presented the adventures of a team of free lance skindivers in Honolulu. *The Islanders* featured the adventures of a pair of handsome pilots and two beautiful women who operated a tiny airline service in the Spice Islands. *Hong Kong* cast Rod Taylor in warmed-over Charlie Chan-type adventures set in the mysterious Orient. One show managed to incorporate two clichéd settings in one season. Premiering in the fall as *Klondike,* it featured Ralph Taeger and James Coburn in a premise that was *The Alaskans* sideways, mixing cut-throat adventures and pure-as-the-snow innocence in the Northland's beautiful but dangerous palace of ice. By mid-season, the producers admitted *Klondike* was a failure and, in a bold programming stroke, put Taeger and Coburn in a new but somehow familiar setting and show, *Acapulco.* The new mixture of cut-throat adventures and pure-as-the-sand innocence in Mexico's beautiful but dangerous seaside paradise didn't last three months.

As failure in the action-adventure format became more frequent, Warner Brothers began transplanting actors from the unsuccessful series to some of its remaining slots. *Cheyenne* became a rotating series, taking the *Sugarfoot* and *Bronco* shows under its banner. Roger Moore moved from the Alaskan frontier of the 1890s to the old West of the 1880s in the improbable role of Beau Maverick, the long-lost British cousin of Bret and Bart. Bret (James Garner) had apparently fallen into the river while panning for gold and was seen only in *Maverick* reruns. Another refugee from *The Alaskans,* Dorothy Provine, brought her nightclub singer character to Warner Brothers' weak imitation of *The Untouchables, The Roaring Twenties.* Rex Reason and Donald May joined her as a pair of investigative reporters always in search of hot scoops on the latest activities of bootleggers and mobsters, but the series was just an empty imitation and a ridiculously unfaithful re-creation of the decade. It relied on a few artifacts of the period (raccoon coats, cars, the Charleston), acceptable Twenties-style music, and supposedly timely phrases ("Twenty-three skidoo," "hotcha") to cover the predictable plots and feeble characters, accepting at face value a few common clichés about the Twenties but failing to exhibit any insight into the era. Just as the Seventies' *Happy Days* would pale in comparison to the Fifties' own *Dobie Gillis, The Roaring Twenties* was a mere shadow of the sharply produced *Untouchables,* and it faded after two seasons. One other new Warner Brothers action-adventure series, *Surfside Six,* also managed to hang on for two seasons while serving as yet another haven for members of the studio's action-adventure acting company. Van Williams moved in from *Bourbon Street Beat* while his partner, Troy Donahue, eventually moved on to *Hawaiian Eye.* Apparently Warners had run out of exotic foreign spots so it set the usual flip talk and detective pretty boys aboard a houseboat in Miami Beach (address: Surfside Six).

It was too much. After three years of variations on the "two parts private eye, one part cutie pie" formula, the public had had enough. As the 1960–61 season progressed, the Warner Brothers-ABC-action-adventure structure began sliding into the ocean. The other networks quickly shifted their energies back to other formats, but ABC had nowhere else to go. It had stumbled upon this formula almost by accident and the network was on the verge of returning to its pre-action-adventure number three status. Though ABC might still produce an occasional, isolated hit, it could no longer automatically count on a continuing source of new programs. As the network began drawing up plans for the next season (a process which, at the time, was usually completed by March), it frantically searched for any formula that might provide a steady stream of shows, hoping that blind chance might strike again. ABC even tried expanding the dubious concept of bringing so-called "adult cartoons" to prime time, a format that had had a disappointing debut in 1960 with *The Flintstones.*

Through the summer and early fall of 1960, ABC's advance publicity touted *The Flintstones* as the "first adult cartoon show" and promised that it would be a satire on suburban life that would appeal to grownups as well as children. Rarely had a show been so erroneously hyped. When the program hit the airwaves in late September, it was immediately apparent that *The Flintstones* was actually just another kiddie cartoon series from the TV animation mill of Bill Hanna and Joseph Barbera, a team responsible for such characters as Tom and Jerry and Yogi Bear. Nonetheless, ABC's placement of the show at 8:30 P.M. (past the traditional kiddie hour), its choice of sponsor (Winston cigarettes), and its continuing ballyhoo indicated that the network was seriously aiming *The Flintstones* at adults. Unfortunately, while the program's faults might have been quietly passed over in a Saturday morning children's slot, they couldn't withstand the direct comparisons with other prime time fare.

Ironically, at the same time ABC was plugging *The Flintstones* as a cartoon series capable of entertaining all age groups, it was almost ignoring another prime time cartoon show on its schedule that really could, *The Bugs Bunny Show.* The series had been developed after Ollie Treyz discovered that an independent station in Chicago (WGN) had been running old Bugs Bunny cartoons in prime time (6:30 P.M. in the Midwest) with considerable success. Hoping to duplicate that success on the network, ABC bought the last of the Warner Brothers theatrical cartoons not yet released to television and presented them in a format that featured brand new introductions and transitions by Bugs and other popular Warner characters such as Daffy Duck, Elmer Fudd, Foghorn Leghorn, and Porky Pig. Because these cartoons were originally intended for release with Warner Brothers movies, the cartoonists had specifically aimed at entertaining the adults as well as the children with playful lampoons of Hollywood stars, popular movies, and then-current events. The animation, scripts, and characters reflected more than thirty years of sophisticated development by some of the best animators in Hollywood and they hopelessly outclassed anything produced specifically for television.

Hanna-Barbera could not possibly match the high standards of Warner Brothers' best cartoons, but in attempting to develop its own cartoon series for adults, the company did begin with a sensible strategy. It took the successful characters from a regular adult sitcom (in this case, *The Honeymooners*) and created animated caricatures. To increase the potential for gags and satire, the cartoon characters were placed in a fully developed suburban community that happened to be set in the Stone Age. Veteran character actors such as Mel Blanc and Bea Benaderet were cast to do some of the voices. The series held great promise that was never realized. All the appealing elements of *The Honeymooners'* characters were lost in the transition to animation, and *The Flintstones* emerged

The *Checkmate* detective team of Jed Sills (Doug McClure, *l.*) and Don Corey (Anthony George, *r.*) always turned to the talents of professional criminologist-consultant Carl Hyatt (Sebastian Cabot). (*From* Checkmate. *Courtesy of MCA Television Limited*)

as a dimwitted interpolation in a Stone Age setting. Fred Flintstone was noisy, boastful, and stupid. His neighbor, Barney Rubble, was a dolt. The interaction and scheming of the two lacked the wit, energy, humor, and deep affection of the Jackie Gleason–Art Carney original. Fred's wife, Wilma, possessed none of the intelligence, personality, and understanding of Alice Kramden. All of the characters were flat, empty, and nearly impossible to like. Perhaps the weak characters might have been tolerable if the promised satire on American life had come through. It didn't. All Hanna-Barbera did was effect a one-to-one transplant of modern mechanical devices to Stone Age animal equivalents. Fred and Barney operated enormous dinosaurs instead of mechanical bulldozers. Fred drove a car powered by his own two feet. Pterodactyls with seats strapped to their backs served as airplanes. That was it. No satire. Very little wit. The animation, characters, stories, and humor of *The Flintstones* were all second class and lame. Nonetheless, the series lasted six seasons on ABC, though the characters of Fred, Wilma, Pebbles (their daughter), Barney, Betty Rubble, and Bamm Bamm (their son) reached their most effective penetration of the market when the show ended its prime time run and moved to the Saturday morning kiddie circuit and then into syndication, spawning several spinoff series along the way.

For ABC's immediate future, *The Flintstones* provided a quick program fad for the network to exploit, and by the 1961–62 season, it had three additional "adult" cartoon series that followed *The Flintstones* style: *Top Cat* (a *Sergeant Bilko* imitation), *Calvin and the Colonel* (*Amos and Andy* of the animal world), and *The Jetsons* (*The Flintstones* backwards). Of course, the cartoon format was much too limited in appeal to serve as a substitute for the fading action-adventure series, but it underscored the return to ABC's patchwork style of filling its prime time schedule with virtually

anything, in the hope that a flash hit would take hold.

For a change, ABC was not alone in feeling the absence of high quality new shows. All three networks had reached the bottom of a programming slump in 1960–61. Only two new series made it into the top ten, ABC's leisurely *My Three Sons* and CBS's rural-oriented *Andy Griffith Show. My Three Sons* was just a routine family comedy featuring Fred MacMurray, while CBS's show effectively reunited the "No Time for Sergeants" movie team of Andy Griffith and Don Knotts. Their roles were essentially continuations of their film characters, grown a bit older and relocated in the small town of Mayberry, North Carolina. Andy played an understanding and mature good ol' boy who served as the town's sheriff, and Knotts was the hysterically bug-eyed paranoiac deputy, Barney Fife, who constantly tried, and failed, to fit his own image of the traditional tough cop. Barney never understood that big city high pressure tactics were unnecessary in Mayberry because it was virtually crime free. The program's tempo reflected the slow-as-molasses life of a small rural town and a good deal of time was devoted to warm family segments featuring Andy as a gentle widower trying to raise his young son, Opie (Ronny Howard), with the help of his aunt, Bee Taylor (Frances Bavier). These vignettes followed *The Rifleman* pattern of a father-son relationship as Opie learned homey lessons about life either on his own or from his dad. The comedic foundation of the show, though, rested with the contrast between this very normal family life and the crackpot notions of a handful of citizens who had long ago lost the fight for mental stability. Mayberry's serenity was inevitably shaken by the outbreaks of hysteria led by Barney; Otis, the town drunk; Floyd, the barber; and the two ultimate personifications of country naivete, Gomer and Goober Pyle. Through it all, Andy was never ruffled and didn't bother to carry a gun. He knew that nothing had ever happened in that town and that nothing ever would. The calm hominess of the program, combined with the balance between sanity and insanity, proved very popular with viewers and they followed the story of Mayberry for eleven years.

There were also a few outstanding dramatic shows that season, including the expanded hour version of *Naked City* (with a new leading man, Paul Burke), the surprisingly serious private eye drama of *Checkmate* (with fat and jolly Sebastian Cabot as a professional criminologist who was the guiding genius behind prettyboy detectives Anthony George and Doug McClure), and the offbeat character studies of *Route 66*. Eight years before "Easy Rider" brought the drifting anti-hero into vogue, George Maharis and Martin Milner set out on U.S. highway 66 "in search of America" and some direction for their lives. Milner played a clean-cut college boy who had lost his family fortune with the death of his father and Maharis portrayed a reformed juvenile delinquent from the ghetto. The two had pooled their funds, purchased a Corvette (the show was sponsored by Chevrolet), and become drifters who cruised the country, inevitably drawn along the way into the lives of people who were facing some crisis. The wide open format allowed the series' chief writer, Stirling Silliphant, the opportunity to introduce a varied assortment of slightly off-beat personalities and place them into modern morality plays. These people were good at heart, but slightly warped or evil, and it was up to Maharis and Milner (acting as unofficial social workers and psychoanalysts) to help them face the consequences of their actions and reassert their goodness. Filmed on location, *Route 66* was a good show due to its strong cast, good writing, and flexible format. The only aspect that made no sense was how episodes taking place in Butte, Montana, or rural Mississippi could be part of a series named after a road that ran from Chicago to Los Angeles.

These series provided a few moments of high quality entertainment in an otherwise depressingly mediocre season. Effluvia such as *Peter Loves Mary, National Velvet, The Tab Hunter Show, Pete and Gladys,* and *Guestward Ho!* filled the airwaves. Westerns reached a new level of sadism with the gory vengeance killings and intrafamily homicides of *Whispering Smith,* and the sadistic white slavers and threats of brutal mutilation in *The Westerner* (produced and directed by Sam Peckinpah). Even two former television greats, Jackie Gleason and Milton Berle, turned up in roles that were embarrassing and demeaning to their tremendous talents.

Gleason returned to television as the host of an insipid quiz show, *You're in the Picture.* Contestants behind a large picture canvas stuck their faces through cutouts in the scene and tried to identify the situation in the picture, using clues provided by Gleason. This format lasted one week. Gleason scrapped it and took over the show himself, announcing on the second program that the premiere had, "laid, without a doubt, the biggest bomb in history." He devoted the entire program that week and the next to a thirty-minute comedy monologue based on the frantic meetings by the show's producers as they desperately tried to salvage something from the venture. They finally wrote it off as a total loss and Gleason used the two remaining months of the program's run to feature whatever friends he could talk into helping him out. Even though Gleason's show was an obvious loser, it remained on the air for two more months because, at that time, the networks didn't bother with wholesale mid-season schedule changes and replacements. They felt that a show doing poorly in January couldn't possibly improve dramatically before the season ended, so to try to promote and improve it would be a waste of time and money. It was much wiser to write off the bad shows, let them finish their run, and concentrate instead on assembling the new fall schedule by the end of February.

Milton Berle's reappearance was not as disastrous as Jackie Gleason's, but it was no less degrading. Mr. Television, the man whose talents had enticed many Americans into purchasing their first sets, was relegated to providing patter for *Jackpot Bowling.* Each week, sportscaster Chick Hearn did the play-by-play and Berle appeared at the beginning, middle, and end of the show to tell a few jokes and hand out a few thousand dollars in prize money. The comedown of Gleason and Berle was staggering but representative. The great geniuses of television's early years were becoming cheapened pawns whose name value was callously exploited. Where would it all end? Would Sid Caesar turn up as a carnival clown on a kiddie show? Would Fred Coe begin producing laxative commercials? Would Pat Weaver wind up running a UHF station in Arkansas? Would Tony Miner start working for Soupy Sales? No esthetic genius appeared invulnerable. Television seemed hell-bent on eradicating any quality it had developed. Though the networks pointed with justifiable pride to their highly praised documentaries and news shows, programs such as *Jackpot Bowling, Surfside Six,* and *The Flintstones* more accurately reflected the true state of the industry.

Television's critics had all but given up complaining that the networks had gone too far in sacrificing program quality to viewer quantity, realizing that their protests would be brushed aside with the latest statistics indicating that viewing totals were up again. After all, the network chiefs responded, the public cast its vote of support every day by tuning in whatever they churned out. Among themselves, though, even broadcasters admitted that the 1960–61 season was less-than-exceptional, and there were plans to tinker with a few programs and perhaps introduce a few new programming wrinkles—but there was no hurry. Improvements

might take place eventually, but in laying out the schedules for the 1961–62 season the emphasis remained on gaining a competitive edge, not upgrading quality. A few mundane programs were accepted as a necessary part of broadcasting along with the desperate rating battles and unstable program formats. It was all business as usual. Each of the networks totaled their profits and losses for the season and prepared for the annual convention of the National Association of Broadcasters.

Every year broadcast executives met to discuss the state of the industry, pat themselves on the back, and listen to a bland, cliché-ridden speech by an important government figure (usually from the FCC) who did little to dispel the convention euphoria or the notion that everyone there was doing a great job "serving the public interest." Newly appointed FCC chairman Newton Minow was scheduled to deliver the address on May 9, 1961, before that year's NAB gathering in Washington. Coming only two months after he took office, Minow's speech would be his first chance to express his ideas about broadcasting directly to its important executives and leaders. Though the thirty-five-year-old former law partner of Adlai Stevenson was an unknown quantity, it was assumed that he would probably follow the usual pattern of praise tempered with vague exhortations that the industry do even better in the future. All of the bigwigs of network TV were in the audience: Bob Sarnoff and Robert Kinter of NBC, Leonard Goldenson and Ollie Treyz of ABC, and Frank Stanton and James Aubrey of CBS. They were not prepared for what Minow chose to say:

> I invite you to sit down in front of your television set when your station [or network] goes on the air and stay there without a book, magazine, newspaper, profit-and-loss sheet, or ratings book to distract you—and keep your eyes glued to that set until the station signs off. I can assure

The pride of Mayberry: (from *l.*) Deputy Barney Fife (Don Knotts), gas station attendant Gomer Pyle (Jim Nabors), and sheriff Andy Taylor (Andy Griffith). *(Photo by Viacom, Hollywood)*

you that you will observe a vast wasteland. You will see a procession of game shows, violence, audience participation shows, formula comedies about totally unbelievable families, blood and thunder, mayhem, violence, sadism, murder, Western badmen, Western goodmen, private eyes, gangsters, more violence, and cartoons, and, endlessly, commercials, many screaming, cajoling, and offending, and, most of all, boredom. True, you will see a few things you enjoy, but they will be very, very few, and if you think I exaggerate, try it.

At this point, Sarnoff's brow (always perpetually wrinkled) showed a few more furrows. Treyz's face had turned white, while Stanton's was red. The faces of Kinter and Aubrey were frozen in masks, and Goldenson's had iced into a Mona Lisa smile. Minow went on:

Is there one person in this room who claims that broadcasting can't do better? Is there one network president in this room who claims he can't do better? Why is so much of television so bad? . . . We need imagination in programming, not sterility; creativity, not imitation; experimentation, not conformity; excellence, not mediocrity.

The members of the NAB were stunned. No one had ever talked to them that way before. What's more, Minow, as head of the FCC, might actually do something to implement his suggestions and seriously affect the industry. Consequently, no one dared to openly rebuke him as he delivered his speech, though the convention was filled with behind-the-scenes grumbling.

Newspapers picked up Minow's "vast wasteland" phrase and critics used it as a quick condemnation of the entire industry. Though broadcasters grudgingly came to the general consensus that in some respects Minow was right and the 1960–61 season had been exceptionally weak, they were in a bind. Despite the expectation that something should be done immediately to improve television programming after the adverse publicity directed toward it, the 1961–62 schedules had been locked up and sold since March and couldn't be changed in May. The best the networks could do was slot a few more public affairs shows, paint rosy pictures for 1962–63, and prepare to endure the barrage of criticism they felt certain would greet the new season.

21. I Still Have the Stench in My Nose

NETWORK czars were braced for disaster following FCC chairman Newton Minow's roasting of the industry in his "vast wasteland" speech. Lavish reforms were promised by network potentates for the 1962–63 season, but as the 1961–62 season progressed the need for such dramatic action faded. Though some truly terrible television aired in the new season, Minow's speech, almost by accident, marked the rock bottom end of a decline rather than the identification of a permanent, insoluble situation. Ever since the rise of the big money quiz shows in 1955 and 1956, the quality of TV had been eroding steadily as the industry put aside many high quality drama, comedy, and news shows which drew only adequate ratings in favor of programs that offered the promise of flashy, but unstable, instant success. In searching for possible new hit formats for the 1961–62 season, network executives had developed, by chance or instinct, several concepts and programs that sparked a revival of some of television's best work of the previous decade, updated for the Sixties. Major breakthroughs took place in legal, medical, movie, and sitcom formats with programs that set the pattern television shows of both high and low quality would follow for the remainder of the decade. There was only a handful of these new shows that fall, but they provided enough good new television to take some of the immediate sting from the vast wasteland description and to convince people that, after one of the most uninspired seasons in TV history, something was being done to improve programming.

The legal drama of *The Defenders* came directly from the so-called golden age of television. Back in February, 1957, *Studio One* had presented a two-part story of a father-and-son legal team that had to overcome both intrafamily disagreements and judicial obstacles. Written by Reginald Rose and produced by Herb Brodkin, "The Defenders" offered a situation far more complex than the average TV crime show. As lawyer *père,* Ralph Bellamy found himself torn between his distaste for the defendant, a repulsive young hoodlum played by Steve McQueen, and his responsibilities to the legal profession. His bright but idealistic son, played by William Shatner, insisted that their client receive the best defense possible, even though he was probably guilty. The story received high critical acclaim and, four years later with *Perry Mason* a successful series, Brodkin and Rose teamed up again to produce a new lawyer series based on the play. They brought their high dramatic standards to *The Defenders* and treated it like the drama anthology shows of old, with one important difference.

Drama anthologies such as *Studio One* had demanded that viewers accept a whole new world every week, without offering any identifiable continuing characters to provide a much-needed personal link. Even if the shows were first rate and dealt with themes and issues that hit home, many viewers felt it just wasn't worth the constant effort required to follow the maze of new faces and settings. Instead they turned increasingly to continuing series with familiar central characters or, at best, anthology series with stable, well-known hosts such as Alfred Hitchcock and Rod Serling. In the waning days of the drama anthology genre, producers used big name Hollywood guest stars in an attempt to overcome the continuity gap, but the tactic was not very successful because the format problem still remained: in the intimate world of television, the public preferred familiar characters and settings.

In *The Defenders,* Brodkin and Rose tied together their high quality writing, production, and selection of guest stars with a strong pair of central characters: E. G. Marshall as trial lawyer Lawrence Preston and Robert Reed as his son, Kenneth. Within the very accessible framework of courtroom drama, they presented tight character studies as well as the public debate of controversial topics television normally never dealt with. Nonetheless, it still looked for all the world like just another good lawyer show and CBS slotted it on Saturday night following *Perry Mason.* The placement was perfect because the two programs complemented each other. *Perry Mason* was a well-directed murder melodrama while *The Defenders* focused on characters and issues. The treatment of touchy subjects was never obvious and overbearing because Brodkin and Rose carefully incorporated it into each week's case. The trial process became a full-scale debate presenting both pro and con arguments through Marshall, Reed, and the supporting characters and guest stars as they planned the best ways to handle the legal strategy. Through all the topical discussions, however, the program still maintained the basics of good drama with strong characters and entertaining scripts.

The Defenders was the first TV series to examine the effects and implications of entertainment blacklisting. Jack Klugman por-

MONDAY

	7:00	7:30	8:00	8:30	9:00	9:30	10:00	10:30	
	Expedition	Cheyenne		The Rifleman	Surfside Six		BEN CASEY		ABC
	local	To Tell The Truth	Pete And Gladys	WINDOW ON MAIN STREET	Danny Thomas Show	Andy Griffith Show	Hennessey	I've Got A Secret	CBS
	local		National Velvet	The Price Is Right	87TH PRECINCT		Thriller		NBC

TUESDAY

	7:00	7:30	8:00	8:30	9:00	9:30	10:00	10:30	
	local	Bugs Bunny Show	Bachelor Father	CALVIN AND THE COLONEL	THE NEW BREED		ALCOA PREMIERE	Bell And Howell Close-Up	ABC
	local	Marshal Dillon	DICK VAN DYKE SHOW	The Many Loves Of Dobie Gillis	Red Skelton Show	ICHABOD AND ME	Garry Moore Show		CBS
	local	Laramie		Alfred Hitchcock Presents	DICK POWELL SHOW		CAIN'S HUNDRED		NBC

WEDNESDAY

	7:00	7:30	8:00	8:30	9:00	9:30	10:00	10:30	
	local	STEVE ALLEN SHOW		TOP CAT	Hawaiian Eye		Naked City		ABC
	local	THE ALVIN SHOW	Father Knows Best	Checkmate		MRS. G GOES TO COLLEGE	U.S. Steel Hour / Armstrong Circle Theater		CBS
	local	Wagon Train		JOEY BISHOP SHOW	Perry Como's Kraft Music Hall		BOB NEWHART SHOW	DAVID BRINKLEY'S JOURNAL	NBC

THURSDAY

	7:00	7:30	8:00	8:30	9:00	9:30	10:00	10:30	
	local	The Adventures Of Ozzie And Harriet	Donna Reed Show	The Real McCoys	My Three Sons	MARGIE	The Untouchables		ABC
	local	FRONTIER CIRCUS		NEW BOB CUMMINGS SHOW	THE INVESTIGATORS		CBS Reports		CBS
	local	The Outlaws		DR. KILDARE		HAZEL	Sing Along With Mitch		NBC

FRIDAY

	7:00	7:30	8:00	8:30	9:00	9:30	10:00	10:30	
	local	STRAIGHTAWAY	THE HATHAWAYS	The Flintstones	77 Sunset Strip		TARGET: THE CORRUPTORS		ABC
	local	Rawhide		Route 66		FATHER OF THE BRIDE	The Twilight Zone	Eyewitness	CBS
	local	INTERNATIONAL SHOWTIME		Robert Taylor's Detectives		Bell Telephone Hour / Dinah Shore Show		FRANK McGEE'S HERE AND NOW	NBC

SATURDAY

	7:00	7:30	8:00	8:30	9:00	9:30	10:00	10:30	
	Matty's Funday Funnies	The Roaring Twenties		Leave It To Beaver	Lawrence Welk Show		Fight Of The Week	Make That Spare	ABC
	local	Perry Mason		THE DEFENDERS		Have Gun, Will Travel	Gunsmoke		CBS
	local	Tales Of Wells Fargo		The Tall Man	NBC SATURDAY NIGHT AT THE MOVIES				NBC

SUNDAY

	7:00	7:30	8:00	8:30	9:00	9:30	10:00	10:30	
	Maverick [from 6:30]	FOLLOW THE SUN		Lawman	BUS STOP				ABC
	Lassie	Dennis The Menace	Ed Sullivan Show		General Electric Theater	Jack Benny Program	Candid Camera	What's My Line	CBS
	The Bullwinkle Show	Walt Disney's Wonderful World Of Color		CAR 54, WHERE ARE YOU?	Bonanza		DuPont Show Of The Week		NBC

trayed a John Henry Faulk-type character who found his broadcasting career ended after his sponsor was frightened by a small pressure group. Another episode, "Voices of Death," scrutinized the flaws in the judicial system itself and raised the possibility that an innocent person could be sentenced to death. The first episode of the series thrashed out the issue of mercy killing while another installment, "The Benefactor," dealt openly with abortion, then illegal and barely acknowledged. This episode, in which a doctor spoke out in favor of the practice, caused a public controversy in which eleven of the 180 stations that normally carried the program, as well as the regular sponsor, pulled out for that week. Despite such a daring (yet evenhanded) approach to important issues, *The Defenders* was an immediate ratings winner for CBS. Throughout its four-year run it maintained high standards of production quality while attracting a large and faithful audience that didn't seem to mind "serious drama" on a weekly basis.

NBC and ABC turned to a different profession, medicine, in their pursuit of ratings success. Aside from *Medic* (Worthington Miner's 1954 series for NBC starring Richard Boone), doctors had been largely ignored by television until these two networks realized that the medical profession offered the opportunity to present romantic, good-looking heroes in situations that were literally matters of life and death. For its medical drama, NBC reached back two decades and came up with *Dr. Kildare,* based on the old MGM film series that starred Lew Ayres and Lionel Barrymore. For the TV update, Raymond Massey portrayed the Barrymore character of crusty but compassionate Dr. Leonard Gillespie, the senior medical guru at Blair General Hospital, and Richard Chamberlain played the young idealistic intern, James Kildare. The two central characters established a relationship similar to the father-and-son lawyer team of *The Defenders* in which they consistently disagreed on operating policy for each week's patients. Gillespie, the experienced veteran, preached patience and understanding while the young, impetuous Kildare put principle before tradition, often making the innocent mistakes of youthful inexperience. Unlike *The Defenders,* though, the stories emerging from their conflicts were not in-depth discussions of complex issues but rather high class soap opera. While a very good soap opera, *Dr. Kildare* was still just a sugar-coated view of life with inordinately good-looking people experiencing one heightened dramatic crisis after another. There always seemed to be some beautiful woman dying of leukemia who fell in love with Kildare, or a visiting specialist who threatened to have Kildare suspended over some minor procedural infraction. Chamberlain, while a fine dramatic actor, projected a choir-boy image of goodness in these situations. He was almost too good. He never seemed to have an impure thought or a desire to do anything in life other than cure disease. The steady stream of guest stars, as the patients and visiting doctors, suffered from the same inherent limitations of the soap opera plots. All the characters and situations were neatly wrapped up in a structure that was ridiculously constant: each episode featured three patients suffering different maladies, while an in-house controversy raged among the doctors.

ABC's medical drama, *Ben Casey,* was structured almost identically to *Dr. Kildare.* It had the same soap opera-ish conflicts and diseases, a parade of guest stars as the tormented patients, and the interaction between the handsome young neurosurgeon, Ben Casey (Vincent Edwards), and his crusty but compassionate mentor, Dr. Zorba (Sam Jaffe). The chief difference between the two programs was that Casey was a more rugged character than Kildare. Casey's image was that of a man torn by his conscience as he faced the important decisions at the hospital. In contrast to Kildare's choir-boy goodness, Casey was once described as "the grim doctor who must be cruel to be kind." Despite the minor differences, both *Dr. Kildare* and *Ben Casey* were exactly the same in one important area: both programs seemed designed to appeal specifically to women. The love and death medical themes that had kept housewives entranced for decades on the daytime soap operas were moved, intact, to the nighttime medical soapers. The characters of Kildare and Casey were enticing and charismatic, with Chamberlain appealing primarily to older mothers and young girls, while Edwards attracted more worldly women in their twenties and thirties. Both programs offered competent drama and conflict in addition to the suds and sex, thus extending the appeal to the entire family. Both programs also turned into the smash hits of the season, which was welcome news to both NBC and ABC.

The two networks had faced the 1961–62 season in a depressed state and were moved to innovation out of a desire to dramatically change their situations. ABC was fading rapidly following the collapse of its action-adventure format, and NBC was trying hard to rise from the uncomfortable number three slot. Besides developing the successful new medical dramas, the two competitors also revived the idea of prime time feature films and this, too, provided both with welcome ratings boosts.

Films had been regularly aired in network prime time before 1961, but no network had ever presented relatively recent domestic feature films in the slots. At first, the major Hollywood studios had been very reluctant to release their old films to television because they feared this would destroy the market for rerelease and would offer, free on television, competition for new material then at the theaters. Consequently, the *CBS Film Theater of the Air* in the Forties had run ancient two-reelers more to fill empty hours than to attract an audience. In the Fifties, ABC's *Famous Film Festival* was forced to belie its title by featuring moldy unknown British product rather than well-known American films. The network's *Hollywood Film Theater* managed to secure American material from RKO, but the films were largely stale and forgettable. By 1957, the major American studios had changed their policies and released most of the pre-1948 films to the home viewing market. By then, the networks feared that these high quality films would make their weekly series look bad, so they didn't pick up the available films; instead, these became the private cache of late afternoon and late night local programmers.

In 1961, NBC decided to take a shot at scheduling old movies in prime time as part of its effort to raise itself from the doldrums of last place. The network paid 20th Century-Fox $25 million for fifty post-1950 films to be aired in prime time on Saturday night,

though the network protected itself against the possibility of a disastrous failure with a clause in the contract that gave it the right to "bug out" after sixteen weeks if the film series proved a flop. Unlike every previous prime time film effort, *NBC Saturday Night at the Movies* quickly established itself as a ratings contender, though it didn't come to dominate Saturday night for several more years. The series succeeded where previous efforts had failed for two reasons: The films were relatively new and the package contained a fair portion of outright box office hits. What's more, nearly half of the films were in color, and with color set sales continuing a slow and steady advance, such an attraction was beginning to have some meaning.

ABC noted NBC's success, quickly purchased fifteen post-1948 films from United Artists, and in April, 1962, premiered its own prime time movie slot, *Hollywood Special* (soon renamed *The ABC Sunday Night Movie*). After years of bitter rivalry between network television and the Hollywood studios, the two looked to each other as important partners in the entertainment industry. The battle was over and their marriage was nearly complete.

As the power at the top, CBS did not have to chase every program fad and unproven concept, but could develop shows at a more leisurely pace in its traditional strengths such as drama and situation comedy. The network had been the home of high quality situation comedies since the early Fifties with programs such as *I Love Lucy, The Honeymooners,* and *The Phil Silvers Show,* but as the decade progressed it had turned from this format to emphasize other forms such as Westerns, quiz shows, and sixty-minute adventure series. Consequently, CBS had not actively searched for successors to the great sitcoms of the decade and had been content with keeping the top ten vehicles of its established stars such as Jack Benny and Danny Thomas. When the other formats faded,

September 17, 1961
DuPont Show of the Week. (NBC). After four years as a series of floating dramatic specials for CBS, the DuPont program switches to NBC, changing formats as well. The weekly series now includes drama, documentary, and variety presentations ranging from "The Wonderful World of Christmas" (with Carol Burnett and Harpo Marx) to "Hemingway" (narrated by Chet Huntley).

September 24, 1961
Walt Disney's Wonderful World of Color. (NBC). Robert Kinter, who has signed Disney to television when he was with ABC, brings the popular family program with him to NBC. For the first time, the show airs in color (which ABC always shied away from), beginning with the premiere episode, "Mathmagic Land," featuring Donald Duck and a new animated character, Professor Ludwig Von Drake.

September 30, 1961
Gunsmoke expands to sixty minutes, while the cream of six years of the half-hour shows are rerun on Tuesday nights under the title *Marshal Dillon.*

October 2, 1961
Calendar. (CBS). Harry Reasoner hosts a thirty-minute morning show combining hard news and soft features. Reasoner's wry essays, co-written with Andrew Rooney, are a high point of the program.

December 11, 1961
The Mike Douglas Show. The former band singer starts a ninety-minute afternoon talk show on Westinghouse's KYW in Cleveland. By October, 1963, the show is syndicated nationally.

the network turned again to comedy for new material. With the obvious success of such programs as *Dennis the Menace,* network president James Aubrey moved to reemphasize this network strength and, in the fall line-ups for 1960 and 1961, one-half of CBS's new programs were situation comedies. Aubrey also encouraged the development of ideas and pilots for additional sitcoms, feeling that the potential for tremendous success rested in this format.

In the summer of 1960, CBS aired *Comedy Spot* which, like many summer filler series, served as a dumping ground for pilot films that had failed to win network support. Occasionally one of the rejected pilots struck a nerve and was picked up for production after all, but most faded away, with the summer broadcast serving as a sad postscript to an aborted idea. The few that were picked up on the rebound sometimes faced special difficulties in production because very often by that time the cast and crew had already committed themselves to other ventures and were no longer interested in the proposed series. One pilot from the summer of 1960 that managed to overcome its initial rejection and find a place in the 1961–62 schedule was a pet project of Sid Caesar's old cohort, Carl Reiner, called *Head of the Family,* which depicted the home and office life of Rob Petrie, the head writer for a television comedy show.

In the pilot episode aired on *Comedy Spot,* Petrie (played by Reiner) and his wife Laura (Barbara Britton) had to convince their son Ritchie (Gary Morgan) that his father's job was as interesting and important as those of the other kids' fathers. To prove his point, Rob brought Ritchie to the office to see firsthand how valuable he was to the other two writers, Sally Rogers (Sylvia Miles) and Buddy Sorrell (Morty Gunty), and the show's host, Alan Sturdy (Jack Wakefield). The format seemed workable, the cast adequate, and the writing mildly clever, but it just didn't click. Reiner refused to give up on the idea after the initial rejection and reworked the series, keeping the format intact but assembling a new cast. He remained an occasional performer as the Alan

Sturdy character (renamed Alan Brady), but concentrated on writing and production, relinquishing the lead role of Rob Petrie to Dick Van Dyke (who had bounced about CBS for five years as a host for cartoon and morning programming). Mary Tyler Moore (David Janssen's secretary in *Richard Diamond, Private Detective*) assumed the part of Laura, and Larry Matthews played Ritchie. In a stroke of genius, veteran comics Morey Amsterdam and Rose Marie, who had labored for years in the wilderness after some success in the very early days of broadcasting, were cast as the new Buddy and Sally. Amsterdam had been a frequent performer in network television's early days and Rose Marie had begun singing on the NBC radio network when she was three years old (as Baby Rose Marie), and both brought a much needed sharp comic edge to their characters. CBS was convinced and scheduled the new series, renamed *The Dick Van Dyke Show,* to begin in October, 1961. The new cast lifted the program's highly workable format far above its original promise and—combined with the work of executive producer Sheldon Leonard, directors John Rich and Jerry Paris, and writers Bill Persky, Sam Denoff, and Reiner himself—made *The Dick Van Dyke Show* a worthy successor to *Lucy* and *Bilko*. Though it took several seasons to catch on, the program eventually outdistanced its competition and built a large and loyal audience.

The Dick Van Dyke Show set its action in both the Petrie home in suburban New Rochelle and Rob's office in Manhattan. The home scenes were generally along the lines of traditional TV comedies, with adequate support for the domestic situations provided by the Petries' next door neighbors, Millie and Jerry Helper (played by Ann Morgan Guilbert and director Jerry Paris), but the office scenes were bits of inspired brilliance that gave the show its drive. Borrowing a hook from another Sheldon Leonard program, *The Danny Thomas Show,* Reiner, Persky, and Denoff set Dick Van Dyke in an "I Me Mine" format, once removed: Van Dyke, the star of a TV sitcom, portrayed a writer for a TV comedy series, in a part written for him by writers of a TV sitcom. By working with a world they faced every day (writing for a TV comedy show), Reiner, Persky, and Denoff infused the office scenes with sharp, animated humor as Rob, Buddy, and Sally tossed quips back and forth in a rapid-fire style reminiscent of an old vaudeville stage show. The writers also directed some effective barbs against television itself in scenes that involved the show's vain star, Alan Brady (Reiner), and its flunky producer, Brady's brother-in-law, Mel Cooley (Richard Deacon). Whether the comedy was set at work or at home, the situations were always humorous and exaggerated, but still basically real, if highly unlikely. The stories were not a relevant satire on the times, but the effective presentation of crises and complications that a television writer living and working in New York might face.

Series such as *I Love Lucy* and *Leave It to Beaver* had symbolized life in the Fifties, and *The Dick Van Dyke Show* did much the same for the first half of the Sixties, perfectly capturing the feeling and sense of the Kennedy years. (With her bouffant hairdo, Mary Tyler Moore even looked a little like Jackie Kennedy in those days.) The series presented a range of characters living out exaggerated views of everyday life in a world not very different from the one that most viewers faced. Rob and Laura lived in a real middle class town in which real people commuted to and from real jobs. He was a decent, intelligent, hard-working father and she was a helpful and clever wife who was neither wacky, gorgeous, nor conniving. The program effectively replaced the interchangeable blandness of the Fifties with a generally real view of the successful middle class life of the early Sixties.

The Dick Van Dyke Show, The Defenders, Dr. Kildare, Ben Casey, and prime time movies were important signs that television was improving and had broken out of the disastrous state of the 1960–61 season. Nonetheless, they were only a handful among the new shows that premiered in the fall. Most of the new entries were weak vehicles for talented performers, mindless fluff, or just very bad television. For the most part, the 1961–62 season still carried the unmistakable marks of a vast wasteland.

Several new sitcoms merely maintained the mold of late Fifties blandness: *Window on Main Street* reactivated Robert Young in his favorite role as thoughtful patriarch; *Room for One More,* starring Andrew Duggan, continued television's fascination with families enlarged by adoption or remarriage; *Hazel* (based on the long-running *Saturday Evening Post* cartoon) cast Shirley Booth as maid to possibly the dumbest family in TV history; and *Mrs. G. Goes to College* provided an unfairly pathetic swan song for Gertrude Berg.

Two promising young comics, Bob Newhart and Joey Bishop, made misdirected, undistinguished debuts as comedy headliners. Newhart, whose comedy album *The Button Down Mind* had been a 1960 sleeper hit, was miscast as a genial host of a half-hour variety show. Bishop, who had made a name for himself with his ad-lib witicisms on TV panel and talk shows, found himself playing a public relations man in a ploddingly scripted sitcom that wasted his quick wit.

Nat Hiken, the creator of Sergeant Bilko, tried unsuccessfully to duplicate the formula of that series with *Car 54, Where Are You?* Two excellent character actors, Joe E. Ross and Fred Gwynne, were cast as the bumbling policemen who cruised the Big Apple in squad car 54, but it was *Bilko* without Bilko. Ross, as Gunther Toody, faithfully duplicated his bumbling oo-oo-ooing *Bilko* character of Mess Sergeant Rupert Ritzik, but it wasn't enough. Though he and Gwynne, as the drab, earlobe-pulling Francis Muldoon, provided hilarious caricatures of the Jack Webb look-alikes that appeared to populate nearly every cop show, the two worked best as supporting actors. They couldn't match the mad energy of Phil Silvers, whose domineering personality had held the *Bilko* show together, and *Car 54, Where Are You?* seemed constantly in search of a main character. Hiken had slipped up on the basics of a good sitcom and as a result the program provided merely adequate diversion, rarely matching the energy of its catchy opening theme song.

One new sitcom, though, managed to top all these minor artistic flaws with a premise that seemed designed to epitomize the term "vast wasteland"—*The Hathaways,* possibly the worst series ever to air on network TV. The show marked the last step in television's vilification of American parenthood, presenting Jack Weston and Peggy Cass as surrogate parents to three chimpanzees, Enoch, Charley, and Candy. Weston and Cass treated the three chimps as human children, dressing them in children's clothes and encouraging them to imitate human actions such as dancing, eating, and playing. The scripts, acting, and production were horrible, and the premise itself was utterly degrading to both the audience and the actors. (Weston often wore an expression that made him look like a befuddled monkey.) *The Hathaways* more than justified the network executives' early apprehension about the new season and, though it lasted only one year, it stood as an embarrassing example of the depths programmers had reached in their desperate search for a chance hit in any format or premise.

Despite the total worthlessness of sitcoms such as *The Hathaways,* the programs that attracted the heaviest criticism in the 1961–62 season were the so-called "realistic" crime shows. Under the guise of drama, these programs presented violence that was at best merely gratuitous but at its worst sordid, morbid, and gruesome. Among the merely gratuitous shows were *Cain's Hundred* and *Target: The Corruptors,* two inferior permutations of *The Untouchables* set in the present. In *Cain's Hundred,* Mark Richman portrayed Nicholas Cain, a former mob lawyer who came over to the side of the law and helped track down his former employers, the nation's one hundred top mobsters. Though the series bore some surface resemblance to *The Untouchables* (Richman's Cain

The Dick Van Dyke Show home setting: (from *l.*) Dick Van Dyke as Rob Petrie, Larry Matthews as son Ritchie, and Mary Tyler Moore as Laura Petrie. *(Photo by Viacom, Hollywood)*

personality was very similar to Robert Stack's Eliot Ness; and Paul Monash, executive producer of *Cain*, had worked on the pilot for "The Untouchables"), it lacked high quality supporting characters and any feel for realism. The series focused on little else but gunplay. *Target: The Corruptors* set its violent gunplay under the respectable guise of uncovering modern crime by featuring the adventures of an intrepid newspaper reporter who worked with federal agents to weed out and expose corruption. No matter what area of modern life they investigated, though, violence was inevitable. The series began with a dramatization of crime in the field of garbage collecting and within the first twenty seconds of the premiere episode, a garbage man was shot.

87th Precinct went beyond violence into morbidity and sexual overtones. It was a bad version of *Naked City*, focusing on the daily grind of New York City law enforcement. Detective Steve Carella (Robert Lansing) led a squad of plainclothes cops who were all morose, shoddy, and dense. The plots emphasized cheap thrills and titillating violence. One episode featured the pursuit of a sadistic murderer who first tattooed, then poisoned, his female victims. After a particularly gruesome chase, he was somehow detained by Carella's beautiful deaf-mute wife and then captured. Such disgusting individuals and plots cast an appropriately somber pall over the entire series.

Of all the exercises in violence, ABC's drama anthology *Bus Stop* provided the most graphic, brutal, and controversial episode, and the one that touched off a wave of outraged reaction among network affiliates as well as in the halls of Congress. Loosely based on the movie of the same name, *Bus Stop* set a small central cast in a tiny Colorado town to await the weekly guest stars who inevitably began each story with their arrival at the town's bus depot.

At the office in *The Dick Van Dyke Show:* (from *l.*) Dick Van Dyke, Morey Amsterdam as Buddy Sorrell, and Rose Marie as Sally Rogers. *(Photo by Viacom, Hollywood)*

At first, the 20th Century-Fox series dealt in light Hollywood fluff such as an errant father returning to defend the honor of his wrongly accused son. To spice up later episodes, the show turned to more sensationalist tabloid material, culminating in "A Lion Walks Among Us" (directed by Robert Altman). *Bus Stop* used Fabian, a former self-acclaimed rock'n'roller who was still popular with teens, as its guest star draw in the story. Though really a very clean-cut young man, Fabian was cast as a degenerate drifter capable only of deceit, betrayal, and murder. To win acquittal of one charge of murder in the town, he had an affair with the D.A.'s alcoholic wife and then used that to blackmail the D.A. Once released, he killed his own lawyers. In a perverse "balance of justice," the D.A.'s wife then killed him.

This sordid episode was labeled "rancid" by one critic and twenty-five stations refused to air it. They claimed it was obscene and that it glorified violence and perversion while deliberately using a teen favorite to entice young viewers. Senator John Pastore of Rhode Island, who was rapidly becoming a vocal new watchdog of television, agreed. He happened to be holding hearings on the very topic of TV violence when the episode aired and he could not get it out of his mind. He brought it up in congressional debate again and again for months as the perfect example of the terrible excesses he was fighting. "I looked at it," he said, "and I haven't felt clean since. I still have the stench in my nose."

In spite of the *Bus Stop* brouhaha, network television weathered its first season following Newton Minow's vast wasteland speech rather well. Westerns no longer saturated each evening's line-up. Action-adventure gave way to medical soap opera. Serious drama returned in the guise of a continuing series. Situation comedy experienced a rebirth. And public affairs programming increased substantially. Overall, television had steered itself away from the mediocre excesses of the immediate past and pulled itself out of the rut it had fallen into after the quiz shows. In the process, TV managed to restore some of the luster to its tarnished respectability. What's more, the public's perception of television quality had risen as well. Consequently, executives planning the 1962–63 season felt no compulsion to implement the full scale changes they had vaguely pledged immediately following Minow's speech. Instead, they slipped back into business as usual and worked at developing imitations and spinoffs of the respectable and successful new doctor, sitcom, and movie formats. At the same time as the networks began seriously considering exactly what to copy for the new fall schedules, television lost one of its true originals, Ernie Kovacs, who died on January 12, 1962, in a car crash.

Kovacs had been the first true *television* comedian. Even back in the *Three to Get Ready* days on a local Philadelphia station, he seemed to understand the visual possibilities inherent in television better than any other performer on the air. Though other comics such as Milton Berle and Sid Caesar were visual performers (that is, their acts had to be seen to be appreciated), they were only doing vaudeville in front of a camera. Kovacs understood the potential for humor in the tricks and effects that were possible only on television. Since his brief stint as a part-time host of the *Tonight* show in the 1956-57 season, Kovacs had been offered few opportunities to perform on network television. He made a few movies in Hollywood while being wasted as host of several low-level ABC series such as *Take a Good Look* (a panel quiz show that used his characters and skits as game clues) and *Silents Please* (in which he supplied funny voice-over comments to cut-downs of silent film classics).

In early 1961, Kovacs talked his sponsor, Dutch Masters, into

One year after the death of *Amos and Andy* on the radio, Freeman Gosden and Charles Correll again bring their characters to television in the less controversial setting of the animated *Calvin and the Colonel:* (from *l.*) Colonel Montgomery J. Klaxton (voice by Gosden) and Calvin Burnside (voice by Correll). (*From* Calvin and the Colonel. *Courtesy of MCA Television Limited*)

allowing him to produce, write, and act in a series of monthly specials in the company's regular Thursday night *Silents Please* slot. The cigar makers enjoyed having the cigar-chomping Kovacs as host to that show and agreed to support the experiment. On an absurdly small budget for the project he envisioned ($15,000 per show), Kovacs launched his series. From the very first special in April, he totally departed from the then established form of TV comedy (monologues followed by skits) and presented instead short unconnected bits of humor (blackouts) with an emphasis on visual, often abstract, tricks of TV technology. One thirty-minute program consisted of the visual interpretation of sound, with no narration whatsoever. For instance, instead of showing an orchestra playing "The 1812 Overture," Kovacs used snapping celery stalks and slamming desk drawers as visual accompaniment to the music. He also directed digs at his regular show, *Silents Please,* by taking the logical next step in his manipulation of the old films. Instead of providing just voice-over comments, he used a special effect to physically step into the picture as a frustrated director calling out humorous and absurd orders to the performers.

The program also featured the Kovacs cast of continuing characters who were quite funny even without the aid of his technological tricks. The most familiar was Percy Dovetonsils, an effeminate, permanently soused poet who read nonsense verse with ludicrous titles such as "Ode to an Emotional Knight Who Once Wore the Suit of Medieval Armor Now in the Metropolitan Museum of Art While Engaged to One of Botticelli's Models." Others included Miklos Molnar, a Hungarian chef also "under the influence," who presented cooking tips; Auntie Gruesome, a dolled-up host to a creature features-type TV show, who ended up scaring himself with his long and gruesome descriptions of the horror stories; and Wolfgang Sauerbraten, a German radio DJ who introduced the latest hits in gibberish German-English clearly aimed at lampooning American broadcasters. Even such sacred objects as the closing credits fell to Kovacs's wit: Once they appeared as writing in a sink and were washed down the drain after each name.

Kovacs turned out eight such specials on ABC before he died and, though hampered by a meager budget, he nevertheless tried to do something different with television. Many viewers were frankly befuddled by what they saw and, truth be told, much of it wasn't very funny. What was vitally important was that in an industry content with blandness and imitation, Kovacs dared to challenge the limits of TV technology and steer it into previously unexplored territories. He pioneered a style that would completely alter television comedy, but that wouldn't occur until years later, when his approach and technique were used to form the basis of *Rowan and Martin's Laugh-In.* Long after his ABC specials were aired and forgotten, the entire country at last understood just what he had been trying to accomplish, and applauded.

22. CBS + RFD = $$$

DESPITE all the promises of programming reform made by television executives in May, 1961, the 1962–63 schedule turned out to be just business as usual. The improvements during the 1961–62 season had blunted Newton Minow's vast wasteland charge and diffused criticism by the government and the public. Profits and ratings once again became the chief concerns of network programmers and they began to cast a critical eye at the overabundance of news and public affairs shows which had proliferated chiefly as a public relations device to shore up television's respectability. By the 1962–63 season, six prime time programs, two on each network, provided a total of four hours of material weekly: *Howard K. Smith—News and Comment* and *Bell and Howell Closeup* on ABC; *CBS Reports* and *Eyewitness* on CBS; and *David Brinkley's Journal* and *Chet Huntley Reporting* on NBC. These programs were generally well done but there were too many of them and their sheer number diluted the audience and stretched resources far too thin to allow quality productions each week. Nonetheless, several hard-hitting news reports reached prime time in the process, giving the network news departments the opportunity to flex their muscles.

CBS, with a sideways glance at the *cinéma vérité* style of ABC's *Closeup* documentary series, had hired Jay McMullen in 1961 as its own roving *vérité* reporter. Even though at the time the networks had serious reservations about investigative news reporting for television (preferring traditional public affairs documentaries and discussions instead), McMullen was assigned to dig for unusual and controversial material. His first (and best) piece for CBS, "Biography of a Bookie Joint," managed to overcome most network objections to the form and demonstrated the effective impact of investigative TV journalism. McMullen found a key shop in Boston's Back Bay area that was visited by nearly 1,000 people each day, including many policemen. Further investigation revealed that the key shop was actually a bookie joint. He set up an observation post in a room across the street from the shop and, over a period of months, watched and filmed the comings and goings of the key shop's customers and even managed to shoot (admittedly jerky) footage of the shop's interior using an 8mm camera hidden in a false lunch box. Federal agents were informed of the illegal operations by McMullen and they, in turn, apparently tipped off the crew with the time of their impending raid on the shop, giving McMullen the opportunity to film it. "Biography of a Bookie Joint" emerged as an engrossing, real life crime thriller, complete with

a dramatic sweep by the Feds as a climax, and it was widely acclaimed by viewers across the country.

In the city of Boston itself, the report caused immediate and long lasting convulsions. The local affiliate did not air it for one and one-half years, while legal wrangling took place. The city's police commissioner was forced to resign, and the Massachusetts legislators censured one member for the disparaging remarks he made on the program about his colleagues. In the ensuing trial, the police, tarnished by the evidence on film of their participation in the illegal gambling joint, tried to disprove the facts and dates contained in the story. Others contended that the show revealed blatant news mismanagement and biased reporting. The accuracy and objectivity of McMullen's story was proved correct at every step, though the charge of bias would be leveled with increasing frequency as investigative TV journalism developed through the decade.

In 1962, NBC presented its own real life dramatic news adventure, "The Tunnel," a ninety-minute war story set in Berlin. Most foreign issue documentaries of the time inevitably settled for fluff travelogue visits ("This Is Monaco") and innocuous insights ("Mouamba—Land in Conflict") but "The Tunnel" presented the desperate scheme of some brave heroes in conflict with clear-cut bad guys. The program followed the daring escape of fifty-nine East Berliners through a 450-foot tunnel dug by twenty-one West Berliners. The constant fear of exposure and capture hung over everyone until the exciting climax of the story when the joyful East Berliners successfully made their way under the Berlin wall to freedom. So potent was this story that, due to the international tensions resulting from the Cuban missile crisis in October, "The Tunnel" (originally scheduled to air in October) was delayed two months. When it played in December, it earned critical acclaim, registered surprisingly strong ratings, and proved to be far more dramatic than the artificial action shows that usually filled prime time.

Besides offering a crime exposé and war drama, the networks also displayed more daring in traditional documentaries and news reports. *CBS Reports* tackled such previously taboo subjects as birth control and teenage smoking as well as new concerns such as ecology. In "The Silent Spring of Rachel Carson" (broadcast in April of 1963), CBS presented an evenhanded examination of the heavy use of pesticides and their possible disruption of the balance of nature, which Carson described in a book she had written. Because the issue wasn't familiar to most Americans, exposure in a network documentary tremendously aided Carson's side, much as the great debates in 1960 had helped relative unknown John Kennedy achieve an equal footing with Richard Nixon in the eyes of the public. Simply by acknowledging and interviewing spokesmen of a cause, television could inadvertently aid one side or another and make it almost impossible to ignore an issue or personality. One of the season's major TV controversies, in fact, developed when ABC's Howard K. Smith examined the personality and then-fading career of former Vice President Richard Nixon.

Smith had quit CBS, his long-time home, at the end of 1961 after a phrase comparing Southern bigots to Nazi storm troopers had been blipped from one of his occasional commentaries on the network's nightly TV news (oddly enough, the comment was left in the radio version). CBS said that Smith had crossed the line between analysis and editorial opinion, so Smith said *adios,* signed with ABC in the beginning of 1962, and immediately received his own program, *Howard K. Smith—News and Comment.* Unlike *David Brinkley's Journal, Chet Huntley Reporting,* and *Eyewitness* (with Walter Cronkite and Charles Kuralt), which all mixed feature reports and in-depth news reviews in the style of the Seventies' *60 Minutes,* Smith attempted to revive the spirit of the radio news commentators of the Thirties and Forties. Other respected commentators including Quincy Howe and Drew Pearson had tried to bring that style of news analysis from network radio to television in the late Forties and early Fifties, but the format always seemed too static for television. Smith set his program in a homey living room and embellished the commentary with charts, maps, occasional film clips, and interviews. Despite all the window dressing, it remained essentially just "talking heads" with little visual impact for television. Nonetheless, the program created quite a fuss in November, 1962, with "The Political Obituary of Richard Nixon."

Only two years after his unsuccessful bid for the presidency, Nixon had lost a bitter campaign for the governorship of California, and it appeared that he was, in fact, through with politics (or vice versa). Following his latest defeat he proclaimed to the reporters gathered in California that they would not "have Nixon to kick around any more because, gentlemen, this is my last press conference." Smith took Nixon at his word and devoted his program on November 11 to a review of the man's political career, presenting observations from both supporters and detractors. Among those critical of Nixon was Alger Hiss, a former state department official who had been labeled a "Red subversive" in the late Forties by then Representative Nixon and who eventually served time for perjury. In a one-minute film interview, Hiss said that Nixon's main motivation for doggedly pursuing him had been pure personal and political ambition. Hiss's charges were immediately followed by four minutes of filmed praise for Nixon by Representative Gerald Ford. Despite the careful balance of opinions, the very appearance of Hiss ignited a firestorm of protest. One of the show's sponsors, Kemper Insurance, pulled out. Conservative politicians and some publications, particularly the *Chicago Tribune,* kept the story alive for months, constantly issuing shocked statements asking how a TV network such as ABC could allow a convicted liar on the air. "Mr. Hiss is news," Smith replied, "and we're in the news business. I'm not running a Sunday school program." Other sponsors stuck by the program and ABC sued Kemper for violating its contract (the network eventually won its case). In spite of ABC's vigorous defense, though, it did not appreciate the trouble Smith had stirred up and the veteran newsman was by-passed for major assignments for the next year, and his *News and Comment* disappeared in the summer.

Smith's program joined most of the other public affairs shows that were dropped or lost their regular prime time slot as the networks modified their commitments to news throughout 1963. Executives pointed out that there had been too many shows appearing at once and the reduced frequency would loosen budgets and allow higher quality presentations. Besides, the special public affairs programs had already served their chief function very well by contributing to the overall prestige of television and apparently proving to the FCC that the medium was no longer a vast wasteland. No new government regulations had been imposed and none appeared on the horizon. There was therefore no overwhelming reason to continue to carry too many unprofitable shows with generally unspectacular ratings in prime time, though the networks insisted that they strongly supported the continuing growth of their individual news departments.

Even at the season's high water mark in prime time public affairs, many of television's critics saw a network retreat from the form as inevitable. Though they applauded the material carried by ABC, CBS, and NBC, they began searching for some way to break the iron grip of network influence and control over programming. The UHF system and educational television were two potential tools to that end and both exhibited long overdue development in the 1962–63 season. They had been created by the FCC in 1952 as the freeze on TV station construction was lifted, but had remained catatonic for nearly a decade.

The commission launched educational television in 1952 with a bold stroke—setting aside 242 station allocations specifically for noncommercial broadcasting. Despite this promising beginning, educational broadcasting experienced very little growth over the next ten years. By 1960, there were only forty-eight educational stations

September 10, 1962
Hugh Downs replaces John Chancellor as major domo of *Today.*

September 10, 1962
Mal Goode becomes the first black network correspondent, covering the United Nations for ABC.

September 19, 1962
The Virginian. (NBC). The first ninety-minute television Western and, like *Bonanza,* it is broadcast in color. Though the series has a strong central cast (Lee J. Cobb, James Drury, and Doug McClure), the stories frequently focus on the weekly guest stars.

September 23, 1962
The Jetsons. (ABC). ABC at last airs its *first* program in color, the premiere of another Hanna-Barbera cartoon series. Essentially *The Flintstones* backwards, the new show is a simple animated family sitcom with the setting moved from the stone age to the twenty-first century.

September 27, 1962
The Andy Williams Show. (NBC). Mr. Easy Listening enters the limelight in a series produced by Bud Yorkin and Norman Lear. Andy's television "family" includes the four singing Osmond Brothers (ages 7 through 12) who open with "I'm a Ding Dong Daddy from Dumas."

October 1, 1962
The Merv Griffin Show. (NBC). The former singer and game show host tries his hand at an hour-long afternoon talk show, with help from such writers as Pat McCormick and Dick Cavett. This daytime version of *Tonight* fades by April.

FALL 1962 SCHEDULE

MONDAY

	7:00	7:30	8:00	8:30	9:00	9:30	10:00	10:30	
	local	Cheyenne		The Rifleman	STONEY BURKE		Ben Casey		ABC
	local	To Tell The Truth	I've Got A Secret	THE LUCY SHOW	Danny Thomas Show	Andy Griffith Show	LORETTA YOUNG SHOW	STUMP THE STARS	CBS
	local	IT'S A MAN'S WORLD		SAINTS AND SINNERS		The Price Is Right	David Brinkley's Journal	local	NBC

TUESDAY

	7:00	7:30	8:00	8:30	9:00	9:30	10:00	10:30	
	local	COMBAT!		Hawaiian Eye		The Untouchables		Bell And Howell Close-Up	ABC
	local	Marshal Dillon	LLOYD BRIDGES SHOW	Red Skelton Hour		Jack Benny Program	Garry Moore Show		CBS
	local	Laramie		EMPIRE		Dick Powell Show		Chet Huntley Reporting	NBC

WEDNESDAY

	7:00	7:30	8:00	8:30	9:00	9:30	10:00	10:30	
	local	Wagon Train		GOING MY WAY		OUR MAN HIGGINS	Naked City		ABC
	local	CBS Reports / CBS News Specials		The Many Loves Of Dobie Gillis	THE BEVERLY HILLBILLIES	Dick Van Dyke Show	U.S. Steel Hour / Armstrong Circle Theater		CBS
	local	THE VIRGINIAN			Perry Como's Kraft Music Hall		THE ELEVENTH HOUR		NBC

THURSDAY

	7:00	7:30	8:00	8:30	9:00	9:30	10:00	10:30	
	local	The Adventures Of Ozzie And Harriet	Donna Reed Show	Leave It To Beaver	My Three Sons	McHALE'S NAVY	Alcoa Premiere / Fred Astaire Presenting		ABC
	local	Mr. Ed	Perry Mason		THE NURSES		Alfred Hitchcock Hour		CBS
	local	WIDE COUNTRY		Dr. Kildare		Hazel	ANDY WILLIAMS SHOW		NBC

FRIDAY

	7:00	7:30	8:00	8:30	9:00	9:30	10:00	10:30	
	local	THE GALLANT MEN		The Flintstones	I'M DICKENS – HE'S FENSTER	77 Sunset Strip		local	ABC
	local	Rawhide		Route 66		FAIR EXCHANGE		Eyewitness	CBS
	local	International Showtime		Sing Along With Mitch		DON'T CALL ME CHARLIE	JACK PAAR SHOW		NBC

SATURDAY

	7:00	7:30	8:00	8:30	9:00	9:30	10:00	10:30	
	Beany And Cecil	ROY ROGERS AND DALE EVANS SHOW		MR. SMITH GOES TO WASHINGTON	Lawrence Welk Show		Fight Of The Week	Make That Spare	ABC
	local	JACKIE GLEASON SHOW		The Defenders		Have Gun, Will Travel	Gunsmoke		CBS
	local	SAM BENEDICT		The New Joey Bishop Show	NBC Saturday Night At The Movies				NBC

SUNDAY

	7:00	7:30	8:00	8:30	9:00	9:30	10:00	10:30	
	Father Knows Best	THE JETSONS	The ABC Sunday Night Movie				Voice Of Firestone	Howard K. Smith – News And Comment	ABC
	Lassie	Dennis The Menace	Ed Sullivan Show		The Real McCoys	General Electric True	Candid Camera	What's My Line	CBS
	ENISGN O'TOOLE	Walt Disney's Wonderful World Of Color		Car 54, Where Are You?	Bonanza		DuPont Show Of The Week @Dinah Shore Show		NBC

on the air. All but four of them were associated with the fledgling National Educational Television network, but that only produced eight hours of programming each week. What's more, expensive coaxial cable connections were out of the question, so the filmed shows were sent to the affiliates through the mail. Such cost-cutting measures were necessary because in setting up noncommercial stations the FCC had left one important problem unresolved—funding. If the stations were to be noncommercial but also independent of the government, where was the money for operational expenses to come from? A few private corporations, particularly the Ford Foundation, stepped in from the beginning and contributed millions, but it was nowhere near the amount necessary to launch a national chain of stations that could be taken seriously by viewers.

There was an additional problem. Viewers. Many of the frequencies so generously earmarked by the FCC for noncommercial use were on the UHF band. None of the eighteen million television sets in use in 1952 were capable of receiving UHF signals. Stations in a few markets such as KQED in San Francisco and WGBH in Boston were lucky enough to receive VHF allocations, but for the most part viewers couldn't tune in the educational stations, so there was virtually no audience. More importantly, by the end of the Fifties, major markets such as New York, Los Angeles, Cleveland, and Washington still had no educational station at all. The near invisible status of noncommercial television reduced it to a very expensive laboratory and made it impossible to stir any interest in improving the situation. Until the important figures in broadcasting and government living in New York, Los Angeles, and Washington could see educational television in operation, a solution to the funding problem would never be worked out.

In order to provide a noncommerical outlet in New York City, a group of New York-based forces (calling themselves Educational Television for the Metropolitan Area) decided to buy an existing commercial VHF station and set it up as a showpiece for educational TV. After protracted delays and legal challenges, the group purchased Newark's WNTA, channel 13, for $6.2 million. One-third of the money was donated by CBS, NBC, and ABC, who saw educational television as an excellent way to answer the criticisms leveled at the commercial networks. They could point to their generosity in supporting the noble project even as they continued to concentrate on more profitable popular appeal entertainment. As long as educational television stuck to classroom type programming aimed at the "egghead" fringe, they knew it would never provide any real competition for the mass audience.

WNTA was renamed WNDT (later changed to WNET) and it hit the New York airwaves on September 16, 1962, as the sixty-eighth educational station in the country. Newton Minow and Ed Murrow hosted the gala opening festivities which were attended by representatives from all three commercial networks. Yet there were conflicting priorities and philosophies among the many divergent interests that had united to establish the new station and these immediately surfaced during the chaotic two-and-one-half-hour premiere broadcast. The networks were most upset by an eighty-three-minute British film which extolled the BBC and labeled American television as 80% junk. They felt the film was a stab in the back after all the support they had given the new station and CBS, NBC, and ABC executives went away angry. The station also faced union problems and had to shut down for two weeks immediately following the premiere telecast in order to resolve them.

When WNDT returned, New Yorkers had an opportunity to see, at last, the wonders of noncommercial television. It was a direct throwback to the very early days of commercial television. Aside from the expected educational fare for children, there were boring discussion shows (*Books for Our Times, Invitation to Art*), attempts at educational fare for adults (*Russian for Beginners, Face of Sweden*), an overload of British films, and the inevitable, excruciatingly detailed thirty-minute studies of esoteric subjects such as Japanese brushstroke painting. All were numbing and not very entertaining, but channel 13 was new to broadcasting, short of money, and uncertain which tricks of the trade would work in the world of noncommercial television.

The increased visibility of educational television did bring about important changes, though. The federal government began handing out small yearly subsidies and the Ford Foundation increased the amount of its continuing support. Educational stations started broadcasting (though on UHF) in Washington and Los Angeles, and the NET network developed its first quasi-hits. *International Magazine* was a weekly news feature program put together by foreign broadcasters (chiefly from the BBC) who covered world events as well as the commercial networks, and sometimes surpassed them. In February, 1963, WGBH in Boston began producing *The French Chef,* which featured Julia Child demonstrating elaborate cooking techniques. Within a few months, she became the network's first star as her imposing figure and distinctive voice appeared on NET stations across the country. Despite these impressive gains, the fate of educational television ultimately rested with the development of UHF, because that's where most of the educational stations were located.

The UHF system had also begun in 1952 and it faced a long struggle to win support among set manufacturers, viewers, and sponsors. From the beginning, manufacturers saw no reason to spend extra money to include UHF capabilities unless their customers demanded it. The public wouldn't demand UHF until there was something worth watching on the system. Until there were enough sponsors to pay for exciting new programs, there couldn't be anything worth watching, and with so few viewers, what sponsor would make the investment? For more than two years the status of UHF remained unchanged. In September, 1954, following gov-

The Clampett clan: (from *l.*) Jed (Buddy Ebsen), Granny (Irene Ryan), Jethro (Max Baer), and Elly May (Donna Douglas). *(Photo by Viacom, Hollywood)*

In the fourth season of *McHale's Navy,* the setting shifted from the South Pacific to Italy, but the central character conflicts remained unchanged. Headliners for the series were Joe Flynn (2nd from *l.*), Tim Conway (*c.* kneeling), and Ernest Borgnine (*r.*). (*From* McHale's Navy. *Courtesy of MCA Television Limited*)

ernment and industry pressure on the FCC to do something to help the system, the commission amended its rules and increased the number of owned and operated stations a network could possess from five to seven—as long as two were UHF stations. It was assumed that if a network affiliate in a major city were on UHF, there would be sufficient demand by the public to push set manufacturers into beginning production of sets capable of receiving both UHF and VHF signals, thus breaking the stagnant situation. Within two years, CBS and NBC had purchased two UHF stations each and began offering their shows on UHF only to viewers in Milwaukee, Wisconsin and Hartford, Connecticut (CBS), and New Britain, Connecticut, and Buffalo, New York (NBC). This did not cause any increased demand for UHF sets. Instead, a few interested people purchased expensive special converters that allowed their old sets to pick up both UHF and VHF signals while most simply tuned to another network.

The FCC then decided to attempt a much more sweeping change and announced that it would suggest ordering cities throughout the country to be designated as either all-UHF or all-VHF markets. The problem with "deintermixture" (as the proposed policy was

labeled) was that no city wanted to be converted to an all-UHF market, rendering every television set in town useless. The FCC faced intensive lobbying for and against deintermixture, and wavered back and forth throughout 1956 and 1957, though Peoria, Illinois; Madison, Wisconsin; Evansville, Indiana; and Hartford, Connecticut were actually designated as deintermixture test cities. In late 1957, the commission opted for "undeintermixture" and allowed the UHF situation to remain unchanged, thus ending any serious efforts for expansion. By 1959, NBC and CBS had sold their UHF stations and the problem remained unsolved for nearly three more years.

In February, 1962, the FCC took up the question again and decided to aim directly at the chief stumbling block to the growth of the UHF system, the home receivers themselves. Instead of counting on the subtle pressures of supply and demand to motivate television set manufacturers into including UHF reception capabilities on their sets, the commission proposed to Congress that a law be passsed *requiring* the feature on all new American televisions. Throughout the spring, FCC chairman Newton Minow carried on an effective lobbying effort, with help from the White House, and salvaged the bill after most observers had given it up for dead. To underscore its strong belief that the proposed law offered the best possible solution to the UHF problem, the FCC announced that if the bill were not passed, it would deintermix eight major markets—immediately. A few days later, Congress passed the bill and the commission set April 30, 1964, as the day the law would take effect. Due to manufacturing production schedules, this meant that the 1965 model sets would be the first with both VHF and UHF capabilities. Though it would take years for the full ramifications of the new law to be felt, it was obvious that changes in American broadcasting would be monumental. Eventually, most television sets in the country would be capable of receiving UHF signals, thus allowing many more independent commercial stations, as well as most of the country's educational stations, the opportunity to survive and grow. The slow but steady growth of UHF in the late 1960s also solved ABC's long-standing problem of not having enough affiliates. By the end of the decade, ABC, for the first time, had stations carrying its programming into every major American city. Minow's work with the "all-channel" bill changed the shape of American television far more than his vast wasteland speech. Its passage provided a satisfying conclusion to his tenure as commissioner and he resigned from the FCC in 1963, having set into motion forces in television that would continue to grow through the next two decades.

After the period of uncertainty and confusion that culminated in the disastrous vast wasteland season, the commercial networks themselves were at last coasting into the new decade with confidence, several hit formats, and a sense of control. The 1962–63 season presented a nod toward medical drama (following the success of the previous season's *Ben Casey* and *Dr. Kildare*), several series set in World War II, a surprise revival in variety formats, and an incredibly successful new sitcom. These were added to a schedule that already included strong holdovers in several different formats and some outstanding individual news programs, producing what was, overall, a very good season.

After ABC's performance in the 1961–62 season sent the network back into the cellar, action-adventure whiz Ollie Treyz was forced to walk the plank in March, 1962, and the new president, Tom Moore, continued the search for another successful format to bring ABC back into contention. He brought in a revamped schedule for the 1962–63 season which contained the usual ABC potpourri of gimmicks, adding one new one, war. With World War II nearly two decades in the past, it seemed safe for television to restage the conflict so ABC presented *Gallant Men, Combat!,* and *McHale's Navy.* Warner Brothers' *Gallant Men* was pure grade-B movie pap that followed the 1943 Italian Campaign through the eyes of an American war correspondent who accompanied an infantry squad on vital "suicide" missions that never seemed to endanger him or any other members of the regular cast. The Robert Altman directed series, *Combat!,* was more realistic, focusing on the continuing struggles of average soldiers in an infantry unit winding through Europe after D-Day, rather than on supposedly momentous battles that could decide the outcome of the entire war. *Combat!* drew on a consistently good cast of regulars, guest stars, and a first class production unit to develop the personal conflict of men at war into tight drama. The war setting also allowed a good deal of violence and ABC knew that couldn't hurt in the ratings.

McHale's Navy offered an entirely different view of the same war in a "briny Bilko" situation comedy set on an island in the South Pacific. In the true *Bilko* style, the members of the crew under Lieutenant Commander Quinton McHale (Ernest Borgnine) spent most of their time bickering among themselves, gambling,

and hatching money-making schemes rather than facing the enemy. Of course, Bilko's adventures had been set in a peacetime Army but McHale's were close enough—the Japanese were usually presented as an unseen threat or convenient plot device rather than a dedicated, visible foe. Borgnine was cast as a lovable conniver, Joe Flynn as the perpetually befuddled C.O., and Tim Conway as the head of McHale's crew of flunkies. Unfortuniately, the show suffered from pathetically weak scripting and, as if to compensate, most of the characters seemed to be trying too hard to be funny, and their antics paled in comparison to their obvious *Bilko* counterparts. They didn't have the depth to transcend the show's many weaknesses. Nonetheless, the series did excel at physical humor and many of the Borgnine-Conway interactions bordered on classic slapstick, often saving the program. The inspired moments of *McHale's Navy* made it funnier than many comedies then on the air (two other new military sitcoms, NBC's *Don't Call Me Charlie* and *Ensign O'Toole,* could barely muster a laugh between them), and the crew managed to survive four seasons, a transplant to the European front, and two theatrical feature films ("McHale's Navy" and "McHale's Navy Joins the Air Force").

As usual, ABC drew on the new theme for several more seasons, eventually exploiting nearly every theater of conflict from World War II. Surprisingly, though, the network all but ignored the successful medical format of the previous season and left it to NBC and CBS to produce predictable imitations. *The Nurses* (on CBS) brought the familiar sudsy style of romantic serials to such topical

---

October 6, 1962
Phase two of *The Avengers* in Britain. Patrick Macnee continues his role as a dapper adventurer, but he is now identified as government agent John Steed, and teamed up with a beautiful woman, the ultra-cool widow Mrs. Catherine Gale (played by Honor Blackman). The writing for the revamped format is much sharper and more innovative: On the first new episode, a double agent is killed while appearing on a television talk show.

October 14, 1962
The Saint. Former Maverick brother Roger Moore portrays yet another Anglican spy, the very handsome Simon Templar a.k.a. The Saint, for Britain's ATV network.

April 1, 1963
Twenty-six-year-old Fred Silverman, who did his masters thesis at Ohio State in the late 1950s on ABC's programming schedule, becomes chief daytime programmer for CBS.

May 12, 1963
CBS bars twenty-one-year-old Bob Dylan from singing "Talkin' John Birch Society Blues" on *The Ed Sullivan Show,* even though Sullivan approved it. Dylan takes a hike and refuses to appear at all.

May 14, 1963
Newton Minow resigns as FCC chairman.

May 15, 1963
Gordon Cooper sends the first live television pictures from an American astronaut in orbit, but NASA refuses to allow the networks to show them.

August 30, 1963
The final weekday appearance of *American Bandstand.* Beginning September 7, the program will appear only on Saturday afternoons.

James Drury, star of the ninety-minute weekly series *The Virginian,* which ran for nine years on NBC. (*From* The Virginian. *Courtesy of MCA Television Limited*)

issues as syphilis, thalidomide babies, black nurses, and drug abuse, featuring an idealistic student nurse and the crusty but compassionate head nurse. For NBC, MGM sent medical drama down the road taken by Warner Brothers in the late Fifties (when it produced a Western that wasn't a Western, *77 Sunset Strip*) by offering a doctor show that wasn't quite a doctor show, *The Eleventh Hour.* Though they didn't stray far from the operating room, the stories of psychiatrist Theodore Bassett (Wendell Corey) demonstrated that the life, death, and romance found in television's hospitals could be presented within the structure of other occupations as well in so-called career dramas. The new series managed to incorporate topical and titillating angles such as a frigid woman and her unfaithful husband, illegitimate teenage pregnancy, abortion, and even the murder and rape of a girl by a young boy with taints of homosexuality. It was obvious that the format of career drama could be just as soapy as straight medical fare and the studios made plans to develop other spinoffs in the future.

Perhaps the season's biggest surprise was the successful revival of Jackie Gleason's old variety show after several misfired comebacks over the previous five years. It was virtually the same program Gleason had brought to CBS from DuMont a decade earlier (even Art Carney dropped by occasionally) and there was no reason for its revival to work this time. More than likely, the almost total absence of such material from TV for several years, combined with the position Gleason had achieved as one of the medium's immortals, generated enough energy and interest to make the show appear fresh and new again. In any case, there were a few new

wrinkles: Most of the skits were placed within the so-called "American Scene Magazine" and Gleason's Joe the Bartender character was joined every week by comedian Frank Fontaine as the slightly smashed Crazy Guggenheim, whose slurred speech and halfwit manner gave way to a deep operatic voice when he was asked to sing a song. Gleason once again registered high ratings on Saturday night and, within two years, used his clout to move the entire show to "the sun and fun capital of the world," Miami Beach.

Another TV veteran, *Tonight* host Jack Paar, decided the daily routine was too much and moved his variety format intact from his late night slot to prime time on Friday night. During his five years on the *Tonight* show, Paar had cultivated a peculiarly ambivalent image and, in an era of very predictable leading men, was practically the only unpredictable character on TV. He fluctuated between images of a "good-little-boy-who-loves-everybody" and a snarling, slightly blue, cobra that was liable to lash out at enemies, real and imagined, forever prompting the gossip columns to wonder: "What is Jack Paar *really* like?" During his heyday at the turn of the decade, he carried on innumerable public feuds on the air, insulting nationally known entertainers and columnists that had crossed him, even walking off his own show once after an NBC censor had arbitrarily blipped a mildly risque joke from the day's tape. He made the NBC brass come begging for his return and thereafter he seemed ready and willing to walk off again over other issues, such as his salary and work schedule. Paar had clout with NBC and he knew it. Though his move to prime time left a gaping hole in a slot the network had always found difficult to fill, NBC agreed to it. In prime time, Paar continued his successful approach to variety and interviews, which included a bevy of showbiz celebrity guests (Zsa Zsa Gabor, Jayne Mansfield), up-and-coming young talent (such as writer-turner-comic Woody Allen), nationally known public figures (Richard Nixon was a frequent guest), and home movies depicting his travels to exotic locales of the world. NBC was left with the problem of finding a late night successor.

The network chose Johnny Carson, the host of an ABC daytime game show, *Who Do You Trust?,* for the difficult job of maintaining NBC's lock on late night viewing. Though he had substituted for Paar on the *Tonight* show a number of times, Carson had a very different style and the network was not sure that he could maintain the program's consistently high ratings. NBC brass realized that Paar himself had been in a similar situation in 1957 when he took over the program, and had responded by shaping it to his own style and taste—and a ratings winner. They felt that Carson probably had the right instincts for the tough job and hoped for similar success. There was one important complication, however. Jack Paar had scheduled his departure from *Tonight* for April, 1962, and Carson's contract with ABC did not expire until October. Though he had been allowed to moonlight as host on a part time basis in the past, ABC refused to let him start a permanent stint on another network before his contract ran out. This resulted in a five-month interregnum that provided a golden opportunity for anyone else to attempt to snatch the late night audience from NBC. The network hung tight with guest hosts joining Paar's number two man, Hugh Downs, who remained on hand to provide some continuity. The expected challenge to the *Tonight* show came, ironically, from a former host of the program, Steve Allen, whose latest variety show for ABC had been foundering. Allen was signed by the Westinghouse (Group W) stations to host a pre-taped late night talk show that was syndicated across the country and run in direct competition with NBC. With a few months head start on Carson, Allen's new show, produced by Allan Sherman, managed to maintain respectable ratings even without his old familiar family of supporting performers. It was clear that Carson's task would not be easy.

Carson took over *Tonight* on October 1, 1962, bringing along his game show cohort, Ed McMahon, as his number two man. (Hugh Downs left the show in September to become the host of the morning *Today* program.) Like Paar, Carson grew comfortably into the job and tailored the show to fit his style, shifting the emphasis from variety to light talk. He carefully limited his involvement as a central performer to his daily monologue and occasional sketches, preferring instead the role of overall program manipulator whose main job was to keep up the pace by steering guests into productive areas of conversation (interesting, funny, ribald) and injecting humorous barbs. By not overextending himself, Carson was able to maintain viewer interest in his personality (a mixture of Midwestern farm boy naivete and Hollywood brashness), even without a familiar family of guests (McMahon and the band were the only regulars). He brought a relaxing charisma to the late night slot and was soon known to all simply as "Johnny." The *Tonight* show withstood challenges mounted both in syndication (Mike Douglas and Merv Griffin) and on the other networks (Les Crane and Joey Bishop), and Carson remained as host of the slot longer than Jerry Lester, Steve Allen, and Jack Paar combined, giving NBC unquestioned supremacy in late night programming into the 1980s.

For the rest of the broadcast day, though, CBS ruled the ratings. At one time in the 1962-63 season, CBS had all ten of the top ten daytime shows and eighteen of the top twenty prime time shows. Network president James Aubrey's decision to develop CBS's traditional strength, situation comedy, paid off far beyond his expectations. Though there were a few flops such as *Fair Exchange* (an attempt to expand sitcoms to a sixty-minute format) and the transplanted *Real McCoys* (with only Luke, Grandpa, and Pepino left), the new vehicle for Lucille Ball was an outright smash. She was reunited with Vivian Vance and played yet another TV widow trying to raise her children, outfox her boss (the omnipresent Gale Gordon), and earn extra money. Lucy quickly returned to the top ten with Jack Benny, Andy Griffith, and Danny Thomas. By February, the increasingly popular Dick Van Dyke joined their ranks. And then there were the Clampetts.

The Beverly Hillbillies opened to some of the worst reviews in TV history. Critics tore the show apart for its many obvious faults: The plots were abysmal, the dialogue childish, and the production Hollywood-to-the-core. What they failed to recognize or perhaps refused to accept was that the program was extremely funny. Viewers apparently had no difficulty detecting the comic strengths of the show because, within six weeks of its premiere, it became the number one show in the nation. Not since *The $64,000 Question* had a new program risen to the top so fast.

Like *Lucy, Bilko,* and *The Honeymooners, The Beverly Hillbillies* respected the basics of situation comedy. It contained both a humorous premise and central characters who had the potential for continuous exploitation week after week. Another product of the mind of Paul Henning (a refugee from *The Real McCoys*), the show presented a family of Ozark hillbillies who moved to California after striking oil on their property and becoming fabulously wealthy. The dichotomy of a hillbilly clan living in a sumptuous Beverly Hills mansion provided two important sources of humor: the naivete of the Clampetts as they persisted in their backwoods manners and morals in posh Beverly Hills, and the specious sham of Beverly Hills itself as snobby rich people put aside their exclusive

standards and bowed to the Clampett fortune. A careful mixture of craziness and sanity in the cast of characters allowed this setup to work perfectly as Henning took the make up of *I Love Lucy* and turned it on its head. In *I Love Lucy,* the generally realistic premise set Lucy as the "zany but lovable madcap" in a normally sane world. *The Beverly Hillbillies* was just the opposite. The premise was virtually impossible, so Henning used a dash of normality to set off the insanity, placing one rational mind in a totally lunatic world.

Jed Clampett (Buddy Ebsen) provided the oasis of reason among the loco characters. Jed was a good ol' boy who possessed most of the admirable traits connected with rural folks—he was decent, unpretentious, and sagacious. More than anyone else in the show, Jed understood not only his immediate family but the strange breed of people living in Beverly Hills as well. He quickly figured out how the big city folks operated, but he never assimilated, keeping his mountain clothes and downhome drawl despite his new-found wealth. Only Jed, the family and neighborhood peacemaker, kept his head while everyone else engaged in heated spats and irrational flights of fancy. Without him, the Clampett house and the program itself would have collapsed into an anarchistic rubble.

With Jed as a central hub of normality, the lunatic characters of the show could take off, as the philosophies and manners of Beverly Hills met those of the Ozark Mountains head on. Jed's mother-in-law, Granny (Irene Ryan), was an unreconstructed Confederate always ready to fly into a rage against the forces of modern America. She never accepted her new surroundings as her real home, remaining convinced that nothing in California would ever come close to what she had left behind in the hills. Granny made no attempt to hide her disdain for the city folks and she waged a never-ending war with anyone she saw attempting to upset her way of life. That included practically everybody.

Elly May (Donna Douglas), Jed's beautiful but unmarried daughter, was also off in a world of her own, though she had no quarrel with normal society as long as it played by the rules she was familiar with. Consequently, she continued to act the way she felt any normal girl should act, perpetually dumbfounding potential suitors by ignoring the traditional shy demure pose of young debutantes and persisting in her tomboyish independence. Elly May loved animals, from horned toads to goats, and was also proud to display her physical strength, easily outwrestling any prospective husband. She never appreciated the fact that she had moved into an entirely new world and she could never understand why she had so little success in finding a mate in the wilds of Beverly Hills.

Elly May was a clarion of clarity compared to her cousin, Jethro Bodine (Max Baer, son of the former heavyweight champ), the ultimate country rube, a refugee from the sixth grade with no connections to reality. Jethro had no difficulty understanding the big city—it was one huge playground. Very much a ten-year-old mind in a twenty-year-old body, he engaged in childish mischief playing with such Beverly Hills toys as hot rods, swimmin' pools, and movie stars. More than anyone else, Jethro needed the constant attention of his Uncle Jed for discipline and guidance, so that he wouldn't be swept away by the distractions and excitement of the city and lose his hillbilly roots.

Trying to uphold the reputation of Beverly Hills were Jed's banker, Milburn Drysdale (Raymond Bailey), and his secretary, Jane Hathaway (Nancy Kulp). The pair provided an upper class mirror of the Clampetts, funny in their own marvelously lampooned world and even funnier when they tried to imitate the hillbilly ways of their clients. Drysdale filled the traditional sitcom image of a business executive: He was a dimwitted, amoral schemer driven totally by the possession and acquisition of money. Beyond that, Drysdale constantly humiliated himself to satisfy every whim of the Clampetts. He couldn't risk the possibility that they might move their boodle elsewhere, so he willingly bent every rule of genteel conduct for them. Miss Hathaway was a stuck-up, over-educated snobbish big business secretary who was as totally dedicated to pleasing the Clampetts as her boss and she effectively bullied anyone who dared cross her path. The two were models of self-serving dedication and they stood at the center of high society's world as it fell to the hillbillies.

In spite of all the reviewers who told viewers *The Beverly Hillbillies* was a stupid show, the audience laughed. It really didn't matter that the plots were innocuous and the dialogue quite silly. The characters were genuinely amusing and it was a joy to see them go through their paces. The program was an exaggerated farce, in the tradition of television's most cherished comedy shows. And it was funny.

The overwhelming success of *The Beverly Hillbillies,* and comedy in general in 1962–63, propelled CBS to an astounding lead in nighttime ratings. On the average, CBS's prime time schedule earned higher ratings that year than any other network schedule in television's past. Added to its total domination of daytime programming, the season's prime time success made CBS appear invincible, and most of the hit shows looked as if they could last for years. More importantly, the success of *The Beverly Hillbillies* and veteran *Andy Griffith* convinced not only CBS, but the industry at large, that rural-based situation comedies were the new key to the public's heart. Once again, the networks stood ready to give the public exactly what it wanted—in abundance.

23. Hands Across the Ocean

CBS REIGNED as the undisputed king of television entertainment programming in 1963 and network president James Aubrey aimed to consolidate that position in the new fall line-up. He shifted the time slots of a few veterans, added several new drama and variety programs, and began the seemingly endless procession of country clones from the wildly successful *Beverly Hillbillies.* As Aubrey was fine-tuning the prime time schedule, CBS News moved to regain its preeminence in the nightly news race, one of the few program periods in which the network wasn't number one. Though CBS was the acknowledged leader in producing news documentaries, the much more commercially lucrative nightly news slot was then consistently dominated by NBC's *Huntley-Brinkley Report.*

The perpetual battle between the CBS and NBC news departments had begun on the radio in the late Thirties. In an era dominated by a reliance on outside wire services for the latest headlines, CBS had taken the lead in developing its own news-gathering operation. During World War II, Edward R. Murrow's live on-the-spot reports from the front allowed the entire country to share the dramatic events in Europe, and put CBS far out in front of NBC in news prestige and ratings. As the networks set up their television news operations in the Forties, CBS took the lead in this new medium by using a constant, familiar figure as its nightly news anchor—young Douglas Edwards. By 1950, NBC's slick professional newsreel show, *Camel News Caravan* with John Cameron Swayze, had passed Edwards and had remained at the top for several years, fading from number one in the mid-Fifties as the public tired of Swayze's overly theatrical style. In 1956, NBC replaced him with Chet Huntley and David Brinkley, a news team that had proved very popular covering the political conventions that year, and by 1958 it was on top once again with *The Huntley-Brinkley Report,* retaining that lead into the Sixties.

Despite the strong competition between the two networks, their fifteen-minute TV news programs were remarkably similar and stuck to the simple formula of a news anchor reading the headlines for major news items and covering a few stories in moderate detail, possibly with accompanying film. The network news departments could cover scheduled special events such as presidential elections quite well, but were limited to a handful of cities for breaking stories. The two news giants had only recently begun acting like independent news organizations at all by setting up their own camera crews and bureaus in their New York, Washington, and Chicago locations, but it remained virtually impossible for them to cover adequately events in most other American cities. The networks still had to rely on local affiliates for film footage and reports from out in the hustings. In December, 1961, CBS announced a major change in its news-gathering operation as it established four additional domestic bureaus—in Los Angeles, Denver, Atlanta, and Dallas—to give the network the capability of covering, on its own, almost any news event in the United States. The expansion allowed the CBS nightly news program to shift from the leisurely newsreel style of the past to a roving reporter format that encouraged its bureau heads, such as Dan Rather in Dallas (newly hired from Houston's KHOU), to dig for stories and move immediately on major events. Accompanying this behind-the-scenes reorganization was an important on-camera substitution. After sixteen years as anchor, Douglas Edwards was deftly deposed by CBS and replaced by Walter Cronkite, a newsman who had been CBS's man at political conventions, elections, and space shots for over a decade and who had already become, in the public's eye, Mr. CBS News. Cronkite took over the show in April, 1962, and CBS hoped that his proven ability to engender public trust would attract more viewers than the effective but somehow distant Edwards. These changes set the stage for the most important move of all—expanding the length of the nightly news show, which had remained at fifteen minutes since its inception in the Forties. With the number of network bureaus more than doubled, fifteen minutes wasn't enough time to present all the stories they could turn out. Though affiliates were reluctant to surrender lucrative local news time to an expanded national newscast, after intensive lobbying by the network, the locals agreed.

On September 2, 1963, CBS launched its expanded news program with a new set, a new regular feature, a special opening night interview, and an intense publicity campaign usually reserved only for fall premieres of entertainment programs. In a departure from the traditional sparse studio news set, CBS placed Cronkite at a desk directly in the newsroom itself, with other people working at their own desks visible in the background, and the noise of the news teletype machines audible as well. He was joined by Eric Sevareid, who began fourteen years of nightly commentary and analysis that evening. As a special opening night attraction, Cronkite conducted a lengthy, exclusive interview with President Kennedy in which they discussed Vietnam, civil rights, and the 1964 election—topics that the expanded news programs could begin

MONDAY

	7:30	8:00	8:30	9:00	9:30	10:00	10:30	
	THE OUTER LIMITS			Wagon Train		BREAKING POINT		ABC
	To Tell The Truth	I've Got A Secret	The Lucy Show	Danny Thomas Show	Andy Griffith Show	EAST SIDE, WEST SIDE		CBS
	NBC Monday Night At The Movies				HOLLYWOOD AND THE STARS	Sing Along With Mitch		NBC

TUESDAY

	7:30	8:00	8:30	9:00	9:30	10:00	10:30	
	Combat!		McHale's Navy	THE GREATEST SHOW ON EARTH		THE FUGITIVE		ABC
	Marshal Dillon	Red Skelton Hour		PETTICOAT JUNCTION	Jack Benny Program	Garry Moore Show		CBS
	MR. NOVAK		Redigo	RICHARD BOONE SHOW		Andy Williams Show / The Bell Telephone Hour		NBC

WEDNESDAY

	7:30	8:00	8:30	9:00	9:30	10:00	10:30	
	The Adventures Of Ozzie And Harriet	PATTY DUKE SHOW	The Price Is Right	Ben Casey		CHANNING		ABC
	CBS Reports / CHRONICLES		GLYNIS	The Beverly Hillbillies	Dick Van Dyke Show	DANNY KAYE SHOW		CBS
	The Virginian			ESPIONAGE		The Eleventh Hour		NBC

THURSDAY

	7:30	8:00	8:30	9:00	9:30	10:00	10:30	
	The Flintstones	Donna Reed Show	My Three Sons	THE JIMMY DEAN SHOW		Sid Caesar Show / EDIE ADAMS SHOW	local	ABC
	Password	Rawhide		Perry Mason		The Nurses		CBS
	TEMPLE HOUSTON		Dr. Kildare		Hazel	THE KRAFT SUSPENSE THEATER @Perry Como's Kraft Music Hall		NBC

FRIDAY

	7:30	8:00	8:30	9:00	9:30	10:00	10:30	
	77 Sunset Strip		BURKE'S LAW		THE FARMER'S DAUGHTER	Fight Of The Week	Make That Spare	ABC
	GREAT ADVENTURE		Route 66		The Twilight Zone	Alfred Hitchcock Hour		CBS
	International Showtime		BOB HOPE PRESENTS THE CHRYSLER THEATER @The Bob Hope Show		HARRY'S GIRLS	Jack Paar Show		NBC

SATURDAY

	7:30	8:00	8:30	9:00	9:30	10:00	10:30	
	Hootenanny		Lawrence Welk Show		THE JERRY LEWIS SHOW [to 11:30]			ABC
	Jackie Gleason Show		THE NEW PHIL SILVERS SHOW	The Defenders		Gunsmoke		CBS
	THE LIEUTENANT		Joey Bishop Show	NBC Saturday Night At The Movies				NBC

SUNDAY

	7:00	7:30	8:00	8:30	9:00	9:30	10:00	10:30	
	local	THE TRAVELS OF JAMIE McPHEETERS		ARREST AND TRIAL			100 GRAND	ABC News Reports	ABC
	Lassie	MY FAVORITE MARTIAN	Ed Sullivan Show		JUDY GARLAND SHOW		Candid Camera	What's My Line	CBS
	BILL DANA SHOW	Walt Disney's Wonderful World Of Color		GRINDL	Bonanza		DuPont Show Of The Week / NBC Specials		NBC

to cover with regularity and depth never before possible on television. One week later, NBC expanded *The Huntley-Brinkley Report* to thirty minutes (including its own exclusive interview with President Kennedy), and joined the shift to the more comprehensive approach to the news. Network news had done more that double in length; its quality had improved tremendously in the process.

When the fall's new entertainment programs appeared, though, news once again receded into the background and viewers began selecting their favorites for the season. To no one's surprise, CBS continued its domination of prime time television with *The Beverly Hillbillies* again in the number one spot and situation comedy in general thriving. There was also considerable interest in variety because two major entertainment figures who had for years avoided television series commitments signed up for new weekly programs: Judy Garland and Jerry Lewis. Neither survived the season.

Judy Garland had triumphed the previous season in a lowkey, easy-going special with friends Frank Sinatra and Dean Martin, and she had agreed to try the weekly grind for CBS by continuing that same style of program with Norman Jewison as producer. Unfortunately, this mood was not successfully transplanted to her series which suffered from weak writing and bad casting. In a disastrous mismatch, Jerry Van Dyke (younger brother of Dick) was given the "show-within-a-show" role of Judy's teacher in TV technique. The boisterous Van Dyke personality was completely

at odds with Garland's and the hoped-for humorous interactions between the two fell flat. Occasionally particular guest star segments of the show worked well, such as Garland's numbers with her young daughter, Liza Minnelli, and up-and-coming young singer Barbra Streisand, but the success of the program rested on the weekly scripts and Garland's overall performance, and both were far too erratic. Against the steadily increasing strength of NBC's *Bonanza*, the show brought in embarrassingly low ratings, despite the strong lead-in provided by Ed Sullivan. Garland went through several producers before her program quietly expired in the spring.

ABC took the biggest variety gamble of the season by providing a 120-minute vehicle for TV's *enfant terrible*, Jerry Lewis. The network invested nearly $9 million in the project, including a share of the expensive, extensive remodeling of the El Capitan theater in Hollywood (scene of Richard Nixon's Checkers speech) to serve as the locale for the show. Besides being live (in an era when nearly every other show was on film or tape), the series violated several unwritten laws of prime time television. Variety shows were usually given a one-hour block to fill—Lewis's new live show was two hours every week. Network prime time schedules normally ended at 11:00 P.M.—Lewis's show ran from 9:30 P.M. until 11:30 P.M. Most variety shows stocked themselves with a family of secondary comics and singers to help ease the pressure on the host— Lewis tried to carry the whole show by himself, relying only on guest appearances by his well-known showbiz friends for support. Lewis was certainly funny enough to carry his own television show but, in this case, he tried too many innovations at once, and the program fell flat in its premiere. On the very first show everybody was very tense. Camera shots and mike cues were off. A huge screen set up so that the studio audience could see the show just as it was seen by the home audience failed to work and ended up blocking their view. With the audience blinded, Lewis's timing was thrown off. Worst of all, the skits were bad. Reviewers labeled it a "tasteless flop" and the program never recovered. The harder Lewis worked, the more frantic the show seemed to get, never settling down to acquire any style, pace, or direction. Instead of being an "informal two hours of fun, entertainment, discussion, and interviews in a spontaneous atmosphere" it took on the appearance of a weekly Jerry Lewis telethon without the cripples, containing a few entertaining performances by superstar guests amid extended stretches of filler. Perhaps *The Jerry Lewis Show* might have had a chance if it had been only one hour long so that the writers wouldn't have been so desperate for material, or if it had been prerecorded on tape so that some of the more complicated bits could have been staged several times and reworked. Even against such tough competition as *Gunsmoke* and the NBC movie, Lewis might have then triumphed instead of being clobbered by them. In December, ABC, making the best of a bad situation, paid Lewis $2 million to tear up the contract for forty shows. Lewis closed his final show in anger, blaming his failure on the networks and sponsors who, he said, didn't like his "non-conformist ideas." "I don't like to do like I'm supposed to!" he explained.

Though Lewis was gone, ABC was still stuck with the remodeled El Capitan theater. In a surprise move, the network decided to replace the flopped Jerry Lewis variety show with another variety show from the same theater. What's more, *The Hollywood Palace* (as both the series and theater were rechristened) didn't even have a regular host. Instead, the program used guest stars as hosts to what was essentially a sixty-minute vaudeo show straight out of the *Toast of the Town* mold, featuring eight different acts that were presented in the lavish, almost garish, setting of the cavernous Hollywood Palace. Although originating in Hollywood, the show brought the look and feel of Las Vegas-style revues back to network television. Apparently, the absence of such material and the wide range of guest hosts (from Bing Crosby to Phyllis Diller) made the show appear fresh and exciting because, against all odds, it caught on and lasted until the end of the decade.

The Hollywood Palace was another case of a classic format being revived and updated for a new generation of viewers, just as sitcoms such as *The Dick Van Dyke Show* and drama programs such as *The Defenders* had successfully brought these forms into the Sixties. Though some mourned the passing of the originals, especially in live drama, it was necessary and inevitable for television to move on. In June of 1963, the *U.S. Steel Hour* and the *Armstrong Circle Theater* were axed, and at the end of the 1963–64 season, the last of the New York-based drama series, David Susskind's *DuPont Show of the Week,* was also canceled. The concept of weekly live drama (or live-on-tape) had fit well with television's early years but seemed an anachronism in an age of mass entertainment shows and high pressure ratings races. More importantly, though the golden age of television produced many priceless moments, it had been elevated, in memory, to a higher position than it ever deserved. There were, after all, many very bad live dramas, and the productions were often not really the thrilling challenge many people fondly looked back on. Upon the demise of his *DuPont Show,* David Susskind, who had carried on live drama almost single-handedly for the past few years, candidly acknowledged that the excitement of staging such drama was mostly "hallucinatory—like the kicks induced by cocaine, it's not worth the hangover." With the avenues opened by filmed series, it seemed ridiculous to endure the physical limitations of the studio, the omnipresent feeling of claustrophobia, and the occasional minor but distracting fluffs of live productions. Film was easier to work with, cost about the same, and, if handled with discipline and skill, could rival the best work from the golden age of television.

Susskind's Talent Associates achieved artistic success in a filmed series that very season with *East Side, West Side,* a career drama modeled somewhat after *The Defenders.* The series was shot in New York City and dealt with contemporary social problems faced by a Manhattan social worker, Neil Brock (George C. Scott) and his secretary, Jane Foster (Cicely Tyson). Each week's episode focused on a particular aspect of the seamy side of the big city such as prostitution, juvenile delinquency, and inadequate housing, and often developed into something of a social docudrama on the injustices of American life, with Scott and Tyson sometimes used only peripherally as part of the discussion. In spite of such a potentially dry format, many episodes were gems of insight and warmth (such as James Earl Jones's portrayal of an enraged but powerless Harlem father whose baby had died of a rat bite) and the series emerged as one of the best attempts ever to combine dramatic entertainment with social commentary. Nonetheless, there was not very much latitude in the show's premise; as a mere social worker Scott could do little but offer words of advice when confronted with yet another problem. In a mid-season attempt to remedy this

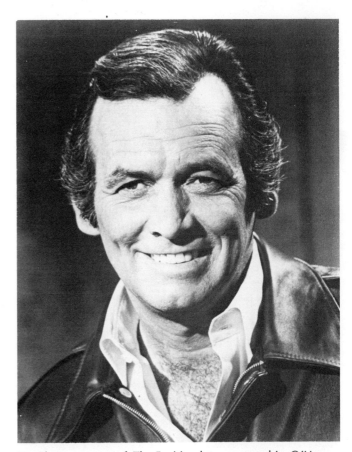

David Janssen, star of *The Fugitive,* later appeared in *O'Hara U.S. Treasury* and *Harry-O.* (From *O'Hara U.S. Treasury.* Courtesy of MCA Television Limited)

shortcoming, Scott's character went to work for a local congressman so that possible solutions could be presented. Despite the first class writing and production, and the variation in format, the show never succeeded in shaking off its generally maudlin tone and vanished after only one season.

The most successful new dramatic show of the season came from ABC and producer Quinn Martin and, rather than trying to expose all the social ills of the country, it focused on the intense struggle of one man, Dr. Richard Kimble, an outlaw that society was actually out to destroy. Loosely based on Victor Hugo's *Les Misérables* (with a bit of *Route 66* thrown in), *The Fugitive* followed the flight of Dr. Kimble (David Janssen), who had been unjustly accused and convicted of murdering his wife, but who had managed to escape his police guard and execution in the confusion following the wreck of the train carrying him to the death house. Though free, Kimble faced the twin tasks of finding a mysterious one-armed man he had seen leaving the scene of the crime (but who could not be found at the time of the trial) and evading the pursuit of police Lieutenant Philip Gerard (Barry Morse) who was "obsessed with his capture."

In a TV world populated almost exclusively by winners, Kimble was a loser, free to go anywhere he wanted in the United States, but living in constant fear of capture. He was a prisoner of the entire country because anyone, even those he befriended in his travels, could turn him in, wittingly or unwittingly. Whenever Kimble found himself becoming too involved in people's lives, he would "clam up" and attempt to fade into the background, unnoticed. As a convicted murderer under a death sentence, any move that made him stand out—however briefly—was literally a life-and-death gamble. Yet despite the risks, he was inevitably drawn into other people's lives because he needed them in order to evade

the law, track the one-armed man, and escape his own loneliness. Janssen's lowkey acting style captured perfectly the behavior of a man on the run, down to the guarded mannerisms and nervous tics of a fugitive. His sad, quick smile (a brief rise in one corner of his mouth while the rest of his face remained immobile) said it all: Dr. Kimble could never find true peace, even if he met people who believed in his innocence; he had to keep running and to find the one-armed man because the alternative for him was death. No amount of human kindness could change that cold, hard fact. The tension created by this setup gave the series an underlying dramatic edge that was skillfully underplayed but constantly present.

In many ways, *The Fugitive* was a program ahead of its time, presenting the intense struggle of a truly alienated American years before the phrase became popular. Other characters such as Maverick and Paladin had operated on a different moral plane than traditional society, but they had chosen that life, thrived on it, and could one day probably settle somewhere without much difficulty. Richard Kimble could never let down his guard, relax, and rejoin normal society. He had been forced outside its boundaries by its legal machinery even though he was innocent, and his only chance for survival rested with his own individual strength and determination. Until he could find a man the police forces had been unable to locate, even while dodging these same forces himself, Kimble was an outcast, a hunted man as well as a hunter. In the late Sixties, television and movies tried to exploit the feeling of alienation that seemed to grip many people in the country then, but most of those vehicles were shallow and failed to grasp the scope of emotions involved. *The Fugitive* managed to handle the concept of alienation with considerably more success and at the same time treat more complex themes of justice, guilt, and justified paranoia as well. Though such themes had previously appeared on TV, chiefly in the extinct drama anthologies, *The Fugitive* developed them over time in a well produced weekly series. It took four years for Richard Kimble to come face-to-face with the one-armed man. Through it all, the series maintained strong ratings (it was frequently in the top ten) and a loyal audience that found itself caught up in both the characters and the premise, as the series seemed to touch an almost hidden vein of American sympathies.

The refinement of themes and formats from television's early days was not limited to entertainment programs. One of the devastating issues of the Fifties, blacklisting, was also modified, renamed, and ushered into the Sixties, even though it had been assumed that the triumph of John Henry Faulk in 1962 had marked the end of the odious practice. It hadn't.

In early 1963, ABC decided to latch onto the latest teen music fad, folk music, with *Hootenanny,* a weekly series taped on various college campuses. For the April premiere program, the reigning queen of American folk music, Joan Baez, was slated to appear with Pete Seeger, the man who had invented the word "hootenanny" along with Woody Guthrie. Then ABC announced that it would not accept Seeger because of his well-known leftist politics and, in particular, because on August 18, 1955, during the height of blacklisting, he had refused to answer questions put to him by the House Un-American Activities Committee on his Communist party ties. Blacklisting was not dead, and ABC was not alone in its apprehension over Seeger. In January, 1962, NBC had vetoed a scheduled appearance by Seeger on *The Jack Paar Show* and, in early 1963, CBS had done the same to his planned participation in a folk music special. The networks were still wary of controversial figures and allegations of subversive activities, and now relied on a policy of "network censorship" (the phrase seemed less McCarthy-esque than blacklisting) to protect themselves. Though Seeger and the issue of blacklisting were very soon forgotten, the issue of censorship remained and, six years later, Seeger would once again bring it to a head.

Hootenanny went on without Seeger—and without Joan Baez, the Greenbriar Boys, Tom Paxton, and Ramblin' Jack Elliott, who all refused to perform on the program in protest. Despite this disastrous beginning, the show recovered and became a surprise hit, hanging on through the spring and summer to earn a niche in ABC's fall schedule for 1963. *Hootenanny* was an effective outlet for folk music and introduced many performers previously unknown to the American public, including Canada's Ian and Sylvia, Ireland's Clancy Brothers, and natives such as the Simon Sisters (Carly and Lucy), the Smothers Brothers, and the very all-American Chad Mitchell Trio. At the same time, the show displayed little musical and emotional connection with the new wave of folk protest then in vogue. It was the folk equivalent to the Dick Clark *Beechnut Show,* presenting a new form of music in an antiseptic forum. Host Jack Linkletter (Art's son) was, like Dick Clark, more a clean-cut announcer than someone in tune with the spirit of the music. He and the producers were content with the happy-go-lucky song-around-a-campfire style of such safe singers as Glenn Yarbrough and the Limeliters, the Rooftop Singers, and the New Christy Minstrels, and they tried to avoid the controversy inherent in protest figures like Bob Dylan, Phil Ochs, and Pete Seeger. Though *Hootenanny* lasted the season, it, and the entire folk music boom, was soon outdistanced by a seemingly brand new musical style that slipped in over the horizon.

In October, 1963, *The Ed Sullivan Show* featured British singer Cliff Richard, who had been the reigning king of rock'n'roll in Britain for five years, but had never made a dent in the American charts. Then, early in November, Sullivan presented Billy J. Kramer and the Dakotas, a group managed by young British impresario Brian Epstein. Something was up. Sullivan, a man who had made his name in television by being one step ahead of the public's mood, was devoting his attention to the British brand of rock'n'roll, a form usually ridiculed, if not completely ignored, in America.

Sullivan had actually been a little late in picking up on the last major teen phenomenon, Elvis Presley, so perhaps he was especially sensitive to the success in Britain of a new generation of home-grown rockers which he saw first-hand while on vacation the previous summer. The frantic teenage airport receptions and the extensive play in the British media left him totally nonplussed and he decided to take the lead in bringing this new British sound to America, assuming that it could be just as big in the U.S., if not bigger. In the last week of November, 1963, he agreed to present Brian Epstein's premiere group, the Beatles, as headliners on his show in February, 1964. At that point, American music circles considered the Beatles just another British group that had been successful in England but unable to stir any interest in the United States, and the first class treatment accorded the band seemed highly unusual. After all, they had never performed in America and three singles and an album released in the States in 1963 had gone nowhere. By the time Sullivan introduced the Beatles to his audience on February 9, 1964, his agreement seemed nothing short of brilliant. They were the number one group in the nation with records topping both the single and album charts. In just over two months, an extensive push by their new American record company, Capitol, had turned the Beatles into a national mania and their song "I Want To Hold Your Hand" had become one of the fastest selling records ever released. Millions of Americans were eager to see the group perform live for the first time.

It was a peculiar evening. Police stations dutifully reported an amazing dropoff of teenage crime during the show as between sixty and seventy percent of the American television audience (over twenty-five million homes) tuned to CBS. The Beatles opened and closed the show and in the space of one hour were transformed from motionless publicity photos to real live human beings with distinct individual personalities: Ringo Starr, the plain one with the big nose, sat in the back, pounding them skins. George Harrison, the quiet mysterious one, played lead guitar while Paul McCartney and John Lennon handled (respectively) bass and rhythm guitars as well as the lead vocals. Paul was the cute one while John ("sorry girls, he's married") projected more of a tough guy image. Just as Presley had his hip swivel, the Beatles displayed their own distinctive symbol—a mop-top hair style that shook as they sang, "Yeah! Yeah! Yeah!" Besides seeing and hearing the group perform, viewers were also exposed to their first direct dose of Beatlemania as the studio cameras focused on hundreds of teenage girls in the audience weeping, screaming, and even fainting. Parents didn't know whether to laugh at the group and the screaming fans or condemn them, but kids across the country drank it all in. In that one night, as television once again allowed millions to share an experience as one, the medium created a musical and cultural supergroup.

The Beatles were not really doing anything brand new. They were just British musicians who were playing their own version of American rock'n'roll from the Presley era. Nonetheless, their distinctive accents and dress made them appear new, and their

September 24, 1963
Petticoat Junction. (CBS). Paul Henning begins spinning off successful series from *The Beverly Hillbillies.*

September 24, 1963
Mr. Novak. (NBC). James Franciscus plays the Dr. Kildare of the classroom, with Dean Jagger in the Dr. Gillespie role of mentor-principal.

December 30, 1963
Let's Make a Deal. (NBC). Monty Hall begins exploiting basic human greed every weekday afternoon.

January 21, 1964
Ed Murrow resigns as director of the U.S. Information Agency due to poor health.

March 2, 1964
Fred Friendly replaces Dick Salant as president of CBS News. Salant moves to a more amorphous position, CBS vice president for corporate affairs.

March 25, 1964
Live trans-Pacific television begins, via the Relay II satellite.

April 30, 1964
UHF Day. From this point on, all new television sets must be capable of receiving channels 14 through 83.

August 13, 1964
CBS buys the New York Yankees.

September 11, 1964
After twenty years, boxing vanishes from weekly network television as ABC's *Fight of the Week* expires in Cleveland. Don Dunphy calls the last fight: Dick Tiger beats Don Fullmer in ten rounds.

Ed Sullivan *(c.)* brought the Beatles into millions of American homes. (The Beatles: from *l.* Ringo Starr, George Harrison, John Lennon, Paul McCartney.) *(Courtesy Capitol Records)*

overnight exposure to millions of Americans helped create an instant interest in other British rock groups such as the Dave Clark Five and the Rolling Stones, who soon turned up on shows such as Sullivan's and *The Hollywood Palace.* In addition, the desire for *anything* English, which had been building with the increasingly successful series of the theatrical films featuring British secret agent James Bond, exploded into nearly every aspect of American culture with the coming of the Beatles. American television executives, who had begun casting eyes at Britain as a source of possible inspiration for programming, took a closer look, sensing the possibility of uncovering a first class hit for the American market. This was a distinct change from the image British television had carried throughout the Fifties.

Under the watchful eye of the British government, the noncommercial British Broadcasting Corporation had always followed a philosophy that steered away from the strong concentration of pure entertainment programs that shaped American television and focused instead on material that was relatively bland in comparison. In September, 1955, after much wrangling, commercial television came to Britain and began to compete with the BBC. At first, the newcomers relied heavily on tons of imported American filmed series, turning out only a few shows of their own that made the return trip to the States (those shows such as *The Adventures of Robin Hood* and *Ivanhoe* dealt with traditional American views of England: knights, castles, robber barons, and the like). By 1960,

British television began producing its own programs that equalled, and sometimes surpassed, American fare.

Britain's first major homegrown hit was Granada TV's *Coronation Street,* a soap opera. Instead of dealing with beautiful rich people, as traditional American soapers did, the program centered on the exploits of just plain folk in the working class city of Manchester, the sort that might be found in America in *The Honeymooners.* Gleason's show was an exception, though, to the general American view of TV heroes. In Britain, *Coronation Street* quickly became the top-rated show and working class settings became commonplace in other series.

One and one-half years later, the BBC (aiming to meet its commercial competition head-on) presented a successful sitcom version of *Coronation Street, Steptoe and Son,* starring Wilfrid Brambell (later cast as Paul McCartney's grandfather in the Beatles' film "A Hard Day's Night") and Harry Corbett. The two portrayed Albert and Harold Steptoe, father and son junk dealers who were forever squabbling over money and the future. As the elder Steptoe, Brambell played to perfection the garrulous and possessive aging father determined to prevent his son from leaving the homestead; he often resorted to underhanded tricks to break up Harold's budding romances or inclinations to venture into a new business on his own. He always succeeded as Harold inevitably decided to remain in the junk business, at home, with his dad, despite the constant interference. The vibrancy of Brambell and Corbett in their characters, as well as the unique nature of the setting, quickly caught on with the British public and by late 1963 *Steptoe and Son* replaced *Coronation Street* for a while as the country's most popular program. It was one of the first important British programs to catch an American network's attention and NBC showed a few *Steptoe and Son* clips on *The Jack Paar Show* in April, 1964, while subcontracting with Embassy Pictures to produce a pilot for an American version of the show. The pilot, however, was rejected and plans for the series eventually shelved. Even adapted for American tastes, the "life among the lowly" concept just didn't seem quite right for the Stateside audience, which had been weaned on solid middle class heroes.

British television's first major success in the American market was with its own particular brand of spy adventures, a field that had been remarkably unsuccessful in the U.S. Throughout the Fifties, American producers had insisted on presenting hackneyed run-throughs of stereotyped cold war clashes between square-jawed Americans upholding democracy and freedom and Communist forces made up of unbelievably stupid agents with heavy foreign accents, in such vehicles as *I Led Three Lives* (starring Richard Carlson), *Biff Baker, USA* (starring Alan Hale, Jr.), and *The Hunter* (starring Barry Nelson). None of these were very successful and the networks were convinced that spy shows just didn't sell. Ironically, James Bond, the smooth, sophisticated spy whose adventure novels launched the British passion for international intrigue, was nearly made into an American television series several times during the decade.

In 1954, shortly after the publication of the first James Bond novel, *Casino Royale,* CBS paid author Ian Fleming $1,000 for the rights to do a special one-hour live TV drama production of the story. The network cast veteran TV spy Barry Nelson as agent-playboy James Bond (a role almost identical to Nelson's U.S. agent-playboy character from the old *Hunter* series) and Peter Lorre as a ruthless Soviet operative, and on October 21 presented the adaptation on its *Climax* anthology series. CBS wasn't interested in any further adventures, so Fleming sold the theatrical film rights to that story and turned out two more novels. The next year, working with NBC producer Henry Morganthau III, he began writing a new half-hour TV adventure series to be filmed on location in Jamaica, *Commander Jamaica.* James Bond served as a model for the main character in the pilot script, but the project fell through so Fleming used the script as a basis for the next book in the Bond series, *Dr. No,* instead. Several years later, in 1958, CBS decided to try a TV series featuring the actual Bond character (titled, appropriately, *James Bond, Secret Agent*), and Fleming wrote plot outlines for six episodes. Once again, the planned series was shelved, so he adapted three of the TV treatments for his anthology of James Bond short stories, *For Your Eyes Only,* and concentrated his energies on using the character as the basis for a series of theatrical films. (The *Casino Royale* film project had never materialized.) Fleming at last succeeded in selling the options to his remaining Bond novels in 1961 to producers Harry Saltzman and Albert Broccoli who, in turn, convinced United Artists to finance the project, and in 1962 the first James Bond film, "Dr. No," appeared. It earned over $1 million in Britain alone and the 1963 followup, "From Russia With Love," was released at the height of the spy craze in Britain, and became a major box office success in the U.S.

British television had begun to cash in on the increasing interest in spies and international espionage at the turn of the decade, and each of its three major spy programs (*Danger Man, The Saint,* *The Avengers*) eventually made it to American television. In September, 1960, ATV, a British commercial network, produced its own version of James Bond, secret agent John Drake (Patrick McGoohan) in *Danger Man.* Unlike America's old spy vehicles, the series showed the enemies of democracy as intelligent equals to the government's agents, and their elaborate plans of subversion unfolded in well-written, engrossing adventures (specific politics were, of course, downplayed). McGoohan's punchy independent persona gave the show an extra lift that attracted American attention and CBS picked it up for a brief run in the summer of 1961, when it attracted critical acclaim but few viewers.

One year later, another series featuring global intrigue began in Britain, Leslie Charteris's *The Saint,* starring Roger Moore as Simon Templar. Templar was presented as a handsome, wealthy, sophisticated playboy in the Bond mold, but the program was really quite bland. The villains were usually involved in moderately elaborate but routine crimes and, very often, Templar emerged as nothing more than a vintage private eye updated for the Sixties. Nonetheless, Moore was already a familiar figure to American audiences from his stint in several Warner Brothers action-adventure series and *The Saint* was picked up for the American market rather quickly—first through syndication to individual stations in 1963 and, four years later, by NBC for a network run. The more traditional approach of the program made it much more attractive to American programmers interested in exploiting the spy craze with a fairly safe product. A more unconventional British spy series, *The Avengers,* had to wait until 1966 for its extraordinary style and premise to reach American viewers.

The Avengers began in January, 1961, as a moderately straightforward spy show featuring Patrick Macnee and Ian Hendry as dilettante men-about-town involved in solving crimes and avenging evil. In October, 1962, the premise was revamped and the show began displaying a distinctively different tone that turned it into a British cult favorite with a small but rapidly growing legion of fans. Macnee was identified as government agent John Steed and joined in his adventures by Mrs. Catherine Gale, a widow (played by Honor Blackman). The two were thrust into complicated plots hatched by peculiar villains and the series began adopting a subtle, tongue-in-cheek approach that produced bizarre yet intriguing stories. Not only were the cases highly unusual, but the relationship between Steed and Mrs. Gale was completely unheard of. They operated as a team and she was his equal in every way. They both defended themselves with skill and finesse, never losing their British cool and sly smiles even in the most dire situations, and neither was dependent on the other for constant rescue. What's more, the romantic connection between the two was kept deliciously unclear; there were hints of *amour* but the viewer was left to decide whether there was, in fact, a liaison or not.

Only a few months after *The Avengers* shifted to its more offbeat style, full-bodied satire came to the BBC with *That Was The Week That Was.* Premiering in December, 1962, *TW3* (as it was known) marked a major step forward in British broadcasting because it was the first show to poke fun at, and actually ridicule, well-known politicians and office holders. A stock company of players, hosted by David Frost and featuring singer Millicent Martin, performed generally irreverent skits to press their points, occasionally even indulging in shock tactics (such as name calling) to catch viewers' attention. The writers based the words and music of the show on the events of the previous week, giving *TW3* a feeling of immediacy akin to a cabaret comedy ensemble. The program was biting, controversial, very funny, and alternately admired and resented by viewers, depending on who was the latest target of abuse. Nonetheless, while a shock to Britain, such satire seemed unthinkable for American television. If any series was unlikely to appear in the United States, *That Was The Week That Was* was it. Yet on Sunday, November 10, 1963, NBC presented a one-hour special-pilot for an American version of *TW3*. Obviously, something had changed.

The mood of the country had grown less somber and less paranoid since 1960. The new spirit was due partly to the reduction in cold war tensions and also to the youth and humor of the Kennedy administration. People simply felt more like laughing. In this atmosphere, NBC decided to take a chance on satire in America. Produced by Leland Hayward and hosted by Henry Fonda, the pilot for *TW3* wasn't as flip or as rough as its British cousin, but it presented some of the freshest, funniest material to hit U.S. TV in years. The guests on the special were traditional humorists including Mike Nichols and Elaine May, Henry Morgan, and Charly Manna, but their humor was much more topical than usual. In one hour they directed barbs at President Kennedy, Richard Nixon, Barry Goldwater, Nelson Rockefeller, crime leaders, dirty books, funeral costs, and left-wing folk songs. The reaction was so strong and positive that NBC called for immediate production of the series, which it had originally considered as a possible new entry in the fall of 1964. Instead, the network planned on a premiere in January. All that remained was to convince skeptical sponsors that the public was ready for such humor. Then something happened.

CBS was in the midst of *As the World Turns* on Friday, November 22, when Walter Cronkite broke in to announce that President Kennedy had been shot in Dallas. Within a few minutes, all three networks suspended regular programming and began what became four days of noncommercial television (at a loss of $40 million in advertising revenue). By presenting, live, all the far-flung events of that weekend at a moment's notice, television news proved itself truly deserving of both serious attention and popular acclaim. People throughout the country looked to television for the news of the tragedy. They saw the official announcement that the President was dead, as well as the first appearance of the new President, Lyndon Johnson. They followed the return to Washington and the formal ceremonies of the state funeral. Many newsmen on each network distinguished themselves throughout the long hours on the air and several new faces became instant "news celebrities."

On CBS, Dan Rather, who scooped all others in reporting Kennedy's death, became unofficial anchorman of the network's Dallas reports, while Roger Mudd and Harry Reasoner, two veteran network reporters who had worked largely unnoticed for years, came to the forefront with their handling of the events in Washington.

On ABC, Howard K. Smith returned from oblivion and teamed up with a new addition to the ABC news staff, Edward P. Morgan. They were so effective together that they became the regular ABC anchor team for the political specials of 1964. Through it all, television treated the events of the Kennedy assassination with a dignity and style many had thought impossible. For the first time, people across the country began to appreciate how much television really meant to them and just what it was capable of. Even well-known critics such as former FCC chairman Newton Minow marveled:

> Only through television could the whole country grasp the tragedy, and at the same time the strength of the democratic process that passed the administration from one president to another within two hours. Television's treatment was sensitive, mature, and dignified. We always hear that television is a young medium. If so, it grew up in a couple of days.

More than any other event to that point, the Kennedy assassination cemented television's role as national information source and national unifier.

As disturbing as the assasination was, television faced an even more unsettling event two days after the President had been shot, as the medium immediately discovered the dangers and conflicts of its increased stature. Lee Harvey Oswald, the accused assassin, was to be transferred from one jail to another on Sunday morning, November 24, and the press, especially television, demanded to witness the event. It was no longer sufficient to merely report that something had happened, the activity had to take place before the cameras. Dallas police complied with the request by making their plans public so that reporters, or anyone, could see Oswald leave the city jail. At 11:20 A.M., at the end of a memorial service for Kennedy in Washington, NBC cut live to Dallas just in time to show the first real-life murder on television as it occurred: A man in a dark suit and hat came out of the crowd, there was a pop, and Oswald dropped from sight, fatally shot. CBS and ABC both just missed also telecasting the event live, but a new device developed for TV sports coverage allowed all three to show the murder again and again with the added impact of slow motion playback.

In demanding access to Oswald, a man who had become an instant media figure, television had focused attention and publicity on what should have been a routine procedure, the prison transfer. Unknowingly, television and television news had crossed a line into a new situation in which it would become increasingly difficult to view the medium as just another reporter. Television was beginning to affect the course of events, transforming seemingly inconsequential actions into important moments in history merely by its presence.

24. The Unloved Messenger

TELEVISION became the object of increasing vilification throughout 1964 for both its entertainment and news programming. The more effective and complete coverage of developing issues and special events by the network news departments upset people of every ideology. They resented the growing encroachment by TV news upon their personal lives and beliefs as well as the unsettling nature of the news itself, often equating the bearer of bad tidings with the disturbing events it reported. At the same time, a move to pure escapism in entertainment programming triggered by the huge success of CBS's rural-based comedy line-up offended the sensibilities of many viewers who found the tube pandering more and more to the lowest common denominator. In contrast to the fondly remembered high drama of TV's golden days, the networks' fall schedules offered country bumpkins, ridiculous settings, childish plots, witches, Martians, and pure soap opera. It all seemed deliberately designed to appeal to viewers who looked at television as a mindless escape tool. Critics pointed to the continuing number one status of *The Beverly Hillbillies* as irrefutable evidence that quality television had fallen on hard times.

The Beverly Hillbillies never deserved all the public defilement it received, but the program was a symbol of the direction television entertainment had taken under the guidance of CBS president James Aubrey. His rural comedy philosophy had kept CBS number one in the ratings and it cleared the path for a host of inferior successors launched by all three networks, with CBS leading the way. Most of the new programs lacked the comic energy of the hillbilly original and were responsible for generally humorless TV. As parent to the trend, though, *The Beverly Hillbillies* received its share of the blame for the sins of its offspring. Even though imitations of successful formats were expected as a normal part of the industry, the blatant, almost incestuous, development of the new sitcom spinoff shows struck many as going too far.

Spinoffs had been an accepted practice in broadcasting for decades, especially in the field of variety. Popular personalities such as Phil Harris and Dennis Day (from *The Jack Benny Program*), Julius La Rosa and Pat Boone (from Arthur Godfrey's shows), and Gisele MacKenzie (from *Your Hit Parade*) had all been promoted from the second string to programs of their own because their association with an established hit gave them an instant advantage over the competition. Situation comedies had certainly followed program trends in the past (wacky housewives, talking animals, showbiz widowers) but in courting the rural themes television developed a very systematic approach to the spin-off process. A specific character or gimmick from a successful sitcom was carefully eased into a new setting and show, as close to the original as possible. Sometimes there were even cross-over cast appearances from the established hit. Unfortunately, many of the new series failed to develop past the surface gimmicks and did not deliver the strong secondary characters and good scripts necessary for support. Yet with the momentum provided by familiar hooks and faces, simple-minded escapist fare prospered.

Beverly Hillbillies producer Paul Henning had started the cloning process in the 1963–64 season with *Petticoat Junction,* which presented the adventures of the folks "back in the hills." Henning took veteran character actor Bea Benaderet, who played cousin Pearl Bodine, Jethro's widowed mother (a minor role in *The Beverly Hillbillies*), rechristened her Kate Bradley (also a widow), and put her in charge of the Shady Rest Hotel in the mythical backwoods town of Hooterville. Though *Petticoat Junction* had the outward trappings of *The Beverly Hillbillies,* there were no creative crazies or charged conflicts in it. The setting was much too restrictive. Gone was the incongruity of the progenitor between rich and poor, socialite and hillbilly. Hooterville was a one-horse town. Even occasional invasions by city slickers such as Homer Bedloe (Charles Lane as a railroad executive determined to scrap the town's ancient train, the Cannonball) were doomed from the start. The aseptic peace of Fifties TV had been transported to the hills and nothing could disturb it. Worst of all, the characters were far too bland to be funny. While Benaderet was usually an excellent supporting character (in roles such as Blanche Morton, the crazy neighbor to George Burns and Gracie Allen), her warm mother figure of Kate Bradley wasn't credible either as a comic center or cagey manipulator. Her three daughters were as interchangeable as their names: Billie Jo, Bobbie Jo, and Betty Jo. Gravelly voiced Edgar Buchanan tried his best in the role of a scheming moneymaker, Joe Carson (the hotel's self-proclaimed manager), but Uncle Joe's ventures usually produced little more than a few good senility jokes. In short, the series was harmless fluff, not at all offensive, but not very funny either. It was pure escapism, a sort of "chewing gum for the eyes and mind," not only far removed from the everyday grim reality of the big city, but also a world apart from rural reality as well.

Nonetheless, the hillbilly connection worked and *Petticoat Junction* was an instant hit—its premiere episode came in as the number

FALL 1964 SCHEDULE

MONDAY

	7:30	8:00	8:30	9:00	9:30	10:00	10:30	
	VOYAGE TO THE BOTTOM OF THE SEA		NO TIME FOR SERGEANTS	WENDY AND ME	BING CROSBY SHOW	Ben Casey		**ABC**
	To Tell The Truth	I've Got A Secret	Andy Griffith Show	The Lucy Show	MANY HAPPY RETURNS	SLATTERY'S PEOPLE		**CBS**
	90 BRISTOL COURT (KAREN; HARRIS AGAINST THE WORLD; TOM, DICK AND MARY)			Andy Williams Show @JONATHAN WINTERS SHOW		Alfred Hitchcock Hour		**NBC**

TUESDAY

	7:30	8:00	8:30	9:00	9:30	10:00	10:30	
	Combat!		McHale's Navy	TYCOON	PEYTON PLACE I	The Fugitive		**ABC**
	local	WORLD WAR ONE	Red Skelton Hour		Petticoat Junction	The Doctors And The Nurses		**CBS**
	Mr. Novak		THE MAN FROM U.N.C.L.E.		That Was The Week That Was	Bell Telephone Hour / NBC News Specials		**NBC**

WEDNESDAY

	7:30	8:00	8:30	9:00	9:30	10:00	10:30	
	The Adventures Of Ozzie And Harriet	Patty Duke Show	SHINDIG	MICKEY	Burke's Law		ABC Scope	**ABC**
	CBS Reports / CBS News Specials		The Beverly Hillbillies	Dick Van Dyke Show	CARA WILLIAMS SHOW	Danny Kaye Show		**CBS**
	The Virginian			NBC Wednesday Night At The Movies				**NBC**

THURSDAY

	7:30	8:00	8:30	9:00	9:30	10:00	10:30	
	The Flintstones	Donna Reed Show	My Three Sons	BEWITCHED	PEYTON PLACE II	Jimmy Dean Show		**ABC**
	THE MUNSTERS	Perry Mason		Password	THE BAILEYS OF BALBOA	The Defenders		**CBS**
	DANIEL BOONE		Dr. Kildare		Hazel	Kraft Suspense Theater @Perry Como's Kraft Music Hall		**NBC**

FRIDAY

	7:30	8:00	8:30	9:00	9:30	10:00	10:30	
	JONNY QUEST	The Farmer's Daughter	THE ADDAMS FAMILY	VALENTINE'S DAY	TWELVE O'CLOCK HIGH		local	**ABC**
	Rawhide		THE ENTERTAINERS		GOMER PYLE, U.S.M.C.	THE REPORTER		**CBS**
	International Showtime		Bob Hope Presents Chrysler Theater @Bob Hope Show		Jack Benny Program	Jack Paar Show		**NBC**

SATURDAY

	7:30	8:00	8:30	9:00	9:30	10:00	10:30	
	The Outer Limits		Lawrence Welk Show		Hollywood Palace		local	**ABC**
	Jackie Gleason Show		GILLIGAN'S ISLAND	MR. BROADWAY		Gunsmoke		**CBS**
	FLIPPER	FAMOUS ADVENTURES OF MR. MAGOO	KENTUCKY JONES	NBC Saturday Night At The Movies				**NBC**

SUNDAY

	7:00	7:30	8:00	8:30	9:00	9:30	10:00	10:30	
	local	Wagon Train		BROADSIDE	The ABC Sunday Night Movie				**ABC**
	Lassie	My Favorite Martian	Ed Sullivan Show		MY LIVING DOLL	Joey Bishop Show	Candid Camera	What's My Line	**CBS**
	PROFILES IN COURAGE [from 6:30]	Walt Disney's Wonderful World Of Color		Bill Dana Show	Bonanza		THE ROGUES		**NBC**

---

five show of the week. Hooterville was undeniably popular and the program lasted seven seasons. In 1965, the show spawned its own calculated clone, *Green Acres*. For that series, Henning took the spinoff formula one step further by keeping the same setting (Hooterville), using many of the same characters (there were frequent crossovers with *Petticoat Junction*), and introducing a premise that was a mirror image of *The Beverly Hillbillies*: two city slickers (Eddie Albert and Eva Gabor) moved to the country. Once again, home viewers were entranced and *Green Acres* clucked on for six years.

Following the success of *Petticoat Junction* in the 1963–64 season, CBS turned to another popular series, *The Andy Griffith Show,* for a spinoff in the fall of 1964, *Gomer Pyle, U.S.M.C.* The Gomer Pyle character of a halfwit gas station attendant (played by Jim Nabors) was drafted by Uncle Aubrey, taken from Mayberry, North Carolina, and placed in a Marine base in California. There, under the tutelage of the often infuriated Sergeant Vincent Carter (Frank Sutton), the simple country rube constantly exasperated yet outwitted the military minds. The setting and premise were nearly identical to Andy Griffith's first major vehicle, "No Time for Sergeants," in 1955. To complete the circle (and to make certain the spinoff was properly launched) Andy accompanied Gomer from Mayberry, taking him into his new setting, and keeping a watchful eye on him throughout the first episode. Gomer clicked and the

series stood as further proof that spinoffs from established hits were a valuable tool that, if handled properly, could produce another equally potent program. Gomer's success was especially impressive because the show not only outscored the direct competition of veteran Jack Benny (who had moved to NBC that year following a contract dispute) but also easily outperformed the same premise on ABC. As a very familiar character, Gomer stood out in the madness of the fall premieres and found it much easier to gain a toehold and build an audience than the unknowns (Sammy Jackson and Harry Hickox) of the ABC version, which even took the *No Time for Sergeants* title. The country took Gomer to heart in his new job, making Nabors a star in his own right as the series remained in the top ten through the Sixties. Gomer's wide-eyed innocence also presented a reassuring view of the military in an era when people were beginning to become aware of the presence of real Marines in a real war. Gomer Pyle was always the all-American country boy.

Some critics, however, found the character to be the personification of everything objectionable about the rural slant being pursued by CBS. Gomer was a naive country bumpkin who obviously read and enjoyed nothing more challenging than *Captain Marvel* comic books (as his cry of "Shazam!" indicated), yet he was one of television's new heroes. His character might have been acceptable as a second banana but as a lead his effusive manner and familiar expressions such as "Sur-*prise!* Sur-*prise!* Sur-*prise!*" and "Gaul-lee Sergeant Carter!" were particularly discordant and grating to some. Nonetheless, the program was well done and very funny, and such reactions more likely reflected deep resentment at the near total domination by escapist fare in entertainment programming. The style seemed as pervasive as Westerns and quizzes had been at their saturation points, but it looked as if the spinoff potential and continued high ratings earned by the silly gimmicks and simpleton heroes would assure them spots in the network schedules for years. While some viewers were upset, most people clearly enjoyed the programs. They were light, uncomplicated, and a welcome haven from bad news.

Just as action-adventure shows in the late Fifties had given the networks Westerns that weren't Westerns, the escapist sitcoms quickly expanded beyond strictly rural settings. Though not direct spinoffs from any established hit, the premises of these new shows were just as unlikely as millionaire hillbillies and included such hooks as Martians, monsters, and witches. Of these, the program that showcased Aubrey escapism at its worst was *Gilligan's Island,* which followed the adventures of the passengers and crew of a sight-seeing charter boat that was shipwrecked on an uncharted South Pacific island. The show literally went to the ends of the earth to avoid reality in a premise that seemed to overwhelm the writers with its limitations. With the castaways confined to a tiny island (they could never be rescued or the program was kaput), the writers settled on a handful of obvious plots and jokes (gorillas, angry natives, other lost souls). They couldn't come up with imaginative and credible ways to introduce new characters and conflicts from the outside world and consequently the scripts were atrocious. Even with the paucity of good material, the cast members might have been able to overcome the tremendous handicap of bad writing by developing a sharp comic insanity in each of their characters. Instead, most of them just overacted and settled into the uninteresting plastic caricatures they had been given: the hard working skipper (Alan Hale, Jr.), his well-meaning but bumbling first mate (Bob Denver), a dumb but beautiful movie star (Tina Louise), a pretty homespun Midwestern girl (Dawn Wells), a brilliant research professor (Russell Johnson), a multimillionaire (Jim Backus) and his pampered wife (Natalie Schafer). Hale, Backus, and Denver made valiant attempts to bring life to their roles, but even they usually fell short. Denver brought the spacey, naive innocence of his Maynard G. Krebs character to first mate Gilligan, but what had worked well in a supporting role to Dobie Gillis could not carry an entire series. He was just another lost child on the island. Backus and Hale flashed moments of wit, but it was a losing battle. Overall, the show resembled nothing so much as a kiddie cartoon and it seemed designed to capture the interest of young children by presenting cardboard adults who acted like children in grown-up bodies. This strategy attracted a fair size audience and allowed the program to survive for three seasons, though it rarely elicited more than an audible groan from most of the nation's adults.

Other new gimmicks might have appeared as silly as *Gilligan's Island* on the surface, but the better ones kept a tighter rein on the initial premise. Rather than building a sweeping but all-too-limiting setting that could prematurely strangle the series, other producers settled for a slight wrinkle to reality that could be continuously exploited. In this vein, a Martian and a witch were incorporated into moderately normal situations and acceptable, if not outstanding, TV fare resulted. Both *My Favorite Martian* (starring Ray Walston as a Martian shipwrecked on Earth) and *Bewitched* (Elizabeth Montgomery as a suburban housewife who happened to be a witch) used their zany hooks primarily as an excuse to display entertaining visual tricks in that week's situation. Once the complications were introduced, the actors and scripts, not the gimmicks, carried the episodes.

Still, a totally bizarre setting could succeed as long as it stuck to the basics of comedy. If the characters and atmosphere on *Gilligan's Island* had been developed beyond dull caricature and cheap tropical sets, the program might have been able to transcend the pathetic scripts. ABC proved it could be done that season with the hilarious adventures of an entire family that came directly out of the world of late night creature features, *The Addams Family* (based on the characters created by cartoonist Charles Addams). Though the plots for the series were usually just adequate, the characters and setting were devilishly sharp. Gomez (John Astin) and his wife Morticia (Carolyn Jones) headed the freaky family that lived in an appropriately spooky old family mansion just outside of town. Rather than limiting the program to predictable monster jokes or half-hearted attempts to make the characters appear a normal part of society (in spite of their background), the producers accepted the members of the family for what they were and stretched the premise to the limit. The Addams family were ghoulish eccentrics and proud of it. They flaunted their behavior in characters that were bristling with energy. Morticia and Gomez cultivated man-eating plants, stayed in on sunny days, and reveled in hurricane winds. To relax, family members enjoyed stretching each other out on the basement rack and, at play, the children experimented with dynamite. The household also included live-in relations Uncle Fester (Jackie Coogan), Grandmama Addams (Blossom Rock), and cousin Itt (a four-foot-tall ball of hair), as well as the ultra basso butler, Lurch (Ted Cassidy), and the ultimate right hand helper, Thing. For all of them, the question of conforming to normal society never came up; the most important task was maintaining family traditions and an awareness of the Addams family roots, which stretched back hundreds of years. They were aristocrats with highly unusual tastes and no doubts about their proper station in life. Gomez and Morticia were passionate, but proper, and their strict adherence to traditional upper class role models resulted in a marvelous caricature of the aristocratic lifestyle. Ever the ardent lover (the slightest word of French by Morticia sent him into an uncontrolled fury), Gomez found himself constantly frustrated by his wife's insistence on abiding by the rules of public decorum ("not now dear—it wouldn't be right"). They were ghoulish in their preferences, but always socially correct.

Such a rich collection of characters, added to the colorful household accouterments, gave the program a comic verve which was even more striking when contrasted with the mundane monster fare of CBS's family of freaks, *The Munsters.* Unlike the Addams household, the Munster family looked like classic horror film creatures: Fred Gwynne played a Frankenstein father; Yvonne De Carlo, the vampire mother; and Al Lewis, Count Dracula. Unfortunately, the attempts at humor in the show never rose above the physical incongruity of the Munsters as they tried to act like an average, if somewhat odd, middle class family. Once the "shock value" of a collection of monsters had worn off, the routine nature of the scripts became painfully evident. Visitors from the outside world would leave the Addams home in a terrified daze; intruders in the Munster mansion merely faced grownups in Halloween costumes. Both series lasted only two seasons, but *The Addams Family* brought a touch of class to escapist television.

Escapism was certainly not limited to situation comedy nor new to television under Aubrey, but rarely had the networks pursued the concept with such a vengeance. TV critics, upset at the trend to rural settings and mindless heroes, were positively aghast at

The arrival of U.S. marines in Vietnam in March 1965 brought about an increase in TV coverage of the war. *(U.S. Army)*

the move by ABC to bring daytime soap opera, intact, to prime time. Television's cultural slide seemed undeniable and complete in the fall of 1964 with the premiere of *Peyton Place.*

Actually, pseudo-soap operas had been in prime time for years in the guise of drama anthologies *(Lux Video Theater),* situation comedies *(Ozzie and Harriet),* epic Westerns *(Bonanza* and *Wagon Train),* and career dramas *(Dr. Kildare* and *Ben Casey),* so much of the disgust was in reaction to the term "soap opera" itself. The networks had found that the label carried a certain stigma that turned off large segments of viewers, so they generally kept the soapy aspects of their prime time programs discretely in the background and adhered to an unwritten rule limiting blatant soap operas to the afternoon "housewife" hours. ABC's move marked a major break from this policy. *Peyton Place* was a regular soaper following characters through a continuing story line, rather than the usual self-contained episodes of other prime time series. The program brazenly displayed the sudsy staples of life, love, and scandal.

For the number three network, the soap opera strategy made a great deal of sense. After all, CBS had made a fortune in daytime TV with such long running classics as *Love of Life, As the World Turns, Search for Tomorrow,* and *The Guiding Light,* and ABC saw no reason to limit its assault on the field to the daytime.

Potential ratings points were just sitting there and, if *Peyton Place* caught on, the network would have two hit shows at once because the series was on twice each week. ABC boldly ballyhooed the show as a novel for television (it was based on a successful book as well as a movie), ignored the cries of anguish from outraged critics, and launched the series with high hopes. It was a smash, though its individual success didn't alter the bias against soaps. *Peyton Place* was the exception that gave soap opera fans a chance for an evening dose of bathos.

The program was a classic soaper with the usual conflicts stemming from guilt associated with extramarital and premarital sex. Though such themes were bold and titillating for prime time, they were familiar stuff to afternoon viewers who studied the cast and conflicts in the New England town of Peyton Place and nodded their approval. Constance MacKenzie (Dorothy Malone) feared the devastating humiliation she felt would occur if anyone discovered her dark secret: Eighteen years before she had "made a terrible mistake" and, nine months later, given birth to an illegitimate child, Allison MacKenzie (Mia Farrow). Now, Dr. Rossi (Ed Nelson), who had delivered the baby (and who probably knew "the secret"), was in love with Constance while Rodney Harrington (Ryan O'Neal) was in love with Allison (only he probably *didn't* know "the secret"). There was much, much more and the story continued with ripening teenagers, broken marriages, adultery, more illegitimate kids (the *ne plus ultra* development in soap opera scripts), and an endless string of coincidences.

In its first season, *Peyton Place* often landed in the top ten, and in the summer of 1965 ABC launched a third night, which lasted through the following summer. At the same time, CBS gave *Our Private World,* an off-shoot of *As the World Turns,* a twice-each-week prime time tryout, but this ran only for one summer. In the fall of 1965, NBC converted *Dr. Kildare* into a twice-each-week serial, recognizing that the program easily matched the sudsiest of daytime soaps. After one year in this guise, *Kildare* also disappeared. Obviously, *Peyton Place* was a one-of-a-kind hit. TV viewers were apparently unwilling to devote themselves to several prime time soaps simultaneously, though they followed *Peyton Place* for nearly five years.

A much more imaginative form of escapist entertainment was the spy craze, led by the phenomenally successful James Bond films and books. Americans had been a bit slower than the British in embracing such larger-than-life international adventures, but by 1964 they, too, were hooked and the networks responded with a parade of Bond-like TV spies. Spies had never been handled very well by American television and the task of bringing the delicate balance of refined wit, cruel violence, desirable women, expensive gimmicks, and occasional self-parody to television seemed especially difficult. NBC was the first to jump on the bandwagon, enlisting James Bond's creator, Ian Fleming, for *Mr. Solo,* a very Bond-ish TV spy series. Fleming had to drop out of the project due to ill health, but the show made it to the air in the fall of 1964 as *The Man from U.N.C.L.E.*

Though obviously working with a substantially smaller budget than the multimillion-dollar Bond film epics, the series was a very good television equivalent, comfortably adopting many of the most attractive Bond gimmicks. The United Network Command for Law Enforcement was a large, powerful CIA-type organization headquartered in the bowels of New York City, with a secret entrance hidden behind a fake wall in a dry cleaning store. U.N.C.L.E. deployed a world-wide network of agents and an arsenal of elaborate gadgets, specially designed guns, and exotic electronic gear including miniature communicators, tiny listening devices, and coded identification badges. Concerns over world domination, the balance of power, and freedom were bandied about, but this was a cosmetic device to give the scripts a topical flavor for what amounted to a weekly battle between good and evil. Just as Bond's British secret service squared off against Spectre, U.N.C.L.E. faced the highly skilled forces of Thrush (the Technological Hierarchy for the Removal of Undesirables and the Subjugation of Humanity) in a never-ending struggle that appeared more a high-powered chess game between the two superpowers than a fight for world domination. Particular schemes assumed important propaganda value and served as an arena for a perverse, sportsmanlike competition between the best agents from both sides. Napoleon Solo (played by Robert Vaughn) was U.N.C.L.E.'s top agent. Like Bond, he was a company man who flaunted the rules of discipline to pursue his own pleasures, placing more trust in his instincts than in standard operating procedures. Solo was a highly refined, highly educated boy-next-door type who fell somewhere in between the aristocratic aloofness of Sherlock Holmes and the gritty earthiness of Sam Spade. He was an excellent Bond surrogate.

The chief difference between the man from U.N.C.L.E. and James Bond was that Bond operated solo but Solo had a partner. At first, Illya Kuryakin (David McCallum) was little more than a right-hand flunky to Solo. (He was featured for all of five seconds in the pilot episode for the series.) In February, however, McCallum was sent on a promotional tour of eight major cities with low *U.N.C.L.E.* ratings during which he earned the right to become an equal partner to Solo. Now only did the ratings go up in the cities he visited, but to the surprise (and delight) of the producers, it became obvious by the enthusiastic response of female fans that the Kuryakin character had become a teen heart-throb. From then on, McCallum's sensitive, intellectual, continental allure was used as an excellent complement to Vaughn's middle-American goodness.

In contrast to the James Bond films, *The Man from U.N.C.L.E.* downplayed cynical sadism and violence in favor of a stronger emphasis on tongue-in-cheek humor and character interaction. An innocent bystander (usually a beautiful woman) was always introduced into the plot to bring the high-level conflict down to a less obtuse level—if the future of mankind didn't mean anything to viewers, then a damsel in distress certainly did. More importantly, with the increased visibility of Kuryakin, the men from U.N.C.L.E. developed a natural repartee, very much in the style of John Steed and Kathy Gale in Britain's *The Avengers.* Because the world of international intrigue all too often involved plots that threatened "the fate of the entire Western world," such an approach was vital to prevent overkill and made the weekly life-and-death perils much easier to take. Though occasionally the program went overboard and turned the entire episode into one long joke ("The Jingle Bells Affair"), when kept in check the lighter touch lifted *The Man from U.N.C.L.E.* far above the level of mundane TV melodrama into a first class escapist spy adventure.

ABC and CBS didn't get their spy programs out until the next season, though in April CBS, perhaps spurred by *U.N.C.L.E.*'s

---

September 16, 1964

Shindig. (ABC). Britain's pioneer of television rock'n'roll, Jack Good, shows America how it's done. His fast-paced showcase for rock talent not only features top artists such as the Beatles, but also presents up-and-coming performers such as Billy Preston and Bobby Sherman.

September 19–25, 1964

"NBC Week." Following ABC's lead, NBC put all its fall premieres into one easy-to-publicize week. NBC also emphasizes the fact that it is the first network to have more than 50% of its prime time fare in color.

October 5, 1964

90 Bristol Court. (NBC). An experiment in program packaging. NBC presents three standard sitcoms as part of one ninety-minute show. The hook? All the characters in *Karen, Harris against the World,* and *Tom, Dick, and Mary* live in the same apartment complex: 90 Bristol Court. Only *Karen* survives past January.

October 7, 1964

NBC and Universal studios present the first two-hour made-for-television movie, "See How They Run," starring John Forsythe and Jane Wyatt. This film—and a few others like it aired this season—receives very little publicity and registers mediocre ratings.

November 8, 1964

Profiles in Courage. (NBC). Robert Saudek, former *Omnibus* guru, presents a series of twenty-six historical dramatizations inspired by John Kennedy's 1956 Pulitzer Prize winning book.

mid-season surge, brought back the British spy series, *Danger Man*, under a new title, *Secret Agent* (featuring a catchy new theme song by Johnny Rivers). The new hour-long version of the program had begun in Britain in October with Patrick McGoohan still in his role of agent John Drake, though he had softened the character a bit to emphasize a wry sense of humor. It proved only slightly less successful than *U.N.C.L.E.* and confirmed that TV spies were a viable commodity.

One marvelous tongue-in-check series somehow lost in this season of escapist fare was *The Rogues*. Produced by Four Star Television, the program was developed as a sophisticated, high quality vehicle for a troupe of veteran performers led by two of the company's own star-owners, Charles Boyer and David Niven. (The two had also participated in the Fifties drama anthology series, *Four Star Playhouse*, the company's first venture.) Set in London, *The Rogues* presented the complicated schemes and crimes of an international family of con artists, led by Niven (as Alec Fleming), who rotated the lead each week with Boyer (as French cousin, Marcel) and Gig Young (as American cousin, Tony). Occasionally, all three would join forces for exceptionally challenging plots, and they often enlisted the aid of British cousins Timmy (Robert Coote) and *grande dame* Margaret (Gladys Cooper). Naturally, the Fleming family only chiseled victims that deserved it (bad guys such as a South American dictator played by Telly Savalas), often leaving them embarrassed and humiliated as well as fleeced. Despite rave reviews and a strong lead-in (the number one rated *Bonanza*), the program failed to register high ratings and was dropped by NBC after only one season. To those disgusted by what they saw as the abysmal level of entertainment programming, such a decision was not surprising—*Gilligan's Island* and *Petticoat Junction* lived on, but a witty, sophisticated program was not even given a second chance.

The critical blasts labeling TV's entertainment programming as childish and unimaginative were ironic because, at the same time, the medium was also being lambasted for its aggressive (some said intrusive) approach to the news. In either direction, television faced outraged viewers, though objections to the news were far more serious. Television entertainment was a matter of taste and tastes differed and changed. Television news touched deeply held and long-standing personal beliefs, and it was becoming increasingly apparent that some people would have been pleased to see network news completely disappear from their lives.

Resentment of the news had grown out of its increased visibility and the exposure it gave to developing controversial issues. Some of the additional coverage was merely a function of time: Over fifteen years viewers had grown accustomed to fifteen-minute nightly newscasts. In 1963 the programs had doubled in length. The number of bureaus and correspondents had also increased substantially. Resources available for normal coverage of an average news event allowed much more depth and detail than before, so by just following everyday procedures correspondents produced more extensive reports. Though the reporters were not "fighting for" a particular cause, some viewers felt that the additional attention made certain issues seem much more important than ever before.

It was also true, however, that the network news departments had been specifically devoting portions of the additional nightly news time to an examination of social and political issues previously left undiscussed. That was one of the reasons they had fought for the longer news time in the first place—to win the opportunity to deal, at length, with important issues. Viewers did not necessarily want to face some of these issues, though, and many resented what they saw as an intrusion on their lives. There were countless special interest newspapers and magazines catering to every ideolog-

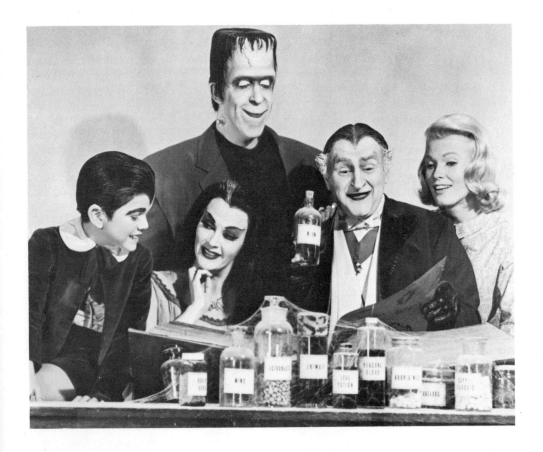

The Munsters: (from *l.*) Butch Patrick as Eddie, Yvonne De Carlo as Lily, Fred Gwynne as Herman, Al Lewis as Grandpa, and Pat Priest as family oddball Marilyn. (*From* The Munsters. *Courtesy of MCA Television Limited*)

ical slant (not everyone had to read the *New York Times*), but if people chose to watch network news at all they had a choice of only three similar programs. Each one tried to present a survey of all the important national news events of the day. The structure of the network news programs made it all but impossible to skip disturbing news items; they came unpredictably into the home before an irked viewer could stop them. Despite the networks' efforts to take an unbiased stance in the reporting, what seemed cool and objective in one region of the country could touch a very sensitive spot in another. It wasn't like radio either. That had permitted the individual listener to form a picture to fit preconceived notions based merely on sounds and narration. Television, with its increasing emphasis on "on the spot" news film, brought profoundly disturbing sounds and pictures into the home and these were difficult to ignore. The period of the mid-Sixties was one of volatile social change anyway and many people resented being forced to confront so many different issues each night in their own living rooms. More and more, they linked their growing resentment of the changes in the country with television, television news, and the networks—the messengers that had, at first, merely carried the word of a new order soon became interchangeable with it. As in the old story of the king who punished the messenger who brought him bad news, viewers reacted to the alterations in their lives by turning on the tube and attacking it. A convenient event to choose as the first to spark the wave of such negative viewer reaction was the mass protest march on Washington led by Dr. Martin Luther King, Jr. on August 28, 1963.

The protest was the largest such assembly in Washington since the impoverished World War I veterans (dubbed the "bonus marchers") had gathered in 1932. The networks, which had been slowly increasing the amount of their civil rights coverage through the early Sixties, treated the assembly as a major national event, equivalent to a space shot or presidential election. There were special live reports throughout the day, prime time specials, and late night wrapups. The coverage showed more than 200,000 civil rights supporters as peaceful, reasonable people gathered together in support of a righteous cause. The Reverend King's impassioned and eloquent "I Have a Dream" speech in favor of civil rights and integration served as the emotional high point to the day and it was carried live to people across the nation. Favorable public reaction to the presentation provided a tremendous boost to civil rights legislation before Congress; legislators began to think that, perhaps, passage of a civil rights bill would not be political suicide. Defenders of segregation, however, saw the changing mood as disastrous and television's participation as unforgivable.

In a three-hour NBC prime time special on civil rights broadcast five days after King's speech, Mississippi Governor Ross Barnett said that television was to blame for civil disorder in America. By raising the expectations of America's blacks too rapidly, he said, the medium had created the climate that allowed "rabble rousers" such as King to gain power. Though Barnett might have been somewhat biased, having felt the sting of bad TV publicity in his own moves against civil rights activities (his efforts to block the admission of a young black man, James Meredith, to the University of Mississippi in 1962 had received extensive TV coverage), he was by no means alone in his beliefs. In the spring and summer of 1964, Alabama's Governor George C. Wallace, in his first run at the presidency, pointed very specifically to the extended civil rights coverage by CBS, NBC, and ABC, as well as the *New York Times* and the *Washington Post*, as "unnecessary." Publicity given to civil rights activities, he contended, not any underlying social injustice, was responsible for the civil rights problem.

November 9, 1964
The Les Crane Show. (ABC). Johnny Carson at last faces some network competition in the late night talk show game. Thirty-year-old Les Crane generally steers his ninety-minute show towards substantive issues rather than celebrity chit chat, using an "in the round" setting and a shotgun microphone to take questions from the audience.

January 1, 1965
After four years, ABC gives up its Monday-through-Friday fifteen-minute late night news program and instead institutes a similar format on weekends only.

January 12, 1965
Hullabaloo. (NBC). A glitzy copy of ABC's *Shindig,* emphasizing scantily-clad, wildly gyrating "go-go" dancers and using mainstream pop stars such as Annette Funicello and Frankie Avalon as guest hosts.

February 1, 1965
Canadian newsman Peter Jennings replaces Ron Cochran as the anchor of ABC's nightly fifteen-minute news show.

April 27, 1965
Edward R. Murrow, 57, dies of lung cancer.

May 10, 1965
The Merv Griffin Show. Group W revamps its syndicated late night talk show, installing Merv Griffin and his sidekick, Arthur Treacher.

June 7, 1965
Sony introduces the first commercial home video tape recorder. Price: $995.

On July 18, 1964, the problem of minor disorders resulting from the push for civil rights exploded into a much more dramatic confrontation as the first major inner city race riot in decades erupted in New York City's Harlem. TV crews rushed to the scene and were shocked to discover that both sides hated reporters. Police, sensitive to the possibility of bad publicity for the force, did not welcome the presence of the news crews, but neither did the rioters. To them, television, with its fancy remote trucks and equipment, was just another arm of what they saw as a white power structure, which was ready to distort their viewpoint and the meaning of their actions. Both sides, during the night, beat up reporters. For the remainder of the summer, thoughtful documentaries and discussions filled the airwaves, as people bravely searched for the complex, underlying causes of the problem, but they usually reached the predictable general conclusion that exceptional slum living conditions and police brutality had touched off the violence. In this light, "Harlem: Test for a Nation" (on NBC) naively cited two cities as models of how to avoid riots: Detroit and Los Angeles. Detroit had an integrated police force; and the black section of Los Angeles, Watts, didn't even look like a slum, it was almost a heavenly suburb. One year later, this "suburb" erupted into violence that totally overshadowed the Harlem riot of 1964.

All three networks picked up dramatic and mildly sensationalist overhead shots of the riot in Watts from a helicamera devised by the crew from an independent Los Angeles station, KTLA (whose grimly appropriate news motto had been: "If hell breaks loose, turn to KTLA!"). Helicopter pilot Hal Fishman provided a blow-by-blow description of the rampaging mobs, audacious looters, burning buildings, and police-civilian confrontations. Thirty-five people died and more than $200 million in property damage took place. At the same time, the network crews were stoned by the mob, equipment was stolen, and a number of $10,000 mobile vans were torched. The beleaguered police displayed little concern for representatives of a medium many felt was glorifying violence with its reporting anyway. In covering Watts, television was once again caught in a no-win situation.

TV conveyed the terror of a volatile situation in a way no other news medium could. The expanded scope of network news had dovetailed almost exactly with the rapidly developing issue of civil rights, in both its peaceful and violent forms. In general, TV failed to satisfy anyone with its coverage. Many people saw it as an all-too-willing forum for anti-establishment figures out to win converts and propagate violence, while many frustrated blacks found it insensitive and ignorant.

With the country reeling from racial tensions and the after-effects of the Kennedy assassination, it took a great deal of guts for NBC to go ahead with its plans for an American version of the popular British satire program *That Was The Week That Was*. The BBC had, in fact dropped its version of the program at the end of 1963 because, it explained, 1964 was an election year and it wouldn't be right for the BBC to make fun of politicians. Despite the fact that the U.S. also faced elections that year, NBC didn't follow suit and instead set about convincing both Madison Avenue and the American public that topical, political humor could be entertaining and profitable.

One fortunate result of the cancellation of the British *TW3* was that it allowed David Frost to join the American version when it premiered in January, 1964 (though at first he remained in the background as just another member of the *TW3* family). Elliott Reid acted as the host and he was joined by Frost, Henry Morgan, Phyllis Newman, Buck Henry, puppeteer Burr Tillstrom, and Nancy Ames, the singing "TW3 Girl." At first, the writers were unsure of their ground (satire was certainly new to American television) and settled for standard TV jokes with topical names plugged in. By the late spring, they began to find their mark and the show picked up noticeably in both pacing and overall quality. The writers developed satirical approaches to topical issues and events while also poking fun at television itself, especially its commercials. Variety shows had been doing sendups of overplayed, all-too-familiar commercials for years (at the time, Danny Kaye's were among the best), but *TW3* did them one better. In one instance, a silly but genuine catsup commercial was run as scheduled. It featured talking hamburger buns that, at the spot's end, joyfully threw their tops into the air when they heard the brand of catsup to be used. When the show resumed, the cast added an unexpected coda: As David Frost began talking to the audience, dozens of hamburger bun tops fell from above and covered him.

The program was at its best, though, in its semi-serious and topical moments. Guest comics Sandy Baron and Alan Alda appeared as a pair of singing segregationist plumbers. Puppeteer Tillstrom staged an award-winning detente of East and West hand puppets that met atop the Berlin wall. President Lyndon Johnson's infamous beagle episode (in which the President lifted one of his pet dogs by its ears) inspired a sendup featuring handpuppet HBJ (Him Beagle Johnson) being snatched by giant presidential hands before it could reveal LBJ's choice for his vice presidential running mate. Johnson was a godsend to the writers because he had so many easily caricatured qualities: he was tall, earthy, and a Texan with an obvious accent. As humorous a target as Johnson was, Barry Goldwater, a Republican presidential candidate in 1964, was even more tempting. One of the most effective (and disturbing) putdowns of Goldwater came in the form of a puppet reading various quotes from the candidate's public statements.

In its first half season (January through June of 1964), *TW3* did fairly well as a Friday night lead-in to Jack Paar. When David Frost took over as host in the fall of 1964, however, NBC moved the program to perhaps the toughest spot on its schedule, Tuesday night against *Petticoat Junction* and *Peyton Place*. Besides facing two top ten shows, *TW3* came into direct conflict with the 1964 presidential campaign. Just as the elections in Britain had caused the end of the BBC version of *TW3*, the American presidential elections effectively doomed the U.S. counterpart, though in a very unusual way. The fate of *TW3*, however, was just one minor skirmish in a running battle over the proper role of television in the contest. As in its civil rights reporting, the medium's own actions were as severely scrutinized as the candidates' campaign strategies. Once again, a deep resentment of television reporting was revealed.

The competition between the network news departments (especially between CBS and NBC) was particularly fierce that year as *The Huntley-Brinkley Report* found itself at the start of a year-long deadlock with Walter Cronkite for nightly news supremacy. Traditional wisdom in broadcasting circles held that the network which won the convention and election coverage would carry the momentum into the lucrative nightly news shows and probably remain on top for the next four years. An increased interest in the early spring primaries provided a convenient warm-up arena, and all three networks took the opportunity to roll out their latest gimmick, computers, to help them make "instant vote projections." John Kennedy's dramatic primary victories in 1960 had alerted reporters to the potential importance of these local contests and, with larger staffs and new technological tricks available, it seemed strategically wise to cover them. As the votes in these elections came in, CBS, NBC, and ABC raced with each other to be the first to declare a winner, using their fancy new equipment. The speed techniques did more than impress the regular viewers and politicians watching; it left them flabbergasted. How could the networks declare a winner with only a minuscule percentage of the vote totals in? CBS, for example, declared Senator Barry Goldwater the victor in the crucial California primary in June with only 2% of the state's vote totals listed on the tote board.

Actually, the feat was illusory. The network computers didn't rely on the official vote tallies for the projections because these not only took hours to trickle in, they were often quite misleading as well (an area strongly supporting one candidate might report in first and show a huge lead that would be wiped out by subsequent reports). Instead, each of the networks employed statistical analysis techniques using the results from a handful of key precincts that had been targeted (from past voting patterns) to provide a highly educated projection of what the final totals for the state would be. Stringers were placed in these precincts and they called the networks directly as soon as the votes were counted, allowing television to call a race often within two hours after the polls closed, compared to a turn-over time of six hours in the past. Instant vote projection was really the result of long hard work and calculated preparation, but the shorthand label stuck and the audience saw the final product in that light. Though there was nothing dishonest about the technique, it nonetheless irked people and raised vague suspicions and resentments. With instant vote projections, the networks had taken away much of the fun from election night with its ever-changing see-saw totals that hinged on every vote. In fact, they also seemed to reduce the importance of each individual vote by using just a sample to pronounce an election decided. To some this was TV news at its most arrogant and intrusive, appointing itself national election judge and showing off its influence on the perception of politics and current events, reducing everything to just more programming fodder.

Anger at the network news operations surfaced unexpectedly at the Republican National Convention at San Francisco's Cow Palace in July, during a speech by former president Dwight Eisenhower, the grand old man of the GOP. In the course of a traditional pep talk address, Eisenhower touched off a spontaneous roar when he unexpectedly condemned "sensation seeking columnists and commentators" (an ironic generalization because Eisenhower was serving as a commentator for ABC at the time). The phrase had been inserted at the very last minute and the delegates eagerly took the opportunity to express their deep distrust (even hate) for TV news to the nation at large. For five minutes they jeered and screamed, shaking their fists at Huntley and Brinkley who were encased in the NBC glass booth high above the arena floor, looking down. Many of the supporters of Senator Goldwater, whose conservative forces controlled the convention (as the result of a brilliant state-by-state primary and caucus strategy), honestly felt that TV news was a disrupting influence on America. If there were any doubters among them, they were convinced by a report carried by CBS while the convention was still in progress. The CBS correspondent in Germany, Daniel Schorr, reported that Goldwater had plans to visit West Germany after the convention and meet with his "counter-part" right wingers. Very few people missed the Nazi allusion, intended or not, and Goldwater was forced to cancel the trip to prevent the negative association from sinking in any deeper. He was rightly incensed and CBS was properly embarrassed.

CBS also lost in the ratings race at the Republican convention, with Huntley and Brinkley clobbering Walter Cronkite by a wide margin. In a desperate move to improve the ratings at the Democratic convention in Atlantic City the next month, CBS executives replaced Cronkite (CBS's sole anchor at special events since 1952) with the team of Robert Trout and Roger Mudd. Though Cronkite insisted he didn't take the action as an insult, people throughout the nation did. "We Want Cronkite" buttons popped up all through the Democratic gathering and viewers across the nation complained bitterly. CBS reinstated him for the election coverage in November, apparently deciding that it was best not to tamper with a national personality so obviously loved and admired. Besides, the Trout-Mudd team had fared no better than Cronkite anyway.

The campaign in the fall between Goldwater and President Johnson was one of the most bitter and vicious races in years, and television was the forum for one of the major battles—imagery. Using some campaign commercials that bordered on being downright unethical, the Democratic party subtly (and not so subtly) painted Goldwater as a man likely to kill little children by irresponsibly and indiscriminately using nuclear power. In September, the message relied on subtle implication: A cute little girl was shown gathering daisies in a field and counting to herself as she picked the petals from the flowers. Her counting blended with and was replaced by the countdown to an atomic bomb explosion. At detonation, the fiery blast replaced the little girl on the screen. Then,

an announcer intoned: "These are the stakes—to make a world in which all God's children can live, or go into the dark." A final message urged viewers to vote for Johnson on election day. Not voting for Johnson apparently would lead to nuclear disaster.

Another commercial, aired soon after this, left less to the imagination. Another cute little girl was shown licking an ice cream cone as a voice-over announcer calmly explained that the girl could be in serious trouble. The ice cream could contain some dangerous strontium 90 radiation from nuclear fallout because Barry Goldwater had opposed the nuclear test ban treaty. If he were elected, there was no telling how long the little girl might last. Though the Democrats pulled the spot after Republican complaints, the damage had been done. Millions had already seen it.

The Republicans, through the Mothers for a Moral America, presented their own lapse in taste, a thirty-minute film, "Choice." The movie painted a picture of the U.S. on the edge of moral collapse with images of topless bathing suits, pornographic book covers, and frenzied black rioters as illustration. It was scheduled to run on NBC on October 22, but at the last minute Goldwater repudiated the production as "nothing but a racist film" in its portrayal of blacks and canceled it.

Goldwater's personal TV presentations were remarkably traditional in comparison to such titillating fare, but he managed to stage his own bit of subtle media manipulation in the process. He arranged for his thirty-minute programs to be scheduled, as often as possible, on Tuesdays at 9:30 P.M. on NBC, preempting *That Was The Week That Was,* which constantly ribbed the senator in its skits. The September 22, 1964, season premiere of *TW3* was replaced by Goldwater's program. The September 29 episode would also have been preempted but NBC had already agreed to sell a sixty-second spot on the show to the Democrats, so *TW3* began its new season only a week late. However, the Republicans managed to buy out the October 6, October 13, and October 27 slots. When they were unable to preempt the show on October 20, they bought a half-hour of time on CBS, to compete with *TW3.* Tuesday, November 3, was election day, so NBC's election coverage wiped out the evening's regular programs. At last, on November 10, a week after the election and President Johnson's landslide victory, *TW3* responded to Goldwater's shenanigans by beginning that week's episode with a film of his concession speech with a voice-over announcer substituting the words:

Due to circumstances beyond control, the regularly scheduled political broadcast scheduled for this time is pre-empted.

It was an appropriate, very funny response, but *TW3* had already been mortally crippled in its quest for even passable ratings. In the vital first weeks of the season, it had rarely been on. *Peyton Place* and *Petticoat Junction* were top ten hits and it was doubtful that many viewers would turn to NBC instead, except perhaps by accident. By spring, *TW3* was gone, a victim of low ratings—and a change in attitudes. In the seventeen months since the enthusiastic reception given the *TW3* pilot, the mood in the country had changed. There were deep feelings of confusion, frustration, and resentment among viewers. Fewer and fewer people felt like laughing at anything so close to home as the news.

25. The Second Season

IN THE fall of 1965, for the first time in television history, all three networks presented their entire set of new season premieres in one week. For seven nights, beginning September 12, viewers were faced with a staggering selection of thirty-five new programs, and more than sixty returning shows. This insane competition marked a complete turnaround from the previous network practice of stringing out the season premieres from late September through mid-October, a procedure that had been in effect for nearly two decades. The reason for the change was quite simple: the CBS ratings romp of the early Sixties had turned into a tight, three-way race and none of the networks could afford to allow their competitors the slightest advantage.

ABC had initiated the practice of a single week for the premieres of its new shows in the fall of 1963. When the network repeated the strategy in the fall of 1964, it scooted to the number one position for the first two ratings reports of the 1964–65 season. Even though CBS regained the lead by November, ABC remained in its best position in years. Building on the advantage provided by its strong early returns, ABC nosed out NBC as the number two network for the season. NBC and CBS had no intention of allowing ABC to repeat its success in the 1965–66 season and both entered the September melée with their own premiere weeks.

The old practice of scattering the premieres of new programs over one month, starting in late September, had begun in the early days of network radio and had been automatically carried over to TV. It was said that such a leisurely pace gave viewers plenty of time to notice and tune in new shows while continuing to follow their old favorites. Consequently, the best way to launch a new show was to slot it either before or after a proven hit in order to catch the spill-over audience. Such a policy obviously favored the network with the greatest number of established hit shows and left most of the new programs on the others unwatched and unnoticed. An industry rule-of-thumb developed: The network with the greatest number of new shows in the fall would probably be the network that came in last. Since the early Sixties, ABC had been in the position of changing nearly one-half of its schedule every fall, and, more than any other network, it had to constantly combat viewer indifference to its unfamiliar new programs. As a result, the network had become locked in the number three position and was desperate for a way to break out. The experimental premiere weeks in 1963 and 1964 were just another ploy in its search for a solution.

ABC's placement of all its new shows in one eye-catching dramatic seven-day sweep made a great deal of sense. With NBC and CBS still in summer reruns, viewers were more inclined to give ABC a chance. As a result, several of its new shows such as *Twelve O'Clock High, The Addams Family, Bewitched, Voyage to the Bottom of the Sea,* and *Shindig* became hits early in the 1964–65 season. Some programs even managed to maintain their momentum once the other two networks unveiled their own new offerings. For example, *Peyton Place,* ABC's experiment in prime time soap opera, received an invaluable boost when viewers tuned in the first week "just to see what all the fuss was about" and became hooked by the dramatic complications and character conflicts. What's more, old ABC programs benefited as well. *Ben Casey,* for instance, had nearly been canceled after a very weak performance against *The Dick Van Dyke Show* and *The Beverly Hillbillies* in the 1963–64 season but, with the head start provided by the premiere week, it found its old audience and became a hit again in a new time period. In short, ABC's plan worked and the network broke the vicious cycle that had helped condemn it to last place.

The quick lead and continued strength of ABC through the 1964–65 season were a dramatic slap to CBS and its president, James Aubrey. Though, technically, a number of specials and preemptions (for the summer Olympics and presidential election campaign) had provided the extra boost that took ABC to the top in its premiere week, there was no denying that the unchallenged king of TV had been seriously shaken. Worse yet, of CBS's own new programs for the 1964–65 season, only *Gomer Pyle* and *Gilligan's Island* were major successes; many of the others were disasters. Drawing on the strength of its veteran hits, CBS regained the ratings lead by Thanksgiving, but by a very slim margin. Faced with the very real possibility of presiding over the network's first losing season in more than a decade, Aubrey boldly broke another industry tradition himself and began a major mid-season overhaul of the CBS schedule.

For years, the networks had operated under the assumption that it was meaningless to tamper with their schedules once the season had begun. It was felt that viewing patterns for the year were formed and set by late November and wouldn't change until the summer break and the next fall. Certainly there had been alterations in the network schedules between January and March in the past, but they were usually a stop-gap maneuver and never part of an overall programming strategy. Aubrey's actions were a calculated effort to repair the damage suffered in the fall and to steer CBS back to undisputed control of first place.

The underlying assumption of Aubrey's mid-season revamping was that the new CBS shows were good, but the schedule had not been put together quite right. He made eleven changes for the winter of 1965, focusing his efforts on shifting time slots rather than introducing new shows. For example, *Slattery's People,* a traditional lawyer drama starring Richard Crenna and featuring Ed Asner, was shifted from Monday night opposite the resuscitated *Ben Casey* to Friday night following *Gomer Pyle,* replacing the weak newspaper melodrama of *The Reporter.* The reasoning was simple: *Slattery's People* had received good critical reviews and should have been able to develop into a hit against a fading veteran, but the show had faltered when *Ben Casey* experienced its surprise revival. With Gomer as a new lead-in, *Slattery's People* could benefit from his spillover audience and slow down the progress of *Twelve O'Clock High,* a new but increasingly popular ABC show. Aubrey discarded the mediocre *Reporter* series and even managed to reduce the ratings damage on Monday night. Though he conceded the slot to *Ben Casey* and ABC by moving in *CBS Reports,* he stripped the news program of all national advertising, realizing that the Nielsen company didn't count unsponsored shows in the ratings. Other shifts followed a similar pattern and involved such "deserving" programs as *My Living Doll* and *The Entertainers.*

Aubrey's frantic mid-season changes worked no miracles, though CBS's ratings improved slightly and it managed to eke out a slim victory for the 1964–65 season. At the end of February, 1965, Aubrey was fired. Rarely in television history had any executive fallen so far, so fast. Yet there were suggestions that Aubrey had undercut his own position by allowing three very weak programs (*The Reporter, The Baileys of Balboa,* and *The Cara Williams Show*) onto CBS's 1964–65 schedule because he had a financial interest in their production outfit. What's more, the poor showing by all three was seen as the central reason CBS had begun to slip in

the fall of 1964. When Aubrey's winter tinkering failed to magically restore the network to its previously unquestioned supremacy, he became a marked man under a cloud of suspicion. Aubrey was replaced by Jack Schneider, whose main background was in sales and administration, rather than programming. He faced the task of keeping CBS on top for the 1965–66 season in what promised to be another tight race.

With all three networks launching the 1965–66 season the same week in head-to-head competition, any small advantage was seen as potentially decisive. NBC and CBS focused on color as the gimmick that could provide the edge necessary for victory because, a decade after color TV sets first went on sale, consumers were buying them in great numbers at last. The long-hoped-for color boom had begun with set sales and color broadcasting growing dramatically in just two years. During 1964 there was a 77% increase in color set purchases. In the fall of 1964, NBC launched the first major color season, with more than 50% of its programming in full tint. During the summer of 1965, the networks began covering live news events such as space shots in color. In the fall of 1965, NBC became the first nearly all-color network with only two of its shows, *I Dream of Jeannie* and *Convoy,* in black and white. At the same time, CBS reached the 50% color mark in its schedule. ABC lagged far behind both and felt the pinch immediately as the ratings for the 1965 fall premieres came in. Not only had it lost the advantage of having the only premiere week on television, it also hadn't moved fast enough on color. For the first time ever, all of the top ten shows were in color. Six percent of American TV homes had color sets and, not surprisingly, people with color sets watched color shows more than the national average. ABC found its black and white stalwarts such as *Peyton Place* and *Ben Casey* sliding lower and lower in the ratings.

CBS and NBC took a strong lead in the new season and once again ABC was in the cellar, facing the grim prospect of a major overhaul of its schedule for the 1966–67 season. Driven by despera-

The camp adventures of *Batman* launched the first "second season": (from *l.*) The Mad Hatter (David Wayne), Batman (Adam West), and Robin (Burt Ward). *(Courtesy of Twentieth Century-Fox)*

	7:30	8:00	8:30	9:00	9:30	10:00	10:30	
MONDAY	Twelve O'Clock High		THE LEGEND OF JESSE JAMES	A MAN CALLED SHENANDOAH	The Farmer's Daughter	Ben Casey		**ABC**
	To Tell The Truth	I've Got A Secret	The Lucy Show	Andy Griffith Show	Hazel	STEVE LAWRENCE SHOW		**CBS**
	Hullabaloo	JOHN FORSYTHE SHOW	Dr. Kildare I	Andy Williams Show @Perry Como's Kraft Music Hall		RUN FOR YOUR LIFE		**NBC**

	7:30	8:00	8:30	9:00	9:30	10:00	10:30	
TUESDAY	Combat!		McHale's Navy	F TROOP	Peyton Place I	The Fugitive		**ABC**
	Rawhide		Red Skelton Show		Petticoat Junction	CBS News Specials / CBS Reports		**CBS**
	MY MOTHER THE CAR	PLEASE DON'T EAT THE DAISIES	Dr. Kildare II	NBC Tuesday Night At The Movies				**NBC**

	7:30	8:00	8:30	9:00	9:30	10:00	10:30	
WEDNESDAY	The Adventures Of Ozzie And Harriet	Patty Duke Show	GIDGET	THE BIG VALLEY		Amos Burke, Secret Agent		**ABC**
	LOST IN SPACE		The Beverly Hillbillies	GREEN ACRES	Dick Van Dyke Show	Danny Kaye Show		**CBS**
	The Virginian			Bob Hope Presents The Chrysler Theater @Bob Hope Show		I SPY		**NBC**

	7:30	8:00	8:30	9:00	9:30	10:00	10:30	
THURSDAY	Shindig I	Donna Reed Show	O.K. CRACKERBY	Bewitched	Peyton Place II	THE LONG HOT SUMMER		**ABC**
	The Munsters	Gilligan's Island	My Three Sons	CBS THURSDAY NIGHT MOVIES				**CBS**
	Daniel Boone		LAREDO		MONA McCLUSKEY	DEAN-MARTIN SHOW		**NBC**

	7:30	8:00	8:30	9:00	9:30	10:00	10:30	
FRIDAY	The Flintstones	TAMMY	The Addams Family	HONEY WEST	Peyton Place III	Jimmy Dean Show		**ABC**
	THE WILD, WILD WEST		HOGAN'S HEROES	Gomer Pyle, U.S.M.C.	SMOTHERS BROTHERS SHOW	Slattery's People		**CBS**
	CAMP RUNAMUCK	HANK	CONVOY		MR. ROBERTS	The Man From U.N.C.L.E.		**NBC**

	7:30	8:00	8:30	9:00	9:30	10:00	10:30	
SATURDAY	Shindig II	The King Family	Lawrence Welk Show		Hollywood Palace		ABC Scope	**ABC**
	Jackie Gleason Show		TRIALS OF O'BRIEN		THE LONER	Gunsmoke		**CBS**
	Flipper	I DREAM OF JEANNIE	GET SMART	NBC Satuday Night At The Movies				**NBC**

	7:00	7:30	8:00	8:30	9:00	9:30	10:00	10:30	
SUNDAY	Voyage To The Bottom Of The Sea		THE F.B.I.		The ABC Sunday Night Movie				**ABC**
	Lassie	My Favorite Martian	Ed Sullivan Show		Perry Mason		Candid Camera	What's My Line	**CBS**
[from 6:30]	Bell Telephone Hour NBC News Specials	Walt Disney's Wonderful World Of Color		Branded	Bonanza		THE WACKIEST SHIP IN THE ARMY		**NBC**

tion, the network decided to discard another industry tradition in the hope of salvaging the 1965–66 season. After the fall premieres, the networks usually focused their attention on setting up the next season's schedule, locking it up by February, and letting unsuccessful shows run their course. If Aubrey had achieved moderate success for CBS in 1964–65 with his mid-season tinkering, why not go one step further: treat January like a new season, with both new programs and major time shifts. A house cleaning would be necessary anyway, so why wait until the next fall? Thus, in January, 1966, ABC launched "the second season."

The early September premiere week made a so-called second season possible. In the early Sixties, the bible of network TV, the Nielsen ratings book (published twice each month), took almost a week to compile, print, and distribute. For example, the book covering the period of September 5 through September 19 (called the "first September" book) would not be in the hands of eager executives until the last days of the month. The book covering September 20 through October 3 (called the "second September") would arrive in mid-October. Each month contained a "first" and "second" book with similar delays, so that when the fall premieres stretched from mid-September through October, the first Nielsen book to take into account all of the new shows for the fall was the second October report, which wasn't in print until the first week of November. With the new season completely launched by

mid-September, the second September ratings book could function as the first gauge of a program's popularity, and thus reliable information on program performance was available an entire month earlier than before. There was enough time to plan and produce shows for a second season that could begin in January.

The obvious ramification of a formal second season was that more programs were given a chance to air. This was a double-edged development because, at the same time, a potentially popular show with low ratings at the start might be yanked off the air before it had a chance to build an audience. A new season in January also marked the beginning of the end of the traditional nine-month television season, stretching from September to May. In the process it delayed until March final decisions on the next fall's line-ups because programmers wanted to see how well second season entries performed.

ABC unveiled its second season amid great fanfare ("The excitement of the fall starts all over again!"), but most of the new shows bombed, which wasn't surprising because most new ABC shows at the time bombed. Despite the additional month available to prepare, many of ABC's new shows were thrown together at the last minute or quickly imported from England. Nonetheless, some of the time shifts worked well. *Peyton Place,* for instance, changed from a Tuesday-Thursday-Friday rotation to a Monday-Tuesday-Friday arrangement, and its ratings returned to the level of the

1964–65 season. In addition, the network increased its percentage of color programming. More importantly, ABC came up with a smash hit to revitalize the schedule, the camp adventures of *Batman*.

Critics had often complained that television was filled with comic-book-type characters. *Batman* accepted the comic book roots of its hero not as a putdown but an inspiration, and proudly flaunted them, though in a very different manner from its fraternal crime stopper, Superman. The syndicated *Adventures of Superman* television series of the Fifties had the trappings of the comic book adventures (the man of steel's colorful costume, invulnerability, power to fly, and super-strength), but ultimately it was just a traditional kiddie-cop adventure presenting Superman as an exceptional, but in many ways typical, stalwart crime fighter. He usually faced the same faceless hoods and routine crimes encountered by his colleagues in the police force and private detective agencies. Batman (billed in the comics as "the world's greatest detective") could have easily fit into the same mold, but producer William Dozier realized that such a formula would probably not work in an age of superhero-type spies and secret agents. Instead, he looked not so much at the character of Batman but at the gimmicks surrounding him and, more importantly, at the style of the comic book medium itself with its flashy colors, impossible gadgets, and unusual action sequences. Dozier decided to stage the series as a television comic book, but with one important difference: all the comic book elements were grossly exaggerated and the program turned into one huge tongue-in-cheek joke. After all, could two adults in leotards and capes really be taken seriously?

Adam West (as Batman and the caped crusader's alter ego, aristocrat-goldbrick Bruce Wayne) and Burt Ward (as Robin the Boy Wonder and Dick Grayson, Wayne's young ward) played the heroes as marvelous caricatures of the gung-ho, power of positive thinking super patriots that had dominated comics since World War II. Batman and Robin were very, *very* serious about fighting crime in Gotham City but, though they never cracked jokes, much of what they said was hilarious. With a perfectly straight face, Batman would wax prosaic on the evils of crime and the importance of good citizenship, even while struggling to escape from a seemingly foolproof trap. Robin greeted every challenge with boyish enthusiasm and shamelessly displayed his perception of the obvious with such phrases as "Holy ice cubes, Batman! It's getting cold!" It was too ridiculous to be true; so naive that it was preposterous; so bad that it was good. That was Dozier's trump card. By hopelessly exaggerating every aspect of the show, he fashioned an insane environment that re-created the comic book world for children but also offered "camp" humor for the teenagers and adults. The style touched every aspect of the show, from the full-screen comic book captions that adorned every fight (matching each punch to some "Crunch!," "Pow!," "ZAP!," or "Ka-zonk" type graphic superimposed on the scene) to the dramatically hokey voice-over announcer-narrator (Dozier himself) who solemnly posed the inevitable question in each episode: "Is this the end of Batman and Robin?" The series ran twice each week, on Wednesday and Thursday nights, and Dozier ended the Wednesday episodes with absurd cliff-hangers designed to lure even the most incredulous audience back for part two—"same bat-time, same bat-channel!" The exaggerated perils were a direct sendup of the many vapid kiddie serials that had run on the radio and in the movie theaters during the Thirties and Forties, using the cliff-hanger come-on to coax fans back for the next episode. At various mid-week climaxes, Batman and Robin were on the verge of being frozen, fried, eaten by lions, unmasked, or turned into postage stamps. The two heroes used a

ludicrous arsenal of "bat" gimmicks in their weekly skirmishes including the batmobile, batcopter, batcomputer, batpole, and batarang—all housed, of course, in the batcave. Best of all, they faced the most colorful array of guest villains a program could ever hope for as some of Hollywood's top character actors donned the garb of Batman's most popular comic book opponents. Unlike the dynamic duo, the villains in the series obviously were having a great time and relished the opportunity to taunt their hated adversaries with clues to their impending crimes. For them, the thrill of battle mattered more than the cold hard cash. Burgess Meredith (the Penguin), Cesar Romero (the Joker), and Frank Gorshin (the Riddler) were the most popular guest stars, though others such as Art Carney (the Archer), George Sanders (Mr. Freeze), David Wayne (Mad Hatter), Victor Buono (King Tut), and, at various times, Julie Newmar, Eartha Kitt, and Lee Ann Meriwether (Catwoman) were equally entertaining. Each performer brought a frenzied lunacy to the role (mad laughter was the most common trait among them) and their antics were the effective balance to the mock-deadpan of Batman and Robin.

Dozier's comic book for television combined superb guests, camp humor, colorful costumes, unusual camera work (emphasizing weird angles), and pure imagination. The result was an instant hit that justified ABC's second season gamble and gave viewers something unusual to laugh at, something beyond the thick-headed antics of Gomer Pyle and Gilligan. *Batman* relied on the traditional battle between good and evil, but treated the melodramatic conflict as a very silly game in which the villains were the most appealing characters. (Batman and Robin were far too serious and the police were incredibly dumb.) Though by no means the only tongue-in-cheek program that season, *Batman* was undoubtedly the most

Chances are even the pizza held by Colonel Robert Hogan (Bob Crane, *l.*) came from an oven hidden beneath Stalag 13 on *Hogan's Heroes*. (Photo by Viacom, Hollywood)

September 12, 1965

After building a following for five years on ABC, the American Football League jumps to NBC.

September 14, 1965

My Mother the Car. (NBC). Jerry Van Dyke plays a suburban hubby who discovers his dead mother reincarnated as a decrepit automobile on a used car lot. Ann Sothern supplies the voice for "mother," who speaks to her son through the car radio.

September 15, 1965

Green Acres. (CBS). Eddie Albert and Eva Gabor play backwards Clampetts (city slickers that move to the country) in a third-generation Paul Henning hillbilly spinoff.

September 16, 1965

The Dean Martin Show. (NBC). Martin returns to television in an easy-going variety hour carried almost completely by his relaxed, slightly naughty personality.

September 18, 1965

I Dream of Jeannie. (NBC). Barbara Eden plays a beautiful 2,000-year-old magical genie who attaches herself to an American astronaut (played by Larry Hagman). As "lord and master" he gets as many wishes as he wants.

September 19, 1965

The F.B.I. (ABC). Quinn Martin presents Efrem Zimbalist, Jr. in a series based on actual cases from the F.B.I.'s files.

October 24, 1965

NBC becomes the first television network with thirty minutes of nightly news seven days a week.

---

distinctive. It launched a nationwide bat-craze, inspired countless parodies in every medium (most never matching the original), and revealed a willingness among viewers to laugh at square-jawed heroics and pillars of authority.

The late-blooming success of *The Man from U.N.C.L.E.* the previous season had set the stage for the influx of tongue-in-cheek heroes starting in the fall of 1965, as all three networks rushed to follow the lead of Napoleon Solo and Illya Kuryakin. Not since ABC's overdose of action-adventure clones from *Maverick* and *77 Sunset Strip* had so many flippant characters appeared. Unlike the insipid productions at the turn of the decade, the new wave of programs contained first class writing, clever situations, and very talented performers.

Foremost among these programs was Britain's *The Avengers* which ABC brought to America as part of its second season line-up. Honor Blackman had departed from the series and Patrick Macnee (as John Steed) had a new cohort, the lovely, leggy Diana Rigg (as Mrs. Emma Peel), who picked up the saucy, flippant interplay and the deliciously ambiguous relationship with Steed. Like Mrs. Gale, she was a strong, sexy, independent woman who could fight crime as well as any man. Such a notion was practically unheard of at the time in American television (the best the Stateside networks could offer was Anne Francis as a female private eye, *Honey West*), and *The Avengers* began building a strong American cult following and winning high critical praise.

Homegrown productions included both tongue-in-cheek spy thrillers and sharp sitcom spoofs that marked a return to the quality of such classics as *Sergeant Bilko*. The two adventure series that came directly out of the *U.N.C.L.E.* mold were NBC's *I Spy* and CBS's *The Wild, Wild West,* which both featured pairs of witty, resourceful agents. *I Spy* presented Robert Culp and Bill Cosby as U.S. government agents (posing as an international tennis star and his trainer) roaming the world in search of Russian, Oriental, and mobster bigwigs. Though eschewing the Bond-U.N.C.L.E. device of a fictional super-secret non-aligned organization of evil in favor of more realistic foes and dramatic situations, the program's location shots and humorous edge were its chief attractions. Cosby, a veteran black comic and nightclub entertainer, worked in some hilarious dialogues with Culp (often about Cosby's ghetto youth in Philadelphia) as they engaged in typical spy shenanigans throughout the world. At first it had been feared that Cosby's co-starring status would be a possible trouble spot for the show, but the mere presence of a black performer on television was no longer automatically a major risk. Only three NBC affiliates refused to air the series (in Albany, Georgia; Savannah, Georgia; and Daytona Beach, Florida). Television was improving its attitude toward blacks and, in fact, the industry felt comfortable enough to award Cosby an Emmy for his *I Spy* role.

CBS's *The Wild, Wild West* offered a unique combination of espionage and Western adventure by reaching all the way back to the *Maverick* roots of flippant cowboys for its unlikely premise of two spies operating in the American West of the 1870s. President Ulysses S. Grant personally assigned special U.S. government agents James T. West (Robert Conrad) and Artemus Gordon (Ross Martin) to the Western frontier, though it was never made quite clear exactly who or what menace he detected as a threat to the nation—certainly the country was in no danger from a foreign power out amid the sagebrush and tumbling tumbleweeds. The producers and writers never let that bother them, nor did they feel obligated to explain what some of the best electronic gadgets of the twentieth century were doing in the 1870s (thinly disguised as "contemporary" inventions of the time). Instead, they used the unique hook provided by the combination of genres to gently spoof both Westerns and spy formats while, at the same time, developing exceptionally off-beat and intriguing stories. Conrad and Martin displayed the required light banter in the face of danger and even managed to "save the Western world" (of the nineteenth century) from the schemes of crazed madmen such as their most frequent foe, Dr. Miguelito Loveless (Michael Dunn), a midget. With its fabulous cast and crew, *The Wild, Wild West* rose above a ridiculous premise to become a solid, entertaining hybrid and a CBS Friday night staple for four seasons.

Action and humor had teamed up earlier in television history in such series as *Maverick,* but in the new programs the line between adventure and comedy grew increasingly fuzzy. The season's best adventure shows were tongue-in-cheek while the best new sitcoms were spoofs of familiar dramatic settings. In the comedies the stories were certainly exaggerated and silly, but they still retained enough action, mock-horror shootouts, and plot complications to function as adequate, though absurd, dramatic adventures. Among the most resilient of the new comedy-adventures was the marvelously mad put-on of *Get Smart,* which managed to outlast all of the other new video spies.

A product of the collective dementia of Buck Henry, Mel Brooks, and Howard Morris, *Get Smart* featured Don Adams as the bumbling, over-confident klutz, Maxwell Smart, secret agent 86 for a CIA-type organization, Control. *Get Smart* used the passion for absurd spy gimmicks as the launching pad for its gags and built from there. U.N.C.L.E. headquarters was hidden behind a false wall in a dry cleaning store, so to gain entrance to Control, Smart had to drop through the false floor of a phone booth. While Solo

in the Gulf of Tonkin. In response, Congress had passed, almost unanimously, the "blank check" Gulf of Tonkin Resolution giving President Johnson virtual wartime powers to "take all necessary measures to r[e]peal any armed attack against the forces of the U.S. and to preve[n]t further aggression." In March, 1965, the first U.S. combat Mar[in]es landed in South Vietnam as the American Air Force bega[n] [c]ontinuous bombing raids throughout the North. Without ev[er] having declared it, the United States was at war with a cou[ntry] most Americans couldn't even pronounce. The networks, how[ev]er, were ready to apply their growing technical expertise to the [diffi]cult challenge of covering the overseas jungle conflict.

It was [ass]umed that the American intervention would last only a few mo[nth]s, so much of the reporting in 1965 reflected an excited, almost a[dven]turous spirit. Unlike the Korean war, with its clumsy battle f[ootag]e (often provided by the U.S. government itself), the Vietna[m con]flict offered a unique opportunity for television to place its cor[respon]dents in an exotic jungle setting as they filmed their stories [for t]he nightly news programs. CBS's Walter Cronkite took a thre[e-wee]k tour of Vietnam in July of 1965 and filed reports of the v[ar t]hat focused on the sophisticated hardware and know-how [of th]e American forces. One segment featured Cronkite aboard a pl[ane z]ooming through the sky while the American pilots aboard pro[udly] explained the bombing apparatus as if it were some shiny ne[w ca]r. For the most part, though, network reports of battle ac[tion] usually consisted of film of a squad of Marines slogging th[rough] some jungle and firing at an unseen enemy somewhere i[n the b]ush. Secretary of Defense Robert McNamara had stated t[hat th]e troops would be home by Christmas, and the need to [dig de]eper into the story didn't seem that pressing.

[Alth]ough many newsmen (like most other Americans) were slow [to re]alize the ramifications of the steadily growing American in[volv]ement in Vietnam, the truly remarkable aspect of the coverage [was] that, despite some government pressure and secrecy, the net[wo]rks were largely free to cover the venture as they wished. For [the] first time in history, a government conducting an overseas [w]ar relinquished control of the way the war was perceived back home. Vietnam became a true "television war" as many people in the country received most of their information on it from the nightly news coverage and occasional specials on the three networks. Such reports rarely examined the underlying purposes of the war and mostly emphasized very popular and visual aspects such as superficial combat footage, the American GIs adjusting to life overseas, and trivial battle statistics and graphs. Still, the fact was that the power of government rhetoric had been usurped and replaced by pictures brought directly into the privacy of individual homes across the country.

It was inevitable that such power over forming public opinion on a foreign policy matter would eventually upset the government. In August, 1965, just a few months after the Dominican Republic conflict, CBS aired a dramatic film report by Morley Safer that deeply disturbed officials. On the August 5 edition of the *CBS Evening News,* viewers were shown the story of an American outfit destroying some huts in the small Vietnamese village of Cam Ne. It wasn't so much what was said in the report that bothered the government, but rather the impression the film left behind. While the residents of the village stood by meekly, crying and begging for a reprieve, the Marines methodically set the huts on fire, many using Zippo cigarette lighters to ignite the straw roofs. The image left by the film was potent and needed no elaboration: The United States, a powerful mechanized society, had sent its Marines into a backward rural country and, with virtually no provocation, was systematically destroying it. Whether there had been any enemy

activity (by the Viet Cong) in Cam Ne became unimportant. The chilling efficiency and lack of moral qualms displayed by the Marines (who were obviously in no immediate danger from the civilians) couldn't help but raise doubts among puzzled citizens as to what the U.S. was really doing there. Other people reacted with anger at CBS, criticizing the network for distorting the story, putting sensationalism above patriotism, and undermining morale. Safer even received mysterious threats on his life. Fred Friendly observed, in response to the protests, "As the power of the [news] medium increases, the power used to suppress it will increase."

The government began to exert more and more pressure on network reporters to "go along with the party line" on war dispatches. Such pressure was usually indirect and couched in appeals for teamwork, patriotism, and common sense understanding that were filtered through the networks' own channels to be conveyed by immediate superiors. This was not very difficult because many top broadcast officials had direct ties to the government and were actually "on the same team." Yet the pressure applied through influential company men rarely came in the form of some heavy-handed demand for the suppression of information, but usually appeared as a polite request to be more restrained, balanced, and sensitive to the possibly damaging repercussions of adverse war reports. Nevertheless, the "reasonable desire" for a more "evenhanded" approach to the news merely added to the tension that was always present between the network news departments and the profit-minded network executives who often viewed the news as an extravagant loss leader necessary merely for prestige.

In spite of the pressure from the top, all three networks presented competent but generally uninciteful war specials throughout 1965. These usually consisted of carefully balanced panel discussions between supporters of the war (such as Harvard professors Henry Kissinger and Zbigniew Brzezinski) and anti-war critics (usually foreign war correspondents because there were not very many homegrown critics available). In a perverse way, TV's evenhandedness in these debates served to help the anti-war cause the most because in 1965 many viewers had never heard arguments against the government's policy expressed at all. As the war intensified, though, the networks began putting more emphasis on the government's side of the story.

In response to the storm of protest over Safer's Cam Ne report, CBS, later that August, aired *Vietnam Perspective,* a series of four hour-long specials that examined several different viewpoints on the war, though it generally presented the government line as basically correct. NBC also began a weekly war program (on Sunday afternoons, hosted by Garrick Utley), *Vietnam Weekly Review,* but this was merely a well produced yet essentially meaningless review of the week's battle reports, focusing on ultimately pointless jungle skirmishes and hill assaults.

Surprisingly, ABC, the network with the weakest news department, provided the best overall coverage of the war within its weekly public affairs series, *ABC Scope.* This program had run, under a variety of titles, in weird hours since 1963. Starting in Februrary, 1966, it devoted all of its time to the Vietnam war. Realizing that the weekly battle statistics were given more than enough coverage on the nightly news (they were as familiar and as meaningless to most viewers as the stock market reports), the producers of *ABC Scope* concentrated instead on one particular aspect of the war each week. Using filmed reports usually produced on location in Vietnam, they tried to make sense of the increasingly perplexing conflict. Some of the programs included: A study of the role of blacks in Vietnam (comparing the views of black militants such as Stokely Carmichael with the views of blacks doing the fighting); film of North Vietnam itself, shot by a French crew on location; and thoughtful, on-the-spot analysis by Howard K. Smith, one of the most eloquent supporters of the war. These programs offered an important perspective to the jumble of general war news available and provided the opportunity for viewers to form intelligent and informed opinions on the issue.

Nobody watched these shows. All of the Vietnam specials regularly turned up at the very bottom of the ratings charts and *ABC Scope* in particular registered the worst ratings of any network program in modern television history. In September, 1965, before it changed formats to become a weekly Vietnam show, only 28% of the more than 150 ABC affiliates aired the program. By 1966, only 27 affiliates bothered to show it at all and not one ABC station in the top fifty markets carried the program at its scheduled slot in prime time (Saturday night at 10:30 P.M.). Most of the ABC stations in major cities stuck the program in some obscure corner of the weekly schedule. WABC in New York aired it Sunday afternoon at 2 P.M. WFAA in Dallas aired it Sunday morning at 9 A.M. WNAC in Boston topped them all; it aired each episode eight days after its scheduled broadcast date, at 1 A.M. Sunday morning. Viewers never complained about the ridiculous time slots because they didn't care. Whether for or against the war, a majority of viewers found any coverage of Vietnam generally upsetting and they fervently avoided anything more than the short clips on the nightly news.

Keenly aware of the public's disinterest in special coverage of the Vietnam war, the networks faced the difficult policy question of how to balance the guaranteed low ratings of Vietnam specials with their unwritten obligation to adequately present such a major story. The question came to a head in early 1966 when it became necessary to decide the best way to cover the public hearings that were being held by Senator William Fulbright's Foreign Relations Committee on the government's handling of the war. Fulbright had become one of the best known congressional war critics and had turned the hearings into the first high level public discussion of the real aims and ultimate goals of the Vietnam conflict. In late January he began by publicly roasting top administration witnesses such as Secretary of State Dean Rusk in days of long, tough questioning. The early sessions were briefly covered on the nightly news but, as the hearings progressed, it was clear that they deserved more extensive airtime. The event was certainly newsworthy, but in what manner would most people prefer to follow it? Live coverage of the actual testimony during the day? The familiar two-or three-minute reports on the nightly news? A special late night half-hour wrap up? A weekend special reviewing the events of the entire week, featuring a discussion panel to analyze the significant developments?

Network executives argued that live coverage preempted the most profitable part of the day and would be wasted anyway; most people interested in the hearings wouldn't be able to watch them. As head of CBS News, Fred Friendly strongly supported blanket live coverage, feeling that the hearings were important and that TV had a responsibility to present them to the millions of viewers who would "bother" to tune in. With NBC's president and long-time supporter of extensive news coverage, Bob Kinter, recently deposed, Friendly was virtually alone among top brass in advocating complete live coverage. He grudgingly agreed to follow a compromise "day-to-day decision process" that called for live coverage on days important witnesses testified and evening highlights for the rest. Without too much trouble, both NBC and CBS followed this course in early February, but on February 10, while NBC went ahead with its planned broadcast of the testimony of George Kennan, former ambassador to Russia, CBS coverage plans were vetoed by network president Schneider. With that action, Schneider saved CBS $175,000 but lost the most respected name in contemporary TV journalism. Friendly quit CBS in protest and was replaced by the man he had succeeded in the first place, Richard Salant.

Though both CBS and NBC wound up carrying two days of hearings live the very next week, an important turning point had been reached in television's handling of the Vietnam war. Friendly's resignation marked the beginning of a swing away from extensive coverage and, while American involvement in the war rapidly increased over the next year, the number of Vietnam specials dropped sharply. Investigative reporting and discussions including spokesmen for "all points of view" were also downplayed. It was not worth the trouble, both internally and with the government, to follow a story viewers did not seem to care about anyway. So even as the United States committed more than 100,000 additional troops to the war effort, the chief source of information on the war for most Americans became nothing more than short repetitive news clips dished out nightly at suppertime.

26. Same Is the Name of the Game

VARIETY, the entertainment industry's own weekly trade magazine, labeled 1966 and 1967 as the era of "no guts journalism" in television. Though ABC continued to produce the rarely seen *ABC Scope* and CBS offered the *CBS News Hour* in prime time, the number of documentaries based on hard news events was down drastically. For example, between September 12 and November 22, 1966, NBC broadcast only three prime time news documentaries of any sort, and ABC offered only two. The news departments at the commercial networks seemed afraid to turn out anything that might possibly provoke official displeasure or viewer indifference.

All three networks practically ignored a new round of hearings on the Vietnam war held in early 1967 by Senator William Fulbright's Foreign Relations Committee. Only the noncommercial NET network gave the discussions extensive coverage, instituting a policy of presenting one-hour cutdowns of the day's live hearings for prime time viewing each night. Instead, NBC stuck to puff travelogue-type features like "The Royal Palace" and "Thoroughbred." ABC covered the war, but turned out some material that resembled gung-ho propaganda films openly endorsing the Vietnam action rather than serious independent assessments of a complex news subject. These efforts were often sponsored by major defense contractors such as the 3M corporation for "Our Time in Hell" (the Marines at war) and B. F. Goodrich for "War in the Skies" (with retired Brigadier General James Stewart as narrator for the exploits of the Air Force in Southeast Asia). CBS came up with "The People of South Vietnam: How They Feel About the War," in which the network attempted to analyze the effects of the war in Vietnam by conducting an on-the-spot public opinion poll. Such a technique was safe, noncontroversial, and hopelessly misdirected, treating the problems facing uneducated peasant farmers in the war-torn country like political or fashion trends in middle class American suburbs.

Yet the "no guts journalism" label wasn't only limited to the apparent hands-off policy toward the Vietnam war. The commercial networks seemed to be ignoring a wide range of controversial subjects, once again leaving NET as the only force apparently willing to produce incisive programs. On shows such as *At Issue* and *NET Journal,* the noncommercial network tackled such topics as misleading advertising, defects in American medical care, the manipulation of the press by President Johnson's administration, and overcharges levied against the poor by supermarkets, credit unions, and the phone company. Serious questions began to be raised on the integrity and independence of the commercial networks' news operations. Was the toning down of controversy deliberate? Were the networks fearful of reprisals by government and industry? Were they somehow too closely aligned to those same forces in government and industry? Or was all this just a comparative cooling off of coverage in contrast to the dramatic news events of 1963, 1964, and 1965?

In January, 1966, ABC brought the discussion to a very concrete level when it announced its desire to be absorbed by ITT, one of the nation's largest conglomerates, and one with extensive government ties. In its petition to the FCC, the network effusively promised that the proposed merger would be a tremendous benefit to broadcasting. With the new corporate money that would be available, ABC could, for instance, expand its public affairs programming. In addition, the increased stature of the network could only help the still struggling UHF system because ABC had the greatest number of UHF affiliates. Thus, as the fortunes of ABC improved, the status of UHF would have to rise as well. At first, the commission appeared to accept all the grand promises at face value and the merger seemed destined for a quick approval. Then, unexpectedly, serious opposition from within both the FCC and the Department of Justice developed and the matter grew more complicated. Asked by the commission for a legal opinion on the case, the Justice Department pointed out that the merger would quite probably lead to some violations of the anti-trust law and would also discourage ITT from going ahead with a backburner notion to start a new television network on its own. Within the FCC, newly appointed commissioner Nicholas Johnson put aside the traditional FCC policy of giving big business the benefit of the doubt, cut through the self-serving gobbledygook and vague promises dished out by ABC, and stated quite bluntly that he saw the merger as motivated solely by economic self-interests that had nothing to do with better serving the public. Johnson also raised the disturbing possibility that ITT, with its extensive government war contracts, might attempt to influence the ABC news department. Though

FALL 1966 SCHEDULE

MONDAY

	7:30	8:00	8:30	9:00	9:30	10:00	10:30	
	IRON HORSE		THE RAT PATROL	THE FELONY SQUAD	Peyton Place I	The Big Valley		ABC
	Gilligan's Island	RUN, BUDDY, RUN	The Lucy Show	Andy Griffith Show	FAMILY AFFAIR	JEAN ARTHUR SHOW	I've Got A Secret	CBS
	THE MONKEES	I Dream Of Jeannie	ROGER MILLER SHOW	THE ROAD WEST @Perry Como's Kraft Music Hall		Run For Your Life		NBC

TUESDAY

	7:30	8:00	8:30	9:00	9:30	10:00	10:30	
	Combat!		THE ROUNDERS	THE PRUITTS OF SOUTHAMPTON	LOVE ON A ROOFTOP	The Fugitive		ABC
	Daktari		Red Skelton Hour		Petticoat Junction	CBS News Hour		CBS
	THE GIRL FROM U.N.C.L.E.		OCCASIONAL WIFE	NBC Tuesday Night At The Movies				NBC

WEDNESDAY

	7:30	8:00	8:30	9:00	9:30	10:00	10:30	
	Batman I	THE MONROES		THE MAN WHO NEVER WAS	Peyton Place II	ABC STAGE '67		ABC
	Lost In Space		The Beverly Hillbillies	Green Acres	Gomer Pyle, U.S.M.C.	Danny Kaye Show		CBS
	The Virginian			Bob Hope Presents The Chrysler Theater @Bob Hope Show		I Spy		NBC

THURSDAY

	7:30	8:00	8:30	9:00	9:30	10:00	10:30	
	Batman II	F Troop	TAMMY GRIMES SHOW	Bewitched	THAT GIRL	HAWK		ABC
	JERICHO		My Three Sons	CBS Thursday Night Movies				CBS
	Daniel Boone		STAR TREK		THE HERO	Dean Martin Show		NBC

FRIDAY

	7:30	8:00	8:30	9:00	9:30	10:00	10:30	
	THE GREEN HORNET	THE TIME TUNNEL		MILTON BERLE SHOW		Twelve O'Clock High		ABC
	The Wild, Wild West		Hogan's Heroes	CBS FRIDAY NIGHT MOVIES				CBS
	TARZAN		The Man From U.N.C.L.E.		T.H.E. CAT	Laredo		NBC

SATURDAY

	7:30	8:00	8:30	9:00	9:30	10:00	10:30	
	SHANE		Lawrence Welk Show		Hollywood Palace		ABC Scope	ABC
	Jackie Gleason Show		PISTOLS 'N' PETTICOATS	MISSION: IMPOSSIBLE		Gunsmoke		CBS
	Flipper	Please Don't Eat The Daisies	Get Smart	NBC Saturday Night At The Movies				NBC

SUNDAY

	7:00	7:30	8:00	8:30	9:00	9:30	10:00	10:30	
	Voyage To The Bottom Of The Sea		The F.B.I.		The ABC Sunday Night Movie				ABC
	Lassie	IT'S ABOUT TIME	Ed Sullivan Show		Garry Moore Show		Candid Camera	What's My Line	CBS
[from 6:30]	Bell Telephone Hour NBC News Specials	Walt Disney's Wonderful World Of Color		HEY LANDLORD	Bonanza		Andy Williams Show		NBC

ITT pledged a three-year "hands off" policy in changing the ABC executive personnel, there were serious doubts that this would be sufficient restraint. In the course of the public hearings on the case, newspaper reporters testified that ITT had pressured their papers to kill stories considered detrimental to the proposed merger. Critics quickly pointed out that if ITT would attempt to distort the news in outlets over which it had no control, what would it do to a wholly owned subsidiary?

In spite of all the objections, the FCC voted to approve the merger by a 4–3 margin, twice (December 1966 and June 1967). Miffed that its warnings had been dismissed so cavalierly, the Department of Justice took the ruling to the U.S. Court of Appeals, further delaying the procedure that by then had dragged through nearly two years of hearings. On January 1, 1968, ITT called off the merger, citing the extensive opposition within the government as the reason for its pullout. Some observers, however, said that the continued mediocre ratings performance by ABC had as much to do with the withdrawal as the expensive, embarrassing legal delays.

As the usual number three network, ABC was constantly searching for gimmicks to attract attention and boost its ratings. Such innovations as the second season premieres of January, 1966, usually brought a brief burst of success, but the glow soon faded as people returned to their old favorites. Nonetheless, ABC's gim-

micks kept the overall network race tight for a while each year and forced CBS and NBC to seriously consider the latest ABC flash and decide whether or not to adopt it for their own schedules. For the fall of 1966, ABC's strategy hinged on two stunts: First, the network moved up its fall premiere week to begin just after Labor Day, giving the shows a week's head start against the premieres on the other networks. Second, ABC slotted blockbuster films such as "Bridge on the River Kwai" for the first weeks of the new season, thereby "front loading" its new schedule with exceptionally attractive specials. The strategy worked and ABC ran away with the psychologically important first ratings period. "Bridge on the River Kwai" was especially potent and captured an impressive 60% of the audience, making it the most popular film then ever seen on television. Though ABC's ratings once again faded as the 1966–67 season progressed, another weapon had been discovered in the battle for ratings success both in the fall and in key ratings sweep weeks throughout the season: hit movies.

All three networks had been pursuing a growing love affair with prime time movies since 1961, but "Bridge on the River Kwai" underscored the dramatic ratings boost a box office smash could provide in a week's competition. Even moderate box office hits could be counted on to score rather well against the more limited formats of weekly series because they were, in comparison, high-budget specials. By early 1967, each network had two nights of movies per week, leaving only Monday without a theatrical production. At the same time, the growing popularity of feature films began to alter the face of network programming in more subtle ways. Though the three other celluloid smashes of the 1966–67 season were "The Robe," "Lillies of the Field," and "PT 109," network purchases for future broadcast included such films as "Tom Jones," "Cat on a Hot Tin Roof," and "Never on Sunday." Even edited for television, they formed the vanguard of a movement to present more "mature" themes (usually of a sexual nature) on TV, dealing with them in a manner no regular series then dared to try. In addition, the continuing success of two-hour films offered solid evidence that the home audience would accept longer programs on a regular basis and the networks increased the number of extra-length series, which sometimes ran up to ninety minutes.

There were some drawbacks in the ratings bonanza, though. The spectacular performance by "Bridge on the River Kwai" guaranteed that the price tags on future film purchases would begin to increase substantially, because there were only so many blockbuster movies available. Facing the prospect of filling six movie slots each week, it was only natural for the networks to search for a guaranteed source of future films. Logically, the search led back to Hollywood and this resulted in the long-postponed consummation of the marriage between television and the major film studios, with NBC and Universal leading the way.

Actually, since the fall of 1962, NBC and Universal had been presenting feature length material each week with the epic Western, *The Virginian*. The ninety-minute series used a core of continuing cast members, but the extra length provided the time for both the stories and guest star performers to develop. Consequently, *The Virginian* was much closer in feel to an anthology of Western films rather than a regular Western TV series. Audiences obviously accepted feature length television shows and enjoyed seeing movies on TV. There was not much difference between a ninety-minute Western and a two-hour melodrama, so the next step was practically inevitable. NBC contracted with Universal to begin producing feature length films that were not part of a series but meant to stand on their own in the regular network movie slots, by-passing any traditional theatrical release. The first batch premiered on NBC in the fall of 1964, but failed to generate either viewer or critical enthusiasm. After more than a year, NBC and Universal came back with new films, but this time backed them with higher budgets and more elaborate publicity.

The first of these new made-for-TV movies was "Fame Is the Name of the Game," which aired on NBC's *Saturday Night at the Movies* during the Thanksgiving weekend of 1966. It was not a major motion picture event by any means. Tony Franciosa played a wise-cracking investigative reporter with a soft heart beneath his cool exterior (a role almost identical to his character in the short-lived *Valentine's Day* series) and Susan Saint James played his wise-cracking cynical gal Friday with a soft heart beneath *her* cool exterior. It was the same as any of Universal's other TV productions, only with a bigger budget. Though well produced, the film was a typical TV action-adventure story with the same gimmicks, characters, and plot twists found in dozens of television series and grade B pictures. (In fact, the plot displayed a remarkable similarity to the 1949 reporter saga, "Chicago Deadline.") Nonetheless, "Fame Is the Name of the Game" stood out as a special event, a "world premiere" movie, and did fantastically well. Three months later, the second new Universal made-for-TV film, "Doomsday Flight," topped these excellent ratings.

"Doomsday Flight" was a much better film, a TV thriller with a clever premise and effective pacing. Written by Rod Serling,

the story focused on the ever-increasing sense of hysteria among the crew members (led by Van Johnson), passengers, and ground personnel of a flight from Los Angeles to New York City upon the discovery that a bomb had been planted aboard the plane. A mad bomber (Edmund O'Brien) had hidden the device before take-off and perversely armed it with an altitude-sensitive explosive set to detonate whenever the plane dropped below a height of 4,000 feet. Luckily, Denver, the "mile high" city (5,280 feet above sea level) was on their flight path, so. . . It wasn't Academy Award material either, but the film was certainly a cut above the average TV adventure stories of the time. The presence of Rod Serling served as an appropriate reminder that made-for-TV movies were really a combination of several familiar TV formats: drama anthology, high-budget special, feature length film, and television melodrama.

Both "Fame Is the Name of the Game" and "Doomsday Flight" turned up among the ten most popular films on TV that season, assuring made-for-TV movies a firm spot in plans for the future by all three networks. NBC was happy with new material from an old friend and Universal, in turn, was pleased to have the jump on its competition in a lucrative new market. Viewers, too, were treated to something special that was, at the same time, very familiar. By the end of the decade, with popular TV movies as a base, Universal became one of the most important individual sources of prime time material on television. Its high percentage of programs on the networks marked the ironic triumph of the Hollywood studios over the upstart television and assured viewers a never-ending flow of standard West Coast productions.

While NBC was experimenting with feature length made-for-

"Fame Is the Name of the Game" scored well as a specially promoted NBC "world premiere movie." Two years later, it returned as the weekly series *Name of the Game,* starring (from *l.*) Robert Stack, Gene Barry, Tony Franciosa. (*From* Name of the Game. *Courtesy of MCA Television Limited*)

TV movie specials, ABC launched its own showcase for special programming, *ABC Stage '67.* This series was considerably more ambitious than NBC's movies, embracing the spirit of Pat Weaver's mixed-bag spectaculars of the Fifties. Under producer Hubbell Robinson, *ABC Stage '67* presented a one-hour drama, comedy, variety, or documentary program each week. The opening episode, "The Love Song of Barney Kempinsky," was a comedy with Alan Arkin (fresh from his comic lead in the hit movie "The Russians Are Coming, The Russians Are Coming") as a scheming, amoral New Yorker trying to raise money by any means possible for his vacation. In the field of drama, Truman Capote wrote and narrated a re-creation of his youth in Alabama, "A Christmas Memory." Former comedy writer Dick Cavett presided over a variety format, "Where It's At," a schizophrenic mix of songs, standard jokes, dance, and parody. Documentaries stuck to safe topics such as the death of Marilyn Monroe and the wit of John Kennedy.

ABC Stage '67 tried to break out of the confines of continuing situations and characters by reviving the one-hour anthology structure, but it failed. Critics, perhaps secretly hoping for a program totally dedicated to serious drama (Bob Hope's *Chrysler Theater* hardly qualified), were only lukewarm in their support of the unpredictable anthology approach that was as likely to showcase Rick Nelson as William Shakespeare. More importantly, *ABC Stage '67* was crippled at birth by the network affiliates, many of which didn't bother to carry the program at all, fearing that it was too 'highbrow.' It was almost mathematically impossible for a show to become a ratings hit unless at least 90% of the television audience could tune in. With so many local defections, *ABC Stage '67* came

in well below the 90% mark and was doomed before its first telecast. Slotted against the very popular *Danny Kaye Show* and *I Spy,* the program was gone within a year. As Pat Weaver had discovered with his spectaculars the decade before, the format demanded patience, fine-tuning, and gradual viewer acceptance, as well as entertaining material. Eventually his spectaculars clicked in such triumphant broadcasts as "Peter Pan." ABC, too, would prosper with the format, but not until the early Seventies when it packaged the eclectic mix in the more accessible made-for-TV movie setting.

Pat Weaver himself was back in network television on CBS (following aborted ventures into a pay television service in California and an ill-conceived fourth network) as executive producer for the revived Garry Moore show. Moore, returning to TV after a two-year absence, was set in a format identical to his successful, long-running variety show of the early Sixties: music, sketches, Durward Kirby, and a fresh family of supporting players including Jackie Vernon, John Byner, Chuck McCann, Lily Tomlin, and Ron Carey. The program was fairly good, but it failed to make a dent in the ratings of its competition, the number one show on television, *Bonanza.* CBS brass, eager for instant success, refused to give the show time to build a following and instead, in November, they fired the supporting players and replaced Weaver. A new format, in which Moore presented tired retreads of old Broadway musical comedies such as "High Button Shoes," was an even bigger flop and the program was axed in January.

To replace the veteran Moore, CBS brought in a pair of young comics who had failed in a situation comedy the previous season, the Smothers Brothers. Tom and Dick Smothers were successful nightclub performers and recording artists who had been given a stupid permutation of *My Favorite Martian* to work with in their 1965–66 sitcom. Tom played Dick's dead brother (lost at sea) who returned to Earth as an inept apprentice angel assigned to aid people in trouble. Even before the show's premiere, CBS wanted to scrap the silly sitcom and use the pair to host a half-hour youth-oriented comedy-variety program instead, but the sponsor owned the program and refused to change formats. *The Smothers Brothers Show* opened to strong ratings, then collapsed. To CBS, this was proof that viewers liked the Smothers Brothers but could not stand the nonsense premise. The network canceled their sitcom but planned to use them in the variety format as soon as possible. The rapid demise of Garry Moore provided the opportune, though unenviable, slot—against number one *Bonanza.*

The Smothers Brothers Comedy Hour began as a very traditional comedy-variety show that just happened to be geared to younger viewers. The team's laid-back style was first described as similar to Dean Martin's: casual to the point of apparent sloppiness, but masking a very deliberate, controlled approach to comedy. They were the fresh new kids of television, bringing along youth-oriented acts such as Harry Nilsson, the Doors, the Who, Mason Williams, and John Hartford, and it was expected that they would slowly build a strong young audience as a base while continuing the variety show traditions of such veterans as Danny Kaye, Red Skelton, and even the recently departed Garry Moore. The unassuming Smothers surprised everyone—within a few weeks of their February premiere they had drawn away enough viewers to knock *Bonanza* out of the number one slot. A large number of youthful viewers who normally stayed away from variety shows tuned in to catch the Smothers Brothers. Almost immediately the Smothers demanded, and received, more latitude in the show and began to adopt a decidedly controversial, anti-establishment, politically topical tone that was appropriate to the new audience but quite different from anything else on television. It turned into the closest thing to satire on American TV since *That Was The Week That Was* but, unlike *TW3, The Smothers Brothers Comedy Hour* was a ratings smash.

Tom and Dick had built their routines on their never-ending sibling rivalry and personal caricatures: Tom was the "dumb" one and Dick was his level-headed, understanding brother. Their monologues had always consisted of Dick trying to straighten out one of Tom's misconceptions, but the source of Tom's confusion began to shift from family frustrations ("Mom always liked you best!") to the government's war policies. Though Dick would eventually "set the record straight," it was clear that Tom's foolish misunderstandings were considered closer to the truth. Supporting cast members Bob Einstein and Pat Paulsen provided additional digs at authority figures through their own deadpan exaggerations. Einstein played a narrow-minded, atonal Los Angeles policeman, Officer Judy, who sauntered on stage whenever the barbs against lawful authority went too far, and callously warned the Smothers that they were under suspicion, arrest, or both for violating some rule of society, usually "abusing" the privilege of free speech. Paulsen mocked much of the foolishness that passed for public debate by solemnly backing absurd notions and supporting familiar issues with ridiculous arguments, usually in the form of program "editorials." He assumed everyone, including himself, was a deliberate liar and not to be trusted; he often paused momentarily and gave a sly smile over particularly blatant distortions in his speeches.

CBS did not quietly accept everything the Smothers wished to present, hit show or not. The network allowed the rarely seen Pete Seeger to appear on the program, but cut out the performance of his new song, "Waist Deep in Big Muddy," a thinly veiled criticism of President Johnson and his war policy. Though the Smothers were very angry, they couldn't do anything about this particular decision. Nevertheless, they continued to stretch the limits of their expression at every opportunity and slowly developed a strong adversary relationship with CBS. The Smothers weren't certain how far they could push their own network, but it seemed that as long as they continued to be funny and successful, they were safe.

In contrast to the new ground being broken by the Smothers Brothers in comedy-variety, the new situation comedies had slipped back into the same well-worn plots, gags, and themes of the early Sixties. More than a dozen new sitcoms premiered in the fall of 1966 and many, such as *Pistols'n'Petticoats, It's About Time,* and *The Tammy Grimes Show,* were still in the grip of the mindless-escapist philosophy of humor. They were worlds apart from the Smothers Brothers and even the clever sitcom parodies of the previous season.

The most popular new sitcom was CBS's *Family Affair,* which featured the tried-and-true formula of a bachelor father adopting and raising orphaned children. Brian Keith played the father figure (he was their uncle, actually) and Sebastian Cabot was his manservant, French. In a very predictable format, the two portrayed refreshingly believable level-headed adults. Keith, as a construction company executive, enjoyed a life apart from his new-found family, and Cabot, despite proper huffing and puffing, grew to love his new charges. The two men were not endowed with a magic instinct for raising children perfectly but, rather, made mistakes, yelled, and were sometimes baffled by the process. Unfortunately, the children, Buffy, Jody, and Cissy, were as mechanical and cardboard as the adults were real. They were children that fulfilled an adult's view of the perfect child: sweet, heartwarming, and innocently profound. No self-respecting kid would ever identify with them. Yet in the same way that *Leave It To Beaver's* realistic children

saved the program from its cardboard adults, *Family Affair's* adults rescued it from the children. Though occasionally overloaded with saccharine plot twists, the series had its heart in the right place. CBS seemed to acknowledge that the show was geared to adult fantasy rather than children's by slotting it rather late in the evening (9:30 P.M.).

Family Affair was the latest example of CBS's continued reliance on traditionalist sitcoms that had kept the network number one, in spite of momentary spurts by the competition, for over a decade. In the 1966–67 season, CBS had fifteen thirty-minute situation comedies on its schedule and, though many of the shows were beginning to age, the network saw no reason to abandon an approach that still worked well. Even if most of the new comedies didn't catch on, the veterans would stay on top until the right successors could be found.

ABC and NBC were also top-heavy in sitcoms, launching ten new comedies of their own that season. A small number of these broke away from the focus of most situation comedies of the past: middle age, middle class families, with preteen or just-teen children. Instead, they attempted to portray an age group usually left out of the equation completely: young adults, some without any children at all!

NBC's most obvious attempt to reach the youth market came in the form of a comedy about a group of struggling rock musicians, *The Monkees*. Michael Nesmith, Micky Dolenz, Davy Jones, and Peter Tork were cast as surrogate Beatles to act and sing amid the thinnest of plots. Most stories were simple, exaggerated melodramas usually carried by a handful of mildly clever camera tricks

April 17, 1967

The Joey Bishop Show. (ABC). Making a return to late night television, ABC teams *Tonight's* regular substitute host, Joey Bishop, and former Group W frontliner, Regis Philbin, for a familiar Monday through Friday desk-and-sofa show. Bishop's first words, after the applause dies down: "Are the ratings out yet?"

May 1, 1967

The Las Vegas Show. (Uni Net). The one-and-only offering in an unsuccessful attempt to launch a fourth commercial network. Bill Dana hosts a late night celebrity talk show that, like the proto-network, lasts only one month.

June 25, 1967

"Our World." (NET). The first truly world-wide television show, consisting of live broadcasts from twenty-six countries on five continents, including a Beatles recording session in London for "All You Need Is Love."

August 27, 1967

After six years as a first run prime time series, two years as a rerun in prime time, three summers as a warm weather prime time fill-in, eight years as a Monday through Friday daytime rerun, two years as a weekend afternoon rerun, and one year as a Saturday morning rerun, *I Love Lucy* is taken off CBS and put into local syndication where it begins rerunning all over again.

August 29, 1967

The Fugitive. (ABC). The day the running stops.

September 3, 1967

What's My Line ends 17½ years on CBS. The final "mystery guest" is the show's moderator, John Charles Daly.

The tense cockpit crew in "Doomsday Flight": (from *l.*) Edward Faulkner, Katherine Crawford, Tom Simcox, Van Johnson. *(From "Doomsday Flight." Courtesy of MCA Television Limited)*

and special effects. Director Jim Frawley won an Emmy for his work in the show, though the techniques were used much more effectively in the obvious models for the series, the Beatles' own films "A Hard Day's Night" (1964) and "Help!" (1965). While particular segments in the program were quite funny, the most talked about aspect of the series was its effectiveness as a promotional tool for rock music. Each episode was, in effect, a half-hour plug for the Monkees' latest disc and their TV image as rock stars became self-fulfilling. Throughout the two-year prime time run of the series, they produced an unbroken string of top ten singles and albums, outselling even the Beatles. When the series ended in 1968, though, their fortunes took an immediate nosedive and the group soon split up. The brief, but intense, success of *The Monkees* was still a minor breakthrough for youth-oriented sitcoms. Even though it was mass consumption TV at its most blatant and commercial, *The Monkees* was the first youth sitcom to directly tap the ever-growing rock'n'roll generation. The comedy was often just traditional slapstick, but the very premise and tempo of the show were a dramatic contrast to the sub-juvenile idiocy of such plodding programs as *It's About Time* and *Gilligan's Island.*

ABC presented the best of the emerging new style of young adult sitcoms with *Love on a Rooftop,* which depicted the first year struggles of young marrieds Julie and Dave Willis. The program featured an excellent mix of personalities with a fine sense of comedy: Judy Carne, as Julie, played her character as a Sixties' variation of Lucy, slightly wacky but also intelligent and level-headed. Julie was the daughter of a wealthy car salesman but she gave up her life of luxury to marry Dave (Peter Duel), a young apprentice architect. Duel portrayed the husband as a likable average guy (not TV average—real world average) who was good looking (but not handsome) and funny (without resorting to cheap slapstick). He just wished that Julie's rich dad (Herbert Voland) would believe that the couple could be happy with his minuscule salary and their tiny rooftop apartment, because they were in love. Rich Little, as their downstairs neighbor, offered his personal sup-

port that alternately helped and further complicated the couple's lives. *Love on a Rooftop* stood apart from the childish humor of rural escapist fare and the exaggerated farce of larger-than-life spoofs. It delivered very human, very funny characters in mildly realistic situations that many young adults could identify with. In doing so, the program was years ahead of its time—and it was totally destroyed by the more familiar competition of NBC's movies and CBS's *Petticoat Junction.* ABC brought the series back five years later for a brief summer rerun and it weathered the test of time well.

Love on a Rooftop might have been the best of the young adult comedies, but *That Girl* was the most successful. Marlo Thomas (Danny's daughter), who had played a stage struck young girl in *The Joey Bishop Show* five years before, played Ann Marie, a stage struck young woman determined to break into showbiz and become an actress. In order to support her single life in New York City, she assumed different odd jobs while searching for that lucky break. A young single working woman trying to fulfill a personal dream offered marvelous possibilities that were never adequately exploited.

Several elements in the stories constantly undercut the premise. For easy laughs, the writers frequently included slapstick scenes that not only shattered the mood and motivation, but also did not work because Thomas was not particularly good at broad physical humor. Ted Bessell played her boyfriend, Don Hollinger, as the epitome of the sexless, stupid males that had populated sitcoms in the Fifties. His dumb, obvious humor further tarnished the credibility of Thomas's character. Worst of all, the series paid only lip service to the premise of an intelligent working woman. Ann Marie was straight out of the TV textbook of daffy women who succeeded in spite of themselves. If Ann was a sharp, sensitive woman who relied on her wits and self motivation to survive, the scripts hid those qualities very well. Instead, *That Girl* relied on Thomas's image as the all-American cutsie-poo sweetheart to carry the show as a safe heart-tug comedy set in the comfortable myths of idealized television romance. In this guise, it lasted five seasons. Even though *That Girl* compromised an innovative premise, its success and its touted image demonstrated that a different type of sitcom *could* work. ABC, NBC, and even CBS soon began tinkering with a slant toward young adults and more realistic settings, but it wouldn't take hold until early in the next decade.

Another concept that wouldn't reach mass acceptance until the Seventies was the peculiar science fiction brainchild of producer Gene Roddenberry, *Star Trek*. Roddenberry had worked on undistinguished series since the mid-Fifties, including an obscure Western in 1960, *Wrangler* (as a writer), and a competent career drama in 1963, *The Lieutenant* (as its producer). In 1964 he turned his attention from the trials and tribulations of young Marines to a more imaginative project he had been toying with for years, a science fiction show. Science fiction had never been handled very well by television, which treated it either as strictly kid stuff such as *Captain Video, Tom Corbett, Space Cadet*, and *Rod Brown of the Rocket Rangers* or in pedantic anthologies such as *Science Fiction Theater, Men into Space*, and *Tales of Tomorrow*. Classier anthologies such as *The Twilight Zone* captured the audience's fancy for a while but suffered from a lack of identifiable continuing characters. In 1963, while Roddenberry was still busy with *The Lieutenant*, ABC launched *The Outer Limits*, a series with substantially better writing than most previous science fiction programs, but it was still mired in the anthology format and it placed too strong an emphasis on frightening, unearthly creatures (bug-eyed monsters). Roddenberry envisioned his project as something different; he called it a "*Wagon Train* to the stars." A small central cast, always on the move, would encounter people with problems (the weekly guest stars) and attempt to resolve them. This was a simple format that had worked well in series such as *Wagon Train, Route 66, The Virginian*, and *The Fugitive*. The only difference was that *Star Trek* would take place in outer space.

By presenting his proposed science fiction show as a saleable adventure series with continuing characters and a slightly different, but exciting, locale, Roddenberry made it easier for the networks to overcome their preconceived notions of science fiction formats as kid stuff and consider the series on its own merits. In April, 1964, the Desilu studios agreed to work on the project and CBS began making favorable noises. The network, though, then decided to stay with science fiction as children's fare and took on Irwin Allen's *Lost in Space* (an average American suburban family of the future launched into the cosmos, but hopelessly lost soon after take-off). Undaunted, Roddenberry continued work on his program and in December, 1964, a one-hour *Star Trek* pilot episode ("The Cage") was completed. It featured Jeffrey Hunter as Christopher Pike, captain of the starship *Enterprise*, and Leonard Nimoy as his chief assistant, Spock, an alien from the planet Vulcan with dark raised eyebrows and pointed ears. They encountered an alien race, humanoid in appearance, with the ability to project illusions so strong that they seemed real. Pike discovered how to sort the truth from illusion, learned the aliens' master plan, and escaped from their planet. NBC expressed interest in the concept, looked at and liked the pilot, but still had some reservations about the series, specifically the cerebral subject matter and the casting. The network was especially bothered by the presentation of the captain's chief assistant as a pointy-eared alien. NBC was sufficiently intrigued with the premise, however, to ask for another pilot, a second shot few producers ever received. Roddenberry took no chances with the new pilot, making the conflicts more obvious and using an almost entirely new cast. William Shatner (who had been playing in the unsuccessful CBS lawyer series *For the People* when the first pilot had been filmed) was recruited as the new captain of the *Enterprise*, James T. Kirk. Leonard Nimoy was kept on as Spock, with his ears intact but the eyebrows softened. Roddenberry finished his revised pilot episode ("Where No Man Has Gone Before") in November, 1965, and presented it to NBC. This time, the network gave him the go-ahead to begin production, setting the series premiere for the fall of 1966.

Actually, Roddenberry had veered somewhat from his promised "*Wagon Train* of the stars" in "The Cage"—the story *had* been a bit "too cerebral," especially for a pilot. With the series in production, though, he set out to prove that science fiction could be accessible, entertaining, and a limitless source of continuing adventures. He imposed strict standards on himself and his production crew, determined to avoid the pitfalls of past TV science fiction ventures by presenting a well thought out, orderly universe for his characters. He had made a very good start in the pilot episodes by eliminating the usual space adventure hardware: space suits, landing craft, and launching pads.

The *Enterprise* had been assembled in space and was not designed to ever land on any planet (gravity and heat friction would have destroyed it), so the ship merely locked into orbit each week. This replaced boring and repetitive lift-off sequences with brief, attractive shots of the ship circling a colorful new world. Kirk and his crew were also assigned to visit only class "M" type planets— those with an atmosphere and inhabitants not very different from Earth. This eliminated bulky space suits and also kept the number of weirdly shaped aliens to a minimum. To transport members of the crew from the spaceship to the planet's surface, some mumbo jumbo about instantaneous matter transfer was devised and an ingenious special effect was used to avoid cumbersome landing vehicles. A landing party would simply stand in the "transporter" device and, within a matter of seconds, their atoms would be broken down, sent to the planet's surface via radio waves, and reassembled with no ill effect. Besides breaking away from the traditional approach to interplanetary exploration, there was a very practical reason for these innovations: money. Weird aliens, space suits, landing gear, and associated hardware involved steep costs in makeup, design, and construction. The technical process used in the transporter sequences was the most expensive continuing device, but it was a bargain compared to the alternative costs. Roddenberry realized that viewers wouldn't be tuning in for a guide to twenty-third-century hardware, so he didn't spend much time explaining them in any great detail. Warp drive engines were just like steam engines—overworked they would overheat and explode. Machines were machines, circuits were circuits, weapons were weapons. They broke down, overloaded, and misfired. The technical details didn't matter. Roddenberry focused his energies instead on telling the story.

He quite firmly dismissed a frequent trash can device of hack science fiction: the unexplained mystery of the future. All too often such stories presented the universe of the future as filled with insanely temperamental villains, heroes who could single-handedly overcome astounding odds, and technical innovations that violated all laws of twentieth-century mechanics. To Roddenberry, it didn't matter that the show took place several hundred years in the future; the audience existed in the present, so everything that happened in *Star Trek* took place for a reason. Aliens required a reason to attack the *Enterprise*. Planets were saved or destroyed for a reason. If the captain and crew embarked on a particular mission, there had to be a reason. The lack of distracting technical gear and jargon, as well as the strict adherence to understandable motivation for each conflict and action, gave the writers and performers the comfortable setting necessary for a solid, dramatic story.

A message from the crew of Apollo 7: (from *l.*) Command module pilot Donn F. Eisele and mission commander Walter Schirra, Jr. *(NASA)*

Star Trek operated under the premise that human nature remained unchanged in the twenty-third-century even though fancy gadgets and technological breakthroughs of astounding scope had taken place. Consequently, the outer galaxy appeared no more foreign than a World War II battalion headquarters or a frontier outpost in the American West of the 1880s. In this tradition, Kirk's immediate supporting crew was a perfect blend of racial and ethnic personalities: a young and impetuous Russian navigator, ensign Pavel Chekov (Walter Koenig); a two-fisted drinker from the Highlands, Lieutenant Commander Montgomery "Scotty" Scott (James Doohan); a beautiful Nubian communications officer, Lieutenant Uhura (Nichelle Nichols); and the efficient, soft-spoken Oriental navigator, Sulu (George Takei).

Kirk stood at the helm, a handsome American man of action, respected by his enemies and loved from afar by women throughout the galaxy. His first love, of course, was the *Enterprise*. Shatner brought just enough lightness and humor to his portrayal of the strong commanding officer to save himself from the horrid clichés inherent in the role. As captain, he constantly faced decisions that required a choice between humanism and official procedure and his two top aides, science officer Spock (Nimoy) and chief medical officer Doctor Leonard "Bones" McCoy (De Forest Kelley) personified his inner struggle. Spock was half Earthling and half Vulcan (an alien race motivated totally by logic) and he calmly analyzed situations based on facts and precedent. He wasn't a cold computer (his human side certainly prevented that) but he would not allow normal human emotions to determine his decisions. On the other hand, McCoy was a country boy from Georgia who put his faith in intuition and man's fallible but essentially generous nature above all rules, logic, and analysis. People came first. Spock and McCoy were constantly at odds with each other, but together they formed a perfect advisor to Kirk as he dealt with each new situation by weighing the two usually conflicting points of view.

By stripping away the peripheral traits of science fiction that other TV presentations had concentrated on, Roddenberry opened up *Star Trek* to the best strain of the sci-fi genre: speculative, symbolic stories. In the guise of an alien setting, *Star Trek* could deal with real twentieth-century Earth problems such as racial antagonism, uncontrolled war, systematic cultural domination, and individual freedom, while not appearing heavyhanded, obvious, or dated. Problems facing humanoid creatures in the far flung future and on distant planets were not as threatening or offensive to people as the same stories in a contemporary setting. The stories became timeless studies of human struggles, often based on familiar folk tales, Biblical stories, and even classical literature. For instance, one of the continuing themes that ran through most *Star Trek* plots was the necessity of a free will and the dangerous illusion of paradise. Though Kirk and his crew usually accepted the fact that each civilization had its own unique style, they were profoundly suspicious of so-called "garden of Eden" planets and deeply disturbed by any force (man or machine, oppressive or benign) that systematically denied its people the right to exercise their free will. Systems that combined paradise with the removal of all complications and conflict were presented as the most tyrannical of all. Freedom without hard choices and responsibility turned a blissful paradise into a very pretty prison. No matter what the theme, however, the scripts were superbly executed. The energy of the cast usually managed to overcome occasional rough spots in the dialogue and plots, and *Star Trek* attained the high standards Roddenberry had set for it.

Unfortunately, the program's ratings never matched this level of artistic success. They were adequate, but never outstanding. NBC tried to cancel the program after the second season, but an outpouring of viewer support won the series a third go-round. This turned out to be merely a brief reprieve and, following the third season, *Star Trek* was canceled, after airing seventy-eight episodes.

Like many other network series, *Star Trek* was put into syndication soon after its axing. Unlike nearly every other syndicated series, *Star Trek* became more popular in off-network repeats than in its network run. Most series actually needed a good syndication stint to turn a profit (the network run usually covered only initial costs), but *Star Trek* went beyond this. Its popularity steadily increased throughout the Seventies and by 1979, ten years after its cancellation, the continued public interest in the program moved Paramount studios to reassemble the entire cast for a feature-length theatrical film. Not since *The Honeymooners* had any series achieved such success so long after it had been dismissed by the networks as past its peak. The themes, production, and characters remained popular long after the "five year mission" of the *Enterprise* had run out.

With *Star Trek, ABC Stage '67, Love on a Rooftop,* and the Smothers Brothers, the 1966–67 season was filled with new shows that were slightly ahead of their time. Appropriately, one of the season's dramatic highlights was the conclusion of a four-year-old series that had once been ahead of *its* time—Quinn Martin's *The Fugitive.* It was an amicable cancellation as Martin, ABC, and David Janssen agreed that, while a fifth season might still be profitable, it was time to move on, but not without resolving the conflicts and questions viewers had been following for over three years. Throughout early 1967, a well-coordinated publicity drive built up suspense over the closed filming sessions for the series' finale. The two-part episode ("The Judgment") was held in secrecy until August, after the full cycle of summer reruns had played. No details were given out prior to air time. No reviewers were allowed to prescreen the show. The final episode was shown the same day throughout the world wherever *The Fugitive* was broadcast.

Part one provided the setup. Police in Los Angeles captured the one-armed man and Lieutenant Gerard knew the publicity would draw Kimble to the area, so he set a trap. Throughout the episode, spurious clues suggested that perhaps the one-armed man was really innocent and that someone else had committed the murder. Perhaps a neighbor, perhaps Gerard, or perhaps even Kimble himself. For seven days the world waited. On August 29, the final episode aired, capturing over 50% of the American audience. Baseball games were delayed. Bars stopped business for one hour. In New Zealand, the International Rugby championship game was delayed as television shared with the world the story of one desperate man in his bid for freedom.

In the final episode, the one-armed man managed to escape police custody, only to be pursued by Kimble. After a dramatic chase through an abandoned amusement park, the two stood face-to-face, alone, atop a high tower. With nowhere else for either man to run, the one-armed man confessed his guilt, but then lunged, determined to kill Kimble. Gerard, arriving on the scene, decided on the spot to trust Kimble, and shot the one-armed man. Only this apparently left Kimble in worse shape than before. No one else had heard the confession, the killer was dead, and Dr. Kimble was in the hands of the law, a doomed man. Then, shamefully, a chicken-hearted neighbor who had seen the murder take place stepped forward. He had been blackmailed into silence and had watched as Richard Kimble was sentenced to die, but he couldn't be held back a second time.

Kimble was exonerated. The final scene showed a triumphant Dr. Kimble leaving the courthouse a free man, accompanied by a good-looking new girlfriend. Narrator William Conrad religiously intoned, "Tuesday, August 29, 1967. The day the running stopped." Real police departments broadcast orders to end the search for both Kimble and the one-armed man. For both men, the running was over. Richard Kimble had found peace at last. Justice and freedom had finally triumphed, at least on television.

There was, however, a postscript. Later that night, on ABC's late night talk show hosted by Joey Bishop, there was a live interview with David Janssen, who was working in Georgia on a new movie. Bishop asked Janssen whether he had anything to say now that he was a free man and beyond the reach of the law. "Yes," Janssen said. "I killed her, Joey. She talked too much."

1967-68 SEASON

27. The Whole World Is Watching

IN THE fall of 1967, TV's top ten list included such venerables as Red Skelton, Ed Sullivan, Jackie Gleason, Lucille Ball, Andy Griffith, *Bonanza, Gunsmoke,* and *The Beverly Hillbillies.* Most had been around for over a decade, some nearly twenty years. Though still popular, they couldn't last forever. Yet programmers were having trouble coming up with a formula to produce durable new replacements and the only bona-fide hits that had emerged from the previous season's new shows were the very traditional *Family Affair,* a revival of *Dragnet,* and the youth-oriented *Smothers Brothers Comedy Hour.* For the 1967–68 season premieres, the networks included a nod to the young adult audience, but for the most part continued to emphasize familiar TV veterans in new but very safe and predictable variety, sitcom, crime, and Western vehicles. Viewers were generally unexcited by it all and, after the flurry of fall premieres passed, they turned back to their old favorites. Though a number of the new shows eventually caught on, none of them became an instant smash. By Christmas, the bucolic saga of *Gentle Ben* (a lovable bear in a Florida game preserve) was the only new program in the top twenty.

As part of the second season revamping in January, another new variety show appeared, hosted by a pair of very familiar show-biz veterans, Dan Rowan and Dick Martin. For years the two had brought their straightforward routines to numerous traditional comedy-variety shows and, in the summer of 1966, had served as competent hosts to one of Dean Martin's summer replacement series. They were unlikely candidates to be pioneers in a new wave of television comedy, yet their new show was truly different. Within four months, *Rowan and Martin's Laugh-In* exploded into a national hit, bringing to mass popularity the innovative television comedy techniques developed years before by Ernie Kovacs.

In the early Sixties, Kovacs had put together a monthly comedy program for ABC in which he replaced the traditional comedy-variety structure with bizarre visuals, off-the-wall sketches, and short unconnected bits (blackouts). The program had fallen short of its innovative premise, though, because Kovacs had been severely limited by a minuscule budget. In 1967, producer George Schlatter, armed with much more money and the latest TV technology, produced a special-pilot for NBC called "Laugh-In," which aired on September 9, 1967. The show reworked and updated the Kovacs

approach to humor, incorporating new video tape tricks and techniques, expanding the crew of writers and performers, and providing viewers with familiar characters to guide them through the maze of images. Blackout bits in the special were edited into a frenzied, machine-gun pace. A gaggle of talented but generally unknown comedians including Ruth Buzzi, Henry Gibson, Arte Johnson, Jo Anne Worley, and Judy Carne delivered the punch lines, catch phrases, puns, and clunkers. The material went by so fast that if there were three good jokes in ten, the laughter from these blotted out the memory of the seven flops. If none of them clicked, there would soon be more flashing by anyway. All the electronic madness was held together by Rowan and Martin, who served as the essentially "square" hosts of the "Laugh-In" special. They had the very important role of anchoring the flights of fancy with their familiar presence and humor. Confounded by everything else, viewers could turn to them for reassurance.

"Laugh-In" was colorful, innovative, and far more exciting than any of the new fall shows premiering that month. When the CBS heavyweights of *Gunsmoke* and *Lucy* swamped the languishing *Man From U.N.C.L.E.* on Monday nights, NBC quickly slotted *Laugh-In* as a mid-season replacement series, though the network feared that the program's unique style might hurt acceptance. Instead, it actually helped. *Laugh-In*'s frantic structure, slightly risque jokes, and many running gags set the show apart from everything else on television and injected life into a format that had seemed catatonic. It attracted many new viewers who had been bored to tears by the familiar variety setup of genial host, light banter, mundane music, and hackneyed sketches. They grew to enjoy the unexpected twists, surprise guest shots, and fresh new characters of *Laugh-In.*

On the very first show in January, Rowan and Martin introduced viewers to the unlikely figure of Tiny Tim, a singer who looked like a cross between a Bowery bum and Tinker Bell. He had a large hook nose, a death-white complexion, and an Arthur Godfrey-type ukulele that he used to accompany his high, lilting falsetto on such traditional ballads as "Tip Toe through the Tulips." Such a bizarre guest was clear evidence that *Laugh-In* was willing to break from the staid and safe traditions of TV variety shows, though even Rowan and Martin acknowledged his extreme peculiarity and

198

turned his presence, actual or threatened, into a running gag ("You're not going to bring back Tiny Tim, are you?").

Other, more traditional, celebrities also appeared on the show, usually delivering quick one-liners in brief cameo shots. Viewers had to be alert to catch such guests as Bob Hope, Sonny Tufts, John Wayne, Zsa Zsa Gabor, and then presidential candidate Richard Nixon, who publicly pondered, "Sock it to *me?*" Frequent guests Sammy Davis, Jr. and Flip Wilson revived the old Pigmeat Markham routine that used the hook line: "Here come de' judge."

Though the guests kept viewers on their toes, the regular cast developed the program's popular continuing bits. A weekly "cocktail party" and the many-shuttered "joke wall" served as the launching pads for timely one-liners by the entire crew, who soon became familiar figures with well-known characterizations. Arte Johnson was a dirty old man forever pestering a spinsterish Ruth Buzzi; Judy Carne was a bikinied go-go dancer with pithy sayings painted on her body; Henry Gibson was a poetry-spouting "flower person"; and announcer Gary Owens was an ear-cupping caricature of radio's deep-voiced announcers of the Thirties. These characters popularized a lexicon of punch lines that soon wound its way into the national language. From Johnson, who also played an unreconstructed Nazi soldier, came the intonation at the end of each show, "Verry interesting. . . ." Whenever Carne was tricked into saying "Sock it to me" (the show's main punch line) she found herself hit by pies, drenched in water, or falling through a trap door. Rowan and Martin themselves added such phrases as "You bet your bippy," "the fickle finger of fate," and "beautiful downtown Burbank." After the show had been a solid hit for more than a year, members of the regular cast moved on and a second generation of *Laugh-In* supporting players arrived including Goldie Hawn, the dumb blonde incarnate; the hippy-dippy Alan Sues; and Lily Tomlin, as the chest-scratching telephone operator, Ernestine.

Like any truly different TV show, *Laugh-In* had to overcome initial uncertainty among viewers, but once they became familiar with the program's style, they found it easy and fun to follow. In one hour, *Laugh-In* squeezed together slapstick, vaudeville, satire, clever visuals, an air of current hipness, and even a few normal guests. The program had everything the other comedy-variety shows had—just more of it, presented with fresh faces and sophisti-

Number 6 (Patrick McGoohan) makes a speech to the residents of the Village as part of his campaign for the post of Number 2 in *The Prisoner.* (© *ITC Entertainment, Inc.*)

MONDAY

Network	7:30	8:00	8:30	9:00	9:30	10:00	10:30
ABC	COWBOY IN AFRICA		The Rat Patrol	The Felony Squad	Peyton Place I	The Big Valley	
CBS	Gunsmoke		The Lucy Show	Andy Griffith Show	Family Affair	CAROL BURNETT SHOW	
NBC	The Monkees	The Man From U.N.C.L.E.		DANNY THOMAS HOUR		I Spy	

TUESDAY

Network	7:30	8:00	8:30	9:00	9:30	10:00	10:30
ABC	GARRISON'S GORILLAS		The Invaders		N.Y.P.D.	Hollywood Palace	
CBS	Daktari		Red Skelton Hour		GOOD MORNING WORLD	CBS News Hour	
NBC	I Dream Of Jeannie	JERRY LEWIS SHOW		NBC Tuesday Night At The Movies			

WEDNESDAY

Network	7:30	8:00	8:30	9:00	9:30	10:00	10:30
ABC	THE LEGEND OF CUSTER		THE SECOND HUNDRED YEARS	The ABC Wednesday Night Movie			
CBS	Lost In Space		The Beverly Hillbillies	Green Acres	HE AND SHE	DUNDEE AND THE CULHANE	
NBC	The Virginian			KRAFT MUSIC HALL @Bob Hope Show		Run For Your Life	

THURSDAY

Network	7:30	8:00	8:30	9:00	9:30	10:00	10:30
ABC	Batman	THE FLYING NUN	Bewitched	That Girl	Peyton Place II	GOOD COMPANY	local
CBS	CIMARRON STRIP			CBS Thursday Night Movies			
NBC	Daniel Boone		IRONSIDE		Dragnet 1968	Dean Martin Show	

FRIDAY

Network	7:30	8:00	8:30	9:00	9:30	10:00	10:30
ABC	OFF TO SEE THE WIZARD		HONDO		THE GUNS OF WILL SONNETT	JUDD, FOR THE DEFENSE	
CBS	The Wild, Wild West		Gomer Pyle, U.S.M.C.	CBS Friday Night Movies			
NBC	Tarzan		Star Trek		ACCIDENTAL FAMILY	Bell Telephone Hour / NBC News Specials	

SATURDAY

Network	7:30	8:00	8:30	9:00	9:30	10:00	10:30
ABC	The Dating Game	The Newlywed Game	Lawrence Welk Show		Iron Horse		ABC Scope
CBS	Jackie Gleason Show		My Three Sons	Hogan's Heroes	Petticoat Junction	MANNIX	
NBC	MAYA		Get Smart	NBC Saturday Night At The Movies			

SUNDAY

Network	7:00	7:30	8:00	8:30	9:00	9:30	10:00	10:30
ABC	Voyage To The Bottom Of The Sea		The F.B.I.		The ABC Sunday Night Movie			
CBS	Lassie	GENTLE BEN	Ed Sullivan Show		Smothers Brothers Comedy Hour		Mission: Impossible	
NBC	A.F.L. Football [from 4:00]	Walt Disney's Wonderful World Of Color		THE MOTHERS-IN-LAW	Bonanza		THE HIGH CHAPARRAL	

cated technical discipline. By May, *Laugh-In* was a solid top ten hit and frequently ended up the number one program on television. Its enormous popularity, along with that of *The Smothers Brothers Comedy Hour,* was tangible evidence that the American TV audience seemed ready for more experimental, sophisticated, and even controversial fare than had been available week in and week out over the previous decade. For still further proof, there was the continuing success of prime time movies.

While most of the new network series struggled near the bottom of the ratings charts, all four movie nights on CBS and NBC rested safely in the top forty. Viewers accepted and supported the more realistic, adult themes in such features as "Never on Sunday," "Tom Jones," "Splendor in the Grass," "Dr. Strangelove," and "King Rat," with such films as "The Birds," "Cat on a Hot Tin Roof," "The Great Escape," and "North by Northwest" racking up extremely high ratings. At mid-season, NBC decided to add a third night of movies in the fall of 1968 so that, for the first time ever, there would be a network movie every night of the week.

Yet over the entire television schedule such changes were taking place slowly, with both viewers and the networks generally moving with caution in shaking up different formats. CBS made a few moves to modernize both its image and schedule for the 1967–68 season, but met solid viewer resistance or indifference in the process.

The network had tried to cancel the oldest oater of them all, *Gunsmoke,* at the end of the 1966–67 season, but an outpouring of public support saved the show from its corporate lynching. Network programmers then stuck it in a new early time slot (Monday at 7:30 P.M.) which was assumed to be an impossible position for an adult Western. Fooling everybody, *Gunsmoke* bounced back into the top ten with even higher ratings than before. However, this didn't signal a revival of interest in the overall Western format and new shows such as *Custer* and *Dundee and the Culhane* quickly faded from view. At the same time, CBS hesitantly experimented in the field of situation comedy with a moderately realistic young adult show, *He and She,* but it met the same fate as ABC's *Love on a Rooftop* from the previous season.

He and She starred the real life husband and wife team of Richard Benjamin and Paula Prentiss, who filled admirably the roles of slightly befuddled, misunderstood husband and slightly wacky, often incomprehensible wife. Paula Prentiss's character (like Judy Carne's in *Love on a Rooftop*) was a genuine step forward in the presentation of women in sitcoms. Though slightly daffy, Paula clearly had a head on her shoulders and was not totally dependent on her husband. They had no children so she was free to pursue her own interests while he worked at his realistic, though certainly uncommon, job as a cartoonist. The two displayed a deep and genuine affection for each other so that even the usual sitcom schemes and complications seemed a reasonable part of being in love.

Besides the strong leads, *He and She* was blessed by a fantastic group of supporting players who should have made the program a smash hit on their talent alone. Former folk singer Hamilton Camp portrayed a gnomish, klutzy apartment superintendent; the venerable Harold Gould was Dick's boss; and Kenneth Mars was a thick-headed but friendly neighborhood fireman who often entered the firehouse by climbing through Dick and Paula's kitchen window. Best of the best, Jack Cassidy played Jetman, the lead character in a television series adaptation of one of Dick's cartoon heroes. Cassidy looked as if he had stepped directly from the comic page and his narcissistic, self-centered manner demonstrated that he truly believed he was a superhero. Creator and character frequently faced off, with Dick's dry drollery serving as the perfect antidote to Jetman's insatiable appetite for self-aggrandizement. Nothing could ultimately shake the star, though, and he thrived on compliments. He instantly responded to one adoring fan's delight at meeting him with the heartfelt observation, "It was worth waiting for, wasn't it?"

He and She was given the advantageous Wednesday night slot that *Gomer Pyle* had recently held (following *The Beverly Hillbillies* and *Green Acres*), but the new sitcom bombed out in the ratings and was canceled after its first season. While very similar programs such as *The Mary Tyler Moore Show* would catch on in another four years, *He and She,* like *Love on a Rooftop,* was guilty of being ahead of its time with a mix of realistic and satirical characters. The most successful new sitcom of the 1967–68 season featured the childish adventures of *The Flying Nun.*

With the failure of *He and She,* and the implied failure of sophisticated sitcoms in general, CBS canceled plans to develop (with American filmmaker Norman Lear as producer) a Stateside version of the relatively daring BBC "working class" sitcom, *Till Death Do Us Part.* For two years that program had been both shocking

and delighting the British audience as the openly bigoted Alf Garnett (Warren Mitchell) violated all known rules of TV decorum. He hurtled epithets at his wife and son-in-law, constantly dropped racial slurs, and called well-known political figures names such as "grammar school twit." Though Britons accepted this behavior in a situation comedy, CBS saw it as obviously too strong for American consumption.

One format that managed a mix of traditional characters and settings with more contemporary concerns was the cop show. With real urban crime on the public's mind and on the nightly news shows, it was often a very short step to the world of fictional police work. The TV crime revival had begun in the 1966–67 season with the return to television of the old *Dragnet* duo of Jack Webb and Ben Alexander, though they appeared in two different programs. Alexander arrived first, in the fall of 1966, with *Felony Squad* for ABC. The program was a very routine cop exercise set in Los Angeles, and its proclivity for scenes of spurting blood ("going heavy on the ketchup") was its only distinguishing feature. Jack Webb, though, made a very conscious effort to appear topical in his revival of *Dragnet* for NBC.

As producer-writer-narrator-star, Webb brought his tight-lipped "just the facts, ma'am" style of drama to a new decade, first in a successful made-for-TV movie, then as a mid-season replacement series, *Dragnet '67* (the year was added to make certain the audience knew this was no rerun). Following its spine-chilling theme song, *Dragnet* had always assured viewers that the story to follow was true—only the names had been changed to protect the innocent—so the format was the perfect front for stories that could appear to be topical. In the very first episode, Webb (as Joe Friday) and his new sidekick, Harry Morgan (as Bill Gannon), relentlessly pursued a crazed LSD pusher who died dramatically of an overdose at the end of the show. Despite the topical trappings, though, *Dragnet*'s chief strengths continued to be its painstaking methodical style and dedicated support for the average cop on the beat. Yet

Chief Robert Ironside (Raymond Burr), confined to a wheelchair, traveled to the scene of a crime in his specially designed van, aided by Detective Sergeant Ed Brown (Don Galloway, far *l.*) and policewoman Eve Whitfield (Barbara Anderson). (*From* Ironside. *Courtesy of MCA Television Limited*)

by focusing on crazed peaceniks and deranged dope fiends, *Dragnet* (and other crime shows such as *The FBI*) could pass off standard grade-B material as hip, modern drama.

The mid-season success of *Dragnet* brought several new crime shows to the 1967–68 line-up. Though they reflected touches of TV topicality, the programs generally presented well produced, high quality stories and conflicts. *N.Y.P.D.* (produced by David Susskind's Talent Associates) was filmed on location in New York City and featured a black and white police duo (played by Robert Hooks and Frank Converse), but the series managed to resist any heavy-handed sociology. *Mannix* (created by Richard Levinson and William Link) cast Mike Connors in the role of the old faithful private eye. At first, the plots in the series centered on the conflict between the lone investigator and the increasingly mechanized job of crime detection. By its second season, though, *Mannix* dropped the computer society angle and slipped into the more familiar rock- 'em sock 'em two-fisted detective mold popular since the days of Mickey Spillane. Raymond Burr settled for a less violent gimmick premise and portrayed a crippled San Francisco police chief in the slickly produced *Ironside.* Though confined to a wheelchair by a sniper's bullet, Robert Ironside could still track down criminals and often use his dominant, snarling personality to intimidate them into surrendering.

As the urban action police shows returned in strength to television, the more fantasy-oriented world of the spies was fading. Over just a few years, the form had been hopelessly diluted in every medium: film, print, and television. For the most part, the gimmicks and humor had completely supplanted the stories, character development, and dramatic confrontations. Even the granddaddy of them all, James Bond, fell victim to gimmick overkill, prompting Sean Connery's departure from the theatrical Bond role after the well-panned "You Only Live Twice." The weekly TV spy series were especially vulnerable to the constant overexposure and had practically become parodies of themselves with conflicts that could

no longer be taken seriously. In Britain, where the spy craze had begun, Diana Rigg (the delectable Mrs. Peel) left TV's best spy series, *The Avengers,* and her replacement, Linda Thorson (as Tara King), adopted a helpless female demeanor that robbed the show of its dramatic tension and unique point of view. Worse yet, the series was revamped so that both John Steed and Tara King lost their free-wheeling independence and were forced to constantly report directly to Mother, an oddball superior in a wheelchair. Yet as super-sleuth TV was in its death rattle, Britain came up with one final spy masterpiece that successfully combined numerous strains of entertainment into one of the best television programs ever devised, *The Prisoner.*

Since 1960, Patrick McGoohan had been portraying secret agent John Drake (a.k.a. Danger Man) and, after seven years, Drake had been involved in almost every possible spy plot. McGoohan felt it was time to take the spy motif one step further and present more dramatically some concepts that were often lurking just under the surface in the *Danger Man-Secret Agent* series. Working under heavy security wraps and backed by Sir Lew Grade's British television network conglomerate, McGoohan, acting as executive producer and star, turned out the seventeen-episode *Prisoner* series. It was the most dazzlingly produced program then on British television and also one of the most expensive, running $168,000 per episode. Such high costs for individual episodes would have been impossible to bear in the open-ended world of American television. There, producers developed ideas into series they hoped would run for years, yet faced the very real possibility of being canceled within weeks. Most British series were designed to end after a set number of weeks anyway, so the total cost of a program was much easier to project. The limited run also allowed more time to concentrate on pacing both in particular episodes and in the entire series. McGoohan constructed each segment of *The Prisoner* with the same care and complexity usually reserved for one-shot feature films and live theatrical productions. As a result, the series achieved a level of artistic success on a par with high quality literature, films, and theater.

The Prisoner took the audience from the supposedly real world of John Drake, the spy, into the symbolic world of The Village, a very pretty prison-resort in which everyone was known only by a number. McGoohan, once again portraying a government agent (presumed to be Drake), found himself in The Village following his abrupt resignation from the British service. He had planned to leave Britain (with a good deal of sensitive security information in his head) and take a soul-searching vacation, but was rendered unconscious and spirited away to the mysterious seaside village before he could finish packing. Once there, McGoohan-Drake was placed in an apartment and given his own number, Six. Number Six faced constant scrutiny and interrogation by Number Two, in charge of the day-to-day operations and security. The contest was simple: In each episode Number Two tried to discover the reason for Number Six's resignation while Number Six tried to thwart him and escape.

This was merely the setup, the logical explanation for the conflict in each episode. The real focus of the series was the concept of independence and free will forever battling authority and submission. Most of the private eyes, spies, and cops presented over the years had been waging the same battle as Number Six, but it had never been so vividly expressed. Philip Marlowe, Sam Spade, Boston Blackie, Martin Kane, Peter Gunn, James Bond, John Drake, and Richard Kimble (on the other side of the law) had been inside-outsiders trying to cope with the encroachments of an increasingly impersonal world. Their unending struggle, though, had always been presented within the convenient and easily identifiable framework of crime and justice. In such a setting, the loner-hero might be insubordinate and a rebel but, in the long run, he still worked for the "legitimate" authority. In reality, the inside-outsider often had more in common with those he pursued than with his superiors. It was just a matter of which side of the fine line of the law one happened to fall on. Ultimately, the most important battle these heroes ever waged was the fight to keep their independent, idiosyncratic ways and not be forced to become average citizens.

In *The Prisoner,* this conflict was laid bare and the dichotomy revealed. Number Six-Drake had spent his adult life tracking down and capturing agents just like him. In The Village he had to face the consequences of his actions and experience first hand the effects of the system he had been working for. The possibility of freedom and escape was constantly dangled as an inducement for him to reveal his real reasons for resigning, but this was an illusion. His personal identity had always come from his own skill and instincts and if he ever dropped his guard, gave in, and accepted such an offer, he would be a beaten man, totally indistinguishable from the faceless, nameless populace at large.

It was never made clear who ran The Village—at various points in the series Soviet, British, and even joint control was suggested. Easily definable good guys and bad guys were thereby eliminated and it was possible that the good guys (the British) weren't so good after all. There might not be any difference between them and the supposed bad guys (the Russians). Perhaps both, as important world powers, were inherently bad. Capitalism and communism lost all meaning and the real, underlying division became clear in *The Prisoner:* control from above or personal free will.

Throughout the fall of 1967 in Britain (and the summer of 1968 in the United States, when CBS presented the series), a surprisingly large number of viewers kept tuning in to observe both McGoohan's splendid performance as a frustrated, but intelligent, caged rat, and the complex plots and elaborate sets that gave the show a level of sophistication far above normal TV fare. The beauty of *The Prisoner,* though, was its simultaneous success on many levels. While a rich, deep program that delved into complex psychological questions, it never ignored the basic rules of good action-adventure television. There was a standard fist fight in almost every episode and, if nothing else, *The Prisoner* could be viewed as an exciting escape story with elaborate gadgets and interesting characters to tickle the imagination. In fact, one episode effectively presented the entire philosophy of the program in the more familiar form of a Western. McGoohan portrayed Number Six as a loner-gunfighter former lawman who refused to become the flunky sheriff in a small town under the thumb of an all-powerful, corrupt judge. In this guise, Number Six seemed almost the same as Matt Dillon and Paladin, and the inside-outsider theme of *The Prisoner* was revealed as a universal one which had already been used by that most basic and durable American morality play, the Western.

The series ended in a tour de force, two-episode finale that revealed still another level of meaning. At the dramatic climax, Number Six discovered that Number One (the boss of all bosses), for whom he had been searching from the beginning, was none other than himself. He was both jailer and prisoner. Hunter and hunted. Persecutor and persecuted. As the characters in the comic strip "Pogo" once explained, "We have met the enemy and he is us."

For a show so different, *The Prisoner* did remarkably well. It became a minor mania in Britain and registered a more than respectable 34% share of the audience in America. The program also received enough critical acclaim to be rerun by CBS the following summer and it eventually turned up as a syndicated series (sans commercials) on public television in the late Seventies.

With the appearance of *The Prisoner,* many American TV observers at last admitted that Britain was outshining America in quality television production on several levels: sitcoms (*Steptoe and Son* and *Till Death Do Us Part*), adventure (*The Prisoner* and *The Avengers*), soap opera (the ever-present *Coronation Street*), and high-class soaps, called historical dramas (such as *The Forsyte Saga,* which was a hit in its first BBC airing during the 1966–67 season). America had few equivalents. For all their good points, programs such as *Ironside* and *Mannix* were not seen as profound expressions of television art. One reason for Britain's superior product was that British televison was guided by a looser set of rules which allowed characters and plots to maintain a more realistic and earthy nature. Another very important reason was the existence of the government-funded, noncommerical BBC that could afford to experiment with forms considered too volatile for commercial broadcasters.

America had nothing to compare with the BBC. For more than ten years, NET had served as a quasi-network for over one hundred educational stations in the United States, but it operated under a severely limited budget and was forced to send its programs through the mail. Instructional shows such as *The French Chef,* children's shows such as *Mr. Rogers' Neighborhood,* and "talking head" public affairs shows such as *Washington Week in Review,* while excellent programs, all reflected very frugal production techniques that constantly pointed up the serious lack of funds available. The programs looked low budget and could never seriously compete with commercial fare for viewer support.

In early 1967, the Carnegie commission issued a report suggesting a radical rethinking of the basics behind educational television. It offered a blueprint for a new concept, public television, that

March 4, 1968
The Dick Cavett Show. (ABC). Former gag writer Dick Cavett conducts a ninety-minute talk show on weekday mornings, with a twist: Not only does he include "serious" non-showbiz guests such as Buckminster Fuller, he brings them out first!

May 21, 1968
"Hunger in America." (CBS). Producer Martin Carr turns out an old-fashioned hard-hitting CBS documentary for *CBS Reports.* Carr focuses on malnutrition among Indians in the Southwest and tenant farmers in Virginia, in the style of Ed Murrow's 1960 "Harvest of Shame." The agriculture industry is quick to criticize the report and even the Secretary of Agriculture, Orville Freeman, finds it necessary to defend the department's hunger policy from the embarrassing footage.

May 27, 1968
After only five months as anchor for *The ABC Evening News,* Bob Young is replaced by Frank Reynolds.

August 5, 1968
The Republican National Convention opens in Miami Beach. ABC opts for "selected coverage" and sticks with regular entertainment fare for the first ninety minutes of prime time.

September 6, 1968
The era of fifteen-minute soap operas, once a staple of daytime radio and television, comes to an end with the final quarter-hour broadcasts of CBS's *Search for Tomorrow* and *The Guiding Light.* Three days later, the two shows return in expanded thirty-minute formats.

would emphasize entertainment and information, not merely instruction. Congress would provide the major funding for public television, but an independent corporation would be established to dispense the money to the local stations in the NET network and act as a buffer between them and Congress. This would allow governmental support but, hopefully, preclude governmental control. President Johnson's strong support of the Carnegie commission's proposals helped push a bill through Congress that made most of the recommendations law. In November, 1967, he signed the Public Broadcasting Act of 1967, which set up the fifteen-member buffer organization called the Corporation for Public Broadcasting. CPB immediately ran into the first of many governmental road blocks. Congress was to grant $9 million for CPB's first year of operation but, in early 1968, both the President and Congress delayed the actual transfer of funds, stalling governmental support for the new system. Instead, as in the past, the largess of many private organizations kept public television afloat until a lower compromise figure could be agreed to by the government. Such haggling over congressional money became a yearly ritual that constantly left the CPB on unsure footing. Even with all its complications, though, the institution of government funding was an important step for the future of public television.

The first program to incorporate the concept of public television was *PBL* (the *Public Broadcast Laboratory*), a weekly, two and one-half hour live news magazine program. The Ford Foundation, which had been channeling money to educational television since NET's inception in 1952, donated $10 million in 1967 for the creation of the program at the urging of former CBS News president, Fred Friendly, who had become the foundation's advisor on television. With the exception of the *CBS News Hour,* the networks had largely given up weekly, hard-hitting news shows, preferring instead safe specials such as "Discover America with Jose Jimenez." *PBL* promised to be unlike anything else then available on television and certainly unlike anything ever seen on NET. It would be live, in color, and use some well-known, highly professional talent drawn from commercial television itself. Edward P. Morgan was granted a two-year leave of absence from ABC to act as *PBL*'s anchorman. Tom Pettit of NBC became head of one of the regional bureaus that produced pieces for the program. CBS News veteran Av Westin was named executive producer. Advance publicity touted the show as a "revolution in broadcasting" and Westin explained the need for it:

> The time has come to put an end to what I call 'music up and under documentaries' in which, as we head into the final commercial, we are reminded that there is a problem and certainly something ought to be done about it—but, please don't ask what.

The premiere of *PBL* in November, 1967, was not quite a revolution, but it was an important landmark in American TV. The first program was a cross between *See It Now* and *Omnibus,* using a mixture of documentary and drama segments all devoted to an overall theme, race relations. The documentary reports examined the Cleveland and Boston mayoral contests, which centered on race; a traditional panel discussion presented appropriately antagonistic extremists from Chicago; and a dramatic production, "A Day of Absence," showed a fantasy world in which all the blacks in America decided to leave, and white society found itself unable to cope with their absence. *PBL* also incorporated sixty-second spots (dubbed "anti-commercials"), placing them at points in the show that their counterparts on a regular commerical program would normally appear. The messages revealed that all the competing brands of aspirin *were* alike, and that the long-longer-longest

fad among cigarette manufacturers only resulted in more-most-mostest tar for the suffering consumer.

The most important aspect of *PBL* was that it successfully adopted the methods and formats used by the commercial networks, signalling a sharp break from the pure educational slant of NET's past. In place of the many drab and deadly boring pseudo-lectures, *PBL* brought in well-known commentators, slick production, and elaborate graphics and sets. It showed that American television could have it both ways, offering programs that were informative and classy as well as entertaining and appealing (a philosophy which eventually produced other successful public television shows such as *Sesame Street*). Unfortunately, *PBL* lasted only two seasons and never became a hit on its own.

PBL was debilitated from its very inception by a series of internecine battles as people at both the Ford Foundation and NET tried to mold the program to fit their own expectations. The thinly veiled anti-white viewpoint of the nearly all black theatrical troupe in the premiere episode rankled a few corporate nerves, so "A Day of Absence" was the only important drama presentation *PBL* ever offered. The anti-commercials were also judged too controversial and dropped after a few weeks, as the program settled into a more traditional documentary format. Even in this approach there was continued disagreement among the *PBL* overseers throughout its first season as the traditional educational faction (led by the dean of the Columbia school of journalism) fought the progressive public wing (headed by Av Westin) for total control of the program. After a showdown in June, 1968, Westin's side retained control, but bitter feelings remained. Money shortages during the second season forced a drastic cutback of in-house production and, after a gallant but losing struggle, *PBL* died on May 18, 1969. Most of its top staff members moved to ABC's news department.

In spite of its troubled history, *PBL* served as an important force in broadcasting. While the commercial networks remained mum, *PBL* examined such issues as a proposed anti-ballistic missile system (ABM), community antenna television (CATV), health care, and the possibility of a second Northeast blackout. It offered independent documentary producers such as Frederick Wiseman invaluable exposure, airing individualistic views of Vietnam, Martin Luther King, Jr., cancer, law and order, and country music. The very existence of *PBL* spurred NBC and CBS to increase their own output of real news documentaries, and the program served as the direct model for NBC's *First Tuesday* and CBS's *60 Minutes,* two newsmagazine shows which premiered in the 1968–69 season.

Despite the prodding from public television in 1967, the commercial networks were still caught in the cautious doldrums of "no guts journalism," especially in their reports on the Vietnam war. Even as American troop strength neared one-half million, network coverage of the war continued practically unchanged, reaching a symbolic low point from late 1967 through January, 1968. Largely due to lobbying by CBS, all three networks tacitly agreed to devote very little attention to the October peace march on Washington by thousands of war protesters, which ended in hundreds of arrests when the group stormed the Pentagon. In January, ABC, accepting the inevitable, canceled its excellently produced, objectively balanced, but rarely seen weekly Vietnam show, *ABC Scope.* In contrast that same month, public television displayed its guts and aired a frankly pro-Viet Cong documentary by Felix Greene, "Inside North Vietnam." Actually, CBS had originally paid for the film but, upon seeing the footage, decided to use only brief excerpts on the nightly news. *NET Journal,* however, presented more than half of the ninety-minute documentary which, though biased, provided a rare look at the North Vietnamese in their homeland.

The film was followed by a one-hour hawk and dove debate but, even so, NET received a great deal of flak for airing the material at all. In April, however, CBS sent its own Charles Collingwood directly to Hanoi for a series of filmed reports. In just a few months, the commercial networks had drastically altered their coverage of the war. The Tet offensive in early February provided the dramatic rallying point for the change and the end of the era of "no guts journalism."

For years, network correspondents had been generally accepting the official government line that the United States was, in fact, winning the war and that the Viet Cong were growing weaker and weaker. Suddenly, this supposedly weakened enemy found the strength to launch a major, well-coordinated offensive throughout South Vietnam. After innumerable evenings of generally pointless jungle combat scenes, Tet gave the networks exciting, street-by-street fighting footage that dramatized the war as never before. The Viet Cong occupied a number of provincial capitals for a few days and the American embassy itself for a few hours. Eventually, the U.S. pushed the Viet Cong back while inflicting heavy casualties, but an important image had been shattered. It was clear that the American government was either ignorant of the Viet Cong's real strength or lying to the American public. For the first time in years, network reporters aggressively and openly questioned the government's position.

The Tet offensive also provided one powerful photographic moment that would forever symbolize the Vietnam war itself. During the height of the offensive, while NBC cameras rolled, the Saigon chief of police calmly raised a small revolver to the temple of a Viet Cong prisoner and pulled the trigger. The V.C. dropped to the ground and blood spurted from his head. It was a quick, passionless act without any great emotions or dramatic words. None were necessary. Though the prisoner was no doubt guilty of something, the real-life execution, taking place without even the niceties of a legal conviction, seemed the final outrage to many Americans. Following the Tet offensive, more and more people joined the reawakened press in publicly questioning the credibility of the government's war policy and the promise of eventual victory.

Network news attention quickly shifted back to the domestic front, as the growing skepticism of the war turned the campaign for the Democratic presidential nomination into a race in which the incumbent President might actually lose. On March 31, in a special television speech, President Johnson announced a reduction in the American bombing of Vietnam, then dramatically withdrew himself from the campaign. Robert Kennedy, Eugene McCarthy, and Vice President Hubert Humphrey were left to vie for the nomination. Among the Republicans, Richard Nixon was well on his way to completing a long personal comeback struggle.

Both parties staged their nominating conventions in August. For the first time, ABC decided to depart from traditional gavel-to-gavel television coverage of the event and opted for ninety-minute "selected coverage" (9:30–11:00 P.M.). This allowed the network to air some of its regular entertainment programs while NBC and CBS vied for the attention of those wrapped up in the convention's

developments. The Republican convention in Miami in early August turned out to be a tedious affair with very few interesting moments anyway. The Democratic convention in Chicago in late August, however, proved an entirely different matter.

A strong feeling of enmity between the press and politicians developed in Chicago even before the convention opened. There was exceptionally tight security due, in part, to the genuine fear which developed after the assassination of Robert Kennedy in June. Beyond that, however, Chicago Mayor Richard Daley seemed determined to prevent anything or anyone, especially the press, from spoiling the traditional convention euphoria. A protracted union dispute (which many network executives felt Daley could have settled if he had really wanted to) wreaked havoc on the networks' plans for live coverage of events throughout the city. Daley and the Democrats also tried to impose strict reductions on the number of press people allowed on the convention floor. What's more, there was obvious tension between pro-administration and anti-war factions, both in the convention hall and gathered on the streets outside. When the convention itself began, the barely contained antagonism broke out into the open.

The anti-war Democrats, while numerous, were out-voted at every turn, and the convention floor often resembled a wrestling ring. The press openly referred to Chicago as an armed camp, even a police state, evoking memories of the Soviet invasion of Czechoslovakia only days before. Despite the security (or because of it), violence broke out both inside and outside. CBS's Dan Rather was shown being punched and dragged from the floor by security forces, prompting Walter Cronkite to proclaim, "I think we've got a bunch of thugs here, Dan." Outside, an eruption of violence between demonstrators and police resulted in the most vivid scenes of U.S. police brutality ever shown. The eerie counter-position of riot footage with convention hall platitudes touched a sensitive nerve in many Americans watching at home.

In the many post-convention inquiries by the FCC and independent organizations, the networks were acquitted of taking a biased point of view in covering the Democratic convention. Nevertheless, television was once again cast in the role of the messenger with the bad news, punished for telling what it knew. The whole world might have been watching, as the street protesters chanted, but the whole world was not getting the same message. People of every point of view were infuriated by what they saw at the Chicago convention, but they adjusted the television images to fit their own preconceived beliefs. Anti-war forces saw Daley as an oriental-style despot who directed the convention from his delegate seat and heckled speakers like a common street hood. At the same time, many others, viewing the same scenes, saw instead a gang of unruly, riotous protesters who provoked the officials into reacting, yet still received free publicity, even open support, from the news media. No matter how the Chicago convention was seen, however, television was accused of a much worse sin: forcing millions of Americans to witness the outrageous events and choose sides.

28. The One Punch Season

THE CHICAGO convention soured Americans not only toward television news but toward the Democratic party as well. As a result, Vice President Hubert Humphrey, who won the presidential nomination in Chicago, began his campaign in September far behind the Republican candidate, former Vice President Richard Nixon. Unlike the 1964 presidential campaign, the 1968 race never appeared openly vicious and cut throat. Nonetheless, behind the scenes there was a great deal of intense activity by the candidates to foster a positive, effective image, especially through television.

Remembering his experience against John Kennedy in 1960, Nixon turned down Humphrey's incessant requests for a series of televised debates. Nixon's TV strategy hinged instead on maintaining complete control over his television environment. When Nixon arrived in a town, he would take part in a staged press conference-discussion program with a supposedly typical cross section of local citizens. Participants in these carefully arranged and highly formatted discussions were gathered in each city by the Nixon advance team as part of its preparation for the candidate's appearance there. Former college football coach Bud Wilkinson traveled along and hosted the local broadcasts. In settings reminiscent of real press conferences, the selected citizens would lob softball questions at Nixon who sharply handled each one. This gambit successfully by-passed Nixon's traditional foes, the working press, and resulted in the appearance of frank and open debate without any of the risks.

Humphrey slowly began fighting his way back, gathering a good deal of sympathy from home viewers who saw the vice president shouted down by anti-war protesters at rally after rally. In an effective Salt Lake City speech broadcast nationwide on September 30, Humphrey broke, ever so slightly, from President Johnson's Vietnam policies, giving him his long-sought image of independence.

Throughout October the gap between the two candidates narrowed and, by November 1, it was a dead heat. On election eve, Monday, November 4, both candidates held separate two-hour national call-in programs on which average citizens phoned in questions to either Nixon (on NBC) or Humphrey (on ABC). Humphrey, ever anxious to debate, had aides monitoring the Nixon broadcast and often took time to respond to charges his opponent had made moments earlier. The Nixon phone-in, as depicted by Joe McGinnis in his book *The Selling of the President, 1968,* was much like the staged regional broadcasts. A member of the production team described the setup:

[Nixon aide Paul] Keyes has a bunch of questions Nixon wants to answer. He's written them in advance to make sure they're properly worded. When someone calls with something similar, they'll use Keyes' question and attribute it to the person who called.

Election night itself proved to be a marathon, the longest election coverage in TV history. Near noon of the following day, Nixon was declared the winner, just barely edging out Humphrey in the popular vote. Six years after his supposed "last press conference," Nixon had completed a remarkable political comeback. Hoping to start fresh, both the President-elect and the press agreed to an initial "hands off" phase, but many doubted the honeymoon would last very long.

With public interest in news events at an election year high, CBS launched its version of *PBL,* called *60 Minutes,* in September. The new show, which alternated with the *CBS News Hour* on Tuesday nights, used the "magazine for television" design quite effectively, even down to the graphics and set. The program was broken into several distinct segments that mixed both hard news and soft feature stories, with veterans Harry Reasoner and Mike Wallace serving as hosts and *See It Now* veteran Don Hewitt as executive producer. On the first show of the series, they presented the views of Italian, German, and British journalists on the American presidential campaign along with an interview with Attorney General Ramsay Clark on American police as the hard news items. These were balanced with warm, homey film essays showing Nixon and Humphrey on the nights they were nominated, and an animated short, "Why Man Creates."

NBC retaliated in January with a similar show, hosted by Sander Vanocur, the two-hour *First Tuesday,* which ran once a month on Tuesday nights. It had a generally softer tone than *60 Minutes,* offering such features as a report on Philip Blaiberg, then the longest-surviving successful heart transplant patient; a portrait of Rita Hayworth at fifty, and an in-depth look at the baton industry. It was *First Tuesday,* however, that came up with the TV news scoop of the year on its second program (February 4, 1969). In a story on the American military's use of chemical warfare, Vanocur reported that in March, 1968, there had been an accident in Dugway, Utah, which resulted in the death of a large number of sheep. *60 Minutes* had done a two-part story on chemical warfare four months earlier, but had allowed the government to review the final product before airing, and its sanitized story produced no such revelations. When the Defense Department offered to help NBC (with the stipulation that it would be able to review the final product), the network turned down the agency and pursued the story on its own. New York Congressman Richard McCarthy happened to be watching NBC February 4 and, wondering why he had never heard of the sheep incident, launched a full scale investigation. Because of the television report and the subsequent congressional investigation, the Department of Defense not only admitted that it had caused the death of the sheep, but also ended all in-air tests of chemicals and gasses for biological warfare.

Congress and television were interacting in a very different way in the upper body as Senator John Pastore of Rhode Island began beating the TV violence drum. The upsurge in crime shows in the previous two years had once again raised the issue of excessive TV violence and fostered another inconclusive round of debate on its possibly harmful effects upon children. The networks feared that in the atmosphere of public outrage following the assassinations of Martin Luther King, Jr. and Robert Kennedy (in April and June of 1968), Senator Pastore might suggest some form of special federal regulation if they did *nothing* about television violence themselves. Therefore, the networks sent out the word in the middle of 1968 to tone down the level of violence in productions planned for the fall.

Assuming this to be just another passing furor, some producers tried to keep their cop and Western formats essentially intact by merely limiting the length and severity of the gun play and fist fights until the congressional heat passed. A star in a new Western series complained that, under the new rules, after an Indian was shot and fell one hundred feet from a cliff, clutching his chest, a follow-up scene had to be added with the gunman leaning over the cliff saying, "He'll live." Even the veterans had to adapt, and the season premiere of *Felony Squad* contained exactly one punch. What's more, there was only one instance of police gunfire and, following that, detective Sam Stone (Howard Duff) leaned over the victim and said, "He's still alive." These strange new rules and illogical twists for action stories gave the 1968–69 season the derogatory nickname of the "one punch season."

With violence out, at least for a while, cop shows had to scrounge for a different hook. *Hawaii Five-O* opted for scenery, much like the early Sixties' *Hawaiian Eye* and *Adventures in Paradise,* and often resembled a well-produced travelogue. Lantern-jawed Steve McGarrett (Jack Lord) headed a team of plainclothes detectives who used all the legal and extra-legal measures necessary to foil any criminal schemes that threatened to disturb the tranquility of their island paradise. Jack Webb, whose police shows had always deemphasized violence, capitalized on the swing away from action and turned out the first in a series of *Dragnet* clones, *Adam-12.* The new program featured a pair of tight-lipped young policemen (played by Martin Milner and Kent McCord) who became involved in three or four unrelated and not very violent crimes each week while on patrol in Los Angeles.

NBC's *Name of the Game* brought the flippant hero back to the forefront in the old but reliable premise of journalist-as-cop. The ninety-minute weekly series, based on the made-for-TV movie, "Fame Is the Name of the Game," presented the story of *Crime* magazine and the exploits of its publisher and reporters who all worked tirelessly to expose the fetid world of organized crime. The show sometimes borrowed the ploy used by *Dragnet* and *The FBI,* grafting a few topical characters onto a well-worn crime story, but the glib-talking performers were the chief draw of the series. Gene Barry, Tony Franciosa, and Robert Stack rotated in the starring role each week, with all three receiving assistance from the magazine's girl Friday, played by Susan Saint James. In spite

of occasional plots based on contemporary issues, at heart *Name of the Game* was pure pulp fiction, with just a few surface trappings of reality. Early in one episode, for instance, Tony Franciosa received a bruise in a fist fight and—violating television's unwritten rule of instantaneous regeneration—he kept that bruise through the rest of the show!

The prime exponent of 1968 television reality, however, was ABC's *Mod Squad* (produced by Aaron Spelling). The series marked the first full-fledged attempt by a network to absorb the look and lingo of the self-proclaimed counter culture and turn them into a standard TV action show. In the face of the deemphasis on violence, ABC wanted a gimmick to keep the action-adventure type format functioning almost undisturbed. With an eye on attracting the younger audience that was boosting the ratings of the youth-flavored comedy-variety shows, the network hoped to create a new sort of TV hero in *Mod Squad.* The three main stars in this cop show were not only young, they were young outcasts.

Preseason ads identified the mod squad as: "One black, one white, and one blonde." Pete Cochran (Michael Cole) was a troubled reject from a wealthy Beverly Hills family, driven to committing petty crimes while racked by the existential angst then so fashionable. Underneath his denim garb, though, lurked the soul of a three-piece suit. Julie Barnes (Peggy Lipton) was a poor white girl who had run away from her prostitute mother. Reflecting the changing times in the world of television, she was a very pretty young woman, but no dummy. Linc Hayes (Clarence Williams III) was an intensely brooding, beautiful black rebel, a veteran of Watts who perpetually wore dark sunglasses. With black consciousness then undergoing a revolution in America, television was beginning a 180-degree turn in its portrayal of blacks. They were

Jack Webb scored another police show hit with the *Dragnet*-like *Adam-12,* starring Kent McCord (*l.*) and Martin Milner. (*From Adam-12. Courtesy of MCA Television Limited*)

MONDAY

	7:30	8:00	8:30	9:00	9:30	10:00	10:30	
ABC	The Avengers		Peyton Place I	THE OUTCASTS		The Big Valley		ABC
CBS	Gunsmoke		HERE'S LUCY	Mayberry R.F.D.	Family Affair	Carol Burnett Show		CBS
NBC	I Dream Of Jeannie	Rowan And Martin's Laugh-In		NBC MONDAY NIGHT AT THE MOVIES				NBC

TUESDAY

	7:30	8:00	8:30	9:00	9:30	10:00	10:30	
ABC	THE MOD SQUAD		It Takes A Thief		N.Y.P.D.	THAT'S LIFE		ABC
CBS	LANCER		Red Skelton Hour		DORIS DAY SHOW	CBS News Hour / 60 MINUTES		CBS
NBC	Jerry Lewis Show		JULIA	NBC Tuesday Night At The Movies				NBC

WEDNESDAY

	7:30	8:00	8:30	9:00	9:30	10:00	10:30	
ABC	HERE COME THE BRIDES		Peyton Place II	The ABC Wednesday Night Movie				ABC
CBS	Daktari		THE GOOD GUYS	The Beverly Hillbillies	Green Acres	Jonathan Winters Show		CBS
NBC	The Virginian			Kraft Music Hall @Bob Hope Show		THE OUTSIDER		NBC

THURSDAY

	7:30	8:00	8:30	9:00	9:30	10:00	10:30	
ABC	THE UGLIEST GIRL IN TOWN	The Flying Nun	Bewitched	That Girl	JOURNEY TO THE UNKNOWN		local	ABC
CBS	BLONDIE	HAWAII FIVE-O		CBS Thursday Night Movies				CBS
NBC	Daniel Boone		Ironside		Dragnet 1969	Dean Martin Show		NBC

FRIDAY

	7:30	8:00	8:30	9:00	9:30	10:00	10:30	
ABC	Operation: Entertainment		The Felony Squad	DON RICKLES SHOW	The Guns Of Will Sonnett	Judd, For The Defense		ABC
CBS	The Wild, Wild West		Gomer Pyle, U.S.M.C.	CBS Friday Night Movies				CBS
NBC	The High Chaparral		THE NAME OF THE GAME			Star Trek		NBC

SATURDAY

	7:30	8:00	8:30	9:00	9:30	10:00	10:30	
ABC	The Dating Game	The Newlywed Game	Lawrence Welk Show		Hollywood Palace		local	ABC
CBS	Jackie Gleason Show		My Three Sons	Hogan's Heroes	Petticoat Junction	Mannix		CBS
NBC	ADAM-12	Get Smart	THE GHOST AND MRS. MUIR	NBC Saturday Night At The Movies				NBC

SUNDAY

	7:00	7:30	8:00	8:30	9:00	9:30	10:00	10:30	
ABC	LAND OF THE GIANTS		The F.B.I.		The ABC Sunday Night Movie				ABC
CBS	Lassie	Gentle Ben	Ed Sullivan Show		Smothers Brothers Comedy Hour		Mission: Impossible		CBS
NBC	NEW ADVENTURES OF HUCK FINN		Walt Disney's Wonderful World Of Color	The Mothers-In-Law	Bonanza		THE BEAUTIFUL PHYLLIS DILLER SHOW		NBC

no longer bumbling, easy-going po' folk like Beulah, but rather articulate neo-philosophers just descended from Olympus, though still spouting streetwise jargon.

The three young demigods had each been arrested on minor charges. Then, middle-aged middle-American police captain Adam Greer (Tige Andrews) talked the reluctant troika into a strange deal. They could do something positive and work within the system as undercover agents who would take on special youth-oriented assignments, possibly even hunting down criminals among their former colleagues. It was a cumbersome, strained premise, but it worked. The three hip, "with it" juvenile detectives were easier for America's teens to identify with than either the square-jawed heroes of *Dragnet* and *The FBI* or the high-living aristocrats of *Name of the Game*. The fact that the trio was secretly working for the establishment mollified the oldsters. With Pete, Julie, and Linc involved in cases as timely as the evening's headlines, ABC could exploit current issues such as youth rebellion, drug abuse, and racial tension while making sure the legitimate authority always triumphed in the end. Now *this* was TV reality.

NBC and CBS, feeling they had been left somewhat behind, quickly turned out a number of soapy "with-it" drama specials that were equally facile at incorporating then current issues into traditional TV plots. The occasional drama series, *CBS Playhouse*, presented a string of stories dealing with ostensibly rebellious young men who pounded their chests and questioned society but, after a talk with a learned elder, saw the light and got a haircut. This symbolic shearing became TV's new happy ending as youth and maturity were reconciled and the prodigal son looked nice for the holidays.

The sudden urge to "tell it like it is" and thus appear "relevant" also began to take hold in the traditional sitcom format as well. NBC patted itself on the back and presented the first modern situation comedy to focus directly on blacks, *Julia*. As if to make up for lost time, though, the series shared the *Mod Squad* approach of raising black characters to nearly divine heights. Julia (Diahann Carroll) was a registered nurse who possessed every possible positive human attribute: she was kind, sweet, forgiving, thoughtful, obedient, and reverent. Befitting the times, her husband had been killed in Vietnam, leaving her to care for their young boy, Corey (Marc Copage). Though head of television's first black family, Julia was actually indistinguishable from dozens of white counterparts such as the Nelsons and the Andersons. She lived in the same aseptically clean expanse of bland suburbia, faced the same predictable family complications, and had a child too adorably cute to be believed. In a perverse sense, *Julia* really did bring true racial equality to television because it was just as real and relevant as any other sitcom then on American television.

What actual relevancy there might have been was still found

only on *The Smothers Brothers Comedy Hour* and *Laugh-In,* both of which had blossomed throughout 1968. The Smothers were feeling their oats, having squeezed *Bonanza* from the number one spot on television while remaining comfortably in the top twenty themselves. Drawing on their hit status, they pushed to include more and more material that was considered unacceptable to the CBS censor, achieving mixed success. Pete Seeger was at last permitted to sing "Waist Deep in Big Muddy," but Harry Belafonte was not allowed to sing "Lord, Don't Stop the Carnival" as accompaniment to video tapes of the Democratic convention's street confrontations. Local CBS affiliates grew increasingly nervous over the Smothers' antics, fearing incensed complaints from viewers and possible government reprimands. To mollify them CBS instituted a closed circuit preview screening of *The Smothers Brothers Comedy Hour* for affiliates, allowing them several days to decide whether they wanted to air that week's program. Yet while the nit-picking by the locals and the CBS censor continued week after week, the Canadian commercial network (CTV) regularly aired the show Sunday nights and never registered any complaints; in fact, it often included the segments excised from American transmission.

The first showdown between the Smothers and CBS came in March, 1969, when the network substituted a Smothers' rerun for that week's scheduled show, claiming the program had been delivered too late for the affiliate preview. The Smothers said that the CBS censor was waging a vendetta against them and demanded that the network change its censorship policy or they'd quit. After all, they pointed out, it had been censorship changes that delayed delivery of the program in question. The network had objected to some remarks by Joan Baez about her husband David (who was then serving a three-year jail sentence for draft evasion), insisting the Smothers delete her line, "Anybody who lays it out in front like that generally gets busted, especially if you organize,

which he did." Tommy Smothers had agreed to the cut under protest but, at the last minute, the censor had raised some additional objections, making it impossible for the Smothers to meet the affiliate preview deadline with the completed show. After heated behind-the-scenes meetings, the Smothers capitulated and the canceled show was aired (as edited by CBS) on March 30. The next week, the two sides reached the breaking point again, and this time the Smothers lost both the battle and the war. On Thursday, April 3, the tape of the program scheduled for broadcast April 6 arrived in New York and CBS objected to two segments: the ribbing of Senator Pastore by Tommy and guest Dan Rowan (should the senator receive the Fickle Finger of Fate award?) and the double-entendre monologue by comedian David Steinberg, who interpreted the Biblical story of Jonah and the whale with lines such as "Then the Gentiles grabbed the Jew by his Old Testament." The Smothers refused to accede to the CBS censorship demands and on April 6, as the controversial episode aired as scheduled in Canada, American viewers were shown a repeat of the November 10 program.

The next morning, the Smothers held an impromptu press conference in the screening room of the Four Seasons restaurant in New York City. TV critics from New York, Boston, and Philadelphia viewed the controversial program and heard an angry outburst by the Smothers against CBS. This was the final straw for the network. Recalcitrant stars could hold out for more money, but calling CBS names in public was something the top brass would not tolerate. That evening's Walter Cronkite news show broke the story that *The Smothers Brothers Comedy Hour* had been canceled, not just for the next fall, but effective immediately. CBS never aired the April 6 show, filling the time slot with reruns until a replacement was ready. (In September, the censored show did air through local syndication by Metromedia.)

The Smothers filed an extensive lawsuit against CBS charging breach of contract, trade libel, and infringement of copyright, but

Hawaii Five-O's tried-and-true crime formula ran for twelve years on CBS. Series star Jack Lord *(r.)* and guest villain George Lazenby. *(Photo by Viacom, Hollywood)*

the case proved inconclusive. The Smothers Brothers had hoped their success would provide them with enough clout to take their fight for principles to the limit, but the truth was that with the national political mood increasingly polarized and watchdogs such as Senator Pastore breathing down broadcasters' necks, none of the networks felt the extra trouble caused by such volatile figures as the Smothers was worth it. By 1970, the Smothers Brothers desperately wanted to return to network television and they turned up in a bland special that won them a brief summer series on ABC. In all their subsequent appearances, though, they seemed much too subdued, especially in contrast to their reputation for generating exciting controversy on their old show.

NBC's *Laugh-In,* though, remained where it was. In spite of occasional political needling, *Laugh-In*'s most revolutionary aspects were its format and pacing. Once the show had become a hit, both were easily accepted and, with the exception of a few ticklish double-entendre jokes, the program was comparatively safe for the network. After its slow start in 1968, *Laugh-In* overtook Lucille Ball and became the top rated TV show on television through most of 1969. Then, surprisingly, nothing happened.

Normally all the networks eagerly jumped on the bandwagon of a new hit format and began turning out formula copies. In the early Sixties, the success of such country hits as *The Andy Griffith Show* and *The Beverly Hillbillies* led to dozens of similar shows throughout prime time and to a strong rural orientation by CBS that remained the backbone of the network's programming even in 1969. *Laugh-In*'s intricate format and image of topicality, however, proved a difficult mixture to match. The networks made several attempts to clone the series, but only one caught on.

In early 1969, ABC launched two *Laugh-In* lookalikes: *What's It All About, World?* and *Turn-On,* which were both total failures. *What's It All About, World?* was a sorry copy that was lost in the netherworld between a standard comedy-variety format and *Laugh-In*'s zaniness. Dean Jones was the program host, but his image was far too straight-laced for the task. The troupe of comedy unknowns could never quite find their mark either, even aided by veteran newsman Alex Dreier. The show tried to be titillating without offending anybody. *Turn-On* was even worse.

Turn-On (Get it? *Laugh-In. Turn-On.*) earned the dubious honor of having the shortest network run in television history—one show. Though it used *Laugh-In*'s own producer, George Schlatter, *Turn-On* showed little of the humor and ingenuity of the original, concentrating instead on mere mechanics of the hit format. Even the human host was eliminated and replaced by a computer, though it was assisted by a guest celebrity (Tim Conway in the first-last episode). The pacing in the program was nothing short of frenetic, modeling itself after the incessant tempo of television commercials: three hundred separate bits were crammed into the half-hour premiere, with the show's credits interspersed randomly throughout. Even with *Laugh-In* an established hit and its fast paced format accepted by the public, *Turn-On* still appeared to many as an incomprehensible mishmash. What's worse, almost every joke fell flat. Two policemen holding Mace cans intoned, "Let us spray." Draft dodgers were shown hitchhiking to Sweden. Maura McGiveney played the slinky, painted Body Politic (ala Judy Carne). "Topical" political comments included such gems as: "The capital of South Vietnam is in Swiss banks!"; "Down with Haya Education!"; and the exchange "I just bought the Washington Senators." "Oh, all I could afford was a Congressman!" The strongest viewer reaction was touched off by several questionable jokes concerning Pope Paul VI and by the sight of a young woman eagerly pulling the lever of a machine dispensing "the pill."

Even before *Turn-On* was aired on Wednesday night, February 5, a number of ABC affiliates expressed their uneasiness over the show, with some either refusing to carry it at all or shifting its local broadcast time to an obscure slot (the type formerly warmed by *ABC Scope*). Though many people missed seeing the show, *Turn-On*'s alleged sacrilegious tenor immediately turned it into a national controversy. An executive of ABC affiliate WEWS in Cleveland sent a wire to the network which stormed, "If you naughty little boys have to write dirty words on the walls, please don't use our walls." This angry missive received a great deal of publicity, though it was later pointed out that the man who sent the wire hadn't seen the program. While ABC's position of last place in the network ratings race gave it more freedom to experiment with new ideas in the hope that one might turn into a hit show, it was, at the same time, in the weakest position to withstand intense public criticism. On February 7, two days after *Turn-On*'s premiere, the program was axed. Three additional shows, already in the can, were never aired. ABC padded the Wednesday night movie to fill *Turn-On*'s slot until it could find a substitute. Taking no chances, the network replaced *Turn-On* with the wholesome musical-variety of *The King Family.*

Laugh-In's George Schlatter had no better luck on NBC. In October, 1968, he produced "Soul," a special-pilot for a series that NBC planned to slot in the fall schedule as a black version of *Laugh-In.* The "Soul" special starred veteran entertainers Lou Rawls, Redd Foxx, Nipsey Russell, and Slappy White, and received acceptable critical reviews, but NBC was unable to sell the projected series to sponsors.

Strangely enough, the only successful copy of *Laugh-In* was one that avoided the liberal-urban slant of the original and settled instead for deep-fried country corn, CBS's *Hee-Haw,* the network's replacement for the canceled Smothers Brothers. While few fans of *Laugh-In* would ever consider watching *Hee-Haw,* both shows were two peas from the same pod, featuring virtually identical formats. *Hee-Haw* merely substituted rural trappings. Familiar country music stars Buck Owens and Roy Clark acted as hosts and they were supported by celebrity guest stars and a comedy troupe of proficient unknowns which soon developed its own familiar characters. Like *Laugh-In,* the pace was rapid, the catch phrases redundant, and the dialogue filled with sexually oriented double-entendres. Ironically, *Hee-Haw* turned out to be the most resilient of all the clones, even outlasting *Laugh-In* itself. At first *Laugh-In* had displayed more wit but, by 1970, the program found itself practically a prisoner of its own catch phrases and format. Even the very name *Laugh-In* seemed anachronistic. *Hee-Haw* suffered from some of the same problems but it was able to maintain a more consistent, if somewhat lower, strain of humor during its many years on the air.

Hee-Haw was originally intended to serve as only a summer filler, but it was such a success that CBS brought it back at the first opportunity. In mid-December of 1969, *Hee-Haw* took the time slot of another successful, but more traditional, down-home comedy-variety show, *The Glen Campbell Goodtime Hour.* That, in turn, switched back to Sunday, taking the old Smothers time period, where it had also begun life (as the Smothers 1968 summer replacement). The Smothers Brothers were gone and these two new hits merely reinforced CBS's decade-old image (going back to the James Aubrey days) as the rural network.

Despite occasional gestures to other forms, CBS inevitably turned to rural-appeal fare for both new season programs and emergency substitutions. Even its copy of the innovative *Laugh-In* followed the same pattern. What's more, the network continued to carry the largest stable of aging veterans which, while still successful, couldn't last indefinitely. CBS needed some fresh faces and formats to maintain traditional viewer loyalty should some of the old favorites begin to depart from the increasingly tight ratings contest. For this season, in fact, only some key mid-season shifts allowed CBS to beat a strong challenge from NBC. Nonetheless, the network continued essentially unchanged into the 1969–70 season, even picking up an old sitcom discarded by NBC *(Get Smart)* for the fall of 1969. After all, though NBC and ABC continued to tinker with unproven formats such as the more topical urban slant of the *Mod Squad* series, CBS still remained number one thanks to its established hits. Though probably inevitable, a major overhaul didn't seem at all urgent to the network brass.

Just as CBS constantly went back to the farm to shore up its programming, ABC, the perpetual third network in ratings, also turned to past strengths such as game shows whenever its latest gimmicks failed. With the exception of an occasional summer replacement, game shows had been largely absent from the networks' prime time schedules since the quiz show scandal of the late Fifties. This policy began to change in the fall of 1966 when, faced with the unmitigated disaster of *The Tammy Grimes Show,* ABC promoted one of its daytime winners, *The Dating Game,* into the nighttime fold to act as a stop gap. Surprisingly, the show earned respectable ratings and, with its low production costs, proved a bargain for advertisers. *The Dating Game* was the first production effort of game show impresario Chuck Barris (a former ABC programming executive), and its prime time success was a breakthrough of sorts in the field. The program dispensed with the all-too-familiar Hollywood celebrity angle of other game shows and instead used nubile young women and handsome young men who were unknowns both to each other and to the audience. The premise was simple: One contestant tried to choose a perfect date from a trio of suitors hidden behind a stage wall by asking a series of specially prepared, slightly suggestive, questions. Though almost

a direct copy of the ancient ABC-Arlene Francis vehicle, *Blind Date,* the loosened moral standards since the late Forties allowed *The Dating Game* to maintain a fairly blatant risque tone. Barris immediately copied his own gimmick and produced the equally successful *Newlywed Game,* which had an even stronger base in double-entendre. The two games became back-to-back brothers on the ABC schedule.

In November, 1968, ABC scored a major game show coup by luring the four-year-old *Let's Make a Deal* from NBC. Although the show was a long-time smash in the daytime, NBC was reluctant to grant it prime time exposure, allowing only a brief summer run in 1967. When the network refused to give the show a second prime time run, its producers defected to ABC. Desperately in need of hit programs to build up its daytime strength, ABC was more than happy to place *Let's Make a Deal* in one of its many open slots in the evening as part of the deal. Though never much of a hit at night, *Let's Make a Deal* carried its loyal daytime audience to ABC and within months the network became number two behind CBS during the daytime.

Let's Make a Deal was a masterpiece in greed, dispensing with challenging questions and specialized knowledge in favor of pure luck. Otherwise respectable citizens stood in line for hours, dressed in ridiculous costumes, hoping for a good seat and the chance to catch host Monty Hall's attention. Monty chose the most oddly attired people in the studio audience as contestants and gave them the chance to wheel and deal their way to big bucks. He awarded them a small prize and then played on their natural greed in a series of increasingly valuable trades, offering visions of untold

---

July 20, 1969. Man walks on the moon. *(NASA)*

ABC's Jules Bergman, NBC's Frank McGee, and CBS's Walter Cronkite had been dutifully reporting the exploits in America's space program since the early Sixties, from the first sub-orbital flights to the launching of the behemoth Saturn V rocket. At first, the space launches produced very long programs that had very few visual highlights once the rocket had been launched. There were only voice transmissions and network mockups to fill the remaining hours. In late 1965, NASA began to allow live transmission of the splashdown and recovery procedure (starting with Gemini 6), but it wasn't until October, 1967, that Americans were treated to the sight of their astronauts, live and in orbit, through signals sent from Apollo 7. The ever-improving technology that permitted live broadcasts from space, even from the capsule itself, at last allowed television to present the full impact and wonder of space exploration.

On the cold and snowy Christmas Eve of 1968, as millions gathered to celebrate Christmas, television shared with the nation, and the world, the excitement and the drama of the flight of Apollo 8, the first manned spaceship ever to orbit the moon. As the ship completed its first lunar orbit and emerged from the far side of the moon, mission control in Houston announced that contact had been reestablished with Apollo 8. Within seconds, an eerie but peaceful black and white image of the moon, close up, appeared on television. It was a sight never before witnessed by human eyes. Later that night, astronauts Frank Borman, Jim Lovell, and Bill Anders presented another panorama of lunar landscape while reading from the book of *Genesis,* closing with, "God bless all of you on the good Earth."

Six months later, the three commercial networks stayed on the air over thirty continuous hours as television showed the first manned landing on the moon. The actual touchdown of the lunar module wasn't televised but, shortly before 11:00 P.M. on July 20, 1969, astronaut Neil Armstrong pulled a string as he began to climb down the ladder of the lunar module to the surface of the moon. A panel opened and a small TV camera began following his descent. The signal was transmitted to the orbiting command module, from there to an Earth-based antenna, then to NASA in Houston, and finally to the networks, thus allowing millions of people to see Armstrong descend the stairs and set man's first step on the moon milliseconds after it actually occurred. If the men who struggled in the early part of the century to create television were to come back to life and ask how their invention was put to use, it would be wise to ignore every entertainment program ever broadcast and show them instead these moments from space. It has been estimated that between 300 million and three-fourths of one billion people either saw or heard Armstrong's descent, live. If ever there was a time that television fulfilled its creators' dreams and brought the world together in peace, this was it.

riches at the end if they would only deal the pittance they had for what lurked behind door number one, door number two, or door number three. Unlike programs such as *Twenty-One,* contestants took all their winnings to each new deal—one bad trade and they could lose everything. Nonetheless, *Let's Make a Deal* tapped the barely subconscious wish to strike it rich quick, and the show became a symbol of the successful excesses of the game show genre. It might not have been great art, but it was pure popular entertainment.

American commercial television has always been the embodiment of both crass and class. In 1969, the gelt gaucherie of *Let's Make a Deal* was the runaway hit of daytime TV, yet at the same time television delivered some of the most historic and poetic moments in its history as it presented the climax to the story of man's conquest of space and the race to the moon.

1969-70 SEASON

29. Effete and Impudent Snobs

SEX AND VIOLENCE: the twin tar babies of American television. No matter how much the public moralists decried what they saw as an excess of sex and violence on TV, as soon as their clamor died down network programmers once again returned to these two familiar standbys. Most of the outraged critics faded after a short time in the public spotlight, while the home audience continued to be drawn by the lure of programs that included healthy doses of sex and violence. So for nearly twenty years, through each cycle of outraged criticism, the networks and producers tried to sneak in as much as possible without disturbing too many vocal viewers or politicians with clout. However, Rhode Island's powerful senator, John Pastore, proved to be one of the more persistent in the long line of television critics. He chaired a series of well-publicized hearings in 1969 and demonstrated that he had no intention of just fading away. Consequently, the new fall schedule for 1969 turned into a schizophrenic mix of strategies devised to bypass governmental intrusion yet still produce hit shows.

Violent police sagas were as easy target for criticism, so the wave of new cop shows was stopped cold. Not one new policeman, spy, private eye, or reporter-as-cop appeared in the fall schedule. There were no new Westerns, either. What's more, even veteran shoot'em-ups such as *The Virginian* continued the one-punch mentality of the previous season, replacing the traditional bar room brawl with nonhuman violence such as turbulent cattle stampedes. The freezing of these two forms still left the networks searching for new ways to present the same sort of emotions. Crime shows and Westerns, with all their violent tendencies, were the perfect vehicles in which to depict basic human crises (love, hate, life, death, greed) in showcases that allowed a natural, dramatic climax of capture and justice. To replace the cowboys and the cops the networks turned to two formats that had flourished on TV in the early Sixties after the demise of the ABC-Warner Brothers action-adventure fad, the doctors and the lawyers. Both professions also dealt with intriguing law breakers and heartbroken beauties, but the drama usually began immediately after the violence had taken place, so the action was verbal rather than physical, often resembling soap operas.

The soapiest of them all were the doctors, presented in three new shows: *Marcus Welby, M.D., Medical Center,* and *The Bold Ones.* These sudsy dramas were aimed directly at young adults and middle-aged women in that desirable 18–34 year-old demographic age group. Each maintained the inviolable Casey-Zorba/

Kildare-Gillespie arrangement of a young handsome medico for sexual interest and a sage mentor to serve as a voice of reason. The standard operating procedure in each episode also remained unchanged from the Casey-Kildare days as the angels in white sought to overcome the illnesses that had struck that week's celebrity guest stars in several unrelated cases. What *had* changed, though, was the by-then prerequisite injection of a hip with-it touch to make the series appear bold and modern. Even the traditional TV doctor conflict between brash youth and experienced elder was viewed as a convenient hook to use in exploiting the then current interest in the "generation gap."

CBS's *Medical Center* had young stalwart Dr. Joe Gannon (Chad Everett) chomping at the bit placed on him by the chief surgeon, Dr. Paul Lochner (James Daly). Both men worked together, though, in dealing with the complex and exotic disorders that came their way—usually in the form of a beautiful, but troubled, woman. *The Doctors* segment of *The Bold Ones* cast E. G. Marshall as a chief neurosurgeon, considered a liberal innovator by his colleagues, who had to keep in check his even more headstrong protégés (John Saxon and David Hartman). On ABC, Marcus Welby, played by the consumate TV parent, Robert Young, fought to control the hot-blooded youthful exuberance of his dashing young aide (who even rode a motorcycle), Dr. Steven Kiley (James Brolin).

Young, a proven hand at dispensing philosophical TV homilies, played Dr. Welby as a father-confessor figure who operated from his own home rather than from a large, impersonal hospital. (The show could have easily been called "Doctor Knows Best.") Though the standard TV doctor illnesses such as amnesia, temporary blindness, and brain tumors received their usual exposure, previously taboo subjects such as abortion and V.D. were added to the plots. The insertion of controversial issues was an ingenious ploy to lure the young audience and seemed to allow frank discussions of complex issues, though in reality the presentations were stacked in advance and the character of Welby was used to spout the established catechisms on the topics. The pregnant woman in the abortion program came to Dr. Welby only after she was almost killed by a sloppy back-alley butcher. Welby, of course, took the injured woman under his care, but was quick to point out that he felt an abortion had been the wrong choice to make in the first place. In facing the problem of V.D., Welby played the consumate guidance counselor, delivering frank but comforting lectures to the youngsters and their parents. They, in turn, responded with appro-

213

FALL 1969 SCHEDULE

	7:30	8:00	8:30	9:00	9:30	10:00	10:30	
MONDAY	THE MUSIC SCENE	THE NEW PEOPLE		THE SURVIVORS		LOVE, AMERICAN STYLE		**ABC**
	Gunsmoke		Here's Lucy	Mayberry R.F.D.	Doris Day Show	Carol Burnett Show		**CBS**
	MY WORLD AND WELCOME TO IT	Rowan And Martin's Laugh-In		NBC Monday Night At The Movies @Bob Hope Show		@NBC Specials		**NBC**

	7:30	8:00	8:30	9:00	9:30	10:00	10:30	
TUESDAY	The Mod Squad		MOVIE OF THE WEEK			MARCUS WELBY, M.D.		**ABC**
	Lancer		Red Skelton Hour		THE GOVERNOR AND J.J.	CBS News Hour 60 Minutes		**CBS**
	I Dream Of Jeannie	DEBBIE REYNOLDS SHOW	Julia	NBC Tuesday Night At The Movies @First Tuesday				**NBC**

	7:30	8:00	8:30	9:00	9:30	10:00	10:30	
WEDNESDAY	The Flying Nun	THE COURTSHIP OF EDDIE'S FATHER	ROOM 222	The ABC Wednesday Night Movie				**ABC**
	Glen Campbell Goodtime Hour		The Beverly Hillbillies	MEDICAL CENTER		Hawaii Five-O		**CBS**
	The Virginian			Kraft Music Hall		THEN CAME BRONSON		**NBC**

	7:30	8:00	8:30	9:00	9:30	10:00	10:30	
THURSDAY	The Ghost And Mrs. Muir	That Girl	Bewitched	This Is Tom Jones		It Takes A Thief		**ABC**
	Family Affair	JIM NABORS HOUR		CBS Thursday Night Movies				**CBS**
	Daniel Boone		Ironside	Dragnet 1970		Dean Martin Show		**NBC**

	7:30	8:00	8:30	9:00	9:30	10:00	10:30	
FRIDAY	Let's Make A Deal	THE BRADY BUNCH	MR. DEEDS GOES TO TOWN	Here Come The Brides		JIMMY DURANTE PRESENTS THE LENNON SISTERS HOUR		**ABC**
	Get Smart	The Good Guys	Hogan's Heroes	CBS Friday Night Movies				**CBS**
	The High Chaparral			The Name Of The Game		BRACKEN'S WORLD		**NBC**

	7:30	8:00	8:30	9:00	9:30	10:00	10:30	
SATURDAY	The Dating Game	The Newlywed Game	Lawrence Welk Show		Hollywood Palace		local	**ABC**
	Jackie Gleason Show		My Three Sons	Green Acres	Petticoat Junction	Mannix		**CBS**
	Andy Williams Show		Adam-12	NBC Saturday Night At The Movies				**NBC**

	7:00	7:30	8:00	8:30	9:00	9:30	10:00	10:30	
SUNDAY	Land Of The Giants		The F.B.I.		The ABC Sunday Night Movie				**ABC**
	Lassie	TO ROME WITH LOVE	Ed Sullivan Show		LESLIE UGGAMS SHOW		Mission: Impossible		**CBS**
	Wild Kingdom	The Wonderful World Of Disney		BILL COSBY SHOW	Bonanza		THE BOLD ONES (THE DOCTORS, THE LAWYERS, THE PROTECTORS)		**NBC**

priate lines like "Who, me?" and "What? *My* child??" The show gave the appearance of presenting progressive drama while actually reducing the issues involved to mere Sunday school lessons.

Though not at all violent, the new doctor shows could sneak in underlying sexual themes in the same way as the afternoon soap operas, by being all talk and no action. Other series, which could not wrap their titillation in the white robes of professional respectability, fared far worse. One of the major victims of the more stringent limitations on TV sex was an elaborately planned ABC series, *The Survivors,* another of the network's forays into the world of novels-for-television. Created by Harold Robbins, a master in the genre of broad-based sexy pulp fiction, the new series proposed to bring to television exciting sex-drenched dramas of the rich and playful jet set. ABC promised that Robbins would be closely involved in the production of the series and that the program would be a true television novel, presenting a different chapter of a continuing story each week. None of this ever happened. Just as the show was about to begin production in mid 1968, the sex and violence controversy flared and *The Survivors* was delayed until the fall of 1969. With the toned down standards still in effect, the series was turned into a traditional television suspense thriller with soap opera touches. Consequently, the exploits of a powerful banking family were mixed with such sudsy

daytime staples as pregnant unmarried damsels trying to hide their shame. The network also abandoned the concept of a TV novel storyline and settled for a stable, celebrity-studded continuing cast (Ralph Bellamy, Lana Turner, Kevin McCarthy, and George Hamilton), but the program didn't survive its forced neutering. The show quickly went through three producers, lost its head star (Bellamy), and, by mid-season, was written off as a full-fledged flop. Despite ABC's major financial investment, the project was quickly disposed of, with an equally unsuccessful spinoff series, *Paris 7000* (starring the only cast holdover, George Hamilton, as an American playboy in Paris), fulfilling certain contractual arrangements between ABC and Universal studios.

Another victim of the tighter production code was an NBC project with 20th Century-Fox, *Bracken's World,* which ostensibly presented the behind-the-scenes lives and loves at a major Hollywood studio but was actually an excuse to expose as much of the nubile young starlets (including Karen Jensen, Linda Harrison, and Laraine Stephens) as the censors would allow. By the time *Bracken's World* began production in the spring of 1969, the stricter rules required the beautiful women to keep most of their clothes on. Though they flitted to and fro complying with the orders given by the off-camera unseen head of the studio, John Bracken (Leslie Nielsen), the stories were quite weak. Forced to rely on its dramatic content without maximum exposure of its aspiring, compliant women, *Bracken's World* folded after only one and a half seasons.

The only new show to succeed with up-front sex in spite of such production limitations was ABC's *Love, American Style*, the first hit comedy anthology program on network TV. Since the early Fifties, the ratings domination by situation comedies in the *I Love Lucy* mold had convinced the networks that stable, familiar characters were essential in order to capture the fickle TV audience. *Love, American Style* broke from this assumption and presented three totally unconnected playlets that used guest stars exclusively. The only group of regulars turned up in the comedy quickies that appeared between the individual playlets. The omni-present theme of love, as portrayed in the different humorous vignettes, held the program together.

Love, American Style did indeed display a freedom in topic and treatment above the traditional situation comedies and it worked hard at cultivating a risque image. At heart, though, it was *very* respectable. There was talk of affairs, sleeping together, and premarital sex, but the Puritan ethic always triumphed and nothing salacious ever occurred either on or off camera. The program was a successful and effective transplant to TV of the Doris Day-Rock Hudson bedroom comedy films of the Fifties, with the same simple underlying premise: The courting rituals in America are in themselves hilarious and will seem so to the viewers when presented in a slightly exaggerated style. With an emphasis on rituals and games over the sex act itself, *Love, American Style* was the most representative example of permissible 1969 TV sex: Not only was it just all talk and no action, even the talk wasn't meant to be taken seriously. Occasionally the sugar-coated view of life became a bit too rich, but the program was generally funny and a genuinely successful innovation by ABC.

ABC and NBC were the only two networks actively experimenting with new forms in the 1969–70 season because CBS had decided to stand pat a while longer with its veteran sixty-minute variety shows and thirty-minute sitcoms. Though it had barely won the previous season, CBS had also experienced noticeable difficulty in coming up with enough new hits during the late Sixties. Instead, the network ended up relying on years of viewer loyalty to familiar formats and stars that would bring people back to CBS after sampling the competition. In the fall of 1969, it looked as if this strategy was going to fail for the first time in over a decade. CBS still had its hits, but there were enough successful regular series, movies, and specials on NBC and ABC to tip the balance in the overall ratings. NBC jumped into first place and remained there until New Year's while ABC's new *Movie of the Week* occasionally hit number one in the weekly ratings. The new *Bill Cosby Show* sitcom and *The Bold Ones* career drama gave NBC a powerful Sunday night line-up. ABC turned out an intelligent new sitcom of its own, *Room 222*, and it received both critical praise and surprisingly good ratings against *The Beverly Hillbillies*.

Room 222 was a sharp break with both the rural slant of CBS's sitcoms and ABC's own trademarks of mindless escapism and cutsie-poo children. The series was topical and humorous while being only slightly sentimental in its portrayal of an integrated middle class urban high school. A largely unknown cast acted out believable stories with the focus on three excellent characters: a daffy white student-teacher (Karen Valentine), an understanding but much put-upon Jewish principal (Michael Constantine), and a black teacher of American history (Lloyd Haynes) whose classes were held in Room 222. They dealt with such dramatic issues as student rights and racial tension, but faced them with humor and more credibility than characters in such series as *The Mod Squad*

or *Marcus Welby, M.D.* With its successful showing in the ratings, *Room 222* at last proved that more up to date settings could work very well in sitcoms, too.

In contrast to this successful momentum, all of CBS's new sitcoms failed, and even variety stalwarts such as Ed Sullivan and newcomer Jim Nabors were in the dumps. In January, NBC felt strong enough to order no changes in its prime time schedule and, by February, it looked as if CBS might lose the season to NBC. Faced with this awesome prospect, CBS's new president, Bob Wood, decided to take drastic steps to stay on top. The first phase was a full-court press to win the season in progress with a game plan designed by veteran CBS programming chief, Mike Dann, and dubbed "Operation 100."

During the one hundred days remaining in the regular season (which ended in April), Dann countered NBC's regular programming and previously announced specials, slot by slot, night by night. He preempted weak shows such as *Get Smart* as often as possible, realizing that even a moderately successful special would probably register better ratings. The most striking aspect of Dann's counterprogramming was that he used some very unusual material: previously run movies such as "Peyton Place" and "The African Queen," specials that had played years before (sometimes on competing networks), and documentary films from National Geographic. By packaging and promoting them as special events, CBS beat NBC at its own game. NBC had aired most of its blockbuster movies in building its fall lead and was unable to effectively counter the CBS moves. Dann's strategy violated CBS's traditional reliance on the strength of its regular series for success, but the plan worked. CBS managed to win by enough each week during the one-hundred

Marcus Welby, M.D. featured TV veteran Robert Young, backed by Elena Verdugo and James Brolin. (*From Marcus Welby, M.D. Courtesy of MCA Television Limited*)

September 22, 1969

Music Scene. (ABC). David Steinberg hosts a rock version of *Your Hit Parade* (with some comedy thrown in), featuring on the first show James Brown, Three Dog Night, and a film of the Beatles hit "Ballad of John and Yoko." The program is one of two back-to-back forty-five-minute shows, but the packaging strategy fails and both vanish by January.

September 26, 1969

The Brady Bunch. (ABC). A vapid suburban sitcom straight out of the 1950s. Robert Reed plays a widower (with three cute sons) who marries a widow (played by Florence Henderson) with three cute daughters. The combined family lives in a typical Los Angeles suburban house, complete with a dog, a cat, and a smart-aleck maid (played by Ann B. Davis).

October 5, 1969

Monty Python's Flying Circus. Meanwhile, back in Britain, the BBC uncovers five *David Frost Show* graduates who take the *Laugh-In* formula beyond the fringe.

December 29, 1969

Dick Cavett becomes ABC's late night replacement for the slumping Joey Bishop.

January 1, 1970

Robert Sarnoff becomes chairman of the board at RCA as his father, seventy-nine-year-old David Sarnoff, is named honorary board chairman.

---

days to boost the network's overall average past NBC's—though just barely.

With his mission accomplished, Dann quit while he was ahead and went to work for public TV's Children's Television Workshop. To replace him, CBS promoted its thirty-two-year-old wunderkind, Fred Silverman, head of the network's daytime programming since 1963. For seven years, Silverman had kept CBS so far ahead in daytime ratings and revenue that the network could afford a few close calls in the nighttime ratings.

The second phase of Wood's plan to retain the number one spot was the surprise axing of three still successful CBS classics at the end of the 1969–70 season: *The Jackie Gleason Show, Petticoat Junction,* and *Red Skelton.* (Skelton moved over to NBC for one last season.) The rationale for these cancellations lay in the new shibboleth of TV programming, demographics. The total number of people viewing a program was no longer the most important consideration, but rather the kind of people watching. While Gleason, Skelton, and *Petticoat Junction* had maintained adequate ratings, they also served to reinforce the image of CBS as the network appealing primarily to old people and country folk rather than the advertisers' favorite segment of society: young marrieds in the 18 to 34-year-old bracket, preferably women because they made most of the domestic purchases. For the sin of appealing to the wrong types of Americans, Gleason, Skelton, and the gang at Hooterville became the first of the CBS veterans to walk the plank.

Though CBS was just coming to grips with the changing reality of television, the other two networks had begun to tinker with some firmly established traditions of prime time TV years before. Since the early Sixties, in fact, a number of network programmers (at NBC in particular) had been sliding back toward the all-but-abandoned anthology format to the extent that even some of the features of the British system, which emphasized limited run series, began turning up on American TV. Ninety-minute Westerns such

as *The Virginian* and *Wagon Train* marked the first tentative moves in this direction because the programs were, in effect, Western anthologies that primarily showcased weekly guest stars while carrying a few continuing characters. NBC's 1964 effort at a situation comedy anthology, *90 Bristol Court,* attempted to incorporate three half-hour sitcoms under one banner, with each segment dealing with that week's particular topic in a different way. It was an intriguing concept, but it turned out to be clumsy, poorly connected, and a total failure.

In the middle and late Sixties, the success of both prime time movies and made-for-TV movies (which were, after all, anthology series) provided the strongest impetus to break from the standard weekly format. *Name of the Game,* a spinoff from the successful made-for-TV movie, used its setup of three major characters alternating in the lead role to have, in effect, three different shows with the same general setting running in the same time slot. NBC extended this concept in 1969 with *The Bold Ones,* a series that alternated separate, totally unrelated segments in the same time slot (*The Doctors, The Lawyers,* and *The Protectors,* the last one eventually replaced by *The Senator*). NBC discovered that major stars such as Gene Barry, Tony Franciosa, Robert Stack *(Name of the Game),* E. G. Marshall *(The Doctors),* Burl Ives *(The Lawyers),* Leslie Nielsen *(The Protectors),* and Hal Holbrook *(The Senator)* were much more likely to agree to do a television series if they didn't have to maintain the insane production pace that a weekly sixty- or ninety-minute TV show required. This very practical consideration resulted in series with both a healthy diversity and many big stars, giving NBC potent programs to capture and keep an audience.

ABC took the almost inevitable next step with made-for-TV movies and gave the format a ninety-minute weekly slot without any continuing segments at all, the Tuesday night *Movie of the Week.* Though not quite a return to *Studio One,* the program in effect brought the full-length weekly anthology format back to television after a decade of limp remnants such as the *U.S. Steel Hour, Armstrong Circle Theater,* and *Chrysler Theater.* The move in the mid-Fifties toward presenting series with popular, continuing characters had, by 1958, marked the end of the TV drama anthologies as an important creative force, but the success of made-for-TV movies demonstrated their renewed viability.

Actually, ABC's *Movie of the Week* more closely resembled the old *ABC Stage '67* show as it incorporated comedy and traditional specials, as well as adventure and drama, under its banner. Thus, material such as David Wolper's documentary film "The Journey of Robert F. Kennedy" joined bread-and-butter adventure-drama features such as "Seven in Darkness," which presented the struggle to safety by seven blind survivors of a jungle plane crash. In addition, the *Movie of the Week* slot served as an excellent showcase for thinly disguised pilot films of proposed regular series; *The Immortal* and *The Young Lawyers* were two such series given the go-ahead for the 1970–71 season following their successful feature film debuts.

NBC also increased its made-for-TV showcases, which the network labeled "world premieres" and inserted in its regular movie slots. Among the presentations were some fairly serious dramas that pulled off the very elusive TV trick of garnering both high ratings and strong critical praise. "Silent Night, Lonely Night," a Christmastime TV adaptation of Robert Anderson's Broadway play, was a tasteful and sensitive study of the pangs of desire between two married people (played by Lloyd Bridges and Shirley Jones) who decided to have a brief affair after one chance meeting. The two lovers were actually shown in bed together and, though they returned to their respective spouses at the end, neither was struck by some divine punishment for the transgression. Outside the daytime soaps (which had been dealing with such encounters, and much more, for years), adultery had never received such favorable treatment in a work for television.

One month later, NBC presented "My Sweet Charlie," a novel-turned-play produced and adapted for television by Richard Levinson and William Link (the creators of *Mannix*). The story was a sensitive portrayal of a chance encounter inter-racial romance—an even more precedent shattering situation than "Silent Night, Lonely Night." Patty Duke played a runaway unwed teenage mother driven by a hurricane to seek shelter in a deserted house. There she encountered a fugitive black activist (Al Freeman) and the two outsiders lovingly shared each other's burdens, discovering that they had a great deal in common. With the passing of the storm, though, their utopia evaporated and the real world entered, breaking them apart. As a sign of the changing times, the kind portrayal of an unwed teenage mother (a very controversial concept only a few years before) was all but overlooked as attention focused on the first black-white romance in TV history. "My Sweet Charlie" won three Emmys and, more importantly, both it and "Silent Night, Lonely Night" did surprisingly well in the ratings. "My Sweet Charlie," in fact, emerged as the highest rated movie on television that year. The message from the ratings success of these innovative stories was that the television audience was evidencing a noticeable rise in the level of its tolerance and sophistication, a development many TV detractors had claimed would never take place.

Accompanying this change was an increase in the number of viewers tuning in programs on public television's NET network. NET had learned from *PBL* that its success as a network rested with shows that were at least structured like commercial network programs so that the audience would give them a chance. In the 1969–70 season it clicked with two such well-produced series, *Sesame Street* and *The Forsyte Saga*. *Sesame Street* was a product of the Children's Television Workshop and began life as an eight million dollar, twenty-nine week television "head start" program aimed at preschool children, especially those in the urban ghettos. The program attempted to teach basic concepts of letters and numbers by using the technique of exciting, constant repetition pioneered by TV commercials. Program headliners such as Jim Henson's colorful muppet characters including the Cookie Monster, Big Bird, Bert, and Ernie elaborated on the basic lessons, adding their own humorous interpretations of the facts. *Sesame Street* was entertaining, educational, and an instant success with adults as well as children. It brought invaluable attention to the other less frenetic features of the NET schedule and boosted the ever-present funding drives as well.

The twenty-six-week *Forsyte Saga* began a Sunday night run on NET in October, 1969, following its smash hit appearances in England in 1967 and, again as a rerun, in 1968. *The Forsyte Saga* was an expensive adaptation of John Galsworthy's novels, following the lives, loves, and losses of a respectable upper class Victorian family over fifty years and three generations. Production and acting in the series were first rate and the historical setting was quite impressive. At heart, though, the series was really just a high-gloss soaper, containing all the ingredients of a period soap opera: dashing young men, beautiful young women, a scheming old skinflint, extra-marital affairs, and a complicated continuing storyline. Nevertheless, American viewers who would never be caught dead watching *As the World Turns* considered *The Forsyte Saga* classy and morally uplifting because it was British and on "educational" TV. They bragged about following the weekly Sun-

day night exploits of the Forsyte family, encouraging their friends to tune in as well. Consequently, the 167 NET stations carrying the program noticed a sizable increase in their Sunday night audiences and they began looking for programs with the same type of attraction. In the fall of 1970, *Masterpiece Theater* was created (with the help of substantial grants from the Mobil Oil Corporation) to present British-made historical dramas on a regular basis, every Sunday night. The program, hosted by *Omnibus* alumnus Alistair Cooke, began with *The First Churchills* and then moved on, in subsequent years, to other Anglophile sagas such as *Elizabeth R* and *Upstairs, Downstairs*. The limited-run imported series brought the individual NET stations large audiences and projected an air of classy success. They also made the expense and bother of producing similar domestic programs seem less and less worthwhile, thus beginning NET's extended parasitic dependence on the BBC.

In 1969, though, the network was still producing several excellent programs of its own, including *The Advocates, NET Playhouse,* and *Hollywood Television Theater. The Advocates* presented a debate of controversial issues argued courtroom style by knowledgeable experts from both sides. *NET Playhouse* turned out dramatic productions such as "The Trail of Tears," an unflinching portrait of American persecution of the Cherokee Indians in the 1830s, starring Johnny Cash and Jack Palance. Perhaps NET's best dramatic production of the year appeared on the May 17, 1969, premiere of *Hollywood Television Theater,* the lavishly funded successor to *NET Playhouse.* George C. Scott directed a new production of "The Andersonville Trial," a 1959 Saul Levitt play that dramatized the Nuremberg-like post-Civil War trial of the commander of an inhuman prisoner of war camp. Scott himself had starred in the original Broadway production but for the new television version,

---

February 4, 1970

After seven years as CBS's daytime programming boss, Fred Silverman is promoted to the nighttime division, as an assistant to chief programmer, Mike Dann.

June 22, 1970

Fred Silverman succeeds Mike Dann as programmer #1 at network #1.

July 8, 1970

The Smothers Brothers Summer Show. (ABC). The brothers sneak back onto television for a summer series with some of their old crew and a few new faces (including Sally Struthers). They avoid becoming embroiled in topical controversies but also fail to rekindle their popularity with viewers. As a result, their program is not picked up for a regular fall season run.

July 16, 1970

Nearly ten years after Ed Murrow's "Harvest of Shame" documentary, Martin Carr shows how little has changed for American migrant workers.

July 31, 1970

Chet Huntley says "goodnight" to David Brinkley for the last time, with the hope that "there will be better and happier news, one day, if we work at it." On August 3, John Chancellor and Frank McGee join Brinkley for the new *NBC Nightly News* format.

September 27, 1970

Ted Mack's *Original Amateur Hour,* television's oldest running entertainment show, gets the gong. Age: 22 years. During its last ten years, the show had been relegated to a Sunday afternoon slot on CBS.

April 30, 1970, President Richard Nixon on prime time announces the U.S. invasion of Cambodia. *(National Archives)*

recorded live on tape, Richard Basehart, Jack Cassidy, and William Shatner took the leads in the thought-provoking debate on moral responsibility.

NET's production style was much closer to the fondly remembered live drama of such vehicles as *Playhouse 90* than the generally action-oriented made-for-TV movies on the commercial networks. Though such programs as *Hollywood Television Theater* were not going to spark a revival of *Studio One* on commercial television, NET's programming was having a greater effect on long-range planning by the commercial television executives. With public television viewing on the rise, they began using NET as a test ground for formats and ideas they feared might not yet be ready for a commercial run. NET had truly become a force to reckon with, not only by the commercial networks but by the government itself.

Since the mid-Sixties, NET had been the boldest network in producing public affairs programs and documentaries. During that time, it managed to avoid most governmental interference because of its minuscule audience and minor budget requirements. As the network became more influential and more dependent on government funding, this began to change. The Corporation for Public Broadcasting (CPB) began to feel pressure from the Nixon administration to reduce clearly anti-administration material. A number of public TV stations became very nervous about airing any possibly inflamatory programs at all. In February, 1970, WETA in Washington refused outright to show "Who Invited Us?" on *NET Journal*. This program was a slightly heavy-handed portrait of America's foreign policy as a strategy strongly influenced by the CIA and private corporations in order to further their own interests—a theme certain to irk the Nixon administration. With governmental funding becoming a major factor in NET finances, it seemed foolish to antagonize the people who had a strong say in just how much money Congress voted for public television. Though home viewers and private corporations such as the Ford Foundation and Mobil Oil still donated freely to NET, the network faced mounting costs such as AT&T line charges as it began to operate more and more like a real network. With the Nixon people sorting out friends

from enemies, the CPB began noticeably kowtowing to the administration in a manner reminiscent of the commercial networks at the height of President Johnson's influence.

In contrast to public television's pullback, the commercial networks, which had been slowly rebuilding their commitment to hard-hitting news after the "no guts journalism" era, regained the courage to air a few truly controversial documentaries. The Black Panthers, a prime target of J. Edgar Hoover's FBI, became the subject of reports on both CBS and ABC in the 1969–70 season. CBS's story led the network into an aggravated battle with the Justice Department, which issued a subpoena for the outtakes from the filmed interviews with Panther leaders. Under protest, CBS surrendered the leftover film, though it's doubtful the FBI found any nefarious plot or revealing off-the-cuff remark in the scraps from the cutting room floor. Nonetheless, when ABC did its report a few months later, the network couldn't guarantee that the same thing wouldn't happen to its films, so only Panther boss David Hilliard agreed to speak on camera. As a final network frustration, the Justice Department then refused to provide anyone to give the government's side of the Panther issue. Despite the limitations, the ABC report was an effective overview of the group and it served as a high point of the network's short-lived new prime time public affairs series, *Now* (hosted by Edward P. Morgan).

NBC, which was usually content to cover safer subjects such as "The Great Barrier Reef," tackled the politically volatile story of migrant farm workers in an *NBC White Paper* produced and directed by Martin Carr, "Migrants." The program was an effective followup to Carr's own previous report (on CBS) in 1968, "Hunger in America," which itself had been a followup to Ed Murrow's 1960 "Harvest of Shame." The most amazing aspect of the new reports was that so little had changed since Murrow's first story on the agricultural workers, both in the fields and behind the scenes. Like its predecessors, "Migrants" took a tough stand and named some major American corporations as being responsible for keeping the migrant workers close to starvation in the world's most bountiful land. It showed a representative of the Coca-Cola company, which owned a large citrus farm, physically breaking up an interview with a tenant who lived in one of the company's filthy shanties. As in the past, the crop growers cried "foul" and exerted intense pressure on NBC to keep the show off the air, labeling it "sneaky journalism." Despite the pressure, the report aired, albeit in the middle of July, without any commercial time sold, and with some affiliates refusing to show it anyway.

In spite of these incidents of bravery, network journalism was forced to take a step backwards in the 1969–70 season as the networks and the Nixon administration locked horns on the most troubling issue of all, the Vietnam war. On October 15, 1969, anti-war forces throughout the country held rallies as part of what was called Moratorium Day. As with the march on the Pentagon two years earlier, CBS was reluctant to devote much coverage to the protests. For Moratorium Day, however, NBC took the initiative and scheduled an 11:30 P.M. wrapup, so CBS did the same. Even this small dose of publicity given to the demonstrators irked Nixon and the President seemed convinced that the press, particularly the television press, was out to sabotage his administration. The next month he saw even further evidence that the "hands off" honeymoon with the news media had certainly come to an end.

On Monday, November 3, Nixon delivered an appeal directly to the viewing public in a half-hour speech that outlined his new Vietnamization policy and asked for support from "the great silent majority of my fellow Americans." Nixon promised his new strategy would eventually lead to the withdrawl of all American ground combat forces and leave South Vietnam to fight the ground war on its own. The speech ended at 10:05 P.M. As usual, the networks had received advance texts of the address a few hours before airtime, and their correspondents stood by for the traditional post-speech commentary and analysis. NBC and CBS devoted ten minutes each to the discussion and then returned to their scheduled programming. One CBS reporter observed that the President's Vietnamization program really offered nothing new and would simply mean an intensification of the American air war. ABC, which ran its report until 10:30, called on other political figures, as well as its own correspondents, for comments, reactions, and analysis. Veteran Democrat Averell Harriman, a former chief negotiator at the Vietnam peace talks, took the opportunity to delivery some harsh criticisms of Nixon's handling of both the war and the ever-stalled peace talks.

This public disagreement and criticism immediately following the President's own speech seemed to be the final straw for Nixon. He decided to launch a strong counter-attack before the networks had a chance to give the protesters any more free air time during the Moratorium II activities scheduled for November 15. The networks were warned that "it would be wise" to cover, live, a speech by Vice President Spiro Agnew at a Republican party conference in Des Moines on November 13. They did. At 7:00 P.M., speaking on CBS, NBC, and ABC, Agnew launched a vituperative attack on these same networks. Before the highly partisan crowd, he criticized the fact that "a small group of men, numbering perhaps no more than a dozen anchormen, commentators, and executive producers" decided what appeared on the nightly network news shows. They comprised, he said, an "unelected elite," an "effete corps of impudent snobs," primarily based in the East, who held a monopoly on the national dissemination of news and opinion. Agnew specifically criticized the "instant analysis" that followed President Nixon's November 3 speech, implying that, coming immediately after the President's address, the remarks were inadequately prepared and therefore of less value to the public. (He did not point out, of course, that the networks had received advance texts of the speech hours before airtime.) Significantly, Agnew exempted the local affiliates from blame because they merely found themselves in the position of broadcasting whatever the networks sent down the line.

The Agnew speech, largely authored by presidential speechwriter Patrick Buchanan, was a deliberate declaration of war by the Nixon administration against the networks. The administration realized that, aside from limited behind-the-scenes pressure, there was very little it could do to force the networks to toe the line. Instead, in a brilliant divide-and-conquer strategy, it aimed for the networks' Achilles' heel. By appealing to the American public and, in particular, to the local affiliates, the administration sought to polarize vague anti-TV news feelings and resentments that had developed throughout the decade, sharpening them into a clear-cut "us versus them" conflict. The networks were thereby outnumbered. If local affiliates began demanding a softening of network tone, then the three majors would have to listen. At the end of Agnew's speech, NBC and ABC immediately returned to regular programming. CBS read a short prepared reply and then pulled out as well. Two days later, there was no special coverage of the Moratorium II activities on any of the networks. On November 20, in Montgomery, Alabama, Agnew added two more names to his enemies' list, identifying the *New York Times* and *Washington Post* as part of the same "Eastern liberal establishment."

For the administration, Agnew's Des Moines speech was a tremendous success. Not only had the networks' tone softened immediately in its aftermath, but the tenor of public debate had turned

In late 1969, Vice President Spiro Agnew launched a strong attack against the networks, criticizing the slant of their news. *(National Archives)*

around. Agnew's speech had touched a responsive nerve in the American public and the networks were on the defensive, trying to prove their innocence while the government called the shots. In January, 1970, the President ended the practice of supplying advance texts of his speeches and distributed them just before air time instead to ensure a reduction in instant analysis. In addition, Nixon aides began leaking stories suggesting that several network reports that placed either the American war effort or the South Vietnamese government in a bad light were trumped up. Richard Salant, president of CBS News, said, "there is an official smear campaign under way to dissuade us from telling the truth as we see it." To counter charges of distortion leveled against one particular story on South Vietnamese atrocities, CBS was fortunate enough to have interviews with the soldiers involved, corroborating the network's story on prisoner mutilation. Nonetheless, the attacks continued and, on another front, individuals with strong ties to the administration (and President Nixon personally) filed a challenge with the FCC to take away a Miami television station owned by the *Washington Post*.

On April 30, the President delivered a prime time address announcing an American invasion of Cambodia. Following the speech, the networks offered almost no commentary at all. A wave of student protests (punctuated by the killing of four students at Kent State University) couldn't be ignored for long, though, and all three networks did prime time wrapups of a major Washington demonstration on May 9, which marked the culmination of the reaction to the invasion. The TV reports presented speakers from both sides and went to extraordinary lengths to appear balanced and non-biased. However, as if to "balance" the very coverage of such an event, CBS (after some outside pressure) agreed to also do a similar prime time wrapup of a pro-administration rally held in Washington on Honor America Day, July 4. NET, also feeling pressure from the White House, gave Honor America Day extensive air time. During all the public reaction to the invasion, both the electronic and print press generally accepted the administration's assertion that the invasion be referred to as the Cambodian "incursion."

Nearly two years after he had vowed to bring the country together, Richard Nixon presided over a highly divided nation, torn apart by the war in Indochina. The television networks were also in a very difficult position, facing pressure from all sides. The government wanted them to "go along" with the official line and was not hesitant to use its muscle. Affiliates were critical and nervous. Yet there was a reawakened conscience in the network news departments and, even in the face of general viewer apathy, they produced incisive news specials and daily reports on the war which only further piqued the administration's anger.

The born-again news team at CBS was especially effective, gathering first hand reports from the war front itself. John Laurence's sixty-minute portrait of an American infantry unit (called C-Company) revealed that there were clear anti-war feelings present even among America's fighting men. Another CBS special, "Where We Stand in Indochina," presented unflattering interviews with Vietnamese generals as CBS's correspondents concluded that, at best, the American invasion of Cambodia was a mistake. Yet in spite of the networks' attempts to reassert their journalistic integrity in covering the important events of the year, all of the season's Vietnam and public affairs specials found their usual place at the very bottom of the ratings tabulations, with the special "Ethics in Government" coming in, somehow appropriately, dead last.

30. Totally Committed and Completely Involved

"WE'RE putting it all together this fall on CBS!" "Let's get together on ABC!" "It's happening on NBC!" That's what the networks told their viewers again and again through the summer of 1970. Campus revolt and the rock generation were reaching a high water mark and youth-oriented shows, which had been bubbling under the surface for about four seasons with increasing success, seemed to hold the key to the new ratings emphasis on audience demographics. The type of person watching television had become increasingly important because the total audience often included a great number of viewers who were judged to be too old or too rural for advertisers' tastes. Determined to win the attention of those in their late teens and twenties, all three networks decided to cast their lot with the kids and they proclaimed the arrival of the new season as heralding something completely different: everything would be Now! Variations on phrases from then current teen slang such as "getting it all together" and "what's happening" filled the networks' ads and show descriptions. This effusive commitment to "telling it like it is" led to one of the shortest format cycles in television history, "relevancy."

Despite all the rhetoric, the networks' self-proclaimed dedication to relevancy in programming really meant TV relevancy—a far cry from anything in the real world. It consisted of grafting the head of topical issues onto the body of standard grade-B drama and restocking familiar forums such as hospitals and court rooms with different, preferably youthful, characters. ABC had attracted lightning with this formula in *The Mod Squad* and *Marcus Welby* and each of the networks rushed to include as many hip phrases, committed characters, and timely conflicts as possible. CBS in particular pursued the trend with a vengeance, apparently out to prove that it was no longer the network of the fuddy-duddies. To the god of youth it offered *Headmaster, The Interns,* and *Storefront Lawyers.* All three received "thumbs down."

Headmaster was a well-intentioned but poorly executed comedy-drama that cast veteran Andy Griffith as Andy Thompson, headmaster at a small private high school in California. In many ways, Griffith was a perfect choice for making relevancy work. He had spent eight years cultivating an image as a warm, level-headed folksy sheriff who was respected by old and young alike, and it was a short step to his new role as a Welby-ish father-confessor.

In a setting reminiscent of ABC's moderately successful high school sitcom of the previous season, *Room 222,* Griffith took on the timely concerns of his troubled wards, trying to guide them through brewing campus revolt and drug overdoses. Unfortunately, the scripts and supporting cast generally lacked the control and subtlety of *Room 222* and the relevant problems clashed with the stock sitcom humor of such characters as the school's athletic coach, played by the slapstick-oriented Jerry Van Dyke. As a result, *Headmaster* emerged as a mish-mash of emotion that made the program appear a cheap vehicle simply attempting to cash in on "today's headlines."

The Interns presented the lives, loves, and labors of five sparkling clean doctors-in-training (three white, one black, one blonde) at a major Los Angeles hospital, and brought the relevancy angle to a format that was quite well suited for soapy topical melodrama. The program religiously adhered to the traditional *Ben Casey-Dr. Kildare* structure including a wise elder statesman and three guest patients each week, but the eternal divinities of youth and relevance raised their unwieldy influence at every turn. As a result, the show was not merely heavy-handed, it was often ludicrous in its emphasis. In their spiffy attire and perfectly set *coiffures,* the interns looked more like demi-god hairdressers than medicos. Their supposedly wise mentor (played by that old highway patrolman, Broderick Crawford) was presented as being no match for the wisdom of youth and he alternated between sagacity and senility. (One critic described his generally dumpy and snarling character as looking like the head of a New Jersey abortion ring.) Above all, the patient ailments were absurd. On one show, they included: a go-go dancer who was bedridden with a twisted foot; a former girlfriend of one of the wavy-haired white interns who begged for the mercy killing of her sick husband; and a meditative monk who not only needed his physical illness cured but his political consciousness reawakened (a task handled by the black intern). For added topicality, this very same episode included a subplot that focused on a bearded orderly who was arrested for peddling pornographic movies. Through it all the happy-go-lucky interns, like their comrades in the Mod Squad, stood by the traditional rules and routine, determined to help trendy youth come to grips with the flawed but manageable establishment.

	7:30	8:00	8:30	9:00	9:30	10:00	10:30	
MONDAY	THE YOUNG LAWYERS		THE SILENT FORCE	ABC NFL MONDAY NIGHT FOOTBALL [to 12 Midnite]				**ABC**
	Gunsmoke		Here's Lucy	Mayberry R.F.D.	Doris Day Show	Carol Burnett Show		**CBS**
	Red Skelton Show	Rowan And Martin's Laugh-In		NBC Monday Night At The Movies @Bob Hope Show		@NBC Specials		**NBC**

	7:30	8:00	8:30	9:00	9:30	10:00	10:30	
TUESDAY	The Mod Squad		Movie Of The Week			Marcus Welby, M.D.		**ABC**
	The Beverly Hillbillies	Green Acres	Hee-Haw		To Rome With Love	CBS News Hour 60 Minutes		**CBS**
	DON KNOTTS SHOW		Julia	NBC Tuesday Night At The Movies @First Tuesday				**NBC**

	7:30	8:00	8:30	9:00	9:30	10:00	10:30	
WEDNESDAY	The Courtship Of Eddie's Father	Make Room For Granddaddy	Room 222	Johnny Cash Show		DAN AUGUST		**ABC**
	STOREFRONT LAWYERS		The Governor And J.J.	Medical Center		Hawaii Five-O		**CBS**
	The Men From Shiloh			Kraft Music Hall		FOUR-IN-ONE (McCLOUD, S.F. INT'L AIRPORT, NIGHT GALLERY, PSYCHIATRIST)		**NBC**

	7:30	8:00	8:30	9:00	9:30	10:00	10:30	
THURSDAY	MATT LINCOLN		Bewitched	BAREFOOT IN THE PARK	THE ODD COUPLE	THE IMMORTAL		**ABC**
	Family Affair	Jim Nabors Hour		CBS Thursday Night Movies				**CBS**
	FLIP WILSON SHOW		Ironside		NANCY	Dean Martin Show		**NBC**

	7:30	8:00	8:30	9:00	9:30	10:00	10:30	
FRIDAY	The Brady Bunch	Nanny And The Professor	THE PARTRIDGE FAMILY	That Girl	Love, American Style	This Is Tom Jones		**ABC**
	THE INTERNS		THE HEADMASTER	CBS Friday Night Movies				**CBS**
	The High Chaparral		The Name Of The Game			Bracken's World		**NBC**

	7:30	8:00	8:30	9:00	9:30	10:00	10:30	
SATURDAY	Let's Make A Deal	The Newlywed Game	Lawrence Welk Show		THE MOST DEADLY GAME		local	**ABC**
	Mission: Impossible		My Three Sons	ARNIE	MARY TYLER MOORE	Mannix		**CBS**
	Andy Williams Show		Adam-12	NBC Saturday Night At The Movies				**NBC**

	7:00	7:30	8:00	8:30	9:00	9:30	10:00	10:30	
SUNDAY	THE YOUNG REBELS		The F.B.I.		The ABC Sunday Night Movie				**ABC**
	Lassie	Hogan's Heroes	Ed Sullivan Show		Glen Campbell Goodtime Hour		TIM CONWAY HOUR		**CBS**
	Wild Kingdom	The Wonderful World Of Disney		Bill Cosby Show	Bonanza		The Bold Ones (The Doctors, The Lawyers, THE SENATOR)		**NBC**

The mixed bag of topical drama, youth, and good old American tradition in these relevant shows aimed at scoring the TV hat trick of *The Mod Squad:* Bring in the oldsters with exciting all-American action; win praise for presenting topical drama; and capture the youth market with stories the kids could relate to. In this approach, *Headmaster* and *The Interns* were merely indelicacies muddled by poorly conceived characters and stories. *Storefront Lawyers,* however, was downright rude and insulting. It epitomized the glaring and obvious contrast between the relevant, realistic world touted in the network ads, and the sugar-coated never-never-land in the programs themselves. The series presented Robert Foxworth, Sheila Larkin, and David Arkin as three young pretty white kids from the safe, liberal suburbs who worked for a law firm uptown but who also set up a storefront office in the ghetto ("where the action is") to aid the poor there for free. The hackneyed scripts never ventured beneath the Naugahyde surface of these 100% plastic kids or into anything even resembling the more sordid side of life among the lowly. Instead, the three legal Samaritans remained oblivious to even the hint of evil or a shred of characterization. In the show's opening credits they blissfully skipped hand-in-hand into the halls of justice, accompanied by a sorry excuse for a contemporary rock theme. Though they constantly battled the establishment, the only motivation ever suggested for their actions came from CBS's incessant plugs that presented the trio as "totally committed and completely involved"—or was it "completely committed and totally involved"?

Storefront Lawyers was easily the worst of the relevancy shows though, ironically, many of the problems with the series reflected problems of the Sixties' youth movement itself. Both were based on a philosophy that merely bringing together "nice" people with "nice" ideas could solve everything: Powerful, entrenched bogeymen of the establishment would roll over and die and some hip jargon would topple a decade of fantasy on television. To this end, *Storefront Lawyers* deliberately oversimplified any complex problems and created a sanitized version of the ghetto populated by evil ogres, helpless po' folk, and noble youth. However, CBS was not alone in the pursuit of relevancy, with both NBC and ABC also offering their own exercises in revolutionary fantasy. To varying degrees, though, nearly every entry suffered from the same problems as *Headmaster, The Interns,* and *Storefront Lawyers.*

NBC's two major relevant offerings were segments in rotating series: *The Senator* in *The Bold Ones* and *The Psychiatrist* in *Four-in-One. The Senator,* starring veteran Hal Holbrook as Senator Hays Stowe, was a commendable effort to treat topical and controversial issues that became bogged down in television's mugwump philosophy on most issues: everybody to a degree is guilty, therefore nobody in particular is guilty. Stowe had won his seat by taking a bold and forthright stand against pollution but, once in office, he emerged as a fuzzy-thinking middle-of-the-road befuddled moderate. The stories therefore couldn't hold together because it was hard to understand why unscrupulous radicals of both the left and right would bother attacking him. Even treatment of issues such as a Kent State-type incident was nothing more than a calculated, camouflaged ambiguity.

The Psychiatrist was similar to *The Interns,* presenting a premise that was traditional Hollywood melodrama featuring forced relevant angles that were almost laughable. Roy Thinnes played a young, semi-hip psychiatrist who used controversial new techniques to bring the day's strung-out acid heads to their senses and guide them to the barber shop for that inevitable haircut. As proof of his success, he was assisted by a former patient-junkie, played by Peter Duel. ABC's *Young Rebels* was even sillier. It modestly tried to restage the American Revolutionary War as if it were a free-speech revolt at Berkeley. The youthful members of the Yankee Doodle Society (two white, one black, one gal) acted as spies behind the British lines, specializing in sabotage and harassment.

Of all the relevant shows presented that fall, ABC's *Young Lawyers* came closest to reaching the touted goal of dealing with contemporary themes and moderately realistic characters. Though its premise was virtually the same as *Storefront Lawyers,* the scripts avoided the tired murder-arson-dope trilogy and centered solely on the learning pangs of two young barristers trying to deal with people caught in the era's uncertainties. For example, in one episode they fought a malpractice suit filed against a young medical intern who had decided to "get involved" and help an auto accident victim. To add further credibility to the series, the team (one white guy, one black gal) received sound but not condescending advice from their mentor, played by veteran Lee J. Cobb. Overall, the stories were much more believable than the fairy tales usually dished out by the other relevant shows and, in a departure from the typical vast expanse of clichéd California adventureland, the action was set in historic Boston.

Ultimately, though, even *The Young Lawyers* fell victim to the essential deception of the entire television relevancy movement. Though ads for the new shows implied the presentation of strongly pro-radical positions, the networks had no intention of taking bold and forthright stands on controversial issues every night in a time of genuine national division—and certainly not on their entertainment programs. This was the soft white underbelly of TV relevancy. Important social problems and contemporary jargon were simply churned into standard television format drama wrapped in love beads. Stories and issues were stacked in advance so that the establishment, aided by clear-thinking moderates, always won. At heart the establishment was right, though occasionally it needed a slight kick to uncover one or two bad apples. Anti-establishment figures usually had some axe to grind and, even if their points were justified, their methods were all wrong. Consequently, the villains in the stories were inevitably demonic bearded hippies or corrupt, long-haired radicals who were, at best, overzealous reformers. The new breed of hero was the former outsider won over to help the establishment correct its own shortcomings in dealing with overly suspicious communities and individuals. Such characters dressed respectably, worked on the side of justice, and, most importantly, had gotten that haircut.

There was certainly nothing new about presenting fantasy as reality on television, nor was there anything morally wrong with exploiting news events and popular fads in television entertainment programming. Such policies had been pursued for years in both good and bad shows. In promoting the 1970–71 season, though, network flaks had presented wholly unrealistic claims that their relevant shows were to be truly different from the past in both substance and image, knowing full well that was not to be the case. By promising a new era in television realism after nearly a decade of escapism and fantasy, but then delivering the same old goods, the networks' new shows had to be judged, however harshly, by a different set of rules. By these rules, the half-hearted poorly written programs of the relevancy craze were artistic failures.

More importantly, the structure of the relevant programs demonstrated that even with a new interest in young adult demographics, the networks had not decided to alienate the silent majority of older viewers overnight. Grownups were still the bread-and-butter of the Nielsen ratings points, so relevancy had been tempered for establishment consumption. By mid-season, it became clear that, in trying to attract two supposedly opposite segments of society, the watered-down relevant programs had failed to excite anyone. The ratings were disastrous. In January, 1971, ABC dropped its *Young Rebels,* and CBS hurried in face-saving format changes on *Headmaster* and *Storefront Lawyers. Headmaster* became *The New Andy Griffith Show* in which Griffith played a town mayor who was a former sheriff, a carbon copy continuation of his old Mayberry series. The storefront lawyers gave up the ghetto, got haircuts, and moved uptown permanently, becoming *Men at Law.* Under the tutelage of sagacious Devlin McNeil (Gerald S. O'Loughlin), they defended more affluent clients such as innocent collegians under attack from the lawyers for the nasty radicals in the Students for a Free America (a barely concealed copy of the SDS). Both of these permutations, as well as *The Young Lawyers, The Senator, The Interns,* and *The Psychiatrist,* expired at the end of the season.

Television's loud and sloppy foray into contemporary drama was a total flop. Yet, almost lost amid the ballyhoo of the 1970 fall premieres, there appeared a saner and more realistic solution for the medium's sudden desire to update its own image. In September of 1970, after half a decade of bland sitcoms that became hits, good sitcoms that flopped, and horrible sitcoms that just hung on, CBS introduced a worthy successor to its comedy classics of the past, *The Mary Tyler Moore Show.* The program was the first out and out hit in the new wave of situation comedies that effectively combined more contemporary attitudes and outlooks with the basic elements of the *I Love Lucy, Honeymooners,* and *Dick Van Dyke* schools. These past sitcoms had used good writing, tight central and supporting casts, and the simplest of sets to present memorable, hilarious comedy. To this strong base, *The Mary Tyler Moore Show* added an important new element: The lead character was an intelligent, unmarried career woman who faced humorous complications and situations that real people often faced.

Mary Tyler Moore played Mary Richards, a small-town girl who came to the big city (Minneapolis-St. Paul, not Los Angeles) to make it on her own. She landed a job in a local TV station (WJM) as an associate producer for the evening news, working behind the scenes in the newsroom with producer Lou Grant (Edward Asner), newswriter Murray Slaughter (Gavin MacLeod), and anchorman Ted Baxter (Ted Knight). There she began to build her confidence and skill as a single woman on her own with a responsible job and personal career goals. The mix of characters and personalities in the office, ranging from generally realistic to broad stereotype, balanced almost perfectly and gave the "young working woman" hook the opportunity to catch on. Very quickly viewers accepted both the novel premise and the first rate cast because they combined to produce a very funny show.

Lou Grant and Mary Richards were presented as the two most realistic characters. Mary obviously took her job as newsperson-producer seriously and was very conscious of her professional man-

The six main performers of *The Mary Tyler Moore Show:* (from *l.*) front: Valerie Harper, Mary Tyler Moore, Cloris Leachman; back: Ted Knight, Ed Asner, Gavin MacLeod. *(MTM Enterprises)*

ner, though she was often a bit too straight, soft-hearted, and trusting for her own good. In some respects, Lou Grant began as the typical blustery-voiced sitcom boss who was really soft as Jello inside, but he soon developed into the nearest thing to a real life boss that could ever be expected in a television comedy. His character was tempered and his emotions presented as more complex, so that he tossed in funny cracks when he was sad and radiated genuine warmth through his anger. Both Lou and Mary certainly delivered their share of punch lines, but they usually carried off their humor as people trying to deal with realistic but confusing situations.

Ted Baxter and Murray Slaughter served as the focus of the more traditional office sitcom barbs. Murray delivered sharp one-liners and putdowns that were primarily directed at Ted, though he departed from these often enough to develop his character somewhat beyond the quick-witted wisecracker type in the style of *Dick Van Dyke*'s Buddy Sorrell. Ted, on the other hand, was all stereotype, but a perfectly marvelous stereotype. Only in Jack Cassidy's Jetman role (in the all-too-brief run of *He and She*) had television ever poked fun at itself so openly. In an era that elevated the blow-dried "happy talk" local newscaster to the forefront (making him the rule, not the exception, in the major markets), the self-obsessed Baxter was a wonderful lampoon of the trend. His rich silver hair and deep-voiced resonance barely camouflaged the near vacuum behind his empty grin. In the program's third season, a new character was added to the office setting, WJM's "Happy Homemaker," Sue Ann Nivens (Betty White), and she provided yet another frontal attack on television's glossy self-image. White, drawing on her background of playing goody-two-shoes characters

over the years, portrayed the sweet-talking pure-as-gold "woman's show" star as a forked-tongued dirty old lady who merely used her bill and coo voice to mask the venom of her pointed remarks.

Such a corps of performers would have been the envy of any sitcom but, just as *The Dick Van Dyke Show* had been staged as essentially a two-set series (the Petrie home and the office), the action in Mary Tyler Moore's program was also split between two settings—the office and Mary's bachelor apartment. At home, two other strong supporting characters, Rhoda and Phyllis, helped to carry a wide range of domestic plots. Rhoda Morgenstern (Valerie Harper) was Mary's upstairs neighbor, a New York City transplant and a fast-talking putdown artist whose barbs were often self-directed. Like Sally Rogers in *Dick Van Dyke* and nearly all other female sidekicks in sitcom history, Rhoda was on the prowl for a husband. Unlike most, though, she was not presented as a de-sexed spinster but as a young, attractive woman who was no dummy. Rhoda was not about to fall for the first clichéd line that came her way and was too intelligent to honestly expect Mr. Right to suddenly walk into her life—but she hadn't given up hoping, either. Though Mary also went out on dates and vaguely planned on marriage, she was in no hurry. Rhoda looked to Mary as a close friend and confidante (practically a sister) and the two shared their feelings on the hopes and frustrations of single life. Rhoda's sharp wit was frequently directed at the manager of their apartment house, Phyllis Lindstrom (Cloris Leachman). Though Rhoda's character was in the more realistic spirit of Lou and Mary, Phyllis was presented as an effective homebody caricature, the epitome of style conscious egoism, who never hesitated to impose on Mary. She eagerly latched onto the latest trends and, while not really evil, usually acted kind and considerate only when she needed something and couldn't just take it.

Lou, Murray, Ted, Sue Ann, Rhoda, and Phyllis were just as much *The Mary Tyler Moore Show* as Mary herself and particular episodes sometimes featured a member of this supporting group as the central character, with Mary relegated to the sidelines. As a true sign of the depth of the individual cast members, it must be noted that all six went on from *The Mary Tyler Moore Show* to star in programs of their own, a feat unmatched by any other sitcom.

Even though the talented cast was the driving force behind the success of *The Mary Tyler Moore Show,* the high level of sophistication in the show's scripts lifted the series above the restrictive confines TV sitcoms were proscribed into during the Sixties. While the writers generally avoided obviously topical issues and fads, they managed to capture the feeling of the Seventies much as *The Dick Van Dyke Show* had done in the Sixties. The three chief characters—Mary, Lou, and Rhoda—were often given the types of problems that real people of the era faced.

Rhoda was caught in the position of many young women at the time: She never tried to hide the fact that she was talented, aggressive, and certainly just as intelligent as many of the men she went out with (probably more so). Though fully aware of the complications in husband hunting that resulted from such a stance, Rhoda had no intention of changing. When she found her ideal candidate for marriage he would have to accept her as she was or not at all. Over the course of the series, Lou became divorced and, as a chunky, middle-aged man whose children had already grown and left home, he really didn't feel like starting to date again. This development added a sensitive edge to his sometimes cantankerous office demeanor because Lou was just as lonely as any former family man, but he didn't want to expose his feelings to strangers or in public. Mary's image as an unmarried career woman with a responsible job other than a secretary or a teacher

was a major break from television tradition. She was not a widow, had no children, and was working because she wanted to build her own life and career. While by no means a diatribe on women's liberation, the program presented, without fanfare, women as being capable of interests beyond housework, marriage, and crazy sitcom schemes. As a true professional, Mary prized her own honesty and integrity very highly. In one episode she even went to jail in order to protect a news source.

Unlike the heavy-handed plots of the flopped relevancy dramas, these serious, sometimes even topical, aspects of *The Mary Tyler Moore Show* never stood out as preachy or phony, but were instead quietly incorporated into the funny scripts and characters, presenting a reality that was tempered by a light and gentle touch that could render it painless, but not forgotten. From the very first episode, the series displayed exceptional production skill and care that set it apart from its competition.

The Mary Tyler Moore Show provided exactly what CBS president Bob Wood had wanted: a new hit show in the traditional CBS groove (a thirty-minute sitcom) that also pulled the network from its old rural rut into new settings that were right for the new decade. Working hand-in-hand with newly chosen program chief Fred Silverman, Wood had made it clear his renovation plans for CBS were serious, including not only a search for new hits, but also the display of new attitudes and strategies in the process of network scheduling as well. In a move considered nothing short of blasphemy for an era that still chiseled network fall schedules in stone in the early spring, Wood approved Silverman's last-minute schedule changes in July, 1970, less than six weeks before the season premieres. This gave Silverman the opportunity to display his later renowned talent for counter-programming and thematic flow, and the new *Mary Tyler Moore Show* emerged with a better time slot than originally planned. *The Beverly Hillbillies* and *Green Acres* were moved to Tuesday, logically preceding *Hee-Haw,* and *Mary Tyler Moore* was shifted to Saturday, joining the company

With all his faults, Archie Bunker (Carroll O'Connor) never became totally unbearable and could even be kind and considerate, especially to his wife, Edith (Jean Stapleton). *(Tandem Productions, Inc.)*

September 17, 1970

The Flip Wilson Show. (NBC). Young black comic Flip Wilson, for years a frequent guest on variety and talk shows, receives his own comedy-variety hour. Armed with such characterizations as the sassy Geraldine Jones and the hustling Rev. Leroy (from the Church of What's Happenin' Now), Wilson turns his new program into an immediate top ten smash.

September 21, 1970

ABC's NFL Monday Night Football. (ABC). Roone Arledge brings professional football back to prime time after nearly two decades. The Cleveland Browns beat "Broadway" Joe Namath and the New York Jets 31 to 21 in Cleveland. Howard Cosell and Keith Jackson do play-by-play while "Dandy Don" Meredith supplies color.

September 24, 1970

The Odd Couple. (ABC). After successful treatments as a hit Broadway play and a feature film, Neil Simon's story of two divorced men sharing an apartment in New York City becomes a hit sitcom for ABC. Under producer Garry Marshall, the show displays consistently good writing and outstanding character acting, led by Tony Randall as the ultra-clean Felix Unger and Jack Klugman as the incurably sloppy Oscar Madison.

October 5, 1970

PBS, the Public Broadcasting System, takes over the non-commercial functions of NET, National Educational Television. New York's WNDT becomes WNET.

of the more sophisticated *Mission: Impossible, Mannix,* and another new "urban" sitcom, *Arnie* (starring Herschel Bernardi). There was more to come. In January, 1971, the second major program component in Wood's modernization drive arrived, *All in the Family.*

For three years, filmmakers Norman Lear and Bud Yorkin had been trying to sell the networks an American version of the BBC hit, *Till Death Do Us Part.* The British series had been on since 1966, offering an irreverent and boisterous view of a working class family that hinged on a crafty old bigot who was forever dominating his wife and daughter and constantly arguing with his liberal son-in-law. In February, 1968, Yorkin and Lear produced a pilot for CBS based on *Till Death Do Us Part,* but CBS turned them down when some moderately innovative domestic sitcoms bombed. Even with the success of the Smothers Brothers and *Laugh-In,* the concept of a lovable bigot tossing off racial epithets and political insults proved too much for the old brass at CBS. In the fall of 1968, Yorkin and Lear approached ABC with a second pilot for the proposed series, called "Justice for All," starring Carroll O'Connor and Jean Stapleton. ABC liked it and scheduled it for January, 1969, but then got cold feet and postponed the series to the fall of 1969. The network at last gave up the idea completely, labeling it too controversial. Sensing failure at marketing the concept as a television series, the two producers prepared to turn it into a film instead but, at the last minute, CBS, under new management, extended some positive feelers. In March, 1970, a revised pilot, "Those Were the Days," was secretly tested on a random audience at the CBS studios in New York City. The reaction was favorable, if somewhat guarded. In July, 1970, in spite of considerable negative pressure from within the CBS hierarchy, network president Bob Wood scheduled the series, renamed *All in the Family,* to premiere at the start of 1971. He said in a press release, "It's time to poke fun at ourselves."

Nonetheless, CBS was quite uncertain how to treat *All in the Family.* Was it satire? Comedy? Social comment? Fearful of a public outcry similar to the one that followed the still not forgotten *Turn-On,* CBS gave the series practically no publicity. It was stuck in a perverse time slot, directly following *Hee-Haw* but right before *60 Minutes.* In either case, pro or con, the network expected a huge reaction the night of the show's debut (January 12, 1971). It never came. Only a few calls were received and most of them were favorable. With so little fanfare, the first ratings for *All in the Family* were naturally quite low.

TV critics and the general public were as confused as the network by the program, uncertain how to react because, in many ways, *All in the Family* was unlike anything Americans had ever seen before. It successfully transferred the spice and life of the controversial British original to an American setting. Archie Bunker (O'Connor) was a "hardhat" racist who disdainfully referred to Yids, Polacks, Spades, and Spics, with his only comeuppance being the protests of his long-haired son-in-law, Mike (Rob Reiner, son of Carl), derisively nicknamed "Meathead" by Archie. The program also dealt with sex—including both blatant verbal references and, for a change, implications of physical activity. Archie and his wife, Edith (Stapleton), who he nicknamed "Dingbat," were shown walking in on their daughter, Gloria (Sally Struthers), and her husband, Mike, just as the two were obviously on the way up to bed to make love. Archie admonished the mini-skirted Gloria, "When you sit down in that thing, the mystery is ended." Because Mike and Gloria lived with Archie and Edith, such ideological and theological clashes were frequent and inevitable. How were viewers to take the racial and sexual references? Blacks in the media were openly split on the *All in the Family* question. Tony Brown, producer of public TV's *Black Journal,* called it "shocking and racist," while Loretta Long, Susan the schoolteacher on *Sesame Street,* said it was "unoffensive and realistic," and Pamela Haynes of the black-oriented *Los Angeles Sentinel* said, "His rantings serve a purpose."

The truth dawned slowly. *All in the Family* wasn't racist, but it wasn't *The Life of Riley,* either. It was a well-written, superbly acted contemporary farce that painted broad stereotyped characters in the best *I Love Lucy* tradition. The difference was that the producers based the stereotypes on real down-to-earth personalities who argued about topics that real people argued about, using words and phrases real people used. After decades of TV shows populated exclusively with stars who were *very* nice, confronting a central character who was not completely lovable came as a shock to many Americans. The Archie Bunker character, in fact, often wasn't lovable at all. Nonetheless, the producers of *All in the Family* did not allow Archie to become totally unbearable, operating under the assumption that everybody had his reasons. He might have been a reactionary stick-in-the-mud spouting a perverse sort of malapropism, but there was another part of him that was genuinely likable. Archie was an honestly simple man who talked about his bigotry but rarely did anything else with it. What's more, it soon became clear that Archie never *won* the arguments. He might remain titular king of his castle (retaining sole rights to his favorite easy chair), but his world of male-WASP domination, simple verities, and America-first-ism was crumbling all about him. Archie fumed and sputtered but always had to concede to the inevitable changes thrust before him by his liberal son-in-law, his feminist daughter, and his black neighbors.

The most amazing thing about *All in the Family* was that its architects succeeded at what the relevancy show producers had seemed to be trying to do: explaining new attitudes in the country to older Americans. TV reviewers were flabbergasted, though, to see such attempts at social realism in the least likely of all formats for national controversy—the television sitcom. The *Mary Tyler Moore* formula had been taken one step further with current issues injected into the very funny, well-written scripts. The combination worked because the producers never forgot the prime rule of showmanship: keep the audience entertained. By carefully mixing the humor and politics, *All in the Family* avoided heavy-handed preaching and became an almost subliminal course in national self-examination. Producer Norman Lear explained:

> [*All in the Family*] holds a mirror up to our prejudices.
> . . . We laugh now, swallowing just the littlest bit of truth about ourselves, and it sits there for the unconscious to toss about later.

Though *All in the Family*'s underlying premise and lively flavor came from its British roots, the show also drew on important American sitcom basics previously used in series such as *The Honeymooners*. The program was essentially a one-set show, with the action taking place in the Bunker living room (with occasional huddles in the kitchen). In a radical departure from then-current TV scripture, *All in the Family* returned to the concept of recording its episodes before a live audience, just as in *The Honeymooners*. The laughs heard at home were actual laughter by live human beings watching the performance as it was being videotaped. This literal liveliness, combined with the Kramden-like working class atmosphere and the inclusion of topical references, served to create a refreshing sense of reality and to make *All in the Family* an actual revolution in American TV. Yet, it was also a revival (in the literal sense of the word) bringing back the basics that had made previous classics so memorable and, at the same time, updating the content for modern consumption.

All in the Family had a very slow start and, like most out of the ordinary TV shows, had to build an audience gradually. By mid-February it sneaked into the top thirty. The first set of episodes ended in March and Silverman wisely chose to begin a full cycle of reruns immediately in order to hook the growing number of new viewers that had only discovered the series in the previous month. It was during this rerun cycle that the show took off. By late May, just before it went off for the summer, *All in the Family* hit number one. The expected viewer reaction to the innovative, controversial program had developed, but the show had also become a big hit. Its characters were accepted and absorbed into everyday language, even appearing in New York City graffiti. "Archie Bunker for President" somebody scrawled on a subway wall, to which another wit added, "He is."

All in the Family marked a turning point in American television programming and it appeared at a time of major change throughout the industry in both commercial and noncommercial broadcasting. In October, 1970, the public television network structure was reorganized, changing NET into PBS, the Public Broadcasting System. More importantly, public television continued to move away from original domestic productions, increasing its reliance on imports from Britain. That fall, PBS presented the thirteen-week BBC series, *Civilization,* hosted by Kenneth Clark and funded by Xerox. The program took viewers on a world-wide tour of Western culture tracing its development over 400 years by focusing on great works of art and architecture. In January, *Masterpiece Theater* picked up where *The Forsyte Saga* left off and offered British made historical dramas every Sunday night. As delightful as these British imports were, they began to spark complaints that PBS was showing signs of practically becoming a BBC subsidiary. Though British programs meant instant class they also discouraged efforts at

homegrown productions. In the winter, PBS presented its last major domestic program for years to come, *The Great American Dream Machine,* hosted by the corpulent Marshall Efron. *Dream Machine* was similar to *PBL*, but humor and satire were added to the "straight" segments (such as a report on FBI-paid provocateurs in radical groups) and, under Efron's guidance, the show reached great heights of wit and irreverence. Levity had always been noticeably absent on public television and this infusion of humor was welcomed by many, though it made the series unpopular with both the Nixon administration and Congress. Poking fun at commercials for frozen pies and Kool-Aid was all right but, when guests such as Woody Allen began ribbing Henry Kissinger, and regular contributor Andy Rooney parodied Nixon's volunteer Army proposal, *Dream Machine* became a walking target for the government. It was shot down in mid-1972. Efron departed with a stinging blast at PBS and New York's WNET, calling them:

> A tight club of relatively rich guys, putting cameras on the poor and asking the middle class for money. What do they say when the middle class asks what channel 13 [WNET] is doing for them? 'We've got some wonderful acquisitions from the BBC . . .'

The commercial networks were also happy to soak up the prestige from British imports. In the summer of 1971, CBS took the unusual step of slotting the six-part British miniseries, *The Six Wives of Henry VIII,* into its Sunday night schedule. It was the only program to eventually air on *Masterpiece Theater* that first found its way to America through a commercial network. NBC even previewed and promoted the *Civilization* series when it ran on PBS in the fall of 1970. At the same time, the network also gave the British

December 7, 1970
After defecting from CBS, Harry Reasoner replaces Frank Reynolds as co-anchor of ABC's nightly news, teaming up with Howard K. Smith.

January 1, 1971
A federally imposed ban on television cigarette ads goes into effect.

June 6, 1971
After twenty-three years of "really big shows," Ed Sullivan is axed. Guests on the final program: Sid Caesar, Carol Channing, Robert Klein, and Gladys Knight and the Pips. "Say goodnight, Eddie . . ."

July 26, 1971
Apollo 15, America's fourth lunar landing mission, sends back the first color television signals from space, using the CBS "spinning disk" system the FCC discarded eighteen years before.

August 16, 1971
John Chancellor becomes the sole anchor on *NBC Nightly News* as Frank McGee leaves the show to replace Hugh Downs on *Today*.

August 29, 1971
After one final season on NBC, Red Skelton ends eighteen years of network television, wishing all "Good health, good life, and may God bless. Goodnight."

September 4, 1971
ABC pulls the plug on Lawrence Welk's bubble machine. The sixteen-year television veteran has the last laugh, though, as his program shifts effortlessly into syndication, continuing with new episodes on a strong line-up of local stations.

limited run series concept a thorough testing in its *Four-in-One* program from Universal studios. Unlike *The Bold Ones*, in which three separate series alternated in the same time slot, *Four-in-One* ran all six episodes of each series before moving on to the next. This was just the style adopted by *Masterpiece Theater* in its presentations.

British limited-run series were usually just that: one premise carried over a set number of episodes and then ended. *Four-in-One* was set up as an extended pilot program for testing new series ideas in prime time against regular shows. At the time, studio pilots were usually aired as single episodes stuck into the movie nights during the spring lull and so rarely faced any strong competition. *Four-in-One* provided a more challenging but realistic face-off. Two of the series failed their tryouts, the silly relevancy of *The Psychiatrist* and the "Airport"-type melodrama of *San Francisco International Airport* (starring Lloyd Bridges and Clu Gulager). *Night Gallery*, a watered down version of *The Twilight Zone*, caught on and became a regular series in 1971 that lasted two seasons. Rod Serling was the host and occasional writer, though he actually had very little control over the choice of material used. The most successful of the miniseries was *McCloud*, starring Dennis Weaver as a Western sheriff somehow assigned to the New York City police force. This series survived for six years, though always remaining a segment in some permutation of *Four-in-One*. Beginning in the 1971–72 season, *Four-in-One* changed to the rotating segment style of *The Bold Ones* and was retitled *The NBC Mystery Movie*.

Though the testing of British concepts from *All in the Family* to miniseries signalled the possibility of important new developments in programs and programming, the government was responsible for the most dramatic changes facing broadcasters. In early 1970, after pressure from Congress, the networks accepted a plan to ban all TV cigarette advertisments. Beginning January 1, 1971, the largest single source of revenue in broadcasting was cut off and television profits were squeezed. To further complicate the situation, a 1970 FCC ruling was put into effect and, starting in the fall of 1971, the networks were required to slice thirty minutes from prime time each night of the week.

Since the mid-Fifties, the FCC had been holding hearings on ways to decrease, if not eliminate, the networks' legal and financial control over programs. Over the years, the networks had voluntarily cut back on the degree of such lucrative control temporarily in order to mollify the FCC, though they returned to near total control as soon as it seemed the commission wouldn't notice. In March, 1965, the FCC drafted a proposed rule that would have limited the networks to 50% control of their prime time schedule, and also virtually banned their profits from domestic and foreign syndication of old shows. This 50–50 proposal was roundly criticized by the networks and bandied about for five years until, in May of 1970, the FCC adopted a Group W-inspired compromise instead

and issued it as a formal rule to take effect in the fall of 1971. The compromise rule still nearly eliminated network profit from syndication, but simply limited to three hours the amount of prime time broadcasting a network could do in one evening. This rule was labeled the "access rule" because it proposed to grant access to the airwaves for independent producers who would be able to go directly to the affiliates to slot their programs in what had previously been network prime time.

The networks, naturally, were aghast at the access rule and CBS filed suit to block it. The Justice Department and the courts, however, upheld the FCC, thus giving legal sanction to the first major inroad in direct governmental control of programming in television history. The FCC's aim, greater access, was quite commendable and the commission no doubt believed the access rule served a wholesome purpose, but the fact was that the rule represented direct governmental control of programming—something the FCC was specifically forbidden to engage in by law. With the precedent set, additional interference could only follow.

Faced with the reality of having to cut three and one-half hours of prime time each week in the fall of 1971, the networks tried to make the best of it. ABC, which had always had more than its share of dead weight, found the access rule a godsend and in January, 1971, jumped the gun by adding two and one-half hours to the half-hour of prime time it already ceded to the local affiliates each week. Freed of the albatross of some of its losers, including remnants of the relevant cycle (*Young Rebels*) and a few flopped crime shows (*Silent Force* and *Most Deadly Game*), ABC's ratings shot up and, in mid-January, the network won one week of the ratings war. It was ABC's first such victory in more than six years.

The second season surge by ABC even further tightened the network competition. CBS had been unable to break away from the incessant challenge by NBC and the two had spent the season locked in a see-saw battle for total ratings superiority. At the end of the 1970–71 season, CBS and NBC were in a dead heat, with both claiming victory. To the CBS leadership, it was clear that more drastic measures had to be taken to ensure supremacy. With the success of two new "urban" sitcoms, president Wood swallowed hard and in one swoop canceled eight stalwarts of the CBS zodiac: *The Ed Sullivan Show* (23 years), *Lassie* (17 years), *Mayberry RFD* (11 years), *The Beverly Hillbillies* (9 years), Jim Nabors (5 years as Gomer Pyle, 2 years as a variety host), *Hogan's Heroes* and *Green Acres* (6 years each), and *Hee-Haw* (2 years). Many of these shows were still very successful but some slots had to be cleared and this was as good a time as any to complete Wood's previously stated plan to steer CBS away from the oldster-yokel image. Wood's purge of so many net vets was the symbolic confirmation that, with the public's acceptance of shows such as *Mary Tyler Moore* and *All in the Family*, the government's forced ban on cigarette commercials, and the appearance of the access rule, 1971 would mark a seismic shift in the equilibrium of American television.

31. Not Just Another Pretty Face

ON SEPTEMBER 13, 1971, prime time shrunk. The FCC's access rule had taken effect and the nightly schedules of all three networks reflected a shakeup far greater than the usual fall season reorganization. The new rules stipulated that the networks could not present more than three hours of prime time fare between 7:00 P.M. and 11:00 P.M. However, the FCC had not specified which three of the four available hours should be used, leaving the choice to the networks themselves. As the traditional domain of news shows (except on Sunday), the 7:00–7:30 P.M. slot was sacrosanct, so the network programmers had to decide between a prime time that would run from 7:30–10:30 P.M. or 8:00–11:00 P.M. Though such a minor shift might have seemed a trivial difference at first, the choice was vitally important because it would determine the tone of network schedules not only for the 1971–72 season but for many seasons to come. If 7:30–10:30 P.M. were selected as prime time, the networks would place even more emphasis on kiddie-oriented productions, and the independent producers would have to develop adult material to fill the resulting late night access time (10:30–11:00 P.M.). The situation would be reversed with 8:00–11:00 P.M. as prime time; the networks would lose a half-hour of kidvid and the earlier access time could be filled with less somber fare such as frothy game shows.

Throughout the spring of 1971, the programming chiefs at CBS, NBC, and ABC engaged in a perverse form of high-level "chicken," using compliance with the access rule as a means to psyche out their competitors and to gain some slight advantage in what promised to be a tight ratings battle in the fall. At first, NBC and ABC seemed to be set on an 8:00–11:00 P.M. prime time so CBS, seeing an irresistible chance for a head start on its competitors, said it would opt for a 7:30 P.M. starting time in which it would schedule sixty-minute shows to kick off every evening. Such a move would have forced the other two to follow suit and change their schedules in order to prevent CBS from nailing down a large audience at the start of each night's viewing. Rumors, tentative plans, and revised proposals filled the air as the networks jockeyed back and forth for two months. Then CBS, which said it really favored the choice of the 8:00–11:00 P.M. slot all along but had suggested 7:30 P.M. only out of competitive zeal, asked the FCC to "suggest" that the networks consider 8:00 P.M. as the start of prime time. The commission went along, issued the proposal, and all three quickly complied. This did not end the pre-fall wrangling, however.

NBC applied for and received a waiver of the access rule so that it could continue sending out three and one-half hours of programming every Sunday night. This exception was granted so that *The Wonderful World of Disney* could continue to provide high quality family entertainment at its usual time. The FCC agreed that *Disney* deserved special treatment, though as penance NBC agreed to cut an extra half-hour from its Friday night schedule. ABC applied for and received a similar waiver for Tuesday night, based on the convoluted reasoning that because Tuesday was its strongest night, cutting part of it out would render the network impotent. In return for an untouched Tuesday line-up, ABC gave up another half-hour on Monday.

Following these byzantine negotiations, which placed an inauspicious reliance on federal umpiring and even invited governmental judgments on program quality, the fall schedules were set. The new boundaries for prime time were from 8:00 P.M. to 11:00 P.M. Wednesday through Saturday and on Monday, and from 7:30 P.M. to 11:00 P.M. (with appropriate gaps) on Sunday and Tuesday. In one final exercise of network brinkmanship, CBS's chief programmer, Fred Silverman, upset the networks' plans again in August, just before the start of the season, by announcing another of his infamous last-minute schedule shifts. *All in the Family,* which had done well in an abominable slot the previous winter, was to be tucked away at 10:30 P.M. Monday, against an NBC movie and ABC's pro football coverage. Playing his trump card, Silverman shifted the proto-hit to the lead-off slot on Saturday night, against very weak competition, in the hope that it would help build Saturday into a CBS sitcom blockbuster night. It worked. *All in the Family* quickly returned to the number one slot in the Nielsen ratings, becoming a solid fall smash and not just a spring fad hit.

Though the boundaries of prime time, and therefore access time, had been established, the question of just what would fill the newly liberated slots was still left up in the air. In announcing the access rule, the FCC had conjured up visions of locally produced public affairs shows, programs offering something nice and wholesome for the kiddies (perhaps a commercial version of *Sesame Street*), and even independently produced serious drama that the networks wouldn't dare touch. Instead, there were game shows. Lots of game shows. Old game shows. Syndicated game shows. Cheap game shows.

MONDAY (7:30 – 10:30)

Network	7:30	8:00	8:30	9:00	9:30	10:00	10:30
ABC	local	Nanny And The Professor	local	ABC NFL Monday Night Football [to 12 Midnite]			
CBS	local	Gunsmoke		Here's Lucy	Doris Day Show	My Three Sons	Arnie
NBC	local	Rowan And Martin's Laugh-In		NBC Monday Night At The Movies			

TUESDAY

Network	7:30	8:00	8:30	9:00	9:30	10:00	10:30
ABC	The Mod Squad		Movie Of The Week			Marcus Welby, M.D.	
CBS	Glen Campbell Goodtime Hour		Hawaii Five-O		CANNON		local
NBC	Ironside		SARGE		THE FUNNY SIDE		local

WEDNESDAY

Network	7:30	8:00	8:30	9:00	9:30	10:00	10:30
ABC	local	Bewitched	The Courtship Of Eddie's Father	The Smith Family	SHIRLEY'S WORLD	THE MAN AND THE CITY	
CBS	local	Carol Burnett Show		Medical Center		Mannix	
NBC	local	Adam-12	NBC Mystery Movie [McCloud, COLUMBO, McMILLAN AND WIFE]			Rod Serling's Night Gallery	

THURSDAY

Network	7:30	8:00	8:30	9:00	9:30	10:00	10:30
ABC	local	Alias Smith And Jones		LONGSTREET		OWEN MARSHALL, COUNSELOR AT LAW	
CBS	local	BEARCATS		CBS Thursday Night Movies @60 Minutes		@CBS News Hour	
NBC	local	Flip Wilson Show		NICHOLS		Dean Martin Show	

FRIDAY

Network	7:30	8:00	8:30	9:00	9:30	10:00	10:30
ABC	local	The Brady Bunch	The Patridge Family	Room 222	The Odd Couple	Love, American Style	
CBS	local	CHICAGO TEDDY BEARS	O'HARA, U.S. TREASURY		THE NEW CBS FRIDAY NIGHT MOVIES		
NBC	local	THE D.A.	NBC World Premiere Movie @Chronolog				local

SATURDAY

Network	7:30	8:00	8:30	9:00	9:30	10:00	10:30
ABC	local	GETTING TOGETHER	MOVIE OF THE WEEKEND			THE PERSUADERS	
CBS	local	All In The Family	FUNNY FACE	THE NEW DICK VAN DYKE SHOW	Mary Tyler Moore	Mission: Impossible	
NBC	local	THE PARTNERS	THE GOOD LIFE	NBC Saturday Night At The Movies			

SUNDAY (7:00 – 10:30)

Network	7:00	7:30	8:00	8:30	9:00	9:30	10:00	10:30
ABC	local		The F.B.I.		The ABC Sunday Night Movie			
CBS	local	CBS Sunday Night Movies			CADE'S COUNTY			local
NBC	local	The Wonderful World Of Disney		JIMMY STEWART	Bonanza @Bob Hope Show		The Bold Ones (The Doctors, The Lawyers)	

Actually, game show producers had begun sliding into syndication five years earlier as they found prime time on the networks, for the most part, closed to them. In September, 1965, *Truth or Consequences,* a veteran of both daytime and nighttime network TV runs, was booted from NBC. One year later, the producers turned down an offer from ABC to revive the show and instead decided to return the program to the air by syndicating new episodes to local stations across the country. Most of the stations were not affiliated with a network, had plenty of time to fill, and were more than happy to broadcast new, first run-episodes of a proven hit in place of their usual steady diet of reruns of old network series. *Truth or Consequences* was soon back in the groove, reuniting long-lost sisters and the like on a jerry-rigged chain of stations throughout the country. Other former network quizzers such as *What's My Line* (fall 1968), *Beat the Clock* and *To Tell the Truth* (September 1969), and *This Is Your Life* (January 1971) followed the lead of *Truth or Consequences* and were resurrected, usually with the word "new" stuck in front of the old title. The appearance of access time in the fall of 1971 opened new vistas for the syndicators as hundreds of network affiliates searched for programs to plug the new gaping holes in their schedules. To serve the expanding market, *Let's Make a Deal* and *Hollywood Squares,* still enjoying successful daytime network runs, joined the fray and began producing additional episodes for evening syndication.

For the most part, local stations chose the syndicated game shows to fill the Monday through Friday access slots. Other material was available such as new syndicated episodes of former network series including *Lassie, Lawrence Welk, Wild Kingdom,* and *Hee-Haw,* but these didn't offer the quick, cheap solution to the weeknight program gap that the quizzes provided and were usually scheduled for the weekends. Nonetheless, as shows that had been dumped by the networks merely for appealing to the wrong audience (either too rural or too old) they were eventually picked up because, like the quiz shows, they supplied familiar entertainment. (*Hee Haw,* in fact, thrived in syndication.) Completely new shows, however, faced an almost insurmountable barrier. Group W, which had pressed the concept of local access with the FCC in the first place, offered a number of its own new entertainment shows in syndication including the satirical *David Frost Revue* and *The Smothers' Organic Prime Time Space Ride,* only to see them die. These programs required larger budgets which made them more expensive to the locals. Consequently, neither the Frost program nor the Smothers show was ever ordered by enough stations to justify the costs involved and both ceased production by the end of the year. More importantly, they could not compete for a mass audience with the plebian appeal of the ever-resilient game show format. With the broadcast day largely filled with network programs, the local stations were not about to sacrifice a potentially lucrative new local time period for material that might not turn a maximum profit. They were even less receptive to innovative concepts than the three networks, a commercial reality that had escaped the FCC's planners. Creative high-quality television might emerge in the long run from the FCC's access rule, but in the short run it just brought more junk.

While the individual stations were filling local access time with game shows, the networks were filling prime time with gumshoes. The most recent movement against television sex and violence had brought to the forefront the less violent figures of doctors, lawyers, and legislators who could act as cop surrogates until the wave of public and governmental pressure lost momentum. While two new Marcus Welby clones did turn up in the fall of 1971, the heat from Washington had sufficiently abated to allow real cops and private eyes to make a comeback. They still avoided violence as much as possible, though, with watered-down settings either in traditional Jack Webb sagas or in equally nonviolent gimmick series featuring a new wave of inside-outsiders.

The Welby imitations came from the good doctor's very own executive producer, David Victor, who adapted the soapy but successful doctor format twice, emerging with one failure, *Man and the City,* and one success, *Owen Marshall: Counselor at Law.* The pilot episode for *Man and the City* cast Anthony Quinn as the mayor of a medium-sized Southwest desert city in a gritty setting that contained innovative touches of reality as part of the mayor's life: a tacky office, an estranged wife, and a devil's advocate for an aide. Once the regular series began, however, the unique desert feel and realistic setting were eliminated and the aseptic Welby world of spiffy offices and beautiful people was substituted instead. Quinn, one of the best tough guy actors of the era, was wasted fighting off-beat emotional causes such as the right of deaf parents to adopt a child who could hear. As a result, the program became merely a lame attempt to create a governmental *Father Knows Best* with pat answers and silly caricatures. *Owen Marshall: Counselor at Law,* with Arthur Hill as a widower-solicitor, was far more successful. Like Welby, Marshall aimed straight for the women: He was an idealized professional who lived in a fancy town and who dealt with the weird problems of the upper middle class, assisted by such gorgeous "hunks" in the supporting cast as Lee Majors and David Soul. The series was awash in bathos as it joined its companion professions in bringing topics previously considered "for soaps only" into prime time. In contrast to the others, though, *Owen Marshall* sometimes attempted a more even-handed treatment of its subjects, such as lesbianism.

The new cops and detectives dispensed with such indulgences and resumed the clear-cut direct pursuit of justice in the never-ending war against crime—albeit still without the physical gusto of the past. Jack Webb's two new entries for the fall continued to follow his standard nonviolent format, emphasizing tight-lipped personalities and the mechanics of crime detection, but neither *The D.A.* nor *O'Hara, U.S. Treasury* proved successful. In an unusual move, Webb used two celebrities that were known for exuding emotion on the screen in the series (Robert Conrad in *The D.A.* and David Janssen in *O'Hara*), but their animated character traits put them in direct conflict with the basis of Webb's unyielding dour format. Consequently, in both shows, the lead character seemed to be visibly straining against the role of tight-lipped hero. Neither program survived the season. Webb was much more successful with a mid-season replacement, *Emergency!,* which returned to his standard character types while increasing the instances of urban style visual action. In fact, *Emergency!* could be considered the perfect Jack Webb program, taking his philosophy of routine

but real-life crime and crime detection and stretching it to the limit. For one hour each week, a succession of unrelated gas explosions, helicopter crashes, arson blazes, bomb threats, and even mundane car crashes bombarded the viewer. It resembled nothing so much as a sixty-minute compilation of short film clips from the very visual disasters local television news directors inevitably featured in their nightly news programs. The show's premise tying the events together was simple: A squad of paramedics from the Los Angeles fire department's rescue division was dispatched to aid the victims, and in each show they drove from disaster to disaster. As with all Jack Webb productions, interspersed in this mayhem were moments of personal banter among the hard-working public servants (including paramedic regulars Robert Fuller, Bobby Troup, Julie London, Kevin Tighe, and Randolph Mantooth). Though the personalities of the paramedics were usually lost in the deadly inferno of disasters each week, *Emergency!* was generally well done, entertaining, and its success in the spring of 1972 began to put the "action" back into crime adventure shows. The program also added immeasurably to the image of Los Angeles as the setting of every horrendous natural or manmade cataclysm ever conceived.

The networks' attempts to be hip the previous season had proven an abysmal failure, so no true outsiders turned up among the new crop of law enforcers in 1971. Instead, there was a collection of characters more acceptable to TV viewers—characters only slightly only of snyc with mainstream society, usually personified as loner cops. Lone guns had thrived in the Fifties (Martin Kane, Peter Gunn, Paladin) but the advent of *77 Sunset Strip* signalled the advance of a more conformist troika-type system. For a decade, law enforcers worked in well-polished teams, sometimes borrowing from the medical format of a young man and his veteran mentor. The success of *Mannix* in the late Sixties began to bring the loner back into vogue and, in the fall of 1971, more than a half dozen such law enforcers appeared. Following in the footpath of the TV Westerns of the late Fifties, many of the new cop shows seemed almost laughable in their desperate search for attractive gimmick

In a 1968 made-for-TV movie, Peter Falk *(l.)* first portrayed Lieutenant Columbo. Gene Barry played Dr. Roy Flemming, a suave psychiatrist who murdered his wife. *(From "Prescription: Murder." Courtesy of MCA Television Limited)*

September 18, 1971

The New Dick Van Dyke Show. (CBS). Dick Van Dyke returns to television in a new, but familiar, sitcom setting, directed by Carl Reiner and slotted immediately before the increasingly successful *Mary Tyler Moore Show.* Van Dyke plays Dick Preston, host of a local television talk show in Phoenix, Arizona.

October 1, 1971

Frank Stanton, president of CBS, Inc. since 1946, moves up to become vice chairman of the CBS board of directors.

October 6, 1971

This Week. (PBS). Bill Moyers, former press secretary to President Lyndon Johnson, begins a weekly documentary essay series. In its second season, the program is renamed *Bill Moyers' Journal.*

October 11, 1971

Upstairs, Downstairs. Britain's London Weekend Television network begins an extended drama series focusing on the social life of Edwardian England. The action is centered at the Bellamy townhouse in a well-to-do district of London. Upstairs: the rich Bellamy family. Downstairs: their servants. The show makes it to the U.S. on *Masterpiece Theater* beginning in January, 1974.

October 13, 1971

The Pittsburgh Pirates beat the Baltimore Orioles 4 to 3 at Pittsburgh in the first World Series night game. NBC urged the later starting time in order to register higher ratings for the contest in prime time and, within a few years, most of baseball's championship games are staged "under the lights."

characters who could mask a generally bland and nonviolent premise. George Kennedy played a policeman turned activist-priest on *Sarge;* James Garner was a cowardly sheriff in the Old West on *Nichols;* and James Franciscus was a blind crusading insurance investigator on *Longstreet.* Several other programs with equally gimmicky characters, though, managed to catch on with viewers and develop into finely crafted adventure series. *Cannon* and the three rotating segments of *The NBC Mystery Movie* (*McCloud, McMillan and Wife,* and *Columbo*) had slightly stronger setups which allowed a wider set of story lines, better scripts, and more effective humor. They could present touches of reality within the ever present fantasy world of television lawmen. At heart, these series were identical in purpose to *Nichols* or *Longstreet,* only they happened to be more successful in overall execution and ratings.

McCloud (a holdover from the previous season's segments of *The NBC Mystery Movie,* then called *Four-in-One*) featured Dennis Weaver as a straight-talking, horse-riding marshal from New Mexico attached to the New York City police force. By using his Western sagacity and common-sense knowledge of people, McCloud constantly broke cases that stumped the locals, thereby exasperating yet amazing his Manhattan precinct chief, played by J. D. Cannon. Weaver was already familiar to viewers as a Western hero from his long stint as Chester, the sidekick in *Gunsmoke,* so he brought some credibility to the task of showing up the smart aleck city slickers—always an appealing notion to beleaguered urban dwellers. Astride his horse and wearing a cowboy hat, McCloud was a literal outsider to the urban New York setting, but his shrewd perception of people's motivations made him a law enforcement insider to be reckoned with. The program thus emerged as a very clever mix of Western and cop formats.

Another segment in *The NBC Mystery Movie* slot, *McMillan and Wife,* also featured off-beat characters—these in a premise

that drew on the old *Mr. and Mrs. North* stories for inspiration. The series presented a pleasant combination of mystery, humor, and police action by the unusual team of Stu McMillan (Rock Hudson), the police commissioner of San Francisco, and his wife, Sally (Susan Saint James). Saint James transferred her wisecracking character from *Name of the Game* to the new setting, mixing her domestic detective work with lighthearted household antics, usually planned with the couple's busybody housekeeper, played by Nancy Walker. Hudson's McMillan was also very down-to-earth and, even though he was the top cop in San Francisco (about as "inside" as possible), he inevitably took to the streets himself in the best loner cop tradition. He and his wife generally discovered and solved most cases themselves with only nominal help from the San Francisco police department, usually represented by McMillan's good-natured aide, Sergeant Enright (John Schuck). *McMillan and Wife*'s emphasis on likable characters and humor was a carefully planned technique used by each of the successful gimmick series. It allowed them to deemphasize violence and also to stand apart from the more traditional police shows which took themselves so seriously in the war against crime.

Still, McCloud and McMillan and his wife were only slight deviations from traditional crime fighters compared to the unlikely characters of Cannon and Columbo, the season's biggest (and sloppiest) successes. *Cannon* brought to the forefront the long-deserving William Conrad, whose rich deep voice had served him well in radio (playing Marshal Dillon in the radio version of *Gunsmoke*) and as a voice-over announcer for television (as in Quinn Martin's *The Fugitive*), but whose stout appearance relegated him to playing criminal heavies on camera. As detective Frank Cannon, Conrad starred in a new series by Quinn Martin that broke two unwritten rules about television heroes: Cannon was fat and he was old. Obviously pushing fifty (if he hadn't already pushed it over), Cannon could never win the hearts of the much-sought-after female audience in the same way as the svelte heroes portrayed by stars such as Craig Stevens, Efrem Zimbalist, Jr., Dennis Weaver, and Rock Hudson. With his heavy gait, Cannon was also not quite the ideal candidate for a frenzied police chase. Since the inception of television cops, such traits were, at best, left to the self-deprecating sidekick and never featured in a leading character. Nonetheless, Conrad, like most of the year's wave of loner cops, played his character strongly but with a slightly humorous touch, keeping the focus on personalities over incidents and appearance. He, too, never let the war on crime overshadow the people most affected by it.

The most visibly eccentric inside-outsider crime fighter introduced that season was Columbo, played by another veteran character actor, Peter Falk, who had been working for years to gain public acceptance for such a hero. In the fall of 1965, Falk starred in the off-beat CBS crime show, *The Trials of O'Brien.* In an era of pretty boy heroes (populated by such good lookers as Richard Chamberlain and Robert Vaughn), Falk's interpretation of attorney Daniel O'Brien as a seedy-looking disheveled little man proved an enigma to most television viewers, who were unable to take the character seriously. When he wasn't in the courtroom, O'Brien was more than likely to be found at the race track playing the horses. How could such a man be a counselor at law? He was even divorced! The mix of humor and drama in *Trials of O'Brien* found little appreciation and support at the time and the series was canceled at mid-season, just another good show that was unfortunately ahead of its time.

A year later, Universal studios began producing a new series of made-for-TV films for NBC, many of which served as pilots

Three years after "Prescription: Murder," Peter Falk returned in
Columbo. (*From* Columbo. *Courtesy of MCA Television Limited*)

for projected new series. In February, 1968, NBC-Universal presented "Prescription: Murder," written by Richard Levinson and William Link. The story traced the unsuccessful scheme of a wealthy psychiatrist (played by Gene Barry) who murdered his wife, but was confronted and eventually unmasked by a deferential detective, Lieutenant Columbo (played by Falk, who essentially carried on the character of O'Brien in this new role). The approach seemed appealing and a second film, a full-fledged pilot, "Ransom for a Deadman," was produced in 1971. In the fall of 1971, *Columbo* was quietly added to the *Mystery Movie* rotation and it slowly, very slowly, built a following. (The series didn't achieve wide public acceptance until well into its second season.) The times had changed since *O'Brien* and the audience was willing to accept a short fuzzy man in a wrinkled raincoat. Though he appeared to be little more than a sloppy, seemingly bumbling policeman, Columbo was actually an alert, perceptive investigator and Falk fleshed out his droll character. Each story became an elaborate cat-and-mouse game between the shuffling, polite detective and the overconfident suspect. *Columbo,* then, was presented not as a traditional whodunit, but rather as a "howzecatchem." At the beginning of each episode the audience was shown the crime as it was committed, so there was never any question of who was guilty. The focus of the stories shifted instead to *how* Columbo would trap the guilty party. Every episode of *Columbo* adhered to this formula but, as in the old *Perry Mason* series, the repetition increased viewers' involvement by making them think, alertly searching for the inevitable fatal error by the villain and the casual, but oh-so-devastating, off-hand remark by Columbo.

The success of these slightly off-beat new shows, as well as the steady number one status of CBS's *All in the Family,* was more tangible economic proof that the American television audience was willing to embrace programs that were somewhat out of the ordinary. Mindful of this, NBC offered at mid-season the first follow-up attempt to the successful style of *All in the Family, Sanford and Son,* another Norman Lear and Bud Yorkin production with British roots and a long history.

In January, 1962, the BBC anthology program *Comedy Playhouse* presented "The Offer," a situation comedy featuring the antics of Albert Steptoe (Wilfrid Brambell), a garrulous and possessive curmudgeon who ran a junk dealership with his son, Harold (Harry Corbett). Albert Steptoe was the archtypical lovable grouch who spent most of his time scheming to break up any plans (such as marriage) his son might have to leave the family business. The public response to the two characters was so strong that in June, 1962, a *Steptoe and Son* series began on the BBC and, by early 1964, it was the number one show in Britain. That same year, excerpts from the program were shown in America on *The Jack Paar Show* and NBC and Embassy Pictures put together a pilot for an Americanized version of the series that was intended to begin in 1965. The pilot, however, was rejected and plans for the series shelved. The British original itself went off the air in November, 1965. Though *Steptoe and Son* was still a highly rated show, its producers admitted frankly that they had run out of ideas and decided to quit while on top. Four and one-half years later, giving in to public demand, the original cast was reassembled and *Steptoe and Son* returned to the BBC with new episodes. Though the series didn't reach the number one slot in this new run, it was successful enough to once again attract American attention. In March, 1971, Norman Lear and Bud Yorkin, who had just finished a long struggle to bring *All in the Family* to television, acquired the rights to produce an American version of *Steptoe and Son.* In September,

---

December 12, 1971

Brig. General David Sarnoff, the father of American television and honorary chairman of the board of RCA, dies in New York at the age of eighty. He worked at the company for sixty-five years.

February 14, 1972

The CBS Late Movie. (CBS). After failing to catch Johnny Carson with Merv Griffin, CBS switches late night formats from talk shows to movies (beginning with "A Patch of Blue"). On March 13, Griffin, still headquartered in Los Angeles, returns to television in afternoon syndication for Metromedia.

April 30, 1972

Arthur Godfrey Time goes off CBS Radio after exactly twenty-seven years.

May 1, 1972

After making numerous West Coast trips over the years, NBC's *Tonight* show moves permanently to Los Angeles.

July 1, 1972

Facing tough new afternoon competition from Merv Griffin's return to syndication, David Frost's syndicated talk program for Group W goes off the air.

July 8–9, 1972

"The Democratic National Telethon." (ABC). On the eve of its nominating convention, the Democratic Party stages an 18½ hour telethon to help cut the party's debt.

July 12, 1972

Thirty-seven-year-old Arthur Taylor becomes president of CBS, Inc., taking Frank Stanton's old job.

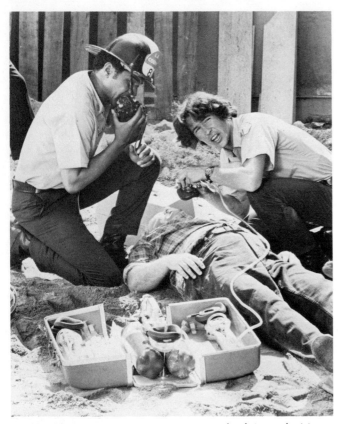

Jack Webb's *Emergency!* put some action back into television crime shows. (*From* Emergency! *Courtesy of MCA Television Limited*)

NBC agreed to put the show into its schedule in January, 1972. By this time, Lear and Yorkin had ceased working as a pair, so while Lear kept his eye on *All in the Family,* Yorkin took control of the new series, called *Sanford and Son.* Like *All in the Family, Sanford and Son* was a one-set show recorded on tape before a live audience. In transferring the junkyard world of *Steptoe and Son* to an American setting, Yorkin kept everything the same as in the original with one major exception: father and son (Fred and Lamont Sanford) were black.

Just as the Bunkers liberated television from the bland stereotypes of white suburbia, the Sanfords led the way in upsetting television's then-current stereotypes of blacks as middle class whites in blackface (such as *Julia*) and Olympian supermen (such as Linc in *The Mod Squad*). Instead, *Sanford and Son* presented blacks in a working class situation set in the ghetto, and used race as a peg for a number of jokes. Just as *All in the Family* was highly derivative of *The Honeymooners, Sanford and Son* was, in many ways, a modern version of *Amos and Andy,* which in the Fifties had cast blacks in a standard wacky *I Love Lucy* style of comedy. Both *Amos and Andy* and *Sanford and Son* presented comic characters who happened to be black living in an essentially all-black world. Within such a setting, the presence of whites was more an emotional feeling than a physical reality so the programs could put aside any awkward preaching and instead thrive in the all-black world with the strengths, stereotypes, and outlandish humor of any other first class American sitcom. Redd Foxx, a patriarch of black vaudeville halls (the so-called chitlin' circuit), portrayed the hypochondriac scheming bumbler, Fred Sanford. Foxx was a master at overacting and, since this was exactly what the character called for, it seemed as if he had spent his entire career preparing

for the role. Son Lamont (Demond Wilson) served the role of believable straightman who, like Jed Clampett in *The Beverly Hillbillies,* was an oasis of sanity necessary to bring the flights of fancy back from the stratosphere. Foxx and Wilson were perfect needles to each other and their love-hate relationship gave the show a secure foundation of humor. The usual sitcom supporting characters rounded out the cast, including a dull-witted accomplice (Whitman Mayo as Fred's pal, Grady) and a female battleaxe (LaWanda Page as Fred's sister-in-law, Esther). At heart, then, *Sanford and Son* was not so much a racial show, but rather a very basic, well-produced contemporary sitcom set in a black ghetto. In fact, all but one of the first year's episodes were simply rewritten *Steptoe and Son* scripts, though in later years Yorkin made a determined effort to use black writers. Fred Sanford might assert his blackness but, more often than not, it was only as part of some scheme or con using his race in much the same way as he used his feigned heart attacks. This television portrayal of working class blacks who were conscious of their race and the problems of ghetto life, but who were also strong humorous characters facing funny situations, was the most important aspect of the success of *Sanford and Son.*

With the American audience softened up after a year of *All in the Family, Sanford and Son* found it much easier to shoot to the top of the Nielsen ratings and managed to place sixth in the compilation of the season's top shows, even though it first appeared in January. Viewers were beginning to understand that *All in the Family* and *Sanford and Son* were not revolutionaries per se, but rather up-to-date continuations of great sitcom traditions of the past. Noting the public's acceptance of the innovative new series, producers and the networks in general grew bolder both in pursuing new formats and reworking old ones. In the process, the formulas for success in the Seventies seemed to be falling into place. Phasing in more contemporary adult concerns, CBS managed to stay on top in the ratings, closely followed by NBC. As usual, ABC was bringing up the rear, though it also joined the movement toward more experimental network ventures.

Miniseries appeared on all three networks, following the success of the CBS presentation of *The Six Wives of Henry VIII* the previous summer. NBC broadcast the BBC's six-part *Search for the Nile,* ABC imported a four-part adaptation of *War and Peace* (produced in Russia), and CBS presented the five-part Italian production of *The Life of Leonardo da Vinci.* Overall, the emphasis on special network programming increased and even the Pat Weaver notion of regularly scheduled specials made a comeback with NBC devoting most of Tuesday night to specials and ABC offering the weekly *Monday Night Special.* ABC also registered impressive success with its expanded schedule of made-for-TV movie presentations. Of the top twenty-three movies aired in the 1971–72 season, eighteen came from ABC's made-for-TV *Movie of the Week* slot. (In fact, only nine of the year's top thirty-two films were traditional theatrical features.) ABC's made-for-television hits included such blockbusters as the spooky crime-tinged "Night Stalker," and the solidly sentimental black-white sports comaraderie of "Brian's Song."

This boldness in entertainment programming was slowly sliding into the news departments as well, especially at CBS. With occasional, but dramatic, bursts of independence even in the face of government irritation and affiliate uneasiness, the network became the unquestioned leader in brave news presentations, particularly after its early 1971 *CBS Reports* episode, "The Selling of the Pentagon." The report examined the American military's public relations efforts that ranged from Pentagon propaganda films (some narrated by nationally known news commentators such as Chet Huntley and CBS's own Walter Cronkite) to elaborate and costly fireworks displays of new battle weapons shown to junketing VIPs. Though the Pentagon claimed the cost of these activities was only $30 million per year, CBS implied that $190 million of the taxpayers' money was a more accurate estimate of the yearly expenses. "The Selling of the Pentagon" did not follow the "on the other hand . . ." tradition of television reporting, adopting instead the best aspects of the subjective muckraking style of journalism newspapers had long practiced. Produced and written by Peter Davis (who later won an Oscar in 1974 for "Hearts and Minds," an admittedly subjective view of the war in Vietnam), the program didn't claim to be an objective study, but rather a hard-nosed TV exposé that examined an issue and reached a conclusion. The program directed criticism not so much at the concept of Pentagon public reations, but at the incredible waste of taxpayers' funds on extravagancies. The military and its congressional friends blasted the show as a "vicious piece of propaganda." Representative Harley O. Staggers, chairman of the House Investigations Subcommittee, kept the issue alive for months by trying to have CBS executive Frank Stanton cited for contempt because he refused the committee's demand for outtakes from the program. In July, 1971, though, the full House turned its back on Staggers and refused to press the contempt issue, and even President Nixon supported CBS in the battle. A few months later, however, the President and CBS were again at loggerheads, this time over a CBS report, "Under Surveillance," that documented FBI spying and wire tapping on domestic radicals.

At the same time, in the fall of 1971, the simmering warfare between the White House and public television at last broke into the open as officials from the Corporation for Public Broadcasting (CPB) publicly complained that Clay Whitehead, chief of the White House's Office of Telecommunications Policy, was trying to inject partisan political considerations into the administration of American public television. In January, 1972, Whitehead went on record as saying that, "there is a real question as to whether public television . . . should be carrying public affairs, news commentary, and that sort of thing." With an election year beginning, the White House preferred a weak, unobtrusive public broadcast system and Whitehead's statement virtually corroborated the charges of administration pressure on public TV. The battle intensified in the summer and, in July, President Nixon vetoed the CPB funding bill that would have granted public television $155 million over the next two years. In August, Nixon forces staged a coup d'etat and the chairman and president of CPB, both appointed by President Johnson, agreed to resign. Public television was rapidly becoming, in effect, the Nixon network. As a result, it offered no commentary at all in its gavel-to-gavel coverage of the August Republican convention in Miami Beach. The cameras simply focused on the podium and followed the scheduled activites, one after another. Recently hired PBS newsmen Robert MacNeil and Sander Vanocur both refused the meaningless wooden role of convention anchor (though they did participate in the nightly convention wrapups), so the job fell to former Johnson press secretary, Bill Moyers. The convetion itself, however, was so well planned (it was literally scripted) that only a few aspects stood out anyway: the fanatically cheering young Nixon supporters and the one vote cast for David Brinkley for vice president.

In contrast, the Democratic convention, held a month earlier in Miami, was extremely disorganized—even for Democrats. Long, rancorous debates on controversial issues such as Vietnam and gay rights filled prime time television and constantly forced the sessions to run overtime. Even on nomination night the delegates failed to restrain themselves and presidential nominee Senator George McGovern was forced to deliver his acceptance speech at 3:00 A.M., when all but the most ardent supporters had already gone to bed.

On the eve of the convention, however, the Democrats managed to coordinate and stage a unique political fund-raising event, an eighteen and one-half hour national telethon, carried on ABC. It was a novel way to erase part of the party's outstanding $9 million debt (from the 1968 campaign) and at the same time reduce the image of dependence on the traditional "fat cats" of politics by appealing directly to millions of "little people." The program was jam-packed with stars and, as such events go, was reasonably well produced and entertaining. It contained humorous partisan "commercials" including a *Mission: Impossible* take-off with a self-destructing tape that instructed Republican agents to bug the Democratic headquarters in Washington. The program was well received and, by the end of the telethon, the Democrats had raised $4 million, enough to pay for the network time and still leave a profit of $2 million.

President Nixon, however, was clearly headed for a second term and, all year, the networks were very wary of crossing him. His February trip to China received heavy coverage, but the May protests to his mining of Vietnam's Haiphong harbor were given minimal exposure. Yet despite this generally cautious manner, Nixon and Nixon supporters continued to be irked at even occasional probing by CBS News. At the Republican convention, for instance, Mike Wallace bravely interviewed Nixon campaign money man Maurice Stans on possible connections to a burglary at the Democratic National Committee headquarters in Washington's Watergate hotel. Reports by Daniel Schorr apparently angered the administration enough that an FBI investigation of Schorr was ordered by White House staffer Chuck Colson. When news of this leaked in November, 1971, and was reported by *Washington Post* reporter Ken Clawson, the government released the patently absurd story that the FBI was checking into Schorr because he was under consideration for an environmental job in the administration. Following the May protests to the Haiphong mining, CBS, the only network to air a prime time special on the activities ("Escalation in Vietnam: Reasons, Risks, and Reactions"), was chastised by the Republican National Committee's publication, *Monday*, which claimed in a headline that: "CBS News accentuates the negative, distorting the facts in reporting Vietnam action." Shortly thereafter, CBS calmly aired films made by Anthony Lewis from the *New York Times* who showed North Vietnamese hospitals, homes, and schools destroyed by American bombs. Ironically, the films were very similar to the Felix Greene footage turned down by the network four years earlier. CBS newsman Don Webster, returning from the war front, said that ever since the American invasion of Cambodia and Laos (which had resulted in some negative comments and reports), the American military displayed open animosity to the press, "especially the radio-TV press and, even more, CBS News."

It wasn't the Vietnam war, however, that produced the season's most exciting combat coverage but, rather, the summer Olympics in Munich, Germany, broadcast on ABC. In 1968, ABC had carried both the summer and winter Olympic games, earning merely satisfactory ratings but demonstrating remarkable professionalism in its handling of the events. NBC's coverage of the 1972 winter Olympics in Japan registered the same "just adequate" Nielsen figures. For the summer Olympics in late August and early September of 1972, the well-trained ABC *Wide World of Sports* production crew, headed by producer Roone Arledge and announcers Jim McKay and Howard Cosell, again turned the often scattered Olympic events into a tight, comprehensible show. Making extensive use of satellite transmissions, ABC scheduled many segments for prime time viewing. The network once more won critical plaudits but this time, surprisingly, very high ratings as well, averaging a 52% share of the audience on Olympic nights.

On Tuesday morning, September 5, the Olympics were dramatically transformed from a highly rated sporting event to an important news story as Palestinian terrorists captured a group of Israeli athletes inside the Olympic compound and held them as hostages. ABC, of course, had a large, professional staff already on the scene to provide extensive day-long coverage of the Munich events, but the network's coverage of the hostage story went beyond being fortunately at the right place at the right time. While CBS and NBC stuck to confusing and poorly produced reports, ABC displayed a strong professional manner and discipline that suddenly made many Americans aware that ABC was a network to be taken seriously. Jim McKay displayed a depth of insight and emotion he had never revealed on *Wide World of Sports* as the events unfolded, live, before the cameras. Newsman Peter Jennings reported from within the cordoned-off compound itself. The terrorists were shown brandishing their weapons and sticking their heads out the window while German paratroopers surrounded the compound and prepared for a possible assault. The possibility that open warfare could erupt at any moment was painfully clear—and undeniably exciting. Both sides waited, tensely, all day. Near 5:00 P.M. (New York time), the terroritsts emerged from the compound with their hostages in tow, stepped into the fuzzy street light, then entered a special bus they had demanded be brought to take them all to the local airport. As the bus disappeared, both the ABC commentators and the home audience could only wait and speculate. At 9:00 P.M. McKay wearily but joyfully announced that, according to the first reports from the airport, all the hostages had been freed. Soon he had to retract this premature happy ending with the ominous phrase, "There will be bad news from the officials." Near 10:30 P.M. McKay, visibly exhausted after his twelve-hour marathon job of anchoring, presented the bad news: All the hostages had died in a violent shoot-out between police and the terrorists. Memorial services were held for the slain athletes and then the games were resumed and completed amid extremely tight security.

ABC's Munich coverage marked an important turning point in the network's image. Not only had it displayed innovation and skill in its excellent production of the Olympic events themselves, it also revealed tremendous adaptability in facing unexpected developments with its presentation of the hostage story. The events in Munich served as a highly visible "coming of age" for what had been derisively labeled for years as "the third network."

32. Ideological Plugola

IN 1973 the FCC finally got around to holding hearings on the first complaints registered against implementation of the 1970 prime time access rule. Despite the howls of protest that had originally greeted the proposal three years earlier, when the hearings actually began no one spoke out in favor of scrapping the new system. The three networks privately confessed that it would take them years to develop a new batch of 7:30 P.M. lead-in programs should the time be returned to them. Independent syndicators and local station owners, who were prospering with profitable game shows in the access slots, had no intention of giving up their new-found bonanza without a fight. In a very short time, a new status quo had taken hold in television. The exemptions granted to ABC and NBC for the 1971–72 season expired and were not renewed. ABC broke up its Tuesday night block while NBC shaved an additional thirty minutes from its Sunday night schedule. For the 1972–73 season, each network adhered to the prescribed three-hour limit on prime time broadcasting every night. At the FCC hearings, NBC publicly conceded that access might actually be a good idea, while ABC had no qualifications—it was ecstatic about the plan. Though still number three, ABC had used the access rule to cut dead weight from its schedule and found itself in a good competitive position, registering a small but healthy ratings jump for the 1971–72 season. Even number one CBS had weathered the storm well, dropping the last of its rural-based programs in its compliance with the access rule.

At the same time, CBS looked to its new smash hit, *All in the Family,* to set the style of comedy for the new decade, and had begun to cultivate the development of similar programs. The network had drawn on sitcoms for ratings success throughout the Fifties and Sixties and prepared to exploit the rejuvenated format again for the Seventies. *All in the Family* was fresh, exciting, provocative, and a rich source to tap for the new wave of humor. The series had expanded its scope from racial themes to deal with other controversial topics such as menopause, impotency, homosexuality, and the Vietnam war. Producer Norman Lear did not just milk the topical issues for a few cheap laughs, but used them as realistic complications faced by generally believable, if somewhat stereotyped, characters. (Lear, in fact, said that he had modeled the Archie Bunker character after his own father.) The popular success of Lear's sitcom style had, within a very short time, effectively changed the focus of situation comedy from the mindless silliness of *Gilligan's Island* to the presentation of human minidramas that had a strong base in comedy.

Irwin Segelstein, a top aide to CBS programmer Fred Silverman, described this approach to comedy as the first major change from the *I Love Lucy* "obstacle course sitcoms." These had presented lovable and wacky characters in absurd situations such as trying to fly a plane without a pilot or falling down a laundry chute. Segelstein said:

> The new comedy always grows out of an identifiable situation, and it involves realism in both life style and dialogue style. It still involves jokes, but the jokes are being made on a different level than before. . . . Where it really departs from the old is that the comedy grows out of the characters themselves rather than out of plot or farcical incidents. The writers start with a serious theme and then develop a comedy about it.

Television drama series had long before melted into a panoply of cops and doctors in soap opera-type action-adventures, so sitcoms had unexpectedly become the driving force in the examination of real-life issues by the medium. Such a development made sense because the framework of comedy defused the omni-present stench of exceeding seriousness and glib solutions that had usually pervaded and ultimately undercut any attempts to deal with real life in the so-called relevant dramas such as *Mod Squad* and the defunct *Storefront Lawyers.* In those, current headlines had merely been grafted onto cliché-ridden plots, shallow characters, and cardboard settings in order to appear up-to-date and topical. Though the characters in sitcoms such as *All in the Family* often fell into stereotypes themselves, the world they were placed in was very real. Consequently, controversial, topical, and realistic issues did not appear as heavy handed intrusions but, rather, as reasonable developments in that setting.

All in the Family had opened its second season with Archie trying to wiggle out of paying for the funeral of a bothersome relative who had died (off-camera) in his house. Such a plot twist was unique to television because characters in traditional TV sitcoms simply didn't die. It worked because the Bunker family faced the situation in character and handled it with humor. This was the key to the continuing success of the series as Norman Lear constantly updated *All in the Family* to reflect the shifts of popular controversy in the Seventies, duplicating the arguments that took

	7:30	8:00	8:30	9:00	9:30	10:00	10:30	
MONDAY	local	THE ROOKIES		ABC NFL Monday Night Football [to 12 Midnite]				**ABC**
	local	Gunsmoke		Here's Lucy	Doris Day Show	THE NEW BILL COSBY SHOW		**CBS**
	local	Rowan And Martin's Laugh-In		NBC Monday Night At The Movies				**NBC**

	7:30	8:00	8:30	9:00	9:30	10:00	10:30	
TUESDAY	local	TEMPERATURE'S RISING	Tuesday Movie Of The Week			Marcus Welby, M.D.		**ABC**
	local	MAUDE	Hawaii Five-O		The New CBS Tuesday Night Movies			**CBS**
	local	Bonanza		The Bold Ones (The Doctors)		NBC REPORTS @First Tuesday		**NBC**

	7:30	8:00	8:30	9:00	9:30	10:00	10:30	
WEDNESDAY	local	PAUL LYNDE SHOW	Wednesday Movie Of The Week			JULIE ANDREWS HOUR		**ABC**
	local	Carol Burnett Show		Medical Center		Cannon		**CBS**
	local	Adam-12	NBC WEDNESDAY NIGHT MYSTERY MOVIE (BANACEK, COOL MILLION, MADIGAN)			SEARCH		**NBC**

	7:30	8:00	8:30	9:00	9:30	10:00	10:30	
THURSDAY	local	The Mod Squad		THE MEN (ASSIGNMENT: VIENNA, DELPHI BUREAU, JIGSAW)		Owen Marshall, Counselor At Law		**ABC**
	local	THE WALTONS		CBS Thursday Night Movies				**CBS**
	local	Flip Wilson Show		Ironside @Bob Hope Show		Dean Martin Show		**NBC**

	7:30	8:00	8:30	9:00	9:30	10:00	10:30	
FRIDAY	local	The Brady Bunch	The Partridge Family	Room 222	The Odd Couple	Love, American Style		**ABC**
	local	Sonny And Cher Comedy Hour		CBS Friday Night Movies				**CBS**
	local	Sanford And Son	THE LITTLE PEOPLE	GHOST STORY		BANYON		**NBC**

	7:30	8:00	8:30	9:00	9:30	10:00	10:30	
SATURDAY	local	Alias Smith And Jones @KUNG FU		STREETS OF SAN FRANCISCO		The Sixth Sense		**ABC**
	local	All In The Family	BRIDGET LOVES BERNIE	Mary Tyler Moore	BOB NEWHART SHOW	Mission: Impossible		**CBS**
	local	Emergency		NBC Saturday Night At The Movies				**NBC**

	7:00	7:30	8:00	8:30	9:00	9:30	10:00	10:30	
SUNDAY	local		The F.B.I.		The ABC Sunday Night Movie				**ABC**
	local	ANNA AND THE KING	M*A*S*H	Sandy Duncan Show	New Dick Van Dyke Show	Mannix		local	**CBS**
	local	The Wonderful World Of Disney		NBC Sunday Mystery Movie (McCloud, Columbo, McMillan And Wife, HEC RAMSEY)			Rod Serling's Night Gallery	local	**NBC**

place in many homes across the country throughout the decade. Originally Archie and son-in-law Mike had passionately disagreed on religious morals, race, and the conduct of the Vietnam war. This expanded to include the ethics of President Nixon's reelection campaign and the investigation into the break-in at the Democratic headquarters in the Watergate. Some episodes went even further and shifted the primary emphasis from comedy to drama. In one such story, the Bunkers and a "Hebrew Defense Association" activist spent the final third of the program arguing the pros and cons of violence as a political tool. Neither side convinced the other. At the conclusion of the argument, the HDA member left the Bunker house and (off-camera) stepped into his car, turned the ignition key, and was instantly killed by a bomb planted under the hood. The episode ended with a silent shot of the stunned Bunkers looking through their doorway at the wreckage.

By 1973, with the Vietnam war ending, the series slowly shifted to playing up the cause of women's liberation. The conflicts between Archie and Gloria, his feminist daughter, were obvious and practically unavoidable. Even though she was a grown woman in her twenties with a job and a husband, to Archie, Gloria would always be his "little girl." It pained him to see her display the independence that signalled not only her rejection of his traditional values but also her inevitable departure from the home roost. A less expected but equally important development was the change in the largely decorative character of Edith. She came forward to demonstrate that older women deserved respect as well. Previously used as a squeaky-voiced butt of all the dumb-Dora housewife jokes ("Stifle it, Dingbat!" Archie would admonish), Edith was emboldened enough to demand consideration of her own needs for love and self-fulfillment. Edith truly cared for Archie and consequently wanted not only his respect for her daily activities but also a little more of the affection he thought years of married life had made unnecessary.

By the mid-1970s the national mood had returned to one of practicality, leaving polemics behind, and *All in the Family* changed again as well. In a television world then filled with *All in the Family*-style spinoffs, it stood as almost a traditional sitcom that focused on such familiar themes as parenthood and grandparenthood. Gloria had a child and she and Mike at last moved out of the Bunker house and set up housekeeping next door. There was still controversy, though it was usually much less strident than in the past. Over the objections of Mike and Gloria, for instance, Archie took their baby, Joey, to a church and baptized him. Lear also kept up the topical flavor of the series with such realistic developments as Archie's getting laid off from his plant (he eventually quit anyway) and Edith fending off a rapist. Archie himself even became a small businessman, mortgaging his house in order to buy his neighborhood bar. Eventually, a mellower and shorter-haired Mike Stivic, like much of his generation, "settled down." He accepted a teaching job in California, taking Gloria and Joey to the other end of the country and leaving Archie and Edith alone in New York. Like much of *their* generation, Archie and Edith carried on in a greatly altered world with their own new interests—and to the end Archie still colorfully griped about whatever was in the headlines.

All in the Family became an American institution of the Seventies, yet at the beginning of the decade its success in dealing with controversy was viewed with amazement. Still, its acceptance should not really have been a complete surprise because over the years viewers had been growing accustomed to seeing more sensitive themes on television through the increasing number of adult-oriented prime time movies. The all-too-obvious double standard between movies and weekly series had to crack eventually as the public became more tolerant of such material. In the fall of 1972, CBS, embracing this new form of sitcom as the key to its continued primacy, launched its first major followups to *All in the Family*, *Maude* and *M*A*S*H*.

Norman Lear's *Maude* was a direct spinoff from *All in the Family* and, on the surface, appeared to be merely a vehicle for an arch-liberal version of Archie Bunker. The character of Maude Findlay (Beatrice Arthur) had been presented in several episodes of *All in the Family* as Edith's cousin whose left wing slant and abrasive manner put her in direct opposition to the outspoken Archie. Maude was quick tempered, rich, and an ardent believer in the right of women to control their own lives. She defended all the planks of liberal dogma and strongly supported freedom of action, freedom of speech, and a big benevolent government that helped others to help themselves. Archie hated her and she despised him. Maude was the perfect focus for a spinoff series and the character was awarded her own program for the 1972–73 season, set in her home environment of a liberal, worldly, upper middle class New York suburban neighborhood. It immediately hit the top ten, joining *All in the Family* and *Sanford and Son*, which had become ensconced at the top of the Nielsen ratings lists (occasionally taking the number one and two slots together). Unlike the Sixties' *Petticoat*

Junction and *Green Acres, Maude* was not a cheap obvious cash-in on a successful hit formula. Lear used the different setting and liberal characters to tackle a whole new range of topics in treatments that matched *All in the Family* in daring and sensitivity.

Perhaps the most revolutionary aspect of *Maude* was that it freed middle-aged women from the TV stereotype of addlebrained spinsters, just as Mary Tyler Moore's program had upset the traditional TV image of a young woman. Though certainly not a raving beauty, Maude was an attractive woman with an active sex life and apparently boundless self-confidence. Despite three unsuccessful marriages that had ended in divorce, she had married again. Her latest husband, Walter (Bill Macy), possessed an intelligent pragmatism and he recognized that Maude needed not only love and reassurance but the opportunity to assert herself, so he usually bowed to her wishes. Walter's business was successful enough that Maude did not have to work, so she devoted her time to a myriad of liberal and women's causes, leaving basic household chores to her maid, Florida (Esther Rolle). Carol (Adrienne Barbeau), Maude's daughter from a previous marriage, and her son, Phillip (Brian Morrison), also lived with Maude and Walter.

Maude was one of the first programs to take advantage of the networks' grudging acceptance of divorce as a fact of life and to successfully incorporate it into a series premise. In 1970, ABC's *The Odd Couple,* featuring a pair of divorced men living together, had marked the beginning of the end of television's parade of widows and widowers, but Maude outdid them both. She had been divorced three times herself and daughter Carol had been divorced once as well.

Despite her exaggerated liberal tendencies and loud-mouthed caricature, Maude was a strong complex character who faced very difficult and very realistic problems. When the issue of personal freedom hit her in areas close to home (such as the possible involvement in premarital sex by her grandson and some obvious affairs by her daughter), she found herself falling into the traditional role of overbearing suspicious mother. She tried to control her instincts, often to no avail. When a series of business mishaps pushed Walter, a normally heavy drinker anyway, into a fling with alcoholism,

The early episodes of *M*A*S*H* emphasized the playboy surgeon theme, as in this hot-tub frolic: (from *l.*) McLean Stevenson, Alan Alda, Wayne Rogers. *(Courtesy of Twentieth Century-Fox)*

September 16, 1972

Bridget Loves Bernie. (CBS). Meredith Baxter is Bridget, a rich Irish-Catholic. David Birney is Bernie, a poor New York Jew. The two fall in love, get married, and have to overcome opposition from both sides of the family. Placed between *All in the Family* and *The Mary Tyler Moore Show,* the program registers good ratings, but also stirs the ire of some religious groups objecting to the positive portrait of inter-marriage. As a result, CBS axes the show after only one season. Life, however, triumphs over art. Baxter and Birney later marry each other in real life.

November 8, 1972

Time-Life's Home Box Office cable television system begins its programming with a National Hockey League contest from Madison Square Garden followed by a movie, "Sometimes a Great Notion." At first, HBO is limited to just 365 cable subscribers in Wilkes-Barre, Pennsylvania.

November 24, 1972

In Concert. (ABC). Don Kirshner produces a late Friday night special-pilot of live rock acts, taped in concert. First up is shock-rocker Alice Cooper. After about twenty minutes of Cooper's mock horror tactics and gyrations with a snake, WPRC in Cincinnati pulls out of the show, saying, "This stopped being music and art and had turned into pornography." On January 19, *In Concert* becomes a regular, once-every-other-week ABC late night series.

January 4, 1973

CBS sells the New York Yankees to George Steinbrenner.

she fought her own panic and his depression to help them both weather the crisis. Perhaps the most painful personal decision she ever faced took place in one of the series' first episodes, a two-part story on abortion, shown in November, 1972. Maude discovered that she was pregnant at an age in which she had no intention of becoming a mother again, and had to decide whether or not to have an abortion. After an agonizing soul search, she concluded that an abortion was the only realistic alternative open to her, but despite her liberal philosophies, this was not presented as an easy choice. The program was the strongest pro-abortion statement made on network TV at the time and it set off a brief public controversy in which a number of CBS affiliates refused to air the episodes. Such actions had formerly been taken only in reaction to documentaries, dramas, or an occasional topical variety format. The *Maude* protests were a symbolic confirmation of the full-fledged serious status being accorded sitcoms.

CBS's other new wave hopeful, *M*A*S*H,* also successfully combined drama with comedy, though it took several years to refine and develop its presentation. The series was based on the popular 1970 Robert Altman film that followed the adventures of two merry playboy combat surgeons (played by Elliott Gould and Donald Sutherland) assigned to an overseas American Mobile Army Surgical Hospital (M*A*S*H) unit during the Korean war. Altman used the twin shock tactics of excessive blood and explicit language to set his film apart from typical war comedies and to stress the cruelty of combat. The television adaptation toned down both the language and obvious bloodletting but, within the limits of television, kept both the gore of war and the joy of sex as major themes. In its first season, though, TV's *M*A*S*H* was, for the most part, a traditional war-is-funny comedy that owed as much to *Hogan's Heroes* and *Sergeant Bilko* as Altman's film. Alan Alda (as Hawkeye Pierce) and Wayne Rogers (as Trapper John McIntyre) emphasized the playboy-surgeon aspect of their characters, drinking too much and perpetually chasing nurses. They were excellent medicos (and knew it) who constantly manipulated their nominal commander, Lieutenant Colonel Henry Blake (McLean Stevenson), while thumbing their noses at military regulations and discipline. Such themes and characters were basic to every war comedy film since World War II and the initial TV treatment offered little evidence that the series was in the same league as Norman Lear's comedies.

*M*A*S*H* did very poorly in the fall of 1972. It was stuck in a hell-hole of a slot: Sunday, between the anemic *Anna and the King* and *The Sandy Duncan Show,* and against ABC's *The FBI* and NBC's *Wonderful World of Disney.* Yet, premiering as it did at the tail end of the Vietnamese war, its mocking of military regimentation and futile war strategies appeared timely and close to home. The program's demographics indicated that while the overall ratings were terrible, *M*A*S*H* was very popular among young adults. CBS executives therefore decided to allow the show time to build an audience. In January, *M*A*S*H* was given slightly more respectable company (Dick Van Dyke and Mannix) and it broke into the top thirty, winning renewal for a second season. CBS program chief Fred Silverman gave it the royal treatment in the fall of 1973 and placed *M*A*S*H* between two comedy blockbusters on Saturday night, *All in the Family* and *The Mary Tyler Moore Show.* The series then rocketed to the top ten and remained there into the Eighties.

Along with its new ratings success, *M*A*S*H* began displaying a remarkable improvement in content. Alan Alda took on added duties such as occasional script writing and directing, and members of the supporting cast began to develop their characters into more complex individuals. The image of merry doctors on the loose was replaced by the intricate relationships among people thrown together in a unique war situation. The writers began shifting the focus of the scripts from straight sitcom into the world of comedy-drama. By the third season, they hit their stride as *M*A*S*H* developed a dramatic style similar to, yet distinct from, Norman Lear's programs. While the Bunkers and Maude very often grappled with topical headline issues, the individuals in *M*A*S*H* faced intimate, personal conflicts of a more timeless nature that were set against the equally real backdrop of a hospital unit trying desperately to save as many lives as possible in a war zone. Very often, particular episodes replaced the traditional sitcom structure of rapid-fire punch lines leading to a hilarious denouement with three occasionally interweaving plot threads, of which one or two were usually serious. A device sometimes used to make the rambling plots less jarring was the composition of a letter home. In effect, this allowed a member of the cast to act as narrator of recent developments at the base, which were shown in flashback as the note bound for the States took shape. Besides serving as a convenient plot hook, these "letters" also allowed the individual cast members to tell the story from their own point of view, adding some depth to the character traits already familiar to the viewers.

Character development became the most impressive feature of *M*A*S*H* and the cast soon raised the TV series far beyond the meat-axe humor and caricatures of the feature film—in a rare instance of the TV copy surpassing the film original. Gary Burghoff, the only performer from the film that made the crossover to television, fleshed out his role of Corporal Radar O'Reilly, Colonel Blake's young aide with an extraordinary sixth sense (he anticipated events moments before they took place). Though Radar possessed an instinctive understanding of the intricate twists in military bureaucracy and his knowledge of procedure actually kept the base running, in many respects he remained the terribly naive Iowa farm boy who sometimes found himself a bit jealous of the swinging lifestyle of Hawkeye and Trapper. Larry Linville and Loretta Swit assumed the roles of Major Frank Burns and chief nurse Major Margaret "Hot Lips" Houlihan, two officers carrying on a torrid affair with each other but determined to follow "proper procedure" whenever possible in the meatloaf surgery world of Korea. They both suffered mercilessly as foils to Hawkeye and Trapper, but they also displayed more humanity and depth than their feature film counterparts (Robert Duvall and Sally Kellerman). Two characters substantially upgraded in the move to television were Father Mulcahy (William Christopher), the company chaplain, and Henry Blake. As camp commander, the TV Henry Blake realized that it wasn't worth the aggravation involved to try to stop the pranks of Hawkeye and Trapper, so he wisely chose to ignore them in the interests of company harmony (and his own peace of mind). The TV Blake was a pushover but he realized it and knew when it was really important to draw the line. Altman's Blake had been just plain stupid. His Mulcahy had been even worse, set up as an ignorant sissy priest. Christopher portrayed the character as a realistic Army chaplain, just as likely to be found in an all-night poker party as in a formal chapel setting. Each of these characters could step in with complications, conflicts, and problems of their own, thus breaking up the strain of constantly focusing on Hawkeye and Trapper.

Good as this cast and the show were by 1974, both aspects improved even further in the fourth season as M*A*S*H revitalized itself with two important cast changes. McLean Stevenson decided to quit the program and move into the comedy-variety field on his own, so his character was written out of the series. The final episode of the 1974–75 season featured a happy farewell party for Henry Blake, who had received his orders shipping him back to the States. A short postscript ended the episode: the death of Henry Blake. In one brilliant stroke, the simple departure of a series regular was transformed into a tragic, ironic twist of war—one of the main themes of the show anyway. After months at the front lines, Blake was killed on the way home in an offshore crash as his plane was struck by random enemy fire. A tearful Radar announced the news in the operating room and, between stitches, the doctors and nurses cried. Before production for the next season began, Wayne Rogers also decided to depart. He had found himself trapped in a character almost identical to Alda's and had been severely limited by the duplication (there was room for only one super-intelligent Yankee anarchist in Korea). As a result, in the fall of 1975, M*A*S*H was practically a brand new program with two-thirds of its central cast altered. Both replacements turned out to be even stronger characters than their predecessors and the quality of the series once again increased dramatically.

Veteran series actor Harry Morgan portrayed the new C.O., Colonel Sherman Potter, an experienced soldier, surgeon, and a much more creditable Army figure than Colonel Blake. Unlike Blake, Potter not only grew angry at his charges, he occasionally even disciplined them. This made his role as benign ruler, inclined to overlook harmless pranks and unnecessary procedure, much more believable. Mike Farrell played Hawkeye's new sidekick, Captain B. J. Hunnicutt, a pure product of the San Francisco way of life. Unlike Trapper, B. J. was different from Hawkeye, yet the two still became fast friends. B. J. was a cool West Coast high-liver with a wife and family and no desire to upset his stable home with promiscuous behavior in Korea. Their personalities complemented each other perfectly, giving both characters plenty of room to shine.

With its basic cast further strengthened, M*A*S*H grew even bolder in its departure from standard sitcom structure. One episode centered solely on the crew trying to watch a film (the old horse opera, "My Darling Clementine") that constantly jammed in the camp projector. To continue the entertainment while the projector was being fixed, they launched an impromptu sing-along talent show. The program reached no dramatic climax; the party simply ended with the inevitable arrival of the new wounded. Another episode brought the series to a level of visual, lyrical poetry as it recreated Ed Murrow's almost legendary 1952 See It Now show from Korea. The performers were allowed to ad-lib in character when responding to questions from the traveling "newsman" and never was their grasp of their roles more evident. Radar blushed at the opportunity to say "hello" to the folks back home. Colonel Potter called the whole Korean escapade stupid. Hawkeye nearly broke down trying to explain how he dealt with keeping a measure of sanity through the war. Father Mulcahy gasped at the recollection of doctors fighting the cold Korean air by subconsciously warming their hands from the heat of open body wounds.

With such powerful descriptions, complex characters, and the very real terror of dealing so closely and continuously with death, M*A*S*H became one of the best sitcom-drama combinations ever on television. It joined All in the Family and Maude in focusing dramatic interest on character development, not slam-bang action and cheap slapstick.

In the fall of 1972, along with the appearance of M*A*S*H, CBS applied this same respect for characters to a new dramatic program as well, in an attempt to revive the moribund format of family drama with The Waltons. Series such as Mama and One Man's Family had flourished in the early Fifties, but had vanished with the development of filmed series and Westerns. With film, action became the goal and so-called Western drama led to crime

January 8, 1973
Wide World of Entertainment. (ABC). Revamping its late night schedule after failing to catch Johnny Carson with Dick Cavett's talk show, ABC institutes a complicated new format arrangement and brings in a former late night giant, Jack Paar. Each month, Jack Paar Tonight appears for one week, Cavett runs for one week, and the alternate two weeks are filled with movies, specials, and concerts.

February 2, 1973
The Midnight Special. (NBC). Network television's first late late night show, running from 1:00 A.M. till 2:30 A.M. Friday nights. Hosted by legendary rock DJ Wolfman Jack, the program is NBC's answer to the ABC In Concert show.

March 31, 1973
Frank Stanton, president of CBS, Inc. for twenty-five years and, since 1971, vice chairman of the CBS board, retires upon reaching the age of sixty-five.

May 4, 1973
Bruce Jay Friedman's play "Steambath" is shown on Hollywood Television Theater, but only a few PBS stations are brave enough to carry it. The story offers an unusual portrayal of the afterlife, with God presented as a Puerto Rican steambath attendant. Bill Bixby plays a man who refuses to admit that he has died, and Valerie Perrine becomes the first woman to display her nipples on American network television.

August 6, 1973
Following a tremendous publicity campaign, CBS unveils its new morning news line-up consisting of veteran television newsman Hughes Rudd and newspaper reporter-TV neophyte Sally Quinn.

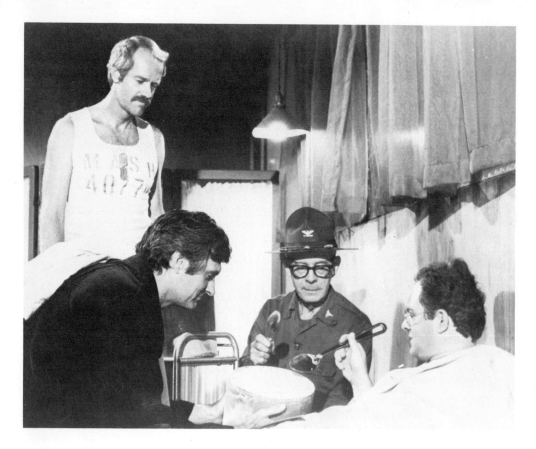

The "second generation" of *M*A*S*H* included: (from *l.*) Mike Farrell as B. J. Hunnicutt, Alan Alda as Hawkeye Pierce, Harry Morgan as Sherman Potter, and Gary Burghoff as Radar. *(Courtesy of Twentieth Century-Fox)*

drama, adventure drama, war drama, and so forth. In these, "drama" really meant "action" (itself a euphemism for "violence"), and producers saw no place for what they regarded as the comparatively dull, extremely limited action in family drama. After a numbing decade of cops, cowboys, and killings, the simple peace of personal family conflict began to appear quite attractive, at least for an occasional contrast. CBS gave *Playhouse 90* graduate Martin Manulis and writer Earl Hamner the go-ahead in 1969 to try such a theme and in October, 1969, *CBS Playhouse* presented "Appalachian Autumn." The story was set in modern times but focused on the experiences of a Vista volunteer working with a close-knit family in a poor Virginia mountain town. Watching the family deal with a devastating coal mine disaster, the volunteer learned that even though they were poor, the members of the mountain clan still retained enough strength and dignity to refuse to beg for help. Reviewers at the time praised the play and its theme, but pointed out that the dialogue was somewhat hokey. The criticism was tempered with encouragement; one reviewer observed, "All it needs is practice."

Just before Christmas, 1971, CBS presented another play with a strong Appalachian family theme, "The Homecoming." Earl Hamner was again the writer and another live drama great, Fielder Cook, served as the director. Hamner based the play on his own autobiography and set the scene in the time period of his own boyhood, the day before Christmas, 1933, in the home of a large poor family from rural Virginia, the Waltons. John Boy (Richard Thomas), the oldest son in the clan, acted as narrator for the story, which took the form of his personal reminiscence of that Depression-era Christmas. The gathering was very important to his own personal growth because it was the first time the family members faced the real possibility of losing John Walton (Andrew Duggan), the head of the family and provider for seven children, his wife Olivia (Patricia Neal), and his own parents (Edgar Bergen

and Ellen Corby). John had been caught in a bus wreck fifty miles from home, but that's all the news the rest of the family had received. As the play unfolded, each member came to grips with the significance of the potential tragedy and its far-reaching aftershocks. If the father was dead or even badly injured, it would be more than just the loss of a loved one; already financially pressed, the family would be pushed into a severe economic pinch. John Boy became acutely aware of his own responsibilities as the oldest son and went to the site of the accident to see if he could help his father, while the rest of the family waited, gripped by fear and trepidation. The story ended happily with the father, safe and sound, reunited with the family in a tearful, heartfelt welcome.

"The Homecoming's" straightforward, unembarrassed sentimentality touched a responsive nerve in the American psyche and the play was judged successful enough to be turned into a series. In spite of several major cast changes (Ralph Waite took the role of John Walton, Michael Learned the role of Olivia, and Will Geer the role of Grandpa Walton), *The Waltons* retained the strength of the Christmas special. The program was sometimes overly sentimental, but the characters carried their emotions well and a strong strain of reality woven through each episode tempered this tendency. Rather than degenerating into a maudlin tear-jerker soap opera, *The Waltons* emerged as a nostalgic re-creation of a much simpler era with clear-cut choices and obvious good guys and bad guys. Within this world, the strong cast presented their characters as proud, realistic people struggling through hard times. Even the Walton children were believable and, during the long run of the series, they grew up, became young adults, and began to move out on their own as America turned from a depression to a world war.

At its premiere in the fall of 1972, *The Waltons* was nearly buried by the competition. The program contained no action-packed gunplay, screeching tires, crime czars, or murder. Few viewers gave it a chance, preferring instead the flashy humor of black comedian Flip Wilson on NBC and the popular but routine gunplay of ABC's *Mod Squad*. Encouraged by some ecstatic reviews and hopeful demographic data, CBS stuck with *The Waltons* even though the program barely nudged the top fifty through the fall. Then slowly, very slowly, it began to catch on. By the spring, it beat Flip Wilson's show for the first time. Just before it went into reruns, the program reached the top ten.

Both *The Waltons* and *M*A*S*H* had been saved by demographics. With the networks beginning to focus on the makeup of the audience a program attracted rather than merely the total number of viewers, they allowed some shows more time to develop a following. Though shows that appealed to the *wrong* audience (too old, too rural) faced the prospect of a much quicker cancellation than before, the new priorities opened up television to the whims of affluent young adults and allowed the introduction of more daring themes to network entertainment programming. Previously, trying to reach the greatest number of people possible had precluded shows containing anything that anyone might have found offensive. The networks now dared to risk a few unusual themes designed to appeal to a particular segment of the audience. They were surprised to discover that sometimes these gambles paid off in high ratings as well.

On November 1, 1972, ABC's *Wednesday Movie of the Week* offered one of these innovative programs, the first straightforward, sympathetic portrayal of homosexuality on American television, the made-for-TV film, "That Certain Summer." Hal Holbrook played a building contractor and Martin Sheen a sound engineer, two very masculine figures, who became homosexual lovers. "That Certain Summer" avoided all the usual clichés and stereotypes of homosexual behavior and focused instead on the personal struggle of Holbrook's character as he tried to explain his lifestyle to his teenage son (by his former wife). Despite the complications the father decided to follow his own feelings and, while his son tried very hard to understand the radical alteration in his father, he couldn't quite accept it. There were no simple solutions offered nor glib putdowns presented. The program was simply a sensitive slice of life featuring normal people caught in a difficult situation yet trying to make the best of it. The program was also a ratings smash.

The networks could "get away" with such innovative entertainment fare because, as the ratings indicated, the public seemed more willing to accept it. At the same time, governmental watchdog Senator John Pastore had faded from view so, for the moment, there was no major anti-sex and violence advocate on the public scene to crusade against the networks. However, the situation was far different in the realm of public affairs. There, the Nixon administration carefully monitored the output from all of the networks and was ready to pounce on any item that presented something disturbing to the White House. Such situations seemed to occur more and more often as the administration, fresh from a landslide victory over Senator George McGovern in November, 1972, stepped up its attack on both commercial and public television. Richard Nixon was at the peak of his power and appeared ready to make the most of the situation.

Just one month after the election, Nixon aide Clay Whitehead delivered a stinging anti-network speech to the executives of local TV stations, spelling out the theories Vice President Spiro Agnew had only implied in his attacks three years before. Whitehead called for more pressure by local affiliates against the networks, especially in the area of news, urging them to delete the segments of the network feed that they didn't care for (which would, presumably,

be the same segments the administration didn't like). He labeled the networks' news and public affairs presentations as consisting chiefly of "elitist gossip" and "intellectual plugola." In exchange for more aggressive action, Whitehead dangled the prospect of affiliate station licenses that would be much more difficult to take away and also remain valid for five years (two years more than the law then allowed). Even ABC's Howard K. Smith, long a supporter of President Nixon, began to worry, saying, "It begins to look like a general assault on reporters."

With such a concerted campaign against them, it was understandable that the networks began to retreat from their aggressive pre-election news style. Nixon was clearly playing for keeps. Consequently, CBS announced the elimination of the well-publicized practice of "instant analysis" that usually followed presidential addresses and delayed its commentary until the next regularly scheduled news program. All three networks failed to present any news specials at all on the controversial Christmas bombings of North Vietnam that took place just a few weeks after Whitehead's speech.

Early in 1973, the administration negotiated a face-saving treaty with the North Vietnamese which ended direct American involvement in the war and secured the release of American prisoners of war. Yet the end of the combat did not mark an end to the pressure on the networks. Almost immediately, both the government and the public indicated that they wanted to put the memories and effects of the war behind them—instantly. Responding to this mood, CBS postponed the television adaptation of a timely new Broadway play concerning the return to the States of a blinded

As *Maude*, Beatrice Arthur freed middle-aged women from the stereotype of addlebrain. *(Tandem Productions, Inc.)*

Vietnam veteran, David Rabe's "Sticks and Bones." The production was a flawed but well-crafted and effective treatment of the gap between the returning soldier (ruined both mentally and physically by the war) and his peaches and cream family (unable to accept the way the war had changed him). Despite his desperate need for help and understanding, the soldier's family chose to virtually ignore him, vainly hoping that he would just disappear from their lives.

"Sticks and Bones" had been scheduled for Friday, March 9, as the second production in a series of thirteen specials for CBS by Joseph Papp's New York Shakespeare company (the first, "Much Ado About Nothing," had played in February), but then the network realized in horror that the program would air in the middle of the return of the real-life POWs from Vietnam. The drama was a far cry from the image the administration had cultivated for the men coming home and CBS decided its placement was inappropriate and rescheduled it for a later date. After all, President Nixon had billed the return of the POWs as a joyful celebration of the conclusion to the war and it seemed foolish to risk antagonizing him with the downbeat theme of the play. Papp was furious at the delay and canceled his four-year agreement with CBS, charging the network with censorship. CBS did air the play months later, stuck in the summer viewing ghetto (August 17) and without any commercials. Only 94 of the usual 200 CBS affiliates chose to air it and some delayed their telecast until late at night.

The situation was even worse over on public television, which found itself almost swallowed whole by the Nixon administration. The top two posts in public TV were held by Nixon appointees after the previous officials had been forced from office. Former Representative Thomas Curtis of Missouri was installed as chairman of the Corporation for Public Broadcasting, the organization that served as the liaison between the Public Broadcasting System and Congress, and Henry Loomis, a former deputy director of the U.S. Information Agency, was appointed president of CPB. Loomis seemed particularly insensitive to the concept of an activist approach to public broadcasting. During Congressional confirmation hearings, Loomis acknowledged that he had never seen an episode of *The Great American Dream Machine,* PBS's most important recent production, and could not even pick up the PBS affiliate in Washington because his set couldn't receive its UHF signal. His concept of "vital programming" topped even the uninterrupted coverage of the Republican convention in 1972. He announced that PBS would offer twenty-one hours of live coverage of the Apollo 17 moonshot in December of 1972, an expensive project that could only duplicate network broadcasts of a fairly dull expedition and would probably serve as nothing more than a good source of pro-administration publicity. Loomis was talked out of this particular proposal, but it was clear that public broadcasting's priorities had been hopelessly distorted as it was placed firmly under the thumb of the administration. It was at this particularly gruesome stage that the Watergate scandal broke into the news and things began to change.

The break-in at the Democratic National Committee's Washington offices in the Watergate building had taken place back in June of 1972, but through the summer and beyond election day, most people had accepted the administration's dismissal of it as a "third rate burglary." Democratic presidential candidate George McGovern had tried to make it a campaign issue by contending that the Nixon administration was tied in with the burglars, but most people dismissed that as a desperate political ploy by a candidate hopelessly behind in the polls. *Washington Post* reporters Bob

Woodward and Carl Bernstein had turned out a steady stream of stories also suggesting a tie-in between the White House and the burglary but, without substantial documentation, no one cared. Television virtually ignored the story. CBS was the only network to do anything important with Watergate before the election, scheduling two fifteen-minute reports on the topic for Walter Cronkite's evening news show during the last week of the campaign. Most Americans were indifferent to the story but, after viewing the first report, presidential aide Charles Colson tried to pressure CBS chairman William Paley into canceling the second report. The second story aired anyway, despite Colson's efforts, though it was cut in half.

In March, 1973, the Senate set up a select committee, under Senator Sam Ervin of North Carolina, to look into the numerous charges of impropriety that had been raised by then. The committee scheduled public hearings for the spring and summer and the networks were faced with a familiar, perplexing problem: What was the best way to cover congressional hearings on a topic that was suddenly very important? They feared that the procedure might drag on for months and gavel-to-gavel coverage would cost a small fortune in lost revenue, estimated at $300,000 per network per day. All three broadcast the opening week's sessions in May and then they agreed to a simple but practical solution: They would rotate coverage. Each day, one network would take its turn showing the hearings while the other two maintained their normal schedules—though they both had the option to carry the session as well if they wished to. This wonderfully obvious solution satisfied nearly everybody. People who didn't care about Watergate could find a soap opera or game show on another network. No one network was backed into a corner and forced to carry the burden alone. Viewers who were interested in the hearings were guaranteed that one network (at least) would have the story. For public television, however, the problem was not so easily resolved.

As soon as the hearings were announced, the administration put strong pressure on PBS stations, discouraging live coverage. For awhile it looked as if the tactic might succeed, but the audacity of the action struck some of the larger stations as going too far. WETA in Washington, WGBH in Boston, WNET in New York, KCET in Los Angeles, and KQED in San Francisco staged their own counter-revolution and formed the so-called salvation network, a group determined to oppose White House efforts to control public television. In April, forces from the salvation network seized control of the PBS board and immediately launched an attack on the Nixon-controlled CPB parent organization. This counter-pressure led to an attempt to reach a compromise, with Tom Curtis acting as chief negotiator, but the CPB board rejected the truce proposal. Curtis resigned as CPB chairman, charging that his efforts had been undermined by administration interference. Board member James Killian, who had been appointed by President Johnson, assumed the post of CPB chairman as an official with no obvious ties to the White House. In spite of continued administration pressure to prevent coverage of the hearings, the newly rejuvenated PBS decided instead to provide extensive coverage, using its Washington-based production agency, NPACT, the National Public Affairs Center for Television (responsible for such programs as *Washington Week in Review*). Via NPACT, PBS sent out both gavel-to-gavel daytime coverage and, more importantly, taped replays in prime time. The evening rebroadcasts, hosted by Robert MacNeil and Jim Lehrer, allowed millions of working people the opportunity to see the actual hearings virtually intact and to judge for themselves the importance of what had taken place that day.

Just as in the Army-McCarthy hearings of 1954, interest in the

Watergate hearings was low at first, but picked up as the public became familiar with the personalities involved and began to appreciate the gravity of the charges. All through the summer, major figures from the administration appeared before the committee. Some confessed to minor infractions while others "stonewalled" and denied any wrongdoing whatsoever. At the end of June, former Nixon counsel John Dean testified for five consecutive days, laying out the most detailed, damaging charges of the summer in which he stated his belief that President Nixon had not only known of the cover-up, but had probably directed it. All three commercial networks chose to cover his testimony and the public was inundated with Watergate stories. The continuing characters of the Ervin committee became national celebrities, with the Bible-quoting Southern drawl of Senator Ervin himself the biggest hit of all. Catch phrases such as "At that point in time," "To the best of my recollection," and "Deep-six" wound their way from witnesses's testimony to become common slang across the nation.

Much to the amazement of the networks, the usual summer dropoff in TV viewing never took place. People couldn't seem to get enough of Watergate. In response, NBC began to include a weekly two-hour Watergate wrapup in prime time every Friday. CBS averaged three sixty-minute prime time wrapups each week, covering the days the other networks handled the daytime rotation. The prime time PBS coverage brought in staggeringly high ratings for public television stations across the country, with some almost reaching the level of a low-rated commercial network show. Daytime coverage regularly topped the game shows and soap operas offered by the other networks, which turned out to be no competition to the real-life drama unfolding every day as the committee (and the public) tried to answer the question: What did the President know and when did he know it? On July 16, the investigation reached a dramatic high point as former Nixon aide Alexander Butterfield revealed that an elaborate secret taping system had been set up in the White House and that there were probably recordings of the many meetings and conversations that had been cited throughout the committee's hearings. The committee requested access to the tapes. President Nixon refused to release them. One month later, after hearing from almost everyone involved in White House affairs, the Ervin committee adjourned for a fall vacation. The networks returned to their normal broadcasting schedules and prepared to launch the 1973–74 season.

Technically, the months of testimony had produced no tangible results or hard evidence. Those who ardently believed in Nixon's innocence remained unconvinced by the testimony. Even those who felt that the entire administration, from Nixon on down, had been proved guilty many times over acknowledged that there didn't appear to be enough clear evidence that could be used to support a vote for impeachment by the House and a trial by the Senate. In reality, though, the testimony resulted in a monumental change in attitude among the American people. Public confidence in the President had plummetted during the televised hearings. The Ervin committee had presided over a struggle for the hearts and minds of the American public similar to the Army-McCarthy hearings two decades before. Once again, television had expanded the forum and allowed the entire nation, as one, to examine a vital issue. Though it still seemed that Nixon would be around for "four more years," he had lost his most powerful tool, the confidence of the nation. He might still be President, but he was no longer in a position to make the press jump.

33. The New Centurions

THE TIMING of the Senate Watergate hearings in the summer of 1973 had been perfect for the networks. Not only did the proceedings end just in time to avoid interfering with the fall premieres, they also helped fill the void in a summer schedule that was leaner than usual. As the result of a three and one-half month strike by television writers in the spring of 1973, program production had ground to a halt. There was an obvious absence of new material for the summer months and the networks relied on news specials and reruns of old series to carry them through to the fall. The major effect of the strike, though, was felt in September.

Most programs airing in September normally began preproduction work in March, immediately after the networks announced the next fall's schedule. Filming followed in June and most series were ready well before the early September premiere week. The writers' strike didn't end until June, so the entire process was thrown off. Despite the frantic work by the writers and crews all through the summer of 1973 once the strike was settled, there just wasn't enough time. Consequently, the networks were forced to ease into the 1973–74 season and, for the first time in a decade, their season premieres had to be strung out over a month. The new series and new episodes of returning programs were aired as they came in. Hastily assembled specials and more reruns filled the remaining gaps. Amid this confusion, CBS was pleasantly surprised with the high ratings scored by *Dan August,* a loner cop series starring Burt Reynolds, which had flopped on ABC in 1970. CBS had picked it up as just another writers' strike filler for the summer, but the program outscored not only the other summer reruns but even some new fall series as well. *Dan August* remained on the air long enough to serve as a strong warmup for the program that was delayed the longest by the writers' strike, another cop show, *Kojak,* which didn't premiere until October 24, the last new series of 1973–74 to arrive.

There were high hopes for *Kojak* among critics and programmers who built their expectations on the quality of the feature-length pilot that had aired the previous March, "The Marcus-Nelson Murders." The three-hour TV film, based on the real life Wylie-Hoffert murder case in New York City, introduced Telly Savalas as Lieutenant Theo Kojak, a radiantly bald, fiercely independent Greek plainclothes detective on the New York City force who fought the establishment he worked for—and lost. Savalas had spent the better part of his career playing an assortment of criminal roles and he

brought a gritty edge to his portrayal of the tough realistic cop. In the pilot, Kojak saw the methods the police had used to railroad a black Brooklyn kid, falsely accused of rape, into confessing to a completely unrelated crime, a double-murder, and he set about to prove the confession baseless. After tedious legwork by Kojak and a lengthy trial, the youth was exonerated of the murders and Kojak joined the happy family to celebrate. Their triumph was short lived. Determined to salvage some "law and order" publicity, the police and prosecutors resurrected the original rape charge and forced the boy back into court to defend himself. Though technically a different case, it was really the same trial all over again, only the prosecution had refined its presentation while the boy, shocked at the turn of events, had lost his confidence and composure. Stunned, Kojak watched helplessly as a new jury delivered a verdict of guilty. The boy was sent to jail and, this time, there was no last minute reprieve. Kojak had been outmaneuvered and couldn't do anything to change things—even his own resignation would have been meaningless. He remained at his post, keenly aware of his own limitations but determined to continue the sometimes hopeless fight for justice.

"The Marcus-Nelson Murders" set very high standards for the series and it soon became apparent that the exceptionally late premiere date reflected time well spent in production. Though it made concessions to the reality of the weekly TV grind (Kojak usually *won* his new cases), the program was the best scripted, directed, and acted cop show on TV, and it maintained the spirit of the highly praised pilot. Kojak remained the people's champion, confident, tough, and willing to defend neighborhoods and individuals battered by crime and injustice. In addition, the writers expanded on some themes implicit in the pilot: In the Seventies, the easily understood and clearly identified mobsters and crime czars of the past had been replaced in the public's mind by more amorphous, but equally frightening, forces. Criminals were often violent madmen and urban delinquents with no stake in society and who attacked randomly for no discernible reason. Even worse, the machinery of justice itself seemed to break down with increasing frequency, often looming as a greater threat than the criminals it was supposed to punish. Kojak was presented as a reassuring figure capable of taking on both of these elements. He was cool under pressure, streetwise, and always in control. At the same time, he was too smart to let his distrust of the bureaucracy blind him to the most effective ways to use it. Kojak could confront a self-serving bureaucrat and a trigger-happy punk with the same unflinching determination, never wasting his anger on meaningless macho stunts. He out-maneuvered his opponents, waited for the perfect moment, and then exploded. When Kojak let loose, his personal energy crackled. He obviously enjoyed both his verbal and physical confrontations because they sometimes provided the only opportunity for justice to triumph. Savalas infused Kojak with a saucy independent personality that dominated the program and gave the scripts added punch. His portrayal of the confident bald man who brandished a lollipop instead of a cigar turned him into a very unlikely national sex symbol and attracted viewers that otherwise had only mild interest in cop shows.

The most controversial aspect of Kojak, however, was its use of violence, and some people brushed aside the excellent acting, writing, and directing to denounce the show as dangerous and harmful. Actually, there was a noticeable upswing in violent action throughout the networks' crime formats this season, reflecting the popularity of violent theatrical cop films such as "The French Connection." Kojak admittedly contained its share of violence, but the writers and producers handled it well. Just as The Untouchables had used violent shoot-outs to underscore the brutality of gangland activity in the Thirties, Kojak used violence as an artful illustration of the frustration of the Seventies. The entire program was as carefully controlled as Kojak himself, with violent interludes used to punctuate the conflicts and emotions. To ignore violence in a program that attempted to present a gritty, realistic picture of New York City urban crime contradicted its very premise. Nonetheless, over the years the level of violent action in the program was reduced somewhat in response to protests from organized pressure groups strongly opposed to TV violence in any form, no matter how artistically effective. In order to restore some of the lost energy in later years, the producers tried to compensate in other ways, such as filming on location in New York City to accentuate the urban atmosphere of the program.

Kojak became an immediate hit in the fall of 1973 and the newest star in a solid line-up of crime programs on all three networks. For decades, such shows had served as basic bread-and-butter programming, occasionally slumping due to overexposure or claims of excessive violence, but inevitably returning with some slight twist, unusual setting, gimmick hero, or outstanding performer as a new draw. Network number one, CBS, for instance, always liked to mix in a few crime dramas with its sitcom strategy because while hit sitcoms scored very well, flopped sitcoms were equally big losers, landing at the very bottom of the ratings charts. Crime shows usually hugged the middle positions in the ratings, turning in a generally stable if not outstanding performance. There were ten new crime shows in the fall of 1973 and, as evidenced by Kojak, the loner cop format was still on the upswing that had begun in the 1971–72 season. Many of the new entries were obvious imitations of the latest gimmick variations to the form. In the 1972–73 season, veteran Buddy Ebsen had taken his down-home country charm into the fight against urban crime in Quinn Martin's Barnaby Jones, and the show had become a second season CBS hit. In the fall of 1973, veteran lowkey charmers Jimmy Stewart and Lorne Greene tried their hands in, respectively, Hawkins (a common sense criminal attorney) and Griff (an L.A. private eye), but they both flopped. Banacek, another hit show from the previous season, had featured a more off-beat ethnic hero—a dapper Polish insurance company detective played by George Peppard. In the usually WASP world of TV cops, such a character was a rarity and, sure enough, several other ethnic detectives appeared along

with Kojak in the fall of 1973. With the exception of Kojak, however, most of these programs had serious inherent flaws and floundered in the ratings despite the ethnic hook.

There was already an obvious model for the new black TV detectives in the wildly successful black Superman-type that appeared in such theatrical films as "Superfly" and "Shaft." NBC's Tenafly consciously avoided this image while CBS brought Shaft himself to network television. Both interpretations left viewers with the uncomfortable feeling that something was missing. In the case of Shaft, it seemed obvious. Despite the fact that the film's star, Richard Roundtree, repeated the title role of New York City private detective John Shaft for the TV series, he had to leave his violent, sexy world behind. Instead, Shaft was given a carbon copy of Columbo's structure in which, at the beginning of each episode, the crime was shown as it took place and the rest of the story focused on Shaft's investigation. Unlike Columbo, who talked the villains to death, Shaft had always depended on direct, violent methods of persuasion, but all the tough talk, blazing gun battles, and beautiful women had to be sanitized for television. Yet the program's problem was more basic than that—Shaft was already played out. The original "Shaft" film had depended on a unique combination of stylistic devices and shock tactics to overcome a weak plot and generally unimpressive acting. It was a brutal story of revenge that gleefully celebrated the hero's legitimate distaste for whites, but it was also a formula that worked well only once. Two theatrical followups ("Shaft's Big Score" and "Shaft in Africa") had demonstrated that both the character and the plot devices could not hold up to repeated exploitation. By the time Roundtree began Shaft's television adventures, he was already just a pale imitation of himself, and it showed.

Telly Savalas as Theo Kojak, a dedicated police detective who brandished a lollipop instead of a cigar. (From Kojak. Courtesy of MCA Television Limited)

MONDAY — Times: 7:30, 8:00, 8:30, 9:00, 9:30, 10:00, 10:30

	7:30	8:00	8:30	9:00	9:30	10:00	10:30	
	local	The Rookies		ABC NFL Monday Night Football [to 12 Midnite]				ABC
	local	Gunsmoke		Here's Lucy	New Dick Van Dyke Show	Medical Center		CBS
	local	LOTSA LUCK	DIANA	NBC Monday Night At The Movies				NBC

TUESDAY

	7:30	8:00	8:30	9:00	9:30	10:00	10:30	
	local	New Temperature's Rising Show	Tuesday Movie Of The Week			Marcus Welby, M.D.		ABC
	local	Maude	Hawaii Five-O	The New CBS Tuesday Night Movies — SHAFT / HAWKINS				CBS
	local	CHASE		THE MAGICIAN		POLICE STORY		NBC

WEDNESDAY

	7:30	8:00	8:30	9:00	9:30	10:00	10:30	
	local	BOB AND CAROL AND TED AND ALICE	Wednesday Movie Of The Week			Owen Marshall, Counselor At Law @DOC ELLIOT		ABC
	local	Sonny And Cher Comedy Hour		Cannon		KOJAK		CBS
	local	Adam-12	NBC Wednesday Mystery Movie (Banacek, TENAFLY, FARADAY AND CO., SNOOP SISTERS)			LOVE STORY		NBC

THURSDAY

	7:30	8:00	8:30	9:00	9:30	10:00	10:30	
	local	TOMA		Kung Fu		Streets Of San Francisco		ABC
	local	The Waltons		CBS Thursday Night Movies				CBS
	local	Flip Wilson Show		Ironside @Bob Hope Show		NBC FOLLIES		NBC

FRIDAY

	7:30	8:00	8:30	9:00	9:30	10:00	10:30	
	local	The Brady Bunch	The Odd Couple	Room 222	ADAM'S RIB	Love, American Style		ABC
	local	CALUCCI'S DEPARTMENT	ROLL OUT	CBS Friday Night Movies				CBS
	local	Sanford And Son	THE GIRL WITH SOMETHING EXTRA	NEEDLES AND PINS	Brian Keith Show	Dean Martin Comedy Hour		NBC

SATURDAY

	7:30	8:00	8:30	9:00	9:30	10:00	10:30	
	local	The Partridge Family	ABC SUSPENSE MOVIE @SIX MILLION DOLLAR MAN			GRIFF		ABC
	local	All In The Family	M*A*S*H	Mary Tyler Moore	Bob Newhart Show	Carol Burnett Show		CBS
	local	Emergency!		NBC Saturday Night At The Movies				NBC

SUNDAY — Times: 7:00, 7:30, 8:00, 8:30, 9:00, 9:30, 10:00, 10:30

	7:00	7:30	8:00	8:30	9:00	9:30	10:00	10:30	
	local	The F.B.I.		The ABC Sunday Night Movie			local		ABC
	local	NEW ADVENTURES OF PERRY MASON		Mannix		Barnaby Jones		local	CBS
	local	The Wonderful World of Disney		NBC Sunday Mystery Movie (McCloud, Columbo, McMillan And Wife, Hec Ramsey)			local @NBC Reports [10:00–11:00]		NBC

NBC's *Tenafly* tried so hard to avoid the simplistic dead-end clichés of the black superdudes that it went too far in the other direction. Richard Levinson and William Link, the team responsible for *Columbo,* presented private detective Harry Tenafly (James McEachin) as just a regular Joe, an average family man with few exciting or distinguishing characteristics. Each episode of the series devoted nearly as much time to his middle class home life and family (a wife and two children) as to the case at hand. Tenafly was not so much an Oreo character (black on the outside, all white inside) as just plain bland. Though characters such as Superfly were two-dimensional caricatures, they were, at least, undeniably exciting.

One ethnic series that did manage to bring the world of violent exploitation movies to television with some success was ABC's *Toma,* loosely based on the exploits of Dave Toma (played by Tony Musante), an actual undercover Italian policeman from Newark, New Jersey. Though the stories made superficial nods to real life drama (Toma had a home life and was shown in bed with his wife), they had none of the class of *Kojak* and resorted instead to cheap violence, brutal sex, and Toma's foul mouth. This was accomplished within the confines of television through implication; the audience was shown everything except the violent acts themselves. For example, one episode featured a kinky rapist with a talcum powder fetish. His frenzied attacks were conveyed by vivid closeups of each victim's face, flashes of talcum powder, and screams, grunts, and gasps which built to a ferocious climax. Without focusing on anything more explicit than the look of terror on the woman's face, these scenes could satisfy a viewer's voyeuristic fantasies nearly as well as the more explicit brutality of the theatrical films. *Toma* also captured the spirit of the abusive language of these films with snarling putdowns such as "If that hooker of yours doesn't shut her mouth, I'll stuff it full of dead fish." *Kojak* proved that television violence could be done artistically and used it to reinforce generally realistic themes and settings. *Toma* did not bother with such complexities. It too often embraced some of the worst features of the era's cheap violent formula films: degrading characters, offensive plots, and rancid dialogue. The series was roundly panned by critics and viewers alike, and, even with its ethnic and violent hooks, *Toma* lasted only one season.

Ethnic detectives were, of course, just another strain in the continuing crime format boom. As in most fads, a rash of them appeared over a few seasons, a few outstanding ones survived, and then another gimmick surfaced. The crime genre was so resilient because, within the gimmick setups, countless minor variations could be incorporated into the same plots. Innovations that led to an entirely new approach to crime were rare. Jack Webb's presentation of policemen as intricate professionals using brains, not brawn, had been such a dramatic departure in the Fifties. Its after-effects were still being felt in television twenty years later when it stood as a television staple. In 1973–74, another such fundamental change in the portrayal of policework occurred at the hands of Joseph Wambaugh, a Los Angeles policeman who moonlighted as a very successful writer. (His police novel, *The New Centurions*, had been turned into a feature film.)

Over the years, the incessant repetition of Webb's stock characters had turned his innovation into a cliché of its own. Cops in programs such as *Adam-12* had become monotonous automatons that talked in clipped phrases and never seemed to entertain an evil thought. Wambaugh knew better. There were bad cops, good cops who made terrible mistakes in judgment, and outstanding officers who performed brilliantly under tremendous pressure. He felt each of the categories offered the potential for rich drama, so he created an anthology series for NBC, *Police Story*, in order to exploit these possibilities. By adopting the anthology format, Wambaugh freed himself from the limitations of one central character who couldn't possibly incorporate every nuance of police action and remain creditable. Instead, he used different guest celebrities in weekly stories that dealt with every aspect of policework. They all shared a sharp, realistic style of dialogue (which was a welcome change from Webb's officialese) as well as an affection for the common cop on the beat who, despite his faults, was usually presented as doing the best job possible. *Police Story* opened a rich new field of police drama that focused on more realistic characters who also faced personal problems that sometimes affected their on-the-job performance. As with any innovative series, *Police Story* caught on very slowly. Though it never became a big hit, it continued in the tradition of TV's best cop shows, delivering solid dependable ratings in its time slot while inspiring a number of spinoffs and imitations such as *Police Woman, Joe Forrester,* and *David Cassidy—Man Undercover.*

Even as he launched his anthology series, Wambaugh was hard at work on another innovative project, a four-part miniseries focusing on the career of one cop, Bumper Morgan (William Holden), who was rapidly approaching retirement age. *The Blue Knight* ostensibly traced the investigation following the murder of a prostitute, but the crux of the story was Morgan's battle with advancing age. He painfully acknowledged that he was too old to do all the legwork necessary to the case, but he insisted that, mentally, he was just as sharp as ever. In any case, he feared retirement because he knew he wasn't ready to cope with such a drastic change in this life. The program was an extended display of Wambaugh's cop philosophy and could have easily played on consecutive weeks of *Police Story* as a series within the series. Instead, NBC ran the four-hour drama on four consecutive nights beginning Tuesday, November 13, in a bold experiment that marked a breakthrough in television programming. Reactions ranged from mild surprise to outright ridicule. Some people snidely suggested that such a programming decision demanded far too much attention from home viewers to succeed. The ratings from the miniseries proved somewhat inconclusive. *The Blue Knight* averaged a 30% share of the audience which, while respectable, was no vindication of the concept. It was left to ABC with its two-part presentation of *QB VII* at the end of April to prove the concept could be very successful.

QB VII was a six-hour adaptation of the lengthly Leon Uris novel that followed the post-war life of a Polish doctor who had performed experiments on inmates in a Nazi concentration camp. Part one focused on the war trial of the doctor while part two examined his life through 1972. The first episode attracted a healthy 38% share and the following night's wrapup did even better, winding up the fifth highest rated show of the week. Buoyed by this

success, ABC announced plans for the presentation of multi-part adaptations of other major works such as *Rich Man, Poor Man, Eleanor and Franklin,* and the as-then unpublished *Roots.* The network had been mumbling about "novels for television" ever since *Peyton Place* and the disastrous Harold Robbins series of 1969, *The Survivors,* but the success of *QB VII* and *The Blue Knight* convinced ABC that the development of several miniseries could provide occasional boosts to ratings in much the same manner as blockbuster movies such as "Bridge on the River Kwai" and "Airport."

ABC was still patching together a prime time schedule that included just about anything that might hype ratings, even on a one-shot basis, because it had once again begun slipping from contention. In many ways, the situation was reminiscent of the network's woes in the mid-Sixties when it instituted the attention-grabbing concepts of an early premiere week and the second season. The major difference was that few such tactics were left. Even the "third season" that was possible with the Nielsen company's new "overnight" ratings service didn't have the popular impact of the previous gimmicks.

ABC had again repeated one of its most frequent programming sins, loading its schedule with too many spinoffs of a hit gimmick, thus diluting its strength. Made-for-TV movie slots occupied the greater part of three nights of the network schedule, but they were no longer sure-fire ratings winners. In addition, attempts to exploit the new strain of sitcoms pioneered by CBS proved disastrous in such series as *Adam's Rib* and *Bob and Carol and Ted and Alice.* ABC's highest rated show (18th) was its *Monday Night Football* broadcast. Its greatest individual successes came in the form of

In the world of super-hero pulp adventures, ABC's *The Six Million Dollar Man* starred Lee Majors. (*From* The Six Million Dollar Man. *Courtesy of MCA Television Limited*)

sports-related programs, comic book-type heroes, and sexual innuendo. For example, in its made-for-TV movie slots, ABC regularly presented stories of prostitution, homosexuality, bigamy, and rape, a line-up best described as tabloid television.

ABC realized very early in the season that it might be possible to combine sex appeal with one of the few areas in which the network was a respected leader, sports, and so it filled one of the writers' strike gaps in September with "Tennis—The Battle of the Sexes." This silly "confrontation" between fifty-five-year-old over-the-hill tennis boor Bobby Riggs and up-and-coming twenty-nine-year-old Billie Jean King was no contest (King won easily), but ABC treated the match with the same intense coverage television usually reserved for such events as the World Series or political nominating conventions. The fluff contest was set, appropriately, in the 100% artificial Houston Astrodome, in prime time, and ballyhooed as the monumental resolution of the perpetual battle between men and women. In order to insure a "balanced" presentation of such an important event, the network assigned one male and one female to serve as color commentators. They supplemented the "play-by-play" reporting by the front line team of Frank Gifford and Howard Cosell, whose malapropisms (such as "making assurance doubly sure") were particularly humorous that night. Despite strong counterprogramming by CBS, "The Battle of the Sexes" registered lovely ratings for ABC and demonstrated the viability of sexual hooks and pseudo sports events. The show also pointed to a general formula that the network had decided to exploit.

With CBS cornering the audience for reality-oriented programs, ABC chose to concentrate on the fantasy world of tabloids and pulp adventure as its antidote to the ratings strength of the competi-

tion. The network's brightest hopes were two larger-than-life heroic caricatures, Kwai Chang Caine and Steve Austin.

Caine's adventures had begun in the 1972–73 season on a once a month series, *Kung-Fu.* David Carradine played a one-half Chinese, one-half American martial arts master who roamed the American West of the 1870s as a veritable Jove of Justice in a premise that mixed bits of *The Fugitive,* "Lost Horizon," and "Billy Jack." Like *The Fugitive* he was on the run, having fled China after deliberately (but in his eyes, justifiably) killing a member of the Royal Family. His thoughts frequently returned to the rigorous training of his youth in far away China as he attempted to serve the cause of justice in the lawless West. Caine took himself very, very seriously, spouting Oriental wisdom and platitudes of peace in the preachy self-righteous style of Tom Laughlin's Billy Jack. He was a bona-fide priest within his obscure Oriental religious sect that preached non-violence, and there wasn't anything resembling a flaw presented in his character. All of this effluvia was a mask, however, for a scrumptiously violent program in the tradition of ABC's action-adventure sagas. Despite his "best efforts" to avoid violent confrontations, Caine constantly ran into nasty villains that had to be disposed of, prompting one reviewer to describe the show as: "Pacifist vegetarian priest beats the holy bejeezus out of frontier bullies." The fights were presented in slow motion, adding to the comic caricature style of the program. In early 1973, *Kung-Fu* was promoted to a weekly slot, though it didn't become a hit until late in the year. The program displayed enough promise in its first season, however, to encourage ABC to approve development of a somewhat similar project for the 1973–74 season, *The Six Million Dollar Man.*

Like *Kung-Fu,* the new series began in the fall as a once a month series and, by January 1974, it was awarded weekly status. The show moved the slow motion battle scenes from the past to the immediate future, featuring the exploits of Steve Austin (Lee Majors), an astronaut who had been horribly crushed in an Air Force jet crash. Rescued from the rubble, he was reconstructed at great government expense (six million dollars) and outfitted with nuclear powered limbs that gave him powers and abilities far beyond those of most mortal men, in an effective update of the ever-popular Superman legend. Unlike *Kung-Fu,* the scripts for *The Six Million Dollar Man* were not burdened with excessive simplistic philosophical preaching. Austin willingly joined the government's Office of Strategic Operations (a thinly disguised CIA-style organization) and fought America's enemies at home and abroad in the best tradition of such wartime comic book patriots as Captain America. The show delivered exciting fantasy and demonstrated that airy comic book television could be done well. When ABC moved Austin into a weekly slot as part of the 1973–74 mid-season shakeup, *The Six Million Dollar Man* became the network's top rated show.

The second season shuffling also resulted in another welcome hit for ABC, the nostalgic *Happy Days* (produced by Garry Marshall, who had adapted *The Odd Couple* for television). As its name implied, *Happy Days* turned from the grim reality of the turbulent early Seventies to the simple rituals of teenage life in the already legendary Fifties. *Andy Griffith Show* veteran Ron Howard played cute-but-shy Richie Cunningham, a very average, very bland teenager living in the very bland city of Milwaukee with his nondescript family: a kind and bumbling father (Tom Bosley), a cardboard mother (Marion Ross), and a cute-but-devilish younger sister, Joanie (Erin Moran). The sitcom usually focused on the escapades of Richie and his bosom buddy, Potsie Weber (Anson Williams), two struggling high school innocents who shared teenage fantasies about sock hops, girls, and hot rods. The *Happy Days*

Richard Nixon prepares to board the helicopter that will take him to Air Force One: (from *l.*) Vice President Gerald Ford, Betty Ford, Pat Nixon, and President Nixon. *(National Archives)*

pilot episode had run on *Love, American Style* in February, 1972, and the show's premise was far removed from the new wave of comedy of CBS, led by Norman Lear's stable of characters. Nonetheless, *Happy Days* immediately entered the top twenty, right behind *The Six Million Dollar Man* in the ratings.

Happy Days owed much of its initial success to momentum from the theatrical film "American Graffiti" (the surprise blockbuster of 1973), in which Howard (the only cast member carried over to the TV series) had played Steve Bolander, a character very similar to Richie Cunningham. Unlike the film, though, the TV series lacked a strong central character (such as Richard Dreyfuss's Curt Henderson) to carry the plots. Howard's Richie was made far too weak and Potsie was a klutz. There was a token hood, Fonzie (Henry Winkler), similar to the John Milner character of the film (played by Paul LeMat), but unlike LeMat, Winkler had only a minor role in the stories.

Happy Days presented itself as an entertaining relic of the less troubled Fifties, but in reality the program failed to rise above the simplistic humor of its nondescript setting, settling into the mold of the Archie and Jughead comic strip or the Aldrich Family radio show. Just as ABC's *Roaring Twenties* had relied completely on the outward trappings of period topicality to carry the entire series, *Happy Days* settled for the increasingly popular revisionist interpretation of the Fifties as an era filled with jive-talking pseudo-juvenile delinquents, mindless adults, and prophetic rock'n'rollers. Viewers found the revamped image easy to comprehend and a convenient substitute for the rapidly fading memories of the bygone era.

Happy Days began to mythologize the Fifties just as two real relics of the era were passing from the scene. They both owed their success to television and both had continued to use it successfully for two decades. Only one went out in triumph.

After twenty-three years of almost continuous production, Lucille Ball gave up the weekly TV grind forever. She had taken her character through several different settings, but the format had remained the same for all of them: wacky redhead against the world. The final permutation, *Here's Lucy,* featured her real-life children as co-stars (Lucie and Desi Arnaz, Jr.) and it was a highly appropriate way for the original queen of television to depart—alongside the young man whose birth had marked the beginning of modern TV. Lucy ended her sitcom run with style and class. Her contemporary, Richard M. Nixon, had experienced an equally long (though considerably rockier) television career, but he left his profession in shame and disgrace.

The Ervin committee had adjourned in August of 1973 and it appeared that President Nixon would have a breathing spell after months of public inquiry. Instead, a new unrelated scandal rocked his administration, touching the one man who had gone through Watergate unscathed, Vice President Sprio Agnew. An investigation into general corruption in Maryland led to allegations of brib-

January 31, 1974
"The Autobiography of Miss Jane Pittman." (CBS). Richard Rosenberg and Robert Christiansen adapt a successful novel into a powerful television drama special spanning black American history from slavery to the civil rights marches. Cicely Tyson portrays Jane Pittman, a proud black woman, in four stages of her life: from young womanhood to the age of 110. The highly praised program wins nine Emmy Awards.

February 1, 1974
Sally Quinn quietly departs *The CBS Morning News,* confessing that she was not really prepared for the job.

April 17, 1974
Frank McGee, fifty-two, host of NBC's *Today,* dies of cancer.

July 4, 1974
Bicentennial Minute. (CBS). The first sixty-second program in television history. Once each night, for more than two years, a celebrity reports on "the way it was" in American history on that date 200 years earlier.

July 29, 1974
Jim Hartz becomes the new host of *Today.*

September 2, 1974
After starring in a CBS television series for twenty-one of the previous twenty-three years, Lucille Ball calls it quits. *Here's Lucy* joins *The Lucy Show* and *I Love Lucy* in the never-ending world of reruns.

ABC's *Toma* was loosely based on the real-life exploits of an undercover Italian-American policeman from Newark, New Jersey: (from *l.*) Tony Musante, Simon Oakland, and Susan Strasberg. (*From* Toma. *Courtesy of MCA Television Limited*)

ery payments to Agnew going back to the days when he had served as the Baltimore county executive. Determined to meet the challenge to his integrity head on, Agnew embarked upon a nationwide speaking tour in the hope of stirring his supporters into pressuring the Maryland prosecutor to call off his dogs. An old hand at manipulating television, Agnew knew his rhetoric would make news and he convinced NBC to carry, nationwide, a speech before a group of Republican women in California on September 29. Looking straight into the camera without batting an eye (as only an honest person could), Agnew proclaimed, "I will not resign if indicted! I will *not* resign if indicted!" On October 10, Agnew resigned, pleading *nolo contendere* ("no contest," an equivalent to guilty) to charges of tax evasion on the bribery payments made to him by Maryland contractors. He was sentenced to three years' probation and fined $10,000. Five days after Agnew's resignation, all three commercial networks, for the first time in history, gave thirty minutes of free prime time to a convicted felon charged with extortion, bribery, and conspiracy. In this last appearance before the public, Agnew ignored his *nolo contendere* plea and pronounced himself innocent. NBC's legal correspondent, Carl Stern, was incredulous and, in the network analysis immediately following the speech, compared Agnew's courtroom admissions of guilt with his TV plea to be judged innocent. Stern pointed out that the two-faced stance wasn't supported by the facts. CBS allowed Agnew's speech to stand on its own, though, as the network continued to exclude instant analysis from its news operations.

Agnew's case had nothing to do with Watergate, but it furthered the perception of total corruption waiting to be unearthed in the Nixon administration. Ten days after Agnew's resignation, Nixon

fired Archibald Cox, the special Watergate prosecutor. This touched off the first serious calls for the President's impeachment.

In mid-November, following publication of an old memo in which Nixon aide Charles Colson bragged of intimidating CBS chairman William Paley, CBS sheepishly announced it would immediately resume providing analysis following Presidential addresses. PBS also exhibited a renewed independence and presented some new public affairs programming such as the excellent "Essay on Watergate" on *Bill Moyers' Journal,* a fair but opinionated one-hour primer on the complex and sometimes confusing events of Watergate. On the evening news shows, new sources of suspicion constantly appeared before the public. Seven top White House aides were indicted for their role in the coverup. One of the tapes Nixon was pressured into releasing contained a mysterious $18\frac{1}{2}$-minute gap during a key conversation. The possibility was even raised that Nixon had deliberately claimed illegal deductions on his income tax.

As he had done so often throughout his career, Nixon turned to television as a means of appealing directly to the people and possibly blunting negative sentiment building against him. President Nixon went on a nation-wide speaking tour and the networks covered, live, his appearances before sympathetic audiences and he scored a few minor points. Nixon was obviously feeling the pressure, however, and openly sniped at reporters and the commercial networks during the tour. At one televised press conference he nervously exclaimed, "I am not a crook." At another, he pointed out that he wasn't really angry at the press because "you can only be angry at those you respect." On April 29, 1974, the President at last delivered his first truly effective television speech on Watergate. Pleading with the nation to move on to more important business and put Watergate aside ("One year of Watergate is enough"), Nixon proudly displayed a huge stack of notebooks which contained hundreds of pages of edited transcripts from most of the White House tapes that had been requested by the courts and by the House impeachment committee. He explained that the unprecedented disclosure of private presidential conversations demonstrated his willingness to cooperate in the various investigations and proved he had nothing to hide. It was a very successful speech, but its positive effects quickly dissipated as people examined the text of the transcripts.

Television's treatment of the mountain of material proved particularly devastating. Instead of being overwhelmed by the sheer volume of the release, the network reporters who had been covering Watergate for months zeroed in on several very important conversations and all three networks presented specials featuring oral readings of transcript excerpts. The results were devastating to Nixon's image. Even heavily edited, the transcripts revealed Richard Nixon as a petty, self-centered man with little concern for justice and an obvious contempt for those he regarded as his enemies. After carefully studying the conversations, even previously friendly newspapers such as the *Chicago Tribune* (which had rushed to print the transcripts verbatim for free distribution to its readers) sadly but firmly called for the President's resignation. Others called for impeachment, convinced that Nixon would never succumb to the calls that he should step down.

After months of deliberation behind closed doors, the House Judiciary Committee opened the formal impeachment hearings to the public, including television, on July 24 and the reality of impeachment hit everyone in the country. As with the Senate hearings the previous year, the mid-summer timing was perfect for the networks and they once again set up rotating coverage while PBS (through NPACT) presented prime time replays. The sense of jocularity that had often lightened the mood of the Ervin committee's actitivities was absent. The House Judiciary Committee was engaged in a serious debate that could well lead to the impeachment of the President of the United States.

For three days, the members of the committee debated the pros and cons of the articles of impeachment, and television carried it all. It became clear that the members of the committee were not engaged in the partisan rhetoric that usually marked such televised hearings. Each committee member displayed a deep personal anguish in trying to determine the truth of the charges and the proper course of action. Lacking clear evidence of a specific crime ("a smoking gun"), they were forced to examine cumulative impressions, general attitudes, strategies, and policies of the President. On Saturday, July 27, the debate reached a dramatic climax, the formal vote on the first article of impeachment. In a scene reminiscent of *Studio One*'s "Twelve Angry Men," the TV cameras focused on each member's face for the roll call voice vote. Throughout the country, viewers shared the drama and tallied the score as the camera panned from member to member, each speaking only one word: "yes" or "no." The motion passed, 27–11.

Two additional articles of impeachment were voted and it appeared almost certain that the full House would approve the resolution of impeachment, which would lead to a trial in the Senate in the fall unless Nixon stepped down voluntarily before then. At first, the President looked as if he would "tough it out" and the networks nervously stood by, ready to cover the lengthly procedure live, fully aware that the process would wreak havoc on their new fall programming.

On August 5, Nixon released an additional tape transcript which served as the long-sought smoking gun and proved to nearly everyone that he had participated in an obstruction of justice. Three days later, Richard Nixon announced his resignation in a prime time address carried live by the networks. They canceled all regular programming for the evening and devoted four hours to the resignation and reactions to it. Nixon's speech was rather restrained and, though lacking both an adequate explanation for his decision to step down and any admission of guilt, it was remarkably free of recrimination. It was so straight that in the analysis that immediately followed, CBS correspondent Dan Rather, a frequent target of Nixon's ire, gushed that the speech contained "nobility" and "a touch of class," before colleague Roger Mudd began to pick apart its vapid content. Some die-hard Nixon supporters such as South Carolina Senator Strom Thurmond went even further and described Nixon's tenure as President in glowing terms, dismissing Watergate as a minor aberration. Roger Mudd pointedly responded, "Well, Senator, if he was so wonderful, why did he have to resign?"

The next morning Nixon was anything but classy. Before leaving the White House, he delivered a pathetic, maudlin farewell to the staff—and he couldn't resist allowing the TV cameras in for one last time. With tears in his eyes, he spoke of his family and middle class background. He pleaded for understanding and forgiveness, but never acknowledged that he had done anything wrong. It was the 1952 Checkers speech all over again. Nixon had come full circle, only it no longer worked. The man who had reached fame and power through a very personal medium could not use it to draw support from the people any more. He still knew the right words but they no longer touched the emotions of the American public. They had supported him with the greatest popular mandate in American history and he had betrayed their trust and consistently lied to them. The people no longer believed Richard Nixon and in his final TV speech he appeared as an empty, broken man who was not worthy of their support, only their pity.

One-half hour later, Nixon flashed the "double V" victory symbol one more time to the cameras, climbed into a helicopter, and flew away.

34. Affirmative Access

RICHARD NIXON'S resignation saved the networks from a lengthy impeachment trial that would have thrown their fall schedules into total chaos. This reprieve was a welcome relief to executives who had been forced to rip up and redraw their schedules once already that summer in response to official rulings from Washington. Government bureaucrats had decided it was again time to do something that would raise the standards of television and promote the kinds of programs they felt were in the public's best interest. In January, 1974, the FCC unveiled Access II, targeted to take effect with the 1974 fall season.

The commission had emerged looking quite foolish following implementation of its 1970 prime time access rule. With a great deal of ballyhoo about increasing the quality of television, it had taken the potentially dangerous step of instigating backhand controls over some prime time programming—only to see an embarrassing proliferation of cheap game shows emerge as a result of Access I. Not taking any chances with its new rule, the FCC moved from merely hoping that producers would gear their new efforts to the commission's taste to a system that demanded it. Two hours each week (7:00–8:00 P.M. Saturday and Sunday) would be returned to network control, but only if the time were filled with news, public affairs, and FCC approved kidvid. The offer was too tempting for ABC, CBS, and NBC to resist. Even though the networks had frankly admitted in 1973 that it would probably be impossible for them to resume control of all seven nights of access time, they were perfectly willing to attempt to fill the lucrative weekend slots. They quickly agreed to the commission's ground rules and in the spring announced line-ups for the fall that included the necessary quota of FCC sanctioned programs. The independent producers were furious and they took the FCC to court. In June, a U.S. District Court ruled in their favor, declaring Access II illegal on the grounds that the new rule did not allow program producers enough time to prepare for its implementation (the 1970 access rule had provided sixteen months for industry adjustment). The court also strongly implied that there were other entire sections of the rule it didn't like. Rather than offer to extend the lead-in time to meet the court's stated objection, the FCC took the opportunity to reexamine its entire strategy and to prepare a completely new proposal. In the meantime, with Access II declared illegal, the original access rule was once again in force. Ironically, this left producers and local stations facing an even tighter situation than before. They had only ninety days to fill the two hours sud-

denly returned to their control. In order to make the September deadline, everyone turned to the quickest, cheapest programs available: more game shows.

The networks faced the opposite task. Each one had to reshuffle its schedule in order to absorb the loss of two hours of programming. The weekend public affairs, news, and kidvid material was all excised. Additionally, six new thirty-minute sitcoms (two on each network) were temporarily shelved, though all of them eventually aired in one form or another later in the season. They included: NBC's *Sunshine* and *The Bob Crane Show*, CBS's *We'll Get By* and *The Love Nest*, and ABC's *Where's The Fire?* and *Everything Money Can't Buy*.

In spite of the last minute legal wrangling and the across the board program purge, the overall tone of the new season's prime time line-up remained unchanged. Though a half dozen sitcoms had been cut from the September schedule, there were still six left among the new fall shows as situation comedy continued to experience a renaissance that had begun in the early Seventies. Success in this "new wave" of comedy, however, eluded all but a handful of producers. Some of the best minds in American TV comedy had already tried and failed to ride this upswing, and the major casualties included Alan King's *The Corner Bar,* Carl Reiner's *A Touch of Grace,* Rob Reiner's *The Super,* and Sam Denoff's *Lotsa Luck.* Many of these vehicles had started with promising concepts, but few had the necessary accompaniment of standout actors and top notch writing to make the premises come alive. They also relied too heavily on all too obvious *All in the Family* production traits such as a live audience, British origin, and proletariat struggle to cover their weaknesses. Most of the producers cited the difficulty of finding good writers for the shows as the major reason for their failure.

Though there was an increasing demand for new wave-style comedy programs, an entire generation of TV sitcom writers had grown up on obstacle-course comedy, never dealing with situations such as a lead character's decision to have an abortion. Consequently, when they were asked to deliver scripts for series that were conceived in the Norman Lear-Bud Yorkin mold, the writers drew on the superficial elements of the new shows and therefore inserted as many racial putdowns and topical references as possible. They failed to realize that the so-called new wave of sitcoms was based on the same strains of humor that had worked for decades, from the vaudeville stage to *I Love Lucy*. Though the subject matter and settings might be more realistic than in the past, clever plot twists, funny situations, sharp dialogue, and interesting characters were still essential. Abandoning these in favor of a half-hour of cheap putdowns and racial slurs underscored the fact that many people in the industry still failed to understand the subtle interplay of traditional humor and realistic settings at work in the shows. This combination was very difficult to handle, even by those who championed the trend, and, at first, Lear and Yorkin had found it necessary to write most of their scripts themselves. Yorkin explained, "You can't take those young guys off shows like *Doris Day* and expect them to do this kind of comedy."

By 1974, Lear had groomed an entire stable of writers proficient in this new form of sitcom and he was able to fuel an amazingly successful strategy of spinoffs and new shows, most of which wore the distinct stamp of *All in the Family.* Though even he couldn't *guarantee* a winner every time (Lear's adaptation of the off-Broadway hit "The Hot 1 Baltimore" flopped on ABC in the spring of 1975), he had worked out a very reliable formula for the success that had eluded so many others. Lear carefully selected supporting characters from his established hits and placed them in their own vehicles, building a chain of ratings champs for CBS in the process. Just as CBS president James Aubrey had directed a parade of rural spinoffs from *The Beverly Hillbillies* and *The Andy Griffith Show* in the early Sixties, Lear took race, topicality, and occasional forays into serious issues and ran with them through the Seventies. His techniques were just as blatant as Aubrey's, but a steady supply of top notch scripts maintained a generally high level of quality with each succeeding series. While perhaps not quite as good as the *All in the Family* original, his new programs were certainly well done and, to his credit, Lear tried to give each one its own special focus.

First out of the *All in the Family* mold was *Maude,* begun in the fall of 1972 as a spinoff series for the character of Edith Bunker's cousin, played by Beatrice Arthur. In February, 1974, Lear launched *Good Times,* which showcased Maude's black maid, Florida Evans (Esther Rolle), who left New York and settled with her family in the projects of Chicago. As something of a black

"heart" comedy in the tradition of the Fifties' *Mama, Good Times* emphasized the warm goodness of the hard working parents, Florida and her husband James (John Amos), as they struggled to raise their three children, James Junior "J.J." (Jimmie Walker), Thelma (BernNadette Stanis), and Michael (Ralph Carter). In his update of this once popular form, Lear avoided the saccharine whitewash of the Sixties' "warm black comedy," *Julia,* and presented the characters as a generally believable realistic black family. There were the obligatory putdowns and insults, but most of these were handled by the children, especially J.J., the oldest son. Florida and James saved their energy for the never-ending problem of family survival in the white man's world.

For his next spinoff (in January, 1975) Lear presented the problems faced by a middle class black family that actually "made it," Archie Bunker's next door neighbors, the Jeffersons. The Jefferson family had been introduced in *All in the Family* as a black equivalent to the Bunkers, so a spinoff series was almost inevitable. After all, every important element was already there. George Jefferson (Sherman Hemsley) was a self-centered snob and bigot who intensely disliked whites, Louise (Isabel Sanford) was his long-suffering but forgiving wife, and Lionel (Mike Evans) was his tolerant son who outraged his father (and Archie) by becoming close friends with Mike and Gloria. To launch the new series, the Jeffersons moved from Queens to a fashionable East Side apartment in Manhattan. Though peppered with topical references and characters (an inter-racial couple lived just down the hall), for the most part this new series was far less serious than *All in the Family* and it placed more emphasis on strident insults and blustery confrontations. George Jefferson was an even more pigheaded and preposterous "head of the household" than Archie Bunker, and he was constantly deflated by his business associates and neighbors, the rest of his family, and Florence (Marla Gibbs), their flippant black maid. Nonetheless, as a self-made black businessman he faced racial problems from a perspective totally different from Archie, Maude, and Florida, and the series made use of his special interests and particular point of view.

It was no accident that Lear's two new hit sitcoms focused on

James Garner *(r.)* as Jim Rockford and Noah Beery as his dad, "Rocky." (*From* The Rockford Files. *Courtesy of MCA Television Limited*)

FALL 1974 SCHEDULE

MONDAY

	7:30	8:00	8:30	9:00	9:30	10:00	10:30	
	local	The Rookies		ABC NFL Monday Night Football [to 12 Midnite]				ABC
	local	Gunsmoke		Maude	RHODA	Medical Center		CBS
	local	BORN FREE		NBC Monday Night At The Movies				NBC

TUESDAY

	7:30	8:00	8:30	9:00	9:30	10:00	10:30	
	local	Happy Days	Tuesday Movie Of The Week			Marcus Welby, M.D.		ABC
	local	Good Times	M*A*S*H	Hawaii Five-O		Barnaby Jones		CBS
	local	Adam-12	NBC World Premiere Movie			Police Story		NBC

WEDNESDAY

	7:30	8:00	8:30	9:00	9:30	10:00	10:30	
	local	THAT'S MY MAMA	Wednesday Movie Of The Week			GET CHRISTIE LOVE		ABC
	local	SONS AND DAUGHTERS		Cannon		MANHUNTER		CBS
	local	LITTLE HOUSE ON THE PRAIRIE		LUCAS TANNER @Bob Hope Show		PETROCELLI		NBC

THURSDAY

	7:30	8:00	8:30	9:00	9:30	10:00	10:30	
	local	The Odd Couple	PAPER MOON	Streets Of San Francisco		HARRY O		ABC
	local	The Waltons		CBS Thursday Night Movies				CBS
	local	SIERRA		Ironside		MOVIN' ON		NBC

FRIDAY

	7:30	8:00	8:30	9:00	9:30	10:00	10:30	
	local	KODIAK	Six Million Dollar Man		THE TEXAS WHEELERS	KOLCHAK – THE NIGHT STALKER		ABC
	local	PLANET OF THE APES		CBS Friday Night Movies				CBS
	local	Sanford And Son	CHICO AND THE MAN	THE ROCKFORD FILES		POLICE WOMAN		NBC

SATURDAY

	7:30	8:00	8:30	9:00	9:30	10:00	10:30	
	local	THE NEW LAND		Kung Fu		NAKIA		ABC
	local	All In The Family	PAUL SAND IN FRIENDS AND LOVERS	Mary Tyler Moore	Bob Newhart Show	Carol Burnett Show		CBS
	local	Emergency!		NBC Saturday Night At The Movies				NBC

SUNDAY

	7:00	7:30	8:00	8:30	9:00	9:30	10:00	10:30	
	local	SONNY COMEDY REVUE		The ABC Sunday Night Movie					ABC
	local	Apple's Way		Kojak		Mannix		local	CBS
	local	The Wonderful World Of Disney		NBC Sunday Mystery Movie (McCloud, Columbo, McMillan And Wife, AMY PRENTISS)			local @NBC Reports [10:00–11:00]		NBC

blacks. Perhaps the one aspect of new wave comedy that everyone agreed on was that it had strong ethnic and racial themes. Unfortunately, some writers and producers frequently used the mere presence of minorities as a lazy shortcut that allowed them to sidestep complicated issues and complex drama and settle instead for stories that were "automatically topical" because they featured blacks. Worse yet, their treatment of ethnic groups frequently degenerated into a string of very old stereotypes. For instance, an Archie Bunker type would be set up as a lovable strawman to be torn down after delivering "unintentionally" funny lines that demonstrated what a close-minded bigot he was. This was a crafty combination that allowed warmed-over racial clichés to be used in the inevitable exchange of putdowns, turning what might have been labeled as racist or insulting in the past into an unmistakable sign that the program was "up to date" and "with it." The line between a sophisticated sitcom and a plastic exercise in name calling was often a fine one and, even on the better shows, it was sometimes unclear whether the scripts drew on the putdowns of the bigot or the cheap racial caricatures for the laughs.

One offender in this regard was, surprisingly, Norman Lear's *Good Times* which, by its second season, began shifting the focus more and more to J.J.'s antics. Walker portrayed J.J. as a hip-talking wisecracker, but when he rolled his eyes and exclaimed "Dyn-o-mite!" with a shit-eating grin, it sounded an awful lot like

"Holy Mackeral, Andy." The original scripts had kept his antics in check, with J.J. appearing as nothing worse than a problem child with an enormous ego (certainly a realistic problem) who even poked fun at himself and his shortcomings. However, J.J. soon became a cult figure among pre-teen youth and the writers began playing up his comic caricature more and more. By the end of the third season, John Amos quit the series in disgust, citing his personal frustration at the degeneration in writing and characterization. One year later, Esther Rolle also quit. Both characters were written out of the series (James was killed in an accident in Mississippi and Florida moved to the Southwest for her health) so that, ironically, for one season a warm "family" comedy functioned with no parents at all. Rolle returned in the fall of 1978 when the producers promised to shift back to the original thrust of the show and downplay J.J.'s mindless antics. Even with Rolle back, the program could not recapture its initial spirit and it was canceled only a few months after her reappearance.

Jimmie Walker's sudden rise to cult status was the perfect example of the shaky status of television's newly found social conscience. Here was a young black comic who became a national celebrity, especially among black children, by portraying a shiftless, addle-brained jive-ass—exactly the sort of media character blacks had been complaining about for years. Just because a series centered on a minority group did not guarantee that the characters would necessarily be given enviable and uplifting traits, even within the supposedly sophisticated sitcoms.

No matter what shape they took, though, minority groups were firmly established as the strong hook for television in the Seventies. Despite the many horrible scripts and one-dimensional characters that had appeared in the wake of *All in the Family,* television was slowly absorbing them. After several years of scrutiny, other writers and producers at last began to adapt the Norman Lear formula successfully in their own efforts. In the process, TV completely reshaped its portrait of the world from the aseptic white suburbs of the Fifties, to the new ideal of the Seventies: a totally integrated society with a perfect mixture of every race, color, and creed. This merely reflected the real world, where assorted minority groups were becoming increasingly vocal, demanding additional participation in such diverse fields as politics, labor, and education through programs of "affirmative action" (a euphemism to replace the buzz word "quotas"). Though such profound social changes might take generations in real life and require government legislated mathematical mixes, for network television it meant that the WASP world was suddenly junked in favor of a new money maker, the increasingly popular world of colorful ethnics who promsied high ratings and increased profits. By the 1974–75 season, this new order seemed practically a *fait accompli* (on TV at least) as viewers welcomed *Chico and the Man* and *Barney Miller.* Neither of these shows came from Norman Lear, but both were up to his standards and they signalled that successful, high quality, generally realistic ethnic humor was no longer Lear's exclusive domain.

James Komack's *Chico and the Man* literally followed in the footsteps of *Sanford and Son* and, riding on the strength of such an enviable lead-in, catapulted straight into the top ten. It was a perfect companion show to the story of a father and son junk dealership in the Los Angeles ghetto. Ed Brown (Jack Albertson) and his Chicano assistant Chico Rodriguez (Freddie Prinze) operated a run down garage in a decrepit section of East Los Angeles.

Though one of the first programs to slant itself toward the Mexican-American minority, it was just as much a generation gap comedy as a racial show. Ed ("The Man") was a dyspeptic old coot who one day let a cheerful young Chicano talk him into a job as his assistant at the garage. Very quickly he and Chico became friends, though Ed never publicly dropped his image as a hardnosed quasi-Bunkerish bigot. (He claimed that he didn't like anybody, but it was obvious he really loved everybody.) Unlike the structure in many of the other ethnic based shows, Ed and Chico were not so much characters in conflict as two sides of the same character: one was a buoyant optimistic dreamer who believed anything was possible, and the other was an unreconstructed cynic who had seen too many such hopes turn sour. Neither was set up as an obvious bad guy and both delivered funny one-liners that were closer to vaudeville routines than spiteful putdowns. The energy between the two characters turned merely adequate scripts into highly entertaining encounters as grumpy Ed found himself growing increasingly fond of the enthusiastic Chico, secretly hoping that he would succeed in working his way out of the ghetto.

One reason for the strong chemistry between Ed and Chico was that there seemed to be a touch of real life magic to the setting. Prinze was only twenty when he moved from a brief career as a nightclub stand-up comic to share the lead in a top ten TV show. He seemed remarkably successful at keeping up with veteran trouper Albertson and well on his way to fulfilling "Chico" 's optimistic dream of becoming a Chicano superstar. This fusion of images made Prinze's subsequent suicide in January of 1977 especially shocking, and it punctured the show's premise with a grim dose of reality. Though the producers attempted to continue the series by using twelve-year-old Gabriel Melgar as a new Chicano character (orphan Raul Garcia), Prinze's death had robbed the show of its comic tension. The revamped format lasted only one season, unable to duplicate the special energy that had first propelled the series.

After splitting with her husband, Rhoda (Valerie Harper) once again became an eligible single woman, often double dating with her sister, Brenda (Julie Kavner). (From *r.*) Harper, Ray Buktenica, Kavner, and Ron Silver. *(MTM Enterprises)*

If the champions of affirmative action could have selected the cast for a TV sitcom, they could not have done better than the crew of New York City's 12th police precinct as presented in Danny Arnold's *Barney Miller*. Set in the appropriately diverse district of Greenwich Village, the program showcased a kaleidoscope of distinctive character types: Captain Barney Miller, a level-headed Jewish chief of detectives (Hal Linden); Detective Harris, a cool confident black (Ron Glass); Sgt. Wojehowicz, a beefy hard-working Pole (Max Gail); Sgt. Yemana, a soft-spoken reliable Oriental (Jack Soo); Sgt. Chano Amengual, a voluble Puerto Rican (Gregory Sierra); Sgt. Fish, an aging but dedicated man on the verge of retirement (Abe Vigoda); and Inspector Luger, a pure Hollywood B-movie type complete with fedora and raincoat (James Gregory). Each performer drew on the accepted stereotypes of his character but, for the most part, snide putdowns were kept in check and the group evolved into a close knit company facing realistic, if extremely wacky, situations. The precinct house became the center stage for conflicts between members of the crew as well as for confrontations with the insane world of New York City outside. Despite the very funny plots, *Barney Miller* was a far cry from the pure farce and physical pratfalls of previous "stationhouse sitcoms" such as *Car 54, Where Are You?* Its humor grew out of the characters themselves placed in believable, though exaggerated, situations, rather than from outlandish plots or silly misunderstandings. The program was one of the best new-wave sitcoms to evolve outside the Norman Lear stable, combining topical themes and ethnic concerns with the basics of comedy: a simple set, good acting, and well-written scripts. It was not, however, an instant smash, premiering as part of ABC's second season schedule in January of 1975, slotted against *The Waltons*. Over the years,

though, it went through a number of time shifts and became one of the network's steady, reliable shows, even inspiring a short lived spinoff series, *Fish* (featuring Sgt. Fish after his retirement).

CBS was quite pleased with the success of Norman Lear's spinoffs and eagerly looked to its other hot sitcoms for more winners. The network had slated a program created and produced by *M*A*S*H*'s Alan Alda, *We'll Get By*, for the fall of 1974, but postponed it as part of the cutbacks resulting from the Access II mess. When it finally aired in the late spring, *We'll Get By* proved a disappointment. Audiences expecting the mixture of madcap humor and serious themes of *M*A*S*H* were let down by the lowkey premise of a middle class lawyer and his family living in a New Jersey suburb. The series simply never caught fire. Viewers, as well as the CBS brass, were much happier with the first spinoff from *The Mary Tyler Moore Show*, *Rhoda*, the most successful new sitcom of the season.

Fans of *The Mary Tyler Moore Show* had become quite fond of Mary's wisecracking neighbor with a heart of gold, Rhoda Morgenstern, and they eagerly followed her move from the frozen Midwest back to her home turf of New York City—she was giving it "one last chance." Valerie Harper handled the transition from plumpish second banana to slim, glamorous lead character quite well. She softened Rhoda's slightly out-of-sync personality a bit, giving the character more stability and providing the new supporting crew with opportunities to shine on its own. Rhoda's sister Brenda (Julie Kavner) assumed Rhoda's old role as an overintelligent, overweight young woman, traditional enough to spend most of her time talking about men but modern enough to joke about it. Their mother, Ida Morgenstern (Nancy Walker), played the perfect Jewish mother: pushy, overbearing, self-deprecating, but with the required heart of gold beneath her tough exterior.

Perhaps the most important change in Rhoda's life was that in the very first episode of her own series she met a man and fell in love. Joe Gerard (David Groh) was a nice Jewish boy, handsome, and an eminently respectable young business man on the way up. In short, a "good catch." On October 28, after four years of frustrated single life in Minneapolis, Rhoda got married in a one-hour special that featured the entire crew from *The Mary Tyler Moore Show* as wedding guests. The program was the top-rated special of the season and *Rhoda* stayed in the top ten for two years straight. Yet, there were some Rhoda fans who were unhappy.

Critics complained that marriage had taken the edge from Rhoda and trapped her in stories that were severely limited by the essentially dull character of Joe Gerard. In the fall of 1976, the writers took the critics' advice and began to work Joe out of the series. He and Rhoda were first separated, then, a year later, divorced. Joe admitted that he had only consented to marriage because he knew that Rhoda would never have agreed simply to live together (which was all he had really wanted). During the messy transition year between the separation and divorce, the writers were very uncertain what to focus on for the humor. Consequently, *Rhoda* became more a soap opera than a sitcom and the show's ratings dipped dramatically. It was not until well into the 1977–78 season that the program began to regain some of its old stature as viewers discovered that the generally maudlin plots had been scrapped and the show was once again funny. Rhoda had returned to the role of an attractive, eligible single woman. She and Brenda (who had lost her chubbiness) were set in the very workable premise of independent young women trying to make it on their own, which was what many people had expected of the show from the very beginning.

With such a strong line-up of freshmen, TV comedy was at a

peak virtually unmatched in network history. Nearly a dozen excellent sitcoms aired each week, from veterans such as *All in the Family, M*A*S*H, The Odd Couple,* and *The Mary Tyler Moore Show* to newcomers *Rhoda, Chico and the Man,* and *Barney Miller.* American television had successfully absorbed the British television style of working class humor while it redeveloped some of its best sitcom characters and settings for the Seventies. Appropriately, it was at this point that British television provided a *new* "new wave" style of comedy that made the American Norman Lear type of sitcom seem almost old hat. It was in 1974 that Americans discovered *Monty Python's Flying Circus.*

The program had begun its run on the BBC in October, 1969, as British TV humor began to move away from working class comedy (which had flourished there in the mid-Sixties) to its own interpretation of the Ernie Kovacs style of television. *Rowan and Martin's Laugh-In* was the obvious catalyst for the show, as the BBC gathered a group of talented graduates from David Frost's many comedy series and offered them the opportunity to write and perform in their own weekly half-hour comedy series. They responded with a mad collection of blackouts, outrageous skits, old fashioned physical humor, and rapid-fire editing that surpassed even *Laugh-In* in bringing the Kovacs style to high-quality realization. Sketches were interrupted by other sketches as well as by flashes of music, phony "program announcements," reactions by "outraged government officials," and animated cartoon cutout characters (designed by an American, Terry Gilliam). Each episode ran without commercials so the dizzy pace never let up. It appeared to be total anarchy, but was actually a very careful mixture of bread-and-butter physical comedy with high class word play, shock-tactic humor, and parodies of television itself. Within the same half-hour, punch lines and sketches were reworked several times, presenting different approaches to the same jokes. As writers and editors as well as performers, the Python crew understood the necessity of setting up contrasts to punctuate the comedy and to help the pacing.

The physical humor was loud and flashy, in the best tradition of Milton Berle burlesque. Characters walked funny, donned ridiculous costumes, dressed in drag, and screamed. Word play ranged from slightly restrained vulgarity ("filthy bastard") to complicated allusions to great works of literature. The animated cutouts included a variety of unlikely subjects: nude women, government leaders, nude men, cricket players, and giant animals. Just for variety, "taboo" subjects such as death, sex, and canabalism were discussed as casually as royal pronouncements. Biting its own BBC hand, the crew lampooned the mainstays of noncommercial British television: pretentious documentaries and boring talk shows. Participants in the Python permutations were either perversely handicapped (unable to speak English or, worse, simply dead) or stuck in the wrong panel ("Che Guevara" was questioned about obscure cricket championship matches). Documentary narrators inevitably missed the obvious and focused on ridiculous subjects such as flying sheep. The BBC was quite uncertain about the monster it had unleashed, convinced that only a lunatic fringe could possibly enjoy such an eclectic mess. Instead, the program went beyond the fringe and became a big enough success for the BBC to call the Python crew back for three more seasons.

American television would not touch *Monty Python's Flying Circus* at first. Not only was it a censor's nightmare, the humor seemed too idiosyncratic—who outside Britain *cared* about cricket? The initial reaction by the American public seemed to confirm this judgment. Two record albums and a film ("And Now for Something Completely Different"), consisting of selected sketches from the

series, flopped in the early Seventies. Members of the cast made a few U.S. TV appearances but they failed to have any impact on the American market, and *Monty Python* seemed destined to the same obscurity in the United States as Britain's *Goon Show* in the Fifties. In 1974, Time-Life Films sold the Python series to the Eastern Educational Network and that fall, five years after its British premiere, *Monty Python's Flying Circus* appeared on a handful of public TV stations. Much to the surprise of everyone, the show took off and became one of public TV's highest rated programs. Viewers simply ignored the occasional inscrutable allusions to obscure British interests and enjoyed the fresh, daring insanity. As a British import on public television, *Monty Python* aired intact the outrageous treatment of topics that American performers would have been booted off the air for even suggesting (such as eating your dead mother). By mid-1975, the group's second film ("Monty Python and the Holy Grail") opened to an enthusiastic Stateside reception. By then, the TV series itself was on 120 stations across the country, including KPRC, Houston, the first commercial station to carry it—complete with commercials. *Monty Python's Flying Circus* provided a lively change of pace from the equally funny but fervently realistic sitcoms then on American network television. It allowed viewers the opportunity for a direct dose of a completely different style and the program became a long-running staple of public television. Over the next few years, *Monty Python*-style humor also turned up in some American television shows, most notably in a venture outside of network prime time, NBC's *Saturday Night Live.*

Though situation comedy served as the primary component for the 1974–75 season, the crime show format was close behind. In exploiting the form, the networks relied on the most successful gimmicks of the previous season, loner ethnic cops and violence. The plots in many of the new shows, however, drew chiefly on

January 6, 1975
NBC's eleven-year-old daytime hit, *Another World,* becomes the first soap opera to expand to one hour, five days a week.

January 24, 1975
Hot l Baltimore. (ABC). Norman Lear's first major flop, an off-beat sitcom based on a popular off-Broadway play. Set in a seedy Baltimore hotel (with a permanently burned out light behind the *e* of the "hotel" sign), the program focuses on a wide range of controversial character types (from pimpless hookers to a pair of male homosexual lovers). Some people object to the treatment of such risque topics in prime time, but, unlike Lear's other ventures, the show does not generate any great following from the protests. One reviewer observes that the so-called "adult" series is really just bad caricature and "as shocking as last week's bread."

April 29, 1975
To mark the fall of Saigon, all three commercial networks present documentary reports. CBS: "Vietnam: A War That Is Finished"; NBC: "7,382 Days in Vietnam"; and ABC: "Vietnam: Lessons Learned, Prices Paid."

August 6, 1975
NBC News Update. (NBC). NBC begins inserting a sixty-second news summary into prime time.

September 1, 1975
The oldest oater of them all, *Gunsmoke,* fades from CBS after twenty years, leaving prime time virtually devoid of Westerns.

the cheap and obvious aspects of these gimmicks and failed to generate an ounce of original excitement. In fact, most of the new "individualistic loners" were practically dead on arrival. *Archer* (Brian Keith as a 1930s Sam Spade-style investigator) and *Khan!* (featuring perennial *Hawaii Five-O* villain Khigh Dhiegh as an Oriental private eye in San Francisco) ran only four weeks each. *Nakia* and *Caribe* lasted a few months. *Get Christie Love* (Teresa Graves as a sassy, sexy black undercover police agent) eked out nearly one complete season. *Petrocelli* (a Harvard-educated Italian working as a private eye in Arizona) and *Harry O* (David Janssen as a disabled former cop turned private eye) actually managed to hold on for two dull seasons each.

The only instant hit among the new crime shows really wasn't a new show at all. James Garner dusted off his old Maverick character, moved from the amorphous West of the 1870s to the amorphous West Coast of the 1970s, and became Jim Rockford, a smart-talking ex-con with a wry sense of humor who worked as a private investigator. *The Rockford Files* followed the *Maverick* formula to the letter, downplaying life-and-death confrontations in favor of lighter, less wearisome complications between Rockford and his clients, his dad (played by Noah Beery), and various collection agencies (he always seemed on the verge of bankruptcy). It was one of the smoothest crime shows in years, as the writers tailored the scripts to match Garner's relaxed character perfectly, and the program remained one of NBC's most consistent ratings winners for half a decade.

Three other crime shows also became hits that season, but unlike *The Rockford Files*, NBC's *Police Woman* and ABC's *Baretta* and *S.W.A.T.* each took more time to build an audience, not catching on until the spring rerun cycle. They were different from *The Rockford Files* in one other important respect: each was very violent.

Police Woman (which followed *The Rockford Files*) was a spinoff from Joseph Wambaugh's *Police Story* anthology series, but it was not very faithful to the original's concept of focusing on more realistic, human aspects of police work. The "unflinching look at the real world of police women" devoted much of its attention to gratuitous violence such as savage death scenes or closeups of traumatized rape victims. Pepper Anderson (Angie Dickinson) was played up primarily as a titillating sex symbol, with frequent shots of her in revealing costumes, legs apart, pistol pointed. One reviewer described the show as the epitome of the crime genre's new excesses, saying its motto was, "Shoot now, talk dirty later." *Kojak* had demonstrated that violence could be used very effectively in order to underscore the grim reality of urban crime, but the writers on that program generally turned in scripts that gave Telly Savalas excellent material to work with. *Police Woman* rarely offered Dickinson the same opportunity. *Baretta* was even worse, presenting stories that could be accurately summarized as: Smash! Bang! Crash! Boom! Screech! Zoom!

Baretta was a new attempt by the producers of *Toma* to cash in, more gracefully, on the violent cop show trend. Robert Blake was cast as an out-of-the-ordinary cop who was streetwise and ready to defend the little people from hardnosed police harassment as well as from violent urban criminals. Blake's interpretation of the role was the high point of the show as he hammered Tony Baretta into an intriguing off-beat character. He took the cheap gimmicks of the premise—Baretta was a master at disguise and owned a talking cockatoo for a pet—and transformed them into engaging traits of the little fellow's personality. Occasionally some interesting plot twists surfaced, but Blake usually found himself struggling with merely average scripts, sometimes even "rewriting" a scene on the set by refining Baretta's actions himself. His energy

carried over into the overall production, raising *Baretta* to the level of a good, straight-forward, well-produced cop show. This helped to smooth over the excessive violence that formed the nucleus for nearly every episode. Though Tony Baretta might have been engaged in a constant battle against urban crime, he still took the time to care for individual victims and was not afraid to show honest, gut emotions. *S.W.A.T.*, ABC's other late-rising cop show of the season, took a completely different approach, carrying the theme of urban guerrilla warfare to its final, depersonalized conclusion.

Producers Aaron Spelling and Leonard Goldberg (of *The Mod Squad* and *The Rookies*) set up *S.W.A.T.* as the ultimate crime-action program, portraying Los Angeles (where else?) as one huge battleground populated by raving lunatics, crazed maniacs, and helpless citizens. To protect the populace from the madmen poised to ravage the city, a five-man Special Weapons and Tactics (S.W.A.T.) squad stood ready, led by Lieutenant Hondo Harrelson (Steve Forrest). Every week, just when it appeared as if the city were doomed, an ominous green truck would come howling into view. As the truck screeched to a halt, a small army of faceless men in flak suits threw open its doors and leaped out, ready to face a threat no average citizen or normal policeman could handle. It was a perverse combination of grade-B war and Western films, with the S.W.A.T. team riding in like the cavalry of old to overwhelm the enemy. However, instead of using six-shooters, they rode in with an arsenal of bazooka-type weapons that could demolish a small country. The enemy wasn't beaten, it was blown away.

Such total war completely eliminated the chance for a slice of humanity and left little room in the field for the personal one-to-one confrontations of such Sam Spade surrogates as Columbo, Cannon, and Mannix or of such hard working outsiders as Kojak and Baretta. *S.W.A.T.* literally turned the war on crime into an all-out war between society and its enemies. In such a war, anything was allowed. Even Jack Webb's fiercely pro-cop series, from *Dragnet* to *Emergency*, had shown more restraint. *S.W.A.T.* celebrated overkill and massive retaliation, briefly touching a sensitive nerve among viewers. The program flashed into the top ten in the summer, but disappeared after its second season. As its legacy, the series left behind an unmistakable sign of television's ability to influence taste and modify values of separate communities across the country simultaneously. In dozens of small, previously peaceful towns such as Bloomington, Indiana, local officials began setting aside huge sums of local revenue to finance their own smartly dressed S.W.A.T. teams. After all, there was more glamour to be found in training for such a squad than merely concentrating on humdrum, routine police work.

S.W.A.T. marked a symbolic peak in television violence, coming as it did at the end of more than a decade of real life uncontrolled violence that television had brought into everyone's living room. Americans had viewed graphic confrontations on the home front and on the war front with increasing frustration at their inability to do anything about them. *S.W.A.T.*, in effect, restaged the Vietnam war and the riots in the streets, but returned ultimate control to the righteous forces of law and order for a satisfying conclusion. It was a bitterly ironic contrast to the confusion and desperation that marked the end of the real war that seemed to have caused so many of the problems in the first place.

Following the 1973 Paris Peace Accord, the United States had rushed to sweep the Vietnam war under the carpet. American combat troops were withdrawn by the fall of 1973 and the South Vietnamese army assumed responsibility for keeping order in the countryside and maintaining security. They faced a series of widespread guerrilla attacks which kept the war percolating at a low but constant level. In the spring of 1975, the South Vietnamese forces collapsed and the American public was given a visual jolt more shocking that the years of combat footage and bombing statistics. As Communist forces swept through the country and assumed control over village after village, the network cameras focused on the stream of refugees fleeing to the south for safety. By the end of April, uncontrolled panic had set in—supposedly safe enclaves protected by the South Vietnamese forces had fallen in rapid succession and the Communist drive south became a rout. A Communist takeover of the countryside seemed inevitable. Bureaucrats, soldiers, merchants, and thousands of average people who had built their lives around the American presence in Vietnam feared for their own survival. Everyone began scrambling for the apparent safety of the capital city of Saigon itself, determined to get there by any means possible. Near the end, the only way out was by American airplanes.

On the last flight out of DaNang, a CBS camera crew captured the incredible scene. Frightened men (chiefly South Vietnamese soldiers) shoved women and children aside in a desperate bid to climb aboard an already overcrowded airplane. The plane was so jammed with refugees that it had to take off with the stairway ramp still hanging out, open, and the crew had to push people off as the craft taxied down the runway. Some of those who couldn't make it aboard began shooting at the plane in anger and frustration. Others clung to the stairs even after takeoff, with most falling off once the plane was airborne. Soon after their arrival in Saigon, those who had made it discovered that their escape to freedom was short lived. The collapse of Saigon itself was imminent. Once again, there was a hectic evacuation, starting at the U.S. embassy. Once again, the TV crews focused on the desperate crowds trying to reach safety. At the embassy, they clawed at the gates while helicopters took the last of the staff and press to boats waiting offshore. At the harbor, thousands pressed to climb aboard one of the departing ships. South Vietnamese pilots hijacked expensive American-built Army helicopters and ditched them in the sea near the American carriers, hoping to make it on board. The final hours at the Saigon airport were a repeat of the desperation of DaNang.

No matter what position they had taken on the war, individual Americans found the news clips a sobering, gut-wrenching experience. The United States was leaving behind, defenseless, a great number of people who had staked their lives on America's ultimate success in South Vietnam, either on the battlefield or at the negotiating table. In return, they had been abandoned. The graphic television reports were something of an emotional penance, as Americans watched the traumatic mess of Vietnam conclude right before their eyes, forced to confront at their dinner tables the reality of what their country had done to a small group of people half a world away.

35. Freddie or Not?

ON TUESDAY, September 10, 1974, NBC kicked off a new series of made-for-TV movies for the 1974–75 season with "Born Innocent," a tough presentation of the effects of reform school on a naive teenage girl. It was produced by Richard Rosenberg and Robert Christiansen, the team responsible earlier that year for the highly acclaimed civil rights drama, "Autobiography of Miss Jane Pittman," a successful vehicle for Cicely Tyson. In "Born Innocent" they cast Linda Blair, the young star of the hit theatrical horror film "The Exorcist," as fourteen-year-old Chris Parker, a gentle and confused child placed in a juvenile detention home by her parents for being an incorrigible runaway. Though Chris had run away six times in two years, it was clear that, with an alcoholic mother and a weak, sadistic father at home, she was an unfortunate victim needing help and understanding, not punishment. Instead, she was made a ward of the state and locked up with drug addicts and child prostitutes in the women's section of a state reform school. There, Chris was cruelly and insensitively handled by the authorities and mercilessly taunted by the other girls. For the most part, the producers managed to handle the entire story with a minimum of graphic horror. The film did not set up any easily identifiable devils or angels but rather concerned itself with the deadend hopeless condition of the prison and its dehumanizing influence on everyone there. At the climax of the story, the innocent Chris was gang raped in the shower by a group of girls using a wooden plunger. They triumphantly cried, "Now you're one of us!"

"Born Innocent" was practically swallowed up amid the fall premiere hoopla. It did not receive much on-air promotion and, up against the season premieres of CBS's hit *Good Times* and ABC's mildly successful *Happy Days*, it registered only fair ratings. Afterward, many TV critics did not bother to review it, though those who did tended to be largely complimentary. Ron Powers of the *Chicago Sun-Times* praised the program as "courageous, honest, and intelligently crafted television drama." The *Hollywood Reporter* called it "a massive, brutal indictment of the juvenile justice system." A few years earlier, the serious topic and brutal setting of "Born Innocent" might have sent shock waves throughout the industry but, by the fall of 1974, even rape scenes were almost passé on television. Still, the clearly adult-oriented film had been particularly accessible to a young audience, airing relatively early in the evening (8:00–10:00 P.M.) and appearing at the start of the new fall season when youthful viewing levels were high.

A few days after the "Born Innocent" telecast, a San Francisco teenage girl was assaulted on a deserted stretch of California beach by a gang of girls, who used a coke bottle to rape her. The parents of the attacked girl sued NBC, claiming the violence on the tube had been the instigator of the violence on the beach. NBC denied any connection or responsibility, but the legal wrangling lasted four years. (NBC eventually won the case.) Even before it ever reached the courts, though, the real life incident of rape provided a very visible rallying point for the small but vocal group of viewers who, for years, had protested what they saw as excessive levels of sex and violence on television. At last, they said, here was proof of the harmful effects of unrestrained television on impressionable minds.

Throughout the previous cycles of public protest that had accompanied the heydays of Western, crime, and action-adventure shows during the Fifties and Sixties, the networks had been able to blunt the criticism and avoid any serious threats of anti-network legislation. In the Seventies, the anti-gore groups grew more sophisticated and organized their scattered interests into a number of dedicated lobbying groups, moving beyond outraged letters to the editor and appearances at inconsequential congressional hearings. They took careful aim at lawmakers, television moguls, and the news media in general. As a result, the protests that followed the "Born Innocent" case could not be brushed aside with a few vague promises by the networks. In the fall of 1974, the intensified protests reached the House and Senate committees that controlled the FCC's purse strings and they ordered the commission to take some sort of action on the complicated matter of the influence of television sex and violence on children.

The FCC was hesitant to impose an outright ban. Access rules that "encouraged" quality programming (however heavy-handedly) were one thing, but an out-and-out veto of sex and violence in programming ventured onto very shaky legal grounds that the commission preferred to avoid. Instead, it passed the buck to the networks, urging them to solve the problem for everyone by coming up with strong self-imposed guidelines to mollify the public protesters. In the meantime, the FCC continued to work on its revised prime time access rules and in January, 1975, it unveiled Access III, a complicated set of specific guidelines loaded with exemptions and clarifications, and scheduled to take effect that fall. On a practical level, the complex new rules translated into the return to network control of one hour of prime time each week (Sunday, 7:00–8:00 P.M.), as long as it was filled with FCC-approved kidvid or public affairs. There were the expected challenges to the new regulations, but the courts were more receptive than they had been to Access II the previous year, not even objecting to the mere nine months lead time allowed for industry adjustment. By the spring, the arguments against the new formula for prime time had been turned down and the FCC had a legally approved right to sit as judge and censor over a specific slice of network prime time programming.

That was only one hour from the schedule, hardly enough to assuage the critics of sex and violence. In the face of the tremendous pressure from the FCC, Congress, and the public, the networks needed to do something specific to blunt the criticism and take the sting from the continuing accusations.

In late December, 1974, nearly four months after "Born Innocent" aired, CBS president Arthur Taylor proposed that all three networks agree to observe a "family hour" between 8:00 P.M. and 9:00 P.M. each night, during which they would air only material suitable for the entire family. Taylor promised that CBS would lead the way and urged the other networks to follow. One month later, the NAB, the National Association of Broadcasters (the self-regulating organization of the television industry), voted overwhelmingly to make the family hour quasi-legal, revising its general code of practices established in the Fifties to include adherence to the concept. Its new rules required that "programming inappropriate for viewing by a general family audience" not be aired in the family hour and, beyond that, shows which "contain material that could be disturbing to significant segments of the audience" would have to be preceded by a warning that the program was intended for mature viewers—no matter what time of day it aired.

Other TV executives were furious but helpless. What network could dare openly say, "No, we are not going to adhere to the family hour. We'd rather fill our time with gratuitous sex and violence." That would be public relations suicide. So ABC and NBC joined CBS in setting up their schedules for the fall of 1975 in light of both Access III and the family hour. Congress was happy. The FCC was happy. Sponsors felt relieved. Adoption of the rule diffused the most intense public pressure, though it didn't lay the issues to rest. With the family hour in effect, watchdog groups had very specific criteria by which to judge eight of each network's twenty-two prime time hours every week, as well as the encouragement to scan the remaining time for other offenses. Far from being a final solution, then, the rule created a myriad of other production and planning problems.

One question was obvious: Just what was appropriate for a general family audience? When dealing with the Sunday night kidvid slot in its access rules, the FCC specifically cited *The Wonderful World of Disney* as the kind of programming it wanted. *Disney*, however, was in a unique situation that really didn't offer much help in planning other series. Its producers could draw on more than forty years of studio material, from beautifully photographed nature films to dozens of hit movies specifically aimed at kids—as well as some of the best cartoon animation ever done. For twenty years the networks had tried and failed to generate just one program in this style; they certainly could not produce eight each in one season. A more practical model was CBS's *The Waltons* which offered an obvious hook: programs in the family hour could focus on . . . families! Consequently, *Joe and Sons* (the struggles of a widower-sheet metal worker trying to raise his two teenage sons), *Three for the Road* (the travels of a widower-photographer who roamed the country in a motor home with his two young sons), *Swiss Family Robinson* (Irwin Allen's suburban-family-lost-in-space motif shifted back to a desert island), and *The Family Holvak* (the struggles of the Holvak family in a small Southern town during the Depression) appeared in the fall line-up. They were simple, sanitized, and saccharine with obvious heavy-handed morals handed down by preachy adults. None of these programs even

Fay Stewart (Lee Grant) relives old times with her former husband, Jack (Joe Silver). (*From* Fay. *Courtesy of MCA Television Limited*)

FALL 1975 SCHEDULE

	7:30	8:00	8:30	9:00	9:30	10:00	10:30	
MONDAY	local	BARBARY COAST			ABC NFL Monday Night Football [to 12 Midnite]			**ABC**
	local	Rhoda	PHYLLIS	All In The Family	Maude	Medical Center		**CBS**
	local	THE INVISIBLE MAN		NBC Monday Night At The Movies				**NBC**

	7:30	8:00	8:30	9:00	9:30	10:00	10:30	
TUESDAY	local	Happy Days	WELCOME BACK KOTTER	The Rookies		Marcus Welby, M. D.		**ABC**
	local	Good Times	JOE AND SONS	SWITCH		BEACON HILL		**CBS**
	local	Movin' On		Police Story		JOE FORRESTER		**NBC**

	7:30	8:00	8:30	9:00	9:30	10:00	10:30	
WEDNESDAY	local	WHEN THINGS WERE ROTTEN	That's My Mama	Baretta		STARSKY AND HUTCH		**ABC**
	local	Tony Orlando And Dawn Show		Cannon		KATE McSHANE		**CBS**
	local	Little House On The Prairie		DOCTORS HOSPITAL		Petrocelli		**NBC**

	7:30	8:00	8:30	9:00	9:30	10:00	10:30	
THURSDAY	local	Barney Miller	ON THE ROCKS	Streets Of San Francisco		Harry O		**ABC**
	local	The Waltons		CBS Thursday Night Movies				**CBS**
	local	THE MONTEFUSCOS	FAY	ELLERY QUEEN		MEDICAL STORY		**NBC**

	7:30	8:00	8:30	9:00	9:30	10:00	10:30	
FRIDAY	local	MOBILE ONE		The ABC Friday Night Movie				**ABC**
	local	BIG EDDIE	M*A*S*H	Hawaii Five-O		Barnaby Jones		**CBS**
	local	Sanford And Son	Chico And The Man	The Rockford Files		Police Woman		**NBC**

	7:30	8:00	8:30	9:00	9:30	10:00	10:30	
SATURDAY	local	SATURDAY NIGHT LIVE WITH HOWARD COSELL		S.W.A.T.		MATT HELM		**ABC**
	local	The Jeffersons	DOC	Mary Tyler Moore	Bob Newhart Show	Carol Burnett Show		**CBS**
	local	Emergency!		NBC Saturday Night At The Movies				**NBC**

	7:00	7:30	8:00	8:30	9:00	9:30	10:00	10:30	
SUNDAY	SWISS FAMILY ROBINSON		The Six Million Dollar Man		The ABC Sunday Night Movie				**ABC**
	THREE FOR THE ROAD		Cher		Kojak		BRONK		**CBS**
	The Wonderful World Of Disney		THE FAMILY HOLVAK		NBC Sunday Mystery Movie [McCloud, Columbo, McMillan And Wife, McCOY]				**NBC**

made it to January. In fact, the only successful family hour copy of *The Waltons* was NBC's *Little House on the Prairie,* which had begun the previous fall.

Though *Little House on the Prairie* presented an incredibly sentimental view of the West of the 1870s, the cast was strong and the stories were interesting character studies of the individual members of the Ingalls family, told from the perspective of the second oldest daughter, Laura (Melissa Gilbert). The series was based on the *Little House* books written by the real life Laura Ingalls Wilder and, overall, the program downplayed violent action, presenting it as an aberration rather than the main thread of family life in the Old West. Unlike *The Waltons,* which had started out slowly in its first season, *Little House on the Prairie* popped into the top ten within weeks of its fall premiere and remained a consistent winner for NBC through the decade. The program was given a strong boost from the very beginning by the credibility of Michael Landon in the lead role of Charles Ingalls, the young father. He eased his Little Joe character from *Bonanza* into the role of a struggling homesteader in the Minnesota frontier who was loved by his family and respected by his fellow pioneers. Like the Waltons, the Ingalls family had to adapt to the changing demands of life in an uncertain period of American history. They also faced difficult personal crises such as the sudden blindness of daughter Mary in the show's fourth season. Though it had been conceived well

before the family hour concept was developed, *Little House on the Prairie* was an ideal show for the time period.

For the most part, however, the networks were extremely unsuccessful not only with new family-oriented programs for the family hour, but with practically all their other new offerings in those slots. Nineteen of the twenty-six new family hour programs from the 1975–76 season were axed by the next fall. Actually, this percentage was not that much worse than the failure rate for most new shows, but these were spectacular failures with extremely low ratings and muddy, insipid episodes. CBS and NBC were particularly uncertain of just what sort of show was suitable for the family hour and they groped for guidelines that would help sort through the maze of inconsistency. *All in the Family* was moved to a later slot, but *The Jeffersons* was kept in place. The warm family humor of *Good Times* remained in the family hour, but so did the realistic comedy-drama of *M*A*S*H.* Sex was to be downplayed, yet Cher wore low-cut, revealing outfits on her variety show.

Against such a mish-mash of contradictory interpretations of the new rule, writers and producers struggled to turn out their programs. Some managed to roll with the punches, such as the ever-resourceful crew of *M*A*S*H* who used the de-emphasis on sex as a plot springboard to end the overplayed torrid love affair between Major Burns and Major "Hot Lips" Houlihan. Other shows found their concepts crippled beyond repair, and many in the industry pointed to *Fay* as the best example of a potentially good show done in by the family hour.

Fay was created by Norman Lear graduate Susan Harris, who had written a number of episodes for *All in the Family* and *Maude,* including the two-part story of Maude's abortion. She conceived *Fay* as a free-wheeling realistic comedy about a middle-aged divorcee (Lee Grant) attempting to adjust to life after marriage. Instead, the program was stuffed into the family hour and Fay's adult concerns (such as the pursuit of an active sex life) were reduced to adolescent pap. Grant angrily lashed out at NBC for the change and for supporting the family hour in general, saying that, "they all think the American people have no intelligence whatsoever . . . the family hour is a form of childish censorship." Following the family hour guidelines, *Fay* became a hopeless bland mess that was canceled by NBC programming chief Marvin Antonowsky after only three weeks. Grant, appearing on the non-family hour *Tonight* show, heard the news backstage and, once on camera, labeled Antonowsky "the mad programmer" and then proceeded to "give him the finger."

Other people were just as outraged, but they expressed their anger through the courts, hoping to get the rule declared illegal. Right after the family hour took effect, the Writers Guild, the Directors Guild, the Screen Actors Guild, and top producers such as Bill Persky, Sam Denoff, and Norman Lear filed suit, claiming the family hour violated the First Amendment to the Constitution by infringing on free speech and setting up governmental intervention in programming. They pointed to the pressure from Congress and the FCC that had led to the "voluntary" inception of the rule and argued that it was created illegally. More importantly, they said it "chilled the creative activity" of TV and threatened to "set back television's move toward realism and social importance." They held these goals as more important than "protecting" impressionable children by shielding them from the slightest whiff of controversy. In fact, if violent shows were to be judged as dangerous because they fostered distorted concepts among children (such as violence being an acceptable solution to life's problems), then overly sentimental idealized programs could be accused of the same sin—they, too, presented goals and values out of sync with real life. While filming *Fay,* Lee Grant had touched on this concept: "I think it's dangerous and cruel to tell people that such a [sweet sentimental] world exists. It's simply not true."

In addition to these lofty motives, there was a very important financial threat perceived. The lucrative post-network syndication rerun value for shows such as *Kojak* and *Baretta* would most likely be greatly reduced by the tone set in the family hour rule. If such material was unsuitable in the early evening, could it possibly survive public scrutiny in the later afternoons when many children would certainly be watching?

The family hour case lasted until the end of May, 1976, but Judge Warren J. Ferguson withheld ruling immediately, hoping that an out-of-court settlement could be worked out in the meantime. He feared that if he ruled against the family hour, the court would be compounding the problem by sticking its nose into programming decisions. In November, 1976, when it became clear that an out-of-court compromise would never be reached, Judge Ferguson issued his ruling. He blasted the FCC, CBS, NBC, ABC, and the NAB for walking all over First Amendment rights, but he did not overturn the family hour rules. Instead, he issued a stern warning to the government to stay out of program control and urged the networks to dismantle the family hour if they wanted to. Despite the strong condemnation of the family hour by the court, the networks were still in the same bind: They could not

eliminate the family hour without a great deal of embarrassing negative publicity. For the rule to disappear, it would have to do so quietly, probably just fading away due to a lack of public and network interest. For the foreseeable future, that possibility was unlikely and the family hour rapidly became part of the networks' status quo, despite the obvious flaws and contradictions that had surfaced.

Perhaps the most appropriate by-product of the family hour was its effect on the remainder of the schedule. Both old and new programs that were deemed too violent, sexy, or controversial for the family slot were all squeezed into the 9:00–11:00 P.M. period every night, prompting one TV critic to label it "Slime at Nine." This was more than just a cute phrase; it served as a cutting reminder of the ludicrous fallacy behind 8:00–9:00 P.M. as an off-limits area to supposedly noxious adult fare: Many kids were not ushered off to bed at 9:00 P.M. (8:00 P.M. in the Central time zone). The Nielsen audience figures revealed that the number of children that watched *Baretta* was greater than the number that watched *The Waltons.* Before long, the self-appointed guardians of public morality concluded that the family hour was inadequate protection for impressionable children and they began to search for a more effective solution, though for the time being their intense public pressure on broadcasters eased.

Lindsay Wagner played Jamie Sommers, another super-powered hero for ABC. (*From* The Bionic Woman. *Courtesy of MCA Television Limited*)

September 20, 1975

Saturday Night Live with Howard Cosell. (ABC). Roone Arledge and Cosell team up for a wide world of entertainment specifically designed to duplicate the successful Ed Sullivan formula.

September 21, 1975

Space: 1999. A British outer space series rejected by the American networks but successfully sold into syndication. Martin Landau, Barbara Bain, and Barry Morse play Earth scientists set adrift in space after a lunar explosion blows their base into the inky deep. After a strong start, the program falters as viewers complain about its wooden characterizations and weak storylines.

September 30, 1975

Home Box Office goes national via a satellite hook-up.

October 2, 1975

"Fear on Trial." (CBS). Twenty years after firing John Henry Faulk, CBS airs a two-hour docudrama on the famous blacklisting case. William Devane plays Faulk, George C. Scott plays lawyer Louis Nizer, and David Susskind and Mark Goodson appear as themselves. The *real* John Henry Faulk, meanwhile, has returned to television as a storyteller on the syndicated *Hee-Haw.*

October 2, 1975

ABC Late Night. (ABC). In a new move to compete with Johnny Carson, ABC begins airing repeats of old network series, beginning with episodes from its own *Movie of the Week* program and CBS's *Mannix.*

October 20, 1975

Robert MacNeil Report. A thirty-minute in-depth study of one news item a day begins on the East Coast public television stations. On January 5, it goes on the full PBS network. Later in 1976, Washington co-anchor Jim Lehrer receives co-billing.

Ironically, CBS, the network that had proposed the family hour concept, suffered the most from it. In one swoop, CBS corporate president Taylor had undermined the philosophies and formulas of the sophisticated, generally realistic programs such as *Kojak, All in the Family, M*A*S*H,* and *Maude* which had kept CBS number one through the Seventies. In doing so, he stopped the network's momentum cold and, in effect, completely changed the direction of television for the remainder of the decade. Rather than flourishing with further developments of adult themes, the networks had to redirect one-third of their efforts to kidvid programming. CBS and NBC were caught unprepared for that form. ABC, however, was ready.

Kidvid had been an important cornerstone of ABC strategy for more than twenty years, from *Disneyland* to *The Six Million Dollar Man.* While NBC and CBS floundered trying to devise programs suitable for the entire family for the fall of 1975, ABC quickly realized that its usual kidvid fare would be perfect for the family hour.

Taylor's tactical blunder had given ABC the opportunity to excel in a format that drew on one of its proven strengths. He then compounded his mistake by letting Fred Silverman, his chief programmer, slip away to ABC. This double stroke of good fortune could not have come at a more opportune time for the perennial third place ABC. In the fall of 1974, Fred Pierce had become president of the ABC network and he immediately launched a shakeup designed to pull ABC from its doldrums. He overhauled the fall schedule only a month after it began, determined to build on traditional ABC strengths and expand the network's horizons.

In the second season reshuffling, Pierce reduced the frequency of made-for-TV movies (which were no longer sure-fire blockbusters), brought forward one of the network's rare new-wave sitcoms (*Barney Miller*), and placed a renewed emphasis on the urban action-adventure format with *Baretta* and *S.W.A.T.* There was no immediate dramatic rise in ABC's fortunes, but Pierce clearly demonstrated that he had strong programming instincts. In the spring of 1975, he and his chief programmer, Martin Starger, put together one of the strongest ABC fall schedules in years. They placed their popular crime-action shows (*The Rookies, Baretta, S.W.A.T., Streets of San Francisco*) in the pivotal post-family hour 9:00–10:00 P.M. swing shift and built around them: crime and medical drama at 10:00 P.M.; variety, kidvid adventure, and sitcoms at 8:00 P.M. It was a solid schedule in theory, but many ABC master plans of the past had looked good on paper, only to fail in the field. Perhaps this one would have failed as well, but in June, 1975, Fred Silverman joined ABC and the new schedule was placed in the hands of one of the sharpest programmers in television.

Silverman had written his master's thesis at Ohio State University in the late Fifties on ABC's prime time programming strategy. At age twenty-five he had become the wizard behind CBS's daytime programming success, and in the early Seventies had helped keep the network number one by modernizing its prime time line-up. In early 1975, with his contract about to expire, Silverman asked for an increase in official power at CBS, feeling he deserved the recognition. CBS president Taylor disagreed over this relatively modest request and let Silverman take his talents to ABC instead. One network insider observed that "giving Freddie just one more limousine might have kept him home."

Silverman did not make a single change in ABC's fall 1975 schedule, but his manipulative skills were put to the test immediately. ABC had scheduled its new season premieres for late September while both NBC and CBS had targeted their push to begin right on the heels of Labor Day with special "sneak preview" episodes, so it was possible for ABC to fall behind before one of its programs ever aired. In order to prevent NBC and CBS from developing runaway hits against weak ABC rerun competition, Silverman slotted clusters of flashy specials against these previews. His strategy worked. ABC held on until its own premieres and turned in its best ratings performance in more than a decade. The network jumped into second place, right behind CBS.

Of course, there were some immediate failures, including several shows that had "looked good on paper." Mel Brooks had interrupted a string of red hot genre parodies in film to create a TV parody of Robin Hood, *When Things Were Rotten,* but his combination of broad comedy and mild obscenity was forced to fly on television without the obscenity and flopped. Howard Cosell tried to revive the Ed Sullivan combination of a non-performing host and a mixed bag of live variety acts, but he lacked the savvy and restraint to pull it off. And despite the continued popularity of *Star Trek* in syndicated reruns, William Shatner failed to attract a sufficiently large audience to carry the kidvid Western adventure yarns of *Barbary Coast.* For a change, though, ABC found good news mixed with the bad, and its new *Welcome Back, Kotter* and *Starsky and Hutch* joined the revitalized *Happy Days* as new season hits.

Very often in the past, ABC had stumbled upon good programming ideas, but was unable to slot them effectively or cultivate them into major hits. One of Fred Silverman's talents was spotting sometimes hidden potential in marginally successful shows and bringing it out into the open. For the fall of 1975, *Happy Days* was given a complete body job and began its third season sporting a new, more up-to-date theme song, flashier production, and a live audience. More importantly, the theretofore minor figure of Arthur "Fonzie" Fonzarelli was promoted to co-star status. When the series had begun in early 1974, ABC had been wary of focusing too much attention on a proto-hoodlum wearing a leather jacket, so Fonzie had been restricted to brief appearances in the stories. When on-camera, he was shown with his motorcycle—which somehow served as an acceptable excuse for the menacing leather jacket. In the revised premise for *Happy Days,* Fonzie was liberated from his bike and moved into the garage apartment of the Cunningham home, becoming, in effect, a member of the family. Fonzie's expanded role provided the series with a sorely needed strong central character to contrast with the bland world that had been set up. To stand out in this setting, Henry Winkler played his Fonzie character as a more exaggerated macho-bravado hero, who was not merely the toughest, sharpest teenager around, but also protector, counselor, and guru to both adults and teenagers in the neighborhood. They naturally turned to him because "the Fonz" always appeared to be on top of things and in control—he was "cool" in the face of virtually any challenge. This dichotomy between cool control and witless confusion charged the series with new energy and gave both the bland teens and hapless adults the motivation to assert themselves in order to win Fonzie's respect and approval. (Ron Howard's character of Richie improved the most in this manner.)

Setting up a dropout auto mechanic as the smartest guy in town was patently absurd, but the show needed such a larger-than-life caricature. The Fifties nostalgia hook that had first served as the basis for the series had worn thin very quickly. There wasn't any reason to be interested in the unexciting, slightly nurdish characters of Richie and Potsie, nor in the bumbling good intentions of Mr. and Mrs. Cunningham. Besides, *Happy Days* had never been a very good representation of teenage life in the Fifties anyway; it had merely imitated the bland world of Fifties TV sitcoms. With the elevation of Fonzie to the driving force in the *Happy Days* world, the series became the past as people wished to remember it, whether it was the Fifties, Forties, or even the Seventies. In such memories, Fonzie was the perfect hero: He drew on his natural wits rather than formal schooling and could handle any situation better than stuffy, over-educated adults. Fonzie also became a hero to contemporary teens who were entranced by his cool control, and they turned Henry Winkler into a heart-throb of the Seventies.

The revitalized *Happy Days* registered a strong upsurge in ratings and served as an unexpectedly potent lead-in to a new teen sitcom, *Welcome Back, Kotter.* Stand-up comic Gabe Kaplan played a young teacher (Gabe Kotter) who accepted a post at his old high school in Brooklyn to teach a special remedial class of disruptive juvenile delinquents, nicknamed "the sweathogs." They consisted of an appropriately diverse group of ethnic types, including: Vinnie Barbarino, a dumb but handsome Italian (John Travolta); Juan Epstein, a Jewish-Chicano muscleman with a head full of get-rich-quick schemes (Robert Hegyes); Frederick "Boom Boom" Washington, a confident, jive-talking black (Lawrence-Hilton Jacobs); and Arnold Horshack, a naive, ingratiating kid with a high pitched, squeaky voice (Ron Palillo). Kotter recognized their antics from his days as a class troublemaker ten years before and realized that the special class was their last chance—if he failed to win their trust and cooperation, they would probably leave high school without the basic skills for survival.

Welcome Back, Kotter had all the trappings of an insightful, topical study of ghetto education, only the producer (*Chico and the Man*'s James Komack) had no desire to take the series in that direction. It was intended as light family hour humor aimed at the kids, so the conflicts and crises at James Buchanan High School owed much more to *Our Miss Brooks* than Norman Lear. Occasionally there were a few serious message episodes on such topics as the dangers of drugs, the importance of a high school diploma, and sex education but, for the most part, the show consisted of stand-up comedy exchanges between Kotter and the sweathogs, very loosely tied together by minor plot complications. Of course, Kotter never seemed to teach anything, rarely asking questions much harder than "Who discovered America?" Instead, the sweathogs were always involved in "special educational activities" outside the classroom. The program fulfilled every child's secret fantasy of the perfect class: field trips, a comedian for a teacher, and no work. Yet despite the ancient jokes and simple plots, the series worked. The cast members had an excellent sense of timing and their personal interaction covered the many obvious flaws of the series quite well. After awhile, *Welcome Back, Kotter* produced its own teen idol, as Travolta's sexy Vinnie Barbarino began competing with Winkler's Fonz for pinup space in the teen magazines. Travolta parlayed this attention into an unusually successful transition to motion pictures, a feat rarely accomplished by TV stars.

With *Welcome Back, Kotter,* ABC showed how an old fashioned kidvid sitcom could handle the family hour requirements quite nicely, leaving the high-gloss violence to thrive after nine. ABC's big new success in this style of post-family hour programming was *Starsky and Hutch,* placed immediately after the increasingly popular *Baretta.* In order to breathe life into the familiar setting of two plainclothes detectives (Paul Michael Glaser as Dave Starsky and David Soul as Ken "Hutch" Hutchinson), producers Aaron Spelling and Leonard Goldberg took the Maverick formula of witty comaraderie under fire and mixed it with the Seventies world of urban crime and violence. Starsky and Hutch needed to be near-

---

November 3, 1975
    Good Morning America. (ABC). A complete facelift for ABC's version of *Today,* including new hosts (David Hartman and Nancy Dussault) and a new newsman (Steve Bell).

November 5, 1975
    End of the Sarnoff era at RCA as Robert Sarnoff, age fifty-seven, is deposed as RCA's chairman of the board and chief executive officer.

February 2, 1976
    Jackie Gleason brings back the Honeymooners, on ABC, as an occasional special. Audrey Meadows returns to the role of Alice Kramden as she and Ralph celebrate their 25th wedding anniversary.

April 12, 1976
    ABC takes over Monday night baseball from NBC.

June 14, 1976
    The Gong Show. (NBC). Game show whiz Chuck Barris steps in front of the cameras as the last-minute choice for hosting his latest daytime project: a zany update of the *Original Amateur Hour* format. Aspiring amateur talent performs for a panel of celebrity judges, any of whom can eliminate the would-be stars by "giving them the gong."

July 10, 1976
    Time-Life's Home Box Office system gets a competitor in the pay-cable television field in the form of Viacom's Showtime.

Supermen to survive the endless car chases and shoot-outs that filled each episode, so their light banter, personal putdowns, and sly sideways glances at beautiful women were necessary to keep viewers interested in their lives. This obvious scenario had been in the ABC schedule for years in various action-adventure series, but it represented a major change by Spelling and Goldberg. They toned down their reliance on the Jack Webb style of super-efficient, flawless, gung-ho cops (their *S.W.A.T.* had been a souped-up version of Webb's *Emergency*) in favor of more casual characters that didn't necessarily adhere to the law themselves. Thus, Starsky and Hutch resembled the street punks they fought more than other members of the police force. Though the program proved to be quite popular with many viewers, some critics pointed to the sleazier aspects of the package as the perfect example of "Slime at Nine" programming.

Nonetheless, with *Starsky and Hutch, Welcome Back, Kotter,* and *Happy Days,* ABC coasted through the early fall in second place, well behind CBS but far ahead of NBC. In a panic, NBC tore up its schedule and began making plans for wholesale changes in January. In mid-October, however, it received a welcome but unexpected boost from the World Series. The dramatic battle between the Boston Red Sox and Cincinnati Reds extended over seven games, most played in prime time, and brought in the highest sports ratings in television history at the time. On the strength of those two weeks of baseball competition, NBC jumped back into contention in the cumulative ratings contest. By December, less than one ratings point separated the three networks.

At this critical juncture in the season's ratings competition, Fred Silverman's instincts and expertise came into play as he analyzed ABC's position. Silverman reasoned that with the three networks virtually even, implementing successful mid-season changes was more important than planning the next fall's line-ups. The network that jumped ahead in January would have the momentum to carry it through the next season. After all, finishing first in 1975–76 meant starting the next season at number one. Consequently, Silverman treated January, 1976, like a brand-new season. He not only introduced a cluster of second season hopefuls, he also slotted special programming designed to keep the competition constantly off balance.

CBS executives chose to follow the strategy that had worked for twenty years: wait out the competition. They felt that ultimately viewers would return to their old favorites on CBS after the novelty of the new programs wore off. The public had remained loyal to CBS for two decades; the network still had more than half the shows in the top ten; and there was no reason to assume that ABC, even with Fred Silverman, could keep pace through the winter and spring. Therefore, CBS made only a few minor adjustments in its schedule for the second season. By early February, it was clear that CBS had underestimated the competition, as ABC began winning week after week of the ratings battle.

Silverman finetuned the ABC schedule, building strong lead-in shows perfect for the family hour. The biggest new hit of the second season was a spinoff from *Happy Days* featuring two young women, friends of the Fonz, Laverne (Penny Marshall, sister of the show's producer, Garry Marshall) and Shirley (Cindy Williams), who had graduated high school and were striking off on their own. They were aggressive working class characters employed at a Milwaukee brewery, but with a very active social life that frequently put them in conflict with snotty upper-class types. Like Fonzie, they drew on their natural instincts and know-how rather than formal education in successfully facing these situations. Though set in the late Fifties (like *Happy Days*), *Laverne and Shirley* presented women

in a role unheard of in television twenty years before: They were strong, self-sufficient, and in control of their lives—as well as being lovable, wacky, and searching for eligible men. They were just as likely to pull their klutzy male co-workers, Lenny (Michael McKean) and Squiggy (David Lander), from some dumb misunderstanding as to need rescuing themselves. At the same time, the series also marked a return to the Fifties *I Love Lucy* style of physical comedy and slapstick humor, continuing the move from realism precipitated by the family hour.

Practically overnight, the thrust of new comedy shows had changed. Though *Welcome Back, Kotter, Happy Days,* and *Laverne and Shirley* had serious moments, their humor was straightforward, physical, and not very sophisticated or overly concerned with relevant social issues. Comic caricatures and super-"cool" heroes such as the Fonz and Barbarino became the important new hooks for the plots and laughs. This marked the beginning of the end of the dominance of Norman Lear's style of comedy, and his new entry for CBS, *One Day at a Time,* was his last new network series to become a top ten hit in the Seventies. *Laverne and Shirley* was placed in the hot slot following *Happy Days* (*Welcome Back, Kotter* was moved to lead into *Barney Miller* on Thursday), and both series immediately jumped into the top ten. They were joined there by another ABC clone, *The Bionic Woman,* who was literally raised from the dead and given her own show.

In the spring of 1975, a two-part story on *The Six Million Dollar Man* introduced Jaime Sommers (Lindsay Wagner), an old flame of Steve Austin's who, after an accident, was also given nuclear powered limbs. The ratings for the episodes had been extremely high and the public obviously wanted to see more of the Bionic Woman; however, she had been killed at the end of that story. Such minor considerations had never stopped comic book writers in the past, so she was brought back in the fall of 1975 in another two-part episode of *The Six Million Dollar Man.* In January, *The Bionic Woman* became a weekly family hour series of its own. In order to help boost the new program's ratings, both Steve Austin and Jaime Sommers occasionally appeared in each other's stories, and both series were plugged in the coming attractions at the end of every episode. Anyone who was interested in one of the shows would end up watching both. Just to be safe, Silverman also flip-flopped the two series a few times, running *The Bionic Woman* in *The Six Million Dollar Man*'s time slot, and vice versa.

ABC had unlocked the secret of the family hour, going straight for the motherlode: kids from two through seventeen. The kids responded and turned ABC's family hour fare into certified hits on five of the seven nights of programming. Suddenly, ABC was dominating most nights of the week, combining its family hour success with solid action-adventure shows.

In the past, ABC had blown ratings leads by finding one program type and working it to death. Silverman did not let this happen and seemed determined to develop winning programs in many directions so that ABC could build its own well-rounded stable of hits and draw viewer loyalty similar to the support that had taken CBS through season after season of success. Even as the new ABC hits became familiar to more and more people, Silverman began inserting special programming to lure new viewers who would then hopefully stick around for the regular series.

In early February, ABC devoted thirty and one-half hours of prime time to coverage of the winter Olympics in Innsbruck, Austria. NBC's coverage of the winter games four years earlier had bombed, so many television insiders regarded this as a foolhardy risk, but it paid off. Roone Arledge's *Wide World of Sports* crew, led by Howard Cosell, Frank Gifford, and Chris Schenkel, clearly explained each event. They produced "up close and personal" profiles of standout performers, filmed in the athletes' home towns before the formal competition, to give viewers human background information in addition to the usual endless statistics. Bewildering events such as a cross-country ski and shoot competition became comprehensible and exciting contests with heroes the home audience could cheer on. The winter Olympics coverage won most of its time slots, even up against established entertainment hits.

Immediately after the winter Olympics, ABC introduced its first major followup to the successful 1974 novel-for-television, *QB VII*, the twelve-hour adaptation of Irwin Shaw's *Rich Man, Poor Man*. Like the British historical dramas presented on public television's *Masterpiece Theater, Rich Man, Poor Man* was a high-gloss soap opera. It traced the lives, loves, and intrigues of a high-class family over the span of one generation, focusing on two fiercely antagonistic brothers (played by Peter Strauss and Nick Nolte). Like the Olympics, this miniseries also cracked the top ten.

In the spring, Silverman gave producers Aaron Spelling and Leonard Goldberg the chance to move from the cop mold to more serious themes in *Family*. The series' concept had been kicked about at ABC for three years but landed nowhere because the network had been afraid that the average viewer would not be able to identify with the Lawrence family: they "lived too well, dressed too well, and spoke too well," one executive said. In short, they were portrayed as real people who talked about serious matters such as death, divorce, alcoholism, and homosexuality without wrapping the discussions in vicious putdowns or simpleminded caricatures. Silverman had enough faith in the series to give it an extended tryout against first-run competition in early March, rather than waiting for the late spring and summer rerun season. With practically no publicity, it replaced the ailing *Marcus Welby,*

M.D. and captured a 40% share of the audience against CBS's gimmicky "Sting" rip-off, *Switch,* earning a spot in the fall line-up.

The Olympics were supposed to bomb. *Rich Man, Poor Man* wasn't supposed to be a big hit. *Family* was not even noticed at first. But they all clicked. CBS and NBC executives had felt certain that once the flashy specials were out of the way, ABC's new viewers would melt away. They didn't. For eleven weeks in a row, through the winter and into the spring, ABC won the weekly ratings race, not just with its specials, but with growing viewer loyalty to its regular series. During the second season, ABC had four of the top five shows, nine of the top twenty, and thirteen of the top thirty. It was steadily chipping away at the cumulative ratings lead CBS had built at the start of the season.

In the summer, ABC carried the summer Olympic games in Montreal and these proved more successful than the incredible 1972 Olympics in Munich. For two weeks, the network junked its prime time schedule and presented the Olympics all night, every night. It won every time slot every night, with an average 49% share of the audience. With this sports blockbuster, ABC matched and passed CBS's seasonal average. In one amazing season, ABC had become the number one network, ending years of programming frustration.

Fred Silverman appeared to be a miracle man, with everything he touched turning to gold. Actually, he still had not proved himself in creating new programs from scratch—he had relied on spinoffs and series already under development before he came to ABC. However, there was no denying his ability to program the material at hand into the best possible slots. Fred Silverman had taken his new network to the top and there was no one in the industry better equipped to keep it there.

36. The Big Event

DESPITE ABC's incredible performance from January to August of 1976, the network had just barely edged out CBS in the cumulative ratings for the entire 1975–76 season. CBS, in fact, had technically won the "regular" season (September to April), losing only when the summer rerun period was averaged in to the total. The fall of 1976 was therefore expected to mark the beginning of a very tight season-long ratings battle. To counter the revitalized ABC, NBC turned to special event programs while CBS eased in a handful of new shows, still convinced that, in the new season, viewers would return once again to their old favorites. As the network temporarily on top, ABC planned to build on the momentum of last season's dramatic come-from-behind victory, confident that it had won viewer loyalty with its new hits and frequent specials.

Just as he had done in keeping CBS on top earlier in the decade, Fred Silverman carefully arranged ABC's series, stars, and special events for the fall, yet he remained flexible enough to make last minute changes to counter the competition with the strongest possible line-up. He shifted a variety series featuring the musical duo of the Captain and Tennille from a scheduled summer tryout period directly into the fall line-up where it could serve as both an ideal family hour program and an ABC promotional device. Then, at the end of August, he changed the announced time slots of five series, including new episodes of the popular *Rich Man, Poor Man* story. He rescheduled that series (labeled *Book II*) from a Saturday night slot to the frontlines on Tuesday at 9:00 P.M., right after *Laverne and Shirley.*

Counting on the strength of its familiar veterans, CBS held firm. NBC, however, juggled its own schedule in response, changing the announced time slots of six shows, eliminating *Snip* (a situation comedy based on the film "Shampoo"), and postponing the John O'Hara-inspired drama *Gibbsville* until an appropriate second season slot opened. These changes took place so close to the opening of the new season that the special fall preview edition of *TV Guide* (which hit the stands in mid-September) still contained close-up background information on these two NBC proto-series. The editors apologized and explained that the text, graphs, and writeups in that issue reflected the new season as it stood at press deadline time, but that everything could change at any moment. Even the once sacrosanct fall schedules had succumbed to the increasingly common last-minute network brinkmanship aimed at scoring the season's first ratings blow.

Attempting to gain an additional edge, each of the networks also jammed September with special events such as blockbuster films, extended length series premiere episodes, TV movies, and celebrity-studded variety shows. The previous fall Silverman had used such "stunting" and "frontloading" techniques extensively in order to keep the other networks from building an insurmountable ratings lead over then number three ABC. This season, all three networks stressed such programming both to pump up their ratings on particular nights and also to tout their overall schedules by using regular series stars as special headliners and guests. Such cross-pollination encouraged viewers to follow a network's entire line-up to see their favorite series stars in action.

During premiere week, variety star Sonny Bono played a ruthless rock manager and record promoter on CBS's *Switch,* while the casts of both *Switch* and *One Day at a Time* appeared on the season opener of *The Tony Orlando and Dawn Rainbow Hour.* Freddie Prinze, from *Chico and the Man,* played a character similar in spirit to his fast-talking Chico in a new NBC made-for-television movie, "The Million Dollar Ripoff." On ABC, stars such as Penny Marshall and Cindy Williams from *Laverne and Shirley* and the sweathogs of *Welcome Back, Kotter* appeared throughout the week. They ushered in the new Captain and Tennille variety show as well as new series from Bill Cosby *(Cos)* and *Kotter*'s producer, James Komack *(Mr. T and Tina).* To plug the one-hour season premiere of *Happy Days* featuring Roz Kelly as Pinky Tuscadero (a tough-talking woman with her eyes on the Fonz), Kelly also appeared the night before as a special guest on *The Captain and Tennille.*

Once viewers had sampled the many new offerings and specials, they did just as CBS had predicted and returned to their old favorites. However, these favorites now included Lee Majors, Henry Winkler, John Travolta, Robert Blake, Peter Strauss, Lindsay Wagner, Penny Marshall, Cindy Williams, and Gabe Kaplan—all stars of series on ABC.

Fred Silverman had analyzed the network situation perfectly the previous season. The special events and flashy changes in the early months of 1976 had lured viewers and introduced them to the regular ABC stars and series. As these shows began winning week after week in the ratings, more and more people fell into the habit of looking in on the programs presented by the new number one network. These new viewer habits carried over into the fall and the expected tight three-way race never developed.

Instead, ABC quickly jumped out in front and stayed there, dominating four or five nights a week. It was soon clear that ABC had solidified its position as the number one network and would win the 1976–77 season with ease. The real fight became the contest for the number two spot.

Of course, ABC had its share of clunkers including *Holmes and Yo Yo, The Nancy Walker Show,* and *Mr. T and Tina*—which never caught on even with all the hype. Overall, however, the network did extremely well with its returning shows and even managed to come up with the only new regular series to break into the top ten, *Charlie's Angels.*

Produced by crime show veterans Aaron Spelling and Leonard Goldberg (of *Starsky and Hutch* and *The Mod Squad*). *Charlie's Angels* featured a trio of beautiful women taken from routine police-work and assigned to special undercover detective duty by a man known only as Charlie (John Forsythe). He dubbed them his squad of "angels" and used them for dangerous undercover missions suited to their particular talents. Charlie never appeared in person, but gave his instructions over a speaker phone, outlining the details of each high-priority mission. When not near a phone, the angels took orders from Charlie's flunky, John Bosley (David Doyle). Despite the familiar cloak and dagger trappings, *Charlie's Angels* was far more than a routine detective-adventure show. It was an excuse to show sixty minutes of suggestive poses by walking, talking pin-up girls.

Each of Charlie's angels waged her battles in form-fitting clothes, a bikini, or nightgown, soundly thrashing international spies, deranged maniacs, and other strawmen-villains without ever working up a sweat. Yet they also willingly responded to the orders from their off-camera male superior, creating the perfect male sexual fantasy with a dream woman for every man: Sabrina (Kate Jackson) was the lowkey intelligent type that combined brains and beauty; Kelly (Jaclyn Smith) symbolized the traditional high society charmer who was always in style; and Jill (Farrah Fawcett) brought up images of torrid backstreet passion with her windswept coiffure and knowing smile.

Television critics gasped in horror when they realized that the suggestive soft-core porn of ABC's latest hit was the most popular new series of the season. They rushed to point out the obvious flaws of *Charlie's Angels,* panning the show as "dreadful," "schlock" and "stupid." Yet just as the general public had ignored the critical lambasting of *The Beverly Hillbillies* the decade before, viewers (male and female) eagerly followed the adventures of the three scantily clad glamour lovelies despite the knocks. The threadbare plots, papier-mâché characters, and wooden dialogue did not matter. Women were pleased to see a team of female adventurers more than hold their own in a standard television setting. The men were more than happy to ogle. Besides, nothing explicit ever took place on the screen.

The sex on *Charlie's Angels* was really just suggestive titillation—squeaky clean TV sex. Even with their bra-less wardrobe, Sabrina, Kelly, and Jill were, in truth, just like previous television glamour girls such as the genie (Barbara Eden) of *I Dream of Jeannie,* the perfectly constructed female robot (Julie Newmar) of *My Living Doll,* and the aspiring starlets of *Bracken's World.* They never appeared in scenes of torrid physical passion, just in revealing costumes. The active imaginations of the viewers filled in the rest with whatever fantasy seemed appropriate.

With *Charlie's Angels* ABC had once again struck ratings gold and the reality of the network's competitive position at last hit home at CBS. After the first month of the new season, though CBS still had twelve of the top forty shows (including the very

successful *All in the Family* and *M*A*S*H*) the former number one found itself in the cellar. With the exception of a new blue collar working sitcom, *Alice* (based on the hit movie "Alice Doesn't Live Here Anymore"), all the new CBS shows bombed. More importantly, many previously solid CBS hits such as *Phyllis, Kojak,* and *Sonny and Cher* were dropping even as the ABC line-up soared.

Part of CBS's problem could be traced directly to the family hour, which CBS corporate president Arthur Taylor had originally proposed and championed. Overnight it had shifted the emphasis in prime time programming away from relatively adult fare such as *Kojak* to the types of teen-oriented material that ABC had specialized in for years. While ABC rolled on with shows such as *Laverne and Shirley,* CBS was unable to develop new programs that could adapt its strengths to the demands of a television world less interested in topical issues and realistic violence.

A more important cause of CBS's downfall, however, was that while on top the network had become complacent and overconfident. Instead of developing a wide range of pilots and new shows as back-up inventory, the network had stagnated. Since the fall of 1974 CBS had come up with only three new hit shows (*Rhoda, The Jeffersons,* and *One Day at a Time*) to step in and share some of the load. As a result, CBS's success depended almost entirely on an increasingly old line-up. ABC, in contrast, had only one program—*The Streets of San Francisco*—that had been on before the fall of 1973.

In the late 1960s, CBS management had committed the same sin with an over-reliance on aging rural series, but then-network president Bob Wood and his chief programmer Fred Silverman had been able to snap CBS back to life by pruning the schedule and ushering in the Norman Lear-*All in the Family* era. That action had come just in time. Now, it was too late to save the 1976–77 season. As one CBS insider put it, "We're running out of gas."

In October, CBS's Arthur Taylor walked the plank and the network began a top-to-bottom executive housecleaning. The new management team, led by Gene Jankowski, faced both the long-term task of rebuilding the network's schedule and the immediate challenge of trying to salvage the current season by at least moving ahead of NBC into the number two spot.

NBC found itself in a much better competitive position going into the fall of 1976. Not only did the network have high hopes for two special prime time vehicles (dramatic miniseries and "big event" specials), it had also developed a new comedy-variety show the previous season that had become the talk of television: *Saturday Night Live.*

Since the early Fifties, NBC had consistently turned to comedy-variety as an important television programming strategy. Stars such as Bob Hope, Dean Martin and Jerry Lewis, Sid Caesar, Flip Wilson, and Dan Rowan and Dick Martin had headlined some of the network's most successful programs. Though Bob Hope and Dean Martin continued to do occasional specials, NBC had been unable to find successful new headliners for a weekly series going into the mid-Seventies. The network had brought in the Smothers Brothers as mid-season replacements in 1974–75, but—after strong opening ratings in January, 1975—their series failed. Despite fresh talent such as Steve Martin, Don Novello (as Vatican correspondent Father Guido Sarducci), and writer Chevy Chase, the Smothers seemed unable to adapt to the new decade. They fluctuated between familiar rehashes of bits from their late Sixties show (with Pat Paulsen and Bob "Officer Judy" Einstein) and bland new skits with guests such as Ringo Starr.

For the fall of 1975, the network turned to former *Laugh-In*

FALL 1976 SCHEDULE

	7:30	8:00	8:30	9:00	9:30	10:00	10:30	
MONDAY	local	THE CAPTAIN AND TENNILLE		ABC NFL Monday Night Football [to 12 Midnite]				**ABC**
	local	Rhoda	Phyllis	Maude	ALL'S FAIR	EXECUTIVE SUITE		**CBS**
	local	Little House On The Prairie		NBC Monday Night At The Movies				**NBC**

	7:30	8:00	8:30	9:00	9:30	10:00	10:30	
TUESDAY	local	Happy Days	Laverne And Shirley	Rich Man, Poor Man – Book II		Family		**ABC**
	local	Tony Orlando And Dawn Rainbow Hour		M*A*S*H	One Day At A Time	Switch		**CBS**
	local	BAA BAA BLACK SHEEP		Police Woman		Police Story		**NBC**

	7:30	8:00	8:30	9:00	9:30	10:00	10:30	
WEDNESDAY	local	The Bionic Woman		Baretta		CHARLIE'S ANGELS		**ABC**
	local	Good Times	BALL FOUR	All In The Family	ALICE	The Blue Knight		**CBS**
	local	The Practice	NBC Movie Of The Week			THE QUEST		**NBC**

	7:30	8:00	8:30	9:00	9:30	10:00	10:30	
THURSDAY	local	Welcome Back Kotter	Barney Miller	TONY RANDALL SHOW	NANCY WALKER SHOW	Streets Of San Francisco		**ABC**
	local	The Waltons		Hawaii Five-O		Barnaby Jones		**CBS**
	local	THE GEMINI MAN		BEST SELLERS (THE CAPTAINS AND THE KINGS, ONCE AN EAGLE)		VAN DYKE AND COMPANY		**NBC**

	7:30	8:00	8:30	9:00	9:30	10:00	10:30	
FRIDAY	local	Donny And Marie		The ABC Friday Night Movie				**ABC**
	CAMPAIGN '76: RACE FOR THE WHITE HOUSE	SPENCER'S PILOTS		CBS Friday Night Movies				**CBS**
	local	Sanford And Son	Chico And The Man	The Rockford Files		SERPICO		**NBC**

	7:30	8:00	8:30	9:00	9:30	10:00	10:30	
SATURDAY	local	HOLMES AND YOYO	MR. T. AND TINA @THE NEW, ORIGINAL WONDER WOMAN	Starsky And Hutch		MOST WANTED		**ABC**
	local	The Jeffersons	Doc	Mary Tyler Moore	Bob Newhart Show	Carol Burnett Show		**CBS**
	local	Emergency!		NBC Saturday Night At The Movies				**NBC**

	7:00	7:30	8:00	8:30	9:00	9:30	10:00	10:30	
SUNDAY	COS		The Six Million Dollar Man		The ABC Sunday Night Movie				**ABC**
	60 Minutes		Sonny And Cher Show		Kojak		DELVECCHIO		**CBS**
	The Wonderful World Of Disney		NBC Sunday Mystery Movie (McCloud, Columbo, McMillan, QUINCY, M.E.)			THE BIG EVENT			**NBC**

writer Lorne Michaels to supervise a new comedy-variety show. (Over the previous two seasons Michaels had worked on two successful comedy-variety specials starring another *Laugh-In* graduate, Lily Tomlin, first as a writer, then as a producer.) Because the proposed new NBC series was viewed as somewhat experimental, it was slotted to appear late night on Saturdays, 11:30 P.M. to 1:00 A.M., three times a month. This placement was also aimed at tapping the young adult audience, a long-ignored but growing group of viewers that the networks had begun to pursue during the 1972–73 season.

The initial shows targeted for this demographic group featured rock music. ABC was first in November, 1972, with a late Friday night special, *In Concert*. The program soon became a twice-monthly fixture and NBC followed in early 1973 with its own weekly late night series, *The Midnight Special* (hosted by legendary rock disk jockey Wolfman Jack). That program also broke new ground by becoming the latest-starting network show in television history, beginning after the Friday night *Tonight* show (1:00 A.M. Saturday morning). Though rock had rarely been able to capture sufficiently high ratings to succeed in prime time, the late Friday night exposure attracted a solid audience consisting primarily of young adults that shunned prime time (going out for the evening instead) but who returned to catch their favorite acts before turning in.

In the fall of 1974, NBC slotted a monthly news and public affairs program, *Weekend*, in the Saturday night slot of 11:30 P.M. Its slightly tongue-in-cheek style catered toward this same young adult crowd. For the fall of 1975, NBC's new Saturday night comedy-variety show was to fill in the remaining three weekends of each month.

In setting up the new program, Michaels was determined to develop *Saturday Night Live* as a special entity, different from standard prime time network variety. Like NBC's *Your Show of Shows* from the early 1950s, there would be guest stars, but they would be generally limited to a guest host that would work with a continuing company of writers and supporting players. Like the late night rock shows, the musical guests (rock, jazz, and folk-oriented) would be presented straight, performing one or two songs without engaging in banal "transition" patter. Like *Laugh-In* and the original *Smothers Brothers Comedy Hour*, there would be topical references and satirical jabs, as well as parodies of television, movies, and commercials. And, like the fondly remembered golden age of television, the program would be presented *live*, from New York City, before a real studio audience.

The decision to do the program as a live New York production immediately gave the project a distinct flavor and generated high expectations, while the late night weekend slot provided the much needed time to work out the rough spots. The first broadcast of

NBC's *Saturday Night Live* took place on October 11, 1975, with veteran comic George Carlin as host and Billy Preston and Janis Ian as the musical guests. It was very uneven. Singer-songwriter Paul Simon hosted the second show and, in effect, turned it into a Paul Simon musical special. (He had three guest singers and together they performed nearly a dozen numbers.) Yet in just a few months, working with subsequent hosts such as Rob Reiner, Lily Tomlin, Candice Bergen, Richard Pryor, Buck Henry, and Dick Cavett, the program's crew jelled and the show began to develop its style, a reputation, and a following.

High school and college students were among the first to latch on to the show, partially because the program was deliberately outrageous, sometimes even tasteless, in the style of the increasingly popular BBC import, *Monty Python's Flying Circus,* and the home-grown radio, stage, and magazine efforts of the *National Lampoon.* The opening joke on the very first show involved the Python-ish premise of two men dying of heart attacks, capped with the punch-line: *"Live, from New York, it's Saturday Night!"*

As with *Your Shows of Shows,* the company of regular performers evolved into the real stars of the series. Dubbed "The Not Ready for Prime Time Players," Dan Aykroyd, John Belushi, Chevy Chase, Jane Curtin, Garrett Morris, Laraine Newman, and Gilda Radner each developed their own distinctive character types and caricatures. Chase was the first to attract a following, based chiefly on his mock newscasts ("Weekend Update") and his portrayal of a bumbling, dull-witted President Gerald Ford.

Aykroyd, Belushi, and Chase also served as program writers, joining *National Lampoon* co-founder Michael O'Donoghue, Lorne Michaels himself, and nearly a dozen others. They produced the expected excellent movie and television parodies, including a re-make of "Citizen Kane" (revealing Kane's last words to be: "Roast Beef on Rye with Mustard"), *Star Trek*'s final voyage, and a "Jaws"-like urban killer, the "Land Shark." Political and topical subjects ranged from President Richard Nixon's final days in office to Claudine Longet's "accidental" shooting of a number of helpless skiers on the slopes. (The latter prompted an on-the-air apology.) Yet there were also very effective mood pieces such as a chance coffee shop encounter between a young man and a woman he had admired from afar years before, in high school. By the spring of 1976, *Saturday Night Live* had gained such a following that even Gerald Ford's press secretary, Ron Nessen (a former NBC news correspondent), agreed to serve as host, bringing along film inserts of President Ford himself.

For the next four years, *Saturday Night Live* grew in popularity and quality. Though the very nature of a live weekly show meant that any particular episode might be weak, overall the series emerged as the most daring and innovative television program of the late Seventies. Hosts such as consumer advocate Ralph Nader, football star O. J. Simpson, and rock star Frank Zappa, as well as more traditional Hollywood actors such as Cecily Tyson, Richard Benjamin, and Elliott Gould, turned in excellent performances as headliners. Though Chevy Chase left the cast in the program's second season to pursue a solo career in films (he was replaced by another of the show's writers, Bill Murray), the rest of the players remained, further developing their stock of characters and routines. Skits became increasingly complex and sophisticated with such presentations as "The Pepsi-Syndrome" (based on the nuclear accident at Three Mile Island and the film "The China Syndrome") running nearly twenty minutes.

After five seasons, all the players as well as Lorne Michaels himself left the show. (A completely new cast took over in the fall of 1980.) Most attempted solo film projects, with Chevy Chase

and John Belushi scoring the biggest successes (Chase in "Foul Play" and Belushi in "National Lampoon's Animal House" and—with Dan Aykroyd—in "The Blues Brothers"). One of the biggest stars to emerge from *Saturday Night Live,* though, was comic Steve Martin. He hosted the show a half dozen times (beginning in the second season), launching a fabulously successful concert, film, and writing career in the process.

Unlike *Your Show of Shows,* all *Saturday Night Live* episodes were preserved on video tape and could be rerun during the summer or during the regular season to give the cast a few weeks off. In the show's fifth season, NBC took highlights from these tapes and turned them into a brief prime time series, *The Best of Saturday Night Live.*

NBC's 1975 late night comedy-variety experiment was quickly recognized as an unqualified success and, for the fall of 1976, the network hoped for similar success in prime time with another traditional NBC programming strength, blockbuster special events.

Ever since the Pat Weaver days of the early Fifties when NBC had last been on top, the network had done very well with special programming. In the 1975–76 season, for instance, the prime time World Series broadcasts had kept NBC in contention for number one through December. For the 1976–77 season, NBC set aside a specific weekly slot for prime time sports extravaganzas, blockbuster movies, special dramatic presentations, and even nostalgic retrospectives. Dubbed *The Big Event,* this Sunday night series was designed to expand or shrink to accommodate different types of programs. Some nights it ran ninety minutes; on others it filled the entire Sunday night prime time block. Occasionally *The Big Event* extended to other nights as well. This was the most flexible, extensive use of irregularly scheduled programming any network had attempted in years.

Jack Klugman as Quincy, a stubborn and dedicated medical examiner. (*From* Quincy, M.E. *Courtesy of MCA Television Limited*)

The Big Event got off to an inauspicious start with "The Big Party," a boring collection of live and taped clips from a number of "exciting and glamorous showbiz parties" throughout New York City. Rather than perform, most of the celebrities merely plugged their latest projects before waving the camera on. Dick Cavett, host of the confusing, fractured format, said at one point, "I'm absolutely humiliated because I don't know what I'm supposed to be doing." Shortly thereafter, he began doing impromptu hand-shadows.

Subsequent *Big Event* presentations were much better shows, offering viewers many exciting television programs, from the annual World Series contest to the American network debut of the 1939 movie classic, "Gone With the Wind." The *Saturday Night Live* cast made its first prime time appearance in February with "Live from the Mardi Gras—It's *Saturday Night* on Sunday!" Among the special dramatic presentations were several docudramas including "Raid on Entebbe" (the Israeli commando rescue mission to Africa), "Tail Gunner Joe" (a silly and self-righteous review of McCarthyism), and "Jesus of Nazareth" (a special Easter presentation of the life of Christ, directed by Franco Zeffirelli). There were also well produced retrospectives that gave producers and writers the chance to rummage through movie studio and network archives and to share, on the air, the nostalgic treasure trove they uncovered. Two of the best of this type were the three-hour "*Life* Goes to the Movies" (a dandy review of cinematic history hosted by Shirley MacLaine, Liza Minnelli, and Henry Fonda) and the four-and-one-half-hour "NBC: The First Fifty Years" (NBC's own history presented through the eyes of Greg Garrison, Dean Martin's producer, and hosted by Orson Welles, the era's consummate voice of history).

The Big Event gave NBC a tremendous weekly ratings boost that pushed it past CBS and into brief head-to-head competition with ABC, largely due to the record-breaking audience for "Gone With the Wind," telecast over two nights in early November. At

the time, the film won the distinction of being the highest rated program in television history.

The chief problem with *The Big Event* was the one that always followed such special series, from Pat Weaver's spectaculars to ABC's made-for-TV movies: There were only so many special events. What's more, each episode had to stand on its own with less carryover than for a regular series with returning characters and a consistent situation. Viewers did not automatically follow *The Big Event* but rather tuned in special programs that had caught their attention. In subsequent seasons, then, the emphasis of *The Big Event* shifted somewhat to more frequent use of theatrical features, special made-for-TV movies, and miniseries, mixed in with occasional specials.

Even with its shortcomings, *The Big Event* was a welcome success for NBC and became one of the top ten shows for the 1976–77 season. It demonstrated that viewers would tune to special events, even those carried over an entire evening or running several nights. Lacking many regular series hits, NBC frequently billed special events on other nights as "Big Events" and began to further develop this "event programming" strategy as its answer to ABC's success. This dovetailed perfectly with the network's increasing interest in miniseries, begun that season with the *Best Sellers* anthology.

Best Sellers was an obvious attempt to cash in on the success of ABC's novel-for-television hit *Rich Man, Poor Man* by using the approach taken by public television's *Masterpiece Theater* to present several "novels" in one season. Since 1970, *Masterpiece Theater* had served as the weekly slot for such miniseries as *The Pallisers* and *Upstairs, Downstairs,* running one entire work before moving on to the next title. These sweeping, romantic dynasty epics (chiefly British series, usually set in the 1800s) pulled in surprisingly high ratings for PBS and had even inspired CBS to attempt an Americanized version in 1975–76, *Beacon Hill.* That series, however, quickly became bogged down by its period production and stilted storyline and lasted for only one-half of a season.

NBC planned to avoid those problems with *Best Sellers* by taking the attractive soap opera hooks of lust and intrigue and wrapping them within the works of slick pulp fiction in the style of Harold Robbins, Jacqueline Susann, and Irwin Shaw. The network turned to Universal studios for production of the series and the studio brought in big name stars as special secondary and cameo players to support the very beautiful but generally unknown newcomers cast in the lead roles. In addition, each story was structured to follow the style of the drawn-out British epics that spanned generations, though these American versions usually focused on World War II.

Best Sellers consisted of four miniseries: Taylor Caldwell's *Captains and the Kings,* Anton Myrer's *Once an Eagle,* Norman Bogner's *Seventh Avenue,* and Robert Ludlum's *The Rhinemann Exchange.* They all did fairly well in the ratings, though overall *Best Sellers* was not a blockbuster, averaging just a 27% share of the audience. This was quite a letdown and far below the top ten performance of *Rich Man, Poor Man* the previous season. One other NBC novel-for-television, however, did much better. Upton Sinclair's *The Moneychangers,* which ran in four parts on *The Big Event* in December, scored a 35% share of the audience presenting exactly the same type of soapy drama as *Best Sellers.* Apparently the weekly *Best Sellers* slot was not the most effective commercial format for these novels-for-television. In fact, a weekly series seemed to reduce the impact of the programs as special events. Incorporating such miniseries within *The Big Event* format, though, seemed to offer the best of both worlds. Not only could each one be touted as a special presentation, there was also no need to churn out "a chapter each week" because other material appeared in the slot as well. NBC therefore dropped the weekly *Best Sellers* after only one season and merged subsequent miniseries into various *Big Event* and movie slots.

Even though NBC had made the most substantial commitment to special events and miniseries for the 1976–77 season, it was number one ABC that scored with the show that was both the season's most successful miniseries and television's biggest big event.

Following the high ratings of one of television's first multi-part docudramas, *QB VII* (presented in April, 1974), ABC had begun work on other historical-type dramas, based both in pure fiction (*Rich Man, Poor Man*) and real life (*Eleanor and Franklin*). One of the books selected for miniseries treatment was *Roots*, a work in progress by black writer Alex Haley, who had distinguished himself with his assistance on the autobiography of black activist Malcolm X in the mid-Sixties. At that time, Haley had become increasingly interested in his own black heritage and, at age forty-four, set about reconstructing his family genealogy, determined to trace his personal roots back to Africa, if possible. His search consumed nearly twelve years and was financed chiefly through the advance sale of every possible permutation of the story he hoped to tell, including an adaptation for television.

Plans for the David Wolper production of *Roots* were already well under way before Fred Silverman came to ABC, but it was Silverman who had to decide the most effective way to present the finished product. Haley's incessant probing had resulted in a story that was potential ratings dynamite, tracing the struggle for freedom by Kunte Kinte, an African hunter brought to America as a slave in colonial days, and his descendents. The twelve-hour adaptation took Haley's story from the kidnapping of the young Kunte Kinte (LeVar Burton), through several generations of slavery to the family's post-Civil War independence on their own farm. Subtitled "The Triumph of an American Family," *Roots* was an epic drama of love, war, and death in the soapy style of the successful *Rich Man, Poor Man*. It was assumed that ABC would place *Roots* in a weekly slot (two or three hours at a time) for a month or two, just as it had done with *Rich Man, Poor Man*. Instead, Silverman chose to transform *Roots* into a special television event and he scheduled it for eight consecutive nights, from Sunday, January 23, through Sunday, January 30, 1977, running one or two hours each night. Such treatment had never been given to an entertainment program before, though it was not totally unprecedented. In its coverage of the Olympics the previous season, ABC had junked its entire prime time schedule for two straight weeks in order to present special sports coverage. The packaging of *Roots* was a simple variation on that strategy.

Silverman was taking a chance with the eight nights of *Roots*, facing either overkill from too much exposure at once on a sensitive topic, or indifference to the entire subject, especially by whites. Of all the networks, though, ABC was in the strongest position and had the most room to maneuver. The continued high ratings of ABC's regular series had given the network a comfortable lead in the cumulative ratings race so even a mediocre performance would not have been disastrous. Just to be safe, though, Silverman made certain that *Roots* ended its run before the vital February ratings "sweeps' began.

Naturally, ABC gave *Roots* a tremendous buildup on the air, emphasizing the star-studded cast that included O. J. Simpson, John Amos, Leslie Uggams, Cicely Tyson, Ben Vereen, Ed Asner, Chuck Connors, Lloyd Bridges, and Lorne Greene. It also encouraged schools and civic groups to participate in special courses and discussions based on the program. Haley himself was already working the lecture-and-talk-show circuit hyping the book, so he started including plugs for the television adaptation as well. Just before the miniseries aired, the hardcover edition of *Roots* topped the bestseller charts. Yet despite all the promotion, no one was prepared for the tremendous surge of interest that exploded across the nation.

Roots began with an unexpectedly large number of viewers on opening night and the interest just kept growing. By the time the series concluded, it had broken practically every ratings record in TV history. One-hundred-thirty million people saw some part of *Roots*, more than any other entertainment program ever aired, topping even the spectacular ratings of NBC's presentation of "Gone With the Wind" two months earlier. ABC won every night *Roots* aired and its ratings average for the week (35.5%) was the highest any network had ever registered. The eight episodes of *Roots* held the top eight ratings positions of the week, boosting all twenty-one of ABC's shows into the top twenty-six as well. The concluding segment snared a 71% share of the audience and was the highest rated entertainment show in TV history. (The other seven segments placed fourth, fifth, sixth, eighth, ninth, tenth, and thirteenth in the all-time ratings compilation.) The first post-*Roots* issue of the showbiz weekly *Variety* epitomized the entertainment industry's reaction to the program as it bluntly headlined: "*Roots* Remakes TV World in Eight Nights!"

The more impulsive analysts and executives went even further, declaring that thirty years of programming tradition had been exploded practically overnight, and that *Roots* marked the passing of regular weekly TV fare in favor of diversified miniseries that

November 11, 1976
"Network," Paddy Chayefsky's film fantasy of television network strategy taken to a deadly extreme, opens in New York. Peter Finch plays Howard Beale, news anchor for the mythical U.B.S. network, who angrily denounces American broadcasting and American life in general, shouting, "I'm mad as hell and I'm not going to take it anymore!" Instead of firing him, the network uses "the mad prophet of the airwaves" to build an audience. When his ratings drop, Beale is assassinated by the network's hired guns.

December 17, 1976
Ted Turner's Atlanta UHF independent station, carried by cable in six Southern states, becomes a "super station" by sending its signal, via satellite, to cable systems nationwide.

December 22, 1976
Paramount Pictures buys the Hughes Television Network.

April 1, 1977
After some abortive efforts in the 1950s and 1960s, over-the-air pay television catches on. KBSC, channel 52 in Los Angeles, institutes a "subscription" television operation called "On TV."

May 4, 1977
After being paid one million dollars, former President Richard Nixon comes out of nearly three years of hibernation to be interviewed by David Frost in the first of five hour-long programs.

May 11, 1977
CBS chairman William Paley relinquishes his other job, chief executive officer, to CBS president John Backe.

June 1, 1977
Roone Arledge, president of ABC Sports, becomes president of ABC News as well.

placed an extra emphasis on reality. Some people even asserted that *Roots,* and *Roots* alone, had made ABC number one for the 1976–77 season. Such contentions conveniently ignored both the merely adequate ratings of other miniseries that season, as well as the strength of ABC's regular line-up.

In reality, ABC had been safely ensconced at the top before *Roots* aired and its ratings never slumped once *Roots* was gone. Regular weekly series were still the backbone of television and *Roots* did not mark the end of that format. It was merely an exceptionally successful special event. Nonetheless, *Roots* had passed beyond being viewed as merely a very successful TV show to the status of a national phenomenon, and the nation's pundits felt obligated to explain every aspect of its success. *Time* magazine confidently labeled its story: "Why *Roots* Hit Home." Other magazines, newspapers, and talk shows rushed to present their own sweeping observations, identifying *Roots* in terms such as "the ultimate admission of white guilt" and "the beginning of a new era of racial harmony."

There was certainly a good deal to analyze. Millions of people had rearranged eight days of their lives in order to follow *Roots* on television. Restaurants, social clubs, and movie houses reported sharp drops in attendance during the broadcast, while bookstores faced mobs of buyers who depleted their stockpiles of the book. Places such as drug stores and newsstands, which normally never touched hardcover editions, sold *Roots.* Beyond that, people from every ethnic group began to take an interest in their own personal roots and thousands followed Haley's lead in digging through state birth records, newspaper files, and old shipping logs. It was obvious that *Roots* had touched Americans in every walk of life, but in their zeal to come to grips with a very special event, people ignored many simple, obvious aspects of the *Roots* phenomenon.

Interest in ethnic pride and U.S. history had been on the upswing for years, reaching a peak in the 1976 American bicentennial cele-brations. Haley, in fact, dedicated the book as his bicentennial gift to the nation. *Roots* was therefore presented to an exceptionally receptive audience which was generally familiar with the highlights of the country's developments. The program was also handed a built-in base audience of sorts: An extended cold weather snap throughout the East and Midwest forced many people to remain home, so television viewing was slightly higher than usual anyway.

Above all, *Roots* attracted and kept its audience because it contained the basics of entertaining television: excellent writing, first rate acting, effective violence, strong relationships, tantalizing sex angles, a clear-cut conflict between good and evil, and an upbeat ending. Although race was its central theme, in structure *Roots* was actually more like a Western in the tradition of *Bonanza* and *Wagon Train* only with blacks as the heroes and whites as the villains. The willingness of whites to identify with the black characters did not reflect an admission of racial guilt as much as the usual desire of the audience to side with the good guys on TV. Their allegiance was perfectly consistent with twenty years of television adventure yarns.

Of course, the presentation of blacks as the good guys was a very important change. Over the eight nights of *Roots,* millions shared the black perspective on very familiar events, seeing the old story of the struggle for personal freedom and the fulfillment of the American dream from a new vantage point. "The triumph of an American family" cheered by the nation was, for the first time, the triumph of black Americans. In a way no lecture, preacher, or textbook ever could, *Roots* conveyed the essence of black pride and black culture to millions of Americans. *Roots,* in that sense, *did* become far more than just a successful television show. It came to serve as a respected national rallying point for all black Americans, transforming Alex Haley's personal "obsession" into a symbol of ethnic pride.

37. T & A TV

IN EARLY 1975, despite the success of *All in the Family, Sanford and Son, Maude, The Jeffersons,* and *Good Times,* producer Norman Lear found himself unable to convince any of the three commercial networks to pick up one of his new program projects: a spoof of soap operas. Even CBS, which had financed the pilot, declined to exercise its option on the material. Lear was convinced he had another potential hit on his hands, so he decided to use his contacts and prestige to deal directly with local television programmers, by-passing the networks completely in order to syndicate the show. He met with nearly two dozen of the country's top station managers in late summer, 1975, offering them rights to *Mary Hartman, Mary Hartman.*

Pitching a show too hot for the networks directly to the locals went against the conventional programming wisdom. Traditionally, local programmers were viewed as even more fearful of controversy than the networks. Yet local executives were also interested in getting the larger slice of the television advertising pie possible when the "middle men" (the networks) were eliminated. Earlier that year more than 100 stations had purchased an original science fiction series, *Space: 1999,* directly from a British production company that had offered it to them following rejection by all three networks. Lear was then one of the most successful program producers in television, so the locals gave his proposal serious consideration. After viewing a few sample episodes, several stations agreed to sign on, though Lear did not woo everyone. WNBC and independent WPIX from New York City turned down *Mary Hartman, Mary Hartman* before Metromedia's WNEW bought it. Chicago's top VHF independent, WGN, decided to pass on the offer as well, so the series went to a low-rated UHF station instead. By *Mary Hartman*'s premiere in January 1976, though, Lear had assembled a complement of fifty-four stations to run the series, five days a week.

At first, many stations placed *Mary Hartman* in the afternoon, the time when other television soaps played. Other programmers discovered that *Mary Hartman* worked quite well in a late night slot and many placed the show just after prime time. It was there that, unexpectedly, the series took off and became a national hit. For the first time, a syndicated program became the most talked about series on television.

Mary Hartman, Mary Hartman built a following by walking the delicate line between reality and farce in presenting the adventures of characters from the mythical town of Fernwood, Ohio.

The program was funny, clever, satirical, sometimes outrageous, and sometimes touching. In form, it played more like a regular soap opera than a sitcom: There was a complicated continuing storyline, no laugh track, and an absence of typical comedy one-liners. Yet the pacing was faster than the usual soaper and the expected plot complications of illicit sex, love triangles, and dreams of showbiz success were set slightly but effectively askew by exaggerating both the soap opera style and soap opera plot twists.

Mary Hartman (Louise Lasser) was a typical middle class housewife and mother, only she wore a little girl's Pollyanna housedress and pigtails. Her husband Tom (Greg Mullavey) was temporarily impotent, her young daughter Heather (Claudia Lamb) was ready to run away, her promiscuous sister Cathy (Debralee Scott) was suicidal, and her grandfather Raymond (Victor Kilian) had been identified as the neighborhood flasher. Mary's deepest concern in the opening episode, however, was over the waxy yellow buildup on her kitchen floor.

In subsequent weeks as the storyline evolved, viewers found themselves hooked on the characters of Mary, her family, and her friends, as well as on the program's quickly won reputation for unusual plot twists. At the end of the first season, Mary was chosen the year's "average American housewife" and invited to appear on television on *The David Susskind Show.* As the definitive consumer housewife who had accepted and modeled her real life on the commercial images of the perfect television household, she found herself unable to cope with actually crossing over to become a part of the world of television. In the studio she suffered a mental breakdown on the air.

With such stories, *Mary Hartman, Mary Hartman* regularly topped its competition, often at the expense of the lucrative local news shows running against it on the network affiliates. In March, Metromedia found itself doing so well with *Mary Hartman* that the company ripped up its contract with Norman Lear and wrote a new one for a higher rate.

While *Mary Hartman, Mary Hartman* never duplicated its frantic first year following, the show did last for two more seasons, never losing its feel for outlandish plot twists. Mary began her second season in a mental hospital, recuperating from her on-the-air breakdown. This facility turned out to have another function: It was one of the "average TV households" selected by the Nielsen television ratings service for estimating national viewing habits. Back home, Mary's friend Loretta Haggers (Mary Kay Place) achieved

FALL 1977 SCHEDULE

	7:30	8:00	8:30	9:00	9:30	10:00	10:30	
MONDAY	local	THE SAN PEDRO BEACH BUMS		ABC NFL Monday Night Football [to 12 Midnite]				**ABC**
	local	YOUNG DAN'L BOONE		BETTY WHITE SHOW	Maude	RAFFERTY		**CBS**
	local	Little House On The Prairie @Laugh-In		NBC Monday Night At The Movies @Columbo				**NBC**

	7:30	8:00	8:30	9:00	9:30	10:00	10:30	
TUESDAY	local	Happy Days	Laverne And Shirley	Three's Company	SOAP	Family		**ABC**
	local	THE FITZPATRICKS		M*A*S*H	One Day At A Time	LOU GRANT		**CBS**
	local	THE RICHARD PRYOR SHOW		MULLIGAN'S STEW		Police Woman		**NBC**

	7:30	8:00	8:30	9:00	9:30	10:00	10:30	
WEDNESDAY	local	Eight Is Enough		Charlie's Angels		Baretta		**ABC**
	local	Good Times	Busting Loose	CBS Wednesday Night Movies				**CBS**
	local	The Life And Times Of Grizzly Adams		THE OREGON TRAIL		BIG HAWAII		**NBC**

	7:30	8:00	8:30	9:00	9:30	10:00	10:30	
THURSDAY	local	Welcome Back Kotter	What's Happening?	Barney Miller	CARTER COUNTRY	REDD FOXX		**ABC**
	local	The Waltons		Hawaii Five-O		Barnaby Jones		**CBS**
	local	CHiPs		THE MAN FROM ATLANTIS		ROSETTI AND RYAN		**NBC**

	7:30	8:00	8:30	9:00	9:30	10:00	10:30	
FRIDAY	local	Donny And Marie		The ABC Friday Night Movie				**ABC**
	local	The New Adventures Of Wonder Woman		LOGAN'S RUN		Switch		**CBS**
	local	Sanford Arms	Chico And The Man	The Rockford Files		Quincy, M.E.		**NBC**

	7:30	8:00	8:30	9:00	9:30	10:00	10:30	
SATURDAY	local	Fish	OPERATION PETTICOAT	Starsky And Hutch		THE LOVE BOAT		**ABC**
	local	Bob Newhart Show	WE'VE GOT EACH OTHER	The Jeffersons	Tony Randall Show	Carol Burnett Show		**CBS**
	local	The Bionic Woman		NBC Saturday Night At The Movies				**NBC**

	7:00	7:30	8:00	8:30	9:00	9:30	10:00	10:30	
SUNDAY	Hardy Boys/Nancy Drew Mysteries		The Six Million Dollar Man		The ABC Sunday Night Movie				**ABC**
	60 Minutes		Rhoda	ON OUR OWN	All In The Family	Alice	Kojak		**CBS**
	The Wonderful World Of Disney				THE BIG EVENT @Police Story				**NBC**

her dream of recording a hit Country and Western record ("Baby Boy"), but was tricked into signing over her career management from her husband Charlie (Graham Jarvis) to a slick con man, Barth Gimble (Martin Mull). Neighbor Merle Jeeter (Dabney Coleman) managed to stage a successful campaign for mayor by proving that he had nothing to hide: He stood before a town assembly wearing only a raincoat. Mary's father, George Shumway (Philip Bruns) topped them all. Much to the confusion—but eventual delight—of his wife Martha (Dody Goodman), George came out of necessary plastic surgery following a plant accident looking exactly like Tab Hunter, from head to toe. (Tab Hunter himself took over the role.)

Louise Lasser decided to leave the show at the end of the second season, so the title changed to *Forever Fernwood* in the fall of 1977. To set up her departure, Mary abandoned her family and left Fernwood to elope with a handsome policeman, Sergeant Dennis Foley (Bruce Solomon). The final episode with Lasser showed Mary's new life as a virtual replay of her old, even down to concern over the waxy yellow buildup on her floor.

The message of *Mary Hartman, Mary Hartman* went out loud and clear to both local station programmers and program producers: Popular new programs could be successfully sold and promoted without any involvement by ABC, CBS, or NBC. In 1977, Lear himself launched two other syndicated ventures, *All That Glitters*

(a humorous soap opera on sexual role reversal) and a *Mary Hartman* spinoff/summer substitute that spoofed late night talk shows, *Fernwood 2-Nite* (later called *America 2-Nite*). Universal studios and Mobil Oil were even more successful with their respective first-run projects: Operation Prime Time (OPT) and the Mobil Showcase Network. These ad-hoc networks were set up for a limited but effective penetration of prime time, including placement on network affiliates. The first OPT presentation, a six-hour miniseries (*Testimony of Two Men*), scored well on ninety stations during the May, 1977, sweeps. Mobil's first series, a ten-part program the company purchased from the BBC (*The Explorers*—retitled *Ten Who Dared*), ran over ten weeks on forty stations, twenty-five of which were network affiliates. Each success guaranteed that there would be further challenges to the established networks' hold on programming, even in prime time.

While all three networks had been embarrassed by the acceptance of *Mary Hartman* in syndication after they had turned it down, ABC was the only one to try a similar format in prime time, slotting its own soap opera spoof for the fall of 1977. Thirty-five-year-old Susan Harris, who had written the abortion episodes of *Maude* and created the short-lived *Fay* for NBC, was the creator and chief writer for this new program, called *Soap*. The series setup was simple: the trials and tribulations of two sisters and their families, one wealthy (the Tates) and one middle class (the

Campbells). The plots would focus on the usual grist of soaps, with a heavy emphasis on sex.

Even with the acceptance of *Mary Hartman*, ABC was nervous about *Soap* and held a private screening of two episodes for affiliate executives at an ABC convention in May, 1977. While the reaction was generally favorable (much to the relief of the network), the affiliate programmers convinced ABC to allow stations in the Central time zone to delay the show an hour so that it would not appear before 9:00 P.M. The network also promised to add a "viewer discretion" warning at the beginning of each episode identifying the series as more adult-oriented. Then something strange happened. Months before an episode of *Soap* ever hit the air, the series became the subject of heated criticism across the country.

Advance word about the show clearly conveyed the point that *Soap*, like *Mary Hartman*, would be a sexually oriented comedy, but no one seemed to know just how far it would go. Speculation based on plot summaries and hearsay touched off a wave of charges and counter-charges. *Newsweek* magazine, giving an advance synopsis of one of the episodes already produced, reported that *Soap* would present the seduction of a priest in church. This set off alarms in Catholic parishes throughout the country, and letters began pouring in to ABC demanding that the network take the show off the air—even before it aired one episode. *The Tiding*, the official weekly of the Los Angeles archdiocese, observed that ABC's decision to schedule *Soap* showed little respect for the audience and that the network's initials really stood for "Absolutely Brazen Contempt." Citizens of Memphis, Tennessee, picketed local ABC affiliate WHBQ with placards that read: "Protect our children from evil!" and "We don't want *Soap!*" The U.S. Catholic Conference labeled *Soap* "morally reprehensible," saying the program would be "publicly challenged" and should be "removed from television."

Even some of those select few that had already seen *Soap* joined in the criticism. Westinghouse's only ABC affiliate (WJZ in Baltimore) decided not to air *Soap* because, "it presented a variety of subject matter which does not lend itself to comedic episodic form." The executive vice president of WOWK in Huntington, West Virginia, called it, "One long dirty joke."

As public protests mounted through the summer, ABC and its chief programmer, Fred Silverman, began to fight back. The network described *Soap* as more than just a soap opera: It was "an adult character comedy with a continuing storyline." More importantly, Silverman stressed that "no character in *Soap* is ever rewarded for immoral behavior, and, in the final analysis, there will be retribution for such behavior."

Regarding the controversy over the show itself, Fred Silverman pointedly remarked:

> The summer of 1977 may well go down in television history as the summer of *Soap*. Never have so many words been written about a television pilot which so few people have actually seen.

The Reverend Bob Spencer, an Atlanta Baptist minister, explained the validity, in his eyes, of the protests against the program before it aired:

> We don't have to see the show to know it's indecent. We believe what we have read in national and local publications.
> . . . I believe in the Bible and I don't have to see certain things to know they are wrong.

By August, fifteen ABC affiliates said they would not show the program, and two advertisers had pulled out. In early September, both the *New York Times* and the *Washington Post* ran editorials on the *Soap* controversy. The *Times* backed the protesters, asking how else could people object. The *Post* defended the right to object but said that people should wait until the show was on before registering their complaints.

Through all the rumpus, ABC held firm. On the day before

Louise Lasser as Mary Hartman and Greg Mullavey as her husband, Tom, in Norman Lear's humorous soap opera, *Mary Hartman, Mary Hartman. (Tandem Productions, Inc.)*

the premiere, the *ABC Evening News* covered the *Soap* controversy as a news story and, on September 13, the special one-hour first episode aired. It was quite a letdown.

People expecting a sophisticated sexy show that would upset the traditional television taboos were given instead a series of silly slapstick scenes and sophomoric one-liners. Unlike *Mary Hartman, Mary Hartman,* everything in *Soap* was played for cheap laughs. The characters were one-dimensional and relegated to delivering leering putdowns on such topics as homosexuals, extra-marital affairs, impotency, transvestites, and sex-change operations. Even the much-discussed seduction of the priest turned out to be just a double-entendre proposition which produced a few moments of embarrassment for the cleric but no violation of his vows. *Soap* was not the promised outrageous adult satire, just a tiresomely childish program.

Nonetheless, with all the advance publicity, *Soap* became the season's first big hit, immediately landing in the top ten. As the season wore on, the program slipped a bit in the ratings, but several important revisions then took place. The scripts moved away from being a collection of scandalous topics and innuendo to focus instead on developing both the comic characters and plotline. Though still much more joke-oriented than *Mary Hartman, Soap* began to mix in less boisterous, more human moments. There was still a tremendous emphasis on sex, but the characters began to care for each other.

With this new approach, *Soap* began to build solid audience support presenting likable characters in funny situations. The high-

light of the first season was the trial of Jessica Tate (Katherine Helmond) for the murder of her tennis-pro lover (played by Robert Urich). Certain of her innocence, she spent most of the time trying to cheer up her household, including her promiscuous husband Chester (Robert Mandan), their daughters Corinne (Diana Canova) and Eunice (Jennifer Salt), son Billy (Jimmy Baio), and Benson (Robert Guillaume), their sharp-tongued black butler. Though pronounced guilty, Jessica was saved from imprisonment at the start of the second season when Chester confessed to the crime, explaining that he had been temporarily out of his mind when he did it. Jessica's sister, Mary Campbell (Cathryn Damon), spent much of the first season trying to prevent the murder of her new husband, Burt (Richard Mulligan), by her son, Danny (Ted Wass), who had become involved in organized crime.

The best example of the improvement in *Soap* could be found in the character development of Mary's other son from her first marriage, Jodie Dallas (Billy Crystal), a homosexual. At the start of the series, Jodie served chiefly as the focus for every "gay" joke the writers felt they could get away with. Then Jodie's character was fleshed out and softened. He decided against a sex-change operation, had an unsuccessful affair with a football player, and, to his own amazement, found himself involved with a woman, even becoming a father. This eventually led to an emotional legal battle at the close of the third season in which Jodie gave a powerful, impassioned courtroom speech in defense of his attempt to win custody of the child. By then, all that remained of the original *Soap* controversy was ABC's continued policy of airing the summer reruns of the show in late night slots instead of its usual prime time period. The network had quietly dropped both the time delay feed to the Midwest and the viewer discretion warning in December, 1977, as *Soap* shifted focus.

Perhaps the most important aspect of the public controversy surrounding the premiere of *Soap* was that it served as a dramatic illustration of the networks' increased emphasis on sex as a replacement for violence—and a rallying point for reaction against this policy. This new wave of sexual hooks had begun with the success of *Charlie's Angels* for ABC in the fall of 1976 and the number one network had the most success in exploiting it in other shows for the 1977–78 season, especially in comedies. As with *Charlie's Angels,* these programs took an ogler's approach to sex, emphasizing well-built bodies and suggestive comments over any real sex. The perfect example of this ABC formula for sexual comedy was *Three's Company,* a carry-over hit that had begun in the spring of 1977.

Three's Company presented three young singles living together in the same apartment: Jack Tripper (John Ritter), an easy-going part-time professional cook; Janet Wood (Joyce DeWitt), a level-headed brunette florist; and Chrissy Snow (Suzanne Somers), a sexy "dumb blonde" office secretary. Despite the scandalous setup, nothing ever happened between them. The three were "just good friends" sharing the apartment in order to split the rent. To assure Stanley Roper (Norman Fell), their apartment landlord, that their activities were perfectly harmless, they convinced him that Jack was gay and had no interest in either woman.

As a mater of fact, Jack would eye both—and practically any other pretty woman that crossed his path. In addition, everyone else in *Three's Company* was always thinking about and talking about sex, so a typical program would consist of some simple complication (usually resulting from a misunderstanding involving Chrissy) giving the men a chance to leer and deliver risque lines, and the women a chance to strike suggestive poses and deliver risque lines. The series was an obstacle course sitcom right out of the all-talk-no-action mode of *Love, American Style* from the 1960s and the Rock Hudson-Doris Day "pillow talk" theatrical comedies of the 1950s, playing it squeaky clean but hinting dirty.

While *Three's Company* merely carried on the *Love, American Style* philosophy, two other of the season's new hit ABC series followed that actual program format. Produced by Aaron Spelling and Leonard Goldberg (of *Charlie's Angels*), both *The Love Boat* and *Fantasy Island* (a mid-season replacement) were mildly titillating anthologies, interweaving several light romantic tales to make an hour show. Unlike *Love, American Style*, though, there were also series regulars that appeared each week to tie the individual segments together as part of the same overall story: *Mary Tyler Moore* alumnus Gavin MacLeod acted as the skipper of the *Pacific Princess*, *Love Boat*'s romantic cruise ship, while Ricardo Montalban played the mysterious Mr. Roarke, owner of the tropical island resort where fantasies seemed to come true.

ABC was comfortably on top, propelled by the tremendous performance of its sitcoms, both the established series such as *Happy Days* and the new hits including *Love Boat*, *Soap*, and *Three's Company*. Even against this competition, former number one CBS still had solid top ten performances from *M*A*S*H*, *All in the Family*, *One Day at a Time*, and newcomer *Alice*, but the network was very eager to develop new shows itself as part of a concerted rebuilding effort. One of the companies it placed strong hope in was Mary Tyler Moore's production company, MTM. Like Norman Lear's company, MTM had developed a specific approach to comedy that could be used to spawn other shows. For seven years, *The Mary Tyler Moore Show* and its immediate spinoffs (*Rhoda* and *Phyllis*) stood as the base of the company, but when Moore called it quits at the end of the 1976–77 season, the company needed to work in earnest to create series successors to these hits.

MTM had developed *The Mary Tyler Moore Show* as the model of an adult-oriented ensemble comedy for the Seventies, with very strong supporting players and excellent writing. While Norman Lear usually set his stories in a formal family situation (such as the Bunkers or the Jeffersons) and would "do a show on rape" (or some other topical issue), Moore's ensemble formed a "professional family" of individuals that worked together and grew to love, respect, and depend on each other. Such an approach, however, needed time for the writers and performers to develop the pacing of the series and for the audience to become familiar with the characters.

MTM's first attempt at a new companion comedy was *The Bob Newhart Show*, which began in the fall of 1972, slotted immediately after Moore's show. This placement gave it a spillover audience that found another good show similar to but distinct from *Mary Tyler Moore*. Developed by David Davis and Lorenzo Music, *The Bob Newhart Show* focused on the home and office life of a lowkey Chicago psychologist, Bob Hartley (Bob Newhart), and his loving but strongly independent wife Emily (Suzanne Pleshette), a grammar school teacher. The excellent supporting cast included Bill Daily as neighbor-sidekick Howard Borden, Marcia Wallace as office receptionist Carol, Peter Bonerz as orthodontist Jerry Robinson, and Jack Riley as Elliott Carlin, an incurable neurotic. Like *The Mary Tyler Moore Show*, Newhart's series improved each season as the cast members developed their characters and personalities.

Besides *Bob Newhart* and the two direct *Mary Tyler Moore* spinoffs (*Rhoda* and *Phyllis*), MTM had found that the ensemble comedy formula—while easy to outline in theory—was very tricky to successfully duplicate with totally new characters and settings. Three promising MTM shows—*Paul Sand in Friends and Lovers*

(a bass violinist with the Boston Philharmonic), *We've Got Each Other* (a husband-wife role reversal) and *Texas Wheelers* (Jack Elam, Gary Busey, and Mark Hamill as fun-loving ranch hands in modern rural Texas)—flopped, hurt chiefly by either unfamiliar characters or a difficult premise to develop. Yet at the same time the ensemble approach was still working quite well in *M*A*S*H* and *Barney Miller*, which both survived major cast changes by drawing on the strength of their respective companies of players. Obviously, the formula was resilient once the show got off the ground: The difficulty was in trying to quickly acquaint viewers with a totally new world. For the 1977–78 season, then, the company placed tremendous hope on a careful combination of the old and the new for what looked like a sure-fire comedy winner: *The Betty White Show*.

The new program carefully drew basic elements from *The Mary Tyler Moore Show*, including two former cast members, Betty White and Georgia Engel. White played Joyce Whitman, a sweet-faced woman with a biting tongue (just like Sue Ann Nivens) and Engel was Mitzi Maloney, Joyce's dumb but kind-hearted apartmentmate (just like Georgette Franklin). Like *Mary Tyler Moore*, the series included a show-within-a-show. Joyce was the star of a new CBS television cop show called *Undercover Woman* (a take-off on the popular NBC series *Police Woman* starring Angie Dickinson) and the stories focused on both her home life and behind-the-scenes production activity, including anxious reports on the show's ratings. Included in the support cast were John Hillerman as acerbic show director John Elliot, Joyce's former husband; Caren Kaye as Tracy Garrett, a sexy young actress on the make; and Alex Henteloff as Doug Porterfield, the insecure liaison from the network.

The Betty White Show started strong in a tough slot (against

November 14, 1977
   Walter Cronkite interviews both Egyptian President Anwar Sadat and Israeli Prime Minister Menachem Begin, via satellite, on his nightly news show. Sadat says he might visit Jerusalem. Cronkite asks Begin if that would be all right with Israel. Begin says yes. Five days later, Sadat flies to Israel with Cronkite, NBC's John Chancellor, and ABC's Barbara Walters in tow.

November 30, 1977
   Eric Sevareid, a thirty-eight-year CBS veteran, retires upon reaching age sixty-five.

January 22, 1978
   Sportsworld. (NBC). A new weekend afternoon sports anthology, modeled after ABC's *Wide World of Sports*.

March 10, 1978
   The Incredible Hulk. (CBS). Bill Bixby plays Dr. David Banner who, when angered, turns into Lou Ferrigno as the big green Hulk. The series is loosely based on the Marvel Comics hero.

March 19, 1978
   Mike Stivic, wife Gloria, and baby Joey leave Archie and Edith Bunker and Queens for a new home in California.

April 10, 1978
   America 2-Night. Norman Lear's satiric view of late night television moves intact from Fernwood, Ohio, to Alta Coma, California (the unfinished furniture capital of the world). Martin Mull is Barth Gimble, the self-centered host; Fred Willard plays the Ed McMahon role of sidekick Jerry Hubbard; and musical veteran Frank DeVol is band leader Happy Kyne, director of the off-key Mirth-makers.

Bill Bixby *(l.)* played David Banner, who, when angered, turned into the Incredible Hulk (Lou Ferrigno). (*From* The Incredible Hulk. *Courtesy of MCA Television Limited*)

Monday Night Football and an NBC movie), but then collapsed completely and was gone by January. Even with so many "surefire" hooks, the mixture had failed to jell, hurt chiefly by two flaws in the setup: White's caustic character, while a good foil in a supporting role, did not provide a very likable lead; and the angle of Joyce's former husband being the director of *Undercover Woman* was a silly gimmick that just got in the way of the inevitable conflicts between the two working on opposite sides of the camera.

The failure of *The Betty White Show* was a great disappointment to MTM, which had pegged the series as its front line comedy successor to Moore's show. It was also more bad news for CBS, which wanted some quick success to counter ABC's increasing number of successful comedies. With this latest failure, the prospect for quickly regaining the top spot looked increasingly bleak. Neither Norman Lear nor MTM, which had been the main sources for CBS's success in the early Seventies, seemed able to come up with new hits to replace their successful older shows when they inevitably ended their runs.

As ABC continued securely in its number one spot, NBC and CBS went on the offensive and became more openly critical of ABC's programming. This dovetailed perfectly with the protests by pressure groups which had suddenly realized that their crusades against violent television had ushered in the increased emphasis on sex. As the top network with the top shows, ABC was the obvious target for their renewed protests. CBS and NBC just joined in the chorus.

Robert Wussler, president of CBS television, said during the height of the *Soap* controversy that his network would *never* have aired the program, and then went on to call ABC's shows:

> . . . comic book stuff, cartoon style without the cartooning, and I say it is junk . . . they're all clever and well done, but they're like junk food.

NBC's new programming whiz, Paul Klein, introduced a shorthand description of ABC's programming gimmick: "jiggling." Referring to the bra-less, bouncy breasts of such ABC stars as Suzanne Somers and Farah Fawcett, he said, "You can get an audience from jiggling."

What neither network pointed out, of course, was that both were scrambling for that same audience and were looking for ways to adapt such ABC hooks as comic book adventures, teen comedy, and sexual-orientation to their own schedules. When ABC's Fred Silverman decided in early 1977 to cut the still successful *Bionic Woman* and *The Adventures of Wonder Woman* from the ABC schedule (feeling they had probably peaked), NBC and CBS (respectively) were more than willing to pick them up for the fall of 1977. Besides *The New Adventures of Wonder Woman,* CBS also added another comic book series to its schedule, *The Incredible Hulk.*

NBC was even more blatant in playing up sexual hooks. The World War II adventure series *Black Sheep Squadron* (a revival of the previous season's *Baa Baa Blacksheep*) introduced four nubile nurses to the cast, dubbed "Pappy's Lambs" (a dig at *Charlie's Angels* which ran opposite the show). A relatively straightforward drama series, *James at 15,* was forced to pump up the scripts with sex angles, culminating with the day James turned sixteen and lost his virginity. There was even a male equivalent of *Charlie's Angels, CHiPs,* featuring two gorgeous "hunks" (Larry Wilcox and Erik Estrada) for the women to admire.

NBC's sex angle surfaced most often, however, in the network's schedule of miniseries, which formed the cornerstone of its programming strategy. One NBC insider said, only partly tongue-in-cheek, "If ABC is doing kiddie porn, NBC will give the audience adult porn." The soapy drama of *The Moneychangers* had done well the previous season taking such an approach, so the network touted *79 Park Avenue, Aspen, Loose Change,* and *Wheels* as spicy special events. These "novels for television" usually ran over consecutive nights on NBC's Saturday movie, the Sunday *Big Event,* and the Monday movie, and all featured steamy sex (frequent thrashing in bed), seamy characters, and unbridled ambition. Though not actually showing much more than ABC's sex comedies, the presentation in these pulpy stories was far more direct: Illicit sex was just another requirement for success and advancement in corporate America.

These programs did well in the ratings, to an extent proving that the success of *Roots* and *Rich Man, Poor Man* was no fluke. Nonetheless, the grand pronouncements regarding miniseries toned down considerably from the euphoria following *Roots.* NBC was the only network committed to miniseries on a continuing basis. The other networks regarded them more as extended specials to be used sparingly as blockbuster lures during the ratings sweeps or to open the season. ABC, for example, slotted the six-part *Washington: Behind Closed Doors,* a political drama loosely based on John Ehrlichman's *The Company,* as its premiere week lure. That series did all right, but was not an exceptional blockbuster like *Roots.*

NBC scored much better in November with *The Godfather Saga,* a combination of the two theatrical "Godfather" films plus nearly an hour of previously unused footage. "Godfather" director Francis Ford Coppola himself supervised the entire project, including the necessary adjustment of particularly violent scenes to the limitations of television. The finished product ran nine hours over four nights and was dubbed: *Mario Puzo's "The Godfather": The Complete Novel for Television.* By presenting the saga of the Corleone family in chronological order, the chilling evolution of gangland power from young Vito Corleone's first kill to Michael Corleone's calculated murder of his own brother clearly emerged. For once, the television version of a theatrical feature was more effective and powerful than the original presentation.

NBC's success with such special events helped the network cover the fact that it had very few hit series. *Little House on the Prairie* was the network's only top ten entry, and *CHiPs,* its highest rated new show, did not even make the top twenty. NBC was in even worse shape than CBS, which was at least trying its best at a concerted rebuilding effort.

As the season wore on, the problems with NBC's event strategy became increasingly apparent as the problems of miniseries became clear. Miniseries were much more expensive to produce than regular series, yet generally they did not do well in reruns. Unlike the interchangeable segments of a regular series, the episodes of a miniseries had to be shown in order, preferably over consecutive nights. Yet this meant either setting aside weekly slots for miniseries—thus reducing their "specialness" by making them part of the weekly program routine—or constant preemption (which undercut attempts to develop strong regular series).

The most dramatic flaw in the miniseries scheme was that the best time to slot a series could instantly become the worst. A new story had to do well on opening night or the network was stuck with a multiple-night failure because it was hard to convince people to join the events in mid-run. NBC's biggest miniseries bomb took place during the February sweeps when ABC's *How the West Was Won* and CBS's Sunday movie, "Gator," soundly defeated an episode of *King,* a highly touted three-part story on the life of Dr. Martin Luther King, Jr.

King became the symbol of an unsuccessful miniseries. It was well-written and featured excellent performances (Paul Winfield as Martin Luther King, Jr.; Ossie Davis as Martin Luther King, Sr.; and Cicely Tyson as Coretta Scott King). Nonetheless, it lacked the sexy hooks of shows such as *79 Park Avenue* or the built-in violence of *The Godfather Saga.* Consequently, NBC was very careful with its final miniseries of the season, *Holocaust,* scheduling it before the spring sweeps and against chiefly rerun material by CBS and ABC. Network programming boss Paul Klein even downplayed network expectations because *Holocaust* seemed the perfect candidate for a ratings flop. It was a depressing story of the persecution and systematic murder of six million Jews by the Nazis in World War II. There was no happy ending and all the heroic characters—with a few exceptions—were gassed or shot by the end of the story.

Despite all these apparent handicaps, the four nights of *Holocaust* became the most-watched entertainment show in NBC's history, drawing nearly 120 million viewers. It became the number two miniseries in television, right behind *Roots.* And, like *Roots,* it used the basics of good television drama to hit home in a very special way.

Holocaust transformed a nearly incomprehensible crime against humanity into a personal war drama, focusing on an ambitious young German lawyer, Erik Dorf (Michael Moriarty), and an upper-middle-class Jewish doctor in Berlin, Josef Weiss (Fritz Weaver), and his family (Rosemary Harris as his wife Berta; Joseph Bottoms as their younger son, Rudi; Blanche Baker as their daughter, Anna; James Woods as their son, Karl; and Meryl Streep as Karl's Aryan wife, Inga). Both were caught up in the rise of Nazism: Dorf as a legal henchman for the party and Dr. Weiss as an innocent man fighting to hang on to his family, his dignity, and his life. Over the four nights of *Holocaust* he was stripped of them all.

Like *Roots, Holocaust* acted as a catalyst for ethnic pride and even anger. Throughout the country, millions watched the re-creation of events that had been a frightening part of their lives. For another, much younger, generation, *Holocaust* conveyed the horror of events they had never really thought about as anything more than another page of history.

Despite the surprising performance of *Holocaust,* NBC's basic programming problems remained unchanged. The network's decision to commit itself to developing expensive miniseries over weekly shows locked it into that "longform" pattern. Without strong new series to plug in, NBC would have to continue to stress "event programming." This, in turn, seemed to guarantee a long stint by NBC at number three and the beginning of a long reign by ABC as number one.

ABC's formulas ruled the airwaves.

CBS continued to arrange and rearrange its old hits.

NBC produced great special events, but was a prisoner of its abysmal lack of strong regular series.

Then, in one bold move, this network equation changed.

On January 20, 1978, the man who had guided ABC to the top, Fred Silverman, announced his defection to NBC. The broadcast industry wondered: Could Silverman pull the TV hat trick and make NBC his third number one network?

38. Born Again Broadcasting

THE ANNOUNCEMENT of Fred Silverman's jump from ABC to NBC not only sent shock waves through the broadcast industry but also attracted a great deal of coverage by the general news media. Like his move from CBS to ABC three years before, the story made good copy. Once again, Silverman was leaving a number one television network and taking his tremendous programming expertise to the last place competition. In 1975 that had marked the beginning of a changed television world that soon found ABC at the top of the heap. Comparisons and speculation were inevitable: Could "Freddie" work his magic once again?

Actually, Silverman faced a far more difficult task coming to NBC. ABC in the mid-1970s had been on the verge of breaking out with its kid-oriented shows and was only waiting for a deft hand to guide it. NBC in 1978 was floundering. The network had only a handful of popular prime time shows: *The Big Event, Little House on the Prairie, The Rockford Files, Quincy,* and the moderately successful *CHiPs.* More importantly, NBC was heavily committed to a big-event-miniseries strategy, which placed great reliance on what had proved to be a very unpredictable form.

There were also other weak spots. Late night ratings king Johnny Carson was showing increasing signs of wanting to end his seventeen-year stint on *Tonight.* The previously unassailable *Today* show found its ratings lead being whittled away by ABC's *Good Morning America.* In the nightly news race, ABC's new *World News Tonight* format threatened NBC in the contest for the number two spot behind CBS's Walter Cronkite. And as a result of such overall slippage, NBC was even losing affiliates.

NBC was the perfect new challenge for Fred Silverman, offering him something more important than a hefty new salary and fringe benefits: an impressive boost to his professional pride. Instead of serving as just a sharp prime time programmer, Silverman was hired as president of the entire NBC broadcast corporation, including television, radio, and special projects.

Beyond that, there was the undeniable challenge of once again playing the part of miracle man. Almost single-handedly Silverman had built up the image of a network programmer to someone just as important as the programs and stars themselves. With ABC almost routinely continuing as number one, his day-to-day decisions there seemed far less crucial. Now, at NBC, he was instantly the most important man at the network.

Silverman's contract with ABC ran until June 8, 1978, and the network held him to it. As a result, between January and June,

Silverman was forced into a management limbo of sorts. He could not communicate with NBC personnel yet was no longer part of the ABC team. For five months he vacationed while his new network put together the schedule for the fall of 1978 with absolutely no input from him. This heightened the dramatic effect of Silverman's arrival in June: Who or what would remain?

NBC's emphasis on event programming under Paul Klein ran in direct opposition to Silverman's philosophies. Though he was master at slotting special events, Silverman's base of success at ABC and CBS was regular series, especially sitcoms. NBC did not have one hit sitcom going into the fall of 1978, so it was expected that when Silverman took over there would be an all-out campaign to beat ABC at its own game with teen sitcoms and suggestive sex. Yet when Silverman actually assumed control in June, just the opposite occurred: Fred Silverman suddenly became the champion of "quality" programming. Three days after assuming office, he told NBC affiliates, "I want NBC not only to be the audience leader—but also the most respected network." He also pledged a stronger commitment to news, cultural specials, and family programming.

Obviously, some of this was standard public relations rhetoric, but Silverman also backed such talk with action. During the summer he made several changes in the announced NBC fall schedule, replacing *Coast to Coast* (a sexy adventure-comedy featuring two airline stewardesses and a handsome steward) with *Lifeline* (a cinéma-vérité-style documentary series about real life doctors operating on real patients in real hospitals), and transforming *Legs* (a Garry Marshall sitcom about the backstage life of sexy Las Vegas showgirls) into *Who's Watching the Kids?,* an apartment house sitcom emphasizing Jim Belushi (brother of John) and *Happy Days* alumnus Scott Baio rather than the glamour girls. Though NBC could not cut back overnight on miniseries well into production, Silverman did axe plans for thirty hours of Universal miniseries that he labeled as too sexploitive. These included a sequel to the successful *79 Park Avenue* and a Taylor Caldwell story about a prostitute in ancient Rome.

Such moves seemed quite surprising from the man who had recently presided over a schedule that included *Three's Company, Charlie's Angels,* and *Love Boat.* In a sense, though, this "born again" commitment to quality was about the best counter-programming hook available. Practically speaking, there was little chance of changing NBC's competitive position for the 1978–79 season, so while planning for the future Silverman focused attention on something other than instant ratings success. He ordered at least thirty new pilot concepts to be ready in January, when he could begin to phase in shows more in tune with the long-range Silverman plan for NBC supremacy. Silverman also felt that ABC's approach to television had peaked and it was only a matter of time before viewers grew tired of the ABC schedule as a whole, so he instructed producers to stay away from "jiggling" themes in the new NBC pilot projects.

Following Silverman's schedule adjustments, NBC opened the season a strong number two, temporarily buoyed by good opening ratings for the twenty-five hour miniseries *Centennial* (running as a *Big Event*) and the usual boost provided by the World Series. By November, NBC had begun to slide. *Centennial* fell out of the top twenty and all nine of the network's new fall series flopped. During the November ratings sweeps, NBC finished a distant third with only four programs among the top forty shows.

Though he had promised in June to cut down on last-minute program shuffling, Silverman decided he could not wait any longer to act. At the start of December, he wiped the slate clean and canceled nine of NBC's nineteen series in one day, including all

of the new fall shows that had survived until then. Silverman fell back on the thirty pilots he had ordered and pulled out nine new shows, including three sitcoms. Even hold-over program boss Paul Klein was deposed in the winter shakeup. It was clear the Silverman era at NBC had begun in earnest.

Despite these moves, the rest of the season was a shambles for NBC. From January until May, the network's schedule was a revolving door for new shows that premiered, quickly shifted time slots, and then disappeared. NBC tried virtually any concept for a series, including: a weekly slot for miniseries (*NBC Novels for Television*); a revival of *Columbo* without the Columbo character (*Mrs. Columbo*); a land-locked *Love Boat* (*Supertrain*, produced by NBC itself and featuring a very expensive model train set); an update of the *Millionaire* format (*Sweepstakes*); a cash-in on the fraternity humor success of the film "Animal House" (*Brothers and Sisters*); serialized melodramas (*Cliffhangers*); and even the old *Stand By for Crime* setup of a crime drama mixed with a game show-type panel (*Whodunnit?* with Ed McMahon as host and famed criminal lawyer F. Lee Bailey as a regular panelist).

Even the high-priority search for new hit NBC sitcoms produced only two marginal successes, *Diff'rent Strokes* and *Hello Larry*,

The cast of *Lou Grant:* (from *l.*) Ed Asner, Daryl Anderson, Robert Walden, Linda Kelsey, Jack Bannon, Mason Adams, and (*c.*, seated) Nancy Marchand. *(MTM Enterprises)*

FALL 1978 SCHEDULE

	7:30	8:00	8:30	9:00	9:30	10:00	10:30	
MONDAY	local	Welcome Back Kotter	Operation Petticoat	ABC NFL Monday Night Football [to 12 Midnite]				**ABC**
	local	WKRP IN CINCINNATI	PEOPLE	M*A*S*H	One Day At A Time	Lou Grant		**CBS**
	local	Little House On The Prairie		NBC Monday Night At The Movies				**NBC**

	7:30	8:00	8:30	9:00	9:30	10:00	10:30	
TUESDAY	local	Happy Days	Laverne And Shirley	Three's Company	TAXI	Starsky And Hutch		**ABC**
	local	THE PAPER CHASE		CBS Tuesday Night Movies				**CBS**
	local	GRANDPA GOES TO WASHINGTON		Big Event II				**NBC**

	7:30	8:00	8:30	9:00	9:30	10:00	10:30	
WEDNESDAY	local	Eight Is Enough		Charlie's Angels		VEGA$		**ABC**
	local	The Jeffersons	IN THE BEGINNING	CBS Wednesday Night Movies				**CBS**
	local	DICK CLARK'S LIVE WEDNESDAY		NBC Wednesday Night At The Movies				**NBC**

	7:30	8:00	8:30	9:00	9:30	10:00	10:30	
THURSDAY	local	MORK AND MINDY	What's Happening?	Barney Miller	Soap	Family		**ABC**
	local	The Waltons		Hawaii Five-O		Barnaby Jones		**CBS**
	local	Project U.F.O.		Quincy, M.E.		W.E.B.		**NBC**

	7:30	8:00	8:30	9:00	9:30	10:00	10:30	
FRIDAY	local	Donny And Marie		The ABC Friday Night Movie				**ABC**
	local	The New Adventures Of Wonder Woman		The Incredible Hulk		FLYING HIGH		**CBS**
	local	THE WAVERLY WONDERS	WHO'S WATCHING THE KIDS?	The Rockford Files		THE EDDIE CAPRA MYSTERIES		**NBC**

	7:30	8:00	8:30	9:00	9:30	10:00	10:30	
SATURDAY	local	Carter Country	APPLE PIE	The Love Boat		Fantasy Island		**ABC**
	local	Rhoda	Good Times	THE AMERICAN GIRLS		Dallas		**CBS**
	local	CHiPs		NBC SATURDAY SPECIALS		THE SWORD OF JUSTICE		**NBC**

	7:00	7:30	8:00	8:30	9:00	9:30	10:00	10:30	
SUNDAY	The Hardy Boys Mysteries		BATTLESTAR GALACTICA		The ABC Sunday Night Movie				**ABC**
	60 Minutes		MARY		All In The Family	Alice	KAZ		**CBS**
	The Wonderful World Of Disney		Big Event I				LIFELINE		**NBC**

back-to-back offerings from Norman Lear's TAT/Tandem company. *Hello, Larry* was a male version of *One Day at a Time,* starring McLean Stevenson as a divorced radio talk show host with two teenage daughters. *Diff'rent Strokes* served as a black-infused *Family Affair,* featuring Conrad Bain (of *Maude*) as a wealthy Manhattan millionaire-widower who adopted two black orphans from Harlem, thirteen-year-old Willis Jackson (Todd Bridges) and his eight-year-old brother, Arnold (Gary Coleman). Both series offered warm lessons on growing up and occasionally the two combined for special one-hour joint episodes. Silverman also treated them as a matched set; even during NBC's many schedule shifts the two moved in tandem. Silverman saw Coleman as a potential new network star and he hoped that *Diff'rent Strokes* would help *Hello, Larry* build its audience as well. *Hello, Larry* eventually flopped, but *Diff'rent Strokes* caught on and Coleman became a frequent guest attraction on other NBC series.

NBC wound up finishing the 1978–79 season deep in third place, a full rating point lower than its 1977–78 showing. Silverman eventually admitted that his frantic mid-season juggling was the wrong strategy, saying that a slower transition would have worked better. Most of the chosen pilots had been forced into the weekly schedule far too quickly and suffered from the lack of production time. Still, Silverman carried over into the next season a few shows that had done moderately well and continued with his reorganization

plans, aiming for the 1980 Olympic games in Moscow. NBC had purchased exclusive television rights for them in February 1977 at a price tag of $100 million, and Silverman knew from his ABC success with the 1976 Olympics that the games provided the perfect launching pad for the new season. If NBC had a strong line-up to promote during the Olympics, the network could, with a little luck, be back on top by Christmas, 1980. Informally, that became Silverman's deadline for success.

For the present, however, ABC continued to reign as number one. Silverman had left his former network in very strong shape and ABC president Fred Pierce and Tony Thomopoulos, Silverman's replacement as chief programmer, pursued a vigorous fall campaign, determined not only to keep ABC far ahead of the pack, but also to prove that the network's success had not been due totally to Silverman. Besides touting all the returning ABC hits, they used a rerun of *Roots* to open September and then promoted a championship boxing rematch between Muhammad Ali and Leon Spinks into the number one slot the first week of the new season. Through October ABC continued comfortably on top with eight of the top ten shows and nineteen of the top thirty. Unlike NBC, ABC had little trouble with its new fall shows: Four of the five were in the top fifteen. The only thing close to a ratings disappointment for ABC was the late fall collapse of *Battlestar Galactica,* the network's attempt to cash in on the spectacular success of George Lucas's film for 20th Century-Fox, "Star Wars."

Opening with huge crowds in May 1977, "Star Wars" quickly became the top-grossing movie of all time, appealing to both children and adult audiences. It took a simple space war adventure yarn, reminiscent of the popular Buck Rogers and Flash Gordon film serials of the 1930s and 1940s, and effectively updated it with a witty script and spectacular special effects. Its success led to a host of imitations and a general revival of interest in science fiction adventures.

The first "Star Wars"-inspired television series was NBC's *Quark,* a space comedy (created by Buck Henry) that had just missed earning a spot on the network's fall schedule in 1977. Though *Quark's* May 1977 pilot was set up as a parody of *Star Trek,* the revived series added appropriate "Star Wars" touches and opened in February 1978 with an effective take-off on the hit film, complete with a mysterious power known as "The Source" (actually the voice of Hans Conried). The series regulars included Richard Benjamin as commander Adam Quark, skipper of a garbage ship in the United Galaxy Sanitation Patrol; Conrad Janis as Palindrome, Quark's home base superior; Richard Kelton as Ficus, Quark's Spock-like logical assistant (he was really a plant that looked human); and former Doublemint chewing gum identical twins Cyb and Tricia Barnstable as Betty I and Betty II, the ship's radio crew (one was a clone of the other). Subsequent episodes featured parodies of other popular space tales (including *Star Trek,* "2001: A Space Odyssey," and Flash Gordon), but the premise was far too limited and the series failed to catch on.

For the fall of 1978, Universal came up with *Battlestar Galactica,* a flashy big-budget space effort that took the essential "Star Wars" plot of a space war and combined it with touches of basic science fiction philosophy. (There was a small army of humans, led by Lorne Greene as Commander Adama, fighting the Cylons, a race of robots out to destroy all mankind.) *Battlestar Galactica* opened with a three-hour premiere that so effectively captured the "Star Wars" techniques and rhythm that 20th Century-Fox sued Universal for copyright infringement. *Galactica's* early episodes landed in the top ten and easily clobbered its competition, especially CBS's highly touted new variety hour starring Mary Tyler Moore. This produced a sigh of relief at both ABC and Universal because, in order to duplicate the technical effects audiences had come to expect after "Star Wars," the program's budget for the first few episodes was several million dollars. This success, however, was short-lived.

The scripts for subsequent episodes of *Battlestar Galactica* were far below the quality of the season opener, shifting the emphasis to simple kiddie adventures closer to *Lost in Space* than *Star Trek* or "Star Wars." In November, CBS juggled its Sunday schedule, dropped Moore's show, and placed veteran *All in the Family* against *Battlestar Galactica.* Within one month, Archie and Edith had knocked the space saga out of the top thirty. By the end of the season, ABC dropped the program as an expensive failure. Both the network and Universal attempted a bit of additional mileage from their investment the following season with a short run revival (*Galactica: 1980*) and an update of *Buck Rogers,* but neither registered impressive ratings.

Though *Battlestar Galactica* turned out to be a flop, ABC scored spectacular success with a very different sort of space hero, Mork from Ork, in another spinoff from Garry Marshall's *Happy Days.* Marshall explained that one of his children (no doubt inspired by "Star Wars") suggested it would be fun to do a *Happy Days* episode involving aliens from outer space, so he had the adventure take place in a dream. Dozing off one night, Richie Cunningham dreamt that he met Mork (Robin Williams), a nutty alien with

strange powers, who decided to take him back to his home planet, Ork. To save Richie, the Fonz challenged Mork to a duel and then—Richie woke up. Naturally, neither Richie's friends nor family took his story seriously, yet the episode ended with a knock at the door and the reappearance of Robin Williams, playing a country hick, asking Richie for directions.

The "Mork" episode ran in February 1978 and went over extremely well, so Williams was given his own series for the fall, set in the present. For *Mork and Mindy,* he continued the role of alien Mork, this time sent on a long term fact-finding mission to Earth, landing in Boulder, Colorado, and taken in by a young single woman, Mindy McConnell (Pam Dawber). On the surface, *Mork and Mindy* was just *My Favorite Martian* updated and should have been primarily for kids, but instead it managed the "Star Wars" trick of appealing to all ages. Williams's Mork had a crazy unpredictable manner (he seemed permanently on speed) and at any moment could spout lines (in the appropriate voices) from old movies, TV shows, and even political speeches. These off-the-wall improvisations appealed to young adults, while the physical humor (such as hanging upside down in a closet or drinking orange juice from a pitcher using only his index finger) attracted the kids. Parents found the program good family entertainment because, despite his powers, Mork was very much a little boy exploring a strange new world. Dressed in baggy jeans and suspenders, he innocently wandered into situations and each week learned some basic lesson of life.

Even though Mork lived with Mindy (staying in the attic of her apartment), the two were like brother and sister, with Mork

With *WKRP in Cincinnati,* MTM again turned the premise of an unsuccessful Midwest broadcast operation into a top-notch sitcom: (from *l.*) top: Frank Bonner and Gordon Jump; middle: Richard Sanders, Gary Sandy, Jan Smithers, and Tim Reid; bottom: Loni Anderson and Howard Hesseman. *(MTM Enterprises)*

September 13, 1978

W.E.B. (NBC). Lin Bolen, a former NBC programmer who served as the role model for Faye Dunaway's Diane Christensen character in the film "Network," produces a TV series patterned after the movie. Appropriately, this is the first show canceled in the 1978–79 season.

October 8, 1978

Return of the Saint. ATV in England brings back suave adventurer Simon Templar a.k.a The Saint with a new lead, Ian Ogilvy. CBS airs the revival in a late night slot beginning in December, 1979.

October 14 & 21, 1978

"Rescue from Gilligan's Island." (NBC). After fourteen years on the "uncharted desert isle," the seven shipwrecked refugees from the *Minnow* are rescued at last. This two-part special ends with everyone shipwrecked again on the same island, but the program does well in the ratings so they are rescued once more in a May 1979 sequel.

November 18, 1978

California Congressman Leo Ryan, NBC correspondent Don Harris, and two others are killed in an ambush at the air strip near the religious commune of Jim Jones in Guyana.

December 15, 1978

MCA begins test marketing "DiscoVision," the first video disk player put on sale.

January 28, 1979

Sunday Morning. (CBS). Charles Kuralt comes off the road to host a lowkey, informative ninety-minute news show on early Sunday morning.

February 18–25, 1979

Roots: The Next Generations. (ABC). For twelve hours over seven nights, Alex Haley's search for his family history moves from Reconstruction to Africa in 1967. James Earl Jones plays Haley and Marlon Brando, in a rare television dramatic appearance, plays American Nazi leader George Lincoln Rockwell.

---

running to her arms for a hug whenever he was afraid or confused. In a similar manner, Mindy's father (played by *Quark* veteran Conrad Janis) and grandmother (played by Elizabeth Kerr)—who ran a music shop in town—acted as homespun surrogate parent figures, casting a stern but loving eye on Mork's crazy actions (even after they learned he was an alien).

Though the supporting cast was good, Williams and his manic energy were the obvious focus of the series. He was even allowed to draw on his improvisational background and ad-lib a bit during the filming before the live audience. As a result, when Mork broke into one of his wild spurts of rapid-fire jokes, allusions, and body movements, the show revved up to a pace reminiscent of *Laugh-In.* No one—not even the writers and other performers—knew exactly what was coming next.

Mork and Mindy was launched with a special one-hour episode featuring guest appearances by Henry Winkler and Penny Marshall in a new "flashback" sequence showing how the Fonz and Laverne had actually met alien Mork in the 1950s. With this tie-in from ABC's top superstars, *Mork and Mindy* became an instant smash, adding to ABC's amazing chain of sitcom hits. The network's continuing ratings success, though, prompted cries of anguish by television critics, even those that liked *Mork and Mindy,* because it seemed to guarantee that teen-oriented shows would continue

to dominate programming at the expense of more adult fare for years to come. In particular, the critics pointed to the failure of a prestigious new CBS drama series, *The Paper Chase,* as a sure sign that in this ABC-dominated era of television, a quality show did not stand a chance.

The Paper Chase was based on the 1973 theatrical film starring Timothy Bottoms as a Harvard law student who fell in love with the daughter (played by Lindsay Wagner) of his tyrannical law professor, Charles Kingsfield (John Houseman). For the series, Houseman continued his role of Kingsfield with a new cast of students, but the same focus: the struggles of first-year law students in a study group trying to develop the necessary discipline to become lawyers. The series tackled such obtuse subjects as legal ethics, personal discipline, and legal methodology, as well as flashier matters such as sexual harassment of students and prison reform.

CBS slotted *The Paper Chase* directly opposite *Happy Days* and *Laverne and Shirley* which, at first glance, seemed "suicidal" scheduling. Actually, though, it made sense as perfect counter-programming. *The Waltons,* for instance, had proved to be Flip Wilson's undoing in a similar match-up earlier in the decade. With high quality writing and good characters, *The Paper Chase* could slowly but steadily build an audience and perhaps pull a similar upset. Its placement against the top teen humor shows of television, however, turned the series instead into a symbolic rallying point that was regarded somehow as a barometer of whether the American public wanted quality drama or familiar comedy. Not surprisingly, the public chose familiar comedy. *The Paper Chase* was clobbered in the ratings. Yet, in their eagerness to support a serious drama show, critics ignored many obvious flaws in the series that were just as important as time placement to its failure.

John Houseman was very effective in the lead role of Professor Charles Kingsfield, completely dominating the screen with his presence. James Stephens as James Hart was also good as the hardworking kid from the Midwest waiting on tables to earn his law degree. The rest of the characters, however, were just adequate. Worse yet, the scripts were weak, often sabotaging potentially effective themes with hokey, heavy-handed subplots or preachy dialogue. (In two of the best episodes—one on moot court and another on understanding contract law—the main characters were inexplicably struck by a case of puppy love halfway through the story.) In addition, the scripts seemed very restricted by the setup of classes, the small study group, and trying to involve Houseman in every story.

Still, these flaws might have been overcome by fleshing out the characters. Instead, *The Paper Chase* settled for stiff stereotypes that made most of the characters downright unlikable. Hart's study group included a strident feminist, the son of a prominent lawyer, and a smark-aleck jock. Even beyond that, they were all clever kids studying at a prestigious law school to be rich and successful lawyers. It was very difficult to feel much sympathy for characters whose greatest fear was not finishing at the top of the class. Even Hart, who had to work nights to earn money for school, was exactly the type of student the average person grew to resent: He studied hard, always had the right answers, and held down a job to boot. Stephens, fortunately, was given the opportunity to soften and develop his character. The others were not so lucky. The fact that *The Paper Chase* managed to occasionally overcome so many obstacles for some effective scenes was a tribute to the determination of the cast and the powerful figure of Houseman.

CBS did not let *The Paper Chase* die without a fight. When it appeared obvious that the program was not going to siphon viewers from the ABC comedy blockbusters running against it, the network moved the show for a few weeks to later Tuesday night against much weaker competition (the fading *Starsky and Hutch*). Even given this breathing space, the show's ratings did not change significantly—viewers still did not tune in. The series was canceled soon thereafter, becoming the most glorious television failure in years.

Despite the well publicized flop of *The Paper Chase*, the state of quality programming on television was actually quite healthy. Besides established hits such as CBS's *M*A*S*H*, ABC's *Barney Miller*, and NBC's *Saturday Night Live*, there were several strong newcomers, including four high quality shows from the MTM production family: *Lou Grant, The White Shadow, WKRP in Cincinnati,* and *Taxi.*

Lou Grant had premiered in the fall of 1977, starting very slowly in the ratings and barely hanging on through the winter. The show was a somewhat risky approach to one of the most obvious successors to *The Mary Tyler Moore Show*. Instead of placing Ed Asner's Lou Grant character in another sitcom, MTM used him as the basis for its first hour-long drama program. The premise was simple: After being fired from his management position at WJM-TV in Minneapolis, Lou Grant returned to the newspaper business, becoming city editor of the *Los Angeles Tribune*. Each episode revolved around the investigation and preparation of stories for the daily paper.

MTM applied its comedy ensemble approach to the new drama series, building a large supporting cast behind Asner and a wide range of topical, sometimes controversial, subject matter for the stories. This was a tricky combination and everyone involved needed the opportunity to work out the bugs. Asner's Lou Grant character had been a popular part of *The Mary Tyler Moore Show* for seven years and his presence helped buy the time necessary for development.

At first, the stories and character development focused primarily on Asner. This allowed him some very effective scenes as a middle-aged man suddenly taking on a whole new career in a brand new city, but it left the supporting characters less clearly defined. They seemed more like character types straight out of such theatrical "newspaper film" hits as "The Front Page" and the more recent "All the President's Men" (about the Watergate investigation by Bob Woodward and Carl Bernstein). There was an irascible editor-in-chief (Mason Adams as Charlie Hume), a long-haired photographer (Daryl Anderson as Dennis "Animal" Price), a young woman reporter (Rebecca Balding as Carla Mardigian, soon replaced by Linda Kelsey as Billie Newman), an intense Bernstein-like investigative reporter (Robert Walden as Joe Rossi), a handsome assistant city editor (Jack Bannon as Art Donovan), and an older woman as owner and publisher (Nancy Marchand as Margaret Pynchon). In addition, some of the scripts ended up a bit preachy and self-conscious while others tried to cover too many aspects of some "burning issue" and emerged as just a series of interviews ending in some dramatic headline. For example, in one of the first season's episodes (Billie Newman's investigation into the background of an American Nazi), an otherwise effective drama was undercut at the end by the melodramatic news of the Nazi's suicide as a result of the *Tribune*'s story. (Billie had discovered he was Jewish.)

One of the best episodes of the first season was more restrained and realistic in tackling its problem: Should an aging, possibly senile, judge be removed from the bench? It could have been a flashy exposé, but instead turned into an intense interpersonal confrontation, reaching a dramatic peak during a discussion between the judge, Mrs. Pynchon, Lou Grant, and Charlie Hume in the *Tribune*'s editorial offices. After some serious soul-searching, the judge decided on his own to retire. The *Tribune*'s only story from

the events was a short item in the back of the paper.

This was the heart of the matter: Most newspaper stories are not Watergate-style headliners that help topple governments, but rather consist of small slices of life from the news of the day. Throughout the first season both the writers and the performers sharpened their skills and moved into a more difficult style: tackling issues that often had no flashy ending, glib solution, or obvious bad guys. To do so, the focus shifted away from the exposé orientation to how shades of problems affected people. In the process, the *Lou Grant* ensemble graduated from being merely reporter types to full-fledged interesting characters that just happened to work at a newspaper. The show became an effective equivalent to the legal drama of *The Defenders* from the early Sixties, providing entertaining dramatizations of current topical issues within the framework of a standard TV series.

By the 1978–79 season, *Lou Grant* had stretched, found its style, and flourished. Though Asner's Grant remained the solid rock at the helm of the city desk, more and more time was turned over to the other performers. With this more controlled approach emphasizing characters, *Lou Grant* was able to mix in stories that went beyond merely dealing with controversy, including quiet mood pieces, straightforward character conflicts in the office, and even a sly tribute to Thirties-style Hollywood detective movies (complete with a Sam Spade-type voice-over narration by Asner.) At the same time, particular episodes that did take a strong stand were that much more effective.

In a story dealing with Vietnam veterans, Lou tried to help an

March 5, 1979
NBC's *Another World* becomes the first ninety-minute soap opera.

March 11, 1979
Mr. Dugan. (CBS). The scheduled premiere for the show that never was. At the urging of prominent black leaders, Norman Lear cancels his new sitcom about a black Congressman, even though promotional clips for the show have already aired.

March 19, 1979
The House of Representatives begins allowing TV cameras to broadcast its daily sessions.

April 1, 1979
William Leonard succeeds Richard Salant as president of CBS News. Salant, forced to retire from CBS upon reaching age sixty-five, moves to NBC where he becomes vice chairman in charge of news.

April 20, 1979
Howard K. Smith quits ABC after seventeen years. Angered that his nightly commentary on the evening news had been cut to about three-per-week, Smith leaves his resignation on the ABC bulletin board in Washington and then goes on vacation.

May 12, 1979
Professional soccer returns to American network television as ABC airs the first of five North American Soccer League regular season games per year, plus three playoff games and the "Soccer Bowl" championships.

August 27, 1979
CBS begins inserting a West Coast "update" into its Pacific feed of *The CBS Evening News*. Terry Drinkwater, in Los Angeles, supplies the latest information on developing stories as well as items of special interest to coast residents.

In *Diff'rent Strokes,* a millionaire-widower (Conrad Bain) raises both his daughter (Dana Plato) and two orphaned brothers (Gary Coleman, *l.,* and Todd Bridges). *(Tandem Productions, Inc.)*

unemployed black vet find a job, discovering in the process that there were dramatic differences in the after-effects of World War II (Lou's war) and the Vietnam war on the men who fought. While this naturally led to a *Tribune* series on Vietnam veterans, it also helped Lou to understand the personal pressures affecting a Vietnam veteran on his staff, Animal. The program also made extremely effective use of the *60 Minutes* style of intercutting between separate interviews to underscore points. While Rossi asked officials from a local Veterans Administration office about the unique problems facing those who had fought in Vietnam, Billie posed similar questions to representatives from an organization of Vietnam vets. As each person raised an issue, there was an appropriate comment from the other interview inserted, illustrating how very different the perceptions of the same situation really were. The episode ended with mixed results: Animal solved his problem, the unemployed veteran did not get a job, and all the frustrations discussed in that hour remained unresolved.

A sure sign that *Lou Grant* had inherited the mantle of the golden age of television drama came when a pressure group tried to stop the airing of an episode on nursing homes. The program not only presented an effective look at older Americans, it stirred the ire of the nursing home industry which tried to get the sponsors and CBS not to include the episode in the summer reruns. The story in question focused at first on the shoddy treatment in one particular nursing home where Billie took an undercover job as a nurse's aide. It quickly expanded to the larger issue of growing old with dignity and, on that subject, the program took a clear, unequivocal stand: Nursing homes were not the answer. One character, a seventy-year-old woman, explained that she would rather spend one day at home than ten years in a nursing home—*any* nursing home. Another declared that "even the best of 'em is just a place to wait to die." To its credit, CBS stuck by the series and reran the episode.

Like the MTM ensemble comedies, *Lou Grant* had needed time to grow. Once in the groove, the show managed to pull off the difficult task of presenting thoughtful, well-written, and entertaining drama with class and consistency. It also provided a sharp reminder to CBS that some of its biggest hits had needed time to catch on. From barely adequate ratings early in its first season, *Lou Grant* slowly inched up the charts. It cracked the top thirty by early spring, winning renewal. By the summer of 1978, it took off, consistently finishing in the top ten. Thereafter it scored well enough to be considered both a solid ratings performer and one of the most respected series on television.

Lou Grant's success gave MTM credibility in the drama field and the company followed with another hour-long series, *The White Shadow,* which CBS plugged into the 1978–79 schedule in late November. *The White Shadow* presented Ken Howard as Ken Reeves, a former professional basketball player who was forced to retire following an injury. In order to stay with the game, he took a job as basketball coach for Carver High, a largely black Los Angeles ghetto school. The stories focused on the white coach's efforts—on and off the basketball court—to build the talented but unsuccessful team members into winners by helping them develop self-respect, discipline, responsibility, and a spirit of teamwork. Actually, these goals were quite similar to the ideals behind the ill-fated *Paper Chase,* only in *The White Shadow* everything clicked. The writing, dialogue, and characters at Carver High were solid and believable, especially the students. As a result, the series was able to tackle a wide range of themes in a manner distinct from but every bit as good as *Lou Grant.* Some stories dealt with broad topical issues such as VD, drugs, and teenage pregnancy, while others concentrated on small slices of life such as the team's first airplane flight or each senior's decision whether or not to try college. At the end of the second season, the team won the city basketball championship and—in violation of television's taboo against anyone ever aging—all but four of the players graduated. Like any real high school coach, Reeves had to start all over again the next school year.

MTM's new-found success in the field of drama was welcome news to CBS, but the network was even more pleased when the company at last came up with a sitcom successor to *The Mary Tyler Moore Show, WKRP in Cincinnati.*

Another story of broadcasting in the Midwest, *WKRP* began with Andy Travis (Gary Sandy), a hot-shot program director, being brought in to boost the ratings of a "beautiful music" radio station, WKRP. He immediately changed its format to rock'n'roll, receiving only grudging approval from station manager Arthur Carlson (Gordon Jump), who was worried what his mother might think (she owned WKRP). Andy discovered that one of the station's disk jockeys was a West Coast legend, Dr. Johnny Fever (Howard Hesseman) and instituted the format change during the "Doctor's" morning show. Fever dragged the needle across the instrumental record then playing and kicked into a hard-driving rock song, punctuating the format announcement with the word "Booger!" (He had lost his job in Los Angeles for saying that on the air.) Travis then brought in another rock pro for the evening shift, Venus Flytrap (Tim Reid), a hip but mellow black disk jockey.

The changes in WKRP upset sales manager Herb Tarlek (Frank Bonner) and news director Les Nessman (Richard Sanders), both of whom did not like rock'n'roll. Les was a straight-laced newsman who took his job very, very seriously, especially the hog reports. (He displayed the Silver Sow award proudly and prominently on his desk.) Herb spent most of his time making unsuccessful passes at Jennifer Marlowe (Loni Anderson), the station's beautiful receptionist. Yet they both decided to give the new format a try—it might catch on and possibly boost the station's ratings from dead last in the market.

WKRP's premise and ensemble were MTM's strongest since The Mary Tyler Moore Show and the series won high praise (especially from radio disk jockeys). Like The Mary Tyler Moore Show, WKRP got in some effective digs at the world of broadcasting. For instance, as a Thanksgiving promotion, Carlson decided to release a load of wild turkeys from a helicopter above a shopping mall where Les was stationed to do a live remote broadcast. He failed to realize until it was too late that turkeys cannot fly. Les described the disastrous results in a horrified voice, using lines exactly like those in the live radio report of the crash of the German Zeppelin Hindenburg in 1937.

In spite of such inventiveness, WKRP's ratings were quite low through September and October, and it seemed doomed to die just a popular cult program. CBS, however, came up with an innovative new strategy to give the show a second chance: Instead of canceling WKRP, the network pulled the program from the schedule for a few months. This break gave MTM time to work out the bugs and when WKRP returned in January, CBS gave it the royal treatment, slotting it between M*A*S*H and Lou Grant. WKRP registered the expected better ratings in its new slot and then took off. During the summer, it shot into the top five, outscoring even M*A*S*H.

WKRP was a near-perfect execution of the MTM philosophy of sitcoms, which may be why CBS gave it a second chance. The show had a funny situation with many obvious hooks, yet it also used the setting as a backdrop for developing the humanity of its characters. Jennifer looked like a typical "dumb blonde" but was totally in control of her situation at all times. Leering Herb played up to her but when she called his bluff, he backed down and the two actually became friends. Venus hid behind his on-the-air name because he was AWOL from the Army, yet conservative Arthur Carlson stood by him when that news came out and helped negotiate a compromise settlement with the government. Johnny Fever loved rock music, but admitted that he felt embarrassed living and looking like a college kid when he was almost forty. Lee was an insecure, shy man who hid behind a male supremacy view, yet he learned to accept assistance in his private turf, news gathering, from a woman, Bailey Quarters (Jan Smithers).

The other MTM-family newcomer for the fall of 1978 had a similar high quality set up and cast, but unlike WKRP in Cincinnati, ABC's Taxi became an immediate hit. Technically, Taxi was not an MTM show, but the series had the MTM company style stamped all over it. In early 1977, as The Mary Tyler Moore Show ended its run on CBS, ABC signed four veteran MTM producers to turn out a similar style show. James Brooks (co-creator of Mary Tyler Moore and Rhoda), Ed Weinberger and Stan Daniels (co-producers of Mary Tyler Moore), and David Davis (producer of Rhoda and co-creator of The Bob Newhart Show) came up with Taxi, a comedy set in a New York City taxi company's dispatch garage.

Alex Reiger (Judd Hirsch) was the focus of the series, a cabbie who was perfectly happy driving a taxi as his life's work. The other "hacks" dreamed of grand success in other areas and claimed that the taxi job was just temporary: Bobby Wheeler (Jeff Conaway) wanted to be an actor, Tony Banta (Tony Danza) a boxer, and Elaine Nardo (Marilu Henner) an art dealer. In the meantime, they shared the less glamorous life at the Sunshine Cab Company working with each other, an immigrant mechanic who barely spoke English (Andy Kaufman as Latka Gravas) and a surly, diminutive dispatcher (Danny DeVito as Louie DiPalma). As in every good MTM show, the group developed into a strong ensemble, fleshing out the characters while facing a wide variety of funny situations. Unlike the many other ensemble shows, though, Taxi was an immediate top ten smash, given a tremendous boost by the lead-in of Happy Days, Laverne and Shirley, and Three's Company.

Adding the strong performance of newcomers Taxi, Mork and Mindy, and (in the early fall) Battlestar Galactica to its returning hits, ABC jumped out to a commanding lead at the start of the 1978-79 season. It was painfully obvious to CBS and NBC almost immediately that ABC would walk away with its third straight winning season in the overall ratings. Yet there was still a chance to score an upset victory in a more limited contest, the brief but highly competitive race to win the "sweep" months.

Throughout the year, the Nielsen ratings service measured how well the networks were doing each week, using its sample of some 1,200 "metered" families across the country. Four times each year, for an entire month, the company conducted a much more detailed survey (called a "sweep") that encompassed the performance of more than 700 commercial stations, which then used the results to determine their local advertising rates. In order to calculate these ratings, the company set up a much larger sample (several hundred thousand homes) for November, February, May, and July (representing typical months for their respective seasons).

Because the prime time programming on the network affiliates was in the hands of the networks, the locals pressured them to air the most saleable shows possible during the sweeps. The increasingly fierce ratings wars in the mid-1970s led to the practice of stacking these months (especially the heavy-viewing winter month of February) with blockbuster movies, specials, and flashy gimmicks—in the process, of course, making these supposedly typical months very untypical.

The February, 1979, sweeps were the most intense to that point. The month became a merry-go-round of time shifts, stunts, and specials. One night viewers had to decide between an episode of Roots: The Next Generations on ABC and the network television premieres of two major movies: "American Graffiti" on NBC and "Marathon Man" on CBS. On another February evening, the choice was between "Elvis," ABC's docudrama on the life of Elvis Presley, "Gone With the Wind" on CBS, and "One Flew Over the Cuckoo's Nest" on NBC. There were expanded editions of some series while others completely disappeared. It was an expensive, confusing month that left both viewers and executives unhappy. The concentration of so many blockbuster events running against each other—and disrupting the regular weekly schedule—frustrated and annoyed viewers. At the same time, counter-programming moves and stunts were very expensive for the networks. (One night, February 11, was reported to have cost them $13 million.)

Ironically, after all the moves and countermoves, the February sweeps produced no great surprises and seemed only to confirm the obvious: ABC was on top with CBS and NBC far behind fighting for the number two spot. Every media analyst regarded these results as clear evidence of a television status quo that would be around for a long time to come. ABC's number one position looked unassailable.

They were wrong.

39. Gleam in the Eye

IN MAY 1977 ABC made an unusual personnel shift and appointed Roone Arledge, then president of the network's sports operations, to an additional post: president of ABC News. Though ABC had successfully taken a commanding lead in entertainment programming, it desperately wanted similar triumphs in the less profitable but more prestigious area of news. Arledge had built ABC Sports into a highly respected and tremendously successful arm of the network; and while continuing at that post, he was to do the same in news.

Since coming to ABC from NBC in 1960, Arledge had demonstrated a sharp sense for packaging and presentation, overseeing such operations as ABC's live coverage of the Olympic games and weekly shows such as *Wide World of Sports* and *Monday Night Football.* His news responsibilities required him to apply his expertise to another area of network programming that involved both live on-the-spot events and reports from all over the nation and the world.

One of the key areas for improvement was ABC's nightly news program. In 1976, the network had attracted a great deal of attention by signing away Barbara Walters from NBC for $1 million and making her co-anchor of the evening news with Harry Reasoner. That match-up never jelled, leaving Reasoner unhappy and the ratings virtually unchanged. When Arledge took command of ABC News he realized that trying to find a personality mix to outdraw Walter Cronkite was the wrong strategy—even CBS itself was not sure who could replace Cronkite. Instead, Arledge concentrated on completely reworking ABC's nightly news format to give it a distinctly different feel and appearance from the competition.

Arledge's primary goal was to reduce the incessant focus on the anchor position in the nightly news and, at the start of 1978, *The ABC Evening News* began to change. Two former ABC news anchors, Frank Reynolds and Peter Jennings, appeared more often, acting as "mini-anchors" for stories from their respective beats: Washington (for governmental stories) and London (for foreign news). ABC's news ratings went up, so Arledge decided to develop his concept further. The result was *World News Tonight.*

The new format, which premiered in July 1978, was slick and fast moving. There was less patter between stories, more use of graphic material—including teasers for upcoming reports—and catchy electronic stinger music going into the commercials. Arledge moved the anchors into a newsroom setting and incorporated the control room bank of monitors into the open and close of the program. Moreover, he broke from a hoary news tradition and eliminated the New York anchor position. Frank Reynolds, still in Washington covering the federal government, became the "first among equals" in an anchor triumverate: Reynolds usually opened and closed the show, with the necessary transition comments divided between him, Peter Jennings on the foreign desk in London, and newcomer Max Robinson in Chicago, handling domestic reports outside Washington. Barbara Walters remained in New York, but shifted to special assignments and interviews, her real strengths, while Harry Reasoner jumped to CBS (the network he had left for ABC back in 1970).

World News Tonight did improve in the ratings, but that represented only a first step. If ABC was going to tout itself as a leader in news programming, it needed some dramatic action to build its credibility. The most obvious move was to expand the nightly news slot—a proposal fiercely resisted for years by affiliates from all three networks, even when championed by Walter Cronkite himself. Local programmers knew that an hour of network news, or even forty-five minutes, would take time from their own lucrative newscasts or access slot series. It was unlikely that ABC would have any better luck with a proposal to expand the evening news. There was, however, another way for the network to increase its news programming: use a different slot, such as late night (11:30 P.M.) immediately following the late local news. This was the time all the networks generally used anyway for either their "instant news" special reports on late-breaking developments in big stories or the obligatory obituaries on major political and entertainment figures. The chief problem with the late night slot was that it faced formidable competition: Johnny Carson. Since the mid-Seventies, CBS and ABC had garnered respectable, if not spectacular, ratings against the *Tonight* show with reruns of movies and old network series. No one thought that a regular late night news show would stand a chance against such solid entertainment fare. Then on Sunday, November 4, 1979, Iranian militants seized control of the U.S. embassy in Teheran and, in the process, took more than fifty Americans hostage.

NBC aired the first report on the events in Iran, showing pictures of the embassy takeover during halftime of its Sunday afternoon football game. All three networks immediately rushed correspondents and crews into the country, while drawing on film from European broadcasters in the meantime. In the special late night reports, network correspondents attempted to sort out the events, and their initial explanation of the situation was rather straightforward: Iranian militants had seized the American embassy in angry reaction to the decision by the United States government to admit the exiled Iranian Shah, Mohammed Reza Pahlavi, for medical treatment in New York City. They demanded the extradition of the former Shah in exchange for the hostages.

All three networks did their best to report every available detail on the hostage crisis and, on November 18, each one broadcast its own filmed interview with Iran's religious and secular leader, Ayatollah Ruhollah Khomeini (conducted by Mike Wallace for CBS, John Hart for NBC, and Peter Jennings for ABC—all of whom had to submit questions in advance). After a flurry of late night reports following the embassy seizure, though, both CBS and NBC pulled back, scheduling a late night wrapup only if there were some dramatic developments that day. ABC, however, committed itself to a broadcast at least fifteen minutes long each weeknight "for the duration" (beginning November 8), under the title *The Iran Crisis: America Held Hostage* (anchored first by Frank Reynolds, then by Ted Koppel). In the process, the network not only attracted a huge audience (sometimes outdrawing the entertainment offerings on both CBS and NBC), but also found itself in a position to deal with the story in much greater depth. Instead of merely repeating what had been reported on the nightly news, *The Iran Crisis* featured longer and more detailed presentations on all aspects of the story. At first, the reports covered the obvious questions: What happened today? What do Americans think about it? What can the United States do now? These soon led to a far more difficult question: Why did it happen? In trying to answer that, each evening's report became, in effect, a mini-lesson in basic foreign policy and Mideast history.

The *Iran Crisis* reports served as an all-around unexpected bonus for Roone Arledge and ABC News. The show attracted a large, steady audience and helped viewers to become accustomed to a late night news program. It also established ABC as *the* network with complete coverage of the situation. This boost in credibility and viewership spilled over into other programs. *Good Morning America,* which had been gaining on *Today* for a while, at last pulled ahead with the bonus carryover audience of people who had gone to bed watching ABC and who then woke up with the TV dial still set there. *World News Tonight* also rose in the ratings, moving into a virtual deadlock with NBC for the number two position behind CBS.

The hostage situation lasted far longer than anyone first imagined. Through November, December, and early January, reporters filed hundreds of stories on virtually every movement, rumor, and protest in and around the captured embassy. Media coverage, in fact, became an issue itself both in the States and in Iran. American correspondents complained that many of the "spontaneous" demonstrations against "Western imperialism" probably took place because the Western camera crews stationed outside the embassy were ready and eager to film. Officials in Iran, on the other hand, grew increasingly frustrated at their inability to control the image of their own country sent back by the journalists. In mid-January, Iran ordered all American reporters out of the country, so subsequent stories had to be filed from "listening posts" in nearby countries or through other foreign reporters allowed to remain.

By March, though there were still no end to the hostage situation at hand, ABC decided to change its late night *Iran Crisis* "special reports" into a permanent nightly news show that would cover other stories as well. The show was extended to twenty minutes each night and retitled *Nightline*. The revamped program followed the *Iran Crisis* format, though, concentrating on in-depth coverage of a few items rather than a recap of the earlier nightly news (much like PBS's *MacNeil-Lehrer Report*). While *Nightline* was not as big a draw as the Iran wrapups, four months of late night reports had built a solid base audience for ABC, and the show was able to compete successfully in the slot. ABC News emerged from the crisis with stronger news credibility, an expanded news schedule, and higher ratings overall for its *World News Tonight* program. Arledge had done his job well and now focused on beating CBS. Even the nightly news lead would be up for grabs soon because Walter Cronkite was nearing retirement.

Despite ABC's improved news performance, CBS was still considered the leader in news, based on the tremendous public respect for Cronkite as a credible source, the quality of CBS's own special reports, and its increasingly successful news magazine, *60 Minutes,* which had actually become a top ten show.

60 Minutes had been around since 1968, attracting little attention at first with its deft mix of hard-hitting investigative reporting and softer, entertaining feature pieces. It ran for three seasons in prime time, but was exiled in 1972 to the fringe period of very early Sunday evening where it was preempted every fall by professional football. During the summer of 1975, the show ran in a Sunday prime time slot and managed to land in the top thirty. When it returned in December, following the football season, *60 Minutes* was placed at the beginning of prime time against *The Wonderful World of Disney*. At the same time, correspondent Dan Rather joined Mike Wallace and Morley Safer as one of the program's co-anchors.

Through 1976 and 1977, the program's ratings rose steadily, benefiting from the hefty audience of its fall sports lead-in, NFL football. In April 1977, the CBS news division announced an unheard-of development: Due to the success of *60 Minutes,* it was showing a profit. This was a dramatic change from the long-standing image of news programs as prestigious loss leaders, and for the 1977–78 season CBS made every effort not to have its Sunday afternoon football coverage run overtime and thereby shorten *60 Minutes.*

Going into the fall of 1979, *60 Minutes* was an established top ten show and, by October, it ranked as the number one network show overall. This was no fall ratings fluke as *60 Minutes* hung on through the winter and spring, eventually finishing as the number one program for the 1979–80 season—the first television news show ever to reach those rarefied heights. Such ratings success sent a clear message to all the networks' programming departments: *60 Minutes* was the biggest bargain in television. Not only did it now offer both prestige and high ratings, but, as a news show, its budget was only a small fraction of most entertainment series, thus allowing a tremendous profit margin. Both NBC and ABC joined the bandwagon and reinstituted prime time news shows, with mixed results.

ABC launched *20/20* in the summer of 1978. The June premiere was a disaster and at times seemed almost a bad parody of *60 Minutes*. A pair of ill-at-ease hosts, Harold Hayes and Australian Robert Hughes (two print journalists) introduced an investigative report by Geraldo Rivera on the training of vicious greyhound racing dogs (including gory footage of the animals attacking and eating rabbits); a piece by Sander Vanocur on the threat of homemade nuclear bombs; and puff-piece interviews with California governor Jerry Brown, his sister, and his mother. Hayes and Hughes were canned after the first show and veteran Hugh Downs assumed the hosting chores. The program ran weekly through the remainder of the summer and as a monthly series during the regular season,

FALL 1979 SCHEDULE

	7:30	8:00	8:30	9:00	9:30	10:00	10:30	
MONDAY	local	240-ROBERT			ABC NFL Monday Night Football [to 12 Midnite]			**ABC**
	local	The White Shadow		M*A*S*H	WKRP In Cincinnati	Lou Grant		**CBS**
	local	Little House On The Prairie		NBC Monday Night At The Movies				**NBC**

	7:30	8:00	8:30	9:00	9:30	10:00	10:30	
TUESDAY	local	Happy Days	Angie	Three's Company	Taxi	THE LAZARUS SYNDROME		**ABC**
	local	CALIFORNIA FEVER		CBS Tuesday Night Movies				**CBS**
	local	THE MISADVENTURES OF SHERIFF LOBO		NBC Tuesday Night At The Movies				**NBC**

	7:30	8:00	8:30	9:00	9:30	10:00	10:30	
WEDNESDAY	local	Eight Is Enough		Charlie's Angels		Vega$		**ABC**
	local	THE LAST RESORT	STRUCK BY LIGHTNING	CBS Wednesday Night Movies				**CBS**
	local	Real People		Diff'rent Strokes	Hello, Larry	The Best Of Saturday Night Live		**NBC**

	7:30	8:00	8:30	9:00	9:30	10:00	10:30	
THURSDAY	local	Laverne And Shirley	BENSON	Barney Miller	Soap	20/20		**ABC**
	local	The Waltons		Hawaii Five-O		Barnaby Jones		**CBS**
	local	BUCK ROGERS IN THE 25TH CENTURY		Quincy, M.E.		Kate Loves A Mystery		**NBC**

	7:30	8:00	8:30	9:00	9:30	10:00	10:30	
FRIDAY	local	Fantasy Island		The ABC Friday Night Movie				**ABC**
	local	The Incredible Hulk		The Dukes Of Hazzard		Dallas		**CBS**
	local	CHiPs		The Rockford Files		EISCHIED		**NBC**

	7:30	8:00	8:30	9:00	9:30	10:00	10:30	
SATURDAY	local	The Ropers	Detective School	The Love Boat		SHIRLEY		**ABC**
	local	WORKING STIFFS	The Bad News Bears	BIG SHAMUS, LITTLE SHAMUS		PARIS		**CBS**
	local			B. J. And The Bear		A MAN CALLED SLOANE		**NBC**

	7:00	7:30	8:00	8:30	9:00	9:30	10:00	10:30	
SUNDAY	OUT OF THE BLUE	A NEW KIND OF FAMILY	Mork And Mindy	THE ASSOCIATES	The ABC Sunday Night Movie				**ABC**
	60 Minutes		Archie Bunker's Place	One Day At A Time	Alice	The Jeffersons	TRAPPER JOHN, M.D.		**CBS**
	Disney's Wonderful World		The Sunday Big Event				Prime Time Sunday		**NBC**

hammering out its weak spots and moving away from the much-criticized sensationalist style of the opening episode to a more controlled and focused approach. By the time 20/20 returned as a weekly series in May 1979, the show had developed its own distinctive weekly magazine format, which was generally more feature-oriented than 60 Minutes. As with the nightly news race, ABC gave up trying to beat CBS at its own game and tailored its program to a different style of appeal.

NBC decided to use an existing series for its prime time magazine, promoting Weekend (with Lloyd Dobyns) from a late Saturday night monthly show to a weekly prime time slot beginning in January 1979. Weekend's mix of serious subjects and light, satiric features did not transfer well to the demands of weekly prime time exposure, and the show bombed in its new time period (coming in the lowest rated program on prime time television). In June, NBC brought in another late night star, Tomorrow's Tom Snyder, to host the more serious Prime Time Sunday. Though scoring better than Weekend, this series was also unable to duplicate the success of 60 Minutes or even 20/20. In the fall of 1980, NBC revamped the show again as NBC Magazine with David Brinkley, adding to the usual feature reports a round table discussion between NBC correspondents (much like PBS's Washington Week in Review). However, like its predecessors, NBC Magazine was a ratings flop.

Even CBS had difficulty when it tried to create its own feature-oriented spinoff to 60 Minutes. Back in January 1977, the network launched Who's Who (hosted by Dan Rather and Barbara Howar), built around personalities in the news, much like the weekly feature magazine People. Each program included extended profiles of or interviews with famous writers, performers, and politicians, mixed with short gossipy anecdotes delivered by Rather and Howar. To contrast with these high-powered celebrities, the program also incorporated reporter Charles Kuralt's popular "On the Road" feature from the evening news in which he turned attention to unusual, amusing, and talented non-celebrities throughout the country. Though individual segments occasionally worked (Kuralt's features were consistently the most entertaining), the program never jelled and instead fizzled by June.

For the fall of 1978, CBS went directly to Time Inc., the publisher of People magazine, for a celebrity-oriented feature program called (what else?) People. With David Susskind as executive producer, the half-hour show (hosted by former Miss America Phyllis George) faithfully duplicated its slick, glitzy magazine namesake. That, too, flopped, chiefly because People's print style of dozens of super short articles and picture captions did not adapt well to television. TV's People played like a series of thirty-second commercials sandwiched between title graphics and upbeat disco music.

Ironically, while all three networks had great difficulty in trying to successfully copy *60 Minutes,* another type of news magazine was catching on locally in the prime time access slot. This Monday-through-Friday program began in August 1976 on Group W's KPIX in San Francisco, which axed the syndicated *Concentration, Dealer's Choice, The Price Is Right, The New Treasure Hunt,* and *Name That Tune* from the 7:30–8:00 P.M. access slot in order to run the new locally produced show. Three of the five canceled series had been beating their competition, so the move was not out of desperation at poor ratings. Rather, it reflected a desire by KPIX program manager Bill Hiller to do something different with access time, possibly even developing a program that could itself be profitably syndicated. He made himself executive producer for *Evening: The MTWTF Show* (for *M*onday, *T*uesday, *W*ednesday, *T*hursday, and *F*riday)—soon simplified to *Evening Magazine.*

The format for the new show consisted of a nightly celebrity profile (subjects the first week included Paul McCartney, Bill Cosby, Valerie Perrine, and John Ehrlichman), brief helpful "tips" (such as how to exercise while watering your plants), and a "wild card" feature piece. After only two months, the program was a hit, registering better ratings than the game shows it replaced. Within a year, the Group W stations in Boston, Philadelphia, Pittsburgh, and Baltimore added the program to their schedules. Each followed the basic format, with their own local production crews and hosts, and each was also responsible for doing one piece each week that was offered to the other stations. This gave each show both a local and a national slant. By the fall of 1979, the *Evening Magazine* format was on forty-five stations (running as *PM Magazine* on non-Group W stations) and had become the number one access show in the country.

Television critics, of course, loved *Evening Magazine* and pointed to it as the program that fulfilled the ideal of the FCC's much maligned access rule. While *Evening Magazine* was certainly much more informative than most syndicated game shows, it was not exactly an overnight commitment to educate viewers with hard-hitting public affairs. In essence, all *Evening Magazine* did was take generally non-controversial "soft" features that were typically part of many local newscasts anyway and package them with similar features from other local stations. Yet this familiar feel probably helped account for the program's popularity, especially with its use of local hosts to read transition material and introduce each story. (Most stations that carried the show did at least one or two local pieces each week.) While *Evening Magazine* was born and bred in local access syndication, there was no reason that its basic format could not work in network prime time as well. NBC, in early 1979, became the first network to come up at last with a workable feature and personality-oriented program, *Real People.*

Former *Laugh-In* producer George Schlatter developed *Real People* as a stage for non-celebrities, "real people" who were presented to be as amusing, talented, and entertaining as any showbiz figures. This was the same world of American backroads visited by such reporters as Charles Kuralt, whose stories usually served as an off-beat closing feature for the network news. *Real People* strung together a series of such reports and anecdotes on unusual individuals in strange situations, focusing as much on the personality of the visiting correspondents as on the "ordinary folks" being interviewed. Schlatter enlisted a large cast of entertaining personalities to act as co-hosts, correspondents, and regular guests, including (for the first season) Fred Willard, Jimmy Breslin, Mark Russell, John Barbour, Sarah Purcell, Bill Rafferty, and Skip Stephenson. He also took a cue from Allen Funt's old *Candid Camera* series and set up the show itself as the playback stage for the films and tapes of their stunts and interviews, presented to a studio audience

for laughs and applause. These feature reports included such subjects as an all-male swimsuit competition judged by women, a man in San Francisco named Sherlock Bones who searched for lost pets, and even a *Candid Camera*-type skit featuring real shoppers being asked their opinion of a foul-tasting "new" drink as if they were part of a commercial. (When they thought the camera was on, they praised the drink; when they thought the camera was off, they made faces and admitted it was awful.)

Real People represented one of NBC's few moderate successes from its 1978–79 "revolving door" season, capturing just enough viewers during a six-episode spring run to win renewal for the fall of 1979. Without much fanfare, the ratings for *Real People* crept upward and by Christmas of 1979, the show had sneaked into the top thirty, occasionally beating ABC's *Eight Is Enough* in the time slot. As *Real People* caught on, all three networks were quick to launch copies, turning the format into a brief programming fad labeled "reality shows."

Alan Landsburg, creator of the pseudo-scientific syndicated access show *In Search Of* (which examined such topics as witchcraft and UFOs), produced *That's Incredible* for ABC. The series harkened back to Robert Ripley's *Believe It or Not,* showing "incredible" occurrences that affected real people such as a forest ranger hit by lightning seven times, a woman who allowed herself to be covered with bees, and a Minnesota policeman who reported seeing a UFO. Hosts John Davidson, Cathy Lee Crosby, and Fran Tarkenton presented the stories in an upbeat casual style of wide-eyed amazement ("That's incredible!"). *That's Incredible* turned in incredible ratings, placing in the season's top ten shows, even ahead of *Real People.* Landsburg followed up *That's Incredible* with *Those Amazing Animals,* a similar series for ABC that focused on "incredible" events in the animal kingdom, and *No Holds Barred,* a brief late night CBS show that copied the *Real People* formula but aimed it toward the *Saturday Night Live* audience. CBS also turned to veteran game show producers Mark Goodson and Bill Todman

The *60 Minutes* team: (clockwise from top) Dan Rather, Harry Reasoner, Mike Wallace, and Morley Safer. *(CBS News Photo)*

September 12, 1979

Shelly Hack, who appeared in commercials for "Charlie" perfume, replaces Kate Jackson as one of Charlie's Angels.

September 13, 1979

Benson. (ABC). Robert Guillaume takes his butler character, Benson, from *Soap* to the household of a bumbling governor.

September 23, 1979

Archie Bunker's Place. (CBS). A revamped *All in the Family,* set at Archie's tavern. Martin Balsam joins as Murray, Archie's Jewish partner, and Anne Meara plays the new chef, Veronica.

September 23, 1979

The Associates. (ABC). The four *Mary Tyler Moore* veterans who succeeded with *Taxi* fail with a promising ensemble sitcom focusing on three young members of a powerful Wall Street law firm.

October 8, 1979

David Brinkley gives up his co-anchor chores on *NBC Nightly News* for occasional commentary.

November 4, 1979

Three days before Senator Edward Kennedy announces his candidacy for president, "Teddy" airs on *CBS Reports.* Roger Mudd's questioning of the senator reveals a confused and somewhat inarticulate side to the "last Kennedy son," tarnishing his image as an imposing public figure.

March 4, 1980

The Big Show. (NBC). Nick Vanoff, who produced *The Hollywood Palace,* flops with more old style vaudeo, featuring ninety minutes of singing, dancing, swimming, skating, and comedy.

for a reality show update of *What's My Line* called *That's My Line.* The refurbished program did away with the original's celebrity panel and presented instead on-the-scene reports of real people with oddball occupations.

In spite of the success of *Real People,* NBC had disappointing results with its subsequent reality shows. The in-house *Games People Play* lasted just four months, presenting real people participating in so-called "trash sports" such as beer chugging, tug-of-war, and bar bouncer competition. However, George Schlatter's outlet for the *vox populi, Speak Up, America,* ran only a few episodes. The program offered real people across the country the opportunity to speak up on the issues of the day, but NBC affiliates felt uneasy about the deliberate mix of news, public affairs, and entertainment inherent in such a show.

Even with such problems, NBC embraced the reality programming formula because the network needed some kind of breakthrough in its campaign to climb from the ratings cellar. Nonetheless, going into the fall of 1979, it was still no match for the powerhouse line-up at ABC, which looked as if it would continue to roll right over the competition. Not only were there such returning top ten hits as *Happy Days, Three's Company, Laverne and Shirley, Taxi, Mork and Mindy,* and *The Ropers* (a successful spring spinoff from *Three's Company*), but the network also had the World Series in October and the winter Olympic games in February. There seemed no way ABC could lose.

Buoyed by such assumptions, network president Fred Pierce and chief programmer Tony Thomopoulos confidently decided to go for the kill and move some of ABC's big hits (*Mork and Mindy, Laverne and Shirley, Fantasy Island,* and *The Ropers*) to other

nights in order to spread ABC's ratings strength over all seven nights, and obtain an even larger ratings lead. Though this tactic went against the traditional network strategy of not tampering with established successes, it was not really regarded as that much of a risk. After all, the programs could always be moved back.

CBS's disastrous set of new fall sitcoms (*Working Stiffs, The Last Resort,* and *Struck by Lightning*) only seemed to underscore the security of ABC's position. Yet in the first week of the new season, NBC finished on top—due to Fred Silverman's front-loading with blockbuster movies and specials. NBC also won the third week, due to the baseball playoffs and the prime time broadcast of Johnny Carson's 17th anniversary on the *Tonight* show. At the same time, ABC's former hits were slipping in their new time slots, sometimes dropping completely out of the top twenty. ABC recovered somewhat and pulled into the lead for the season by the fifth week as NBC used up its blockbuster specials and faded. CBS, however, quickly cut off some of its dead weight new shows and bounced back as well, moving ahead of NBC by mid-November and breathing down ABC's neck by Christmas. Part of the reason for this immediate rebound by CBS was the sudden surge by the network's Friday night Southern soul mates, *The Dukes of Hazzard* and *Dallas.*

Dallas began as a little-noticed spring series in April 1978, a product of the Lorimar company (which also turned out *The Waltons*). The program was a high-powered classy soap opera, presenting the oil-rich world of the burgeoning sunbelt as the locale of the Ewing clan, owners of a powerful energy empire. Though each episode of *Dallas* could stand on its own, the series played like a spicy soap opera, with continuing story threads winding in and out all season. Aging John "Jock" Ewing (Jim Davis) was the nominal boss of the company, but he was being steadily usurped by his crafty oldest son, John Junior, better known as J. R. (Larry Hagman.) J. R. was determined to keep as much control as possible over the family business, and he was more than willing to use anyone and anything to increase his personal power and Ewing Oil's profits. In fact, he rather enjoyed stepping on other people. He blithely ignored his high-strung wife, Sue Ellen (Linda Gray), and boldly carried on an affair with Kristin (Mary Crosby), Sue Ellen's sister. Yet, when Kristin tried to turn the tables and have her own affair on the side, J. R. barged into the bedroom, smiled at the couple in bed, and coolly telephoned the boss of Kristin's lover, having the interloper fired on the spot.

Jock's younger and more principled son, Bobby (Patrick Duffy), was married to Pamela Barnes (Victoria Principal), the daughter of "Digger" Barnes (David Wayne, and later, Keenan Wynn), Jock's former partner turned arch-enemy. Pamela's brother, Cliff (Ken Kercheval), carried on the family feud by waging a war against the Ewing empire from his post in the Texas state government. The youngest Ewing, Lucy (Charlene Tilton), Jock's granddaughter (and daughter of the exiled Ewing son, Gary), spent her time seducing Ewing ranch hands and flirting with anything that wore pants. Only the Ewing matriarch, "Miss" Ellie (Barbara Bel Geddes), held no grudge against another main character, and she always acted as confidante and peacemaker.

What made *Dallas* stand out from other soap operas (including recent prime time failures *Executive Suite* and *Big Hawaii*) was its Texas locale (where myths of the old West clashed with the reality of modern day business and morals) and the character of J. R. Most glossy soap operas focused on admirable, if somewhat flawed, heroes. J. R. was *bad* and *mean* and *no good* and he *knew* it. He was a villain people loved to hate, and his personal manipulations added an electricity to *Dallas* that attracted viewers who kept tuning in just to see what J. R. would dare try next.

At first CBS did not quite know what to do with *Dallas,* shifting the show a few times before settling on a Friday night slot beginning in January 1979. There it was teamed with another new Southern-based CBS show, *The Dukes of Hazzard,* a slick television equivalent to the popular 1977 Burt Reynolds film, "Smokey and the Bandit."

The Dukes of Hazzard presented life in the rural South as just good fun with fast cars, beautiful women, and moonshine whiskey. Plots for the shows were simple: Cousins Luke Duke (Tom Wopat) and Bo Duke (John Schneider) and the curvaceous female kin Daisy Duke (Catherine Bach) were out to have a good time in Hazzard county, despite constant run–ins with the corrupt local power boss, J. D. Hogg (Sorrell Booke) and his bumbling police force, sheriff Rosco Coltrane (James Best) and deputy Enos Strate (Sonny Shroyer). The two Duke boys were on probation (from some trumped-up charge) so they had to watch their step, and they never did anything really bad. They were what country singer and program narrator Waylon Jennings described as "gold ol' boys fightin' the system." *The Dukes of Hazzard* pulled off its simple, good-timey premise with light-hearted scripts, a colorful cast, up-beat country music, and non-stop car chases and car crashes.

Dallas and *The Dukes of Hazzard* complemented each other well and made a perfect back-to-back Friday night double feature. One month into their partnership, both shows were into the top thirty. By the end of the 1978–79 season, both were in the top twenty. In the fall of 1979, the team kept rising, and both shows broke into the top ten. CBS had already built winning lineups on Sunday and Monday going into the new season, so the *Dallas-Dukes of Hazzard* combination gave the network three consistently strong nights. This was one of the main reasons CBS rebounded so fast from its weak fall start.

For ABC, something was wrong. The network's seemingly invulnerable position had crumbled practically overnight. Boosted by the World Series and hit movies such as "Jaws," ABC held on to first place in the cumulative ratings through January, though CBS won the November ratings sweep. A season that was supposed to be a rout for ABC had turned into a neck-and-neck race.

Fred Silverman had observed, going into the 1979–80 season, that he expected ABC to fade soon because the network was repeating its most frequent sin, overworking hit formulas. While he had been with ABC, Silverman had stressed diversity in programming (from *Three's Company* to *Family*) and even raised a few eyebrows by canceling shows that were still ratings winners (*The Bionic Woman* and *Wonder Woman*) because he felt they had peaked. Now ABC seemed determined to produce as many teen-oriented sitcoms as possible, while banking on the success of all its older series to continue undiminished. Even the homespun *Mork and Mindy* found itself tinted with titillation in episodes featuring Mork as a Dallas Cowboy cheerleader and Raquel Welch as a sexy alien. Silverman explained that when viewers at last tired of ABC, they would not so much tire of particular shows as of the approach taken by the entire schedule.

Equally important to ABC's slippage, though, was the miscalculation by Fred Pierce and Tony Thomopoulos on the drawing power of particular hit shows. Viewers did not automatically follow them to different nights and different times, so all the programs dropped in their new slots, some immediately, some after a few weeks. (*Mork and Mindy* dropped as low as 41st in the ratings one week; in another, *Laverne and Shirley* sank to 51st.) ABC shifted *Fantasy Island* back to its previous Saturday slot almost immediately and the show regained much of its ratings strength. The network dog-

gedly stuck with its other shifts awhile longer, and that was a fatal mistake.

CBS had made similar scheduling moves in the 1978–79 season, rearranging several moderate hits in mid-season to build strength on other nights. In the process, *The White Shadow, One Day at a Time,* and *The Incredible Hulk* lost their audience and practically dropped from sight. CBS quickly saw its mistake and, within a month, moved them all back to their previous slots, thereby saving the shows.

In the fall of 1979, CBS yanked its fall flops from the schedule right away (including its three new sitcom bombs and such losers as *Big Shamus, Little Shamus, California Fever,* and *Paris*). Some were even gone by the beginning of October. ABC, on the other hand, took until February to finish its moves. By then, shows such as *Laverne and Shirley* and *Mork and Mindy* had lost much of their ratings luster and needed time to rebuild even in their old slot. To have former top five shows occasionally in the Nielsen basement dragged down the entire ABC schedule and CBS pulled ahead in January.

One important reason for ABC's inability to move quickly, cut its losses, and bring in new shows was that the network had failed to develop adequate back-up strength. Earlier in the decade, CBS had fallen from first place for much the same reason: While comfortably on top, it had not built up a solid inventory of replacement shows. CBS, however, had also learned its lesson. In the 1978–79 season, the network was ready with *The White Shadow* and *The Dukes of Hazzard* as early winter replacements. This season, CBS displayed more of its valuable "bench strength" at the end

March 11, 1980
   United States. (NBC). Larry Gelbart, the co-creator of *M*A*S*H,* tries a unique thirty-minute comedy on marriage (starring Beau Bridges and Helen Shaver) reminiscent of Ingmar Bergman's "Scenes from a Marriage" for Swedish TV. The program runs without an opening theme or laugh track, devoting most of each episode to conversations about life, death, and sex.

March 15, 1980
   Sanford. (NBC). Redd Foxx returns as Fred Sanford, sans son, but with a rich girlfriend.

April 11, 1980
   Fridays. (ABC). In a blatant copy of NBC's *Saturday Night Live,* ABC brings together nine young unknowns to serve as the troupe for a seventy-minute live comedy show from Los Angeles.

May 8, 1980
   CBS chairman William Paley fires John D. Backe, his heir apparent. Thomas H. Wyman is named the new president and chief executive officer of CBS, Inc.

June 1, 1980
   Ted Turner's Cable News Network begins twenty-four hours a day of television news.

June 9, 1980
   Independent Network News. WPIX in New York sends a nightly national news show via satellite to twenty-seven unaffiliated stations across the country.

June 30, 1980
   John Davidson Show. Group W dumps Mike Douglas as host of its syndicated talk show for the younger Davidson. Douglas keeps his show going by syndicating it himself.

The *Real People* people: (from *l.*) Byron Allen, Skip Stephenson, Sarah Purcell, John Barbour. *(George Schlatter Productions, Inc./Photo by Larry Shulman)*

of 1979 by quickly replacing failed series with two strong new shows: *Knots Landing* (a *Dallas* spinoff set in California, with Ted Shackelford as Gary Ewing, the exiled son) and *House Calls* (a hospital comedy starring Wayne Rogers and Lynn Redgrave and based on a hit movie). Both series became solid hits and kept up the CBS momentum. In April, CBS temporarily replaced *House Calls* with yet another strong series, *Flo* (a spinoff from *Alice*), which immediately jumped into the top ten as well.

ABC, in contrast, had only one big new mid-season hit, *That's Incredible*. *Tenspeed and Brownshoe,* a well produced new cop show, flashed into the top ten after an intense publicity boost surrounding its premiere, but then faded before the characters had time to catch on. *240-Robert* (a pale copy of *CHiPs* and *Emergency*), *B.A.D. Cats* (worse than *240-Robert*), and a condescending blue collar sitcom, *When the Whistle Blows* (worst of all), were tremendous flops.

Still, ABC planned to hang on for the season by riding the winter Olympics ratings boost, then heavily promoting its key series as they returned to their previous hit slots and plugging in special blockbuster movies. The February Olympics did put ABC back in the lead, but, by March, CBS was rolling with solid performances on Sunday, Monday, and Friday. Veterans such as *Archie Bunker's Place* (the renamed *All in the Family*), *Alice,* and *The Jeffersons* were once again top ten hits. MTM shows such as *Lou Grant, WKRP in Cincinnati,* and *The White Shadow* were also doing well. And then CBS's Friday night headliners exploded.

As the battle for the top spot in network television moved into the spring, *Dallas* and *The Dukes of Hazzard* became the hottest shows on the air, sometimes finishing first and second in the weekly ratings. At the end of March, *Dallas* pumped up fresh viewer interest by closing out its new episodes for the season with the shooting of the dastardly J. R. by a mysterious assailant. Reruns

began the following week and many new *Dallas* viewers, lured by the closing episode, stayed put to fill in character background and catch up on the plot lines and setups they had missed from earlier in the season.

Armed with this line-up of hits, CBS closed the gap on ABC and the two were in a dead heat going into the final week of the regular season (which ended April 20). The cumulative ratings victory rested on the performance of a few blockbuster specials. ABC opened strong on Monday, April 14, with the number one show of the week, the annual Academy Awards program hosted by Johnny Carson. CBS neutralized this by scoring big on Tuesday and Wednesday with the surprisingly well done miniseries, *Guyana Tragedy: The Story of Jim Jones*. On Friday, ABC put in "The Best of *That's Incredible,*" a special edition of its only new big hit. It all came down to the last day, Sunday, April 20. ABC pulled out one of its champion theatrical films, "The Sting," for an encore performance. CBS countered with a special new two-hour episode of *The Dukes of Hazzard*. The downhome Hazzard County crew beat the con men from Chicago. CBS won the night, the week, and the season. The final seasonal averages were CBS: 19.6, ABC: 19.5, and NBC, 17.4. CBS held a party to celebrate its first regular season win since the 1975–76 season, and network chairman William Paley called it one of his "sweetest victories."

In one season, CBS had outscored and outmaneuvered the competition with a varied, versatile schedule ranging from the high gloss soap of *Dallas* to the serious character drama of *Lou Grant*. Yet, this dramatic turnaround also underscored how volatile the network standings had become. Even with one of CBS's strongest line-ups in years, there was little chance that victory in the 1979–80 season, however sweet, marked the beginning of another twenty-five year reign at the top by CBS.

40. The Strike

FOR MORE than three years, NBC's strategy for becoming the number one network hinged on the 1980 summer Olympic games. In February, 1977, even before luring Fred Silverman from ABC, NBC had won the rights to the contests (the first to be held in the Soviet Union) by committing a record-breaking $100 million in its bid. This broke down to approximately $22.4 million for the actual television rights, $50 million for the production facilities in Moscow, $12.6 million to the International Olympic Committee, and $12–$15 million for such miscellaneous items as talent and transportation.

There was a very good reason for this expenditure: The 1976 Olympics had helped push ABC to the number one slot. Even though the summer games took place before the annual ratings battle began for the regular season, they had provided a tremendous opportunity for ABC to promote its upcoming fall schedule. NBC counted on doing the same in 1980, while treating its overall Olympic coverage as an on-going "big event" with frequent on-the-air promotions. When Fred Silverman joined NBC in 1978, he also paced his plans toward the summer and fall of 1980, aiming to have ready a strong program line-up that could ride the momentum of the Olympics and bring NBC to the top by Christmas, 1980.

To coincide with its huge investment, NBC signed ABC's Olympics producer in 1976, Don Ohlmeyer, to supervise both the actual coverage in 1980 and the necessary preparations by NBC's sports department. Ohlmeyer's first NBC project was *Sportsworld,* a weekend afternoon sports anthology modeled after ABC's *Wide World of Sports.* This new program gave NBC's sports production crews the opportunity to sharpen their technical skills while providing the network with the perfect on-air promotional forum to talk up Olympic-type competitive events.

As 1980 drew nearer, NBC also scheduled a host of other tie-in programs, ranging from specials such as the animated "Animalympics" to the NBC-financed movie "Goldengirl" featuring Susan Anton as an American track star at the Moscow games. Ohlmeyer himself produced a four-hour made-for-TV movie on the summer Olympics, "The Golden Moment." NBC announced plans for 152½ hours of Olympic coverage in 1980, pre-empting most of its prime time schedule from July 18 through August 5. Then, on Christmas day, 1979, the entire NBC Olympic project was put in jeopardy as the Soviet Union invaded Afghanistan.

The Russian invasion shocked and angered many Americans who were already frustrated by the continuing stalemate over the hostages taken in the seizure of the American embassy in Iran the previous month. Looking for some way (short of war) to protest the Soviet move, many people focused on the summer Olympic games in Moscow as a symbolic rallying point and they began to call for a boycott of the event. On January 20, 1980, President Jimmy Carter appeared on NBC's *Meet the Press* and expressed his support for such a move. He said that unless the Soviets withdrew their forces from Afghanistan by February 20, he would formally request the U.S. Olympic Committee to officially sanction a boycott. Many athletes, who had been training years for the games, disagreed with that course of action, saying that it unfairly mixed sports and politics in violation of the true spirit of Olympic competition.

While everyone watched for the next move by the Soviets, the 1980 winter Olympics went on as scheduled in Lake Placid, New York, running from February 12 through 24 and carried by ABC. The ratings were even better than ABC's successful 1976 winter Olympics coverage, culminating in a dramatic face-off between the Soviet Union and the United States—on ice. There, for the first time in twenty years, the U.S. hockey team beat the Russians, eliminating them from the Olympic championship series. A video tape replay of the game placed as the number four program of the week and, two days later, the U.S. team went on to beat Finland for the gold medal in hockey.

In the jubilation over the American victory, many people opposed to the boycott were quick to point out that the winter Olympics seemed a perfect illustration of why the United States should participate in the summer games: Confrontations could take place in the sports arena rather than on the battlefield. Nonetheless, the Soviet troops remained in Afghanistan into the spring and, on April 22, the U.S. Olympic Committee voted 1,604 to 797 in favor of the resolution calling for a boycott. Though individual athletes were not specifically ordered to stay home, the committee's vote meant that there would be no official U.S. team sent to Moscow and, therefore, no funds available to defray the tremendous cost of participating.

Throughout the months of public debate on the boycott, NBC found itself in a difficult position and deliberately kept a low profile. Because the Soviets said that the Olympics would go on even without U.S. participation, NBC could still carry them. Realistically, however, such a move would have been a public relations fiasco. The network's financial investment in the games had been widely

FALL 1980 SCHEDULE

	7:30	8:00	8:30	9:00	9:30	10:00	10:30	
MONDAY	local	That's Incredible		ABC NFL Monday Night Football [to 12 Midnite]				**ABC**
	local	CBS Special Presentation		M*A*S*H	WKRP In Cincinnati	Lou Grant		**CBS**
	local	Little House On The Prairie		NBC Monday Night At The Movies				**NBC**

	7:30	8:00	8:30	9:00	9:30	10:00	10:30	
TUESDAY	local	Happy Days	Laverne And Shirley	Three's Company	Taxi	Hart To Hart		**ABC**
	local	CBS Tuesday Night Movies						**CBS**
	local	NBC Tuesday Night At The Movies				NBC Specials		**NBC**

	7:30	8:00	8:30	9:00	9:30	10:00	10:30	
WEDNESDAY	local	Eight Is Enough		Charlie's Angels		Vega$		**ABC**
	local	CBS Special Presentation		CBS Wednesday Night Movies				**CBS**
	local	Real People		NBC Movie Of The Week				**NBC**

	7:30	8:00	8:30	9:00	9:30	10:00	10:30	
THURSDAY	local	Mork And Mindy	Angie	ABC SPECIALS		20/20		**ABC**
	local	The White Shadow		CBS SPECIAL MOVIE PRESENTATION				**CBS**
	local	GAMES PEOPLE PLAY		NBC Thursday Night At The Movies				**NBC**

	7:30	8:00	8:30	9:00	9:30	10:00	10:30	
FRIDAY	local	Benson		The ABC Friday Night Movie				**ABC**
	local	The Incredible Hulk		The Dukes Of Hazzard		Dallas		**CBS**
	local	The Flintstones	Facts Of Life	Speak Up America		NBC MAGAZINE WITH DAVID BRINKLEY		**NBC**

	7:30	8:00	8:30	9:00	9:30	10:00	10:30	
SATURDAY	local	The Love Boat				Fantasy Island		**ABC**
	local	Tim Conway Show	CBS SPECIAL MOVIE PRESENTATION					**CBS**
	local	NBC Saturday Night At The Movies						**NBC**

	7:00	7:30	8:00	8:30	9:00	9:30	10:00	10:30	
SUNDAY	THOSE AMAZING ANIMALS		The ABC Sunday Night Movie						**ABC**
	60 Minutes		Archie Bunker's Place	One Day At A Time	Alice	The Jeffersons	Trapper John, M.D.		**CBS**
	Disney's Wonderful World		CHiPs		The Sunday Big Event				**NBC**

reported and to go through with coverage while the athletes themselves were forced to stay home would have appeared to be the height of cynical self-interest.

In May, NBC announced that its far-flung summer Olympics programming would be drastically cut back. Because the U.S. Olympic Committee decided to go through the formality of naming an American Olympic squad, NBC did cover those team trials in the spring and early summer. For the actual games in Moscow, though, NBC limited itself to short feature reports (of about ninety seconds' duration) during the nightly news. This was virtually indistinguishable from the short clips and summaries offered by ABC and CBS as well as other news organizations. A few individual stations went even further and specifically ignored *any* Olympic news, refusing even to mention winners in major events or new world records. Though most news organizations did not go to that extreme, for most television viewers it was as if the 1980 summer Olympics never took place.

NBC lost more than $50 million in ad revenue as well as money already spent in preparations through April. There was not even a chance to rebound four years later—ABC had already won the bidding for the rights to both the summer and winter Olympic games in 1984. Above all, NBC had lost the promotional vehicle it had counted on for more than three years. Fred Silverman and NBC had been done in by events totally outside their control.

Just a few days after the Moscow Olympics began, though, there was another development outside network control, but this one disrupted all three networks. On July 21, 1980, the members of the American Federation of Television and Radio Artists (AFTRA) and the Screen Actors Guild (SAG) went out on strike. This halted production on theatrical films, made-for-TV movies, and most prime time filmed and taped series. The central issue of the strike was a desire by the unions to win for their members a share of the money earned by producers selling the rights to distribute programs on pay television systems and on prerecorded video cassettes and video disks.

Everyone involved recognized the precedent-setting importance of the negotiations. At the time, actors received nothing from cable, cassette, or disk sales, yet, since the mid-1970s, use of these alternate television systems had grown tremendously. Any new contract would serve as a model for future arrangements both by the actors and other craft unions. Both sides therefore approached the contract talks very carefully and, as a result, an immediate settlement was out of the question. Negotiations dragged on through the remainder of the summer while celebrities walked the picket lines.

When the strike began, the companies supplying program material for the networks were just a few weeks into production for the 1980–81 season and had only a handful of shows "in the can." As September approached, it became clear that, for the first time in television history, the networks would have to begin the new season without most of their regular series.

Though the strike virtually shut down Hollywood, there were a number of areas unaffected. Those performers appearing in commercials, news programs, game shows, sports broadcasts, afternoon soap operas, and variety shows all operated under different contracts. Programs such as the *Tonight* show, *60 Minutes, Monday Night Football, Real People,* and *The Tim Conway Show* could go on as usual. The networks were forced to improvise with what was available for the fall, carefully mixing variety specials, theatrical films, sports events, selected reruns, and the few series episodes completed before the strike began.

By chance, number three NBC appeared to be in the best shape to handle the strike season, which seemed a perverse form of justice to balance its Olympic disaster. NBC had a backlog of both old and new miniseries and "big event" presentations to draw from, including the twenty-five hour *Centennial* from 1978, the combined *Godfather Saga* from 1977, and a new twelve-hour miniseries, an adaptation of James Clavell's novel, *Shōgun.* In addition, the network's "reality shows" such as *Real People* were unaffected, and it even had ready a good number of completed episodes from popular series (including four of *CHiPs* and six of *Little House on the Prairie*). NBC also had the World Series and, if the strike dragged into 1981, the Super Bowl.

With such strong inventory, Fred Silverman went into September very aggressively, touting the NBC schedule as being 75%–80% new material through October. CBS and ABC, more reliant on weekly sitcom and drama series than NBC, were not as fortunate. Though ABC brought in its own reality shows *(Those Amazing Animals* and *That's Incredible)* and reran its 1978 miniseries of *Pearl* during the usual September premiere period, the network essentially continued its summer rerun schedule, occasionally using episodes that were several years old. CBS was squeezed even tighter. Though the network had a few new "pre-strike" episodes of *Lou Grant* and *The White Shadow,* some of its other top series such as *M*A*S*H* and *Archie Bunker's Place (All in the Family)* had already parceled out all but the preceding season's shows into rerun syndication. In addition, short-run winter and spring replacement hits such as *Flo* and *House Calls* had only a handful of episodes at all, and those had already been rerun in the summer. Thus, CBS had to scrap most of its schedule and rely instead on elongated movie presentations and reruns of specials.

NBC sensed the potential for a big victory. Even before the strike, Silverman had planned to open the 1980–81 season with a week of *Shōgun.* He stood by that timetable, figuring that the miniseries could be practically unbeatable without front line series competition from the other networks. Silverman's calculations were perfect. The five episodes of *Shōgun* ranked as the top five shows of the first week of the "new" season, giving NBC the highest rated week in its history. *Shōgun* became the second highest miniseries ever, right behind *Roots.*

Unlike *Roots* or *Holocaust,* which focused on generations and families, *Shōgun* was the story of one man's personal struggle. Richard Chamberlain played the hero, an English sea pilot named John Blackthorne, who found himself shipwrecked in Japan during the early 1600s. Facing vast cultural differences, as well as complex political and religious intrigue, Blackthorne slowly adapted his Western instincts to the Eastern traditions. The Englishman befriended Toranaga (Toshiro Mifune), a Japanese warlord aspiring to be the supreme military dictator (or "shōgun") of the country, and fell in love with his translator, the beautiful Mariko (Yoko Shimada). Along the way, Blackthorne also proved himself in com-

bat and won acceptance in his new land, becoming the first non-Japanese samurai warrior. *Shōgun* was an effective combination of exotic settings, beautiful photography, a love triangle, and effective bursts of violence.

The entire *Shōgun* miniseries was shot on location in Japan at a cost of $20 million. Veteran writer Eric Bercovici (who had done *Washington: Behind Closed Doors*) turned out the script from James Clavell's lengthy novel, and Clavell himself served as executive producer. In a truly daring move, they decided to let the Japanese characters in the story speak in Japanese, without subtitles or translation. This allowed viewers to share Blackthorne's initial confusion at, then growing appreciation for, his new country. The program was challenging, effective, and, much to NBC's delight, an overwhelming success, giving the network a big lead to open the season.

The week after *Shōgun,* the striking unions reached a tentative strike settlement with the producers. However, there still remained two or three weeks for ratification by the rank and file, and then about three or four more weeks before the first new shows would be ready to air. So the ad hoc strike schedule continued until the beginning of November, with new shows, new specials, sports, and theatrical films generally outdrawing rerun competition. ABC's NFL *Monday Night Football* had the best opening ratings in its history. Both the baseball playoffs (on ABC) and the World Series (on NBC) also earned record-high ratings. CBS's highly publicized made-for-TV movie about a Jewish woman in a Nazi concentration camp, "Playing for Time" (starring Vanessa Redgrave), scored as the number one show of its week, giving CBS its only weekly win during the strike.

At the beginning of October, the actors ratified the tentative agreement and, on October 6, series production resumed. For the immediate future, the settlement provided actors with a pay rate boost of 33% for prime time reruns. In the developing new video fields, there were important long-range precedents: Performers were granted 4.5% of the distributor's gross for the first year of a show's play on pay TV, and 4.5% of the producer's gross on prerecorded video disk and video cassette sales above 100,000 units. Though such provisions did not result in any immediate cash, they assured performers a share in the expanding video industries that could eventually prove a bonanza. As more and more material was required by the many competing cable services, cable programmers would have to follow the route taken by the commercial networks years before and develop original movies, variety specials, and even continuing dramatic, adventure, and comedy series to supplement their basic schedule of uncut movies and sporting events. All that was years away, though. The immediate focus following the settlement was to turn out new material for the season already in progress as quickly as possible.

The networks' post-strike schedules in October, November, and December were almost as confusing as the strike period because not every returning series followed the same production timetable. Half-hour videotaped programs were ready much faster than hour-long filmed series, so the networks had to continue to improvise, plugging the holes in their schedules as the shows became available. There were other disruptions as well including election coverage, the November sweeps, and holiday specials for Thanksgiving and Christmas. As a result, some season premieres were practically buried and did not produce the expected instant jump in the ratings. It was not until January, 1981, that the schedules settled down at last. Despite NBC's success during the strike season, though, it was CBS that came out on top, once again propelled by *Dallas.*

CBS had done the worst of the networks during the strike because

September 9, 1980

The FCC creates "secondary stations," a new technical classification that sets up the possibility for thousands of new low-powered local television stations.

September 16, 1980

As part of Johnny Carson's new contract with NBC, *Tonight* shrinks to sixty minutes, but has Carson as host four rather than three nights each week. Tom Snyder's *Tomorrow* expands to ninety minutes to take up the half-hour slack.

October 25, 1980

ABC's *Love Boat* and *Fantasy Island* are the first series to get new episodes on the air after the strike settlement.

October 28, 1980

President Jimmy Carter debates Republican challenger Ronald Reagan in Cleveland before a television audience of forty-six million.

November 2, 1980

In the season premiere of *Archie Bunker's Place,* Archie comes to grips with the death of his wife, Edith. This realistic plot development evolved from Jean Stapleton's desire to leave the series for good.

November 4, 1980

NBC's use of strategic exit polls helps the network to call Ronald Reagan the winner in the presidential election at 8:15 p.m., beating ABC's announcement by more than ninety minutes and CBS's by more than two hours.

November 15, 1980

Under new producer Jean Doumanian, the "next generation" of *Saturday Night Live* debuts with a new cast of six unknowns, but the refurbished program fails to jell. After only four months, NBC installs another producer (Dick Ebersol) and revamps both the crew and format.

---

it did not have as extensive a backlog of flashy "event" programming as NBC. More importantly, this weak start threatened to scuttle CBS's game plan for the entire season because it diffused the momentum of the network's strong come-from-behind victory in the 1979–80 season. CBS had planned to start the 1980–81 season with its winning schedule in place and quickly build its previous razor-thin victory into a healthy lead. The strike nullified those plans and gave NBC the initiative instead. CBS could only sit on the side and wait.

Once the strike ended and program production resumed, CBS set out to quickly win back the audience. Its first move, in mid-October, was to rebuild interest in *Dallas* by rerunning episodes from the show's initial tryout as a spring series in 1978. This innovative ploy worked. Few current *Dallas* fans had followed the series in its original run and the ratings for the program remained strong. Then, going into November, CBS began to rekindle the "Who shot J. R.?" mania that had started with the season finale of *Dallas* the previous March. Since then, the program had turned into a worldwide sensation with a fanatic following. In Britain there was even spirited betting on the identity of the assailant. (Odds were quoted at 20–1 that J. R. shot himself!)

To open November, CBS staged *"Dallas* week," airing four episodes of the program in one week (one on Thursday, two on Friday, and one on Sunday). The first two were reruns of the final episodes from the previous season, featuring some of J. R.'s dirtiest deals and culminating in his shooting. This effectively set the stage for the two-part season premiere in which doctors rushed to save

J. R.'s life. All four episodes finished in the top ten (coming in at number one, two, four, and nine for the week). The regular Friday episode the following week continued the story, dangling spurious clues and suspects. This also finished number one. With interest once again at a peak, the answer to the eight-month-old question "Who shot J. R.?" came at last on Friday, November 21. In the closing moments of the program, Kristin, J. R.'s mistress and personal secretary, confessed that she had done it.

A record number of viewers tuned in to find out the answer, sending *Dallas* through the ratings roof. With a 53.3 rating and a 76 share, it became the highest rated individual show ever on television, topping such sports events as the Super Bowl and World Series and previous TV milestones including the birth of Little Ricky on *I Love Lucy,* the final episode of *The Fugitive,* and even the concluding segment of the original *Roots.*

Dallas also set the tone for several late-starting new series as each of the networks tried to duplicate its successful "prime time soap opera" formula. CBS had actually been first in 1979, turning to Lorimar, the company that created *Dallas,* for the *Knots Landing* spinoff. For the fall of 1980, CBS picked up another Lorimar production, *The Secrets of Midland Heights,* a college-town version of *Dallas. Midland Heights* was aimed at a younger audience than *Dallas,* focusing on promiscuous students as well as on the local J. R. surrogate, Guy Millington (John Christopher), the evil son of the most powerful woman in town.

NBC also turned to Lorimar for a prime time soap, *Flamingo Road,* based on the 1949 movie with Joan Crawford. For the television version, Howard Duff played the obligatory evil force, sheriff Titus Semple, who was the one and only power in the small town of Truro, Florida. ABC's *Dynasty,* from Aaron Spelling, featured John Forsythe (the voice of Charlie in Spelling's *Charlie's Angels*) as Blake Carrington, an aging oil tycoon with a lusty young wife and a promiscuous young daughter.

Even with this influx of prime time soaps, *Dallas* stayed at the front of the television ratings pack for the remainder of the season as the many new viewers stuck around to follow the plot complications introduced while J. R. recovered. As CBS's other regular series fell into place, the network wiped out its ratings deficit from the strike period and by mid-December passed both ABC and NBC in the cumulative ratings race, eventually winning the entire 1980–81 season with relative ease.

One reason that NBC, which had taken the ratings lead during the strike, fell so quickly from the top was that the network could not match CBS's line-up of established hit series. Yet, for a while, it looked as if NBC at least had a chance at making a respectable showing for second place overall by following an innovative three-phase post-strike plan.

First, in November, Fred Silverman quickly set in place NBC's strongest night, Wednesday, bringing back *Diff'rent Strokes, Facts of Life,* and *Quincy* to follow the hit *Real People.* For phase two, he held back most of NBC's other returning shows and new series while ABC and CBS slotted theirs, filling in with short-run series instead. One of these, a variety hour starring country singer Barbara Mandrell, proved successful enough to win instant renewal in January.

At the beginning of January, Silverman launched phase three and brought in the remainder of NBC's regular series. Because CBS and ABC had just finished their delayed fall premieres, NBC had a second-season type limelight all to itself. For the first five weeks of 1981, the NBC strategy seemed to be working as the network beat out ABC and came in second four times. Returning (and revamped) programs such as *Lobo, BJ and the Bear,* and *Buck Rogers* all did well in elongated two-hour openers, and new

"The most trusted personality in America," Walter Cronkite, ended nearly nineteen years as anchor for *The CBS Evening News* on March 6, 1981. *60 Minutes* correspondent Dan Rather took over the post three days later. *(CBS News Photo)*

series such as *Flamingo Road, Harper Valley P.T.A.,* and *Hill Street Blues* turned in impressive ratings.

NBC's three-phase post-strike strategy gave Fred Silverman a chance to demonstrate his greatest strength: effectively juggling hit programs on a schedule in order to entice viewers to give the other shows on the network a chance. However, though such Silverman favorites as *Real People* and *Diff'rent Strokes* had caught on, NBC still had not developed a sufficient number of solid series to fill the entire schedule. In many cases, once viewers were lured to NBC, they found little to keep them there. Instead, NBC still had to depend on big events and specials both to buy time for shows to catch on and also to fill between hits. Here, ironically, Silverman's successful strike strategy took its toll.

In presenting a mostly new schedule during the actors' strike, NBC had not only drawn from its backlog of material, it had also aired many blockbuster movies and specials normally kept until the ratings sweep periods. This tactic put NBC in a very vulnerable position, particularly during the February sweeps. While CBS had such top theatrical movies as "Hooper" (with Burt Reynolds) and "The Amityville Horror," and ABC aired "Norma Rae" and "Jaws 2," NBC was left with tepid made-for-TV films such as "Kent State" and "Elvis and the Beauty Queen." Worse yet, with a shortage of attractive event programming, NBC was forced to throw its regular series against such ABC specials as the three-part, eight-hour sexy miniseries *East of Eden* and the flashy made-for-TV movie "Miracle on Ice" (recreating America's 1980 Olympic hockey triumph). As a result, Fred Silverman presided over his third consecutive losing season at NBC. During the summer he was eased out of power and replaced by Grant Tinker, head of the MTM production company.

Though the two and one-half month actors' strike created one

of the most confusing programming periods in television history, it had a much more significant meaning than merely messing up the networks' plans for the 1980–81 season. The strike also marked the first time ABC, CBS, and NBC were forced to confront head-on the changing reality of television technology and to acknowledge the rapidly growing influence of cable TV and home video attachments. For years, the networks had steadfastly ignored or dismissed advances in these fields, but in 1980 this could no longer be done. Already many established television production outfits had begun to diversify in order to fill the programming needs of the new video outlets. The demands by the actors (and other craft unions) for a share in these new sources of profit reflected the increasing confidence in their inevitable growth. At last, the networks began to embrace the changing times as well. Near the end of 1980, first ABC, then CBS, established new cable television divisions to develop programs exclusively for the new video industries. ABC's were the first to hit the air.

At 9:00 P.M. on Sunday, April 12, 1981, ABC's cultural cable service, the Alpha Repertory Television Service (dubbed "ARTS") began a new era in network television by providing the Warner Brothers Nickelodeon cable system with three hours of original programs three nights each week (rebroadcasts filled the other four nights). Like the sparse schedule of network television four decades before, the ARTS offerings represented only a modest start in a new market. Yet they were an important first step, signaling at last a commitment by an established commercial network to stake out a share in the new video fields.

November 17, 1980
Roger Mudd, passed over by CBS as Walter Cronkite's successor, defects to NBC News.

November 30, 1980
Tanya Roberts joins *Charlie's Angels* as Julie Rogers, replacing Shelly Hack who lasted only one season.

December 20, 1980
As an experiment, NBC televises a football game between the New York Jets and Miami Dolphins without any play-by-play announcers.

January 12, 1981
Tomorrow Coast-to-Coast. (NBC). Rona Barrett, formerly of ABC's *Good Morning America*, joins Tom Snyder as co-host of NBC's revamped late late night talk show.

January 20, 1981
After twenty-nine years as CBS's chief anchor for special events, Walter Cronkite reports his farewell news spectacular: the inauguration of Ronald Reagan as President and the release of the American hostages from Iran.

April 11, 1981
Demands for a share of the profits in the new video industries result in more strike action against TV and film producers as the members of the Writers Guild of America walk out. The first program affected: Johnny Carson's *Tonight* show.

April 12, 1981
Anne Baxter hosts opening night for ARTS, ABC's cultural cable service. The initial offerings include performances by flutist Michel Debost, a concert by the Israel Philharmonic, and a feature on painter Gustav Klimt, kicking off the first week's theme: "Paris: The Dream and the Reality."

CONCLUSION

On Beyond Zebra

THE CONSTANT public attention directed toward which network is number one and what shows are in the top ten fosters the image of television as a wide-open free for all. Actually, from the beginning, network television has borne the stamp of a surprisingly small number of people.

Milton Berle inspired millions to buy their first TV sets in the late Forties. During the early Fifties, *I Love Lucy* launched the Desilu studios and began the domination of filmed sitcoms. Throughout that decade, Louis G. Cowan presented one quiz show after another on all the networks. In the late Fifties, ABC drew more than one-fourth of its schedule from the Warner Brothers film studios. NBC carried a similar reliance on Universal studios through the Sixties and Seventies. CBS's president James Aubrey presided over programming geared toward rural America in the early Sixties, building on the success of Paul Henning's *The Beverly Hillbillies.* Ten years later, producer Norman Lear developed a style of television comedy with *All in the Family* that was more urban-oriented, topical, and controversial. Garry Marshall supplied ABC with a string of hit sitcoms that made the network number one in the mid-Seventies. Ace programmer Fred Silverman directed strategy at all three networks during the Seventies, going from CBS to ABC to NBC.

Though thousands of people work toward the finished products, access in television is really very limited. Ultimately, program material is funneled through just a few networks, studios, and producers. As a result, the race for the top spots is more accurately a contest among those that have already staked out a share of the television pie. Placing a show on television means the opportunity not only to earn huge profits but also to use a vast pulpit to present a particular point of view. In the future, as now, those that have power and influence in television will fight to keep it and those that do not will fight to attain it.

From its creation in the late Twenties, the Federal Communications Commission recognized the special limited nature of the broadcast medium and set up rules that called for use of the airwaves for the public's "interest, convenience, and necessity." The FCC tried to include avenues of access by calling on stations to incorporate a wide range of programming aimed at serving their communities. Though often compliance with the commission's rules consisted only of a few token religious, news, and educational programs, these were important precedents because, from the start of American television until the mid-Sixties, most cities had only a few television stations. For the most part, access to the viewing public was largely limited to those within the New York-Hollywood entertainment axis.

Besides fighting for time on existing channels, others in search of a television forum tried to find new outlets, attempting to multiply choices for viewers and available markets for producers. Over the years, a frequently proposed scheme has been the creation of a fourth commercial network, organizing stations into a force equivalent to ABC, CBS, and NBC.

American television had, in fact, begun with four networks, but that situation lasted only a few years. By the mid-Fifties, the Du-Mont television network foundered and died—largely due to a weak financial foundation and a lack of affiliates. The same problems almost killed ABC as well but the network was able to last out the lean years by merging with United Paramount Theaters in 1953, receiving an important influx of cash and stability. By the mid-Sixties, the number of stations throughout the country had grown. Many major cities had at least three TV stations and UHF reception had been mandated for all TV sets. More viewers were capable of picking up ABC's signals and, as that network grew, serious discussions began on the possibility of starting a new fourth commercial network.

In 1967, the United Network, nicknamed "UniNet," became the only proposed fourth network to, thus far, make it to the air. Co-founded by Ollie Treyz (a former president of ABC-TV), UniNet announced grandiose plans for a seven-day-a-week prime time schedule containing new and varied programming, but the only show to ever reach the public was *The Las Vegas Show,* a clone of Johnny Carson's *Tonight* on NBC. Hosted by Bill Dana (a *Tonight* show regular himself under Steven Allen in the Fifties), *The Las Vegas Show* lasted only one month. Local stations were erratic in their support for the proto-network and the lack of solid sponsorship caused both the series and UniNet to collapse and disappear.

Since the demise of the United Network, several companies have announced plans for beginning new, competitive national networks, but none have been able to turn their plans into reality. The problem with starting a fourth network is still affiliates. Though there are many more stations operating than in the lean years of ABC and DuMont, they are not in the right places. A network needs affiliates in about 200 cities to reach 90–95% of the homes with TV sets, and most of the stations currently unaffiliated with ABC, CBS, and NBC are bunched in only the largest cities. Even with more than 700 commercial TV stations on the air in the United States

From left: Randolph Mantooth, David Birney, and Devon Ericson, appearing in Universal's first project for "Operation Prime Time" (OPT), a two-part miniseries. (*From* Testimony of Two Men. *Courtesy of MCA Television Limited*)

a fourth network cannot reach a large enough audience (90% of the viewing public) to attract support from major advertisers.

Long ago realizing that a fourth commercial TV network was a virtual mathematical and physical impossibility, program producers turned to another form of access: syndication, creating an ad-hoc network of stations for individual programs. During the late Forties and early Fifties, independent producers such as Jerry Fairbanks and companies such as Ziv began selling programs to individual stations to slot during time periods not used by the networks. These efforts stalled in the late Fifties as the networks increased the amount of their programming and the locals began using a greater number of readily available old movies as well as reruns of network filmed series. Syndication producers then joined forces with the networks to produce the new wave of Westerns and action-adventure series that were starting to dominate prime time. These, in turn, wound up as syndicated reruns.

Original material for syndication received a boost in the Sixties when powerful groups of stations such as the Westinghouse, Metromedia, and Avco chains struck gold with talk shows. They supplied member stations and other interested locals with video-taped gabfests hosted by Mike Douglas, Merv Griffin, and Phil Donahue for use in the brief non-network time slots of late afternoon and late night. The government expanded the potential syndication market even further with the "all-channel" bill (requiring all television sets manufactured after 1964 to include UHF reception capabilities). As UHF grew through the decade, independent producers again ventured into the realm of producing entertainment series, though at first they just turned out new versions of old game and quiz shows. The government entered the field again with the FCC's 1971 "access rule" which mandated that all three networks turn back thirty minutes each night to be filled locally

by their affiliates. The commission also forbade the use of off-network reruns in this "prime time access" slot, so independent producers stepped in with more game shows, new versions of canceled network programs, and even a few original series.

Through the Seventies, producers grew bolder in their access ventures, producing new comedy, adventure, and drama programs. Most of these had been rejected by the networks, so they were placed on individual stations, by-passing the networks completely. In 1975, the British-made *Space: 1999* gave local programmers big budget space drama with familiar television stars (Martin Landau and Barbara Bain from the successful *Mission: Impossible* series). In 1976, Norman Lear supplied five episodes weekly of the adult-oriented *Mary Hartman, Mary Hartman* comedy soap opera.

Universal studios, television's largest supplier of prime time network programming, took the next step in 1977 when it set up Operation Prime Time (OPT). Universal aimed to compete directly with prime time network programming, placing a first run drama miniseries on stations throughout the country. The success of the first OPT series, *Testimony of Two Men,* turned the experiment into an ongoing project, with Universal offering about three such miniseries per year since then.

Both Universal's OPT formula and Lear's *Mary Hartman, Mary Hartman* went to the heart of access. Instead of trying to build and maintain a full-time network to compete with the established commercial giants, they wisely concentrated on small slices of time. They allowed subscribing stations flexibility in airing the material and gave the locals a flashy product to use against their competition. However, the success of Universal and Lear only underscored the frustration experienced by "outsiders" trying to gain access to prime time television. Ultimately, Universal and Lear merely offered minor variations of what they were, at the same time, supplying to the networks. They were members of the established clique merely tapping a new market. At the time, Lear had a half dozen hit programs running on the networks and Universal was turning out similar miniseries for NBC (on such programs as *Best Sellers* and *NBC Novels for Television*). Yet, their shows' resemblance to network offerings probably accounted for their success in syndication.

Viewers weaned on action-adventure sagas and soapy dramas have come to expect not only certain levels of production standards but also a familiar approach to entertainment. They will accept new ideas, but such material requires time to build a following. In order to win that time, new series have to at least look like a regular big budget network show. Too often, those outside the normal channels of Hollywood lack the resources to mount such productions. Even if a fourth commercial network got off the ground, it would by-pass unusual new shows and instead simply mimic the forms on the established networks in order to quickly build an audience to satisfy advertisers.

Though a fourth commercial network offers little hope for significantly expanded access to television, there are alternatives possible, especially through legal and technical innovations. The government, in fact, has already created the only system to date with a different motivation from the commercial networks: public television.

Noncommercial television began in the United States in 1952, but due to a lack of funding the system was limited to low budget "educational" fare. Access to public television was almost a joke, because there were very few people watching the cheap-looking, deadly dull programs. In the late Sixties, following passage of the Public Broadcasting Act of 1967, public television began acting more like a full-fledged network as its member stations gained production savvy and the government awarded it a yearly stipend.

During the administration of President Richard Nixon, public television was strong enough as an alternative network power to pique the government with its public affairs analysis of war and domestic policies. As a result, the administration forced the PBS network to decentralize and return more power to the local stations. Oddly enough, the complicated system that emerged turned out to be, overall, very good.

The PBS schedule is set up by a convention of local affiliates that bid on shows and pledge support for new series. Local stations usually do not air PBS shows at a set time, instead fitting them into their own schedules as they choose. The affiliates in larger cities such as New York, Chicago, Washington, Boston, and Los Angeles produce programs and offer them to the entire network. Theoretically, anyone who can navigate the funding bureaucracy can produce a show—usually using one of the PBS affiliates—and offer it for nationwide broadcast.

Once a show is picked up, it is treated far differently than it would be by the commercial networks. Philosophically, PBS is meant to co-exist as an alternative to commercial broadcasting, not to replace or defeat it. As a result, programs are treated as something special. Even a one-shot special may be aired twice during the same week in its original broadcasts, then offered perhaps two or three additional times during the same season, and periodically revived over the years. A limited-run series will not be canceled due to "bad ratings" and may even be rerun immediately by public demand. Movies are often aired without any interruption and there are special dance, drama, and documentary shows.

Though it works well catering to a more educated upper-middle-class audience, there are many types of programs that do not fit into the PBS schedule—light comedy and most sporting events, for instance. In addition, public television stations developed a reliance on British programming in the Sixties and very often will, out of habit, include such shows in much the same way that NBC uses series from Universal studios. Though public television is a strong alternative, it is not the all-encompassing answer to American television's closed nature.

The all-channel bill promoting the growth of UHF, the prime time access rules, and public television have demonstrated how, to a degree, specific governmental intervention can open up the overall television system. Future governmental moves by Congress, the FCC, and the courts are the wild cards of broadcasting. An added factor, however, is the increased national awareness of the tremendous influence and power of the broadcast industry. Recent moves to alter the status quo, therefore, have turned into full-scale public debates. When Representative Lionel Van Deerlin proposed, in 1978, a rewrite of the basic law of American broadcasting, the 1934 Communications Act (including a suggestion that many public service obligations for television be removed), religious leaders throughout the country immediately directed organized protests and objections toward Washington. Eventually the proposed bill was shelved. Broadcasting's legal cases, then, have moved from being in-fighting among business interests to public contests. More importantly, special interest groups have grown more sophisticated in pressuring sponsors and legislators so that sweeping changes are very difficult. The more likely source of a revolution in TV access actually rests with technology. Though it, too, is subject to political manipulation, it is far more capable of stepping over legal complications by altering the very process of television transmission itself.

The chief stumbling block to practically any major change in television access and selection has been the very nature of the commercial television setup. There are a limited number of outlets in competition with each other that have to cater to a huge audience. In addition, because commercial television is beamed to homes indiscriminately, nervous executives tend to remove whatever might be perceived as offensive—even though many people might view the material as high-quality, mature, adult entertainment. Popular theatrical movies are edited to soften language, remove violent and sexual action, and sometimes even change the philosophical thrust. Series are created for the largest possible audience. Because commercial television ad rates are based on the relative standings of the programs against each other, the networks select entertainment formulas that have proven popular and successful in the past and might "knock off" the competition. However, technology is changing the system itself, building on ideas that have been around for decades and are at last starting to take off in the Eighties.

As soon as television caught on with the public in the Fifties, various production outfits pressed to get pay TV started as a competitor to free TV. Hollywood studios, losing box office business to television, were especially interested in a system that would allow charges beyond commercials and the one-time purchase price of the TV set. A few such experimental systems got off the ground in the Fifties and early Sixties, using a signal that was coded and could only be picked up by viewers with a decoding box in their home sets. Zenith had an experimental pay-TV station in Chicago and pay-TV stations stayed on the air for a few years in California and Connecticut. The stations ultimately failed for the same reason that various fourth networks flopped: they could not compete with the selection on the established commercial networks.

Inroads in the concept of pay television took place from another angle during the Fifties with cable TV. Rural residents who lived in fringe reception areas—which could only receive signals from one or two stations (if that many)—willingly signed up to pay for clear reception of the closest free TV stations. Cable companies plugged a cable connection directly into the home sets, delivering a signal that even a rooftop antenna could not supply.

The market for such cable service grew and soon urban stations expanded their total audience by hooking up with nearby rural cable systems. In the mid-Seventies, Atlanta television entrepreneur Ted Turner revolutionized cable TV by taking it a step further and transforming his low-profit non-network UHF station into America's first "superstation," WTBS. Though the programming on WTBS consisted of only old movies, syndicated reruns, and

The success of Time Inc.'s Home Box Office (HBO) service paved the way for the tremendous growth of cable television in the early 1980s. *(Courtesy Home Box Office, Inc.)*

local sporting events, Turner worked to get cable TV systems throughout the Southeast to include his station in their service. He realized that, unlike many city dwellers, rural Southern viewers had rarely been offered a choice beyond network affiliates because there were few independents operating in their areas. As more and more local cable systems added WTBS to their cable service, Turner's station became available throughout the South. Using TV relay satellites to bounce his signal to cable systems throughout the country, Turner eventually transformed WTBS into a virtual national TV station available in almost every state of the Union. Other non-network stations (such as WGN in Chicago) followed Turner's lead and began sending their signals to cable systems throughout their regions. Though these independent superstations might one day effectively form a fourth network, they currently just provide another way for more people to see familiar reruns.

Another branch of cable development, pay cable, combined facets of pay TV and cable technology and this has the potential to produce a true commercial alternative to network programming, providing expanded access for material that could never be run on network television. In 1972, Time Inc. set up Home Box Office (HBO), a program service carried over various cable systems, but one with an important difference. Cable subscribers had to pay an additional fee above their regular costs in order to receive the HBO signal. This income allowed HBO to be noncommercial and still profitable, succeeding with an audience of thousands rather than millions. At first HBO was seen in only a few Eastern cities, and its programming was restricted to recent box office films not yet farmed out to network television, R-rated films considered too racy to air intact on the commercial networks, and live sporting events which the networks had by-passed. By the mid-Seventies, HBO was using TV relay satellites to send its signal coast to coast and had also developed a number of its own original programs to drop in between the films including concerts, comedy-variety acts taped in nightclubs, and independently produced entertainment shows.

The success of HBO and its main rival, Viacom's Showtime, paved the way for other, more specialized, cable networks. Ted Turner launched the Cable News Network, a television version of all-news radio. ESPN (the Entertainment and Sports Programming Network) offered twenty-four hours a day of sports, while other cable systems provided such programming as an all-Spanish schedule or live coverage of Congress. A number of UHF stations in large cities came up with "subscription TV" (STV), resurrecting the old concept of pay TV using decoder boxes on home sets to translate a special scrambled signal—providing, in effect, cable-type programming (usually uncut movies) without the cable.

Such subscription stations and cable networks can offer programming far less restrictive and more diverse than "free" TV because pay-cable does not have to be geared toward the vast general public. Unlike regular network signals that can be picked up by anybody, pay-cable systems reach a more select audience that, in effect, invites the new companies into their homes when they pay the required fee. Much like PBS, these pay-TV systems offer viewers an alternative to, but not a total replacement for, commercial television.

PBS, in fact, could become the big loser in the growth of these services in the Eighties, especially as major producers such as Group W and even the commercial networks themselves turn out special "quality programming" for cable. If Public Television loses its segment of the TV audience to these cable alternatives it will also, in the process, lose a major source of its financing: direct viewer donations. PBS may be beaten at its own game, co-opted by cable technology.

In the late Seventies, technology provided one other important change in the relationship between the public and television: home video attachments. Electronic video games introduced the concept of turning away from any program source, cable or commercial network, and using the television screen as a game board. Though these games (variations of Ping-Pong) quickly faded in popularity, the idea of home control did not fade and people began to consider other attachments to their sets. Home video tape recorders soon caught on and, later, prerecorded video disks were put on sale. The video recorders allowed viewers to tape programs for playback at a later time, especially when there was nothing on television that they felt like watching. Video disks presented hit movies directly from the studios to the consumers. The films could be run again and again at any time without any commercials.

In December, 1977, in Columbus, Ohio, Warner Communications (the corporate outgrowth of the Warner Brothers studios) began to test a new type of cable concept, Qube. This brought all the theories of access and control together into one easily billable form. Qube was a pushbutton computer system hooked into the home set via cable and it provided an almost unlimited number of programming choices: commercial network fare, uncut movies, special events, and various locally produced shows. Qube also offered viewers the ultimate video game: the ability to talk back to their sets. Using their control boards to punch in "yes" or "no" answers, viewers could vote on questions or selections put to them by on-the-air personalities. On Qube's opening day, the parents of a newborn child listed several possible names for their baby and, by majority vote, the citizens of Columbus subscribing to Qube made the decision.

From a commercial point of view, the most important aspect of Qube's central computer is that it electronically scans the audience every six seconds, supplying, in effect, an instant rating. For viewers using Qube, the system provides the basis for the best of all possible television worlds. Once the cable system is installed, additional cable services are easier to introduce over the extensive selection of available channels. Adding assorted hardware such as a video tape recorder, video disk player, home computer, electronic games, a large size wall screen, and even a home camera, viewers are at last given an almost limitless selection of material and producers are given a vast market of new outlets. And with the home camera attachment, everyone can become a TV star at home—if only for ten minutes or so.

The mere existence of more channels of access is a technical certainty for the future. Whether there can be anything substantially different offered is another matter entirely. Even on cable, with less pressure to reach a mass audience, there will have to be *somebody* watching and willing to pay for particular shows. If the number of viewers for the commercial networks should drop—as the audience tries the alternative systems—ABC, CBS, and NBC may shift their emphasis and approach in programming, but not very much. Most likely, while special limited interest features are offered on a few cable channels, network television will continue to present variations and expansions of basic mainstream entertainment. Drama, comedy, variety, and sports have thrived in the past because, essentially, these forms are workable and popular.

The commercial networks long ago realized that there is only so much talent in the world and that it is impossible to have exceptional programming nearly twenty-four hours a day. Instead, they accepted television as being a generally routine endeavor that can occasionally provide very special moments. New gadgets may allow instant talkback, but people have always responded to television by their treatment of advertisers, contact with stations, and, most importantly, using the on-off switch. Segments of the audience have become more vocal and organized in their criticisms of television over the years but, when the dust settles, most Americans accept and enjoy what they see on television, despite the bad marks given to TV by some critics and special interest groups. Fred Silverman, television programming wizard of the Seventies, recognized this fact and observed:

> I wish a few critics would stop putting down the millions of people with whom they obviously disagree night after night, season after season. What makes [them] right and 100 million Americans wrong? Commercial television is synchronized, we are in harmony with the contemporary preferences of an overwhelming majority of the American viewing public. We reflect . . . and often . . . we anticipate these preferences.

Television is the most effective means of mass communication yet devised, reaching millions of people in the privacy of their own homes instantly and simultaneously. The issues of access and control have aroused very strong feelings not only because of the commercial interests involved, but because television forms the popular culture of America. Television is an important mirror of the national personality and self-image, reflecting and affecting the tastes and preferences of the people watching. Even if new technical hardware, changes in the broadcast laws, and expanded access only shift slightly the emphasis in the overall approach to entertainment programming, the fact that more people can have a voice in selecting the images flickering at home is vital. The public has often been told that it gets programming as good, as relevant, and as significant as it asks for. With increased avenues of access it can actually choose to live up to that responsibility, or ignore it.

A sharper awareness of the history, power, and limitations of television also has a very personal, practical application. It helps us to realize the important role television has assumed in our lives. For more than thirty years, television has served as the nation's electronic babysitter, giving us a video vision of the world. On the tube, everything has been organized into tight, easy-to-digest segments. As a result, we tend to wish that our own everyday activities were structured like our favorite TV programs, with catchy music at the beginning, fast-paced action throughout, and a satisfying climax. Lacking that, we look to television as a magical escape. It may not present our lives as they really are, but it does reflect the lives we dare lead only in our dreams.

Index

ACKNOWLEDGMENTS

We would like to thank the following for their help in this project:

The Industry:
AT&T Co. (special thanks to Edna Afiriyie)
George Burns
Bing Crosby Productions, Inc. (special thanks to J. R. Rodgers)
Bret Adams Limited
Capitol Records (special thanks to Randall Davis)
CBS (special thanks to Martin Silverstein, Sallie Jones, Mary Perez, James Sirmans, Robert Mackey, Fred Wing, Anne Nelson)
CBS News (special thanks to David Buksbaum, Geraldine Newton-Sharpe, Robert Levithan)
Danny Thomas Productions
David Shapira and Associates, Inc.
Irving Fein
Filmways, Inc. (special thanks to Robert Mirisch)
George Schlatter Productions (special thanks to Beth Grant)
Herbert Hoover Library (special thanks to J. Patrick Wildenberg)
Historical Pictures Service, Inc. (special thanks to Jeane M. Williams)
Home Box Office, Inc. (special thanks to Michele Morrison, Phyllis D. Levinberg)
ITC Entertainment, Inc. (special thanks to Edward Gilbert, Murray Horowitz)
Jack Barry-Dan Enright Productions (special thanks to Dan Driscoll)
Judy Thomas Management
Library of Congress
Lone Ranger Television, Inc. (special thanks to Margaret Scully)
Lucille Ball Productions, Inc. (special thanks to Gary Morton)
MCA, Inc. (special thanks to Ben Halpern, David Darley, Corinne DeLuca, Maureen Angelinetta, and, of course, Tony Sauber)
MTM Enterprises (special thanks to Patricia Ahmann)
Museum of Broadcasting
NASA
National Archives (special thanks to Doug Thurman, Paul White, Mary Young)
NBC (special thanks to Bob Asman)
New York Telephone (special thanks to George Redington)
Peekskill Enterprises, Inc. (special thanks to Jack Philbin)
Smithsonian Institution (special thanks to Anastasia Atsiknoupas)
Sonny Fox Productions (special thanks to David Eagle)

Ed Sullivan Productions (special thanks to Bob Precht, Carmine Santullo)
Tandem Productions, Inc. (special thanks to Lynne Naylor, Barbara Brogliatti, Virginia Carter)
20th Century-Fox (special thanks to Linda Levine)
Viacom Enterprises, Inc. (special thanks to George Faber in Hollywood)
Walt Disney Productions (special thanks to Michael Russell)
William Morris Agency
WTBS (special thanks to Edwin Jay)

Friends: Al Barr, Frank Bierlein, Cecille Boyce, Carolyn Busch, Mike Class, Carole Cohen, Biff Craine, Cindy Farenga, Greg Farmer, Joe Federici, Betsy Foss, Melanie Frey, Mark Guncheon, Bart Helbling, Bob Hirschfeld, Laura Janis, Art Kosatka, Belinda Kosatka, Jim Krog, Jonathan Lehrer, George Maistrellis, Ed Mann, Holly Mann, John Meehan, Nancy Moon, Mark Nelson, Rich Nelson, John O'Leary, Janet Oliver, Dave Plaut, Margaret Sneeringer, Paula Uscian, Flawn Williams, Sam Wooten, Dean Yannias

VERY SPECIAL THANKS TO:

Tony Sauber for his enthusiastic interest, generous intercession, and timely advice on navigating through the entertainment bureaucracy.

Mike Tiefenbacher for his painstaking layout of our schedule graphs.

Michael Mills for his staunch defense of good grammar, proper usage, and the King's English.

Tom Schultheiss for always being there when we needed him.

PJ Haduch for making it happen.

Above all,
Harry would like to thank Wally and
    Wally would like to thank Harry.

ABOUT THE AUTHORS

Harry Castleman was born in Salem, Massachusetts, in 1953, just seventy-five days after the birth of Little Ricky, and, when young, looked a bit like Theodore Cleaver. While earning a political science degree at Northwestern University, Harry spent most of his time working at the college radio station. Next came a stint at the Democratic National Committee, working in its radio-TV department and on special projects such as the 1975 telethon and the 1976 national convention. Harry then moved to Florida where he served as media assistant in two of Governor Reubin Askew's campaigns and press secretary to the state Democratic Party. He also worked at radio stations in Illinois and Florida. In between jobs, Harry co-authored *All Together Now* and *The Beatles Again* before selling out and entering Boston University law school.
P.S. Harry thanks Fay and Lloyd for letting him watch.

Walter J. Podrazik was born in Chicago on February 23, 1952, at 6:27 P.M. (C.S.T.)—just in time to catch *Beat the Clock* on CBS. He received his bachelor's degree from the radio-TV department of the School of Speech at Northwestern University and then took on several special projects for the Democratic National Committee, including work on its 1975 telethon, 1976 national convention, and 1978 mid-term conference. For the 1980 Democratic National Convention in New York City, Wally was the on-site director for the media set up at Madison Square Garden, responsible for such tasks as safely squeezing twenty-three broadcast trailers onto one city block. In a completely different arena, Wally also co-authored *All Together Now* and *The Beatles Again,* served as a research consultant for the special American edition of the Beatles *Rarities* album, and has lent his expertise to a number of other rock and roll books. Currently, Wally offers his consulting services out of Chicago. He does not reside in a Nielsen household.